# MICKEY MANTLE

## The American Dream
*Comes to Life*®

*The Companion Volume to the*

*Public Television Videography™ Program Special*

by Mickey Mantle
and Lewis Early

Edited, compiled, and sequenced by Douglas A. Mackey

M031593205

Sagamore Publishing Inc.
Champaign, Illinois

© 1994 Lewis Early

All rights reserved.

Supervising editor, compiler, and sequencer: Douglas A. Mackey
Production supervision and interior design: Michelle R. Dressen
Production assistant: Brian J. Moore
Dustjacket design: Michelle R. Dressen
Editor: Susan M. McKinney
Proofreader: Phyllis L. Bannon

Photos by the New York Yankees, *The Sporting News*, *The New York Times*, the Baseball Hall of Fame, the National Archives, Bettman Archives/UPI, Associated Press, the Mickey Mantle Collection, Mark Gallagher, Barry Halper, Raymond Gallo, and other private collectors. Every effort has been made to trace the ownership of copyrighted photos. If we have failed to give adequate credit, we will be pleased to make changes in future printings.

Front cover photograph courtesty of Raymond Gallo. For more information contact Gallo Studios, 41 Rolfe, Cranston, RI, 02910.

Library of Congress Catalog Card Number: 94-65138
ISBN: 0-915611-89-9

Printed in the United States.

*This book is dedicated to the memory of Roger Maris,*
*as good a ballplayer and as good a man as there ever was.*

# Contents

# Acknowledgments

The authors wish to give special acknowledgment to the following individuals for their invaluable contributions:

Merlyn Mantle
Danny Mantle
The Mantle family
Lew Rothgeb
Richard Hall
John F. Lehr, Jr.

Douglas A. Mackey
William A. Remas and family
Joe and Peter Bannon
Lou D'Ermilio
Tom Sturdivant
Steve Janson

The authors wish to thank the following individuals and organizations for their assistance and support.

American Program Service—
    Jan Goldstein
Public Television
The New York Yankees
*The New York Daily News*—
    Hugo Masslich and Dave Kaplan
WABC Yankees Radio—
    Steve Appel
*USA Today*—
    Gene Policinski
The Associated Press
*The Sporting News*
*Sports Illustrated*—
    Stanley Weil
The National Archives
The Bettman Archives/UPI
The National Baseball Hall of Fame
Mickey Mantle's Restaurant (NY)—
    Bill Liederman
WFAN Radio (NY)
Billy Martin
Bill "Moose" Skowron
Carrie Lee Rothgeb and family
Timothy Rothgeb
Roy True and Kathy Hampton
Barry Halper
Mark Gallagher
Andy Strasberg
David Hershkowitz
John and Judy Leavitt
May Masunaga and Scott Alden
Robin Cohen and family
Jesse Raiford
Frank Gannon
Dave and Kellye Parker
President Richard Nixon
President George Bush
President Bill Clinton
Estelle Galeano & Joe Kierland
Leslie Deetken
Dr. Harry Friedman
Video Arts — Kim Salyer, Bob Johns & David Murray

The Oakland A's - Tony La Russa
Dennis and Nancy Eckersley
Jose Canseco
Cusy Canseco
Dave Henderson
Rickey Henderson
Carney and Debbie Lansford
Mark McGwire
Pete Rose
Bruce Jenkins
Bob Costas
Roy Firestone
Larry King
Tony Kornheiser
Marty Zad
Mel Allen
Sonny Slaughter
Phil Rizzuto
Paul Simon
Jay Johnstone
Steve Williams
The S.F. Giants — Ben Oakes
Tom Oakes
Rich Hebert
Randy Ottenberg
Phil and Suzie Donaldson
Chuck and Jo Clessler
Jim Stuckey and family
Barbara Stuckey
John and Jacquie Drucker
Joe and Gail DeSciose
Lynette Sonne
Hugh Andrews
Lincoln Norton
James Joyce
Tom and Kitty Kelly
Allan Kaye
Manuel Rodriguez
Ida Honesty
Dr. James Zucherman
Delmy Marquina

*When in New York visit Mickey Mantle's Restaurant, 42 Central Park South, New York NY 10019  Phone: (212) 688-7777*

# Preface

**by Lewis Early**

I met Mickey Mantle for the first time when I was seven years old. The meeting took place at Griffith Stadium in Washington, D.C. The Yankees were getting ready to play the old Washington Senators.

Mickey was my idol, as he was to millions of kids across the country. I had made a wooden plaque for him, a truly awful piece of handiwork, worse than some craft project a child might bring home from summer camp. It said "MICKEY MANTLE: WORLD'S GREATEST BASEBALL PLAYER." Below those words I had painted a picture of Mickey hitting a home run that I had traced from a magazine photo.

I made my way down to the visiting dugout before the game, proudly showed my plaque to the guard and told him that I wanted to see Mr. Mantle. He studied me and my gift for a moment and then turned into the dugout and called out, "Hey Mick!"

Suddenly, overcome with anxiety, I shoved the plaque into the guard's hands and started back up the stairs toward our seats. I had taken only a few steps when a hand grabbed my shoulder and turned me around. It was the guard. He looked at me sternly and said, "Mr. Mantle wants to see you."

I was terrified. I thought, "Oh boy, I've really done it now." The guard led me back to the dugout, and I saw Mickey waiting for me. I slowly walked up to him and he asked me, "Hey, where're you goin' bud?"

I couldn't speak, but it didn't matter. Mickey reached out and shook my hand and said to me, "This is the nicest thing anybody's ever done for me. Thanks a lot. I'll really treasure it." Then he reached into the dugout, grabbed a bat and ball and handed them to me. As he did this, he asked me my name and I told him.

I turned to go back up to my seat, but Mickey stopped me. "Where're you sittin'?" he asked. I pointed to the upper deck. He looked at the guard and winked and said to him, "These seats here're empty, aren't they?" The guard winked back and said, "Yes sir, they sure are."

"Well Lew, why don't you and your friends come down and sit here by the dugout as my guests?" I couldn't believe it. My three older friends who had brought me to the game were eagerly watching from the top of the aisle. They were in awe of the fact that I was actually talking to Mickey Mantle. I waved to them and signaled for them to come down. When they arrived, I introduced them to Mickey. He spoke to all of us for a few minutes and then turned to leave. Then he stopped for a moment, looked back at me and said, "Lemme see if I can hit one out for you today."

Mickey hit two home runs that day, and drove in four runs. The Yankees won the game. (Of course, they *were* playing the Senators.) Every inning, when the Yankees came in from the field, he waved to me and my friends. It's a memory that is indelibly etched in my mind, and I remember it as if it happened yesterday.

From that time on, I made a point of going to every Yankees game in Washington. I would always go down to the dugout to say hello to Mickey before each game. Sometimes I even went over to the Shoreham Hotel and sat in the lobby until I saw him and the other players. I even went up to Yankee Stadium in New York several times. Over the years he gave me many bats and balls, most of which I still have. The ushers and guards got to know me as, "The Kid Who Knows Mickey Mantle."

The years passed, and as I grew up, I stayed in touch with Mickey. He must have told me hundreds of different stories over the years. When I became a writer, I started keeping notes on the different stories he told. I didn't do this with any particular purpose in mind. All I wanted to do was record the stories so that I could remember them later.

When the opportunity came to act as head writer for the Mantle Videography™ Program, and as co-author of this companion volume, I jumped at the chance. In some ways, it was as if I had been waiting my whole life for that opportunity.

The concept for the program was simple, yet radical: Mickey would sit in his trophy room and tell stories, which would be compiled in the first truly autobiographical program. There would be no narrator. The interviewer (me) and the interviewer's questions would neither be seen nor heard. No one else would be interviewed. It would be strictly Mantle, telling his favorite stories, with supporting archival footage, photos, and memorabilia. Period music would give the viewer a feel for the times during which the events Mickey recounted took place.

The success of the program is now well documented. It turned out exactly as we had envisioned, and hundreds of thousands, if not millions, of people have enjoyed it. No project that I have been associated with has generated as much positive commentary and correspondence. It may be titled **Mickey Mantle: The American Dream *Comes to Life*®**, but for those of us who worked on it, and to the many Mickey Mantle and baseball fans around the country, it's a dream come true.

While we were working on the program, especially during the filming at Mickey's home, I spent a great deal of time with him and his marvelous family. I must acknowledge their cooperation and support, and their warmth and hospitality. I thank them for their kindness and assistance, and most of all for their friendship. I just wish that all kids could grow up and find out that their idol is as good and as wonderful as they always dreamed that he/she would be.

One final note: On the last day of shooting, when Mickey and I had finished the interviews and the crew was stowing away equipment, I took a closer look at the walls of his trophy room. There on one wall, in the midst of his many awards, was a small wooden plaque faded by time that simply said: "MICKEY MANTLE: WORLD'S GREATEST BASEBALL PLAYER."

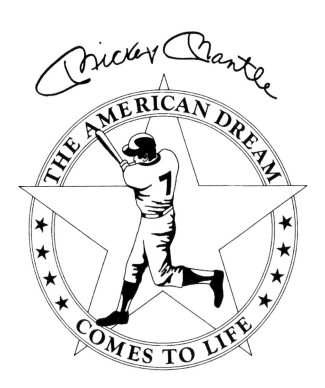

"A magnificent Yankee, the great number 7, Mickey Mantle." — Mel Allen on "Mickey Mantle Day" at Yankee Stadium, June 8, 1969.

This is me in my uniform when I played Sandlot Ball in Miami, Oklahoma. Miami was only a few miles from Commerce, where I grew up.

Me and my Dad, Mutt Mantle. He named me after Mickey Cochrane the great catcher. I'm sure glad he didn't know Mickey's real name was Gordon!

**—I—**
*Introduction*

We were always hunting and fishing when we were kids. This is me and my twin brothers, Ray & Roy, and my sister Barbara. That one fish is almost as big as Barbara!

This is me and my twin brothers, Ray & Roy. They were pretty good athletes, too.

Another one with Ray & Roy. They played for awhile in the Yankees' farm system.

Me and Ray & Roy played just about every sport. Here they're in their football uniforms. In high school, I got kicked in the shin during football practice and ended up in the hospital with osteomyelitis, a bone disease. If it wasn't for penicillin, which had just come out, I might've died or lost my leg. I was never drafted because of this disease.

This is me with my Mom. I guess everybody thinks their Mom is the greatest, and that's how I feel about her. She brought me up right, and when I hurt my leg, she was the one who kept them from amputating it. I owe her a lot.

Tom Greenwade was the Yankees scout who signed me right after I graduated from high school. He first saw me at a game where he'd gone to scout someone else. I hit a couple of home runs into the river at that game. He offered me $400 to play in Joplin for the rest of the summer. My Dad wasn't going for it, so Tom threw in a $1,100 bonus. Later he told me I was the best prospect he ever saw. This picture was taken after the Army wouldn't draft me. He's pointing at one of my injuries.

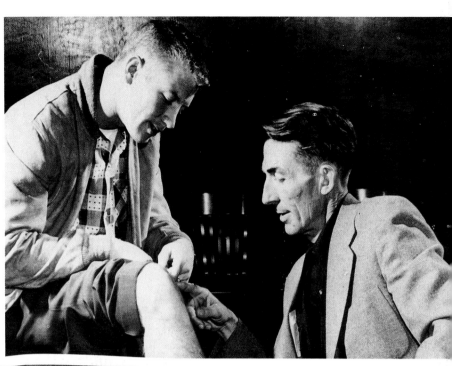

Here I'm relaxing during the off season in Oklahoma. I liked shooting pool and I wasn't too bad at it.

Me and Ray & Roy looking over one of my contracts in the off season. The first contract I signed for the big leagues was at the end of spring training in 1951. Casey Stengel called me in to meet with owners Del Webb and Dan Topping and General Manager George Weiss. Casey really stuck up for me, and got them to give me $7,500, which was $2,500 more than the minimum. It seemed like a fortune to me then. It was probably the biggest moment in my career.

Me and my wife, Merlyn, looking over a contract. I first saw Merlyn at a football game where she was a majorette. A friend set up a triple date with her and two of her friends. We got married December 23, 1951.

I was waiting in Oklahoma for the Yankees to send me my ticket and expense money for spring training in Phoenix in 1951. A reporter came to interview me when I hadn't shown up and the Yankees were trying to find me.

In 1952, they held a "Mickey Mantle Day" for me in Commerce. Folks were really proud of me.

## TULSA HONORS MANTLE

Yankee Gets Griggs Trophy for Bringing Glory to Oklahoma

On "Mickey Mantle Day" in Commerce in 1952, the people lined the streets and we drove through town in a convertible.

Pitcher Ralph Terry, Scout Tom Greenwade, and me. Tom signed both Ralph and me.

This is me sliding into second for a double in my rookie year. Most people don't know it, but I wore number six when I first played with the Yankees. Cliff Mapes wore #7 for the first part of the year, but while I was in the minors, Cliff got traded to the St. Louis Browns.  Bob Cerv took #7 for awhile, but he was sent down to the minors the same day I came back to the Yankees, August 22, 1951.  That's when I got #7.

Me and Casey. This was taken when I first came up with the Yankees. Casey was telling everyone that I was Babe Ruth, Lou Gehrig, and Joe DiMaggio© all rolled into one.

# —II—
# Casey & The Early Days

*Joe DiMaggio was like an idol to me. I think he was probably the best all-around player ever.*

**W**hen I came up to the Yankees, I joined a team that won five straight World Series. I mean, everybody talked about the Bronx Bombers because of all of the great hitters, but we had a great pitching staff, too. We had Allie Reynolds, Vic Rashi, Eddie Lopat, Whitey Ford, and Joe Page in the bullpen. It was just an unbelievable team.

I was hitting pepper one day with three guys. While we were playing, there was a guy who walked behind 'em. Well, I hit one kind of hard, and whoever was supposed to catch it didn't catch it. It hit the guy who was walking behind them in the shins, right on the leg. He turned around and looked and it was Joe DiMaggio! That was the first time I ever saw Joe DiMaggio!

I thought, "Oh My God, I've hit my man!" Because as far as I'm concerned, Joe DiMaggio is probably the greatest all-around baseball player that ever lived. And I had just hit him with the ball!

This is Casey after the Yankees won five straight World Championships, 1949-1953. I don't think any team will do that again. I remember that when I'd make an error or something in a game, one of the players would pull me aside and say "Hey, don't mess around with my money!" They *expected* to play in the World Series, and were all counting on that World Series check.

TUESDAY, SEPTEMBER 15, 1953

# STENGEL AT PEAK OF 44-YEAR CAREER

## First Pilot to Take 5 Flags in Row Was Once Paid for Not Managing Dodgers

# *Casey Stengel*

Casey was a great manager. He was one of the first to platoon his players. I think my Dad saw that coming, because he and my Grandad taught me to switch hit so I'd get to play no matter who was pitching.

Casey became almost like a father to me. He always called me "my boy." He would say "That's my boy there," you know. That's how close we became. He loved to brag to the press about me. He would tell them that I was going to be the next Babe Ruth, Lou Gehrig, and Joe DiMaggio all rolled into one.

I've told the story many times about when I got sent back down to the minor leagues in 1951. We were in Detroit at the time. We had just arrived there, and I'd just had a really terrible series up in Boston. Casey let me get dressed with the rest of the guys and go out on the field. Then he called me back into the clubhouse. He sent the clubhouse man out to get me and he brought me back in. He wanted to tell me alone, by himself.

Well, he had tears in his eyes, and, of course, it broke my heart. He told me, "You've lost all your confidence. I think it would be really good for you to go down for awhile. All we want you to do is just go to Kansas City and get a couple of home runs, a couple of hits, and the first thing you know, you'll get your confidence back, and we'll bring you right back up." Then he said, "You go ahead and get dressed and take off. I'll tell everybody what happened." I've always thought it was really nice of him to let everybody go out of the clubhouse before he told me.

The first time I got up to bat in Kansas City, I laid down a drag bunt and I got a hit. When I came into the dugout after that bunt, George Selkirk, the manager, said "Mick, we know you can bunt. The Yankees didn't send you

down here to learn how to bunt.  They want you to start
hitting the ball so you can get your confidence back.  That's
the only thing you're down here for."

Me and Casey at Yankee
Stadium. Casey became
almost like a father to me.

I struck out a lot my first few years. I made
some errors, too, so I got booed a lot. In 1951,
after I struck out five straight times, they
sent me down to the minors. That was a dark
day for me.

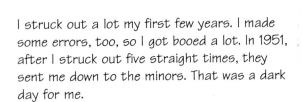

Casey used to do things when he managed that nobody understood when he did them. Most of the time they worked out. If you asked him about it afterward, he always could tell you why he did it, and it usually made sense.

I'm signing another contract with Casey looking on. He always looked after me. He used to call me "my boy."

# MANTLE SENT TO MINORS

*JULY 14, 1951—DETROIT*—Mickey Mantle, the highly regarded rookie outfielder signed by the Yankees earlier this year, was sent down to the Yankees AAA minor league team in Kansas City yesterday. The 19-year-old Mantle has struggled over the past month, seeing his batting average drop from a May 16 high of .308 to his current .261. He reached a new plateau of frustration in Boston when he struck out five consecutive times in the Memorial Day doubleheader against the Red Sox.

When asked if Mantle was through, manager Casey Stengel snapped, "You wish you were through like that kid's through."

Stengel insisted that the move is temporary. "He's been trying to do too much, putting too much pressure on himself. He's striking out too much. He just needs to get his batting eye back, which I'm confident he'll do in Kansas City." Stengel then predicted that Mantle would be back with the team before the season is finished.

Stengel has touted Mantle as the successor to the great Joe DiMaggio. While Mantle has shown flashes of brilliance, particularly with several spectacular home run blasts, he has been mired in a terrible slump over the past month. He leaves the team with seven home runs, 45 RBIs, and a .261 batting average.

Me with my Dad and Cliff Mapes at the lead mines in Oklahoma. Cliff played outfield for the Yankees too. I'll tell you, I'm glad I made it in baseball. Mining is a hard life.

# "I Thought I Raised A Ballplayer!"

Casey was true to his word and brought me back up from the minors later in the '51 season. This picture was taken just after I came up. You can see how happy I was.

After that bunt I didn't get a hit for, like, 22 straight times at bat. I had really reached the bottom. I felt so bad I called my Dad in Commerce, Oklahoma from my hotel room. Commerce is only about 150 miles from Kansas City. I said "Dad, I don't think I can make it. I just can't play ball anymore. Won't you come and get me?"

He asked me where I was and I told him. He said, "I'll be there in a little bit." He drove all the way from Commerce to the hotel in Kansas City. He got there in about three or four hours. He knocked on the door and I let him in, and he got my suitcase and started throwing stuff in it. I said, "What are you doing?" He said, "Well, I'm taking you home." I said, "What do you mean, you're taking me home?" He said, "You said you can't play baseball anymore, so you might as well come on back with me."

Then he said, "I thought I raised a man. You're nothing but a coward. A quitter." I thought he'd come up and pat me on the back and start saying, "Hey, hang in there," or something like that. Instead he really let me have it for about five minutes, calling me a coward and a quitter. He said, "You might as well be a miner like me, so just get your stuff and let's get ready to go." It took me about five minutes to talk him into letting me have another shot at it.

After he left, I went on a tear you couldn't believe. I ended up hitting about .360 or so the rest of the time I was there, and had about 10 or 15 home runs and 60 RBIs. It was unbelievable the way I started hitting. So whatever he did, it was the right thing. And sure enough, later that season the Yankees brought me back up.

Bill Gallo is a famous sports cartoonist. He drew a cartoon of Billy Martin, me and Whitey Ford in the *NY Daily News*. We were sort of like the "Dead End Kids" or something.

# *The King Solomon Story*

**A**nother time I'll never forget was when Casey called me and Billy and Whitey into his office. We were starting to get a reputation, even in the press. For example, Gallo, the *Daily News* cartoonist, came out with one of his cartoons. It showed me and Billy and Whitey standing in front of Casey, and Casey was dressed up like a judge behind the bench, and we were standing there and Billy's got a BB gun behind his back, I've got a sling shot and Whitey had a pea shooter behind him, like the Dead End Kids or somebody like that. And Casey was bawling us out.

About that same time was when Casey called us into his office. He could scare you. I mean, he could get really serious. This time he said, "Do you guys know who King Solomon was?" And we all went, no, not really. We were looking at each other trying to figure out what he was talking about.

He said, "Well, King Solomon was a guy that had a hundred wives, and they couldn't all live in the same house with him, so they had to be scattered all around town. But if he's got all these wives," he said, "he couldn't go get 'em, so he had a guy that lived with him that would run and get the wives and bring 'em to him if he wanted one. Even if he had one way across town that he wanted, this guy had to run and get her and bring her to him. No matter what time of night, even if it was two or three o'clock in the morning, this guy had to run and get her."

"King Solomon lived to be a hundred years old," he said. "Do you know how old this guy that was running and getting King Solomon's wives was when he died? He was 30 years old."

We were all looking at each other. Then he said, "Don't you know what that proves? That just proves that it's not the women that kill you. It's that running after them that does it!"

CHESTERFIELD COUNTY LIBRARY
VIRGINIA

Stan Musial was my first idol. This was when we were getting ready to testify to the Kefauver Committee.  They called me and Stan as well as Ted Williams and Casey Stengel to testify.

Casey loved to talk. He could really get you going with his "Stengelese." This is when he testified to the Kefauver Committee. He talked for a long time, but I don't think anybody really understood what he said.

# The Kefauver Committee

*T*here was a Senate Committee in Washington called the Kefauver Committee and they were trying to prove that baseball was anti-trust or something like that. I never did know what it was, but I was scared to death. They had asked Casey, owner Del Webb, and myself to come from the Yankees, and they had Stan Musial and Ted Williams come too.

We went down there the night before, and we got up early the next morning. All the way on the trip down there, Del Webb was just saying, "Hey, relax," because I was really scared. I was afraid I was going to get thrown in prison or something. I didn't know.

When we got there, the first guy that they swore in was Casey. They asked him, did he think that baseball should be exempt from anti-trust laws or whatever it was, whatever the question was. He started by saying: "I started playing baseball in Kankakee, Illinois, back in 1890," or whatever he said. I really don't know what it was. He talked for about an hour and a half or so — he was really putting the Stengelese to 'em that day.

*Casey Stengel (Excerpt from actual testimony): "Well, I'll tell you, I got a little concerned yesterday in the first three innings when I saw that my three players that I'd gotten rid of, I said, well, if I lose nine what am I gonna do? And when I had a couple of my players that I thought so great of that didn't do so good up to the sixth inning, I was more confused, but I finally had to go and call on a young man in Baltimore that we don't own, and the Yankees don't own him, and he's doing pretty good and I would actually have to tell you that I think we're more the Greta Garbo*

**CONGRESS INVESTIGATES BASEBALL'S MONOPOLY**

Stengel, Mantle, Musial, and Williams to Testify at Kefauver Hearings

*type now from success. We are being hated, I mean from the ownership and all, we are being hated. Every sport that gets too great or one individual . . . "*

They finally asked him to step down. Then they swore me in. I was the next witness. Senator Kefauver said, "Mister Mantle, what do you think? Do you think baseball should be exempt from anti-trust laws?" or whatever. I said, "Sir, I don't really know that much about it, but everything that Casey said, I agree with." And everybody laughed. Then he said, "Mister Mantle, would you mind telling us what Mister Stengel said?" And everyone laughed again.

I got called to testify right after Casey. I was really scared. I thought they might try to put me in jail or something!

Casey getting ready to testify to the Kefauver Committee. He could go on for hours if there was someone there to listen. The sportswriters loved him. When he left the Yankees they had a special dinner for him. I don't think they'd ever done that before.

## Senate Investigates Baseball's Antitrust Status

*JULY 10, 1958, WASHINGTON—* Yesterday the Senate's Antitrust Committee, chaired by Senator Estes Kefauver (Dem., Tenn.) conducted hearings looking into Major League Baseball's exemption from anti-trust legislation. Among those called to testify to the committee were baseball stars Ted Williams, Stan Musial, and Mickey Mantle. New York Yankees owner Del Webb and Manager Casey Stengel also testified.

The highlight of the hearing was Mr. Stengel's testimony, which lasted over an hour. A spellbound, yet highly amused audience listened as Mr. Stengel took them through a circuitous history of major and minor league baseball, the trials and tribulations of managing, offering such unusual commentary as comparing the New York Yankees to Greta Garbo. (see "Kefauver Committee" page 26)

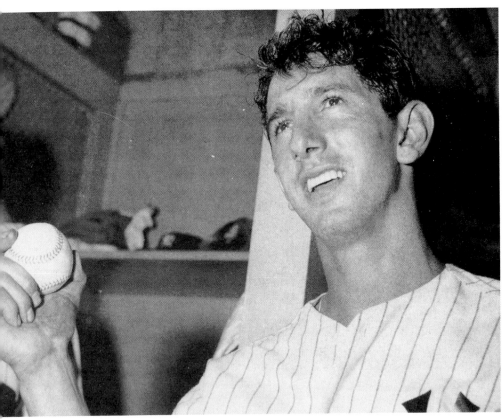

A lot of people don't remember it, but Billy Martin was a pretty good ballplayer, especially when it really counted. His lifetime World Series average was well over .300. One time Harry Byrd, a real hard thrower with the Philadelphia Athletics, was pitching against us. He was getting guys out by pitching inside. Casey told us, "I'll give a hundred bucks to anybody for each time he can get hit by a pitch." Billy got hit three times!

Whitey, me, and Billy.  Whitey won this game just after he'd gotten back from the Army.  I drove in Billy with the winning run.  Here we're celebrating in the clubhouse afterward.  Me and Billy and Whitey were as close as friends could be.

# —III—
# Billy & Whitey

I think Whitey Ford was as good a pitcher as there was. I'll tell you, if the World Series was on the line, I'd give the ball to Whitey every time.

**A**nother question that I get asked a lot is, "What was Billy Martin really like?" I guess people ask me this because me and Billy were such close friends. In fact, I have three brothers, and none of them were any closer to me than Billy was.

Billy was always a great one for jokes. He loved to pull a joke on somebody. He'd get a bigger kick out of that than anybody that I've ever played with.

During my first year with the Yankees, Joe DiMaggio would come to the ballpark in a suit and tie every day. We'd come out in Levis and tennis shoes or anything like that. But Joe was always well dressed.

Billy had one of those prank pens that would spill ink when you went to use it. He'd run up to Joe and ask, "Joe, would you sign this ball for me?" When Joe opened the pen and went to use it, ink would spill all over him. And Joe would grumble, "Oh Billy, how could you have done that?"

The first time I met Whitey was when he married Joanie before the '51 season. It was after our last exhibition game, which was at Ebbets Field in Brooklyn. We all got in buses and went to the wedding. Whitey was in the service then, so I didn't get to know him until he came back later.

This is Whitey, me, and Billy (back row) after we'd gone deep sea fishing. We used to do everything together.

# *"Whiskey Slick"*

Here's "Slick" in action. Usually, when he really needed to get someone out, he could do it.

*T*he first time I met Whitey Ford was in 1951. I remember that we were playing a couple of exhibition games against the Brooklyn Dodgers before the season. Whitey was going to marry Joanie. After one of the games they had a bus to take everybody to Whitey's wedding.

Casey was a great manager. He really knew how to talk to his players. Once we had lost four straight games and he called a clubhouse meeting. Me and Billy and Whitey had probably been partying a little too much. We might've missed a bus or two or been late getting in at night or something.

Casey had a knack of getting on the guys who were going good. We were probably going pretty good at that time, and some of the other guys weren't doing so well. We were kind of his pets, you know, "teacher's pets." After he had gotten on us in front of everybody, as he would walk out, he kind of gave us that wink, like, don't worry about it, you've done all right.

He started the meeting that day by going on about how we needed to get to the ballpark earlier, that guys who weren't hitting too well should come out early for extra hitting, and players should take more infield practice and shag more fly balls. He started getting more serious as he went on with his talk.

Suddenly, he looked right at me and Billy and Whitey and he said, "I'll tell you something else. Some of you guys are getting 'Whiskey Slick.'"

Well nobody had ever heard that expression before, but everybody knew who he was talking about. He went ahead with the meeting, and at the end of the meeting he said, "I'll tell you another thing: Some of you milkshake drinkers better snap out of it, too!"

From that time on, everybody started calling me and Whitey "Slick." And we've called each other "Slick" ever since then. I don't know how come the name didn't stick to Billy. He was just as bad as the two of us, but for some reason or other they just called me and Whitey "Slick." Eventually, it became just Whitey's nickname.

Whitey with some of the guys who served with him in the Army. He missed all of the '51 and '52 seasons.

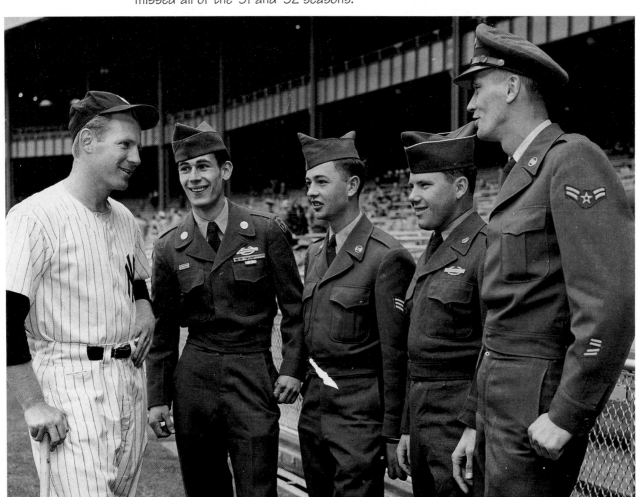

Casey's the one who gave Whitey the nickname "Slick."

Billy loved to play jokes. One time I got a death threat. The guy said that if I played in Boston he would shoot me. Even the FBI got involved. The FBI told me to stay away from the hotel room windows. Billy waited until I was by a window, and then pulled up the blinds and yelled "Look out! Get down!" I dove under the bed. Billy laughed like crazy. But at the ballpark he said, "I'll wear your number and you can wear mine." Nothing scared Billy.

Me and Billy were roommates when he was with the Yankees. Can you
imagine players nowadays carrying their own suitcases?

# The Kenmore Hotel Story

*I* remember that, one day in Boston, we had a day game, and me and Billy Martin went out to a restaurant to eat dinner afterward. The next thing we knew it was about ten 'til twelve, and we had a midnight curfew. But we thought if we really hurried we could make it.

Well, we got stuck in traffic, and we got back to the Kenmore Hotel where the team was staying at about five after twelve. We ran up the steps to the front door and there was Casey Stengel in the lobby with about ten or twelve writers. Casey loved to talk to the writers. He could go on all night.

So we went around back, but the door was locked. But the transom, about a story up, was open. Billy said, "If you get me up on your shoulders I could jump up and get into that window, and then I'll come around and open the door for you."

I had on a brand new sharkskin suit and I really liked it. There he was crawling all over me. I had to stand on one of the trash cans in the back alley to get him up on my shoulders to get him into the window.

He got up into the window, and came around to the door. I could hear him inside, trying to open the door. Then I didn't hear him for awhile. All of a sudden I saw him back up at the window and he said, "Hey, Mick, listen, that door's got a chain and lock on it. I can't get it open. I'll see you tomorrow."

I was still standing out in the alley, all alone.  I had to
stack all those trash cans up and try and get up on them
to get into that window.  I must have fallen off about
four or five times. That sharkskin suit had lettuce and all
kinds of garbage all over it.

Finally I got into the window.  When I got to the room,
Billy was in there already asleep!

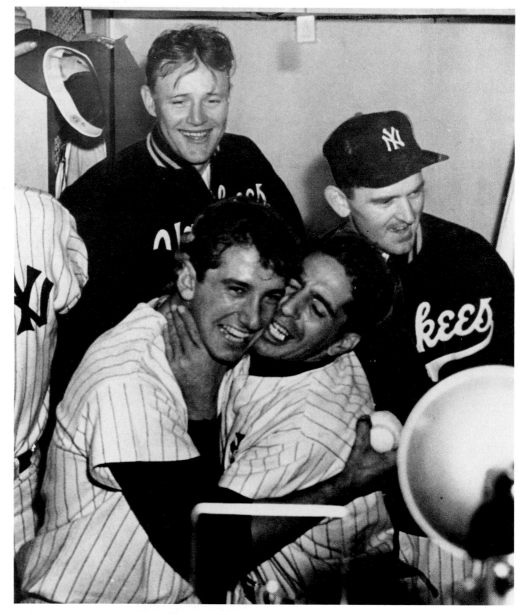

This was after Billy
drove in the winning
run in the bottom of
the ninth in Game 6 of
the '53 World Series.
It won the Series for
us, the Yankees' fifth
straight World
Championship. It was
Billy's twelfth hit in
the Series.

Billy and me did everything together. He used to come live with me during the off season. I remember one time in Oklahoma he left all of his clothes and things in his car when we went to a club one night. He was going to lock his car, but I told him, "Aw, you don't have to do that around here." When we came out all of his stuff was stolen!

Most people think of Billy as a manager, and he was a great one. I'll tell you, he could get guys to run through a wall for him.

Whitey had some great years with the Yankees. His lifetime record was 236 wins against 106 losses. He'd have won a lot more games if he hadn't spent those years in the Army.

Roger Maris, Willie Mays, and me at an All-Star Game. Willie hit something like .400 lifetime off of Whitey, but Whitey did find a way to get him out one particular time.

# The Horace Stoneham All Star Game Story

*T*his story's about after the Giants moved to San Francisco and they had the All Star game there. Everyone remembers that game because Stu Miller was blown off the mound. But I remember it for a different reason.

Whitey always seemed to have a terrible time getting Willie Mays out. I think Willie's lifetime batting average was over .400 against Whitey.

Me and Whitey went out to San Francisco a little early. We got there the day before the All Star game. We wanted to go play golf, so Whitey called Horace Stoneham, the owner of the Giants, and asked him if we could play at his country club. He said, "Sure, just sign for everything. In fact, I'll tell you what I'll do. You just sign for everything and if you get Willie out in the All Star game tomorrow, I'll take care of everything. If you don't, you'll have to pay for it."

Well, we ran up a bill of like $400 or something like that. In 1961 that was really a lot of money. So I told Whitey, "Man, if you get Willie out tomorrow, I'll buy your dinner or anything you want."

Sure enough, Whitey, I think, threw Willie a spitter or something and struck him out. It was one of the few times he ever got Willie out. It was the last out of the inning, too, and everybody said I was jumping up in the air in the outfield. I came running off the field, and grabbed Whitey like it was the last out of a World Series. Nobody could figure it out but Horace Stoneham.

Here we are at the famous "Copacabana"
night club on May 15, 1957. That was quite a
night.

MAY 17, 1957

# YANKEE IS LINKED TO FIGHT IN CAFE

## But Hank Bauer Denies That He Took a Swing at Fan in Copacabana 'Incident'

# The Copacabana Incident

*Y*ou know, everybody asks me about Billy Martin, but the truth is, I never saw him fight. I never saw Billy have a fight.

One of the stories that everybody wants to know about, it seems, is the old Copacabana incident.  On Billy's birthday in 1957, Whitey Ford and I gave him a birthday party.  We'd invited a group of Yankees and their wives.

We went to Danny's Hideaway, which was Billy's favorite place. We had dinner there, and when we finished we decided to go down and catch the ten o'clock show at the Copa with Sammy Davis. They gave us a big table in the middle of the room.

Later, two bowling teams arrived, and they were already feeling pretty good.  They got to talking loud and getting on Sammy, and I think Hank Bauer said, "Hey come on, you guys, cool it. We've got our wives here and you're embarrassing them."

Well, one thing led to another and somebody said, "Meet us in the cloak room."  Of course you didn't have to tell Billy but once, and Hank also.  So the next thing I knew, the cloak room was full of people and everybody was swinging and throwing punches.

Suddenly there was a guy laying right at my feet.  I was in the back just watching everything.  I never hit anybody or got hit. But somebody had hit a guy, because he was laying at my feet.  I thought it was Billy at first.  I picked his head up and saw it wasn't Billy, so I dropped him back down.

The next day the headlines were "Yankees in Copa Fight" and "Billy Martin" this and that. As soon as we got to the ballpark, Billy started packing his bags. I said, "What're you doin'?" He said, "I'm gone. George Weiss (then Yankees General Manager) is just looking for a chance to get rid of me."

Mr. Weiss had warned us a few times about missing planes and trains and stuff like that. Sure enough, Billy got traded. But before that, I'll tell you one of the funniest parts of the whole thing.

One of the guys who'd been in the fight sued Hank Bauer, and we all had to go to court. I'd never been in court before, so I was pretty nervous.

They asked Hank and Whitey and Billy questions, and then they called me to testify. I was sitting there and the judge asked me, "Mr. Mantle, do you have gum in your mouth?" I said, "Yes sir."

I was scared to death. I didn't know what was goin' on. The judge said to me, "Would you do something with it?" I didn't know what to do with it, so I took it out of my mouth and just stuck it under the witness chair.

Then the judge said to me, "Would you tell us what happened?" I said, "Well, I don't know, your honor. I was standing in the back of the cloak room when I saw this guy laying at my feet. I picked him up and it looked like Roy Rogers had ridden through on Trigger, and Trigger had kicked him in the face." Everybody in the courtroom laughed, and the judge said, "Case dismissed."

## YANKEES INVOLVED IN COPACABANA INCIDENT

*MAY 16, 1957—NEW YORK—* Several members of the New York Yankees baseball team reportedly were involved in a fight at the famed Copacabana night club last night here in New York. Players alleged to be involved include Billy Martin, Whitey Ford, Yogi Berra, Hank Bauer, Mickey Mantle and Johnny Kucks.

An eyewitness reported that a group of bowlers had come to the club in a rowdy mood and began shouting obscenities at Sammy Davis, Jr., who was performing at the club. The players had asked the bowlers to stop, whereupon they were challenged to meet the bowling team in the cloakroom to settle their differences.

Police are investigating, but no charges have been filed. Neither the Copacabana nor the New York Yankees could be reached for comment. Witnesses are being questioned (See "Copa Brawl" page 32)

Me, Billy, Hank & Charlene Bauer after Hank won the lawsuit against him. Even though Hank was the one who got sued, Yankees General Manager George Weiss took it out on Billy.

Casey and Billy were real close, too. After Billy got traded they didn't talk to each other for a long time. They did finally make up, though.

# YANKEES MAKE BIG TRADE WITH KANSAS CITY

JUNE 15, 1957, KANSAS CITY— New York officials announced that an eight-player trade has been completed with the Kansas City Athletics. In exchange for second baseman Billy Martin, outfielder/utilityman Woodie Held, pitcher Ralph Terry and outfielder Bob Martyn, the Yankees acquired pitcher Ryne Duren, outfielder Jim Pisoni, second baseman Milt Graff and utilityman Harry Simpson.

The trade came as something of a surprise because it involved fan favorite Billy Martin and the highly regarded Ralph Terry. Yankees officials refused to comment on speculation that Martin may have been traded because of his involvement in the Copacabana night club brawl on May 15th. "We've been watching Ryne Duren," said Yankees General Manager George Weiss, "and we think he can help our pitching staff considerably. We need more (see "Trade" page 28)

Billy was like a brother to me. No one was ever closer. He was my best friend.

# *Billy Gets Traded*

When Billy got traded to Kansas City, it just tore us up. Me and Billy and Whitey were crying and everything. It really was like losing a brother.

Later on that season, Billy was traded to Kansas City. Even though Billy expected it, when they traded Billy, it really tore us up. That was one of the blackest days of my life. We were crying on each other's shoulders and everything. Billy had been my only roommate since I came to the Yankees. So me and Billy and Whitey went out that night planning to souse it up.

I remember that Whitey was pitching the next day, and at one point he said, "I've got to go to bed, because I'm pitching tomorrow." Then he turned to Billy and said, "But I'll tell you what, if I stand straight up tomorrow when I get ready to pitch, it's gonna be a fast ball. If I bend over, it's gonna be a curve ball. But don't go and hit a home run off me." Billy said to Whitey, "Aw, don't worry, don't worry."

Sure enough, Whitey threw him either a fast ball or a slow curve, I really don't remember which it was, but Billy knew what was coming, and I'll be darned if Billy didn't hit a home run. All the way around the bases, he was laughing like hell. The next time Billy was up, Whitey knocked him down!

I've always loved to go hunting. Here I am with my
rifle and my hunting dog.

Me and Billy were always horsing around.
We had a lot of fun together.

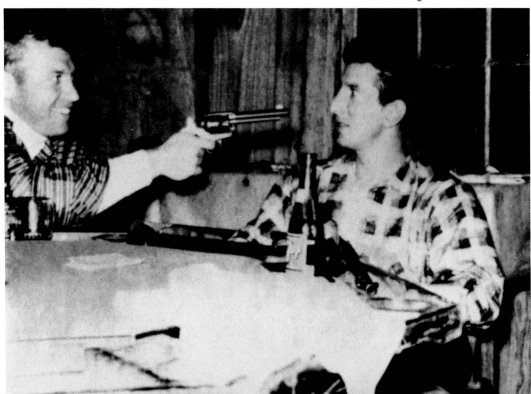

# Billy Shot a Cow

Another question people always seem to ask me is "What made Billy such a good manager?" I always tell them it's because Billy's players knew that if Billy told them to jump off a roof, that Billy would jump off with them. I even have a story to illustrate that point.

When Billy was managing the Texas Rangers, he did such a good job that after the season they gave Billy a new rifle. He wanted to go hunting with it right away. So I told him, "Well, I'll take you hunting. I know a guy with a ranch outside of San Antonio. He's a doctor and a friend of mine, and I think he'll let us hunt on his ranch. But you'll have to get up at four in the morning, because it takes hours to drive there."

Billy said, "I don't care. I want to go deer hunting with my new rifle." So we drove down there and when we got there I said, "You wait in the car and I'll go ask if it's all right for us to go hunting." I went and knocked on the door. The doctor came to the door and said, "Hey, Mick, what are you doing down here?" I said, "I've got Billy Martin out in the car with me. We're wondering if we could go deer hunting on your ranch?"

He said, "Aw, sure, Mick, anytime." I started to walk off, but he said, "By the way, will you do me a favor?" I said, "What's that?" He said, "You see that old mule standing by the barn?"

I looked over by the barn and saw this poor old mule on its last legs. Then the doctor asked me, "Would you shoot that mule for me?" I said, "Aw, Doc, we don't want to shoot your mule. We came down here to hunt deer."

He said to me, "Mick, you'd be doing me a big favor because I just don't have the heart for it. I've had him for about twenty years. He hasn't done any work for at least ten. He's old and suffering. I'm going to have to have him put away. You'd really be doing me a big favor." So I said, "Okay, we'll shoot the mule for you."

Front: Gil McDougald, Jim McDonald, and Gene Woodling. Back: Billy Martin and me. This was after Game 5 of the 1953 World Series when we beat the Dodgers 11-7. Gil McDougald, Billy Martin, and Gene Woodling all homered and I hit a grand slam. Jim McDonald was the winning pitcher.

As I was walking back to the car I thought, "I'm going to pull a joke on Billy." I ran out to the car and yanked the door open and said, "Give me my rifle!" Billy said, "What's the matter?" I said, "We drove four hours to get down here to go deer hunting, and now this guy won't let us. I'm going to shoot his mule!"

Billy said, "Oh, my God, don't do that!" He was trying to grab my rifle back, saying, "We'll get in trouble and go to jail and everything." I said, "Give me the rifle." I finally wrestled the rifle away from him and I ran out to the barn.

Pow! I shot the mule right in the neck. The mule fell over and then, right behind me, I heard, "Bam! Bam! Bam!" I turned around and there was Billy with his gun.

I said, "Billy, what are you doing? He said, "I got three of his cows!"

Billy, Eddie Lopat, and me after me and Billy homered in a '53 World Series game. Eddie'd won the game. He was 4-1 lifetime in the World Series.

Billy and me at Yankee Stadium. We were friends right up until he died. He was a heck of a guy.

1956 was probably my best year. Everything just kind of came together for me. Here I'm getting the "Sultan of Swat" award.

# MANTLE WINS TRIPLE CROWN

OCT. 1, 1956-BOSTON— Mickey Mantle became the first player in nine years to win baseball's Triple Crown, and only the sixth player in history. Mantle finished the season with a final batting average of .353, 52 home runs, and 130 RBIs. He led both leagues in each of the categories, becoming only the fourth player in history to do so.

Mantle finished the season in a dramatic duel with Ted Williams in Boston, where the Yankees played their final series of the regular season. Williams finished the year with an average of .345. Williams is the only player to have won the Triple Crown twice.

When asked how he felt about winning the Triple (see "Triple Crown" page 8)

Here's Casey crowning me with the "Triple Crown," which I won in 1956. On the bats you can see my stats: 52 home runs, 130 RBIs and a .353 batting average.

# —IV—
# *1956: The Turnaround Year*

In this one, I'm sliding in safe at home. Everybody was always talking about my bad legs and all, but it never stopped me from running and sliding when I needed to.

**M**ickey Mantle *(from a 1956 early season interview when asked about breaking Babe Ruth's home run record):* "I think that this year I'd rather lead the league in home runs, runs batted in, and hitting, and that's my goal for this year."

When I first came up there was so much pressure that was brought on me by the media and Casey bragging about me. Like I said, everybody was expecting Babe Ruth and Lou Gehrig and Joe DiMaggio all rolled into one. And it just didn't happen. A lot of people gave me a real hard time at first.

I got booed a lot in Yankee Stadium, because I didn't really do as good as Joe DiMaggio until 1956. He used to hit .323 or .330 every year, and he's probably the greatest living baseball player. So I was trying to take his place, and I wasn't doing it.

Finally, in 1956, I won the Triple Crown, but it wasn't that easy. I remember that the Yankees went into Boston for the last three games of the season. Me and Ted Williams were both hitting .348 or something like that. Of course, I got a couple of bunt hits to protect my average. I was gonna make sure I got some hits. But I hit a couple of other balls pretty good, so it wasn't just the bunts that won me the title.

I think Ted was kinda upset about losing the title. Mostly I think the two bunt hits were what really made him mad. I ended up hitting .353, and I'm not sure what he ended up hitting that year, but he wasn't very far behind me. I remember that they asked him after it was over, "What do you think about Mantle out hitting you?" He said, "If I could run like him, I'd hit .400 every year!" (Mickey laughs.)

I was always a good bunter. Here I'm laying down a drag bunt. I got a couple of bunt hits at the end of 1956 when Ted Williams and I were both trying to win the Batting Title. I bunted because I wanted to make sure I won.

In 1956, I won the Batting Title. I hit .353. In this picture they're giving me the certificate and a silver bat. Al Kaline (left) had won the Title the year before. He'd hit .340.

Casey, Lee MacPhail, me and George Weiss signing my contract in 1957.

On Opening Day in Washington, April 17, 1956, President Eisenhower threw out the first ball. I hit two home runs that day.

TUESDAY, OCTOBER 9, 1956

# LARSEN BEATS DODGERS IN PERFECT GAME; FIRST WORLD SERIES NO-HITTER GIVES YANKS 3-2 LEAD

Yogi Berra celebrating with Don Larsen after Larsen pitched his perfect game in the '56 World Series. That was one of the biggest games I ever played in.

## LARSEN MASTERPIECE—A PERFECT GAME!
### First World Series No-Hitter Gives Yanks Lead

OCT. 9, 1956, NEW YORK— Don Larsen made baseball history yesterday by throwing the first perfect game and no-hitter in World Series history, defeating the Brooklyn Dodgers by a score of 2-0. The victory gave the Yankees a three games to two lead in the Series. The two Yankees runs scored on Mickey Mantle's solo home run to right field with two outs in the fourth inning and Hank Bauer's RBI single in the sixth.

Larsen needed little help in shutting out the Dodgers, throwing only 97 pitches. Two defensive plays were key to preserving the no-hitter. In the second inning, Jackie Robinson hit a hard shot that deflected off third baseman Andy Carey's glove to shortstop Gil McDougal, whose strong throw barely nipped Robinson at first. Later, in the fifth inning, Gil Hodges hit a tremendous sinking line drive about 430 feet into left-center field. Mickey Mantle raced after the ball, lunging at the last second to make a spectacular backhanded catch.

Dodger pitcher Sal Maglie pitched almost as well, retiring the (see "Larsen's Perfect Game" page 3.)

# The Perfect Game

*"Gooney Bird" Don Larsen. During his perfect game he kept trying to talk to everybody about his no-hitter. Ballplayers are real superstitious about that, so nobody wanted to talk to him.*

*I* guess one of the biggest games I ever played in was in the World Series against the Dodgers in 1956, in Don Larsen's perfect game. I remember that in that game, Sal Maglie was pitching a great game for the Dodgers, too.

I'm not sure if I got the first hit or not, but I know that I hit a home run off of Maglie that was right down the right field line and just barely went around the foul pole in Yankee Stadium. It said 296 feet on the outfield wall, but it went further than that. It was hit good enough that it would have been a home run in most ballparks.

Later on, we scraped another run in when someone, I think it was Hank Bauer, got on, and Andy Carey hit a double, something like that. So we scored two runs in the game. Then oh, along about that time was when we started thinking about a no-hitter.

The funny thing about the game, that I remember more than anything else, is that during the game, Larsen was trying to talk to everybody about the no-hitter. Baseball players have a superstition: If a pitcher is pitching a no-hitter, you don't say anything about it. I was down in the corner getting a drink of water and he came over to me. "Gooney Bird" is what we called him, and he said, "Hey Mickey," and I said, "What Gooney?" He said, "Wouldn't it be something if I pitched a no-hitter?" I said, "Come on man, get out of here!" I didn't want to talk about it.

Don Larsen pitching his perfect game in the '56 World Series. That was on October 8, 1956.

Another thing I remember about that game was that I made one of the best catches I've ever made. I wasn't known to be a great fielder or anything, but I could really run, you know, fast. Gil Hodges was at bat and I remember that he hit a ball that would have been way up in the upper deck at Brooklyn's Ebbet's Field. He probably hit it about 450 feet into left center field. It was right at the warning track. But Yankee Stadium was really big in center field, so there was a lot more room than in most ballparks. I had to run a long way, but I caught it. It was one of the best catches I ever made, and it saved his no-hitter.

Gooney's last pitch was a called third strike to Dale Mitchell. The scoreboard tells the story.

I made one of my best catches ever in that game. Gil Hodges hit a long drive to left center. I really had to run a long way to get it. It saved Larsen's no-hitter.

Casey and Larsen after the game in the locker room. People forget that Sal Maglie had pitched a great game for the Dodgers. That day Gooney was better.

Gil McDougald, Gooney Bird, and me after his perfect game. I'd hit a home run to drive in the first run of the game. Gil made a great throw to get Jackie Robinson out in the 2nd inning.

# Jensen Quits Baseball at Age 32
## *Refuses to Fly to Games*

This is Jackie Jensen. Jackie hated to fly. He wasn't the only one. Once we were in a bad storm over the Great Lakes. It was pretty rough. I'm not sure, but I think it was John Blanchard who got scared. He told the stewardess "Put the plane down! Put the plane down!" The stewardess said, "But sir, we can't land, we're over water." John said, "Go ahead and put it down anyway. I can swim, but I can't fly!"

# Jackie Jensen: The Fear of Flying

One year after the season was over, the Yankees went to Japan. Jackie Jensen was scared to death of flying. I mean, even if we were just flying from New York to Boston, much less from San Francisco to Guam to Japan. He used to have to go to a hypnotist, to be able get on an airplane, he was so scared.

On this flight, we had taken off and oh, I guess we were about two hours into the flight and we got into a storm. Of course, Jackie was up in the front of the plane in his trance. I guess he was just relaxing, because he was about half asleep.

Billy Martin was in the back of the plane and we did get into some rough weather and were bouncing around a lot. You've got to know that Jackie was a little bit out of it. The hypnotist had done a good job, I guess. Anyway, Billy put on a Mae West vest, which airplanes had in those days, and he let the air into it - Phhttt! Then he put on an oxygen mask and he went running up front and he grabbed Jackie and shouted, "Jackie! Jackie! Get up! Get up! We're goin' down!"

Of course, the plane was in a storm. It was jumping up and down and going side to side. Jackie jumped up. He was trying to get his vest and his oxygen mask and everything on. All of sudden he looked around. He saw that nobody else was moving, except Billy. It really made Jackie mad when he figured out what Billy'd done. He chased Billy all around the plane trying to catch him. They finally had to stop him, so he never did get back at him.

Here's me and Red Patterson, the Yankees publicity guy. Legend has it that he measured my home run at Griffith Stadium in Washington that I hit on April 17, 1953. It went 565 feet. Red's the one who created the "Tape Measure" home run.

SATURDAY, APRIL 18, 1953

# MANTLE'S 565-FOOT HOME RUN HELPS YANKEES WIN

## 7-3 Defeat of Senators Features Towering Drive by Yank Slugger

This is a diagram of the home run I hit at Griffith Stadium on April 17, 1953. It went where they've marked the picture with the letter "C."

# —V—
# Memorable Home Runs

## The Griffith Stadium Home Run

Another home run at Yankee Stadium. Everybody talked about the short porch in right field, but they forget that center field was 461 feet deep. I think Joe DiMaggio alone probably lost at least 10 home runs a year because of that. He'd hit a long shot to center that would've gone out just about anywhere else. As he came into second he'd see the ball caught way out by the monuments and he'd kick the base in disgust.

When I think about the longest ball or the hardest ball I ever hit, the one that they talk about all the time was the one in Washington at Griffith Stadium that went 565 feet.

Griffith Stadium, in case you don't know, was not like these brand new ballparks. It wasn't three decks and didn't have a dome on it or anything. It was one of the real old ballparks. The wind always seemed to blow out. But it wasn't an easy ballpark to hit home runs in because in right field there was about a ninety foot wall. In center field behind the wall there were some trees where only Larry Doby and myself had hit home runs. I hit two into those trees one year on opening day against Camilo Pascual. So it was not an easy ballpark to hit in.

I remember that Chuck Stobbs was pitching, and I hit the ball real high. There was about a thirty- or forty-mile-an-hour tail wind that day, and it went over the

This home run, #521, off of Tiger pitcher Earl Wilson, tied me with Ted Williams for fourth on the All-Time home run list. The date was April 26, 1968, and we won 5-0.

Joe Pepitone congratulates me after home run #523 on May 30, 1968. This was the first of two home runs I hit that day. It was against the Washington Senators. I went five for five, scored three runs, and had five RBIs. I was playing first base then.

auxiliary scoreboard in left field. It was a long shot. Red Patterson, the Yankees PR man, measured it. It went 565 feet.

The funny thing about the home run is that I had a terrible habit of running around the bases with my head down, because I didn't want to embarrass the pitcher. I knew he was embarrassed enough already. Especially one that long. As I came around second base I was heading to third with my head down. I heard Frank Crosetti, the third base coach, holler, "Hey, look out!" And I looked up and saw Billy Martin, who was on third when I hit the ball. He was tagged up like it was only a long fly, and I almost ran into him. He ran on in to the plate, laughing, with me right behind him. Later he told me, "That's the longest ball I've ever seen hit."

But I think I hit two or three balls harder than that. I know I hit a ball one time over the monuments in the old Yankee Stadium, up into the center field black seats. That was a long shot.

Then there was the one at USC, at Bovard Field during an exhibition game. I think that one went over six hundred feet. The USC ball park wasn't really that big. When the ball went over the fence, I was already going around second, so I didn't see how far it went. It went across a football field too, that was adjacent to the baseball field. And I hit one in San Francisco too, where they said that only DiMaggio had hit one before.

# MANTLE CLOUTS TREMENDOUS HOME RUN

## 565-Foot Blast Clears Griffith Stadium
### Yankees Swarm Nats 7-3

APR. 18, 1953, WASHINGTON— Yankee center fielder Mickey Mantle hit a tremendous home run that may well be the longest ball ever hit. His mammoth wallop came in the fifth inning off Washington pitcher Chuck Stobbs. The ball caromed over the top of the 60-foot auxiliary scoreboard in deep left field and landed several houses away from the ballpark (see photo). Billy Martin was on third base when Mantle launched his spectacular shot.

Yankees Publicity Director Red Patterson immediately left the park and found the ball in the hands of 10-year-old Donald Dunaway, who showed him where the ball had landed. Red then measured the distance, an astonishing 565 feet. Many players wondered afterward just how far the ball would have gone had it not hit the scoreboard. Senators Manager Bucky Harris said "I just wouldn't have believed a ball could be hit that hard. I've never seen anything like it."

During pre-game batting practice, Mantle put on an electrifying show. He hammered several drives deep into the right (see "Mantle's Historic Homer" page C-2)

Bovard Field at the University of Southern California. The arrows show where my home runs went. I hit one from each side of the plate in an exhibition game on March 26, 1951. They say that the one that went across the football field went over 600 feet in the air.

This one, on August 6, 1961, was off Pedro Ramos (then with the Minnesota Twins). It was home run #361, and it put me ahead of Joe DiMaggio in All-Time home runs. It was my second home run of the game off Pedro. I also hit another one in the second game of the American doubleheader. We won both games. That day I went five for nine, scored five runs, drove in four, and walked three times.

# The Pedro Ramos Home Run

This is pitcher Pedro Ramos. Lifetime I hit 12 home runs off Pedro. He was just behind Early Wynn who gave up 13 to me.

One of my favorites was the time I hit the facade off of pitcher Pedro Ramos. We were playing in Washington against the Senators, and one of our pitchers hit some Washington player on purpose. You could tell it was a knock down.

The next inning, I was the lead-off man for the Yankees. I didn't even think anything about it. I just went up to hit, but everybody on our bench and everybody on their bench and even some of the fans knew that Ramos was going to hit me to protect his own players. I didn't blame him. But I hadn't even thought about it.

We were always kind of friendly. I mean, he always wanted to run races with me. And when we would stand around the batting cage before games he used to tease Camilo Pascual, another Washington pitcher, because I had hit a couple of long home runs off of Pascual, and Pascual would tease him about the home runs I had hit off of Ramos. Anyway, he hit me, and I didn't say anything. He didn't try to hit me in the head, he just wanted to hit me because one of their guys got hit.

Well, the next day around the batting cage, he came up to me and said, "Meekie, I'm sorry I had to do that." So I said, "Don't worry about it. But the next time you do it, I'm going to drag a ball down the first base line and run right up your back." He looked at me and said, "You would really do that?"

The funniest thing is that the next time he pitched to me it was in Yankee Stadium, and that's one of the balls I almost hit out of Yankee Stadium.  It hit the facade. After the game he told me, "I'd rather have you run up my back than hit one over the roof!"

This is me in the locker room in Detroit after hitting my 400th home run on September 10, 1962. I was the seventh player to do it. It was a solo home run off Tigers' pitcher Hank Aguirre. We won 3-1.

Somebody should have told me to slide here. I scored the winning run in the eighth inning on a single by Tom Tresh. John Orsino is the catcher, and Stu Miller, the pitcher, is backing him up. We won 4-3.

Pitcher Fred Talbot and Tom Tresh (#15) congratulate me after my first home run of the season on April 29, 1967. I hit it off Angels pitcher Jack Sanford. It was career homer #497. We won 4-3.

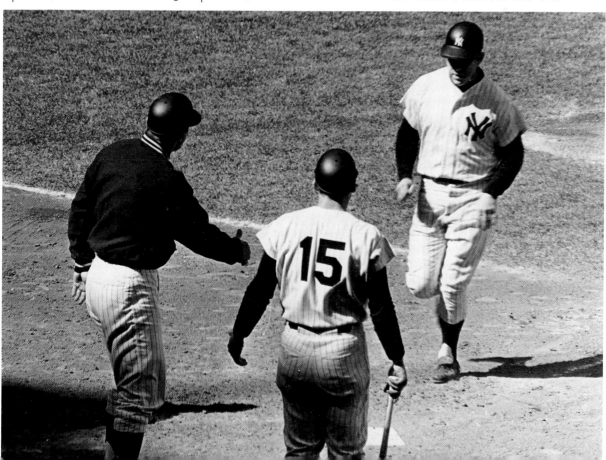

This cartoon came out after I hit the shot off the facade in Yankee Stadium. That was the only home run that I really cared about how far it went. I thought it might go out of the stadium, so I was kind of hoping that it would. No one has ever hit one out of Yankee Stadium.

MAY 23, 1963

## MANTLE'S PRODIGIOUS BLAST NEARLY LEAVES STADIUM
### Yankees Defeat Athletics in 11th, 8-7
#### "Hardest Ball I Ever Hit"

NEW YORK— Mickey Mantle left fans breathless with a titanic solo home run in the 11th inning that not only won the game, but almost became the first home run to be hit out of Yankee Stadium. The blast, which was still rising, hit the right field facade only inches from the top and then bounced all the way back to the infield. The clout came off Kansas City pitcher Bill Fischer (6-1).

The dramatic home run came in a most unexpected manner. The Yankees had taken an early 7-0 lead, only to squander it later in the game to force extra innings. Mantle, leading off the 11th, worked the count to 2 balls and 2 strikes before slamming his tremendous drive. Members of both teams thought the ball would leave the stadium. "It was the hardest ball any man ever hit" according to A's coach Jimmy Dykes. Yogi Berra shouted "My God! That's it!" before realizing that the ball might not clear the decorative facade.

In the locker room afterward, Mickey Mantle said "That was the hardest ball I ever hit. I thought it would go out, I really did." Mantle homered off the facade once before, on May 30, 1956 off then Washington Senators pitcher Pedros Ramos.
(see "Yanks Win in 11," page D-2)

# The Hardest Ball I Ever Hit

*T*he hardest ball I ever hit was in a night game at Yankee Stadium against Kansas City. Bill Fischer was pitching. It was in the eleventh inning, and it also won the game.

It was a line drive, and I thought it had a chance of making it out of Yankee Stadium. This was the only time I think that I ever really cared how far one of my home runs was going. Usually, as long as it was a home run, that was all I cared about. But this time when I hit it, I thought, "This ball might go out of Yankee Stadium." I was kind of watching it and hoping, but it hit the facade, maybe six inches from the top, and then bounced all the way back to the infield. I think that was probably the hardest ball I ever hit.

Here's a diagram of the hardest ball I ever hit. I hit it in the 11th inning of a game on May 22, 1963, and it won the game. It was off pitcher Bill Fischer of Kansas City. They estimated that it would have gone well over 600 feet if it hadn't hit the facade. What they don't show is that the ball bounced all the way back to the infield. (Photo for illustration purposes only.)

This is Joe Collins. He played first base and the outfield for the Yankees from 1948 through 1957.

Someone asked me one time if I ever went up to bat trying to hit a home run. I told them, "Sure, every time!"

# *"Go Chase That One!"*

Joe Collins, Whitey, and Elston Howard after World Series Game 1 in 1955. Whitey was the winning pitcher, Elston hit a two-run home run, and Joe hit two home runs. Joe's two-run homer in the sixth inning put us ahead to stay.

Early in my career, I'd been getting some press about hitting long home runs and the guys on the team had been talking. Every once in a while I'd hit one 440 feet or something at Yankee Stadium and everybody would talk about it.

One day we were playing in Cleveland, and I was in the on-deck circle. Joe Collins was hitting second, and he hit a long home run into the upper deck in Municipal Stadium. But he hit it down the line into the upper deck. When I shook hands with Joe as he came by, he said, "Go chase that one, big boy."

Well, that time at bat I did hit one. There used to be a cigarette ad that was a package stuck on the mezzanine in the upper deck in center field. The one I hit went to the left of it, which was probably about 70 feet farther than Joe's ball. When I had rounded the bases and came back into the dugout, everybody was grinning and clapping and pointing at Joe, and Joe was sitting over on the bench with his cap kind of pulled down. I went over to him and said, "What about that one, Joe?" He said, "Aw, go *@#% in your hat!"

This was on September 1, 1963. Me and Whitey went out the night before, because we knew Whitey wouldn't pitch the day after he'd pitched. I'd just gotten off the disabled list, so I didn't think I'd play either. We stayed out pretty late and overslept. We barely made it to the ballpark on time. Sure enough, in the eighth inning, Ralph Houk had me come in to pinch hit. Hank Bauer was coaching for Baltimore then, and he told pitcher Mike McCormick, "Mantle was out late last night, so he's in no condition to hit. Just fire three hard ones across the plate and strike him out." Meanwhile, Whitey pulled me aside and said, "Hey Mick, whatever you do, just swing at the first pitch. He'll probably throw you a strike." Sure enough, he did, and I swung as hard as I could. They say the home run went about 420 feet. It won the game for us, 5-4.

# The Denny McLain "Gift" Home Run

In 1968, Denny McLain had a great year. He won 31 games and lost only six. He's the last pitcher to win at least 30 games in a season.

This is my home run #535 ball, but the funny thing is that Denny McLain is the one who pitched it to me.

*T*he next to the last home run I hit, number 535, broke Jimmy Foxx's record. But the real story behind it is that Denny McLain is the guy that threw it to me.

We were in Detroit and Denny was pitching that day. He was having a great year. I think he won 31 games that year.

The Tigers were about six to nothing ahead of us. It was late in the game, and when I came up to hit, everyone thought that it was going to be my last time up in Detroit. I had already said that I was thinking about retiring. As it turned out, it was my last time up there.

Denny called time out and walked in toward home plate and called Bill Freehan, the catcher, out from behind the plate. He was about five or six feet in front of the plate and he said to Freehan, "Let's let him hit one. This is probably his last time at bat in Detroit."

Well, I heard him, but you never know whether to believe him or not. So when Freehan came back behind the plate, I asked him, "Did I hear what he said, that he wants me to hit a home run?" Freehan said, "Yeah. I mean, he's not going to work on you, he's just going to throw you fast balls." I thought, "Well, great!"

But I was still a little leery, so the first pitch he threw was right down the middle, but I took it. He looked at me as if to say "Hey, what's the matter?" So then, of course, I knew that he really wanted me to hit one. But on the next pitch, I swung a little too hard and I popped it up. It was a foul ball back in the stands. Freehan just got another ball and threw it back out to Denny.

The next pitch he threw me, he really grooved it, and I really hit it good, up into the upper deck. As I was going around first and second, I kind of peeked out at him and he was looking and grinning. When I came around third, I looked right at him and he gave me a great big wink!

Joe Pepitone was the next hitter. He saw what was going on while he was on deck. So when he came up to hit, he looked out at Denny and he said "Hey, right in here, put me one right in here." The first pitch to Pepitone was right behind his head. Denny knocked him down!

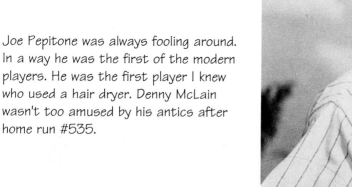

Joe Pepitone was always fooling around. In a way he was the first of the modern players. He was the first player I knew who used a hair dryer. Denny McLain wasn't too amused by his antics after home run #535.

"(Denny McLain)'s thinking, 'I laid one in for you, hit it!' He's saying, 'I'll lay one right in for you, hit it!' And sometimes when you know what's comin' it's tough to hit it. They're all grinnin' — Mickey, McLain, and all of 'em, and all of the, uh, rather, the catcher, Freehan, and OH BOY! THERE IT GOES! IT'S A FAIR BALL AND VERY DEEP! Aw, you gotta give that McLain some credit, I wanna tell ya. He's grinning a mile wide. Boy I tell you, you think these ballplayers don't have heart, Frank, and then — THERE'S MICKEY NODDING TO HIM! THANKING HIM! AND BOY, I TELL YOU, I HAVEN'T SEEN ANYTHING LIKE THIS IN MY LIFE! Mantle has now gone ahead of Jimmy Foxx with 535 home runs. And now McLain is — Pepitone says 'Lay one in for me!' and McLain shakes his head at him and says 'No, Sir!'"
— Phil Rizzuto with Frank Messer, actual game call on Yankees Radio, Sept. 19, 1968

*Season's Greetings*

This was the Yankees'
Christmas Card in 1961. That
was a great year for all of us.

**NEW YORK YANKEES
1961 WORLD CHAMPIONS**

First Row, Left to Right: WHITEY FORD, BILL SKOWRON, HAL RENIFF, JIM HEGAN, FRANK CROSETTI, RALPH HOUK, JOHN SAIN, WALLY MOSES, EARL TORGESON, CLETIS BOYER, YOGI BERRA, MICKEY MANTLE.

Second Row, Left to Right: GUS MAUCH (TRAINER), BILLY GARDNER, BOB HALE, JOE DE MAESTRI, TONY KUBEK, TEX CLEVENGER, RALPH TERRY, HECTOR LOPEZ, BOB CERV, ELSTON HOWARD, ROGER MARIS, BOB TURLEY, JOE SOARES (TRAINER).

Third Row, Left to Right: BOBBY RICHARDSON, AL DOWNING, LUIS ARROYO, JOHN BLANCHARD, BILL STAFFORD, ROLAND SHELDON, JIM COATES, SPUD MURRAY (BATTING PRACTICE PITCHER), BUD DALEY, BRUCE HENRY (TRAVELING SECRETARY).

Seated on Ground in Front: Batboys FRANK PRUDENTI, FRED BENGIS.

# —VI—
# 1961: The Upside Down Year

Ralph Houk, Roy Haney, and me looking over my $100,000 a year contract. I was the first player to make that amount of money a year.

*T*he best team I ever saw in my life, and I really believe this, was the '61 Yankees. We hit 240 home runs, and I think that Whitey Ford won 25 and lost only four. We had Luis Arroyo in the bullpen and Bill Stafford, Ralph Terry, and Art Ditmar.

Everybody had a great year at the same time. Our infield had Cletis Boyer at third, Tony Kubek at short-stop, Bobby Richardson at second, and Moose Skowron at first. Moose hit 27 home runs that year. Our catchers, Yogi Berra, John Blanchard, and Elston Howard, hit over 60 between the three of them. And of course, me and Roger Maris had phenomenal years.

You know, I never got to see the '27 Yankees. Everybody says that was the greatest team ever. But it would have been a good series, I think, if we'd have had the chance to play them.

When we came out of spring training that year, Ralph Houk, our new manager, had told me that I was the team leader and I mean, I was really up. Like a high school football player, you know, you can get up.

Roger Maris and Louis Arroyo. Roger was "Most Valuable Player" in 1961, and Louis was "Fireman of the Year," or Best Relief Pitcher.

He came out, took me aside and told me that he was going to hit Roger third, and me fourth. He thought that it would help Roger hitting third more than it would help me hitting third in front of everybody. Of course, I'd hit third all my life, but he said, "I'll tell you something: you are our leader, and whatever you do is what we're going to do this year." He started making me feel like I really was the best there was.

I took off like a ball of fire, and I really did kind of carry the club for a while. Roger didn't hit a home run for a long time. I must've been ten or so ahead of him at one time. Anyway, all of a sudden, he got on fire and, like I said, that '61 ballclub was just unbelievable.

Roger, Manager Ralph Houk, and me. 1961 was Ralph's first year managing.

We had some kind of line-up that year. Here's Roger (right field), Yogi Berra (left fielder, catcher), me (center field), Elston Howard (catcher), Moose Skowron (first base), and John Blanchard (catcher, outfielder, utility).

Second baseman Bobby Richardson, pitcher Jim Coates, outfielder Hector Lopez, and third baseman Clete Boyer after we clinched the pennant in 1961. That was just a great team. They say the '27 Yankees were the best team ever, but I think it would've been a great series if we could've played them.

It seemed like everybody wanted us to go on their show back then. This was when we went on "The Match Game."

Bobby Richardson loved kids, and he's done a lot of good work with them. He even went on "Captain Kangaroo" once.

Yogi Berra (second row, third from left) and Joe Garagiola (first row on left) grew up in East St. Louis together. They've been friends all their lives. This was one of their first teams.

Yogi was a great catcher. Here he's blocking the plate and getting the out.

# Yogi Berra

Yogi was a great player. He was "Most Valuable Player" three times: 1951, 1954, and 1955.

Joe Garagiola and Tony Kubek. They went on to become the announcers for the "Game of the Week" on NBC.

Yogi was as good a catcher as I ever saw. I'll tell you, he could come from behind the plate on a bunt and almost always throw the guy out. He had a better arm than everybody thought he did. And he could really block the plate.

Yankee Stadium was made for him, with its short porch in right field. He could hit the ball down the right field line better than anybody I ever saw in my life. And he could hit almost anything thrown to him.

Up in Boston one time, they brought in Mickey McDermott, a left handed pitcher, to knock Yogi down. They told him to throw a knockdown pitch at Yogi. Well, the first pitch he threw to Yogi was right at Yogi's head. And Yogi swung at it over his head like he was tomahawking it and hit it right around the right field foul line. It was a fair ball, for a home run! He was unbelievable. He could hit a ball no matter where you threw it.

Most all the stories you hear about Yogi, I think Joe Garagiola made 'em up. Joe made a name for himself by telling Yogi Berra stories. Of course, they grew up together in St. Louis and are great friends. Joe just loves to talk about Yogi.

I have heard Yogi say some funny things. I was standing with him in front of the Gault Ocean Mile during spring training in Fort Lauderdale once and he really looked good. He had on a Hawaiian flowered shirt, a pair of slacks, and a pair of those tong slippers that they wear down in Florida, without any socks.  A little old lady came up to him and said, "Yogi, you look cool today!" And Yogi said, "You don't look too hot yourself!"

One time somebody hollered, "Hey, Yog, what time is it?" He looked at his watch and said, "Oh, you mean right now?"

Everybody always thinks of Yogi as a catcher. What most people don't realize is that in 1961 Yogi was our left fielder. He played the most games of any left fielder. He caught some, too.

Yogi on the "Ed Sullivan Show." A lot of us were invited to go on Sullivan's show over the years.

Yogi went on to manage the Yankees a couple of times. We won the American League pennant under Yogi in 1964.

Yogi catching a foul pop-up. Yogi knew Yankee Stadium so well that, if a foul ball was hit behind him, he could tell where it was going, and he wouldn't even chase it if it was going to be out of reach. He could tell when it was going to be too far back in the stands.

*Yogi and his son, Timmy. Yogi has three sons, Larry, Dale, and Timmy.*

# *"Boy, You Stunk!"*

*I* remember I'd had one of my worst days that I'd ever had, I guess. I'd struck out two or three times with men in scoring position and I dropped a pop fly that cost us the game. Bob Turley was the pitcher. I never will forget that. Of course, he was a nice guy. He came over after the game and said, "Forget it, Mick." I really felt bad. I didn't mind striking out. I was getting used to that by then, but to drop a pop fly and let the winning run in was really bad.

Anyway, I went right straight to my locker and threw my glove and my cap down. I was sitting on my stool in front of my locker with my head in my hands. It was so bad, that the reporters didn't even come in. They knew I was gonna be pretty hot.

As I was just sitting there holding my head, I could feel somebody looking at me. I looked up out from under my hands and there was this little kid standing there. It was Yogi's son, Timmy. Yogi's locker was right next to mine. I looked at him and I said, "Hey, Timmy, how're you doing?" Then I said, "What's the matter?"

He was looking at me really funny. Then he looked me right in the eye and he said, "Boy, you stunk!" Yogi jumped out of his locker and gave him a boot in the butt. He kicked him about four feet out of there and went over and got him and shook him and took him into the player's lounge where he couldn't say anything else!

Roger Maris. A great ballplayer. He was "Most Valuable Player" in 1960 and 1961.

# Roger Maris

In 1961, when Roger broke Babe Ruth's single season home run record, I hit 54 home runs. I won home run titles four times. That year I hit the most I ever hit in a season, but I didn't win the title, Roger did.

P robably one of the questions I get more than anything else is, "What about Roger Maris and yourself?" In 1961, when Roger hit the 61 home runs, there was a lot written that we didn't like each other, that we argued a lot, or fought a lot, or something. That's the farthest thing from the truth. In fact, we lived together on the road. Roger was one of my closest friends, and we used to just joke about all of the headlines that said we were fighting and arguing and mad at each other.

When you think about Roger Maris, the first thing you think about is home runs. I think it's the single hardest thing to do in sports. And to hit 61 of them is *really* hard. But outside of the home runs, the fact that he hit 61 home runs in a single season and nobody else ever has, makes Roger one of the greatest players I've ever seen. I mean, he was as good a fielder as I've ever seen. He had a great arm. He never made a mistake, like throwing a ball too high and letting a guy take an extra base. He was a great base runner. I never saw him make a mistake on the bases. He was always in the game. He was also a good team man. All the guys really liked him, and everyone was really pulling for him at the end.

Roger was a great player. He was a "Gold Glove" outfielder, and he had a great arm. Here he's backing me up on the play, showing me where to throw the ball, just like you're supposed to do.

MARIS' HOME RUN RECORD LOSES ASTERISK

Roger with Roger, Jr. and the "Hickok Belt" for Athlete of the Year.

Roger was invited to the White House, where he met President Kennedy.

Here's Roger receiving his "Gold Glove Award" for the 1960 season.

Roger loved to eat crab, and Maryland is famous for its crab.  When we were in Baltimore we'd buy crabs and beer, fill our bathtub with ice and have a party in our room.  We had some great times in Baltimore. This is a picture of a home run I hit in Baltimore on August 10, 1967 off pitcher Ray Moore.  They said it was the first ball to clear the hedge behind the fence in center field.  I went four for five in that game, scored two runs, drove in three runs, and stole a base.  We won that game 6-3.

# The Roger Maris Swimming Pool Race

It seems like I'm always signing autographs. Most of the time I don't mind doing it, though.

**W**e had an off day in Baltimore and Bob Turley lived in Baltimore. He invited everybody over to his house for a little cookout. We had steak and some beer and stuff, and we were all having a pretty good time.

I used to say, no matter what people were talking about, that I was the Oklahoma State Champion at it. No matter what somebody said. Well, we were sitting around talking by the pool and Roger was telling me about his swimming.

He really was an all-around athlete. He was a great football player in Fargo, North Dakota. And baseball and basketball, and I guess he was a great swimmer. Heck, I can't even swim. But I told him I was the Oklahoma State Champion and I'd like to race him across Turley's pool.

Well, I got Whitey off to the side, and I said, "Hey, Slick, when we dive in the water, get that pool sweep over there, and stick it in the water. I'll grab a hold of it and you run me down to the other end." So he said okay.

Me and Roger got out there in this stance, just like they do in the Olympics, a diving stance. Just as soon as I dived in, Whitey handed me the pole, and ran me down to the other end. But he didn't run straight. He ran kind of sideways, and I was bouncing off of the side of the pool.

Anyway, he got me down there a good ten feet ahead of Roger and I jumped up on the edge of the pool. I was sitting there when Roger got there. I was wiping the water off of my face, shaking my hair and he looks up and he says, "How in the hell did you get here?" He knew he could beat me. He didn't have any idea what happened. Then everybody started laughing and giggling about it.

Pretty soon, he noticed that the whole left side of my arm was almost bleeding from Whitey pulling me against the side. He said, "You son of a gun!" He knew then that I didn't really swim down there.

Roger and his family. His wife Pat is seated. His children (sitting with Mrs. Maris, from left to right) are Kevin, Susan, and Randy. Roger, Jr. is standing. Roger is holding Sandra in his arms.

Me and my family sitting by the pool. (From left to right) There's Danny, David, Billy, Mickey, Jr., and my wife, Merlyn.

Roger and me. Take a look at those hats.

In 1960, I hit 40 home runs and Roger hit 39. They added up to 79, so they had us hold up our jersey numbers to signify the total.

## The M & M Boys

Roger congratulates me after a home run.

*I* can remember that year, once it got far enough into the season, it looked like both me and Roger had a chance of breaking Babe Ruth's record. They called us the "M & M Boys." Almost every newspaper the day after a game would have the M & M Boys in the headline. I don't care if Kubek, Richardson, Cletis Boyer, Moose, Elston, Yogi, or anyone, had hit a home run that won the game, it would still say what the M & M Boys did in the headlines.

The players were so good about it. They made it easy on us, because they would tease us instead of getting mad about it. They didn't say, "Hey, look, I hit a home run and they put the M & M Boys in the headline." They would come around and say, "Hey, what did the M & M Boys do today?" They teased us a lot and they took it really good. They made it a lot easier, especially for Roger after I fell out of the race. I mean, they helped him do it. The whole team did.

They called us the "M & M Boys" in 1961. Papers would write stories saying we didn't get along together, but that's just not true. Roger was one of my best friends.

We got a lot of visitors that year from some really famous people. This is me and Roger with Doris Day.

In 1961, Roger and me combined for 115 home runs. He hit 61 and I hit 54. I don't think any two players will ever hit that many again. After I hit #48, I told Roger, "Well, I beat my guy. Now it's up to you to catch yours." I was talking about Lou Gehrig, who hit 47 in 1927. Babe Ruth hit 60 in 1927.

Roger got a lot of mail that year. Some of it was pretty mean, which I never really understood. Here he's holding telegrams congratulating him for breaking Babe Ruth's record.

Roger, Mrs. Babe Ruth, and me at Yankee Stadium. She came to a lot of the games that year.

## M&M: MANTLE HITS 3 HRs, NOW HAS 43

### *Yankees Sweep Marathon Twinbill, 7-6 & 3-2*

AUG. 7, 1961, NEW YORK— Mickey Mantle continued his torrid pace in quest of Babe Ruth's single season home run record yesterday by homering three times in the Yankees doubleheader against the Minnesota Twins. All three home runs were hit left handed.

Mantle homered twice in the first game off pitcher Pedro Ramos, allowing the Yankees to keep pace and pull out a win in the 15th inning. Mantle's second homer was his 361st, putting him ahead of Joe DiMaggio on the all-time home run list.

After homering is his first two at bats, Mantle doubled in the tying run in the fifth inning to make the score 5-5. The Twins scored the go ahead run in the top of the 10th, only to be tied agin in the bottom of the 10th by John Blanchard's solo home run. In the 15th inning, with runners on 2nd and 3rd, Mantle was intentionally walked to load the bases. Yogi Berra drove in the winning (see "Yankees" page C-3)

## Mickey Clouts #44, Roger #42

### *Yanks Bomb Nats 12-5*

Roger and me heading out to the field. Roger was my roommate on the road. We had a lot of fun together. I'll tell you, I was really pulling for him to break the record at the end of '61. The whole team was.

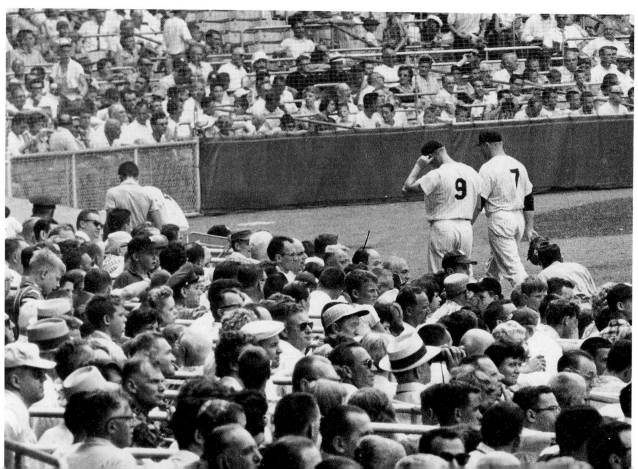

# The Home Run Race

Roger in the locker room after he hit his 61st home run. He hit it on the last day of the season off pitcher Tracy Stallard of the Boston Red Sox. They made a big deal out of the 162-game schedule, but nobody's even come close to his record since he set it.

**Y**ou know, I didn't get to finish the season that year. I had a real bad cold. We were in Boston and one of the announcers told me on the way back home to New York, "You know Mick, those antibiotics that you're taking aren't doing you any good." He said, "I know a doctor that you might be able to go to that can give you a shot that can get rid of that cold. Then you'll feel better and be able to play better."

So I said, "Well, I'll try anything, because I want to stay in the race." I was only two or three home runs behind Roger at that time. Anyway, I went to this doctor and I got a shot in the hip and it turned bad. I got up the next morning and I had a 104 degree temperature. I had to go to the hospital and have it lanced. So I spent the last week and a half of the season watching from my hospital bed.

That made the pressure twice as bad on Roger, because there was only one guy that the reporters could come to. For Roger to have gone ahead and broken the record, I think was just unbelievable. I think it was the greatest thing I've ever seen in sports. I was so proud of him.

And the way he acted. He never ran around the bases jumping up and down, or hit a home run and stood at home plate and watched it go out like they do nowadays. When he hit a home run, he ran around the bases just like he always did. He was a real class act. I even cried when he hit his 61st home run.

"We've only got a handful of people sitting out in left field, but in right field, man, it's hogged out there! And they're standing up! Here's the windup. Fastball. HIT DEEP TO RIGHT! THIS COULD BE IT! WAY BACK THERE. HOLY COW, HE DID IT! 61 FOR MARIS! Look at 'em go for that ball out there. HOLY COW! WHAT A SHOT! Another standing ovation for Roger Maris, and they want him to come out and take a bow. He does. MAN, DO YOU SEE THIS?! HE WANTS TO SIT DOWN AND THEY WON'T LET HIM!"
— Phil Rizzuto, actual game call on Yankees Radio, Oct. 1, 1961

This one tells you a lot about Roger. After he hit his 61st home run, the crowd wanted him to come out for a bow. He didn't want to do it, he was so modest. So the players had to push him out. If you look, you can see one of the guys pushing him.

# The Home Run Record

This is the baseball Roger gave me.

**W**hen Roger hit his 61st home run, he came into the dugout and they were all applauding. I mean, this is something that's only happened once in baseball, right? And the people were all applauding. They wanted him to come back out. He wouldn't come out, so the players had to push him back out. They forced him to come out and take a bow. That's the kind of guy he was. He was great, and I really liked him.

I think it was stupid to have an asterisk behind his home run record, and I'm glad they finally removed it. There have been a lot of guys who have tried since then, and nobody's ever even come close.

I don't know why he hasn't been selected for the Hall of Fame. To me, he's as good as there ever was. I have four boys of my own, and if I could pick somebody for those boys to grow up to be like, it would be Roger.

Out of all the trophies that I have, I think the one thing that I treasure more than anything else is a ball that Roger gave me. It's got his picture on it, and he wrote on it: "To Mickey, the greatest of them all. Best always, Roger Maris."

*Sam Gordon, a restaurant owner in Sacramento, had offered $5,000 for the 61st home run ball. When Sal Durante tried to give the ball to Roger, Roger told Sal he should take the money. Sam gave the ball to Roger, who gave it to the Hall of Fame. That's the kind of guy Roger was. Sal used the money to get married. Here's Roger, Sam Gordon, Sal and Sal's fianceé, Rose Marie.*

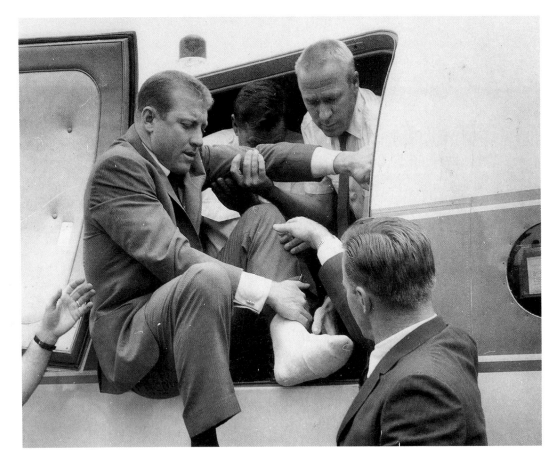

This was after I broke my foot when my spikes caught in the fence in Baltimore in 1963. I did have a lot of injuries. For example, I missed several games at the end of the home run race. That made the pressure twice as bad on Roger. The fact that he went ahead and broke the record is the greatest thing I've ever seen in sports.

Here's another shot of Roger with President Kennedy in the White House.

Norm Cash ("Batting Title"), Roger ("Sultan of Swat Award"), and Whitey ("Cy Young Award").

# MARIS HITS #61!

## *Ruth's Single-Season Record Broken!*
### Commissioner Frick May Attach Asterisk to Mark

OCT. 2, 1961, NEW YORK— Roger Maris set the single-season home run record when he hit his 61st home run, besting Babe Ruth's previous total of 60 in 1927. Maris' blast came off right-hand pitcher Tracy Stallard of the Boston Red Sox in the fourth inning of the Yankees 163rd game.

Maris' home run brings to a head the controversy raging around this year's change from the previous 154-game schedule to the new 162-game schedule. Baseball Commissioner Ford Frick has stated that he is in favor of placing a "distinguishing mark" in record books denoting that Maris' accomplishment took place under the new expanded scheduling.

"It must be taken into account. (See "Maris Sets Record," page 3)

American League President Joe Cronin presents Roger with the Most Valuable Player Award for 1961.

Sunday, March 2, 1969

# MANTLE RETIRES FROM BASEBALL AFTER 18 YEARS

Hanging up #7 for the last time. That was one of the saddest days of my life.

## MICKEY MANTLE RETIRES FROM BASEBALL!

### Baseball Loses a Legendary Player

MARCH 2, 1969—NEW YORK— Baseball legend Mickey Mantle announced his retirement from the game in a tearful press conference. Mantle, who has played 18 seasons for the New York Yankees, said that he was leaving the game because his skills had eroded and "There's just no use trying anymore."

Plagued by injuries throughout his career, the Yankee slugger has become a household name because of his tremendous home runs. His lifetime total of 536 home runs puts him third on the all-time home run list. Mantle has arguably hit some of the longest home runs in baseball history, including a 565-foot drive out of the old Griffith Stadium in Washington, D.C. and two home runs that hit the

facade at Yankee Stadium, almost leaving the park. His list of prodigious home runs in of every ballpark is seemingly endless.

His list of accomplishments and records is impressive. A three-time Most Valuable Player, he led the league in home runs four times. He played in 12 World Series and won seven. He holds the record for the most World Series home runs with 18. His 2,401 games is a New York Yankees record (see "Career Summary" page D-5).

Mantle, a native Oklahoman, was signed by the Yankees in 1949, fresh out of high school. He joined the team in 1951 after an impressive spring training during which he hit .402 with (see "Mantle Retires" page D-5)

# — VII —
## *Reflections*

*From the press conference announcing his retirement:*

**"** *...And I don't hit the ball when I need to, and I can't steal second when I need to.  I can't go from first to third or score from second on base hits.  And I just think it's time that I quit tryin'."*

The press conference where I announced my retirement from baseball on March 1, 1969.

On the first "Mickey Mantle Day" at Yankee Stadium on September 9, 1965 they gave me two quarter horses.

Mayor Wagner proclaimed September 18, 1969 as "Mickey Mantle Day" in New York City.

I was the first to receive the "Hutch Award," named after Fred Hutchinson. The Baseball Writers of America gave it to me in 1965. Hutch, who had managed the Tigers, the Cardinals, and the Reds, had died of cancer the year before. Everyone really liked him.

They gave me the "Hickok Belt" for Professional Athlete of the Year in 1956 when I won the Triple Crown.

Here I am receiving my third "Most Valuable Player Award" for 1962 from American League President Joe Cronin.

Cardinal Spellman gave me this award for some charity work I had done. This was in 1957.

The "Sid Mercer Memorial Award" was given to me on February 13, 1957 by the New York Baseball Writers Association. Sid was the baseball writer the award was named after.

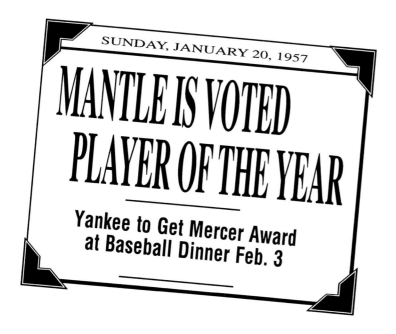

The Philadelphia Sports Writers Association gave me "The Most Courageous Athlete Award" for the 1962 season. You can read the names of some of the other athletes who got it before me.

This was at the beginning of the 1967 season. They made up a blackboard with a list of accomplishments I was nearing.

Me and my family, around 1960. That's my wife Merlyn holding Danny, then Billy, me, David, and Mickey Jr.

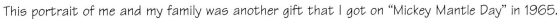

This portrait of me and my family was another gift that I got on "Mickey Mantle Day" in 1965.

"Mickey Mantle Day," June 8, 1969. Yankee Stadium was packed with almost 70,000 people. It won't even hold that many anymore.

# *Mickey Mantle Day*

$\mathcal{I}$ think the biggest thrill I've ever had was in 1969. They declared Mickey Mantle Day at Yankee Stadium. Something like 69,000 or 71,000 people showed up. I don't think the Stadium will even hold that many now.

(From Mickey Mantle Day at Yankee Stadium) *Mel Allen: "A magnificent Yankee, the great number seven, Mickey Mantle!"*

*Mickey Mantle: "When I walked into this stadium 18 years ago, I felt much the same way I do right now. I don't have words to describe how I felt then or how I feel now, but I'll tell you one thing, baseball was real good to me and playing 18 years in Yankee Stadium is the best thing that could ever happen to a ballplayer."*

My wife Merlyn and me at the first "Mickey Mantle Day" in 1965.

At that time they had only retired numbers three, four and five. For Ruth, Gehrig, and DiMaggio. And for a kid from Oklahoma to have his number retired with those three guys is the biggest thrill you could ever have.

I remember that they drove me around Yankee Stadium that day on a golf cart. And the guy that I was driving around with was Danny, one of the ground crew guys who came up at about the same time I did in '51. I'd known him all my life.

As we got to center field or a little past center field, I told him, "Danny, do you know what? This makes me feel like Dolly Parton's little baby when it's nursing. Is this all for me?"

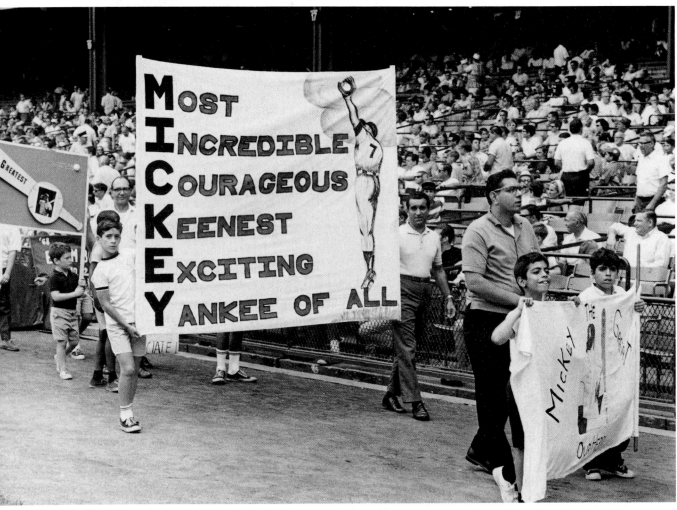

A whole group of kids brought posters on "Mickey Mantle Day" and paraded them around the field. It was really something.

Bobby Kennedy came to the first "Mickey Mantle Day" in 1965.

Here I'm wiping tears from my eyes on "Mickey Mantle Day" on June 8, 1969. That day was one of my greatest thrills.

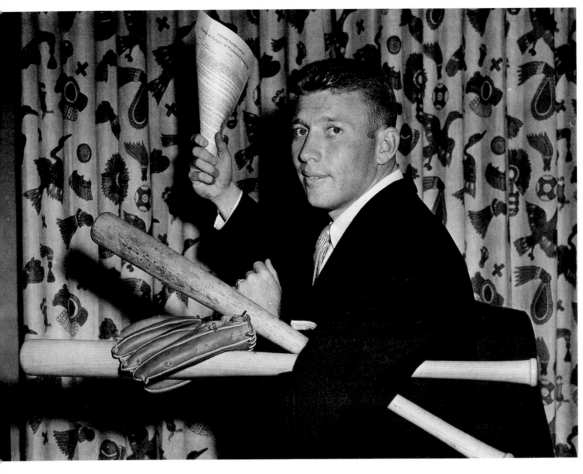

Here I am holding one of my contracts. People always ask me what I think I'd make if I were playing now.

Here I am in the locker room after a game. The press used to gather around my locker, particularly if I'd had a good game. It got really crowded sometimes. I tried to answer their questions. I mean, they were only doing their jobs.

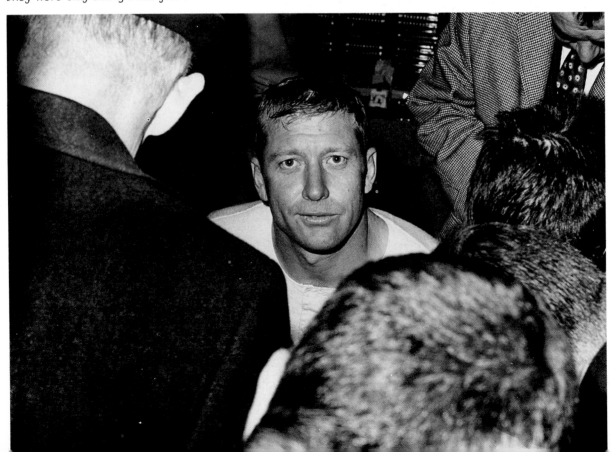

# If I Were Playing Now

Everybody says to me, "Mick, how much do you think you would make now if you were still playing?" I like what Joe DiMaggio said. He said he'd go up and knock on the door at Yankee Stadium. When George Steinbrenner opened the door he'd say, "Hi, pardner." I've always liked that.

Me and Rocky Colavito, the great hitter and outfielder. Rocky played for the Indians and the Tigers mostly, but he spent a little time with Kansas City, the White Sox, the Dodgers, and the Yankees. I think this was taken in 1966 or 1967. He hit 374 home runs in his career.

They held a press conference to announce my contract signing in 1962. You can see manager Ralph Houk to right of me and Howard Cosell sitting next to Ralph. Of course, Howard became famous when he went on "Monday Night Football" years later.

Sometimes it seems like I'm always
signing autographs. I'm not complaining,
but I really don't understand it.

Signing an autograph for Lee Remick and
her son after a game. A lot of celebrities
came by to visit with us and get
autographs.

# One More Autograph

*W*ell, I don't know for what reason, but for some reason or other I seem to be more popular now than I've ever been in my life. I don't know if it's the bubble gum card craze or what. But autograph seekers just seem to come from everywhere.

I know that my bubble gum card sells for thousands of dollars now. Nothing seems to stop 'em, you know.

Not too long ago, I remember they thought I was having a heart attack on an airplane. I had a real bad cold. It was almost like walking pneumonia or something — I could hardly breathe on the plane. I was getting a little scared myself, so I asked the stewardess, "What do you do if somebody has a heart attack?" She looked at me and she said, "My God, you better go sit down. I'll give you some oxygen."

They called the paramedics and they came to the door of the plane when it arrived in Dallas. I still had the oxygen on me that they had put on in the plane. They put me on a stretcher and put the thing in my nose and the oxygen on my face. They were pulling me out of there and some guy was standing outside the door. He yells "Hey, that's Mickey Mantle!" And he says, "Say Mick, would you sign this for me?" He had a piece of paper and pen for me to sign.

Well, they went ahead and took me to the hospital and checked me all over. The next day they gave me an angiogram (a heart test), to see how my heart was. It turned out I was okay, and I just had a very bad cold.

But I got to thinking about that guy wanting an autograph. I mean, as far as he knew, I was dying. I went to New York pretty soon after that, so I made up a story for the New York press.

I told them that I'd dreamed that night that I'd died and gone to heaven. I finally got in to see God and God said, "Well, Mick, I'm sorry, but we can't keep you up here because of the way you acted on Earth." But he said, "Would you do me a favor?" I said, "What's that, God?" He said "Before you go, would you sign those two dozen baseballs there for me?" And I thought that was really funny.

I've signed a lot of autographs for charity. Here I'm signing for St. Vincent's Hospital.

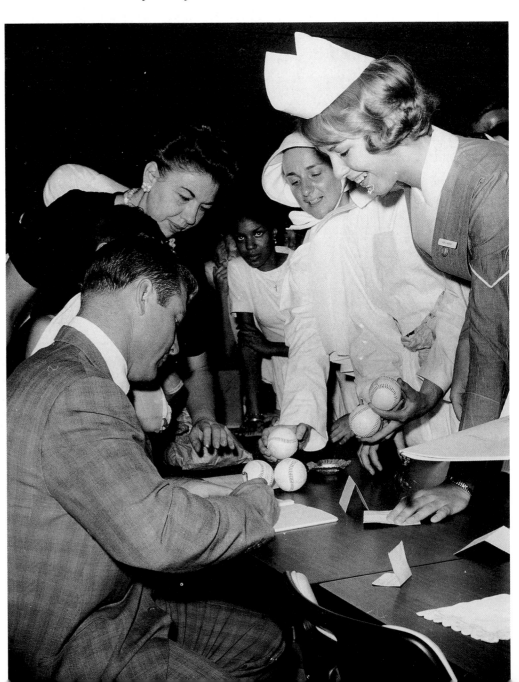

Here I'm signing autographs for some of the kids back in Oklahoma.

I think a lot of kids kind of felt about me the way I'd felt about Stan Musial when I was a kid. I never forgot that, so I always tried to make some time for them.

Posing with a Junior Fire Marshal during spring training in St. Petersburg in 1958.

# The Mick's Message to Kids

*W*ell, that's about it for now. I'd just like to finish up by saying to all you kids out there:

Stay away from drugs and alcohol. Go to school and listen to your teachers. And most of all listen to your moms and dads. You can be anything you want to be in this country of ours, and as good as you set your mind to be. Guys like Stan Musial, Willie Mays, Hank Aaron, all the guys that took care of themselves are up at the top in the stats of life now, not only in baseball. So be sure and take good care of yourselves and go out there and do it. Make us all proud of you.

I did a lot of different things for charity. Here I acted as referee for the Miss Teenage America Turtle Derby one year.

One of the few moments I've had to relax. Nowadays it seems as if I'm busier than I ever was. People seem to recognize me everywhere. Sometimes they don't, though.  Once I was flying in a jet, and we got into some bad weather. This was when the Yankees weren't doing too good. The pilot was a fan, so he took a break and came back to first class to meet me and talk to me. The plane was jumping around, so he got up to go back to the cabin. As he left he said to me, "Boy Mick, we could sure use you today." You know, talking about the Yankees. I guess the guy next to me didn't know me, because he looked at me and asked, "Are you a pilot, too?"

# — VIII —
## *Appendix*

# Lifetime Record

| Year | Club | League | Pos. | G. | AB. | R. | H. | 2B | 3B | HR. | RBI. | B.A. | PO. | A. | E. | F.A |
|------|------|--------|------|----|-----|----|----|----|----|----|----|------|----|----|----|-----|
| 1949 | Independence | K-O-M | SS | 89 | 323 | 54 | 101 | 15 | 7 | 7 | 63 | .313 | 121 | 245 | 47 | .886 |
| 1950 | Joplin | W.A. | SS | 137 | 519 | *141 | *199 | 30 | 12 | 26 | 136 | *.383 | 202 | 340 | 55 | .908 |
| 1951 | New York | Amer. | OF | 96 | 341 | 61 | 91 | 11 | 5 | 13 | 65 | .267 | 135 | 4 | 6 | .959 |
| 1951 | Kansas City | A.A. | OF | 40 | 166 | 32 | 60 | 9 | 3 | 11 | 50 | .361 | 110 | 4 | 4 | .966 |
| 1952 | New York | Amer. | OF-3B | 142 | 549 | 94 | 171 | 37 | 7 | 23 | 87 | .311 | 348 | 16 | *14 | .963 |
| 1953 | New York | Amer. | OF-SS | 127 | 461 | 105 | 136 | 24 | 3 | 21 | 92 | .295 | 322 | 10 | 6 | .982 |
| 1954 | New York | Amer. | OF-1F | 146 | 543 | *129 | 163 | 17 | 12 | 27 | 102 | .300 | 344 | *25 | 9 | .976 |
| 1955 | New York | Amer. | OF-SS | 147 | 517 | 121 | 158 | 25 | 11 | *37 | 99 | .306 | 376 | 11 | 2 | .995 |
| 1956 | New York | Amer. | OF | 150 | 533 | *132 | 188 | 22 | 5 | *52 | *130 | *.353 | 370 | 10 | 4 | .990 |
| 1957 | New York | Amer. | OF | 144 | 474 | *121 | 173 | 28 | 6 | 34 | 94 | .365 | 324 | 6 | 7 | .979 |
| 1958 | New York | Amer. | OF | 150 | 519 | *127 | 158 | 21 | 1 | *42 | 97 | .304 | 331 | 5 | 8 | .977 |
| 1959 | New York | Amer. | OF | 144 | 541 | 104 | 154 | 23 | 4 | 31 | 75 | .285 | 366 | 7 | 2 | *.995 |
| 1960 | New York | Amer. | OF | 153 | 527 | *119 | 145 | 17 | 6 | *40 | 94 | .275 | 326 | 9 | 3 | .991 |
| 1961 | New York | Amer. | OF | 153 | 514 | 132 | 163 | 16 | 6 | 54 | 128 | .317 | 351 | 6 | 6 | .983 |
| 1962 | New York | Amer. | OF | 123 | 377 | 96 | 121 | 15 | 1 | 30 | 89 | .321 | 214 | 4 | 5 | .978 |
| 1963 | New York | Amer. | OF | 65 | 172 | 40 | 54 | 8 | 0 | 15 | 35 | .314 | 99 | 2 | 1 | .990 |
| 1964 | New York | Amer. | OF | 143 | 465 | 92 | 141 | 25 | 2 | 35 | 111 | .303 | 217 | 3 | 5 | .978 |
| 1965 | New York | Amer. | OF | 122 | 361 | 44 | 92 | 12 | 1 | 19 | 46 | .255 | 165 | 3 | 6 | .966 |
| 1966 | New York | Amer. | OF | 108 | 333 | 40 | 96 | 12 | 1 | 23 | 56 | .288 | 172 | 2 | 0 | 1.000 |
| 1967 | New York | Amer. | 1B | 144 | 440 | 63 | 108 | 17 | 0 | 22 | 55 | .245 | 1089 | 91 | 8 | .993 |
| 1968 | New York | Amer. | 1B | 144 | 435 | 57 | 103 | 14 | 1 | 18 | 54 | .237 | 1195 | 76 | 15 | .988 |
| **Major League Totals** | | | | 2,401 | 8,102 | 1,677 | 2,415 | 344 | 72 | 536 | 1,509 | .298 | 6,734 | 290 | 107 | .984 |

*Denotes led league

# World Series Record

| Year | Club | League | Pos. | G. | AB. | R. | H. | 2B | 3B | HR. | RBI. | B.A. | PO. | A. | E. | F.A |
|------|------|--------|------|----|-----|----|----|----|----|-----|------|------|-----|----|----|-----|
| 1951 | New York | Amer. | OF | 2 | 5 | 1 | 1 | 0 | 0 | 0 | 0 | .200 | 4 | 0 | 0 | 1.000 |
| 1952 | New York | Amer. | OF | 7 | 29 | 5 | 10 | 1 | 1 | 2 | 3 | .345 | 16 | 0 | 0 | 1.000 |
| 1953 | New York | Amer. | OF | 6 | 24 | 3 | 5 | 0 | 0 | 2 | 7 | .208 | 14 | 0 | 0 | 1.000 |
| 1955 | New York | Amer. | OF-PH | 3 | 10 | 1 | 2 | 0 | 0 | 1 | 1 | .200 | 4 | 0 | 0 | 1.000 |
| 1956 | New York | Amer. | OF | 7 | 24 | 6 | 6 | 1 | 0 | 3 | 4 | .250 | 18 | 1 | 0 | 1.000 |
| 1957 | New York | Amer. | OF-PH | 6 | 19 | 3 | 5 | 0 | 0 | 1 | 2 | .263 | 8 | 0 | 1 | 1.000 |
| 1958 | New York | Amer. | OF | 7 | 24 | 4 | 6 | 0 | 1 | 2 | 3 | .250 | 16 | 0 | 1 | .889 |
| 1960 | New York | Amer. | OF | 7 | 25 | 8 | 10 | 1 | 0 | 3 | 11 | .400 | 15 | 0 | 0 | 1.000 |
| 1961 | New York | Amer. | OF | 2 | 6 | 0 | 1 | 0 | 0 | 0 | 0 | .167 | 2 | 0 | 0 | 1.000 |
| 1962 | New York | Amer. | OF | 7 | 25 | 2 | 3 | 1 | 0 | 0 | 0 | .120 | 11 | 0 | 0 | 1.000 |
| 1963 | New York | Amer. | OF | 4 | 15 | 1 | 2 | 0 | 0 | 1 | 1 | .133 | 6 | 0 | 0 | 1.000 |
| 1964 | New York | Amer. | OF | 7 | 24 | 8 | 8 | 2 | 0 | 3 | 8 | .333 | 12 | 0 | 2 | .857 |
| **World Series Totals** | | | | 65 | 230 | 42 | 59 | 6 | 2 | 18 | 40 | .257 | 126 | 1 | 3 | .977 |

# All Star Game Record

| Year | League | Pos. | AB. | R. | H. | 2B | 3B | HR. | RBI. | B.A. | PO. | A. | E. | F.A |
|------|--------|------|-----|----|----|----|----|-----|------|------|-----|----|----|-----|
| 1953 | American | OF | 2 | 0 | 0 | 0 | 0 | 0 | 0 | .000 | 0 | 0 | 0 | .000 |
| 1954 | American | OF | 5 | 1 | 2 | 0 | 0 | 0 | 0 | .400 | 2 | 0 | 0 | 1.000 |
| 1955 | American | OF | 6 | 1 | 2 | 0 | 0 | 1 | 3 | .333 | 3 | 0 | 0 | 1.000 |
| 1956 | American | OF | 4 | 1 | 1 | 0 | 0 | 1 | 1 | .250 | 0 | 0 | 0 | .000 |
| 1957 | American | OF | 4 | 1 | 1 | 0 | 0 | 0 | 0 | .250 | 4 | 0 | 0 | 1.000 |
| 1958 | American | OF | 2 | 0 | 1 | 0 | 0 | 0 | 0 | .500 | 3 | 0 | 0 | 1.000 |
| 1959 | American (both games) | OF | 3 | 0 | 1 | 0 | 0 | 0 | 0 | .333 | 3 | 0 | 0 | 1.000 |
| 1960 | American (both games) | OF | 4 | 0 | 1 | 0 | 0 | 0 | 0 | .250 | 5 | 0 | 0 | 1.000 |
| 1961 | American (both games) | OF | 6 | 0 | 0 | 0 | 0 | 0 | 0 | .000 | 5 | 0 | 0 | 1.000 |
| 1962 | American (first game) | OF | 1 | 0 | 0 | 0 | 0 | 0 | 0 | .000 | 0 | 0 | 0 | 1.000 |
| 1964 | American | OF | 4 | 1 | 1 | 0 | 0 | 0 | 0 | .250 | 2 | 0 | 0 | 1.000 |
| 1967 | American | PH | 1 | 0 | 0 | 0 | 0 | 0 | 0 | .000 | 0 | 0 | 0 | .000 |
| **All-Star Game Totals** | | | 42 | 5 | 10 | 0 | 0 | 2 | 4 | .238 | 27 | 0 | 0 | 1.000 |

# Records, Awards, and Achievements *(Partial List)*

## RECORDS *(When He Retired)*:

3rd Highest Career Home Run Total — *536*
Most Games as a Yankee — *2,401*
Most World Series Home Runs — *18*
Most World Series RBIs — *40*
Most World Series Runs — *42*
Most World Series Walks — *43*
Most Home Runs by Position, Career — *OF 496*
Most Home Runs by a Switch Hitter — *536*
Most Games with Switch Hit Home Runs in One Game — *10 (Total 21 HRs)*
Most Extra-Inning Home Runs, Career — *14*
Most Pitch Hit-Hit Home Runs, Career — *7*
Most Home Runs in Final Season — *1968: G 144; AB 435; HR 18*
Most Two Home Run Games — *46*
Longest Measured Home Run in Regular Season Major League Game (565 ft.) — *Griffith Stadium, Washington; April 17, 1953*
Home Runs in Most Consecutive At-Bats, AL (4) — *July 4, 1962 - 2; July 6, 1962 - 2*
Best Home Run Ratio, Career — *HR 536; AB 8102; Ratio 15.12*
Participating Player, Most Players (2) on a Team with 50 or More Home Runs (Single Season), AL — *NY Yankees, 1961: Roger Maris, 61; Mickey Mantle, 54*
Participating Player, Most Players (2) on a Team with 40 or More Home Runs (Single Season), AL — *NY Yankees, 1961: Roger Maris, 61; Mickey Mantle, 54*
Participating Player, Most Players (6) on a Team with 20 or More Home Runs (Single Season), AL — *NY Yankees, 1961: Roger Maris, 61; Mickey Mantle, 54; Bill Skowron, 28; Yogi Berra, 22; Elston Howard, 21; Johnny Blanchard, 21*
Participating Player, Team with Most Home Runs in a Game (7), AL — *NY Yankees, May 30, 1961: Mickey Mantle, 2; Roger Maris, 2; Bill Skowron, 2; Yogi Berra, 1*
Participating Player, Best Home Run Trio, Season, AL — *NY Yankees, 1961: Roger Maris, 61; Mickey Mantle, 54; Bill Skowron, 28; Total 153*
Participating Player, Best Home Run Duo, Season, AL — *NY Yankees, 1961: Roger Maris, 61; Mickey Mantle, 54; Total 115*
Participating Player, Team with Most Home Runs in a Single Season, AL — *NY Yankees, 1961: Total 240*

## AWARDS

Most Valuable Player — *1956, 1957, 1962*
AL Home Run Champion — *1955 (37), 1956 (52), 1958 (42), 1960 (40)*
AL Batting Champion — *1956 (.353)*

AL RBI Champion — *1956 (130)*
AL Slugging Champion — *1956 (.705), 1961 (.687)*
AL Runs Scored Champion — *1954 (129), 1956 (132), 1957 (121), 1958 (127), 1960 (119), 1961 (132)*
Triple Crown Winner — *1956 (52 HRs; .353 Avg.; 130 RBIs) (Led both leagues in each category)*
Hickok Belt Award Winner (Professional Athlete of the Year) - *1956*
Sultan of Swat Award Winner — *1956*
Sid Mercer Memorial Award Winner (Player of the Year) — *1957*
Hutch Award Winner (Baseball Writers of America) — *1965*
Mickey Mantle Day Proclamation, City of New York — *September 18, 1969*
Most Courageous Athlete Award (Philadelphia Sports Writers) — *1962*
Mickey Mantle Day, Yankee Stadium, New York — *September 9, 1965*
Mickey Mantle Day, Yankee Stadium, New York — *June 8, 1969*
Mickey Mantle Day, Commerce, Oklahoma — *1952*
Griggs Trophy (Oklahoma Athlete of the Year) — *1952*
Member, AL Champions — *1951, 1952, 1953, 1955, 1956, 1957, 1958, 1960, 1961, 1962, 1963, 1964*
Member, World Champions — *1951, 1952, 1953, 1956, 1958, 1961, 1962*
Number Retired, NY Yankees, AL — *#7, June 8, 1969*
Elected to Hall of Fame in First Year of Eligibility — *January 16, 1974*
Inducted into Hall of Fame — *August 12, 1974*


## ACHIEVEMENTS

Grand Slam Home Runs, AL (9) — *July 26, 1952; July 29, 1952; July 6, 1953; May 18, 1955; July 30, 1956; May 2, 1961; August 19, 1962; June 18, 1965; July 23, 1966*
World Series Grand Slam Home Runs (1) — *October 6, 1952*
Inside the Park Home Runs (6) — *August 7, 1953; May 9, 1958; May 20, 1958; June 5, 1958; May 12, 1959; June 30, 1961*
Home Runs in Both Games of Doubleheader (11) — *June 19, 1951; July 13, 1952; July 26, 1953; July 10, 1955; May 30, 1956; July 1, 1958; August 16, 1959; August 6, 1961; May 6, 1962; May 6, 1964; July 8, 1966 (Total 25 HRs)*
Back-to-Back Home Runs (With other players) — *39 times*
Pinch Hit Grand Slams, AL (1) — *July 6, 1953, Opponent: Philadelphia Athletics, Pitcher: Frank Fanovich*
Three Home Runs in One Game, AL — *May 13, 1955*
Participating Player, Three Consecutive Home Runs, AL — *June 29, 1966; 3rd Inning: Bobby Richardson, Mickey Mantle, Joe Pepitone*
Career High Season Batting Average — *1957 (.365)*
First Major League Home Run — *May 1, 1951; Left-handed*
Last Major League Home Run — *#536, September 20, 1968; Left-handed*
More Walks than Hits, Season, AL — *1962: BB 122, H 121, BA .321; 1968: BB 106, H 103, BA .237*
Most Combined Hits and Walks, Season, AL — *1956: H 188, BB 122, Total 300; 1957: H 173, BB 146, Total 319*
Career Spent with One Team  — *NY Yankees, 18 years*
Most Home Runs Hit Against (Team) — *1. Washington Senators (80); 2. Detroit Tigers (74); 3. Chicago White Sox (73); 4. Boston Red Sox (69); 5. Cleveland Indians (64)*
Most Home Runs Hit Against (Pitcher) — *1. Early Wynn (13); 2. Pedro Ramos (12); 3. Camilo Pascual (11); 4. Frank Lary (9); 5. (Tie) Chuck Stobbs, Dick Donovan, Billy Pierce, Gary Bell (8)*

# *Home Runs*

### Mickey Mantle's 536 Regular Season Home Runs

**1951**

1.  May 1, 1951,  Comiskey Park vs. Chicago White Sox
2.  May 4, 1951, Sportsman's Park vs.  St. Louis Browns
3.  May 13, 1951, Shibe Park vs. Philadelphia A's
4.  May 16, 1951, Yankee Stadium vs. Cleveland Indians
5.  June 19, 1951, Yankee Stadium vs. Chicago White Sox
6.  June 19, 1951, Yankee Stadium vs. Chicago White Sox
7.  July 7, 1951, Fenway Park vs.  Boston Red Sox
8.  August 25, 1951, Municipal Stadium vs. Cleveland Indians
9.  August 29, 1951, Sportsman's Park vs. St. Louis Browns
10.  September 8, 1951, Yankee Stadium vs. Washington Senators
11.  September 9, 1951, Yankee Stadium vs. Washington Senators
12.  September 12, 1951, Yankee Stadium vs. Detroit Tigers
13.  September 19, 1951, Yankee Stadium vs. Chicago White Sox

**1952**

14.  April 21, 1952, Yankee Stadium vs. Philadelphia A's
15.  April 30, 1952, Yankee Stadium vs. St. Louis Browns
16.  May 30, 1952, Yankee Stadium vs. Philadelphia A's
17.  June 15, 1952, Municipal Stadium vs. Cleveland Indians
18.  June 17, 1952, Briggs Stadium vs. Detroit Tigers
19.  June 22, 1952, Comiskey Park vs. Chicago White Sox
20.  June 27, 1952, Yankee Stadium vs. Philadelphia A's
21.  July 5, 1952, Shibe Park vs. Philadelphia A's
22.  July 6, 1952, Shibe Park vs. Philadelphia A's
23.  July 13, 1952,  Yankee Stadium vs. Detroit Tigers
24.  July 13, 1952, Yankee Stadium vs. Detroit Tigers
25.  July 15, 1952, Yankee Stadium vs. Cleveland Indians
26.  July 17, 1952 Yankee Stadium vs. Cleveland Indians
27.  July 25, 1952, Briggs Stadium vs. Detroit Tigers
28.  July 26, 1952, Briggs Stadium vs. Detroit Tigers
29.  July 29, 1952, Comiskey Park vs. Chicago White Sox
30.  August 11, 1952, Yankee Stadium vs. Boston Red Sox
31.  August 11, 1952, Yankee Stadium vs. Boston Red Sox
32.  August 30, 1952, Yankee Stadium vs. Washington Senators
33.  September 14, 1952, Municipal Stadium vs. Cleveland Indians
34.  September 17, 1952, Briggs Stadium vs. Detroit Tigers
35.  September 24, 1952, Fenway Park vs. Boston Red Sox
36.  September 26, 1952,  Shibe Park vs. Philadelphia A's

**1953**

37.  April 17, 1953, Griffith Stadium vs. Washington Senators
38.  April 23, 1953, Yankee Stadium vs. Boston Red Sox

39.　April 28, 1953, Busch Stadium vs. St. Louis Browns
40.　April 30, 1953, Comiskey Park vs. Chicago White Sox
41.　May 9, 1953, Fenway Park vs. Boston Red Sox
42.　May 25, 1953, Yankee Stadium vs. Boston Red Sox
43.　June 4, 1953, Comiskey Park vs. Chicago White Sox
44.　June 5, 1953, Busch Stadium vs. St. Louis Browns
45.　June 11, 1953,  Briggs Stadium vs. Detroit Tigers
46.　June 18, 1953, Yankee Stadium vs. St. Louis Browns
47.　June 21, 1953, Yankee Stadium vs. Detroit Tigers
48.　June 23, 1953, Yankee Stadium vs. Chicago White Sox
49.　July 16, 1953, Connie Mack Stadium vs. Philadelphia A's
50.　July 26, 1953, Briggs Stadium vs. Detroit Tigers
51.　July 26, 1953, Briggs Stadium vs. Detroit Tigers
52.　August 7, 1953, Yankee Stadium vs. Chicago White Sox
53.　September 1, 1953, Comiskey Park vs. Chicago White Sox
54.　September 7, 1953, Fenway Park vs. Boston Red Sox
55.　September 9, 1953, Yankee Stadium vs. Chicago White Sox
56.　September 12, 1953, Yankee Stadium vs. Detroit Tigers
57.　September 20, 1953, Fenway Park vs. Boston Red Sox

**1954**

58.　April 19, 1954, Fenway Park vs. Boston Red Sox
59.　April 21, 1954, Yankee Stadium vs. Boston Red Sox
60.　May 7, 1954, Yankee Stadium vs. Philadelphia A's
61.　May 21, 1954, Yankee Stadium vs. Boston Red Sox
62.　May 22, 1954, Yankee Stadium vs. Boston Red Sox
63.　May 23, 1954, Yankee Stadium vs. Boston Red Sox
64.　May 25, 1954, Griffith Stadium vs. Washington Senators
65.　May 29, 1954, Fenway Park vs. Boston Red Sox
66.　May 30, 1954, Fenway Park vs. Boston Red Sox
67.　June 6, 1954, Yankee Stadium vs. Baltimore Orioles
68.　June 10, 1954, Yankee Stadium vs. Detroit Tigers
69.　June 20, 1954, Comiskey Park vs. Chicago White Sox
70.　June 26, 1954, Municipal Stadium vs. Cleveland Indians
71.　June 30, 1954, Fenway Park vs. Boston Red Sox
72.　July 1, 1954, Fenway Park vs. Boston Red Sox
73.　July 3, 1954, Yankee Stadium vs. Washington Senators
74.　July 5, 1954, Connie Mack Stadium vs. Philadelphia A's
75.　July 7, 1954, Yankee Stadium vs. Boston Red Sox
76.　July 19, 1954, Yankee Stadium vs. Detroit Tigers
77.　July 22, 1954, Yankee Stadium vs. Chicago White Sox
78.　July 28, 1954, Comiskey Park vs. Chicago White Sox
79.　August 5, 1954, Municipal Stadium vs. Cleveland Indians
80.　August 5, 1954, Municipal Stadium vs. Cleveland Indians
81.　August 8, 1954, Briggs Stadiums vs. Detroit Tigers
82.　August 12, 1954, Yankee Stadium vs. Philadelphia A's
83.　August 15, 1954, Yankee Stadium vs. Boston Red Sox
84.　September 2, 1954, Yankee Stadium vs. Cleveland Indians

**1955**

85.　April 13, 1955, Yankee Stadium vs. Washington Senators
86.　April 18, 1955,  Memorial Stadium vs. Baltimore Orioles
87.　April 28, 1955, Municipal Stadium vs. Kansas City A's
88.　May 3, 1955, Municipal Stadium vs. Cleveland Indians
89.　May 6, 1955, Fenway Park vs. Boston Red Sox
90.　May 7, 1955, Fenway Park vs. Boston Red Sox
91.　May 11, 1955, Yankee Stadium vs. Cleveland Indians

92.    May 13, 1955, Yankee Stadium vs. Detroit Tigers
93.    May 13, 1955, Yankee Stadium vs. Detroit Tigers
94.    May 13, 1955, Yankee Stadium vs. Detroit Tigers
95.    May 18, 1955, Yankee Stadium vs. Chicago White Sox
96.    June 3, 1955, Comiskey Park vs. Chicago White Sox
97.    June 5, 1955, Comiskey Park vs. Chicago White Sox
98.    June 6, 1955, Briggs Stadium vs. Detroit Tigers
99.    June 17, 1955, Yankee Stadium vs. Chicago White Sox
100.   June 19, 1955, Yankee Stadium vs. Chicago White Sox
101.   June 21, 1955, Yankee Stadium vs. Kansas City A's
102.   June 22, 1955, Yankee Stadium vs. Kansas City A's
103.   July 10, 1955, Griffith Stadium vs. Washington Senators
104.   July 10, 1955, Griffith Stadium vs. Washington Senators
105.   July 10, 1955, Griffith Stadium vs. Washington Senators
106.   July 28, 1955, Yankee Stadium vs. Chicago White Sox
107.   July 31, 1955, Yankee Stadium vs. Kansas City A's
108.   August 4, 1955, Yankee Stadium vs. Cleveland Indians
109.   August 7, 1955, Yankee Stadium vs. Detroit Tigers
110.   August 7, 1955, Yankee Stadium vs. Detroit Tigers
111.   August 14, 1955, Memorial Stadium vs. Baltimore Orioles
112.   August 15, 1955, Memorial Stadium vs. Baltimore Orioles
113.   August 15, 1955, Memorial Stadium vs. Baltimore Orioles
114.   August 16, 1955, Fenway Park vs. Boston Red Sox
115.   August 19, 1955, Yankee Stadium vs. Baltimore Orioles
116.   August 21, 1955, Yankee Stadium vs. Baltimore Orioles
117.   August 24, 1955, Briggs Stadium vs. Detroit Tigers
118.   August 28, 1955, Comiskey Park vs. Chicago White Sox
119.   August 31, 1955, Municipal Stadium vs. Kansas City A's
120.   September 2, 1955, Yankee Stadium vs. Washington Senators
121.   September 4, 1955, Yankee Stadium vs. Washington Senators

**1956**
122.   April 17, 1956, Griffith Stadium vs. Washington Senators
123.   April 17, 1956, Griffith Stadium vs. Washington Senators
124.   April 20, 1956, Yankee Stadium vs. Boston Red Sox
125.   April 21, 1956, Yankee Stadium vs. Boston Red Sox
126.   May 1 1956, Yankee Stadium vs. Detroit Tigers
127.   May 2, 1956, Yankee Stadium vs. Detroit Tigers
128.   May 3, 1956, Yankee Stadium vs. Kansas City A's
129.   May 5, 1956, Yankee Stadium vs. Kansas City A's
130.   May 5, 1956, Yankee Stadium vs. Kansas City A's
131.   May 8, 1956, Yankee Stadium vs. Cleveland Indians
132.   May 10, 1956, Yankee Stadium vs. Cleveland Indians
133.   May 14, 1956, Municipal Stadium vs. Cleveland Indians
134.   May 16, 1956, Municipal Stadium vs. Cleveland Indians
135.   May 18, 1956, Comiskey Park vs. Chicago White Sox
136.   May 18, 1956, Comiskey Park vs. Chicago White Sox
137.   May 21, 1956, Municipal Stadium vs. Kansas City A's
138.   May 24, 1956, Briggs Stadium vs. Detroit Tigers
139.   May 29, 1956, Yankee Stadium vs. Boston Red Sox
140.   May 30, 1956, Yankee Stadium vs. Washington Senators
141.   May 30, 1956, Yankee Stadium vs. Washington Senators
142.   June 5, 1956, Yankee Stadium vs. Kansas City A's
143.   June 14, 1956, Yankee Stadium vs. Chicago White Sox
144.   June 15, 1956, Municipal Stadium vs. Cleveland Indians
145.   June 16, 1956, Municipal Stadium vs. Cleveland Indians
146.   June 18, 1956, Briggs Stadium vs. Detroit Tigers

147.  June 20, 1956, Briggs Stadium  vs. Detroit Tigers
148.  June 20, 1956, Briggs Stadium vs. Detroit Tigers
149.  July 1, 1956, Yankee Stadium vs. Washington Senators
150.  July 1, 1956, Yankee Stadium vs. Washington Senators
151.  July 14, 1956, Yankee Stadium vs. Cleveland Indians
152.  July 18, 1956, Yankee Stadium vs. Detroit Tigers
153.  July 22, 1956, Yankee Stadium vs. Kansas City A's
154.  July 30, 1956, Municipal Stadium vs. Cleveland Indians
155.  July 30, 1956, Municipal Stadium vs.  Cleveland Indians
156.  August 4, 1956, Briggs Stadium vs. Detroit Tigers
157.  August 4, 1956, Briggs Stadium vs. Detroit Tigers
158.  August 5, 1956, Briggs Stadium vs. Detroit Tigers
159.  August 8, 1956, Griffith Stadium vs. Washington Senators
160.  August 9, 1956, Griffith Stadium vs. Washington Senators
161.  August 11, 1956, Yankee Stadium vs. Baltimore Orioles
162.  August 12, 1956, Yankee Stadium vs. Baltimore Orioles
163.  August 14, 1956, Yankee Stadium vs. Boston Red Sox
164.  August 23, 1956, Yankee Stadium vs. Chicago White Sox
165.  August 25, 1956, Yankee Stadium vs. Chicago White Sox
166.  August 28, 1956, Yankee Stadium vs. Kansas City A's
167.  August 29, 1956, Yankee Stadium vs. Kansas City A's
168.  August 31, 1956, Griffith Stadium vs. Washington Senators
169.  September 13, 1956, Municipal Stadium vs. Kansas City A's
170.  September 16, 1956, Municipal Stadium vs. Cleveland Indians
171.  September 18, 1956, Comiskey Park vs. Chicago White Sox
172.  September 21, 1956, Fenway Park vs. Boston Red Sox
173.  September 28, 1956, Yankee Stadium vs. Boston Red Sox

**1957**
174.  April 22, 1957, Griffith Stadium vs. Washington Senators
175.  April 24, 1957, Yankee Stadium vs. Baltimore Orioles
176.  May 5, 1957, Comiskey Park vs. Chicago White Sox
177.  May 8, 1957, Municipal Stadium vs. Cleveland Indians
178.  May 12, 1957, Memorial Stadium vs. Baltimore Orioles
179.  May 16, 1957, Yankee Stadium vs. Kansas City A's
180.  May 19, 1957, Yankee Stadium vs. Cleveland Indians
181.  May 25, 1957, Yankee Stadium vs. Washington Senators
182.  May 26, 1957, Yankee Stadium vs. Washington Senators
183.  May 29, 1957, Griffith Stadium vs. Washington Senators
184.  June 2, 1957, Yankee Stadium vs. Baltimore Orioles
185.  June 5, 1957, Municipal Stadium vs. Cleveland Indians
186.  June 6, 1957, Municipal Stadium vs. Cleveland  Indians
187.  June 7, 1957, Briggs Stadium vs.  Detroit Tigers
188.  June 10, 1957, Briggs Stadium vs. Detroit Tigers
189.  June 11, 1957, Comiskey Park vs. Chicago White Sox
190.  June 12, 1957, Comiskey Park vs. Chicago White Sox
191.  June 12, 1957, Comiskey Park vs. Chicago White Sox
192.  June 14, 1957, Municipal Stadium vs. Kansas City A's
193.  June 22, 1957, Yankee Stadium vs. Chicago White Sox
194.  June 23, 1957, Yankee Stadium vs. Chicago White Sox
195.  July 1, 1957, Memorial Stadium vs. Baltimore Orioles
196.  July 11, 1957, Municipal Stadium vs. Kansas City A's
197.  July 12, 1957, Municipal Stadium vs. Kansas City A's
198.  July 21, 1957, Municipal Stadium vs. Kansas City A's
199.  July 23, 1957, Yankee Stadium vs. Chicago White Sox
200.  July 26, 1957, Yankee Stadium vs. Detroit Tigers
201.  July 31, 1957, Yankee Stadium vs. Kansas City A's

202. August 2, 1957, Yankee Stadium vs. Cleveland Indians
203. August 7, 1957, Yankee Stadium vs. Washington Senators
204. August 10, 1957, Memorial Stadium vs. Baltimore Orioles
205. August 13, 1957, Fenway Park vs. Boston Red Sox
206. August 26, 1957, Briggs Stadium vs. Detroit Tigers
207. August 30, 1957, Yankee Stadium vs. Washington Senators

**1958**
208. April 17, 1958, Fenway Park vs. Boston Red Sox
209. May 9, 1958, Yankee Stadium vs. Washington Senators
210. May 18, 1958, Griffith Stadium vs. Washington Senators
211. May 20, 1958, Comiskey Park vs. Chicago White Sox
212. June 2, 1958, Yankee Stadium vs. Chicago White Sox
213. June 3, 1958, Yankee Stadium vs. Chicago White Sox
214. June 4, 1958, Yankee Stadium vs. Chicago White Sox
215. June 5, 1958, Yankee Stadium vs. Chicago White Sox
216. June 6, 1958, Yankee Stadium vs. Cleveland Indians
217. June 6, 1958, Yankee Stadium vs. Cleveland Indians
218. June 8, 1958, Yankee Stadium vs. Cleveland Indians
219. June 13, 1958, Yankee Stadium vs. Detroit Tigers
220. June 24, 1958, Comiskey Park vs. Chicago White Sox
221. June 29, 1958, Municipal Stadium vs. Kansas City A's
222. July 1, 1958, Memorial Stadium vs. Baltimore Orioles
223. July 1, 1958, Memorial Stadium vs. Baltimore Orioles
224. July 3, 1958, Griffith Stadium vs. Washington Senators
225. July 3, 1958, Griffith Stadium vs. Washington Senators
226. July 4, 1958, Griffith Stadium vs. Washington Senators
227. July 5, 1958, Yankee Stadium vs. Boston Red Sox
228. July 6, 1958, Yankee Stadium vs. Boston Red Sox
229. July 11, 1958, Yankee Stadium vs. Cleveland Indians
230. July 14, 1958, Yankee Stadium vs. Chicago White Sox
231. July 15, 1958, Yankee Stadium vs. Detroit Tigers
232. July 23, 1958, Briggs Stadium vs. Detroit Tigers
233. July 24, 1958, Briggs Stadium vs. Detroit Tigers
234. July 28, 1958, Municipal Stadium vs. Kansas City A's
235. July 28, 1958, Municipal Stadium vs. Kansas City A's
236. August 4, 1958, Memorial Stadium vs. Baltimore Orioles
237. August 5, 1958, Memorial Stadium vs. Baltimore Orioles
238. August 9, 1958, Yankee Stadium vs. Boston Red Sox
239. August 11, 1958, Yankee Stadium vs. Baltimore Orioles
240. August 12, 1958, Yankee Stadium vs. Baltimore Orioles
241. August 16, 1958, Fenway Park vs. Boston Red Sox
242. August 17, 1958, Fenway Park vs. Boston Red Sox
243. August 22, 1958, Yankee Stadium vs. Chicago White Sox
244. August 27, 1958, Yankee Stadium vs. Kansas City A's
245. September 2, 1958, Yankee Stadium vs. Boston Red Sox
246. September 3, 1958, Yankee Stadium vs. Boston Red Sox
247. September 9, 1958, Municipal Stadium vs. Cleveland Indians
248. September 17, 1958, Briggs Stadium vs. Detroit Tigers
249. September 24, 1958, Fenway Park vs. Boston Red Sox

**1959**
250. April 21, 1959, Griffith Stadium vs. Washington Senators
251. April 23, 1959, Griffith Stadium vs. Washington Senators
252. April 29, 1959, Comiskey Park vs. Chicago White Sox
253. May 10, 1959, Yankee Stadium vs. Washington Senators
254. May 12, 1959, Yankee Stadium vs. Cleveland Indians

255.   May 20, 1959, Yankee Stadium vs. Detroit Tigers
256.   May 23, 1959, Memorial Stadium vs. Baltimore Orioles
257.   May 24, 1959, Memorial Stadium vs. Baltimore Orioles
258.   May 30, 1959, Griffith Stadium vs. Washington Senators
259.   June 3, 1959, Briggs Stadium vs. Detroit Tigers
260.   June 9, 1959, Yankee Stadium vs. Kansas City A's
261.   June 11, 1959, Yankee Stadium vs. Kansas City A's
262.   June 13, 1959, Yankee Stadium vs. Detroit Tigers
263.   June 17, 1959, Yankee Stadium vs. Chicago White Sox
264.   June 18, 1959, Yankee Stadium vs. Chicago White Sox
265.   June 22, 1959, Municipal Stadium vs. Kansas City A's
266.   June 22, 1959, Municipal Stadium vs. Kansas City A's
267.   June 23, 1959, Municipal Stadium vs. Kansas City A's
268.   July 16, 1959, Yankee Stadium vs. Cleveland Indians
269.   July 19, 1959, Yankee Stadium vs. Chicago White Sox
270.   August 4, 1959, Yankee Stadium vs. Detroit Tigers
271.   August 5, 1959, Yankee Stadium vs. Detroit Tigers
272.   August 16, 1959, Yankee Stadium vs. Boston Red Sox
273.   August 16, 1959, Yankee Stadium vs. Boston Red Sox
274.   August 26, 1959, Municipal Stadium vs. Cleveland Indians
275.   August 29, 1959, Griffith Stadium vs. Washington Senators
276.   September 7, 1959, Fenway Park vs. Boston Red Sox
277.   September 10, 1959, Yankee Stadium vs. Kansas City A's
278.   September 13, 1959, Yankee Stadium vs. Cleveland Indians
279.   September 15, 1959, Yankee Stadium vs. Chicago White Sox
280.   September 15, 1959, Yankee Stadium vs. Chicago White Sox

**1960**
281.   April 22, 1960, Yankee Stadium vs. Baltimore Orioles
282.   May 13, 1960, Griffith Stadium vs. Washington Senators
283.   May 17, 1960, Municipal Stadium vs. Cleveland Indians
284.   May 20, 1960, Comiskey Park vs. Chicago White Sox
285.   May 29, 1960, Yankee Stadium vs. Washington Senators
286.   May 29, 1960, Yankee Stadium vs. Washington Senators
287.   June 1, 1960, Memorial Stadium vs. Baltimore Orioles
288.   June 5, 1960, Yankee Stadium vs. Boston Red Sox
289.   June 8, 1960, Yankee Stadium vs. Chicago White Sox
290.   June 8, 1960, Yankee Stadium vs. Chicago White Sox
291.   June 9, 1960, Yankee Stadium vs. Chicago White Sox
292.   June 10, 1960, Yankee Stadium vs. Cleveland Indians
293.   June 17, 1960, Comiskey Park vs. Chicago White Sox
294.   June 18, 1960, Comiskey Park vs. Chicago White Sox
295.   June 21, 1960, Briggs Stadium vs. Detroit Tigers
296.   June 21, 1960, Briggs Stadium vs. Detroit Tigers
297.   June 28, 1960, Yankee Stadium vs. Kansas City A's
298.   June 30, 1960, Yankee Stadium vs. Kansas City A's
299.   July 3, 1960, Yankee Stadium vs. Detroit Tigers
300.   July 4, 1960, Griffith Stadium vs. Washington Senators
301.   July 15, 1960, Briggs Stadium vs. Detroit Tigers
302.   July 18, 1960, Municipal Stadium vs. Cleveland Indians
303.   July 20, 1960, Municipal Stadium vs. Cleveland Indians
304.   July 24, 1960, Yankee Stadium vs. Chicago White Sox
305.   July 26, 1960, Yankee Stadium vs. Cleveland Indians
306.   July 28, 1960, Yankee Stadium vs. Cleveland Indians
307.   July 31, 1960, Yankee Stadium vs. Kansas City A's
308.   August 15, 1960, Yankee Stadium vs. Baltimore Orioles
309.   August 15, 1960, Yankee Stadium vs. Baltimore Orioles

310. August 26, 1960, Yankee Stadium vs. Cleveland Indians
311. August 28, 1960, Yankee Stadium vs. Detroit Tigers
312. September 6, 1960, Yankee Stadium vs. Boston Red Sox
313. September 10, 1960, Briggs Stadium vs. Detroit Tigers
314. September 11, 1960, Municipal Stadium vs. Cleveland Indians
315. September 17, 1960, Yankee Stadium vs. Baltimore Orioles
316. September 20, 1960, Yankee Stadium vs. Washington Senators
317. September 21, 1960, Yankee Stadium vs. Washington Senators
318. September 24, 1960, Fenway Park vs. Boston Red Sox
319. September 28, 1960, Griffith Stadium vs. Washington Senators
320. September 28, 1960, Griffith Stadium vs. Washington Senators

**1961**

321. April 17, 1961, Yankee Stadium vs. Kansas City A's
322. April 20, 1961, Yankee Stadium vs. Los Angeles Angels
323. April 20, 1961, Yankee Stadium vs. Los Angeles Angels
324. April 21, 1961, Memorial Stadium vs. Baltimore Orioles
325. April 23, 1961, Memorial Stadium vs. Baltimore Orioles
326. April 26, 1961, Tiger Stadium vs. Detroit Tigers
327. April 26, 1961, Tiger Stadium vs. Detroit Tigers
328. May 2, 1961, Metropolitan Stadium vs. Minnesota Twins
329. May 4, 1961, Metropolitan Stadium vs. Minnesota Twins
330. May 16, 1961, Yankee Stadium vs. Washington Senators
331. May 29, 1961, Fenway Park vs. Boston Red Sox
332. May 30, 1961, Fenway Park vs. Boston Red Sox
333. May 30, 1961, Fenway Park vs. Boston Red Sox
334. May 31, 1961, Fenway Park vs. Boston Red Sox
335. June 5, 1961, Yankee Stadium vs. Minnesota Twins
336. June 9, 1961, Yankee Stadium vs. Kansas City A's
337. June 10, 1961, Yankee Stadium vs. Kansas City A's
338. June 11, 1961, Yankee Stadium vs. Los Angeles Angels
339. June 15, 1961, Municipal Stadium vs. Cleveland Indians
340. June 17, 1961, Tiger Stadium vs. Detroit Tigers
341. June 21, 1961, Municipal Stadium vs. Kansas City A's
342. June 21, 1961, Municipal Stadium vs. Kansas City A's
343. June 26, 1961, Wrigley Field vs. Los Angeles Angels
344. June 28, 1961, Wrigley Field vs. Los Angeles Angels
345. June 30, 1961, Yankee Stadium vs. Washington Senators
346. July 1, 1961, Yankee Stadium vs. Washington Senators
347. July 1, 1961, Yankee Stadium vs. Washington Senators
348. July 2, 1961, Yankee Stadium vs. Washington Senators
349. July 8, 1961, Yankee Stadium vs. Boston Red Sox
350. July 13, 1961, Comiskey Park vs. Chicago White Sox
351. July 14, 1961, Comiskey Park vs. Chicago White Sox
352. July 16, 1961, Memorial Stadium vs. Baltimore Orioles
353. July 17, 1961, Memorial Stadium vs. Baltimore Orioles
354. July 18, 1961, Griffith Stadium vs. Washington Senators
355. July 18, 1961, Griffith Stadium vs. Washington Senators
356. July 19, 1961, Griffith Stadium vs. Washington Senators
357. July 21, 1961, Fenway Park vs. Boston Red Sox
358. July 25, 1961, Yankee Stadium vs. Chicago White Sox
359. July 26, 1961, Yankee Stadium vs. Chicago White Sox
360. August 2, 1961, Yankee Stadium vs. Kansas City A's
361. August 6, 1961, Yankee Stadium vs. Minnesota Twins
362. August 6, 1961, Yankee Stadium vs. Minnesota Twins
363. August 6, 1961, Yankee Stadium vs. Minnesota Twins
364. August 11, 1961, Yankee Stadium vs. Washington Senators

365. August 13, 1961, Griffith Stadium vs. Washington Senators
366. August 20, 1961, Municipal Stadium vs. Cleveland Indians
367. August 30, 1961, Metropolitan Stadium vs. Minnesota Twins
368. August 31, 1961, Metropolitan Stadium vs. Minnesota Twins
369. September 3, 1961, Yankee Stadium vs. Detroit Tigers
370. September 3, 1961, Yankee Stadium vs. Detroit Tigers
371. September 5, 1961, Yankee Stadium vs. Washington Senators
372. September 8, 1961, Yankee Stadium vs. Cleveland Indians
373. September 10, 1961, Yankee Stadium vs. Cleveland Indians
374. September 23, 1961, Fenway Park vs. Boston Red Sox

**1962**

375. April 10, 1962, Yankee Stadium vs. Baltimore Orioles
376. April 19, 1962, Memorial Stadium vs. Baltimore Orioles
377. May 5, 1962, Yankee Stadium vs. Washington Senators
378. May 6, 1962, Yankee Stadium vs. Washington Senators
379. May 6, 1962, Yankee Stadium vs. Washington Senators
380. May 6, 1962, Yankee Stadium vs. Washington Senators
381. May 12, 1962, Municipal Stadium vs. Cleveland Indians
382. June 16, 1962, Municipal Stadium vs. Cleveland Indians
383. June 23, 1962, Tiger Stadium vs. Detroit Tigers
384. June 28, 1962, Yankee Stadium vs. Minnesota Twins
385. July 2, 1962, Yankee Stadium vs. Kansas City A's
386. July 3, 1962, Yankee Stadium vs. Kansas City A's
387. July 3, 1962, Yankee Stadium vs. Kansas City A's
388. July 4, 1962, Yankee Stadium vs. Kansas City A's
389. July 4, 1962, Yankee Stadium vs. Kansas City A's
390. July 6, 1962, Metropolitan Stadium vs. Minnesota Twins
391. July 6, 1962, Metropolitan Stadium vs. Minnesota Twins
392. July 18, 1962, Fenway Park vs. Boston Red Sox
393. July 20, 1962, Yankee Stadium vs. Washington Senators
394. July 25, 1962, Yankee Stadium vs. Boston Red Sox
395. July 28, 1962, Yankee Stadium vs. Chicago White Sox
396. August 17, 1962, Municipal Stadium vs. Kansas City A's
397. August 18, 1962, Municipal Stadium vs. Kansas City A's
398. August 19, 1962, Municipal Stadium vs. Kansas City A's
399. August 28, 1962, Yankee Stadium vs. Cleveland Indians
400. September 10, 1962, Tiger Stadium vs. Detroit Tigers
401. September 12, 1962, Municipal Stadium vs. Cleveland Indians
402. September 18, 1962, D.C. Stadium vs. Washington Senators
403. September 18, 1962, D.C. Stadium vs. Washington Senators
404. September 30, 1962, Yankee Stadium vs. Chicago White Sox

**1963**

405. April 10, 1963, Municipal Stadium vs. Kansas City A's
406. April 11, 1963, Yankee Stadium vs. Baltimore Orioles
407. May 4, 1963, Metropolitan Stadium vs. Minnesota Twins
408. May 6, 1963, Tiger Stadium vs. Detroit Tigers
409. May 11, 1963, Memorial Stadium vs. Baltimore Orioles
410. May 15, 1963, Yankee Stadium vs. Minnesota Twins
411. May 21, 1963, Yankee Stadium vs. Kansas City A's
412. May 21, 1963, Yankee Stadium vs. Kansas City A's
413. May 22, 1963, Yankee Stadium vs. Kansas City A's
414. May 26, 1963, Yankee Stadium vs. Washington Senators
415. June 4, 1963, Memorial Stadium vs. Baltimore Orioles
416. August 4, 1963, Yankee Stadium vs. Baltimore Orioles
417. September 1, 1963, Memorial Stadium vs. Baltimore Orioles

418. September 11, 1963, Municipal Stadium vs. Kansas City A's
419. September 21, 1963, Yankee Stadium vs. Kansas City A's

**1964**
420. May 6, 1964, D.C. Stadium vs. Washington Senators
421. May 6, 1964, D.C. Stadium vs. Washington Senators
422. May 8, 1964, Municipal Stadium vs. Cleveland Indians
423. May 9, 1964, Municipal Stadium vs. Cleveland Indians
424. May 16, 1964, Yankee Stadium vs. Kansas City A's
425. May 17, 1964, Yankee Stadium vs. Kansas City A's
426. May 23, 1964, Yankee Stadium vs. Los Angeles Angels
427. May 24, 1964, Yankee Stadium vs. Los Angeles Angels
428. June 11, 1964, Fenway Park vs. Boston Red Sox
429. June 11, 1964, Fenway Park vs. Boston Red Sox
430. June 13, 1964, Yankee Stadium vs. Chicago White Sox
431. June 17, 1964, Yankee Stadium vs. Boston Red Sox
432. June 21, 1964, Comiskey Park vs. Chicago White Sox
433. June 23, 1964, Memorial Stadium vs. Baltimore Orioles
434. June 27, 1964, Yankee Stadium vs. Detroit Tigers
435. July 1, 1964, Yankee Stadium vs. Kansas City A's
436. July 4, 1964, Yankee Stadium vs. Minnesota Twins
437. July 13, 1964, Municipal Stadium vs. Cleveland Indians
438. July 24, 1964, Tiger Stadium vs. Detroit Tigers
439. July 28, 1964, Chavez Ravine vs. Los Angeles Angels
440. August 1, 1964, Metropolitan Stadium vs. Minnesota Twins
441. August 4, 1964, Municipal Stadium vs. Kansas City A's
442. August 11, 1964, Yankee Stadium vs. Chicago White Sox
443. August 12, 1964, Yankee Stadium vs. Chicago White Sox
444. August 12, 1964, Yankee Stadium vs. Chicago White Sox
445. August 22, 1964, Fenway Park vs. Boston Red Sox
446. August 23, 1964, Fenway Park vs. Boston Red Sox
447. August 29, 1964, Yankee Stadium vs. Boston Red Sox
448. September 4, 1964, Municipal Stadium vs. Kansas City A's
449. September 5, 1964, Municipal Stadium vs. Kansas City A's
450. September 17, 1964, Yankee Stadium vs. Los Angeles Angels
451. September 19, 1964, Yankee Stadium vs. Kansas City A's
452. September 22, 1964, Municipal Stadium vs. Cleveland Indians
453. September 27, 1964, D.C. Stadium vs. Washington Senators
454. September 30, 1964, Yankee Stadium vs. Detroit Tigers

**1965**
455. April 17, 1965, Municipal Stadium vs. Kansas City A's
456. April 18, 1965, Municipal Stadium vs. Kansas City A's
457. April 21, 1965, Yankee Stadium vs. Minnesota Twins
458. April 25, 1965, Yankee Stadium vs. Los Angeles Angels
459. May 10, 1965, Fenway Park vs. Boston Red Sox
460. May 11, 1965, Fenway Park vs. Boston Red Sox
461. May 15, 1965, Memorial Stadium vs. Baltimore Orioles
462. May 30, 1965, Comiskey Park vs. Chicago White Sox
463. June 5, 1965, Yankee Stadium vs. Chicago White Sox
464. June 18, 1965, Yankee Stadium vs. Minnesota Twins
465. June 22, 1965, Yankee Stadium vs. Kansas City A's
466. July 15, 1965, Yankee Stadium vs. Washington Senators
467. July 25, 1965, Municipal Stadium vs. Cleveland Indians
468. August 6, 1965, Tiger Stadium vs. Detroit Tigers
469. August 7, 1965, Tiger Stadium vs. Detroit Tigers
470. August 10, 1965, Yankee Stadium vs. Minnesota Twins

471.  August 18, 1965, Yankee Stadium vs. Los Angeles Angels
472.  September 2, 1965, Chavez Ravine vs. Los Angeles Angels
473.  September 4, 1965, Yankee Stadium vs. Boston Red Sox

**1966**
474.  May 9, 1966, Metropolitan Stadium vs. Minnesota Twins
475.  May 14, 1966, Municipal Stadium vs. Kansas City A's
476.  May 25, 1966, Yankee Stadium vs. California Angels
477.  May 25, 1966, Yankee Stadium vs. California Angels
478.  June 1, 1966, Comiskey Park vs. Chicago White Sox
479.  June 16, 1966, Yankee Stadium vs. Cleveland Indians
480.  June 23, 1966, Yankee Stadium vs. Baltimore Orioles
481.  June 28, 1966, Fenway Park vs. Boston Red Sox
482.  June 28, 1966, Fenway Park vs. Boston Red Sox
483.  June 29, 1966, Fenway Park vs. Boston Red Sox
484.  June 29, 1966, Fenway Park vs. Boston Red Sox
485.  July 1, 1966, D.C. Stadium vs. Washington Senators
486.  July 2, 1966, D.C. Stadium vs. Washington Senators
487.  July 2, 1966, D.C. Stadium vs. Washington Senators
488.  July 3, 1966, D.C. Stadium vs. Washington Senators
489.  July 7, 1966, Yankee Stadium vs. Boston Red Sox
490.  July 8, 1966, Yankee Stadium vs. Washington Senators
491.  July 8, 1966, Yankee Stadium vs. Washington Senators
492.  July 23, 1966, Yankee Stadium vs. California Angels
493.  July 24, 1966, Yankee Stadium vs. California Angels
494.  July 29, 1966, Comiskey Park vs. Chicago White Sox
495.  August 14, 1966, Yankee Stadium vs. Cleveland Indians
496.  August 26, 1966, Yankee Stadium vs. Detroit Tigers

**1967**
497.  April 29, 1967, Yankee Stadium vs. California Angels
498.  April 30, 1967, Yankee Stadium vs. California Angels
499.  May 3, 1967, Metropolitan Stadium vs. Minnesota Twins
500.  May 14, 1967, Yankee Stadium vs. Baltimore Orioles
501.  May 17, 1967, Yankee Stadium vs. Cleveland Indians
502.  May 19, 1967, Tiger Stadium vs. Detroit Tigers
503.  May 20, 1967, Tiger Stadium vs. Detroit Tigers
504.  May 21, 1967, Tiger Stadium vs. Detroit Tigers
505.  May 24, 1967, Memorial Stadium vs. Baltimore Orioles
506.  May 27, 1967, Municipal Stadium vs. Cleveland Indians
507.  May 28, 1967, Municipal Stadium vs. Cleveland Indians
508.  June 5, 1967, Yankee Stadium vs. Washington Senators
509.  June 15, 1967, D.C. Stadium vs. Washington Senators
510.  June 24, 1967, Yankee Stadium vs. Detroit Tigers
511.  July 4, 1967, Metropolitan Stadium vs. Minnesota Twins
512.  July 4, 1967, Metropolitan Stadium vs. Minnesota Twins
513.  July 16, 1967, Yankee Stadium vs. Baltimore Orioles
514.  July 22, 1967, Tiger Stadium vs. Detroit Tigers
515.  July 25, 1967, Yankee Stadium vs. Minnesota Twins
516.  August 7, 1967, Anaheim Stadium vs. California Angels
517.  September 2, 1967, Yankee Stadium vs. Washington Senators
518.  September 3, 1967, Yankee Stadium vs. Washington Senators

**1968**
519.  April 18, 1968, Anaheim Stadium vs. California Angels
520.  April 24, 1968, Oakland Coliseum vs. Oakland A's
521.  April 26, 1968, Yankee Stadium vs. Detroit Tigers

522. May 6, 1968, Yankee Stadium vs. Cleveland Indians
523. May 30, 1968, Yankee Stadium vs. Washington Senators
524. May 30, 1968, Yankee Stadium vs. Washington Senators
525. June 7, 1968, Yankee Stadium vs. California Angels
526. June 11, 1968, Yankee Stadium vs. Chicago White Sox
527. June 16, 1968, Anaheim Stadium vs. California Angels
528. June 22, 1968, Metropolitan Stadium vs. Minnesota Twins
529. June 29, 1968, Yankee Stadium vs. Oakland A's
530. August 10, 1968, Yankee Stadium vs. Minnesota Twins
531. August 10, 1968, Yankee Stadium vs. Minnesota Twins
532. August 12, 1968, Anaheim Stadium vs. California Angels
533. August 15, 1968, Oakland Coliseum vs. Oakland A's
534. August 22, 1968, Metropolitan Stadium vs. Minnesota Twins
535. September 19, 1968, Tiger Stadium vs. Detroit Tigers
536. September 20, 1968, Yankee Stadium vs. Boston Red Sox

Total: Left-handed - 372, right-handed - 164


## WORLD SERIES HOME RUNS

1. October 6, 1952, Ebbets Field vs. Brooklyn Dodgers
2. October 7, 1952, Ebbets Field vs. Brooklyn Dodgers
3. October 1, 1953, Yankee Stadium vs. Brooklyn Dodgers
4. October 4, 1953, Ebbets Field vs. Brooklyn Dodgers
5. September 30, 1955, Ebbets Field vs. Brooklyn Dodgers
6. October 3, 1956, Ebbets Field vs. Brooklyn Dodgers
7. October 7, 1956, Yankee Stadium vs. Brooklyn Dodgers
8. October 8, 1956, Yankee Stadium vs. Brooklyn Dodgers
9. October 5, 1957, County Stadium vs. Milwaukee Braves
10. October 2, 1958, County Stadium vs. Milwaukee Braves
11. October 2, 1958, County Stadium vs. Milwaukee Braves
12. October 6, 1960, Forbes Field vs. Pittsburgh Pirates
13. October 6, 1960, Forbes Field vs. Pittsburgh Pirates
14. October 8, 1960, Yankee Stadium vs. Pittsburgh Pirates
15. October 6, 1963, Dodger Stadium vs. Los Angeles Dodgers
16. October 10, 1964, Yankee Stadium vs. St. Louis Cardinals
17. October 14, 1964, Busch Stadium vs. St. Louis Cardinals
18. October 15, 1964, Busch Stadium vs. St. Louis Cardinals

Total: Left-handed - 10, right-handed - 8


## ALL STAR GAME HOME RUNS

1. July 22, 1955, County Stadium, Milwaukee - Pitcher Robin Roberts
2. July 10, 1956, Griffith Stadium, Washington - Pitcher Warren Spahn

Total: Left-handed - 1, right-handed - 1

# ★ ★ ★ ★  Available on Video  ★ ★ ★ ★

**MICKEY MANTLE: The American Dream *Comes to Life*®** — The Original Award-Winning Public Television Videography™ Program Special.  The Mick tells his favorite stories, copiously illustrated with rare archival footage and original artist music by Roy Orbison, Hank Williams, The Coasters, Chuck Berry, and Chubby Checker.  From Casey Stengel and Joe DiMaggio to the Triple Crown in 1956 and the 1961 Home Run Race with Roger Maris, Mickey shares it all.  Includes the famous "Billy Martin Shot a Cow" story.  A must for all baseball fans!

Here's what they're saying about **MICKEY MANTLE: The American Dream *Comes to Life*®**:

---

*The Boston Globe:* "A gem. . . riveting and captivating. . . the best."

*Video Review:* "★★★★ — A home run with the bases loaded."

*The Washington Post:* "Baseball fans should always be this lucky. . . Memorable, delightful and entertaining . .  A thoroughly enjoyable show.  Even non-sports fans will love it."

*USA Today:* "Captures the essence of Mantle. . . the autobiography of the future. . . Interesting and funny. . . one of the very best."

*The Los Angeles Times:* "Exceptionally well done.  It evokes a period of time in baseball's not-too-distant past that is well worth remembering. . .  Mantle is at his finest, and his stories are both humorous and touching."

*The Los Angeles Daily News:* "Captivating. . . worth watching again and again.  It reminds the viewer of how great baseball can be."

*The San Francisco Chronicle:* "Wonderful!  The footage is rare and the interviews are revealing.

*Newsday:* "A hit! Its unique format is a big plus.  A must see."

*The Philadelphia Inquirer:* "Even a Yankee hater will love it."

*The New York Daily News:* "Touching and hilarious.  You can't help but love this program.  The best sports profile ever."

---

Only $29.95 plus $4.50 shipping and handling.  Use the attached order form or
## call 1-800-THE MICK.
(VISA and MasterCard accepted)

# ★ ★ ★ ★  Available on Video  ★ ★ ★ ★

**Also in the *Comes to Life*® Videography™ Program Series**

**JOHN MADDEN: The American Dream *Comes to Life*®**, the second program in this award-winning series.  The Coach recounts stories from his 10-year term as Head Coach of the Oakland Raiders, the inside story of winning Superbowl XI, plus a guided tour of "The Bus," hosting *Saturday Night Live,* and his hilarious Eddie Murphy "Buckwheat" impersonation, his appearance in Paul Simon's "Me & Julio" music video, and much more.

Here's what they're saying about **JOHN MADDEN: The American Dream *Comes to Life*®**:

*The Washington Post:* "A dream video. . . Madden is entertaining and at times outlandish . . . priceless.  More, please!"

*USA Today:* "The cutting edge in video.  The Madden program succeeds where many other sports programs fail. . . Maintains the high standards of (this) series."

*The San Francisco Chronicle:* "One of the great videos. . . priceless.  May even be better than (the Mantle) program, if that's possible."

*The Sacramento Bee:* "60 delightful minutes. . . A must."

*The Baltimore Evening Sun:* "A smash.  Terrific film and tape."

*The San Francisco Examiner:* "Lots of good highlights and the ol' coach is pretty adept at spinning stories.  You'll enjoy (it)."

*The Houston Chronicle:* "Hilarious."

*The Associated Press:* "Entertaining.  That's Madden."

*The Oakland Tribune:* "Madden really makes you feel at home during this program.  One of the best off-the-cuff chats you'll ever hear. . . This is one great video!"

*The New York Daily News:* "Another great program.  These guys (Rothgeb & Hall) really know what they're doing.  Don't miss it!"

Only $29.95 plus $4.50 shipping and handling.  Use the attached order form or
## call 1-800-THE MICK.
(VISA and MasterCard accepted)

# ★ ★ ★ ★  Exclusive Offer!  ★ ★ ★ ★

Fine quality 100% cotton, heavyweight T-shirts and sweatshirts with pocket logo on front and original 4-color design on back.

## T-SHIRTS ONLY $15.95 EACH!

## SWEATSHIRTS ONLY $25.95 EACH!

BACK

FRONT

## OR CALL:
## 1-800-THE MICK
(1-800-843-6425)

- - - - - - - - - - - - - - - - - - - - - - - - - - - - - - - - - - - - - - - - - - - - -

| ITEM | PRICE | QTY | SIZE | POSTAGE | TOTAL |
|------|-------|-----|------|---------|-------|
| T-SHIRT | $15.95 | | | $4.50 | |
| SWEATSHIRT | $25.95 | | | per | |
| MICKEY MANTLE VIDEO | $29.95 | | ███ | item | |
| JOHN MADDEN VIDEO | $29.95 | | ███ | | |
| SIZES:  L • XL • (XXL add $3.00) | | | | TOTAL $ | |

NAME _____     ❏ CHECK    ❏ VISA    ❏ MASTERCARD

ADDRESS _____     CARD. NO. _____

CITY/STATE/ZIP _____     EXP. DATE _____

PHONE _____     SIGNATURE _____

To order send checks payable to The Ark Company, 911 W. Moana Lane, Reno, NV 89509
Please allow 6-8 weeks for delivery. NO P.O. BOXES PLEASE.

M031593205

MANTLE, MICKEY, 1931-
MICKEY MANTLE: THE AMERICAN DREAM COMES TO LIFE.
796.357 M259 MANTLE

Q

CHESTER

CHESTERFIELD COUNTY (VA) PUBLIC LIBRARY

## Chapter 13—Personality     218

# USING THE AP TEACHER MANUAL

This AP Teacher Manual is designed to help you plan for teaching AP Psychology. The elements included in each chapter are suggestions on how to encourage your students to engage with the course content. While the activities presented are by no means exhaustive, they provide a launch point for you to tailor the course to your own classroom.

Our activities are designed with diverse classrooms in mind. Some activities may work better for larger or smaller classes. In all cases, we have tried to ensure that the resources we suggest are widely available at no cost. We hope that this will ensure that all students, regardless of institutional resources, will be able to access these assets.

*Understanding Psychology* is divided first into chapters and then into modules. Each chapter opener provides a short chapter introduction with some main points and guidance on tying this chapter to previous chapters. **AP Essential Questions** help ground each chapter in the AP Course and Exam Description. From there, module outlines provide **AP Learning Targets and Pacing,** which will help you decide how much classroom time to spend on each.

Each module begins with a **Module Summary.** This is a narrative summary of the information that will allow you to quickly orient yourself to each module. The module summary also contains important terminology and concepts that will appear throughout the module.

**AP Key Terms** highlights terminology that students should master in order to prepare for the AP Psychology exam. These terms will also indicate important concepts to master. Some modules also include **AP Key People,** which emphasizes important figures in psychology that students should know before taking the AP Psychology exam.

**Class Discussion Ideas** provide a series of potential discussion topics for students. The suggestions are broadly based, giving you, the AP teacher, a range of options for engaging students on relevant topics in each module.

**Activities** are a series of lessons you could use in order to cover the module material. Students will grow in their ability to interpret research, demonstrate concept knowledge, and increase understanding of how psychological concepts are connected, all of which are tested by the AP Exam.

**Discussion Questions** in most modules provide further opportunities for real-world application of AP Psychology concepts. **Polling Questions** afford another perspective from which to approach these questions, and encourage full-class participation.

**Suggested Media** provide a selection of potential examples of psychological concepts through television, film, and online video resources. While you will want to screen any of these you're considering in order to determine their appropriateness for your classroom, these suggestions provide inspiration for further student engagement. **Additional Readings** provide you with peer-reviewed reading suggestions in order to deepen your subject knowledge.

**AP Student Edition Answer Key** provides a guide for teachers to assess student performance on key questions.

- **Applying Psychology in the 21st Century** is featured once in each chapter, and this AP edition includes questions designed to give students further practice answering AP exam-style questions;

- **Neuroscience in Your Life** is another feature included once per chapter, and is accompanied in the AP edition by questions styled after those on the AP exam;

- **AP Test Practice** provides you with the ability to assess students' knowledge retention in each module, but also to give quick and consistent feedback to students about their preparation for the AP Psychology Exam.

# ABOUT THE AP PSYCHOLOGY COURSE AND EXAM

Welcome to the life-changing study and teaching of *Understanding Psychology*!

In 2019 the College Board made some changes to the Advanced Placement Psychology course and content has been updated to better align with recent developments in the field and to better prepare students for the AP Exam. The course introduces students to the applied and scientific study of human behavior and mental processes. The new College Board Course and Exam Description (CED) provides detailed unit guides with clearly outlined topics, leaving the guesswork of what to cover behind. By familiarizing yourself with the new course framework, you can better prepare your students for success.

The new course framework includes two essential components: course skills and course content. The course skills are central to the study and practice of psychology. Students should develop and apply the described skills on a regular basis over the span of the course.

## Course Framework Components

### COURSE SKILLS

**Skill Category 1: Concept Understanding** Define, explain, and apply concepts, behavior, theories, and perspectives.

- 1.A: Define and/or apply concepts.
- 1.B: Explain behavior in authentic context.
- 1.C: Apply theories and perspectives in authentic contexts.

**Skill Category 2: Data Analysis** Analyze and interpret quantitative data.

**Skill Category 3: Scientific Investigation** Analyze psychological research studies.

### COURSE CONTENT

The course content is now organized into a total of nine units of study that provide a suggested sequence for the course content. Each unit is divided into teachable segments called topics. The topic pages contain the required content for each topic. The changes to the course are quite minimal but noticeable nonetheless.

- Unit 2: Biological Bases of Behavior now includes sleep and dreaming; hypnosis is no longer included.
- Unit 5: Cognitive Psychology now includes intelligence.
- Unit 7: Motivation, Emotion, and Personality—though not apparent by the title of the unit—still requires that students understand and be able to explain the role of stress on the individual. It also includes the study of personality.
- Unit 8: Clinical Psychology now comprises the combination of disorders and the treatment of those disorders.

# Course at a Glance

| Units of Study | Weight on the AP Psychology Exam | *Understanding Psychology* Feldman 14th ed. |
|---|---|---|
| I. Scientific Foundations of Psychology | 10–14% | 14th ed. Chapters 1, 2 |
| II. Biological Bases of Behavior | 8–10% | 14th ed. Chapters 3, 5 |
| III. Sensation and Perception | 6–8% | 14th ed. Chapter 4 |
| IV. Learning | 7–9% | 14th ed. Chapter 6 |
| V. Cognitive Psychology | 13–17% | 14th ed. Chapters 7, 8, 9 |
| VI. Developmental Psychology | 7–9% | 14th ed. Chapter 12 |
| VII. Motivation, Emotion, and Personality | 11–15% | 14th ed. Chapters 10, 11, 13, 14 |
| VIII. Clinical Psychology | 12–16% | 14th ed. Chapters 15, 16 |
| IX. Social Psychology | 8–10% | 14th ed. Chapters 11, 17 |

The breakdown of these units, along with their weight on the AP Exam and corresponding chapters in *Understanding Psychology*, are shown above. If this is your first year teaching the course, organizing the course this way will benefit not only you but also your students. Once you have a feel for teaching the course, units can easily be taught out of the suggested sequence. Make sure to visit College Board's AP Classroom for detailed unit guides, progress checks, and updates to the course!

## Instructional Approaches to the teaching of AP Psychology

Regardless of experience, the place to start is with your calendar. The AP Psychology Exam has traditionally been the first Monday of the test period (check AP Central). Start there and work backward. Use the recommended pacing guide to assist you with this task. Leave about two weeks before the test for intense review and reserve a few days for practice exams. You'll also find a helpful sample syllabus in the front of this manual, and suggestions for timing in each unit. The unit structure respects new AP teachers' time by providing one possible sequence they can adopt or modify rather than having to build from scratch. Keep in mind that the AP Psychology course can be taught in myriad ways, it all depends on the students and communities you serve.

Setting up this calendar will do three things:

1. It will keep you on track. There are some units in psychology that we love to teach and you could easily spend 2 weeks or more teaching if you had time. Stick with the calendar and you will not have to cram in content in April to finish.

2. A calendar will show you at-a-glance when students may be overwhelmed by school wide events, i.e state testing, spirit week, holiday's, etc., and help you to avoid giving a unit test during a busy time.

3. By posting the calendar on your class website, you will help your students stay on track, plan ahead, and know what do to if they miss class.

# Preparing for the AP Psychology Exam

After preparing your own calendar for the year, the next step is to block out time for practicing the Multiple-Choice and Free-Response sections of the exam. Even though you are working with bright students, many of them have never had contact with these types of testing. There are specific phrases ("Evaluate the extent to which . . .") and specific question formats to which students will need to be exposed. You should attempt to have the students work on the application of concepts as often as possible. You can find complete tests and scoring information at AP Central as well as in practice test banks through McGraw-Hill's online resources. There are also practice tests included at the end of each module in the student edition, and a full practice exam at the end of the textbook. The sample essays on the College Board site for all the FRQs (Free Response Questions) allow you and your students to get a good sense of what a strong response should be.

As for the time frames, there are now nine units—each one accounting for a specified percentage of the test. You can find the new CED (Course and Exam Description) at AP Central for a more detailed overview. If you follow the CED and let the units and specified topics guide your teaching, your students will be ready for the test. Remember that the key for excelling on the test is concept understanding and application.

The AP Psychology Exam is 2 hours long. There are two sections to the AP Psychology Exam: a multiple-choice section and a free-response section.

| Section | Question Type | Number of Questions | Timing | Percentage of Total Exam Score |
|---------|--------------|---------------------|--------|-------------------------------|
| I | Multiple-choice questions | 100 | 70 minutes | 66.7% |
| II | Free-response questions | 2<br>Question 1: Concept Application (7 points)<br>Question 2: Research Design (7 points) | 50 minutes | 33.3% |

## Understanding the Format

### MULTIPLE-CHOICE QUESTIONS

There are 100 multiple-choice questions with five answer choices (A–E). Only one answer is correct for each question, and there is no penalty for guessing incorrectly, so encourage students to answer every question even if they don't know the answer or feel uncertain. Students are given 70 minutes to complete this section. All three skill categories are assessed in the multiple-choice section of the AP Exam with the following weighting:

- Skill Category 1: Concept Understanding      75–80%
- Skill Category 2: Data Analysis      8–12%
- Skill Category 3: Scientific Investigation      12–16%

### FREE-RESPONSE QUESTIONS

The free-response section of the Exam includes two questions closely aligned with the course skills that must be answered within 50 minutes (roughly 25 minutes for each question). In question 1: Concept Application, Skill Category 1 is being assessed by students' demonstrating their ability to explain behavior and apply theories and perspectives to authentic contexts. In question 2: Research Design, all three skill categories are being assessed with greater emphasis being placed on Skill Category 3. Students are expected to demonstrate their ability to analyze psychological research studies, including analyzing and interpreting quantitative data.

There will be a plenty of space for students to answer each question. However, student answers must be contained, and no credit will be given for writing outside of the specified area. Student answers must be in complete sentences; bulleted answers will not receive credit which may confuse students since often, the question itself contains bullet points. Make sure students know not to use them in their answers. A thesis statement is not required, and students can separate the response to each part of the question by skipping a line in the examination booklet. Students must be extremely careful to follow the directions and explicitly answer the question they are asked. You can help your students be better prepared for the written portion by incorporating practice FRQ sessions into your course.

When practicing the FRQ for Question 1: Concept Application, have students establish the habit of writing the concept along with its definition. The question rarely asks for the definition, but often a student's response will not score without it. Then, make sure students apply the concept to the situation stated in the question. A good response to each concept usually spans from 3 to 5 sentences in length. Then, have students skip a line or two on their paper before addressing the second concept/bullet. Skipping a line makes it easy for them to insert additional thoughts when reviewing their response, and it makes it easier for the AP Reader to follow and award scores! The same practice should be applied for Question 2 when necessary.

The following is a list of task verbs commonly used in free-response questions: construct/ draw, define, describe, draw a conclusion, explain, and identify/state. It will be helpful to students to have them practice these throughout the year.

# SAMPLE AP PSYCHOLOGY COURSE PLANNER

Schedule will ONLY be adjusted if there are consecutive (ex: more than two "A/B" days) district school closure days.

| Units of Study | Multiple-Choice Coverage on the AP Psychology Exam | Readings | Pacing Guide |
|---|---|---|---|
| I. History & Approaches | 2–4% | 14th ed. Modules #1–3 | Week 1 (August 12–16th) |
| II. Cognition (Memory, Thinking & Language) | 8–10% | 14th ed. Mods. #20–22 & #23–25 | Weeks 2–4 (August 19–Sept. 4th) |
| III. Learning | 7–9% | 14th ed. Mods. #17–19 | Weeks 4–6 (Sept 4–18th) |
| IV. Biological (Nervous System & Brain) | 8–10% | 14th ed. Mods. #7–9 | Weeks 6–9 (Sept 18–Oct. 10th) |
| States of Consciousness | | 14th ed. Mods. #14–16 | |
| V. Testing & Individual Differences (I.Q.) | 5–7% | 14th ed. Mods. #26–28 | Weeks 11–12 (Oct. 21–29th) |
| VI. Sensation & Perception (5 Senses) | 6–8% | 14th ed. Mods. #10–13 | Weeks 12–14 (Oct. 29–Nov. 15th) |
| VII. Development Psychology | 7–9% | 14th ed. Mods. #35–39 | Weeks 15–17 (Nov. 19–Dec. 4th) |
| VIII. Personality | 5–7% | 14th ed. Mods. #40–42 | Weeks 17–19 (Dec. 4–16th) |
| 1st Semester Final *NO test corrections | Cumulative 100 Ques. M/C *NO FRQ | Units #1–8 | |
| IX. M.E.S.H. (Motivation, Emotion, Stress & Health) | 6–8% | 14th ed. Mods. #29–31, 33–34 & 43–45 | Weeks 22–26 (Jan. 7–Feb. 3rd) |
| X. Clinical Psychology | 12–16% | 14th ed. Mods. #46–51 | Weeks 26–30 (Feb. 3rd–Mar. 4th) |
| XI. Social Psychology | 8–10% | 14th ed. Mods. #32, 52–55 | Week 30–33 (Mar. 6–Mar. 25th) |
| XII. Research Methods | 8–10% | 14th ed. Mods. #4–6 | Weeks 33–35 (Mar. 25th–April 8th) |
| 2nd Semester Final | **May 1st** = The final will be cumulative and provide you with a snapshot of what you need to study for the national exam. You will have 70 minutes to answer 100 questions. Worth no more than 20% of your semester grade. There will be no test corrections. The FRQ portion will be during the week of May 4th. | | |

| **Exam Review** (Weeks 33–40) | We will have 5 Days in class to review however it is expected that you are spending time outside of class to review several weeks prior to exam! |
|---|---|
| | ➢ April 15th = Practice Timed M/C (May change) |
| | ➢ April 10th = Practice Timed FRQs (May change) |
| | *AP Psychology exam May 12th, check-in @ 11:00.  Bring a pencil (not mechanical), blue/black ink pen and eraser. |

**AP Exam Format:**

- 100 Multiple Choice Questions
    - 70 minutes
    - 2/3 of total score
    - No guessing penalty!
- 2 Free Response Questions using concepts from any of the 12 topics listed above.
    - 50 minutes (25 minutes per question)
    - Write in paragraphs and complete sentences. NO BULLETS!!
    - Be specific
        - Example If you write "try harder" = doesn't score = too vague. But, "studying two extra hours" = does score.
    - Use the proper psych. vocabulary
    - Underline psych. vocabulary
    - Apply to problem/case study/question presented.
    - Follow the Term, Definition, Application format!

# SAMPLE AP PSYCHOLOGY SYLLABUS

## COURSE DESCRIPTION

The AP Psychology course is a college level <u>survey</u> course designed to introduce students to the systematic and scientific study of the behavior and mental processes of human beings and animals. Students are exposed to the psychological facts, principles and phenomena associated with each of the major subfields within psychology. They also learn about the methods psychologists use in their science and practice. The course is structured to help students obtain and/or strengthen the necessary skills needed to be successful in a college level course. Therefore, assigned reading from the textbook and required note taking will be the expectation nearly every night.

<u>Goals:</u> Students will study human behavior and processes using the scientific method. They will also think critically about psychological claims and studies. Students will learn about psychology at the college level in order to take the AP exam ($97) in May. Students must have organizational, note taking, test taking and study skills all of which will lead to successful completion of the course and the passing of the AP exam which may result in earning college credit (3-4 credits).

## COURSE MATERIALS

Required Text: Feldman, Robert S. (2019). Understanding Psychology (14$^{th}$ ed.) New York: McGraw-Hill Education.

Limited # Available for Check-out: <u>Barron's How to Prepare for the AP Psychology Exam</u> <u>(any edition)</u>

- 3 ring binder (2–2.5")
- Dividers = total of 15
- Index (vocab) Cards
- Pencil Case to submit vocabulary cards
- Highlighters – At least 6
- Colored Pencils/Markers (optional)
- Textbook Cover–JUMBO size
- Loose Leaf Notebook Paper

## GRADES

The 1$^{st}$ & 2$^{nd}$ semester final exam will be worth no more than 20% of your semester grade. Everything else is considered to reflect a "performance" grade for the class. Below are the topics I will use in the gradebook to distinguish between the various forms of "performance."

| | The school grading scale will be followed: |
|---|---|
| **20%** – HW (projects, vocab. cards, textbook notes) | A  90–100% |
| **20%** – Binder Check (lecture note-taking guides, supplemental handouts) | B  80–89% |
| **40%** – Assessments (unit tests, quizzes, FRQs) | C  70–79% |
| | D  60–69% |
| **20%** – Final Exam | F  59–* |

## COURSE SCOPE AND SEQUENCE

- Independent and group projects will be assigned throughout the year.
- There will be 12-unit exams consisting of 50 multiple choice & 1 Free Response Question.
- Course binder, unit vocabulary cards and textbook notes will be collected for a final grade on the day of each unit exam.
- Test corrections can be done on each unit test allowing you the opportunity to recover 1 point of the 2 points assigned for each question that is missed.
- For every unit a homework schedule will be provided. This schedule is reflecting the College Board learning targets, when each module should be read and textbook notes

should be taken, the vocabulary that is required to make flashcards, and when the unit quizzes & test are scheduled to take place.

- The units of study are as follows:
  - History & Research Methods
  - Cognitive Psychology
  - Biological Bases of Behavior
  - Sensation & Perception
  - Learning
  - Testing & Individual Differences
  - Developmental Psychology
  - Motivation, Emotion & Stress
  - Personality
  - Clinical Psychology
  - Social Psychology
- Please see the attached course planner.

## EXTRA CREDIT

➢ May be earned by devoting a free period to the ILC classrooms working with our special needs students. Please see me for additional details and requirements.

➢ May be earned by listening to and completing the assignment on the selected psychology podcast. Please see me for specifics.

➢ May be earned by reading an article and/or book from the approved list of titles. Please see me for specifics.

➢ No extra credit can be received if you have missing assignments in the gradebook.

➢ All extra credit will be weighted the same as homework (20%)

➢ No more than 50 points of extra credit can be earned in a semester.

## SOME OTHER NUGGETS OF INFORMATION

### ✓ All Year:

By maintaining a "B" or better on each unit test, I will grant you the opportunity to take notes using a format that works best for you! Of course, I will continue to collect them on desigated due dates.

### ✓ 2nd–4th Quarters:

Earn a "B" or better on each unit test 1st quarter AND earning an "A" in the class will grant you the opportunity to exempt yourself from either textbook notes or vocabulary cards.

## THE PURPOSE OF TAKING AN AP (*ADVANCED PLACEMENT*) COURSE

"Most colleges and universities in the U.S., as well as colleges and universities in 21 other countries, have an AP policy granting incoming students credit, placement, or both on the basis of their AP Exam grades. Many of these institutions grant up to a full year of college credit (sophomore standing) to students who earn a sufficient number of qualifying AP grades..." (excerpt from AP Psychology *Course Description*)

## OUR COMMITMENT TO THE AP CURRICULUM & TEST

We are in this together. You have my promise that I will do everything possible to prepare you for the AP test. However, your success is entirely up to YOU!!! You must have the **endurance & motivation** to **WANT** to do well. This is a college-level course that will move at a college-level pace; nevertheless, your success is my priority and expectation. As a teacher, and student, I've learned a few things about preparing for tests and I will share with you the tools that I have learned and maintained. I expect everyone to take the AP exam in May (spend $91 now or thousands later). Taking the exam is an excellent prep for what is to come in the future. Why take an AP class and work as hard as I expect you to, if you're not going to take the test? **We will take 2 practice multiple choice AP exams and your second semester final will be a released AP practice test. What about FRQs? By taking all 3, you should have a clear understanding of what you need to do for the AP test.**

CHAPTER **1**
# Introduction to Psychology

## **AP** Introduction

The teaching of psychology is a fascinating, life changing experience (at least it has been for me). This chapter introduces you to the beginnings of psychology and how the science and field of psychology continue to change. The teaching of pre-scientific thought has been eliminated and greater emphasis should be placed on the theoretical approaches in explaining human behavior.

## **AP** Essential Questions

- How does the methodology of the research affect the outcome of a study?
- How do ethical guidelines impact psychological research?

## Module 1: Psychologists at Work

**AP Learning Targets:**

- Distinguish the different domains of psychology
- Describe and compare different theoretical approaches in explaining behavior.

**Pacing:**

½ Block or 1 Traditional Class Period

## Module 2: A Science Evolves: The Past, the Present, and the Future

**AP Learning Targets:**

- Recognize how philosophical and physiological perspectives shaped the development of psychological thought.
- Identify the research contributions of major historical figures in psychology.
- Describe and compare different theoretical approaches in explaining behavior.
- Recognize the strengths and limitations of applying theories to explain behavior.

**Pacing:**

1 Block of 2 Traditional Class Periods

# Module 1: Psychologists at Work

## AP Module Summary

*Psychology* is the scientific study of behavior and mental processes. The phrase "behavior and mental processes" encompasses not just what people do but also their thoughts, emotions, perceptions, reasoning processes, memories, and even the biological activities that maintain bodily functioning.

**THE SUBFIELDS OF PSYCHOLOGY: PSYCHOLOGY'S FAMILY TREE**  The subfields of psychology can be likened to an extended family, with assorted nieces and nephews, aunts and uncles, and cousins who, although they may not interact day to day, are related to one another because they share a common goal: understanding behavior.

**WHAT ARE THE BIOLOGICAL FOUNDATIONS OF BEHAVIOR?**  In the most fundamental sense, people are biological organisms. *Behavioral neuroscience* is the subfield of psychology that mainly examines how the brain and the nervous system—but other biological processes as well—determine behavior.

**HOW DO PEOPLE SENSE, PERCEIVE, LEARN, AND THINK ABOUT THE WORLD?**  Experimental psychology is the branch of psychology that studies the processes of sensing, perceiving, learning, and thinking about the world. Several subspecialties of experimental psychology:

- *Cognitive psychology*—focuses on higher mental processes, including thinking, memory, reasoning, problem solving, judging, decision making, and language.

**WHAT ARE THE SOURCES OF CHANGE AND STABILITY IN BEHAVIOR ACROSS THE LIFE SPAN?**  *Developmental psychology* analyzes how people grow and change from the moment of conception through death. *Personality psychology* focuses on the consistency in people's behavior over time and the traits that differentiate one person from another.

**HOW DO PSYCHOLOGICAL FACTORS AFFECT PHYSICAL AND MENTAL HEALTH?**  *Health psychology* explores the relationship between psychological factors and physical ailments or disease. *Clinical psychology* is the study, diagnosis, and treatment of psychological disorders. Like clinical psychologists, counseling psychologists deal with people's psychological problems, but the problems they deal with are more specific. *Counseling psychology* focuses primarily on educational, social, and career adjustment problems.

**HOW DO OUR SOCIAL NETWORKS AFFECT BEHAVIOR?**  *Social psychology* is the study of how people's thoughts, feelings, and actions are affected by others. Social psychologists concentrate on such diverse topics as human aggression, liking and loving, persuasion, and conformity. *Cross-cultural psychology* investigates the similarities and differences in psychological functioning in and across various cultures and ethnic groups.

**EVOLUTIONARY PSYCHOLOGY**  *Evolutionary psychology* posits that behavior is influenced by our genetic inheritance from our ancestors.

**BEHAVIORAL GENETICS**  *Behavioral genetics* is another rapidly growing area in psychology. It focuses on the biological mechanisms, such as genes and chromosomes, that enable inherited behavior to unfold. Behavioral genetics seeks to understand how we might inherit certain behavioral traits and how the environment influences whether we actually display such traits.

**CLINICAL NEUROPSYCHOLOGY**  *Clinical neuropsychology* unites the areas of neuroscience and clinical psychology: It focuses on the origin of psychological disorders in biological factors.

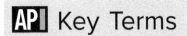 
## Class Discussion Ideas

### The Science of Psychology

**WHAT IS PSYCHOLOGY?** Emphasize that psychologists attempt to describe, predict, and explain behavior. All psychologists use scientific methods to find answers to questions about the causes of behavior.

**DEFINING PSYCHOLOGY** Have the students write down their definitions of psychology. Then go around the room and have them tell you their definitions. Write the main aspects or words of their definitions on the board. You may want to make two columns, one for the science-based definitions and one for media-based definitions. The students will see how media have probably influenced what they think psychology is. You can explain that what the media portray is not necessarily wrong when it comes to psychology, but that there is so much more involved in the scientific aspect of psychology, given that it is based on facts and statistics.

## Activities

**PSYCHOLOGY IS...?** Ask students to write down two or three things that come to their mind when they think of "psychology." Ask students to provide one of their terms out loud & explain their thinking.

**WHAT JOBS ARE THERE OUT THERE?** Break the students into groups and assign each group a couple of the areas of psychology, and then have them research various jobs in those areas. When they are finished, write the areas on the board as headings, and have the students come up to the board to write the various jobs they came up with under the appropriate heading.

**VIRTUAL EXPLORATION OF PSYCHOLOGY CAREERS** In class or as an outside activity, have students go to: http://www.apa.org/careers/resources/guides/careers.aspx. Review the APA brochure for careers in Psychology and identify some of the subfields most interesting to you as well as the job outlook for such a subfield. Then, consider what you can do to help yourself be better prepared to go into such a subfield in the future (Getting ready to work in Psychology). Ask students to list some other job titles they think having a psychology degree in would be useful or required.

## AP Test Practice

### Section I: Multiple Choice

1. **C** *(Skill 1.B, Learning Target 1.E)*

2. **B** *(Skill 1.A, Learning Target 1.E)*

3. **D** *(Skill 1.B, Learning Target 1.E)*

### Section II: Free Response

The clinical domain focuses on the study, diagnosis, and treatment of psychological disorders. Jona might help treat an individual diagnosed with schizophrenia.

The cognitive domain focuses on the study of higher mental processes, such as thinking, memory, reasoning, problem solving, judging, decision making, and language. Jona might study mental strategies for solving complex word problems.

The counseling domain focuses on educational, social, and career adjustment problems. Jona might work with a student to provide organizational skills and study habits to help the student cope with the stress of adjusting to college life.

The developmental domain focuses on how people grow and change from conception through death. Jona might study the age when individuals form their identity.

The educational domain focuses on teaching and learning processes. Jona might study how to effectively motivate high school students to excel in classroom discussions.

The industrial-organizational domain focuses on the psychology of the workplace. Jona might help create a recruiting program to find the best candidates for a specific job title at a large company.

The social domain focuses on the study of how people's thoughts, feelings, and actions are affected by others. Jona might study the influence of violent models on childhood aggression.

# Module 2: A Science Evolves: The Past, The Present, and The Future

## AP Module Summary

This module does a great job of addressing the College Board's Learning Targets. In Module 2, students will be introduced to many important people. It is not necessary to spend considerable time on all the individuals listed in the new CED because several are reintroduced and their work explained in later chapters. Individuals like Mary Whiton Calkins, G. Stanley Hall, and Margaret Floy Washburn only make an appearance in this module, so spend some time reviewing their contributions. In this module it is also important to stress how the theoretical approaches are used to explain human behavior. Knowing the approaches and being able to apply them is vital to a student's understanding of psychology and how it can be used to explain human behavior. The sociocultural perspective is new to the CED for this learning target!

**THE ROOTS OF PSYCHOLOGY**  The formal beginning of psychology as a scientific discipline is generally considered to be in the late 19th century, when Wilhelm Wundt established the first experimental laboratory devoted to psychological phenomena in Leipzig, Germany. His perspective, which came to be known as:

- Structuralism
- Introspection

Over time, psychologists challenged Wundt's approach. Introspection was not a truly scientific technique because there were few ways an outside observer could confirm the accuracy of others' introspections.

- Functionalism
- Gestalt psychology

**WOMEN IN PSYCHOLOGY: FOUNDING MOTHERS**

- Margaret Floy Washburn (1871–1939)
- Mary Calkins (1863–1930)

**TODAY'S FIVE MAJOR PERSPECTIVES**

- Neuroscience/Biological Perspective: Blood, Sweat, and Fears
- Psychodynamic Perspective: Understanding the Inner Person
  - Sigmund Freud

- Behavioral Perspective: Observing the Outer Person
  - John B. Watson
  - B. F. Skinner

- Cognitive Perspective: Identifying the Roots of Understanding
- Humanistic Perspective: The Unique Qualities of the Human Species
  - Carl Rogers
  - Abraham Maslow

## AP Key Terms

behavioral perspective

cognitive perspective

functionalism

Gestalt psychology

humanistic perspective

introspection

neuroscience perspective

psychodynamic perspective

structuralism

## AP Key People

Mary Whiton Calkins

Charles Darwin

Dorothea Dix

Sigmund Freud

G. Stanley Hall

William James

Ivan Pavlov

Jean Piaget

Carl Rogers

B.F. Skinner

Margaret Floy Washburn

John B. Watson

Wilhelm Wundt

## Class Discussion Ideas

Ask students for their strategies on how to remember important people and contributions. If students have taken AP United States History, what strategies did they use to remember all the presidents of the United States? In the memory chapter some methods on how to improve memory will be introduced.

**HELPFUL HINTS FOR STUDENTS** Here are a few ways to help students remember names associated with historical achievements:

"F" (for functionalism) comes before "S" (for structuralism), just as "J" (for James) comes before "W" (for Wundt).

For Gestalt psychology, the "whole is more than the sum of its parts" and the letters "al" (for "all") are in the term's name.

Importance of Perspectives in Psychology

The five perspectives in psychology form a central theme of the course. Alert students to the fact that if they understand these perspectives, they will be in very good shape to understand material presented throughout the course.

**RELATIONSHIPS AMONG DISCIPLINES, PERSPECTIVES, AND ISSUES** By the time you reach this point in the lecture you may want to review with students:

- the differences among the disciplines in psychology,
  - psychologist specialities

- the workplaces in which psychologists are found,
  - where we can find specialities

- the historical and contemporary perspectives, and
  - theoretical positions that a psychologists supports

- the issues
  - different viewpoints among psychologists

Review the difference between:

- "conscious versus unconscious causes of behavior"
  - whether the forces that drive behavior are available to conscious awareness or whether they lie under the surface and are unavailable to the individual's thought processes (unconscious).

- "observable behavior versus internal mental processes"
  - Internal versus observable refers to what is considered acceptable data.
  - Observable side of the issue regard it as inappropriate to use any data other than those that can be objectively recorded.
  - Internal end of the pole believe that is acceptable and appropriate to find out what is going on inside the person (within the "black box").

You can then challenge students to decide, by the end of the course, where they fall on each of the key issues and therefore what perspective lies closest to their beliefs regarding human nature.

## Activities

**ANALYSIS OF A FICTIONAL CHARACTER** Show a brief segment from a movie or television show in which a character displays psychological symptoms. Ask students to discuss the character's symptoms from the five major perspectives.

**HISTORICAL TIMELINE OF PSYCHOLOGY** Have students create a timeline of psychological trends and historical events. This is a good study tool in addition to helping them understand why different schools of thought might have evolved. For example, it makes sense that psychoanalysis came into vogue during the Victorian era, which was a time of repression.

**INTROSPECTION EXERCISE** Read the following to the class:

Wilhelm Wundt founded the first formal psychology laboratory in Leipzig, Germany, in 1879, the date now considered to be the beginning of the science of psychology. A physician and physiologist, Wundt conducted experiments intended to identify the basic nature of human consciousness and experience. His main focus of research was on the senses of vision, touch, and the passage of time; other topics studied in his laboratory included attention, emotion, and memory.

The approach associated with Wundt is structuralism, which seeks to describe the basic building blocks or "structure" of consciousness. The main technique used by Wundt and his colleagues was introspection or "inner sense." In this method, trained subjects are given a stimulus. They then are asked to describe the sensations that made up their conscious experience of that stimulus. In Wundt's laboratory, you might be asked to reflect on your experience of this stimulus for several minutes or even several hours!

Now you can try introspection yourself. Look at the stimulus that will appear on the screen.

- Show a picture of an apple (or hold up any handy object). Ask students, "What is your experience of this apple? How would you describe the sensations of each of the parts of the apple—its colors, its roundness, its shading?"
- Have students write a brief response to the prompt. Once students have done their own introspection, have them discuss their response with a partner. Were their experiences of the apple similar? Different? )

**FUNCTIONALISM EXERCISE** Read the following to the class:

William James opened a small psychology laboratory in 1870 that he used to demonstrate some of the basic processes he taught in his classes at Harvard University. However, the laboratory was for demonstration, not research. James identified himself as a philosopher, not a psychologist. James published *The Principles of Psychology* in 1890. This massive work (two volumes of almost 1,400 pages) contained his theoretical positions in psychology.

Functionalism was the idea that mental processes were useful to living creatures as functional activities in their attempt to maintain and adapt themselves in the world of nature. James developed this position as a reaction against the view of the structuralists that the mind can be divided into units. James's focus on the mind's ability to adapt was derived from Darwin's evolutionary theory that all characteristics of a species must serve some adaptive purpose. According to James, psychology's goal should be to investigate the function, or purpose, of consciousness rather than its structure.

James used the concept of "stream of consciousness" to describe the mind.

Perhaps you are thinking about the instructor in front of you, but if you let your mind wander, you may start to think about where you are going later today, what you did yesterday, the feeling that you are getting hungry and would like something to eat, or perhaps your concern over whether your roommate is still asleep. According to James, these thoughts cannot be separated into component parts as proposed by the structuralists. Instead, they form a stream of the total flow of thoughts, and are not necessarily tied to direct experience.

**Present this instruction:** What are the thoughts going through your mind right now? Take 5 minutes to write about whatever pops into your head.

Gestalt Exercise

Gestalt psychology is based on the observation that we perceive experiences in ways that cannot be reduced simply to a set of basic sensations. The word *Gestalt* comes from the German word for structure, or form. The Gestalt psychologists were represented by, among others, Max Wertheimer, Kurt Koffka, Wolfgang Kohler, and Kurt Lewin, who developed their ideas in the 1920s, having begun their work in Germany and then moving to universities in the United States in the 1930s. They were noted for developing the "laws" of Gestalt psychology, many of which were based on observations derived from studying how people perceived visual illusions.

**Present this instruction:** Now try this experiment from Gestalt psychology. Show student the face/vase image.

What do you see when you look at this picture? Perhaps you noticed two white profiles looking at each other against a black background. Or perhaps you saw a black vase against a white background. Whichever one you saw first, now try to find the other. Gestalt psychologists were interested in the patterns that people saw in stimulus objects and invented a number of illusions designed to learn more about the perceptual assumptions (and errors) that follow from the tendency to view "the whole." Psychologists now call this "top-down" processing.

## Applying Psychology in the 21st Century: Psychology Matters

Answer Suggestions

- Possible behaviors affecting society today include use of technology, bullying, suicide, addiction, etc.
- The neuroscience perspective would explain these behaviors by looking at the brain, nervous system, and other biological functions.
- The psychodynamic perspective would explain these behaviors by looking into unconscious inner forces.
- The behavior perspective would explain these behaviors by objectively measuring observable, external behaviors.
- The cognitive perspective would explain these behaviors by focusing on how people think, understand, and know about the world.
- The humanistic perspective would explain these behaviors by looking into how people grow, develop, or control their lives to gain self-fulfillment.

## AP Test Practice

### Section I: Multiple-Choice

1. **D** *(Skill 1.B, Learning Target 1.A)*

2. **A** *(Skill 1.A, Learning Target 1.B)*

3. **C** *(Skill 1.B, Learning Target 1.C)*

### Section II: Free Response

The neuroscience or biological perspective views behavior from the perspective of biological functioning. Depression could be caused by a lack of the neurotransmitter serotonin.

The behavioral perspective focuses on observable behavior. Depression could be caused by observing a model with similar behaviors or being reinforced for showing signs of depressions.

The cognitive perspective focuses on how people understand and think about the world. Depression could be caused by irrational thoughts.

The humanistic perspective contends that people can control their behavior and that they naturally try to reach their full potential. Depression could be caused by a lack of self-esteem and inability to reach one's full potential.

The psychodynamic perspective views behavior as being motivated by inner, unconscious forces over which a person has little control. Depression could be caused by unconscious childhood conflict.

The evolutionary perspective views behavior has being influenced by our genetic inheritance from our ancestors. Depression would have a genetic influence that helped increase the survival rate of humans' ancient relatives.

# Module 3: Psychology's Key Issues and Controversies

## AP Module Summary

Psychologists address 5 major issues:

**ISSUE 1** Nature (heredity) versus nurture (environment) A psychologist's take on this issue depends partly on which major perspective he or she subscribes to. However, every psychologist would agree that neither nature nor nurture alone is the sole determinant of behavior; rather, it is a combination of the two.

**ISSUE 2** Conscious versus unconscious causes of behavior.
- Great controversies in the field of psychology
- Examples:
  - Clinical psychologists adopting a psychodynamic perspective argue that psychological disorders are brought about by unconscious factors,
  - Cognitive psychologists suggest that psychological disorders largely are the result of faulty thinking processes (cognitive perspective).

**ISSUE 3** Observable behavior versus internal mental processes
- Examples:
  - Behavioral Psychologists, contend that the only legitimate source of information for psychologists is behavior that can be observed directly.
  - Cognitive Psychologists, argue that what goes on inside a person's mind is critical to understanding behavior, and so we must concern ourselves with mental processes.

**ISSUE 4** Free will versus determinism
- How much of our behavior is a matter of **free will** (choices made freely by an individual),
- How much is subject to **determinism**, the notion that behavior is largely produced by factors beyond people's willful control?

**ISSUE 5** Individual differences versus universal principles
- Examples:
  - Neuroscience/Biological perspective tend to look for universal principles of behavior, such as how the nervous system operates or the way certain hormones automatically prime us for sexual activity.
  - Humanistic perspective focus more on the uniqueness of every individual.

Becoming an Informed Consumer of Psychology: Thinking Critically about Psychology: Distinguishing Legitimate Psychology from Pseudo-Psychology

In order to separate accurate information, which is backed by science and objective research, from pseudo-psychology based on anecdotes, opinions, and outright fraud, we need to employ critical thinking techniques.

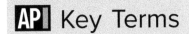 Key Terms

determinism    free will

## Class Discussion Ideas

This module can easily be reviewed by asking students:

- How much of their behavior is caused by heredity and how much is caused by environmental influences?

**POLLING QUESTIONS** Social Media and Psychology: Your text discusses the controversy over whether or not this generation of young adults is more narcissistic than previous generations. Here is your chance to justify what you put on Facebook, Twitter, SnapChat, or other social media sites. How many think that this generation of people is more self-centered and narcissistic than previous ones? How many think that social media is the "cause" for people thinking that they are special and that everyone should be aware of their personal accomplishments and life happenings?

## Activities

**ARE YOU A CRITICAL THINKER?** Pass around various hoax e-mails that state that if the recipients forward the e-mail to 10 people, they will have good luck. (You can give a variety of e-mails that all state about the same thing.) Then ask the students the following questions:

1. Have you ever received an e-mail like the one I handed out? If so, did you follow the directions and forward it on to others?

2. Why do you believe people are gullible and forward the e-mails?

3. Have you ever bought a product because of the statistics associated with the product; for example, some toothpastes state that four out of five dentists choose the toothpaste?

4. Do you question everything or take things at face value?

**SKEPTICISM** Bring in a couple of self-help books from the library. Break the class into groups and have them look through one of these books and choose one of the treatments or suggestions the author gives for a problem. Ask the groups to discuss whether or not the treatment or advice sounds factual. Ask them to write down what credentials the author has. Discuss with the class how self-help books may seem helpful, but should be read and followed carefully. Discuss with them how using the scientific method when conducting research results in more factual conclusions. You may also want to use a self-help website in this activity.

**DRUNK ON CELL PHONES?** Ask students if they agree that driving while using a cell phone is similar to driving drunk. Have them defend their answer. You may want to share with them the Strayer, Drews, and Couch (2006) article listed in the suggested readings.

**SOCIAL MEDIA ADDICTION?** Ask students how many times they check their social media (e.g., Snapchat, Twitter, Facebook, etc.) in any given day. How do they feel when they cannot check their media? Do they think they are addicted? Why or why not?

## Neuroscience in Your Life: Enhancing Your Mind

Answer Suggestions

- Individuals might receive TMS to enhance cognitive abilities. They might explore TMS to increase memory after a stroke, Alzheimer's disease, or a traumatic experience. Perhaps they want to explore increased cognitive abilities for assessments or an employment opportunity.
- In one study, TMS was used to stimulate the hippocampus over one week, which led to increased brain connectivity and improved memory. Questions for the research study might include how large was the sample? What was the composition of the sample (e.g., age, gender)? Was the hippocampus stimulated while encoding or retrieving the memory? What was the operational definition of each variable?

# AP Test Practice

## Section I: Multiple-Choice

1. **B** *(Skill 1.A, Learning Target 1.A)*

2. **E** *(Skill 1.C, Learning Target 1.C)*

3. **E** *(Skill 1.B, Learning Target 1.C)*

## Section II: Free Response

The nature versus nurture debate is centered on the cause of our behaviors being hereditary or the product of the environment. The perspectives that support the nature side of the debate include neuroscience and psychodynamic. The perspectives that support the nurture side of the debate include behavioral and humanistic. The cognitive perspective accepts both sides of the debate.

The conscious versus unconscious debate is centered on how much of our behavior is caused by forces we are aware (conscious) versus how much of our behavior is due to mental process we are unaware (unconscious). The perspectives that support the conscious side of the debate include behavioral and humanistic. The perspectives that support the unconscious side of the debate include neuroscience and psychodynamic. The cognitive perspective accepts both sides of the debate.

The observable versus internal mental processes debate is centered on whether psychology should focus on only behavior that can be seen by others or if the focus should be on internal processes. The behavioral perspective is the only perspective that supports the observable emphasis. The other perspectives (neuroscience, cognitive, humanistic, and psychodynamic) support the internal emphasis.

The free will versus determinism debate is centered on how much of our behavior is a free choice versus how much of our behavior is produced by factors beyond our control. The perspectives that support the free will side of the debate include cognitive and humanistic. The perspectives that support the determinism side of the debate include neuroscience, behavioral, and psychodynamic.

The individual differences versus universal principles debate is centered on behavior being unique to the individual or universal from the culture and society in which we live. The perspectives that support the individual differences side of the debate include cognitive and humanistic. The perspectives that support the universal principles side of the debate include neuroscience and psychodynamic. The behavioral perspective accepts both sides of the debate.

# Psychological Research

## **AP** Introduction

Most students who take psychology often have some general understanding of basic psychology. Mention Pavlov and most likely several students will say dogs, mention Freud and well... But what students often don't realize is that psychology is a science with findings supported by quantifiable data. It is in Chapter 2 that students are reintroduced to the scientific method and, for many, it is their introduction to statistics.

I often refer to this chapter as the money maker. Students who have a strong foundation in their understandings of research design and are able to read and interpret the data perform well on the AP exam. My recommendation for this chapter is to have students read modules 4 and 5 the night before class. Then, take time in class to review and apply the concepts learned especially when it comes to module 5: conducting psychological research. Make sure students know how to read graphs, charts, data, and that they know the different research methods including longitudinal and cross-sectional studies (both of which will reappear in later units). The research of psychologists Bibb Latané and John Darley has been scattered throughout the three modules. Using their research you can introduce students to a phenomenon that still plagues society and at the same time makes learning the concepts a little easier.

## **AP** Essential Questions

- How does the methodology of the research affect the outcome of a study?
- How do ethical guidelines impact psychological research?

## Module 4: The Scientific Method
### AP Learning Targets:

- Discuss the value of reliance on operational definitions and measurement in behavioral research.

### Pacing:

1 Block or 2 Traditional Class Periods

## Module 5: Conducting Psychological Research
### AP Learning Targets:

- Differentiate types of research with regard to purpose, strengths, and weaknesses.
- Discuss the value of reliance on operational definitions and measurements in behavioral research.
- Identify independent, dependent, confounding, and control variables in experimental designs.
- Describe how reseach design drives the reasonable conclusions that can be drawn.

- Distinguish between random assignment of participants to conditions in experiments and random selection of participants, primarily in correlational studies and surveys.
- Predict the validity of behavioral explanations based on the quality of research design.
- Apply basic descriptive statistical concepts, including interpreting and constructing graphs and calculating simple descriptive statistics.
- Distinguish the purpose of descriptive statistics and inferential statistics.

**Pacing:**

3 Blocks or 6 Traditional Class Periods

# Module 6: Critical Research Issues

- Apply basic descriptive statistical concepts, including interpreting and constructing graphs and calculating simple descriptive statistics.
- Identify how ethical issues inform and constrain research practices.
- Describe how ethical and legal guidelines protect research participants and promote sound ethical practice.

**Pacing:**

1 Block or 2 Traditional Class Periods

# Module 4: The Scientific Method

## 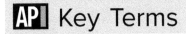 Module Summary

**SCIENTIFIC METHOD** Consists of four main steps: (1) identifying questions of interest, (2) formulating an explanation, (3) carrying out research designed to support or refute the explanation, and (4) communicating the findings. See **Figure 1.**

**THEORIES: SPECIFYING BROAD EXPLANATIONS** Theories are broad explanations and predictions concerning phenomena of interest.

- Example: Psychologists Bibb Latané and John Darley, responding to the failure of bystanders to intervene when Kitty Genovese was murdered in New York, developed what they called a theory of diffusion of responsibility.

**HYPOTHESES: CRAFTING TESTABLE PREDICTIONS**

- *Hypothesis* is a prediction stated in a way that allows it to be tested.
- *Operational definition* is the translation of a hypothesis into specific, testable procedures that can be measured and observed in an experiment.

## AP Key Terms

scientific method

theories

hypothesis

operational definition

## Class Discussion Ideas

Why is it necessary for psychological researchers to use the scientific method?

Think about a psychological issue of interest to you. How would you approach it from a scientific perspective?

Students may have difficulty differentiating theories from hypotheses. Tell them of some different theories you have and ask them to pull out testable hypotheses. For example, you can tell them that a researcher believed that frozen foods do not have calories. Calories are measures of heat. Frozen food, by definition, can't have calories. Therefore, frozen foods are calorie-free. Explain what events this theory might lead to: diets of frozen candy bars, ice cream, Starbucks Frappacinos, frozen cookie dough, and so on that lead to weight gain instead of weight loss. What is the theory? Hypotheses? How can they be tested?

When you see an advertisement, whether it be in a newspaper, magazine, on television, or online, do you pay attention to the statistics that are given? For example, "Four out of five dentists have chosen Brand X toothpaste over other brands." Do you ever think about who those four out of five dentists are and the source of the statistics?

## Polling Questions

**POLLING QUESTION:** Mrs. Smith was found dead in her boarding house. By her side a knife with the initials JB was found. She had one stab wound. Examining the evidence, Inspector Lestrade said, "I believe that John Butcher did it. It's his knife. He knew Mrs. Smith." Is this a theory or hypothesis?

# Activities

**RESEARCH DESIGN:** Have students get into groups and give them the following theory: media violence and adolescent aggression are related. Assign each group to a different research design (correlation, experiment, survey, case study, and naturalistic observation), and ask them to come up with a testable hypothesis and method of testing.

# Suggested Media

*Aspects of Behavior.* CRM/McGraw-Hill, 1971, 26:00. This video introduces the field of psychology. There are also taped interviews with noted historical psychology scholars such as Stanley Milgrim and Abraham Maslow.

The Psych Files. www.thepsychfiles.com. This is a good website housing several free podcasts and videos on various topics related to psychology, including research methods and statistics.

# Additional Readings

Latané, B., & Darley, J. M. (1970). *The unresponsive bystander: Why doesn't he help?* Prentice Hall.

Lillenfield, S. O. (2005). The 10 commandments for helping students distinguish science from pseudoscience in psychology. *APS Observer, 18,* http://people.ucalgary.ca/~mueller/P305/Science-Pseudo.pdf.

Lillenfeld, S. O., Lynn, S. J., Ruscio, J., & Beyerstein, B. L. (2010). *50 great myths of popular psychology: Shattering widespread misconceptions about human behavior.* Wiley-Blackwell.

Mikulak, A. (2014). Using pseudoscience to shine light on good science. *APA Observer, 27.*

# **AP** Student Edition Answer Key

## AP Test Practice

### Section I: Multiple Choice

1. **B** *(Skill 1.A, Learning Target 1.G)*
2. **D** *(Skill 1.B, Learning Target 1.G)*
3. **A** *(Skill 3, Learning Target 1.G)*

### Section II: Free Response

A hypothesis is a testable prediction. If located in a blue room, one's mood will become calm.

An operational definition is the precise description of the procedures so they can be observed and measured in an experiment.

The independent variable is the color and can be operationally defined as baby blue.

The dependent variable is the mood and can be operationally defined as decreased blood pressure.

# Module 5: Conducting Psychological Research

## AP Module Summary

### Naturalistic Observation

- Advantage—we get a sample of what people do in their "natural habitat"
- Disadvantage—the inability to control any of the factors of interest

**SURVEY RESEARCH**
- Advantage—small sample researchers are able to infer with great accuracy
- Disadvantage—sample may not represent the broader population of interest

**THE CASE STUDY**
- Advantage—in-depth and focused
- Disadvantage—if the individuals examined are unique in certain ways, it is impossible to make valid generalizations to a larger population

## Experimental Research (See Figure 2)

- Use the research of Latané and Darley to assist you in teaching the concepts found in this module.
- **Experiment**
  - ○ Example: Latané and Darley, in testing their theory of the diffusion of responsibility in bystander behavior, developed this hypothesis: The higher the number of people who witness an emergency situation, the less likely it is that any of them will help the victim. They then designed an experiment to test this hypothesis. Their first step was to formulate an operational definition of the hypothesis by conceptualizing it in a way that could be tested.

- **Experimental group**
- **Control group**
  - ○ Example: Returning to Latané and Darley's experiment, we see that the researchers needed to translate their hypothesis into something testable. To do this, they decided to create a false emergency situation that would appear to require the aid of a bystander. As their experimental manipulation, they decided to vary the number of bystanders present.

- **Independent variable / Dependent variable**
  - ○ Example: In the case of the Latané and Darley experiment, the independent variable was the number of people present, which was manipulated by the experimenters. For Latané and Darley, the dependent variables were the measure of whether bystanders in each of the groups provided help and the amount of time it took them to do so.

- **Random Assignment of Participants**
  - ○ To make the experiment a valid test of the hypothesis, Latané and Darley needed to add a final step to the design: properly assigning participants to a particular experimental group.
  - ○ How can we ensure that participants in each experimental group will be equally intelligent, extroverted, cooperative, and so forth, when the list of characteristics—any one of which could be important—is potentially endless? The solution is a simple but elegant procedure called random assignment to condition: Participants are assigned to different experimental groups, or "conditions," on the basis of chance and chance alone.

- **Were Latané and Darley right?**
  - To test their hypothesis that increasing the number of bystanders in an emergency situation would lower the degree of helping behavior, Latané and Darley placed the participants in a room and told them that the purpose of the experiment was to talk about personal problems associated with college. The sizes of the discussion groups were two, three, and six people, which constituted the manipulation of the independent variable of group size. Participants were randomly assigned to these groups upon their arrival at the laboratory. Each group included a trained confederate, or employee, of the experimenters. In each two-person group, then, there was only one real "bystander."
  - As the participants in each group were holding their discussion, they suddenly heard through the intercom one of the other participants—the confederate—having what sounded like an epileptic seizure and then calling for help. The participants' behavior was now what counted. The dependent variable was the time that elapsed from the start of the "seizure" to the time a participant began trying to help the "victim."
  - As predicted by the hypothesis, the size of the group had a significant effect on whether a participant provided help. The more people who were present, the less likely it was that someone would supply help (see **Figure 4**).
  - Because these results are straightforward, it seems clear that the experiment confirmed the original hypothesis. However, Latané and Darley could not be sure that the results were truly meaningful until they determined whether the results represented a significant outcome.

- **Moving Beyond the Study**
  - The Latané and Darley study contains all the elements of an experiment: an independent variable, a dependent variable, random assignment to conditions, and multiple experimental groups.
  - Psychologists, like other scientists, require that findings be: **replicated**, or repeated, sometimes using other procedures, in other settings, with other groups of participants, before full confidence can be placed in the results of any single experiment.

## AP Key Terms

| | |
|---|---|
| case study | naturalistic observation |
| control group | random assignment to condition |
| correlational research | replicated research |
| dependent variable | significant outcome |
| experiment | survey research |
| experimental group | treatment |
| experimental manipulation | variables |
| independent variable | |

## Class Discussion Ideas

**Provide students with these examples of naturalistic research:**

Having people of different races drop their books while walking on a campus sidewalk and counting the number of people who stop to help to see if people are more likely to help those of the same race as themselves.

Watching people in a computer lab and counting the number of times that they interrupt their studies to answer email.

Counting the number of times that students versus nonstudents make calls on their cell phones during basketball games.

Recording the number of times that a teacher in a classroom calls on boys and girls to see if boys are more likely to be called on to answer questions.

**Provide students with these examples of survey research:**

Asking a random sample of people to complete an online questionnaire about political attitudes.

Asking people to list their favorite foods to determine if there are geographic differences in food preferences.

Asking people to rate their attitudes toward new television technologies.

Asking about people's experiences in elementary school with male versus female teachers.

**Provide students with these examples of case studies:**

Giving a troubled adolescent a set of lengthy questionnaires and interviews

Asking a mother to talk in-depth about her experiences raising a child with autism

Conducting intensive neurological and neuropsychological testing of a group of children with a rare brain disorder

Documenting progress in psychotherapy with a victim of Hurricane Katrina

**Provide students with these examples of variables to study in correlational studies:**

Self-esteem and height

Depression and length of Internet use

Time spent playing video games and grades

Attractiveness and popularity

Noise level of music and heart rate

**Provide students with these examples of experimental research:**

Determining whether negatively worded advertisements cause people to buy more or less of a product.

Testing people to determine whether memory is better for words or pictures.

Having people take a memory test in a laboratory to determine which conditions are best for promoting short-term memory.

Determining whether people are more likely to lie when they are put in a condition of thinking they need to impress the experimenter compared to a condition in which they do not think they need to impress the experimenter.

**Summary of Descriptive Research Methods**

Have students create a chart to summarize the research methods used in descriptive research, highlighting the advantages and disadvantages of each method. This could be used as a classroom activity in which students work together or independently. In addition to the methods mentioned in the chapter, have students research on their own and include longitudinal and cross-sectional studies

**OPERATIONALLY DEFINE THE VARIABLES** In pairs or small groups, have students operationally define the following: *integrity, generosity, love, maturity, liberal, conservative, exhaustion, stress, attractiveness*. To facilitate discussion, have students share their results with the rest of the class.

**"Psychic Experiments"**

To show the importance of the scientific method, particularly ruling out alternative, competing hypotheses, here are three demonstrations that are very simple to do. It just takes a bit of show"person"ship.

**Experiment 2:**

Prepare three piles of cards:

Pile 1 has three cards,

Pile 2 has four 3's (one from each of the four suits).

Pile 3 the third pile

Put them together at the top of a deck to to create the illusion that you are going to be randomly taking them off the top, but they will have been prearranged.

Now ask for a volunteer and state that you will predict which pile the volunteer will pick because your psychic powers are so strong. In fact, you will write down your prediction ahead of time! Without allowing the volunteer to see what you are doing, write down the number 3 on a large sheet of paper, fold it up, and then turn to the task at hand. Instruct the volunteer to think of a number and really concentrate.

Close your eyes and pretend to be "sensing" what the volunteer is thinking. Then instruct the volunteer to point at the pile she or he has chosen. After pointing to any of the piles, say, "Yes, that is what I predicted! I have written down the number 3!!" Of course you will be right because in Pile #1, there are 3 cards, Pile #2 has all 3's, and the third pile is "Pile #3." After the applause dies down, ask the audience if you have proven you are truly psychic. Of course they won't think you are, but now you can ask them to generate hypotheses about the secret of the trick. Through this process, you will be demonstrating the value of considering alternative hypotheses and being ready to critique a result even if it seems to be dramatically proving a point.

# Activities

**DESIGN AN EXPERIMENT** Explain to students that they are going to study the influence of smiling on social behaviors. The experimental group will interact with a confederate who smiles a lot during the interaction. Ask students: What has to happen in the control group? Would a confederate keep a blank expression?

**PSYCINFO** For a brief assignment, have students use PsycInfo (or Google Scholar) to find a current example of each type of research method (e.g., archival, case study). Briefly describe the method used in each study that students identify.

**MEDIA AND RESEARCH** Have students find a report of research by a media outlet (e.g., TV news, online news source, or radio station) and report to the class what the essence of the report entailed and how the conclusions should be evaluated. Ask students what is missing or what more information they would need before determining the credibility and validity of the research being reported in their media selection.

**STATISTICALLY SIGNIFICANT** Before class, find a few current articles and parse out the results sections. In groups, give students an example of research results and ask them to discuss whether the results were statistically significant and what that means to them. *(Since this is often a difficult concept for students to understand, having them put this in their own words may help clarify the misunderstandings.)*

*Handout: Common Sense or Fact* Use this handout as a way to help students realize that what they think they already know about common everyday occurrences may not actually be true.

This activity involves students reading through a list of common occurrences or common information and stating whether the information is true or false.

*Handout: Correlational Research* (NOTE TO INSTRUCTOR: Edit out the correct answers before distributing to students.)

In correlational research, the relationship between two sets of variables is examined to determine whether they are associated, or correlated. When we find that two variables are strongly correlated with one another, it is tempting to presume that one variable causes the other. The mere fact that two variables occur together does not mean that one causes the other. It is impossible to determine which variable is the "cause" and which is the "result." In addition, there may be a third variable not accounted for that is responsible for the correlation. This principle is known as "correlation is not causation."

In this activity, students will have the chance to learn about the problems involved in making conclusions about causality in correlational research.

*Handout: Experimental Design* (NOTE TO INSTRUCTOR: Edit out the correct answers before distributing to students.)

The only way psychologists can establish cause-and-effect relationships through research is by carrying out an experiment. In a formal experiment, the relationship between two (or more) variables is investigated by deliberately producing a change in one variable in a situation and observing the effects of that change on other aspects of the situation. In an experiment, then, the conditions required to study a question of interest are created by an experimenter, who deliberately makes a change in those conditions in order to observe the effects of that change. The change that an experimenter deliberately produces in a situation is called the "experimental manipulation." Experimental manipulations are used to detect relationships between different variables. In this activity, students will have the chance to explore the factors involved in designing an experimental study.

*Handout: Operational Definitions* Use this handout to have the students find operational definitions in an experiment. In the activity, students are given various segments from actual journal articles and asked to identify the operational definition(s) in each of the articles.

*Handout: Independent and Dependent Variables/Experimental and Control Groups* This activity has different examples of hypotheses for research ideas. The students have to identify both the independent and dependent variables in the hypotheses. They also have to identify who makes up the experimental group and who makes up the control group.

*Handout: Populations and Samples* This handout gives students experience in identifying the population and samples in various examples. Students should be able to differentiate between who the population is and who makes up the sample.

**Survey and Correlational Research**

To demonstrate both survey and correlational methods, conduct a brief study with your students as participants. Have students fill out a brief, simple survey with the following questions (or questions of your choosing):

Favorite ice cream flavor:

Height:

Shoe size:

Number of siblings:

At the next class meeting, present students with the data from their classmates. First, display a figure illustrating the favorite ice cream flavors of students: this is an example of a simple survey question. Second, present the calculated correlation coefficient and display a scatter plot illustrating the correlation between height and shoe size: this is an example of a positive correlation. Finally, present the calculated correlation coefficient and display a scatter plot of the correlation between height and number of siblings: this is an example of a near zero correlation. Correlations can be a difficult topic for students; giving them an example from their own lives can make it easier to understand.

# AP Student Edition Answer Key

## AP Test Practice

### Section I: Multiple-Choice

1. **B** *(Skill 3, Learning Target 1.F)*

2. **A** *(Skill 3, Learning Target 1.H)*

3. **C** *(Skill 2, Learning Target 1.I)*

### Section II: Free Response

In naturalistic observation studies, a researcher simply watches a naturally occurring behavior. Researchers could watch the children play in a natural environment, such as the playground.

An advantage of using a naturalistic observation study includes viewing natural behavior rather than artificial behavior in a laboratory environment.

A disadvantage of using a naturalistic observation study includes being unable to control factors of interest. Also, there is a risk of participants changing their behavior if they are aware of being watched.

In experimental studies, a researcher investigates a relationship between two or more variables by manipulating a variable. Researchers could make an experiment by manipulating the size of the play group and controlling all other variables.

An advantage of the experimental study is it offers the only way to determine a cause-and-effect relationship.

The dependent variable is play and could be operationally defined as time using a toy in the way it was intended to be used.

Operational definitions allow for replication of the study and minimizes different interpretations of play behavior. Also, the use of operational definitions avoids introducing confounding variables.

# Module 6: Critical Research Issues

## AP Module Summary

### The Ethics of Research

Because research has the potential to violate the rights of participants, psychologists are expected to adhere to a strict set of ethical guidelines aimed at protecting participants. Those guidelines involve the following safeguards:

- Protection of participants from physical and mental harm.
- The right of participants to privacy regarding their behavior.
- The assurance that participation in research is completely voluntary.
- The necessity of informing participants about the nature of procedures before their participation in the experiment.
- All experiments must be reviewed by an independent panel before being conducted.

One of psychologists' key ethical principles is *informed consent*. Before participating in an experiment, the participants must sign a document affirming that they have been told the basic outlines of the study and are aware of what their participation will involve, what risks the experiment may hold, and the fact that their participation is purely voluntary and they may terminate it at any time.

Furthermore, after participation in a study, participants must be given a debriefing in which they receive an explanation of the study and the procedures that were involved.

**EXPLORING DIVERSITY: CHOOSING PARTICIPANTS WHO REPRESENT THE SCOPE OF HUMAN BEHAVIOR**

- Example: When Latané and Darley, both college professors, decided who would participate in their experiment, they turned to the people at hand: college students. Using college students as participants has both advantages and drawbacks. The greatest benefit is that because most research occurs in university settings, college students are readily available. The problem is that college students may not represent the general population adequately. In fact, undergraduate research participants are typically a special group of people: relative to the general population, college students tend to be from **W**estern, **e**ducated, **i**ndustrialized, **r**ich, and **d**emocratic cultures (WEIRD).

Because psychology is a science whose goal is to explain all human behavior generally, its studies must use participants who are fully representative of the general population in terms of gender, age, race, ethnicity, socioeconomic status, and educational level. See "Neuroscience in Your Life: The Importance of Using Representative Participants" in the text for an example.

**SHOULD ANIMALS BE USED IN RESEARCH?** Researchers who use nonhuman animals in experiments have their own set of exacting guidelines to ensure that the animals do not suffer. Specifically, researchers must make every effort to minimize discomfort, illness, and pain. Procedures that subject animals to distress are permitted only when an alternative procedure is unavailable and when the research is justified by its prospective value.

Psychological research that employs nonhumans is designed to answer questions differently from those posed in research with humans.

### Threats to Experimental Validity: Avoiding Experimental Bias

- *Experimental bias*—factors that distort the way the independent variable affects the dependent variable in an experiment.
- *Placebo*—a false treatment, such as a pill, "drug," or other substance that has no significant chemical properties or active ingredient.

To overcome the possibility that experimenter expectations will affect the participant, the researcher can use the double-blind procedure. By keeping both the participant and the experimenter who interacts with the participant "blind" to the nature of the treatment that is being administered, researchers can more accurately assess the effects of the treatment.

**BECOMING AN INFORMED CONSUMER OF PSYCHOLOGY: THINKING CRITICALLY ABOUT RESEARCH** Because the field of psychology is based on an accumulated body of research, we must scrutinize thoroughly the methods, results, and claims of researchers. Several basic questions can help us sort through what is valid and what is not. Among the most important questions to ask are these:

- What was the purpose of the research?
- How well was the study conducted?
- Are the results presented fairly?

## AP Key Terms

**experimental bias**

**informed consent**

**placebo**

## Class Discussion Ideas

**ETHICAL CONCERNS** Be sure to differentiate clearly between the need to protect participants from undue risk, the need to inform participants in advance regarding what will take place when they complete the research, and the need to maintain the scientific integrity of the research.

- Example: If Bibb Latané and John Darley (1970) had informed participants of exactly what would transpire in the study on diffusion of responsibility and the bystander effect, their results would not necessarily have provided them with valid results because participants would have known that they were expected to help (this issue relates also to participant expectations).

Another topic of interest to students is that of withholding psychological services in the interests of maintaining the integrity of the experimental design.

**EXPERIMENTAL BIAS** Placebos can be used to minimize the effects of participant expectation, particularly when used in a double-blind procedure. However, placebos can sometimes lead to improvement due to the "placebo effect" (see http://www.nytimes.com/2010/05/04/opinion/04judson.html for an excellent discussion of this issue). Raise the issue of why deception is needed and how best to handle the balance between informed consent and the need to minimize bias.

## Activities

**HANDOUT: ETHICAL DILEMMAS** Use this handout as a way for students to think about ethical considerations when conducting research. This activity gives students research scenarios that deal with ethical concerns. Questions regarding their own ethical considerations follow each scenario.

**APA SUMMIT ON HIGH SCHOOL PSYCHOLOGY EDUCATION** Full of activities and ideas to use in your classroom. I highly recommend checking out Amy Ramponi's "Elephants on Acid" Ethics Research assessment.

**ETHICAL PRINCIPLES** Go to the APA website and look up the Ethical Principles of Psychologists and Code of Conduct: http://www.apa.org/ethics/code/.

**Choose three of the principles and answer the following questions:**

- Why do you think this principle is important?
- What difficulties might psychologists encounter when applying this principle?
- Describe a real-life situation in which this principle might be used.

## Discussion Questions

Do you think psychological research has really controlled for ethnic bias and overcome the problems of ethnicity in research?

Why do you think some individuals are more comfortable with animal testing on rats but uncomfortable with animal tests on dogs?

Ask students to stand up if they believe research on animals is unethical; have them move to stand on the left side of the room. If they believe that it is ethical, have them stand on the right side. If they are unsure, they can stay in the middle. Have the left and right sides discuss their perspectives, and then ask people to move to the part of the room that now represents their stance. Generally, many students will shift views after discussion, and this will illustrate attitude change.

## Polling Questions

**SINCE I CAN USE IT, IT MUST BE OK!** Take a few minutes to review the critical controversy over deception in research. Let's share our own thoughts and ideas about this. How many think that using deception in research is acceptable under any condition? Who thinks that it is not all right to trade one's ethical responsibility, such as informed consent, for advancement in research through deception? How many people in the class have been deceived by someone they trusted?

**POLLING QUESTION:** Do you think it is ethical to use animals in psychological research?

a) Yes

b) No

c) It depends.

**CLIENTS AS FRIENDS, WE'LL SEE?** While many digital immigrants (i.e., older therapists) recoil at the thought of having clients as Facebook friends and too readily call it "unethical," is the answer really that simple? Knowing that the digital age is moving so fast and that access to therapy may have a technological counterpart, what do you think? How many would accept a former client as a *friend* on a social media site once therapy ended? How many think it would be acceptable for a therapist to have a professional social media site and accept friend requests there? Who has had an experience (either their own or that of someone they know) of crossing the boundary lines of ethical behavior with someone in a professional role? Lastly, how many people think it is all right for the therapist to text their clients? Let's discuss the implications of ethical behavior and its effects on others.

# Suggested Media

**AMERICAN PSYCHOLOGICAL ASSOCIATION:** http://www.apa.org/research/index.aspx. This is the official website of the APA. It discusses the ethical regulations and codes of conduct that must be followed when conducting psychological research.

**APA/TOPSS (TEACHERS OF PSYCHOLOGY IN SECONDARY SCHOOLS)** You will need to register for this free resource that is full of resources for all units:
https://www.apa.org/ed/precollege/topss/high-school-summit?tab=4&fbclid=IwAR1FwDV2A-MX5BRmWJeAEkHktYbDujvDyTVYWPVQ1WJEQTKFZRw-U5mkMbw

**ASPECTS OF BEHAVIOR** CRM/McGraw-Hill, 1971, 26:00. This video introduces the field of psychology. There are also taped interviews with noted historical psychology scholars such as Stanley Milgram and Abraham Maslow.

**EPISODES OF THE DISCOVERY CHANNEL'S *MYTHBUSTERS*** Experiments are designed and run in an attempt to debunk common myths, can be found at: https://www.youtube.com/show/mythbusters-show.

**REENACTMENT OF DARLEY AND LATANE'S RESEARCH** http://www.youtube.com/watch?v=KE5YwN4NW5o
Part 3, http://www.youtube.com/watch?v=zIpDPrbRiBo&feature=related.

**SCIENTIFIC AMERICAN FRONTIERS** episode features the ways in which placebo effects can bias research on treatment effectiveness: http://www.chedd-angier.com/frontiers/season13.html.

**ARTICLES, RESEARCH, & RESOURCES IN PSYCHOLOGY:** http://kspope.com/. The site covers a broad range of subjects, including licensing laws, regulation, ethics, medication, military-related issues, suicide and sexual issues, etc. A unique feature that deserves mention is that the website is designed for people with disabilities in accordance with W3C Accessibility Guidelines.

# **AP** Student Edition Answer Key

## AP Test Practice

### Section I: Multiple Choice

1. **D** *(Skill 1.A, Learning Target 1.O)*

2. **E** *(Skill 1.B, Learning Target 1.O)*

3. **E** *(Skill 3, Learning Target 1.I)*

### Section II: Free Response

**A.** Informed consent is a document signed by participants verifying they have been told the basics of the experiment before they participate. This is a key ethical guideline and will need to be put in place for IRB approval. Dr. Cory will need to provide the document that outlines the basics of the study, risks involved, and the right to withdraw at any time.

Debriefing is a process after the experiment in which participants are told about the purpose of the study and the procedures involved. Dr. Cory will debrief participants after the experiment and inform them of the purpose and provide contact information for the results and all future questions.

Confidentiality is the right of participants to privacy regarding their behavior. Dr. Cory will keep all names and results of the study confidential.

**B.** Participant bias can occur when participants think they have figured out what is expected of them in the study. Dr. Cory might use deception to guard against participant expectations.

Experimenter bias can occur if the experimenter unknowingly influences the participant. The researcher might use a double-blind procedure—in which both the experimenter and participant do not know who is in what group—to guard against experimenter expectations.

**C.** The neuroscience perspective views behavior from the perspective of biological functioning. Anxiety could be caused by a lack of a certain neurotransmitter, such as GABA.

The cognitive perspective focuses on how people understand and think about the world. Anxiety could be caused by faulty thinking.

# CHAPTER 3

# Neuroscience and Behavior

## **AP** Introduction

The biological bases of behavior, a topic that often causes much anxiety among many students is one of the most important units in an advanced placement psychology course. Understanding how everything psychological is biological can lead students to better explain why a behavior exists. In this chapter students are introduced to the basic elements of neurons, the nervous and endocrine systems, and the brain. It is important that students know and understand how neurotransmitters influence the biological process and how those chemicals influence behavior and mental processes. Gone are the days of simply knowing where something is located. Instead, students need to be ready to explain and provide evidence and/or reasoning as to how such systems influence behavior.

## **AP** Essential Questions

- How can biology influence our behavior and mental processes?
- What happens when a particular neurotransmitter is absent from the body?
- How do biological and environmental factors interact to influence our behaviors and mental processes?

### Module 7: Neurons: The Basic Elements of Behavior

**AP Learning Targets:**

- Describe the nervous system and its subdivisions and functions.
- Identify basic processes and systems in the biological bases of behavior, including parts of the neuron.
- Identify basic process of transmission of a signal between neurons.
- Discuss the influence of drugs on neurotransmitters.

**Pacing:**

1 Block or 2 Traditional Class Periods

## Module 8: The Nervous System and the Endocrine System: Communicating Within the Body

**AP Learning Targets:**

- Discuss psychology's abiding interest in how heredity, environment, and evolution work together to shape behavior.
- Identify key research contributions of scientists in the area of heredity and environment.
- Predict how traits and behavior can be selected for their adaptive value.
- Discuss the effect of the endocrine system on behavior.
- Describe the nervous system and its subdivisions and functions.
- Identify basic processes and systems in the biological bases of behavior, including parts of the neuron.

**Pacing:**

1 Block or 2 Traditional Class Periods

## Module 9: The Brain

- Describe the nervous system and its subdivisions and functions in the brain.
- Identify the contributions of key researchers to the study of the brain.
- Recount historic and contemporary research strategies and technologies that support research.
- Identify the contributions of key researchers to the development of tools for examining the brain.
- Discuss the role of neuroplasticity in traumatic brain injury.
- Identify the contributions of key researchers to the study of neuroplasticity.

**Pacing:**

2 Blocks for 4 Traditional Class Periods

# Module 7: The Basic Elements of Behavior

## AP Module Summary

*Behavioral neuroscientists* (or biopsychologists) specialize in considering the ways in which the biological structures and functions of the body affect behavior.

### The Structure of the Neuron (See Figure 1)

- *Neurons*, or nerve cells, are the basic elements of the nervous system.
- *Dendrites* look like the twisted branches of a tree, receive messages from other neurons.
- *Axon* is a long, slim, tubelike extension on the opposite side of the cell body that carries messages received by the dendrites to other neurons.
- *Terminal buttons* are located at the of the end of the axon a look like small bulges, they send messages to other neurons.
  - Messages (impulses) that travel through a neuron are electrical in nature and move only in one direction.
  - Impulses begin with the dendrites, continue into the cell body, and lead ultimately along the tubelike extension, the axon, to adjacent neurons.
- *Myelin sheath*, a protective coating of fat and protein that wraps around the axon. The myelin sheath also serves to increase the velocity with which electrical impulses travel through axons.

### How Neurons Fire (See Figure 2 and Figure 3)

- *All-or-none law* - Neurons either fire—that is, transmit an electrical impulse along the axon—or do not fire. They are either on or off, with nothing in between the on state and the off state.
- *Resting potential (state)* - Before a neuron is triggered, it has a negative electrical charge called a resting state.
- *Action potential* - This is the change when an electrical impulse, moves from one end of the axon to the other like a flame moving along a fuse. When a message arrives at a neuron, gates along the cell membrane open briefly to allow positively charged ions to rush in.

### Mirror Neurons

- *Mirror neurons* are specialized neurons that fire not only when a person enacts a particular behavior, but also when a person simply observes another individual carrying out the same behavior.

### Where Neurons Meet: Bridging the Gap (See Figure 4)

- *Synapse* is the space between two neurons where the axon of a sending neuron communicates with the dendrites of a receiving neuron by using chemical messages. When a nerve impulse comes to the end of the axon and reaches a terminal button, the terminal button releases a chemical.
- *Neurotransmitters* are chemicals that carry messages across the synapse to a dendrite (and sometimes the cell body) of a receiving neuron.
- *Excitatory message* is a chemical message that makes it more likely that a receiving neuron will fire and an action potential will travel down its axon.

- *Inhibitory message* does just the opposite; it provides chemical information that prevents or decreases the likelihood that the receiving neuron will fire.
- *Reuptake* neurotransmitters are either deactivated by enzymes or, more commonly, reabsorbed by the terminal button in an example of chemical recycling.

## Neurotransmitters: Multitalented Chemical Couriers (See Figure 5)

Neurotransmitters are a particularly important link between the nervous system and behavior.

- *Acetylcholine* (or ACh, it) transmits messages relating to our skeletal muscles.
- *Glutamate* plays a role in memory.
- *Gamma-amino butyric acid (GABA)* is a primary inhibitory neurotransmitter. It moderates a variety of behaviors, ranging from eating to aggression.
- *Dopamine (DA)* is involved in movement, attention, and learning.
- *Serotonin* is associated with the regulation of sleep, eating, mood, and pain.
- *Endorphins,* another class of neurotransmitters, are a family of chemicals produced by the brain that are similar in structure to painkilling drugs such as morphine.

## **AP** Key Terms

| | |
|---|---|
| action potential | mirror neurons |
| all-or-none law | myelin sheath |
| axon | neurons |
| behavioral neuroscientists (or biopsychologists) | neurotransmitters |
| | resting state |
| dendrite | reuptake |
| excitatory message | synapse |
| inhibitory message | terminal buttons |

## Class Discussion Ideas

**IMPORTANCE OF BIOLOGICAL PSYCHOLOGY** Students often do not initially understand why they have to learn so much biology. To introduce them to the topic of biological psychology, explain to them that everything psychological is biological.

## Parts of the Neuron

- **The Neuron and the Synapse:** Students should be able to identify the various parts of the neuron and the synapse, and be able to explain how information is communicated between neurons.
- **All-or-None Law:** Discuss the implications of the all-or-none law; intense stimuli do not result in higher peaks but more frequent impulses. It is especially important to point out the significance of the fact that the synapse is not a hard-wired connection between neurons. This means that neurons can be more flexible, but it also means that more can "go wrong" in the nervous system, such as if there is too much neurotransmitter present in the synapse (as is the case when cocaine stimulates dopamine receptors), too little (as is the case with dopamine in Parkinson's disease), or too much activity of reuptake enzymes (as is the case with serotonin and psychological disorders such as depression and anxiety). Emphasize the importance of the receptor sites on the postsynaptic surface. Talk about the variety of neurotransmitters and the functions they serve in the nervous system, and the fact that some

neurotransmitters can have different effects (excitatory versus inhibitory), depending on the area of the nervous system in which they are acting.

- **Resting Potential and Action Potential:** Students should be able to describe how ions maintain a resting potential and how a change in the charge of the ion can cause action potential.

## Activities

### Neuroscience

- **Web-Based Learning Neuroscience:** Go to http://faculty.washington.edu/chudler/neurok. html. At this site, you will find a variety of authentic activities such as games, mini-experiments, and creative ways to reinforce nervous system principles for your students. One easy idea from this site is Nervous System Hang-Man.

### Neurons

- **Designing a Neuron from Food:** Go to the local grocery store and pick up the following items: Red Vines licorice (axon), large marshmallows (cell body or myelin), mini M & M's (nucleus or neurotransmitters), mini-pretzel sticks (dendrites) and orange slices candy (terminal button). Pick several other types of candy to represent a neurotransmitter to explain the influence of drugs on neurotransmitters. After lecturing on the various parts of the neuron, have the students design their own neuron with these candy and food items. Design the neurons on paper towels so once finished, students can move their neurons closer to each other without touching (simulating the synapse between neurons) and explain each part and its function. Afterward students can eat their design and enjoy a kinesthetic approach to learning about neural structure and function. *Note: Instructors can substitute any type of food items or candy produces the same concept (e.g., Runt's Candy, with its different shapes and colors, can be used for neurotransmitters to illustrate antagonists/agonists and the "lock-and-key method" of binding onto receptor sites).* *Please check for food allergies prior to planning for this activity. Alternatives to this activity have involved using play-doh, various arts & crafts materials (pipe cleaners).

- **Neural Transmission:** Write the steps for neural transmission on the board. Ask for 12 volunteers. Assign a role to each of the students: electrical stimulus, dendrite, cell body, axon, myelin sheath (use four students for this one), positive ion, negative ion, terminal button, neurotransmitter and neighboring neuron. Line the students up so that they are in the correct order. Go through the steps on the board with the students and have them act out their parts as you go through the steps. Do this a couple of times until you think they have understood it. Next, allow the students to run through the steps by themselves. The students should gain a hands-on idea of how electrical information is passed along an axon for neural transmission to occur. Depending on the size of your class you can also do an entire class act-it-out and video the end product. Then when reviewing for the AP exam show the video to the class this creates a memory with emotion...such a great tool!

- **Neural Activity:** One of the best ways for students to understand neural activity is to "act like a neuron." Have students form two lines of 10 students each in front of the class. For one line, have each student place their right arm on the right leg of the student in front of them. For the other line, have each student place their right arm on the right shoulder of the person in front of them. Instruct the students that when you say, "go," they are to squeeze the right leg of the person in front of them or the right shoulder. When each person feels the squeeze of the person behind him or her, they are to squeeze the person in front of him or her. Record the duration (seconds) it takes for the "message" to travel from the rear of the line to the front of each line. Divide each value by 10 and ask the class to speculate on the difference between these average values. *Reference:* Rozin, P. & Jonides, J. (1977). Mass reaction time: Measurement of the speed of the nerve impulse and the duration of mental processes in class. *Teaching of Psychology, 4,* 91–94.

## Neurotransmitters

- **Parts of the Nervous System:** Have students complete *Handout: Parts of the Nervous System.*
- **Neurotransmitters:** Use *Handout: Neurotransmitters* as a way for students to understand the needs and functions of the various neurotransmitters. The students will have to find, on their own, the purpose for each of the neurotransmitters and determine what could possibly occur if there were a decrease or excess of neurotransmitters.
- **Drugs and Neurotransmitters:** Use *Handout: What's in Your Medicine Cabinet?* This activity will have students examine their own medications to find out if any of them are agonists or antagonists.
- **Electrochemical Transmission:** Have students search on the Internet for a website that talks about epileptic seizures. After the students find and read the page, have them write a one- to two-page paper on how electrical charges are disrupted during a seizure and how this affects information being passed from one area of the brain to the other.

## Discussion Questions

### The Study of the Nervous System in Psychology

- **Nervous System:** Tell students to imagine themselves walking down a dark street late at night when suddenly they think they hear someone following them. Ask them to write down what would be happening to them physiologically as the information they are hearing is going through the nervous system.

### The Neuron and the Synapse

- Are medications for psychological disorders overprescribed?
- What are the implications of the fact that neurons communicate across synapses rather than being directly hard-wired?
- What are the advantages in the nervous system of having neurons fire according to the all-or-none law?

## Polling Questions

**SPEED OF TRANSMISSION**  True or False: All neurons transmit impulses at the same speed.

## Suggested Media

**MIRROR NEURONS. NOVA SCIENCENOW**  Video File, 2006. Video posted to: https://www.youtube.com/watch?v=Xmx1qPyo8Ks.

A 14-minute video that addresses mirror neurons.

**NEURON SYNAPSE**  https://www.youtube.com/watch?v=LT3VKAr4roo.

**RESTING POTENTIAL**  https://www.youtube.com/watch?v=YP_P6bYvEjE.

## AP Test Practice

### Section I: Multiple Choice

1. **C** *(Skill 1.B, Learning Target 2.E)*

2. **B** *(Skill 1.A, Learning Target 2.F)*

3. **A** *(Skill 1.A, Learning Target 2.G)*

### Section II: Free Response

**A.** A lack of acetylcholine has been associated with Alzheimer's disease. A lack of dopamine has been associated with Parkinson's disease.

**B.** Endorphins have been associated with pain reduction. Opiates, such as morphine or oxycodone, mimic the effect of endorphins and reduce pain.

The placebo effect occurs when a participant believes they have received a treatment but a false treatment has been provided. For example, the patient may receive a sugar pill (false treatment) but believes it is making him better, which releases endorphins, leading to the reduction of pain.

# Module 8: The Nervous System and The Endocrine System: Communicating Within the Body

## AP Module Summary

### The Nervous System: Linking Neurons (See Figure 1 and Figure 2)

- *Central nervous system* (CNS) is composed of the brain and spinal cord.
- *Spinal cord*, which is about the thickness of a pencil, contains a bundle of neurons that leaves the brain and runs down the length of the back.
- *Reflex* is an automatic, involuntary response to an incoming stimulus.

Three kinds of neurons are involved in reflexes.

- *Sensory (afferent) neurons* transmit information from the perimeter of the body to the central nervous system.
- *Motor (efferent) neurons* communicate information from the nervous system to muscles and glands.
- *Interneurons* located within the brain and spinal cord communicate internally between motor and sensory neurons.
- *Peripheral nervous system* branches out from the spinal cord and brain and reaches the extremities of the body.

There are two major divisions:

- *Somatic division* specializes in the control of voluntary movements—such as the motion of the eyes to read this sentence or those of the hand to scroll down a page—and the communication of information to and from the sense organs.
- *Autonomic division* controls the parts of the body that keep us alive: the heart, blood vessels, glands, lungs, and other organs that function involuntarily without our awareness.

**ACTIVATING THE DIVISIONS OF THE AUTONOMIC NERVOUS SYSTEM (SEE FIGURE 3)** Autonomic division plays a particularly crucial role during emergencies.
- *Sympathetic division* is the part of the autonomic division of the nervous system that acts to prepare the body for action in stressful situations, engaging all the organism's resources to respond to a threat. This is often called the "fight-or-flight" response.
- *Parasympathetic division* acts to calm the body after the emergency has ended.

**THE EVOLUTIONARY FOUNDATIONS OF THE NERVOUS SYSTEM** The forerunner of the human nervous system is found in the earliest simple organisms to have a spinal cord. Over millions of years, the spinal cord became more specialized, and organisms became capable of distinguishing between different kinds of stimuli and responding appropriately to them. Ultimately, a portion of the spinal cord evolved into what we would consider a primitive brain. Today, the nervous system is hierarchically organized, meaning that relatively newer (from an evolutionary point of view) and more sophisticated regions of the brain regulate the older, and more primitive, parts of the nervous system.
- *Evolutionary psychology* is the branch of psychology that seeks to identify how behavior is influenced and produced by genetic inheritance from our ancestors. Evolutionary psychologists argue that the course of evolution is reflected in the structure and functioning of the nervous system and that evolutionary factors consequently have a significant influence on our everyday behavior.
- *Behavioral genetics* is the study of the effects of heredity on behavior.

## The Endocrine System: Of Chemicals and Glands (See Figure 4)

- *Endocrine system* is a chemical communication network of secreting hormones that send messages throughout the body via the bloodstream.
- *Hormones* are chemicals that circulate through the blood and regulate the functioning or growth of the body.
- *Pituitary gland*, a key component of the endocrine system, is tiny and found near—and regulated by—the hypothalamus in the brain. Sometimes called the "master gland" because it controls the functioning of the rest of the endocrine system.

## AP Key Terms

autonomic division

behavioral genetics

central nervous system (CNS)

endocrine system

evolutionary psychology

hormones

motor (efferent) neurons

parasympathetic division

peripheral nervous system

pituitary gland

reflex

sensory (afferent) neurons

somatic division

spinal cord

sympathetic division

## Class Discussion Ideas

**DNA AND THE BRAIN** Glutamate doesn't function properly in people with schizophrenia, and so they become confused. Restoring glutamate function is the focus of new treatments for schizophrenia.

**CENTRAL AND PERIPHERAL NERVOUS SYSTEMS** The major divisions of the human nervous system, the central and peripheral are to be indicated with a pictorial depiction that also describes the bodily functions that each part controls. The students could be asked to identify each part of both the nervous systems.

## Helpful Hints for Students

- A mnemonic that you may want to share with your students on how they can remember afferent and efferent neurons is SAME (sensory-afferent arrive [at the brain], motor-efferent exit [the brain]). There are many activities to help students learn the parts of the neuron. I have found that the more active a student is when applying the concepts, the better retention.
  - *Autonomic nervous system:* Think of "automatic." This part of the nervous system controls actions that we do not think about and are out of our control.
  - *Sympathetic nervous system:* Think of "sympathetic." When we get emotional ("sympathetic"), we experience arousal and stimulation, exactly the actions of this part of the autonomic nervous system.
  - *Parasympathetic nervous system:* Think of "parachute." Your parasympathetic nervous system works like a parachute in helping you come back down to a normal state of arousal.
  - *Somatic nervous system:* Soma means "body." The somatic nervous system is the "bodily" nervous system, meaning that it translates information received through the bodily senses and gives instructions to the muscles and glands (a long explanation, but if they remember "body," it will help them to remember the term).

# Activities

**ENDOCRINE SYSTEM** Have students complete *Handout: Parts of the Endocrine System.*

**ENDOCRINE AMUSEMENT PARK** Have students form small groups (3-4). Each group is to create an amusement park featuring rides, food, and game attractions for each concept of the nervous and endocrine systems. You can also have students incorporate hormones into this one! Have groups make a poster and then share their amusement parks with the class.

**EXPLORING THE CONNECTIONS BETWEEN THE ENDOCRINE AND NERVOUS SYSTEMS** As a class discussion, explore why and how the endocrine and nervous systems are interconnected. What is the reason for studying the endocrine system in a psychology class? For reference, use the following link to aid in discussion: http://endocrineexplanation.weebly.com/endocrine-explanation.html.

**UNIVERSITY OF UTAH'S LEARN.GENETICS WEBSITE** Useful simulations highlighting areas are of genetics and neuroscience. https://learn.genetics.utah.edu

# AP Student Edition Answer Key

## AP Test Practice

### Section I: Multiple-Choice

1. **A** *(Skill 1.B, Learning Target 2.E)*

2. **A** *(Skill 1.A, Learning Target 2.E)*

3. **B** *(Skill 1.A, Learning Target 2.D)*

### Section II: Free Response

The parasympathetic nervous system acts to calm the body after an emergency and directs the body to store energy for use in emergencies. While Linda is cuddling with her daughter, her parasympathetic nervous system is probably activated. Her pupils are contracted, her heartbeat slows, her blood vessels dilate, and her digestion is stimulated.

Motor neurons send information from the brain and nervous system to the muscles and glands. Linda would use her motor neurons to pick up her daughter and cuddle.

Hormones are the chemical messengers of the endocrine system. For Linda, the hormone oxytocin produces an urge to nurse newborns and cuddle with her daughter. Oxytocin may also be related to the development of trust and effective social interactions with her daughter.

Mirror neurons are specialized cells that fire when a person enacts a particular behavior and when that person observes another individual carrying out the same behavior. Linda may activate her mirror neurons when she smiles or when she watches her daughter smile.

Glutamate is a neurotransmitter that plays a role in memory. Linda may create memories of cuddling with her daughter due to glutamate's role in producing specific biochemical changes at particular synapses.

# Module 9: The Brain

## AP Module Summary

**STUDYING THE BRAIN'S STRUCTURE AND FUNCTIONS: SPYING ON THE BRAIN (SEE FIGURE 1)** The brain has posed a continual challenge to those who would study it. For most of history, its examination was possible only after an individual had died. Today, however, brain-scanning techniques provide a window into the living brain.

- *Electroencephalogram (EEG)* records electrical activity in the brain through electrodes placed on the outside of the skull.
- *Functional magnetic resonance imaging (fMRI)* scans provide a detailed, three-dimensional computer-generated image of brain structures and activity by aiming a powerful magnetic field at the body.
- *Positron emission tomography (PET)* scans show biochemical activity within the brain at a given moment.
- *Transcranial magnetic stimulation (TMS)* is one of the newest types of scan. By exposing a tiny region of the brain to a strong magnetic field, TMS causes a momentary interruption of electrical activity (a "virtual lesion"). Researchers then are able to note the effects of this interruption on normal brain functioning. The enormous advantage of TMS, of course, is that the virtual cut is only temporary.

**THE CENTRAL CORE: OUR "OLD BRAIN" (SEE FIGURE 2 AND FIGURE 3)** *Central core* is quite similar in all vertebrates (species with backbones). The central core is sometimes referred to as the "old brain," because its evolution can be traced back some 500 million years to primitive structures found in nonhuman species.

The first part of the central core of the brain is the hindbrain which contains the:

- *Medulla* controls a number of critical body functions, the most important of which are breathing and heartbeat.
- *Pons* is a bridge in the hindbrain, involved in coordinating muscles and integrating the right and left halves of the body.
- *Cerebellum* regulates motor movements: walking a straight line without staggering and lurching forward, and control balance.
- *Reticular formation* extends from the medulla through the pons, passing through the middle section of the brain—or midbrain—and into the front-most part of the brain, called the forebrain. It is responsible for sleep, arousal, and attention.
- *Thalamus* acts primarily as a relay station for information about the senses.
- *Hypothalamus* is located just below the thalamus. One of its major functions is to maintain homeostasis, a steady internal environment for the body. The hypothalamus helps provide a constant body temperature and monitors the amount of nutrients stored in the cells.

**THE LIMBIC SYSTEM: BEYOND THE CENTRAL CORE (SEE FIGURE 4)** The *limbic system* borders the top of the central core and has connections with the cerebral cortex and is involved in several important functions, including self-preservation, learning, memory, and the experience of pleasure.

- *Amygdala* – emotion
- *Hippocampus* – memory

Injury to the limbic system can produce striking changes in behavior.

**THE CEREBRAL CORTEX: OUR "NEW BRAIN" (SEE FIGURE 5)** *Cerebral cortex* is the "new brain" responsible for the most sophisticated information processing in the brain.
The cortex has four major sections called *lobes*.

- *Frontal lobes* lie at the front center of the cortex and the
- *Parietal lobes* lie behind them
- *Temporal lobes* are found in the lower-center portion of the cortex with the
- *Occipital lobes* lying behind them.

These four sets of lobes are physically separated by deep grooves called sulci.

## Motor Area of the Cortex

- *Motor area* – part of the cortex, responsible for the body's voluntary movement

## Sensory Area of the Cortex

- *Sensory area* – part of the cortex includes three regions:
   - Corresponds primarily to body sensations (including touch and pressure),
   - Relating to sight
   - Relating to sound.

The somatosensory area in the parietal lobe encompasses specific locations associated with the ability to perceive touch and pressure in a particular area of the body. The greater the area devoted to a specific area of the body within the cortex, the more sensitive is that area of the body (see **Figure 6**).

The senses of sound and sight are also represented in specific areas of the cerebral cortex.

- An auditory area located in the temporal lobe is responsible for the sense of hearing.
- The visual area in the cortex, located in the occipital lobe, responds in the same way to electrical stimulation.

**ASSOCIATION AREAS OF THE CORTEX** *Association areas* generally are considered to be the site of higher mental processes such as thinking, language, memory, and speech.

Injuries to the association areas of the brain can produce:

- Aphasia, problems with language.
   - Broca's aphasia, speech becomes halting, laborious, and often ungrammatical, and a speaker is unable to find the right words.
   - Wernicke's aphasia produces difficulties both in understanding others' speech and in the production of language.

## Neuroplasticity and the Brain

- *Neuroplasticity* refers to changes in the brain that occur throughout the life span relating to the addition of new neurons, new interconnections between neurons, and the reorganization of information-processing areas.
- *Neurogenesis* is the creation of new neurons. The ability of neurons to renew themselves during adulthood has significant implications for the potential treatment of disorders of the nervous system.

**THE SPECIALIZATION OF THE HEMISPHERES: TWO BRAINS OR ONE?** Because of the way nerves in the brain are connected to the rest of the body, the two symmetrical left and right mirror-image halves of the brain, called *hemispheres*, control motion in—and receive sensation from—the side of the body opposite their location. The dominance of one hemisphere of the brain in specific functions, such as language, is known as *lateralization*.

**EXPLORING DIVERSITY: HUMAN DIVERSITY AND THE BRAIN** The interplay of biology and environment in behavior is especially clear when we consider evidence suggesting that even in brain structure and function there are both sex and cultural differences. With regard to sex differences, young girls show earlier development in the frontal lobes, which control aggressiveness and language development. On the other hand, boys' brains develop faster in the visual region that facilitates visual and spatial tasks such as geometry. Most males tend to show greater lateralization of language in the left hemisphere. For them, language is clearly relegated largely to the left side of the brain. In contrast, women display less lateralization, with language abilities apt to be more evenly divided between the two hemispheres.

Culture also gives rise to differences in brain lateralization. Native speakers of Japanese seem to process information regarding vowel sounds primarily in the brain's left hemisphere. In contrast, North and South Americans, Europeans, and individuals of Japanese ancestry who learn Japanese later in life handle vowel sounds principally in the right hemisphere.

**THE SPLIT BRAIN: EXPLORING THE TWO HEMISPHERES** It is clear from experiments that the right and left hemispheres of the brain specialize in handling different sorts of information. At the same time, it is important to realize that both hemispheres are capable of understanding, knowing, and being aware of the world, in somewhat different ways. The two hemispheres, then, should be regarded as different in terms of the efficiency with which they process certain kinds of information, rather than as two entirely separate brains. The hemispheres work interdependently to allow the full range and richness of thought of which humans are capable.

## AP Key Terms

| | |
|---|---|
| association areas | limbic system |
| central core | lobes |
| cerebellum (ser-uh-BELL-um) | motor area |
| cerebral cortex | neuroplasticity |
| hemispheres | reticular formation |
| hypothalamus | sensory area |
| lateralization | thalamus |

## Class Discussion Ideas

**H. M. AND THE ROLE OF THE HIPPOCAMPUS** Psychologists learned how essential the hippocampus is in memory and learning through a case study of Henry Molaison (H. M.) who had this structure surgically removed on both sides of the brain.

- **Discussion:** A National Public Radio broadcast of the story of H. M. and the history of memory: http://www.npr.org/templates/story/story.php?storyId=7584970.

**HELPFUL HINTS FOR STUDENTS** Here are some hints to give students to help them remember the terms (Spoiler alert: the puns here are really bad—but effective!):

- *Medulla*: Pound fist on chest to make the impression of your heart is beating while reciting "medulla oblongata"
- *Cerebellum*: You need this for balance—cere-bal (ance)-um.
- *Reticular formation*: Like a military formation, it sends messages up and down within the brain.
- *Thalamus*: You would throw a ball during a relay race. The thalamus is a relay station.
- *Hypothalamus*: Looking at your fist, you have 5 knuckles, label each knuckle with one of the 5-F's (Fight, Flight, Fahrenheit-temperature, Fornication-sexual arousal, Food)
- *Limbic system*: When you dance the limbo, you feel happy (emotion function), and later you remember having a good time (memory function).

- *Hippocampus*: You would remember if you saw a hippo while you were camping in the woods.
- *Broca's area:* Think of Tom Brokaw, the newscaster. Without speech, he would not be able to announce the news.
- *Wernicke's area*: Not Broca's area.

Psychologist Michael Britt has a great podcast you can watch to gain additional strategies. http://www.thepsychfiles.com/2008/09/episode-72-video-memorize-the-parts-of-the-brain/

**BIOGRAPHY OF ROGER SPERRY**  Roger Sperry was born August 20, 1913, in Hartford, Connecticut. He was awarded a Nobel Prize in Physiology or Medicine in 1981 for his more than 40 years of research on the brain. The prize was given specifically for his work on the "split brain," in which he discovered that the two cerebral hemispheres of the brain had distinct functions. The left, usually the dominant side, is involved in reasoning, language, writing, and reading, whereas the right, or less dominant side, is more involved in nonverbal processes, such as art, music, and creative behavior.

In one of his most important studies, Sperry asked subjects who had undergone split-brain surgery to focus on the center of a divided display screen. The word *key* was flashed on the left side of the screen, while the word *ring* was projected on the right side. When asked what they saw, the split-brain patients answered *ring* but denied that any other word was also projected onto the screen. Only the word *ring* went to the speech center in the left hemisphere. Although the right hemisphere cannot verbalize the information (the word *key*) that was projected on the left side of the screen, subjects are able to identify the information nonverbally. Sperry asked subjects to pick up the object just named without looking at it. If subjects were told to use their left hand, they could easily identify a key. However, if asked what they had just touched, they would respond *ring*.

Sperry received his PhD from the University of Chicago in 1941. He did his early research at the Yerkes Laboratories of Primate Biology and the National Institute of Health before joining the staff of the California Institute of Technology in 1954 as Hixon Professor of Psychobiology. He originally studied cats and found that the corpus callosum, or nerve bundle connecting the two cerebral hemispheres, was necessary for the transfer of information from one side of the brain to the other.

Sperry next began to study epileptic patients whose corpus callosum had been severed to prevent seizures. His research on the "syndrome of hemisphere deconnection" has contributed valuable information to the treatment of various brain disorders.

Sperry continued to be an active researcher until his death in 1994.

Source: Pettijohn, T. E. (1998). *Psychology: A ConnecText* (4th ed.). Dushkin/McGraw-Hill.

**THE STORY OF PHINEAS GAGE**  In a freak accident in 1848, an explosion drove a 3-foot-long iron bar completely through the skull of railroad worker Phineas Gage, where it remained after the accident. Amazingly, Gage survived and, despite the rod being lodged through his head, a few minutes later seemed to be fine. But he wasn't. Before the accident, Gage was hardworking and cautious. Afterward, he became irresponsible, drank heavily, and drifted from one wild scheme to another. In the words of one of his physicians, "he was 'no longer Gage.'" Students are often fascinated by the story of Phineas Gage: https://www.youtube.com/watch?v=yXbAMHzYGJ0.

## Key Concepts

- **Limbic System:** The limbic system is instrumental in emotional functioning. What happens when it is damaged? The text outlines the famous case of Phineas Gage but there are more recent, and scientific, outlines of this issue. For example, Bauman, Lavenex, Mason, Capitanio, and Amaral (2004) lesioned different portions of the limbic system in rhesus monkeys and found that specific parts of the limbic system are involved in specific emotional and social be-haviors (e.g., the amygdala is linked with avoiding potential danger). (Example 2.K.4)

# Activities

**PARTS OF THE BRAIN** I recommend that you create a note taker consisting of blank diagrams of the 3 brain regions (central core, limbic system, and cerebral cortex). Have students record information that you review in class by labeling the diagrams, adding specific details and functions. Adding color to each area will also cause neurons to fire. *Handouts 5* and *6* contain assignments.

**LEFT AND RIGHT BRAIN HEMISPHERES** Use *Handout: Which Hemisphere Is It?* Have students identify the hemisphere responsible for different activities. The students will gain an idea of hemispheric differences.

**BRAIN DAMAGE REPAIR** Have students go on the Internet and find cases where neurogenesis has been successful. Have them discuss how the research was conducted and what concerns there are about conducting this type of research in humans.

**SPLIT BRAINS** Have students go on the Internet and find a website that discusses split-brain surgery. Next, have them write a one- to two-page paper summarizing what they read and their feelings on the ethics of conducting split-brain surgery.

**NFL AND TBI** Ask students to think about sports and brain injury. In particular ask them to think about football and brain injury. You may want them to read the article: "NFL needs to aid brain, concussion research." *San Francisco Chronicle*. September 6, 2009. Ask them if sports should be made safer. Ask them who should be held accountable for players who develop dementia early in life.

**PHENOTYPE AND GENOTYPE** Have students look in the mirror and describe what they see (hair color, eye color, hair texture (straight, curly, etc.), and so on. Have them report the same information for their mother and father. Have them discuss genotypes and phenotypes, and outline which of their phenotypic features are dominant and which are recessive. If they want their child to look like them, what phenotype will their partner need to display?

# Discussion Questions

What might be the importance of the fact that the amygdala and the hippocampus, the centers for emotion and memory, are located close together and are both part of the "old brain"?

How might the findings on neuroplasticity be applied to issues such as retraining older workers or helping brain-injured individuals recover lost functions?

Imagine your favorite food. Now imagine taking a bite of that food. What parts of the brain became activated as you ate your favorite food?

What is the importance of considering genetics and the brain when analyzing behavior and mental processes?

What behaviors have been passed on in your family, and how far back can they be traced?

Ask students what they know about the nature-nurture debate. Do they know the current consensus (that genes and environment interact to influence many traits)? Ask students if they understand the concept of a nature and nurture interaction. How much do they believe is nature? How much do they believe is environment? What types of things constitute nature? What types of things constitute environment?

# Polling Questions

**THE BILLON DOLLAR QUEST TO BUILD A SUPER COMPUTER** Researchers are in the process of mapping brain structures, functions, and analyzing data to produce the Human Brain Project, a computer that supersedes our brain power and capacity. Who thinks this project can actually happen? How many would agree that it is possible to make a computer function better than your own brain? If a supercomputer is built, how many of you think that it would be bad for humans?

# Suggested Media

**AMERICAN PSYCHOLOGICAL ASSOCIATION:** http://www.apa.org/research/index.aspx. This is the official website of the APA. It discusses the ethical regulations and codes of conduct that must be followed when conducting psychological research.

**APA/TOPSS (TEACHERS OF PSYCHOLOGY IN SECONDARY SCHOOLS)** You will need to register for this free resource that is full of resources for all units: https://www.apa.org/ed/precollege/topss/high-school-summit?tab=4&fbclid=IwAR1FwDV2A-MX5BRmWJeAEkHktYbDujvDyTVYWPVQ1WJEQTKFZRw-U5mkMbw

**ASPECTS OF BEHAVIOR** CRM/McGraw-Hill, 1971, 26:00. This video introduces the field of psychology. There are also taped interviews with noted historical psychology scholars such as Stanley Milgram and Abraham Maslow.

**REENACTMENT OF DALEY AND LATANE'S RESEARCH** http://www.youtube.com/watch?v=KE5YwN4NW5o Part 3, http://www.youtube.com/watch?v=zIpDPrbRiBo&feature=related.

**SCIENTIFIC AMERICAN FRONTIERS** episode features the ways in which placebo effects can bias research on treatment effectiveness: http://www.chedd-angier.com/frontiers/season13.html.

**ARTICLES, RESEARCH, & RESOURCES IN PSYCHOLOGY:** http://kspope.com/. The site covers a broad range of subjects, including licensing laws, regulation, ethics, medication, military-related issues, suicide and sexual issues, etc. A unique feature that deserves mention is that the website is designed for people with disabilities in accordance with W3C Accessibility Guidelines.

# **AP** Student Edition Answer Key

## Applying Psychology in the 21st Century: Bypassing Broken Neural Pathways with a Chip in the Brain

Answer Suggestions

- Doctors implanted a chip into Ian's skull. The chip was full of tiny electrodes that detected neurons firing in the brain region dedicated to hand movements. The signals were then sent to a port, in Ian's skull, connected to computers in the researcher's lab. Ian spent hours watching videos of hand movements and imagined himself making those movements. After lots of training, Ian used his hand by merely thinking about it. He was the first person to control his muscles using his own neural signals relayed by a computer.
- At this time the neural bypass only works when connected to computers in the lab. The training worked with Ian but may not work with other individuals.

# Neuroscience in Your Life: The Plastic Brain

Answer Suggestions

- After a patient loses a limb the brain can reorganize, and areas of the sensory and motor cortex can take over brain regions that previously controlled functioning of that body part.
- A better understanding of neuroplasticity could help improve human functioning. Drugs could be used to trigger the development of new neurons to treat nervous system disorders. Early experiences could modify the way information is processed. By getting children involved in multiple languages or taking music lessons early in life, it could help change their brains.
- Epileptic patients may undergo split-brain surgery in which their corpus callosum is severed to reduce seizures. After the surgery, the hemispheres are independent. However, with neuroplasticity a hemisphere may take over a function associated with the other hemisphere. For example, the right hemisphere may start to produce and understand language instead of the left hemisphere.

# AP Test Practice

## Section I: Multiple-Choice

1. **E** *(Skill 1.B, Learning Target 2.I)*
2. **B** *(Skill 1.A, Learning Target 2.J)*
3. **B** *(Skill 1.B, Learning Target 1.B)*

## Section II: Free Response

**A.** The cerebellum is in charge of bodily balance. Jamal uses his cerebellum to remain balanced and walk fluidly across the stage.

The motor cortex is in charge of voluntary motor movements. Jamal uses his motor cortex when voluntarily moving his fingers on the keys of the saxophone and turning the sheet music.

The occipital lobe is in charge of processing vision in order to see. Jamal uses his occipital lobe to see the music sheets in front of him while he plays a new song.

**B.** A PET scan shows biochemical activity within the brain at a given moment. Radioactive glucose is injected and tracked by a computer to find the most active brain regions. Jamal would have a PET scan to help find damage associated with brain activity, such as memory or movement.

An fMRI scan shows a computer-generated image of brain structures and activity by using a powerful magnetic field. Jamal would have an fMRI scan to produce a vivid, detailed image of the functioning of his brain.

**C.** The left frontal lobe consists of Broca's area, which is in charge of speech production. If Jamal has damage to his frontal lobe he may have problems producing speech.

The left temporal lobe consists of Wernicke's area, which is in charge of speech comprehension and production. If Jamal has damage to his temporal lobe he may have problems understanding speech.

# CHAPTER 4

# Sensation and Perception

## AP Introduction

One of the most difficult and fascinating chapters in psychology is the study and understanding of our senses and how they aid in our perception of our environment. Similar to chapter 3, students need to continue to make connections between physiology and psychology. Equally important is being able to explain the "how" and "why" of external stimulus gathered from the outside and how our perceptions impact behavior and mental processes. The study of sensation and perception allows for a stronger connection between biological and cognitive perspectives, both helping with explaining how we think and behave. The area of parapsychological phenomena has been eliminated from this chapter and will not appear on the AP exam.

## AP Essential Questions

- How do we process the information we receive from our environments?
- How does our interpretation of the information we receive from the environment influence our behaviors and mental processes?

## Module 10: Sensing the World Around Us

**AP Learning Targets:**

- Discuss basic principles of sensory transduction, including absolute threshold, difference threshold, signal detection, and sensory adaptation.
- Identify the research contributions of major historical figures in sensation and perception.

**Pacing:**

1 Block or 2 Traditional Class Periods

## Module 11: Vision: Shedding Light on the Eye

**AP Learning Targets:**

- Describe general principles of organizing and integrating sensation to promote stable awareness of the external world.
- Describe the vision process, including the specific nature of energy transduction, relevant anatomical structures, and specialized pathways in the brain for each of the senses.
- Explain common sensory conditions.

**Pacing:**

2 Blocks or 4 Traditional Class Periods

# Module 12: Hearing and the Other Senses

**AP Learning Targets**

- Describe the hearing process, including the specific nature of energy transduction, relevant anatomical structures, and specialized pathways in the brain for each of the senses.
- Describe taste and smell processes, including the specific nature of energy transduction, relevant anatomical structures, and specialized pathways in the brain for each of the senses.
- Describe sensory processes, including the specific nature of energy transduction, relevant anatomical structures, and specialized pathways in the brain for each of the body senses.

**Pacing:**

2 Blocks for 4 Traditional Class Periods

# Module 13: Perceptual Organization: Constructing Our View of the World

**AP Learning Targets**

- Describe general principles of organizing and integrating sensation to promote stable awareness of the external world.
- Discuss how experience and culture can influence perceptual processes.
- Explain the role of top-down processing in producing vulnerability to illusion.

**Pacing:**

2 Block or 4 Traditional Class Periods

# Module 10: Sensing the World Around Us

## Module Summary

- *Sensation* is the activation of the sense organs by a source of physical energy.
- *Perception* is the sorting out, interpretation, analysis, and integration of stimuli carried out by the sense organs and brain.
- *Stimulus* is any passing source of physical energy that produces a response in a sense organ.
- *Psychophysics* is the study of the relationship between the physical aspects of stimuli and our psychological experience of them.
  - Psychophysics played a central role in the development of the field of psychology.

### Absolute Thresholds: Detecting What's Out There

- *Absolute threshold* is the smallest intensity of a stimulus that must be present for it to be detected.

Normally, our senses cannot detect stimulation quite as well because of the presence of noise. *Noise,* as defined by psychophysicists, is background stimulation that interferes with the perception of other stimuli. Hence, noise refers not just to auditory stimuli, as the word suggests, but also to unwanted stimuli that interfere with other senses.

### Difference Thresholds: Noticing Distinctions Between Stimuli

- *Difference threshold* is the smallest level of added or reduced stimulation required to sense that a change in stimulation has occurred. Thus, the difference threshold is the minimum change in stimulation required to detect the difference between two stimuli, and so it also is called a *just noticeable difference*.
- *Weber's law* is a basic law of psychophysics stating that a just noticeable difference is a constant proportion of the intensity of an initial stimulus (rather than a constant amount). Weber's law helps explain why a person in a quiet room is more startled by the ringing of a cell phone than is a person in an already noisy room.

### Sensory Adaptation: Turning Down Our Responses

- *Adaptation* is an adjustment in sensory capacity after prolonged exposure to unchanging stimuli. Adaptation occurs as people become accustomed to a stimulus and change their frame of reference.

## AP Key Terms

absolute threshold

adaptation

difference threshold (just noticeable difference)

perception

psychophysics

sensation

stimulus

Weber's law

# Class Discussion Ideas

**CLASS DEMONSTRATION: ABSOLUTE THRESHOLD** Ask for a volunteer. Using a 2-gallon pitcher of water, add 1/8 teaspoon of sugar and continue to add more until the volunteer can taste the sugar. No more than 1 teaspoon should be required.

**CLASS DEMONSTRATION: DIFFERENCE THRESHOLD** Have students touch their own arms with one finger. They should take a second finger and touch a point close to the first finger. When they can feel two distinct touches on their arm, this is the difference threshold for touch. This is more effective if students can do this to each other rather than to themselves.

**CLASS DEMONSTRATION: WEBER'S LAW** Select a volunteer and ask them to say something in a normal voice (such as "I love psychology"). Ask the class if they could hear the volunteer, which they should be able to do very clearly. Then say that you will have the volunteer repeat this phrase but this time while the rest of the class is talking to each other. Then instruct the class to stop talking. Ask if they could hear the volunteer. They should not have been able to hear. Alternatively, ask the volunteer to speak louder and louder over the class's talking until the class can clearly hear their voice. Then ask the volunteer whether they had to talk louder than when the room was silent. The answer should definitely be yes.

# Activities

**DIFFERENCE THRESHOLDS** To demonstrate difference thresholds and the just noticeable difference, bring a pile of books, a blindfold, and some CDs to class and ask for a strong volunteer. Place the blindfold on student volunteer and the stack of books in their arms. Tell them to report when they think you have added another book. Then slowly add CDs to the pile until they say something. Even though weight is constantly being added, they won't notice it until there is a 3% change. You can tell them that when they ask friends to help them move, they can maximize this. Their buddy picks up a box, and they add a few more things on top, saying, "You won't even notice the extra weight," and, in some cases, they'll be right!

# **AP** Discussion Questions

**PSYCHOPHYSICS** Ask students to provide examples from their daily lives of Weber's law and sensory adaptation.

- From an evolutionary standpoint, why might the eye have evolved so that the rods, which we rely on in low light, do not provide sharp images? Are there any advantages to this system?

## AP Test Practice

### Section I: Multiple Choice

1. **D** *(Skill 1.B, Learning Target 3.A/3.C)*

2. **B** *(Skill 1.A, Learning Target 3.B)*

3. **A** *(Skill 1.A, Learning Target 3.B)*

## Section II: Free Response

**A.**

Absolute threshold is the smallest intensity of a stimulus that must be present for the stimulus to be detected. Beau has a very low absolute threshold for taste and can quickly detect when a new spice has been added to the recipe.

Difference threshold is the smallest level of stimulation required to sense a change in stimulation has occurred. Beau has reached the difference threshold when adding more salt to his recipe and can tell that it is getting saltier than usual.

**B.**

Sensory adaptation is an adjustment in sensory after prolonged exposure to unchanging stimuli. Beau has been in the kitchen for hours testing new recipes and cannot detect the burnt smell due to the constant exposure. He is also experiencing sensory adaptation for taste. The initial taste of adding a new ingredient to the recipe can be very strong and distinct, but after several taste tests it no longer has the same effect for Beau.

# Module 11: Vision: Shedding Light on the Eye

## AP Module Summary

Vision starts with light, the physical energy that stimulates the eye. Light is a form of electromagnetic radiation waves. The sizes of wavelengths correspond to different types of energy. The range of wavelengths that humans are sensitive to—called the visual spectrum—is relatively small (see **Figure 1**). Light waves coming from some object outside the body are sensed by the only organ that is capable of responding to the visible spectrum: the eye. Our eyes convert light to a form that can be used by the neurons that serve as messengers to the brain.

## Illuminating the Structure of the Eye (See Figure 2 and Figure 3)

- *Cornea* is a transparent, protective window; its curvature, bends (or refracts) light as it passes through, playing a primary role in focusing the light more sharply.
- *Pupil* is a dark hole in the center of the *iris*, the colored part of the eye. The size of the pupil opening depends on the amount of light in the environment. Light traverses the *pupil*.
- *Lens*, which is directly behind the pupil. The lens acts to bend the rays of light so that they are properly focused on the rear of the eye. The lens focuses light by changing its own thickness, a process called
  - Accommodation: It becomes flatter when viewing distant objects and rounder when looking at closer objects.

## Reaching the Retina

- *Retina* is the part of the eye that converts the electromagnetic energy of light to electrical impulses for transmission to the brain.

There are two kinds of light-sensitive receptor cells in the retina.

- *Rods* are thin, cylindrical receptor cells that are highly sensitive to light.
  - Rods play a key role in peripheral vision—seeing objects that are outside the main center of focus—and in night vision.
  - Dark adaptation is the phenomenon of adjusting to dim light after being in brighter light.
  - Light adaptation is the process of adjusting to bright light after exposure to dim light.

- *Cones* are typically cone-shaped, light-sensitive receptor cells that are responsible for sharp focus and color perception particularly in bright light.
  - Cones are concentrated on the part of the retina called the
    - *Fovea*—a sensitive region of the retina.

**SENDING THE MESSAGE FROM THE EYE TO THE BRAIN** Stimulation of the nerve cells in the eye triggers a neural response that is transmitted to other nerve cells in the retina called *bipolar cells* and *ganglion cells*.

- *Optic nerve* is a bundle of ganglion axons that carry visual information to the brain.

## Processing the Visual Message

- *Ganglion cells*—gather information from a group of rods and cones in a particular area of the eye and compares the amount of light entering the center of that area with the amount of light in the area around it.
- *Feature detection* is the activation of neurons in the cortex by visual stimuli of specific shapes or patterns.

More recent work has added to our knowledge of the complex ways in which visual information coming from individual neurons is combined and processed. Different parts of the brain process nerve impulses simultaneously according to the attributes of the image.

**COLOR VISION AND COLOR BLINDNESS: THE 7-MILLION-COLOR SPECTRUM**  Although the variety of colors that people are generally able to distinguish is vast, there are certain individuals whose ability to perceive color is quite limited—those who are color-blind. Approximately 7% of men and 0.4% of women are color-blind.

## Explaining Color Vision

- *Trichromatic theory of color vision,* which does not explain color vision completely, suggests that there are three kinds of cones in the retina, each of which responds primarily to a specific range of wavelengths:
  - Blue-violet colors,
  - Green,
  - Yellow-red.

According to trichromatic theory, perception of color is influenced by the relative strength with which each of the three kinds of cones is activated.

- *Opponent-process theory of color vision* suggests that receptor cells are linked in pairs, working in opposition to each other. The theory provides a good explanation for afterimages (see **Figure 7**).

## **AP** Key Terms

| | |
|---|---|
| **cones** | **retina** |
| **feature detector** | **rods** |
| **opponent-process theory of color vision** | **trichromatic theory of color vision** |
| **optic nerve** | |

## Class Discussion Ideas

**THE JOY OF VISUAL PERCEPTION**  This website contains several useful visual images and material for preparing your lecture: http://www.yorku.ca/eye/thejoy.htm.

## Visual Pathways

- **Parts of the Eye and Visual Pathways:** Students should be able to identify and describe the structures of the eye. They should also be able to describe the visual pathway for the left and right visual fields.
  - Point out that light reflected off objects is projected onto the retina, traveling first through the structures of the eye, where it is refracted and reversed. Make sure that students understand that the eye is not like a camera in that it does not record exact replicas of objects. Describe the pathway from the retina to the brain showing the crossover at the optic chiasm.
  - *I recommend that you create a note taker consisting of blank diagrams of the eye. Have students record information that you review in class by labeling the diagram, adding specific details and functions. Adding color to each area will also cause neurons to fire.

- **The Eye and Its Structures:** Show an illustration of the eye and its structures, highlighting the parts as follows:
  - After the image leaves the retina in the form of neural transmission, the processing of the image in the brain becomes increasingly complex and sophisticated. Information from the image passes from the rods and cones to the bipolar and ganglion cells and from there travels to the visual cortex of the brain. However, the path taken by these neural signals

is not a direct one. As the optic nerves leave each eyeball, they meet at a point roughly between the two eyes—called the optic chiasm—where each optic nerve then splits. (POINT TO THE OPTIC CHIASM.)

- ○ In order to understand what happens at the optic chiasm, we have to go back to what is happening within the eye. (POINT TO THE RIGHT AND LEFT VISUAL FIELDS AT THE TOP.)
- ○ Our eyes see the world in terms of a "right visual field" and a "left visual field." These correspond to the two halves of all objects, images, and scenes that we look at.
- ○ Each eye can be divided into a right and left retina. (POINT TO THE RIGHT AND LEFT RETINAS.)
- ○ Images on the right half of the visual field cross and are projected onto the left half of each retina. (POINT TO THIS PATHWAY.)
- ○ Similarly, images on the left half of the visual field cross and are projected onto the right half of each retina. (POINT TO THIS PATHWAY.)
- ○ As you can see here, all information from each right half of the retina goes to the right visual cortex. All information from each left half of the retina goes to the left visual cortex.
- ○ In other words, all information from the right visual field ends up being projected onto the left visual cortex. All information from the left visual field ends up being projected onto the right visual cortex. (REVIEW BOTH PATHWAYS.)

## Activities

## Processing of Visual Information

- **Processing of Visual Information:** *Handout: Processing of Visual Information,* reviews the processing of visual information.
- **Bottom-Up and Top-Down Processing:** Use *Handout: Is It Top-Down or Bottom-Up?* This activity has students look at examples and then identify the examples as either bottom-up processing or top-down processing. Students will gain knowledge and experience in recognizing the difference between the two types of processing.
- **Hands-Free:** As you drive, there are many signs reminding you not to text or talk on the phone while driving. Companies have come up with hands-free alternatives. Break the class into groups and have them recall what has been discussed about inattentional blindness, then debate whether or not hand-free devices resolve the concern about distracted driving. Each student or group should then write a summary paper of its findings.

## Color Vision and Color-Blindness

- **Fading Dot:** Direct students to this website: http://www.exploratorium.edu/exhibits/fading_dot/fading_dot.html.
- **Monocular Cues:** Break the class into groups and have the groups give examples of the monocular cues discussed in the chapter, such as familiar size, height in the field of view, linear perspective, overlap, shading, and texture gradient. In their examples, the groups should also include pictures.
- **Afterimages:** Go to http://faculty.washington.edu/chudler/after.html for an interactive afterimage activity.
- **FM 100 Hue Test:** Have students go to http://www.xrite.com/online-color-test-challenge for an online test of color (hue) discrimination. They are presented with rows of colors that they are asked to place in order by dragging and dropping each color. Responses are then scored and compared to one's peer group (by age and gender). This can be used for discussion on thresholds or the visual system.
- **Facial Recognition:** This is a good link that lets students actively participate in facial recognition with a focus on faces that appear upside down: http://faculty.washington.edu/chudler/java/faces.html.

## Discussion Questions

Have students look at the green, black, and yellow flag in the text (**Figure 7**) and then at a blank wall. Ask them the following questions:

- What colors did you see when viewing the afterimage of the green, black, and yellow flag?
- Why is this afterimage used as support for the opponent-process theory?
- How can the opponent process theory be combined with the trichromatic theory into one unified theory of color perception?
- What are some practical problems faced by people who are color-blind? How could people who are color-blind be trained to overcome these problems?

## **AP** Student Edition Answer Key

### Neuroscience in Your Life: Recognizing Faces

Answer Suggestions

- The independent variable is exposure to faces because it is the variable being manipulated. The dependent variable is brain activity for faces because it is being measured.
- Early sensory experience is important for the development of face recognition. Face processing is due to nurture (experience) and nature (genetics).

### AP Test Practice

#### Section I: Multiple-Choice

1. **C** (Skill 2, Learning Target 3.C)

2. **D** (Skill 1.B, Learning Target 3.F)

3. **E** (Skill 1.B, Learning Target 3.G)

#### Section II: Free Response

**A.**
Color vision is associated with cones. Connie could have a problem seeing color due to a deficiency of cones.

Foveal vision is the central part of the eye responsible for acuity or sharpness of vision. Connie might have problems with her fovea, leading to her not being able to see clearly.

Peripheral vision is associated with rods. Connie could have problems with her rods and therefore not be able to see items located in her peripheral vision.

**B.**
The independent variable is the new eye drop medication because it is the variable being manipulated.

The dependent variable is cataracts or the degree that the lens is clouded over because it is the variable being measure.

**C.**
Random assignment allows for cause-and-effect conclusions. If participants were randomly assigned and the results were significant, we could say the new medication caused a reduction in cataracts.

Placebo effect is the beneficial impact of an inert substance by simply believing in the treatment.

Patients in the second group were provided a placebo or saline solution. If they believe they have received the real treatment they may have improved symptoms simply due to believing in the treatment.

# Module 12: Hearing and the Other Senses

## AP Module Summary

**SENSING SOUND (SEE FIGURE 1)** Sound localization is the process by which we identify the direction from which a sound is coming.

- *Sound* is the movement of air molecules brought about by a source of vibration.
- *Eardrum* is aptly named because it operates as a miniature drum, vibrating when sound waves hit it. Vibrations are then transferred into the:
- *Middle ear*, a tiny chamber containing three bones (the *hammer*, the *anvil*, and the *stirrup*) that transmit vibrations to the *oval window*, a thin membrane leading to the inner ear.
- *Inner ear* is the portion of the ear that changes the sound vibrations into a form in which they can be transmitted to the brain. When sound enters the inner ear through the oval window, it moves into the:
  - *Cochlea*, a coiled tube that looks something like a snail and is filled with fluid that vibrates in response to sound. Inside the cochlea is the
  - *Basilar membrane*, a structure that runs through the center of the cochlea, dividing it into an upper chamber and a lower chamber. The basilar membrane is covered with *hair cells*. When the hair cells are bent by the vibrations entering the cochlea, the cells send a neural message to the brain.

## Physical Aspects of Sound

- *Frequency* is the number of wave cycles that occur in a second (see **Figure 2**).
- *Pitch* is the characteristic that makes sound seem "high" or "low."
- *Amplitude* is a feature of wave patterns that allows us to distinguish between loud and soft sounds.

## Explaining Hearing: Listen to the Theories of Sound

- *Place theory of hearing* states that different areas of the basilar membrane respond to different frequencies.
- *Frequency theory of hearing* suggests that the entire basilar membrane acts as a microphone, vibrating as a whole in response to a sound.
- *Echolocation* is the use of sound waves and echoes to determine where objects are. It is a technique that bats and some people with visual impairment use for navigation.

**BALANCE: THE UPS AND DOWNS OF LIFE** Several structures of the ear are related more to our sense of balance than to our hearing. Collectively, these structures are known as the *vestibular system*, which responds to the pull of gravity and allows us to maintain our balance. The main structure of the vestibular system is formed by the *semicircular canals* of the inner ear, which consist of three tubes containing fluid that sloshes through them when the head moves, signaling rotational or angular movement to the brain.

**SMELL** Although many animals have keener abilities to detect odors than we do, the human sense of smell (olfaction) permits us to detect more than 10,000 separate smells. The sense of smell is sparked when the molecules of a substance enter the nasal passages and meet *olfactory cells*, the receptor neurons of the nose, which are spread across the nasal cavity. More than 1,000 separate types of receptors have been identified on those cells so far. Each of these receptors is so specialized that it responds only to a small band of different odors. The responses of the separate olfactory cells are then transmitted to the brain, where they are combined into recognition of a particular smell.

**TASTE** The sense of taste (*gustation*) involves receptor cells that respond to four basic stimulus qualities: sweet, sour, salty, and bitter. A fifth category also exists, a flavor called umami (a meaty or savory taste), although there is controversy about whether it qualifies as a fundamental taste. The receptor cells for taste are located in roughly 10,000 *taste buds*, which are distributed across the tongue and other parts of the mouth and throat. The taste buds wear out and are replaced every 10 days or so.

## The Skin Senses: Touch, Pressure, Temperature, and Pain

- *Skin senses*—touch, pressure, temperature, and pain—play a critical role in survival, making us aware of potential danger to our bodies (see **Figure 5**).
  - One explanation for pain is that it is an outcome of cell injury; when a cell is damaged, regardless of the source of damage, it releases a chemical called *substance P* that transmits pain messages to the brain.
- *Gate-control theory of pain*, particular nerve receptors in the spinal cord lead to specific areas of the brain related to pain. When these receptors are activated because of an injury or problem with a part of the body, a "gate" to the brain is opened, allowing us to experience the sensation of pain. However, another set of neural receptors can, when stimulated, close the "gate" to the brain, thereby reducing the experience of pain.

**HOW OUR SENSES INTERACT** Certain people have an unusual condition known as s*ynesthesia*, in which exposure to one sensation (such as sound) evokes an additional one (such as vision). See the "Neuroscience in Your Life: Synesthesia and the Overconnected Brain" in the text for more details.

## **AP** Key Terms

| | |
|---|---|
| basilar membrane | hair cells |
| cochlea (KOKE-lee-uh) | place theory of hearing |
| eardrum | semicircular canals |
| frequency theory of hearing | skin senses |
| gate-control theory of pain | sound |

## Class Discussion Ideas

**AUDITORY STRUCTURES** Describe each of the organs in the ear, from the outer ear to the cochlea. Contrast the place and frequency theories of hearing by showing the parts of the cochlea that react to different frequencies (the place theory).

**HELPFUL HINTS FOR STUDENTS** Help students to remember the auditory structures by giving them these hints:

- Hammer, anvil, and stirrups: These are the middle ear structures involved in conduction of the sound wave. Paul Revere rode a horse (using the stirrups) to "conduct" information.
- Basilar membrane: Like the strings of a "double bass," this membrane vibrates in response to sound waves.
- Cochlea: This literally means "snail shell," and that is what it looks like. Think of drinking a Coca-Cola on the beach.

**FREQUENCY AND HIGH-PITCHED RINGTONES** Our sensitivity to different frequencies changes as we age. For instance, as we get older, the range of frequencies we can detect declines, particularly for high-pitched sounds. This is why high school students sometimes choose high-pitched ring tones for their cell phones in settings in which cell phone use is forbidden: the ringing sound goes undetected by their aging teachers. To demonstrate this to your class, go to the following website and test their hearing: http://www.freemosquitoringtones.org.

# Activities

## Auditory Information Processing

Have students complete *Handout: Auditory Information Processing.*

**SEMICIRCULAR CANALS AND BALANCE**  To learn about the role of the semicircular canal in balance, have students complete this assignment:

- Have a friend spin you around on a chair seven or eight times. Then have that friend help you stand up on one leg.
- How well were you able to stand up on one leg?
- How did you feel when you were being spun around?
- (Note: This also can be used as a class demonstration.)

**SENSE OF SMELL**  Have students complete *Handout: Smell Rating Activity.* You can tally the results and show them which scents they chose and how they rated them.

**SENSE OF TASTE**  Have students complete *Handout: Taste Rating Activity.* As with the smell ratings, tally the results and give students feedback on their data.

**SENSES CHALLENGE**

- **Exploring Touch:** Ask for three volunteers and send them to the hallway. While the volunteers are in the hallway, arrange the classroom desks to form a maze. Throughout the maze, place various objects on the desks. These objects should represent various aspects of touch, such as something sharp for pain and something hot and something cold for temperature. Blindfold the volunteers and then have them come back into the classroom and work their way through the maze. After they have completed the maze, ask them to explain the senses they experienced as they went through the maze.
- **Taste:** For this activity you will need orange juice and food coloring. You could also use mashed potatoes or rice and food coloring. Paper cups are also necessary. Pour three glasses of orange juice. Color two with food coloring. Varying shades of red work nicely. Any food color will deepen and change the color. Have students taste the drinks and rate how they taste. You may want to ask them which drink is sweeter. Which drink is more bitter? Which has more orange-juice flavor? Students typically rate them differently. After the demo, you may want to put food coloring in water and have them notice that it doesn't change the taste. *Source:* Hoegg, J., & Alba, J. W. (2007). Taste perception: More than meets the tongue. *Journal of Consumer Research, 33,* 301–314.
- **Taste:** For this activity, bring Juicy Fruit Gems (candy) to class for all your students—first checking for any allergies or sensitivities. Pass out the candy. Ask students to hold their noses shut. Have them take a bite of the fruit gem, chew, swallow, and then rate the sweetness. If their noses are shut they should not get any flavor. Have students unplug their noses. They should perceive a burst of flavor. Ask them to rate the flavor and the sweetness. Students should notice a flavor burst caused by movement of air into their mouths that allows the odorants to enter the back of the nose (retronasal olfaction). Did the sweet taste change when they unplugged their noses? *Source:* Bartoshuk, L. (2014). *From supertasters to better tomatoes: What modern taste psychophysics can do.* Presentation at the National Institute for Teaching Psychology, St. Petersburg, FL.
- **Taste:** An activity for taste can be found at http://www.scientificamerican.com/article/bring-science-home-sour-preference-age/.
- **Smell:** Use *Handout: Emotional Smells* as a way for the students to realize and think about how smells set up emotional memories for them.
- **Smell and Taste:** Ask for a class volunteer who has no food allergies. Blindfold the student and plug their noise with a swimming nose plug or something similar. Offer them an apple, pear, or potato and ask them what they taste. This can lead to a discussion of the interaction of taste and smell. You may also mention that as people age, their sense of smell declines. How does this influence their taste sensations? *Source:* Diekhoff, G. M. (1990).

Sensory interdependencies. In V. Parker Makosky, et. al. (Eds.). *Activities handbook for the teaching of psychology—Volume 3*. Washington, DC: American Psychology Association.

- **Researching New Technology**: Have students search for one journal article or magazine article that explains the impact that new technology (e.g., iPods, iPads, ear buds, Kindles, and e-readers) has on the health of our senses. Ask them to write a one- to two-page critique of that article and reflect on what changes they can personally make when using such devices to help protect their senses from damage.
- **Sensory Abilities Survey:** Have students complete the simple true-and-false survey in *Handout: Sensory Abilities Survey.* Comparison data is available to share with students.
- **Sensory Adaptation:** Use *Handout: What Sensory Adaptation Did You Experience Already Today?* The goal of this assignment is to have students realize that they experience sensory adaptation every day, and it often happens without them even being aware of it.

## Discussion Questions

**HEARING DAMAGE** If hearing damage results from exposure to noises such as loud music and iPods, why do people continue to put themselves at risk?

**BIOLOGY AND CULTURE IN SMELL AND TASTE PREFERENCES** It has been said that we taste with our eyes first. Professional chefs give great thought to the presentation of foods. Think about your favorite food and focus not on how it tastes but on how it looks. Now think about how it smells. How do vision, smell, and taste work together to produce the experience of your favorite dish? Would your favorite beef stew be just as appetizing if it were served in a dog food dish?

- Imagine a person standing at a corner. As she starts to cross the street, she hears a car slamming on its brakes and turns her head to see a car hitting a tree. Explain what is occurring both in vision and audition as this person sees and hears the accident.
- Ask students what smells trigger strong childhood memories. Explain why smells create such strong memory cues.

## Polling Questions

**HAVE YOU LOST YOUR...?** Losing one of your senses can be very challenging. Of the five senses we talked about in this chapter, which one of the five do you think you could give up? Cast your vote. Who knows someone who has lost one of their five senses? How many people think that individuals who are deaf or blind perceive life just as someone who has all their senses intact?

**SENSE OR NO SENSE?** Ask students which sense, if they had to choose, they would be most willing to go without for the rest of their lives (you can use the CPS clickers to poll the class). Then ask them why.

**SENSORY ADAPTATION** Ask students if they are wearing a watch, ring, or necklace (you may use CPS to poll the class on this). Now ask them how many of them can feel that piece of jewelry. Most people can't. They might when they first put it on that day, but after a little (very little) time has passed, they may no longer feel it. The same thing happens at pool parties. Some people are in the pool saying the water's "not that bad." Then you jump in and think its freezing! Were they lying? No, they had just already undergone sensory adaptation to the temperature.

**POLLING QUESTION: TOUCH ME, HOLD ME, SQUEEZE ME TIGHT** Often, the focus on our sensory systems is largely dedicated to seeing and hearing. However, there is very strong evidence that suggests touch may be the most important sense we have. Developmental research has shown that touching creates a bond that fosters emotional and physical connections. How many students think that touching is one of the most important parts of developing a relationship with someone? Who would say they are considered "touchy-feely" people by their friends or family?

**POLLING QUESTION: SPICE IT UP!** Culture can influence the experiences of taste. Think about the last time you were out at a restaurant with your friends and you disagreed on whether a particular food item was spicy or not. For some, the experience of spicy foods is introduced slowly into their diet as children so they can learn "what is delicious" at an early age. How many of you like spicy foods and the hotter the better? Which culture do you think has the spiciest foods? (Instructor note: Search Google for "cultures with the spiciest foods" for the most updated list of options for polling). Discuss how cultural influences inform our perceptions of "delicious" or umami.

# AP Student Edition Answer Key

## Applying Psychology in the 21st Century: Sniffing Out Flash Drives

Answer Suggestions

- An absolute threshold is the smallest intensity of a stimulus that must be present for the stimulus to be detected.
- Smell is associated with memory. Stronger smells might have increased memories. A stronger sense of smell might result in hidden means of communication, such as pheromones found in nonhuman species.

## AP Test Practice

### Section I: Multiple-Choice

1.  **E** (Skill 1.B, Learning Target 2.I)

2.  **B** (Skill 1.A, Learning Target 2.J)

3.  **B** (Skill 1.B, Learning Target 1.B)

### Section II: Free Response

**A.**
The cerebellum is in charge of bodily balance. Jamal uses his cerebellum to remain balanced and walk fluidly across the stage.

The motor cortex is in charge of voluntary motor movements. Jamal uses his motor cortex when voluntarily moving his fingers on the buttons of the saxophone and turning the sheet music.

The occipital lobe is in charge of processing vision in order to see. Jamal uses his occipital lobe to see the music sheets in front of him while he plays a new song.

**B.**
A PET scan shows biochemical activity within the brain at a given moment. Radioactive glucose is injected and tracked by a computer to find the most active brain regions. Jamal would have a PET scan to help find damage associated with brain activity, such as memory or movement.

An fMRI scan shows a computer-generated image of brain structures and activity by using a powerful magnetic field. Jamal would have an fMRI scan to produce a vivid, detailed image of the functioning of his brain.

**C.**
The left frontal lobe consists of Broca's area, which is in charge of speech production. If Jamal has damage to his frontal lobe he may have problems producing speech.

The left temporal lobe consists of Wernicke's area, which is in charge of speech comprehension and production. If Jamal has damage to his temporal lobe he may have problems understanding speech.

# Module 13: Perceptual Organization: Constructing Our View of the World

## AP Module Summary

### The Gestalt Laws of Organization (See Figure 1 and Figure 2)

- *Gestalt laws of organization* refer to a series of principles that describe how we organize bits and pieces of information into meaningful wholes.

### Top-Down and Bottom-Up Processing (See Figure 3 and Figure 4)

- *Top-down processing*, perception is guided by higher-level knowledge, experience, expectations, and motivations.
- *Bottom-up processing* consists of the progression of recognizing and processing information from individual components of a stimuli and moving to the perception of the whole.
- Top-down and bottom-up processing occur simultaneously, and interact with each other, in our perception of the world around us.

### Depth Perception: Translating 2-D To 3-D

- *Depth perception*—the ability to view the world in three dimensions and to perceive distance.

Due largely to the fact that we have two eyes and that there is a certain distance between the eyes, a slightly different image reaches each retina. The brain integrates the two images into one view, but it also recognizes the difference in images and uses this difference to estimate the distance of an object from us.

The difference in the images seen by the left eye and the right eye is known as *binocular disparity*.

- *Monocular cues*—a sense of depth and distance with just one eye.
  - *Motion parallax* is the change in position of an object on the retina caused by movement of your body relative to the object.
  - *Relative size* reflects the assumption that if two objects are the same size, the object that makes a smaller image on the retina is farther away than the one that makes a larger image.
  - *Texture gradient* provides information about distance, because the details of things that are far away are less distinct.
  - *Linear perspective* (in which objects in the distance appear to converge) as a monocular cue in estimating distance, allowing the two-dimensional image on the retina to record the three-dimensional world.

### Perceptual Constancy

- *Perceptual constancy* is the recognition that physical objects are unvarying and consistent, even though our sensory input about them varies (e.g. size, shape, color, and brightness).

### Perceptual Illusions: The Deceptions of Perceptions (See Figure 5 and Figure 6)

- *Visual illusions* are physical stimuli that consistently produce errors in perception.

## Subliminal Perception

- *Subliminal perception* is the perception of messages about which we have no awareness.

The stimulus could be a written word, a sound, or even a smell that activates the sensory system but is not intense enough for a person to report having experienced it.

Social psychologists refer to subliminal messages as priming, can influence behavior in subtle ways, there is little evidence that they can lead to major changes in attitudes or behavior.

## AP Key Terms

bottom-up processing

depth perception

Gestalt (geh-SHTALLT)
  laws of organization

perceptual constancy

top-down processing

visual illusions

## Class Discussion Ideas

**MOON ILLUSION DEMONSTRATION** For the moon illusion, conduct the following demonstration: Ask students to write down their answer to this question: You are watching the moon just after it has risen above the horizon. If you were to hold out your hand at arm's length, what object would completely cover the moon from view?

1. Pea
2. Quarter
3. Golf ball
4. Baseball
5. Dinner plate

Ask for a show of hands for each choice. Most students will choose answer 2 or 3 when 1 is the correct answer.

Background information on the moon illusion can be found on this website:

http://science.nasa.gov/science-news/science-at-nasa/2008/16jun_moonillusion/.

**HELPFUL HINTS FOR STUDENTS: NAMES OF ILLUSIONS** To help students remember the names of the illusions, give them these hints:

- Müller-Lyer (two-headed arrows): Müller was a "liar" when he said that two arrows were the same length.
- Ponzo (train tracks): You can take the train to Ponzo, a lovely Italian town.
- Poggendorf (discontinuous line; example is air traffic controller's radar screen): Mr. Poggendorf, an air traffic controller, lost his job when he almost caused a crash.

**OTHER VISUAL ILLUSIONS** Have students explore the following website and discuss the illusions in terms of the visual system: https://www.verywell.com/cool-optical-illusions-2795841.

**DEMONSTRATION: TOP-DOWN PROCESSING** To illustrate top-down processing, show students this paragraph:

> Aoccdrnig to a rscheearch at Cmabrigde Uinervtisy, it deosn't mttaer in waht oredr the ltteers in a wrod are, the olny iprmoetnt tihng is taht the frist and lsat ltteer be at the rghit pclae. The rset can be a toatl mses and you can sitll raed it wouthit porbelm. Tihs is bcuseae the huamn mnid deos not raed ervey lteter by istlef, but the wrod as a wlohe.

To help students remember the difference between top-down and bottom-up, explain that they refer to the direction of processing. Top-down means from the cortex down, and bottom-up means from the senses up to the brain.

# Activities

## The Moon Illusion

Assign *Handout: The Moon Illusion.*

# Discussion and Polling Questions

Ask students to explain how their own perceptual sets might create stereotypes, prejudice, or discrimination.

**SUBLIMINAL PERCEPTION** Do you believe in subliminal perception?

**IT'S EVERYONE ELSE'S FAULT BUT MY OWN** Texting, talking, and driving have become one of the hottest topics in the media. Most of us would say that we are good drivers and that often the other person is at fault for an accident, a near miss, or even road rage. Who has caught themselves yelling at someone because the other person was texting or talking and wasn't paying attention while driving and almost hit you? Let's be honest: how many of you have been the one texting or talking on the phone and almost got into an accident, near miss, or braked hard because you weren't paying attention? Who thinks they can actually multitask without sacrificing quality or concentration on all the tasks at hand? How many people think that the media is making too big of a deal about talking on the phone or texting while driving?

# **AP** Student Edition Answer Key

## AP Test Practice

### Section I: Multiple-Choice

1. **E** *(Skill 1.B, Learning Target 3.A)*

2. **D** *(Skill 1.C, Learning Target 3.D)*

3. **B** *(Skill 1.A, Learning Target 3.H)*

### Section II: Free Response

**A.**
Figure ground is a Gestalt law of organization in which the figure is the object being perceived and the ground is the background or space within the object. As Ariana stares at the animals near the river they are the figure because they have meaning and are being perceived, and the mountains are the ground because they are the background.

The Gestalt principle of proximity states we perceive elements that are closer together as grouped together. According to proximity, Arianna would organize the three animals near each other at the river as belonging to one group.

**B.**
Binocular disparity uses the difference in the images seen by the left and right eye to determine distance. Ariana uses the differences between the images on her two retinas to judge the distance between the river and the mountains.

Relative size provides information about distance by assuming that if two objects are the same size, the object that makes a smaller image on the retina is farther away than the one that makes a larger image. According to relative size, the animals by the river are closer and should appear larger than the animals by the hiking path, which are farther away and smaller.

Texture gradient provides information about distance because items farther away have less distinct details than objects that are closer. According to texture gradient, Ariana should see less detail on the flowers that are farther away in the field and more detail on the flowers that are close to her.

Linear perspective provides information about distance because objects farther away appear to converge. According to linear perspective, animals located near where the hiking path converged will appear farther away.

Motion parallax provides information about distance because as you are moving stable objects in the distance will appear to move at a slower speed and in the same direction as you are. According to motion parallax, while on the moving train the mountains in the distance will appear to move at a slower speed and in the same direction as Ariana is moving.

# CHAPTER 5

# States of Consciousness

## AP Introduction

The one unit that saw the most change with the new College Board Exam and Description Guide for 2019–2020 is the States of Consciousness unit. To begin with, the unit has been consolidated by eliminating the study of hypnosis as a testable topic. And, the unit itself has been added to the second unit in the guide, Biological Bases of Behavior. The topics of study that have remained the same are the ever popular stages of sleep, dreams, and drugs.

## AP Essential Questions

- How can biology influence our behavior and mental processes?
- What happens when a particular neurotransmitter is absent from the body?
- How do biological and environmental factors interact to influence our behaviors and mental processes?

Ask any student what they love to do most and have so little time for and their answer is most likely going to be sleep. This module is sure to create a buzz in your classroom. Students love talking about their dreams and so desparately want to know more about sleep. The only change is that students need to be better prepared with knowing the neural and behavioral characteristics of the sleep cycle and that there are only stages 1, 2, 3 NREM & REM (stage 4 NREM was consolidated into stage 3 NREM several years ago).

## Module 14: Sleep and Dreams

**AP Learning Targets:**

- Describe various states of consciousness and their impact on behavior.
- Identify the contributions of major figures in consciousness research.
- Discuss aspects of sleep and dreaming.

**Pacing:**

½ Block or 1 Traditional Class Period

# Module 15: Hypnosis and Meditation

[Author's note: The most talked about change coming from the College Board is the removal of hypnosis from the Course and Exam Description guide. While you should not ignore the module and the information within, since there will be no questions related to hypnosis on future advanced placement exams, this would be an area to eliminate from the classroom and expect students to learn on their own.]

**AP Learning Targets:**

- Describe various states of consciousness and their impact on behavior.

**Pacing:**

0 Block or 0 Traditional Class Periods

# Module 16: Drug Use: The Highs and Lows of Consciousness

**AP Learning Targets:**

- Discuss the influence of drugs on neurotransmitters.
- Identify the major psychoactive drug categories and classify specific drugs, including their psychological and physiological effects.
- Discuss drug dependence, addiction, tolerance, and withdrawal.

**Pacing:**

1.5 Block or 2.5 Traditional Class periods

# Module 14: Sleep and Dreams

## AP Module Summary

**Consciousness** is the awareness of the sensations, thoughts, and feelings we experience at a given moment. Consciousness is our subjective understanding of both the environment around us and our private internal world, unobservable to outsiders.

Although sleeping is a state that we all experience, many unanswered questions about sleep still remain, along with a considerable number of myths.

**THE STAGES OF SLEEP (SEE FIGURE 2 AND FIGURE 3)** People progress through a series of distinct stages of sleep during a night's rest—known as stage 1 through stage 3 and REM sleep—moving through the stages in cycles lasting about 90 minutes.

- *Stage (NREM) 1 sleep* is characterized by relatively rapid, low-amplitude brain waves.
- *Stage (NREM) 2 sleep* makes up about half of the total sleep of those in their early 20s and is characterized by a slower, more regular wave pattern.
- *Stage 3 (NREM) sleep,* this is when the brain waves become slower, with higher peaks and lower valleys in the wave pattern. During stage 3 people are least responsive to outside stimulation.

## REM Sleep: The Paradox of Sleep

- *Rapid Eye Movement*, or *REM sleep*: Several times a night, when sleepers have cycled back to a shallower state of sleep, their heart rate increases and becomes irregular, their blood pressure rises, and their breathing rate increases. Most characteristic of this period is the back-and-forth movement of the eyes, as if watching an action-filled movie.
- REM sleep is usually accompanied by dreams, which—whether or not people remember them—are experienced by everyone during some part of their night's sleep.
- Paradoxically, while all this activity is occurring, the major muscles of the body appear to be paralyzed.

**WHY DO WE SLEEP, AND HOW MUCH SLEEP IS NECESSARY?** Evolutionary perspective suggests that sleep permitted our ancestors to conserve energy at night, a time when food was relatively hard to come by. Consequently, they were better able to forage for food when the sun was up. Sleep restores and replenishes our brains and bodies. For instance, the reduced activity of the brain during non-REM sleep may give neurons in the brain a chance to repair themselves. Sleep also assists physical growth and brain development in children. For example, the release of growth hormones is associated with deep sleep (Peterfi et al., 2010).

**APPLYING PSYCHOLOGY IN THE 21ST CENTURY: SLEEPING TO FORGET** An interesting amount of evidence suggests that the primary function of sleep is to help us forget. It allows the brian to eliminate unnecessary information, a process called reverse learning (Heller et al., 2014). During this process, the brain prunes back on certain neural connections while we sleep. In a study with mice, when they experienced stress and then were given a chemical to inhibit the pruning process, they awoke the next day to be more fearful of their surroundings. Further, when placed in a new environment, those mice given the inhibitory chemical were less curious and more fearful than those not given this chemical and essentially permitted to sleep normally the night before (Diering et al., 2017).

**THE FUNCTION AND MEANING OF DREAMING (SEE FIGURE 6)** Although dreams tend to be subjective to the person having them, common elements frequently occur in everyone's dreams.

**PSYCHOANALYTIC EXPLANATIONS OF DREAMS: DO DREAMS REPRESENT UNCONSIOUS WISH FULFILLMENT?**

- *Unconscious Wish Fulfillment Theory*—Sigmund Freud proposed that dreams represent unconscious wishes that dreamers desire to see fulfilled (see **Figure 7**).
- Manifest content of the dream—its storyline—is what we remember and report about the dream.
- Latent content, which includes the actual, underlying wishes that the dream represents.

Many psychologists reject Freud's view that dreams typically represent unconscious wishes and that particular objects and events in a dream are symbolic.

**EVOLUTIONARY EXPLANATIONS OF DREAMS: DREAMS-FOR-SURVIVAL THEORY** *Dreams-for-survival theory*, which is based in the evolutionary perspective, dreams permit us to reconsider and reprocess during sleep information that is critical for our daily survival. In the dreams-for-survival theory, dreams represent concerns about our daily lives,

**NEUROSCIENCE EXPLANATIONS OF DREAMS: ACTIVATION-SYNTHESIS THEORY** *Activation-synthesis theory* focuses on the random electrical energy that the brain produces during REM sleep, possibly as a result of changes in the production of particular neurotransmitters.

## Sleep Disturbances: Slumbering Problems

- *Insomnia* is a condition in which people experience difficulty in sleeping. Insomnia is a problem that afflicts as many as one-third of all people. Women and older adults are more likely to suffer from insomnia, as well as people who are unusually thin or are depressed.
- *Sleep apnea* is a condition in which a person has difficulty breathing while sleeping. The result is disturbed, fitful sleep, and a significant loss of REM sleep, as the person is constantly reawakened when the lack of oxygen becomes great enough to trigger a waking response.
- *Night terrors* are sudden awakenings from non-REM sleep that are accompanied by extreme fear, panic, and strong physiological arousal. Usually occurring in stage 3 sleep, night terrors may be so frightening that a sleeper awakens with a shriek.
- *Narcolepsy* is uncontrollable sleeping that occurs for short periods while a person is awake. No matter what the activity—holding a heated conversation, exercising, or driving—a narcoleptic will suddenly fall asleep.
- *Sleep talking* and *sleepwalking*, two sleep disturbances that are usually harmless. Both occur during stage 3 sleep and are more common in children than in adults.

## Circadian Rhythms: Life Cycles

- *Circadian rhythms* are biological processes that occur regularly on approximately a 24-hour cycle.
- Brain's suprachiasmatic nucleus (SCN) controls circadian rhythms. However, the relative amount of light and darkness, which varies with the seasons of the year, also plays a role in regulating circadian rhythms.

## Daydreams: Dreams Without Sleep

- *Daydreams* are fantasies that people construct while awake.

## Becoming an Informed Consumer of Psychology: Sleeping Better

- Exercise during the day (at least 6 hours before bedtime).
- Avoid long naps—but consider taking short ones.
- Choose a regular bedtime and stick to it.

- Avoid drinks with caffeine after lunch.
- Drink a glass of warm milk at bedtime.
- Avoid sleeping pills.
- Try not to sleep.

## **AP** Key Terms

activation-synthesis theory

circadian rhythms

consciousness

daydreams

dreams-for-survival theory

rapid eye movement (REM) sleep

Stage 1 sleep

Stage 2 sleep

Stage 3 sleep

unconscious wish fulfillment theory

## Class Discussion Ideas

**FREUDIAN SYMBOLS IN DREAMS** Show students the following list of Freudian symbols. Do they agree that these symbols have hidden, unconscious meanings?

| Male Symbols | Female Symbols | Symbols of Intercourse |
|---|---|---|
| Bullets | Ovens | Climbing stairs |
| Snakes | Boxes | Crossing a bridge |
| Sticks | Tunnels | Riding an elevator |
| Fire | Caves | Flying in an airplane |
| Umbrellas | Bottles | Walking down a hallway |
| Hoses | Ships | Entering a room |
| Knives | Apples | Traveling through a tunnel |
| Guns | Peaches | |
| Trains and planes | Grapefruits | |

**DREAM THEORY EXAMPLE** Describe one of your recent dreams (one that does not have any obvious sexual or embarrassing content). Use it to contrast the dream theories.

**COMMON DREAM THEMES** Take a poll of the class to find out what the most common dreams are. Assuming that most would have had dreams about common, everyday experiences, ask them what the implications are for the theories of dreaming (i.e., these probably will support the activation-synthesis theory).

**SLEEP DEPRIVATION AND SLEEP DEBT** Talk about sleep deprivation and sleep debt. Present the results of the National Sleep Foundation study, *Sleep in America* (see https://sleepfoundation.org/sleep-polls).

**GUIDELINES FOR A BETTER NIGHT'S SLEEP** In addition to (or instead of) the guidelines provided in the book for getting a better night's sleep, consider this list, from the National Sleep Foundation (see https://sleepfoundation.org/sleep-tools-tips).
- Consume less or no caffeine and avoid alcohol.
- Drink less fluids before going to sleep.
- Avoid heavy meals close to bedtime.
- Avoid nicotine.
- Exercise regularly but do so in the daytime, preferably after noon.

- Try a relaxing routine, such as soaking in hot water (a hot tub or bath) before bedtime.
- Establish a regular bedtime and wake time schedule.

**NEW YORK TIMES ARTICLE: BACKGROUND ON SLEEP AND DREAMS** See Angier, N. (October 23, 2007). In the dreamscape of nightmares, clues to why we dream at all. *The New York Times,* (http://www.nytimes.com/2007/10/23/science/23angi.html?_r=1&pagewanted=all) for an extensive discussion of the functions of sleep and dreams.

## Activities

**STREAM OF CONSCIOUSNESS** Take 20 minutes and document your stream of consciousness. Just write whatever comes into your mind during this period. When you have finished, take a close look at what your stream of consciousness reveals. What topics came up that surprised you? Are the thoughts and feelings you wrote down reflective of your daily life? Your important goals and values? What is *not* mentioned in your stream of consciousness that is surprising to you?

### CONTENT OF DREAMS

- **What Do You Dream?** Have students complete *Handout: What Do You Dream?* which asks them to indicate the nature of their dreams. You can tally up the results and summarize them to the class on a later occasion.
- **Dream Diary:** Keep a dream diary for a few days. When you wake up in the morning, immediately write down all that you can remember about your dreams. Have you had many bizarre or unusual dreams? Are there themes in your dreams that reflect the concerns of your daily life? Compare the content of your dream diary with the stream-of-consciousness document you produced for the stream-of-consciousness exercise above. Are there similarities in the content of your relaxed waking mind and your dreams?

### THEORIES OF DREAMING; MELATONIN

- **Comparing Theories of Dreams:** Have students complete *Handout: Comparing Theories of Dreams.*
- **Melatonin:** Have students complete an Internet search for articles and other websites that concern melatonin. Next, have students decide why melatonin would be particularly helpful for eastward travel but not westward. Finally, have them determine the health safety of taking melatonin for jet lag.

### SLEEP DEBT QUESTIONNAIRE AND THE LIFE OF SLEEP INTERVIEW

- **Sleep Debt:** Have students complete *Handout: Measure Your Sleep Debt,* which contains the sleep debt questionnaire.
- **The Life of Sleep:** Interview one to two people about changes in how much they sleep and the quality of sleep as they have gotten older. Also ask some questions about any experiences they had with children growing up and their sleep patterns. See if you can take the information learned from the interview and create your own image of sleep across the life span

### SLEEP IQ QUIZ AND SLEEP DISORDERS

- **Sleep IQ Quiz:** Have students complete *Handout: What's Your Sleep IQ?,* which contains the sleep IQ quiz.
- **Sleep Disorders:** Use *Handout: Which Sleep Disorder Is It?* The goal of the activity is to have students identify the various sleep disorders. They will read various examples and have to identify which sleep disorder is occurring.

### CIRCADIAN RHYTHMS

- **Circadian Rhythms:** Have students complete *Handout: Morningness-Eveningness Questionnaire.*

# Discussion Questions

**THEORIES OF DREAMS**
- Why do you think that most people forget their dreams?
- Which theory of dreaming do you find most convincing? Why?

**SLEEP**
- Ask students to consider the differences between your family or friends in regard to the number of hours of sleep they require. Is the number of hours different from yours? To what do you attribute the difference? How do you think daily activities such as school, work, and family obligations affect your ability to get a good night's sleep?
- Sleep is very important in learning. Adolescents often do not get enough sleep. Why does high school start so early? Ask students if it would be better to start later. Why or why not? What sorts of problems do they see in trying to change the start times in high schools?
- In many cultures, infants sleep with their parents, and some cultures encourage a family bed in which everyone sleeps together. Ask students whether they think this is a good practice and if they would implement this practice in their home.

# Polling Questions

**POLLING QUESTION: WHAT DO DOGS DREAM ABOUT?** Ever wondered what your dog or pet was dreaming about? An article in *Psychology Today* by Stanley Coren (2010) suggested that at a structural level, the brains of dogs are similar to those of humans. "Also, during sleep the brain wave patterns of dogs are similar to that of people and go through the same stages of electrical activity observed in humans, all of which is consistent with the idea that dogs are dreaming." So, who has wondered what dogs or other animals dream about? How many of you think the purpose of dreaming in animals is similar to the reasons why humans dream? How many of you think that animals other than dogs dream? Of those who have pets, how many of you let your dog or cat sleep in bed with you?

**POLLING QUESTION: SLEEP** Based on what you have learned about sleep, do you believe that schools should have later start times?

# Suggested Media

- *Adolescent Brains Are a Work in Progress. Frontline,* PBS: http://www.pbs.org/wgbh/pages/frontline/shows/teenbrain/work/adolescent.html.
- *American Academy of Sleep Medicine:* www.aasmnet.org.
- *Dopamine: Natural Ways to Increase Dopamine Levels:* http://www.integrativepsychiatry.net/dopamine.html.
- *Dream interpretation:* http://www.dreammoods.com/dreambank/
- *Inside the Teen Brain.* PBS: http://www.pbs.org/wgbh/pages/frontline/video/flv/generic.html?s=frol02p392&continuous=1. Deals with sleep. (Requires Flash 9 or better.)
- *National Institute of Health:* http://nccam.nih.gov/health/meditation/overview.htm. This site provides an overview of meditation including benefits.
- *National Sleep Foundation:* https://sleepfoundation.org.
- *The Science of Sleep. 60 Minutes* (part 1). CBS. 13:02. https://www.cbsnews.com/video/science-of-sleep-part-1/
- *The Science of Sleep.* 60 Minutes (part 2). CBS. 12:37. https://www.cbsnews.com/video/the-science-of-sleep-2-parts/
- *Sleep and Sleep Disorders—CDC:* https://www.cdc.gov/sleep/index.html.

- *Sleepiness: When Your Brain Has a Mind of Its Own.* Insight Media, 2012, 53:00. This program examines the brain and sleep and the importance of sleep.
- *Stages of Sleep:* http://www.youtube.com/watch?v=qEWbu37fH9k. Show this to the class to provide a brief demonstration with animation of the stages of sleep as measured by EEG.

**POPULAR MOVIES**

- **Sleep and Dreams:** Show a scene from a movie in which altered states of consciousness in sleep and dreams are shown, such as *Vanilla Sky* (lucid dreams) and *Minority Report* (precognitions). Your students will most likely be able to give you other suggestions as well if this is not your favorite movie genre. A scene from the movie *Insomnia* can be shown in which the main character suffers from this disturbance. In addition to showing this sleep disturbance, the movie also shows the effects of sleep deprivation on behavior.

## AP Student Edition Answer Key

## Applying Psychology in the 21st Century: Sleeping to Forget

Answer Suggestions

- The hypothesis is that the day's activities trigger increased synaptic growth, which must be pruned back during sleep.
- Researchers examined thin brain slices of mice and found sleeping mice had an 18% reduction in the size of synapses compared to the awake mice. Another study found a drop in surface proteins when mice fell asleep, which is consistent with a reduction in synapses. A final study used a drug to inhibit synaptic pruning and found that this lack of pruning left mice with excessive synapses that produced confused memories.

## Neuroscience in Your Life: Why Are We So Emotional When We Don't Get Enough Sleep?

Answer Suggestions

- Sleep deprivation leads to feeling edgy, slowed reaction time, and lowered performance on academic and physical tasks.
- The independent variable is the amount of sleep because it is the variable being manipulated. The dependent variable is the emotional reactivity because it is the variable being measured.

# AP Test Practice

## Section I: Multiple Choice

1.   **C** *(Skill 1.C, Learning Target 2.R)*

2.   **E** *(Skill 1.B, Learning Target 2.S)*

3.   **E** *(Skill 1.A, Learning Target 2.S)*

## Section II: Free Response

**A.**

The circadian rhythm is the 24-hour biological cycle. John is experiencing jet lag, which disrupted his circadian rhythm. Because his sleep-wake cycle has been disrupted he is having problems falling asleep.

People deprived of REM sleep show a rebound effect when allowed to sleep undisturbed. Significantly more time is spent in REM than normal, which is why John is experiencing crazy dreams in REM.

Insomnia is a sleep disorder associated with problems falling asleep. Sometimes it can be situational. John is unable to fall asleep due to his sleep-wake schedule being disrupted by travel.

**B.**

PET scan research supports the wish fulfillment theory for dreams. During REM sleep the brain areas associated with emotion and motivation—limbic and paralimbic areas—are active. At the same time the areas associated with logical analysis and attention, the association areas of the prefrontal cortex, are not active. This activation sequence makes it more likely that John's dreams reflect his unconscious wishes.

Research supports the dreams-for-survival theory. Certain dreams allow people to focus on and consolidate memories, especially for procedural motor skills. For example, rats seem to dream about mazes they learned to run through during the day. Humans who learned a visual task and were then allowed REM sleep increased their performance on the memory task the following day, but if awakened during REM sleep, their performance declined. Dreaming can help John remember material from his overseas trip.

# Module 15: Hypnosis and Meditation

## AP Module Summary

**HYPNOSIS: A TRANCE-FORMING EXPERIENCE?** *Hypnosis* is a trancelike state of heightened susceptibility to the suggestions of others.

**A DIFFERENT STATE OF CONSCIOUSNESS?** Some psychologists believe that hypnosis represents a state of consciousness that differs significantly from other states. Changes in electrical activity in the brain are associated with hypnosis, supporting the position that hypnosis is a state of consciousness different from normal waking (Hilgard, 1992; Kallio & Revonsuo, 2003; Fingelkurts, Fingelkurts, & Kallio, 2007; Hinterberger, Schöner, & Halsband, 2011). In this view, hypnosis represents a state of divided consciousness.

According to famed hypnosis researcher Ernest Hilgard, hypnosis brings about a dissociation, or division, of consciousness into two simultaneous components. In one stream of consciousness, hypnotized people are following the commands of the hypnotist. Yet on another level of consciousness, they are acting as "hidden observers," aware of what is happening to them.

On the other side of the controversy are psychologists who reject the notion that hypnosis is a state significantly different from normal waking consciousness. They argue that altered brain-wave patterns are not sufficient to demonstrate a qualitative difference because no other specific physiological changes occur when people are in trances.

**MEDITATION: REGULATING OUR OWN STATE OF CONSCIOUSNESS** *Meditation* is a learned technique for refocusing attention that brings about an altered state of consciousness. Meditation typically consists of the repetition of a mantra—a sound, word, or syllable—over and over. In some forms of meditation, the focus is on a picture, flame, or specific part of the body. Regardless of the nature of the particular initial stimulus, the key to the procedure is concentrating on it so thoroughly that the meditator becomes unaware of any outside stimulation and reaches a different state of consciousness. Meditation is a means of altering consciousness that is practiced in many different cultures, though it can take different forms and serve different purposes across cultures.

## AP Key Terms

**Hypnosis**
**meditation**

## Class Discussion Ideas

**CONTINUUM OF DISSOCIATION** As mentioned in the text, there is a continuum of dissociation that includes dissociative disorders (e.g., dissociative amnesia, dissociative fugue, dissociative identity disorder, and depersonalization) and may include mundane phenomena such as dreams, daydreams, and what is called "highway hypnosis."

See also http://hypnoticworld.com/facts/

# Activities

**EVERYDAY TRANCE STATES** Give students *Handout: "Trance" Diary,* which asks them to indicate which everyday trance states they have experienced.

**MEDITATION**
- **Meditation Awareness:** Invite a guest from the local community to lead a guided meditation session for your class (check out local yoga studios for potential guests). After the meditation session, discuss how the students' experience relates to what they have learned about consciousness.
- **Mindful Meditation:** Try out mindful meditation following the guidelines outlined out http://www.learningmeditation.com/. Meditate once a day for a week, keeping track of your mood, health, and behaviors over the course of the week. How did mindful meditation work for you?
- **Guided Imagery Exercise:** In class, have the students get into a physical location of the room where they can be more relaxed. Turn down the lights, turn on some soft, calming music, and begin in a quiet manner helping the students to relax. Have them close their eyes, stretch their limbs, and begin focusing on a particular image (a river, an ocean, a beach). Guide the students through the image: What are they doing there? What does it smell like? Who are they with, and what are they hearing? Using questions like this helps students create their own individualized relaxation experience. This exercise could take up to 20 minutes to complete. Have students reflect on this experience either in writing or orally.

# Discussion Questions

**THE EXPERIENCE OF HYPNOSIS** Ask students the following questions:
- Do you think that hypnosis is real, or is it fake?
- Have you ever been hypnotized? If so, what did that feel like? If not, what do you think it would feel like?
- What have the critics said about the use of hypnosis? In your answer, you should discuss viewpoints of those people who favor the use of hypnosis and of those who don't support the use of hypnosis.

**MEDITATION AND HEALTH** Consider the recent emphasis on living a healthier lifestyle. Dieting, eating right, exercising, and decreasing stress are all very common conversations. How important is meditation and having a cognitive space for personal reflection and growth in living a healthy lifestyle? Or, is meditation a trendier thing to do? What evidence do you base your thinking on?

# Polling Questions

**HYPNOTISM IS JUST AN ACT, REALLY?** According to the American Psychological Association, "Hypnosis is a therapeutic technique in which clinicians make suggestions to individuals who have undergone a procedure designed to relax them and focus their minds. Although hypnosis has been controversial, most clinicians now agree it can be a powerful, effective therapeutic technique for a wide range of conditions, including pain, anxiety, and mood disorders. Hypnosis can also help people change their habits, such as quitting smoking." What do you think? How many think hypnosis is real and can help people? Who is skeptical that hypnosis really works? How many of you can see an advantage of using hypnosis for treatments related to pain, smoking, and other mental health concerns? Who would want to be hypnotized?

**MEDITATION** Do you practice any form of meditation?

## Suggested Media

- *Brain scans and meditation:* http://www.livescience.com/health/070629_naming_emotions.html.
- *David Chamers.* "How Do You Explain Consciousness?" TED Talk, March 2014: http://www.ted.com/talks/david_chalmers_how_do_you_explain_consciousness.
- *Hypnosis—Psychology Today:* https://www.psychologytoday.com/basics/hypnosis.
- *International Society for Hypnosis:* http://www.ishhypnosis.org.
- *Just Trial and Error: Conversations on Consciousness.* M & M Films, 2012, 63:00. Cognitive neuroscientist Brian Butterworth, perceptual neuroscientist Beau Lotto, sculptor Antony Gormley, and others explore the meaning of consciousness as it is understood in their respective fields.

## **AP** Student Edition Answer Key

### AP Test Practice

#### Section I: Multiple Choice

1. **A** *(Skill 1.B, Learning Target 2.O)*

2. **B** *(Skill 1.B, Learning Target 2.O)*

3. **B** *(Skill 2, Learning Target 2.O)*

#### Section II: Free Response

The evolutionary perspective views behavior has been influenced by the genetic inheritance from our ancestors. Meditation would have a genetic influence that helped increase the survival rate of our ancestors.

The neuroscience perspective views behavior from the perspective of biological functioning. During meditation oxygen usage decreases, heart rate and blood pressure decline, and brain-wave patterns change. A neurotransmitter that increases pleasure might also be released.

The behavioral perspective focuses on observable behavior. Meditating with others could result in modeling and healthy behaviors could be reinforced.

The cognitive perspective focuses on how people understand and think about the world. Meditation could alter one's thinking to positive, rational thoughts.

The humanistic perspective contends that people can control their behavior and that they naturally try to reach their full potential. Meditation can be used to meet one's needs and help support one's drive for self-actualization.

The psychodynamic perspective views behavior as being motivated by inner, unconscious forces over which a person has little control. Meditation can be used to help explore the present moment and then unconscious forces.

# Module 16: Drug Use: The Highs and Lows of Consciousness

## **AP** Module Summary

In module 16, the review of several biological concepts become important. Students are expected to know the classification of drugs with the standard stimulants and depressants but new is the category of hallucinogens. I also predict that opiates will be added eventually and so include it as a category for students to know.

Drugs of one sort or another are a part of almost everyone's life. From infancy on, most people take vitamins, aspirin, or cold-relief medicine. However, these drugs rarely produce an altered state of consciousness.

- *Psychoactive drugs* influence a person's emotions, perceptions, and behavior.
  - ○ Example: A cup of coffee or a bottle of beer are examples of psychoactive drugs.
- *Addictive drugs* produce a physiological or psychological dependence (or both) in the user, and withdrawal from them leads to a craving for the drug that, in some cases, may be nearly irresistible.

In physiological dependence, the body becomes so accustomed to functioning in the presence of a drug that it cannot function without it. In psychological dependence, people believe that they need the drug to respond to the stresses of daily living.

**STIMULANTS: DRUG HIGHS (SEE FIGURE 3)** *Stimulants* are drugs that have an arousal effect on the central nervous system, causing a rise in heart rate, blood pressure, and muscular tension.
  - ○ Examples: Caffeine and nicotine
- **Amphetamines** *Amphetamines* stimulate the central nervous system, bringing about a sense of energy and alertness, talkativeness, heightened confidence, and a mood "high."
  - ○ Examples:
    *Methamphetamine* is a white, crystalline drug that U.S. police now say is the most dangerous street drug.

    *Bath salts* are an amphetamine-like stimulant containing chemicals related to cathinone.

- **Cocaine** *Cocaine* is inhaled or snorted through the nose, smoked, or injected directly into the bloodstream. It is rapidly absorbed into the body and takes effect almost immediately. The brain may become permanently rewired, triggering a psychological and physical addiction in which users grow obsessed with obtaining the drug.

**DEPRESSANTS: DRUG LOWS** *Depressants* impede the nervous system by causing neurons to fire more slowly. Small doses result in at least temporary feelings of intoxication—drunkenness—along with a sense of euphoria and joy.
- **Alcohol** *Alcohol* is the most common depressant. It is used by more people than is any other drug. Although alcohol is a depressant, most people claim that it increases their sense of sociability and well-being. The discrepancy between the actual and the perceived effects of alcohol lies in the initial effects it produces in the majority of individuals who use it: release of tension and stress, feelings of happiness, and loss of inhibitions. However, as the dose of alcohol increases, the depressive effects become more pronounced (see **Figure 6**).
- **Barbituates** *Barbiturates* are frequently prescribed by physicians to induce sleep or reduce stress, barbiturates produce a sense of relaxation. Barbiturates are psychologically and physically addictive.

## NARCOTICS, OPIATES, AND OPIOIDS: RELIEVING PAIN AND ANXIETY

- *Narcotics* are drugs that increase relaxation and relieve pain and anxiety. The most powerful narcotics, morphine, heroin and codeine fall into the class of drugs called opiates, or narcotics derived from natural substances.

- Conversely, *opioids* are synthetic forms of narcotics and include medications such as Vicodin, Percocet, Fentanyl, and OxyContin. Both opiates and opioids are involved in the current "opioid crisis," and their use has reached epidemic proportions. The newest opioids are 100 times more potent than heroin.

**HALLUCINOGENS: PSYCHEDELIC DRUGS** Hallucinogens are drugs that alter perceptual processes and are capable of producing hallucinations, or experiences that seem real but are not.

- ○ Example: Marijuana (see **Figure 7**), whose active ingredient—THC—is found in a common weed, cannabis.

- **Marijuana** Marijuana is typically smoked in cigarettes or pipes, although it can be cooked and eaten. The effects of marijuana vary from person to person, but they typically consist of feelings of euphoria and general well-being. Sensory experiences seem more vivid and intense, and a person's sense of self-importance seems to grow. There is little scientific evidence for the popular belief that users "graduate" from marijuana to more dangerous drugs. On the other hand, some research suggests that there are similarities in the way marijuana and drugs such as cocaine and heroin affect the brain, as well as evidence that heavy use may impact negatively on cognitive ability in the long run.

**MDMA (ECSTASY) AND LSD** MDMA ("Ecstasy") and lysergic acid diethylamide (LSD, or "acid") fall into the category of hallucinogens. Both drugs affect the operation of the neurotransmitter serotonin in the brain, causing an alteration in brain-cell activity and perception (Cloud, 2000; Buchert et al., 2004).

**BECOMING AN INFORMED CONSUMER OF PSYCHOLOGY: IDENTIFYING DRUGS AND ALCOHOL PROBLEMS** Many people with drug and alcohol problems deny that they have them, and even close friends and family members may fail to realize when occasional social use of drugs or alcohol has turned into abuse.

Certain signs, however, indicate when use becomes abuse (National Institute on Drug Abuse, 2000). Among them are the following:

- Always getting high to have a good time
- Being high more often than not
- Getting high to get oneself going
- Going to work or class while high
- Missing or being unprepared for class or work because you were high
- Feeling badly later about something you said or did while high
- Driving a car while high
- Coming in conflict with the law because of drugs
- Doing something while high that you would not do otherwise
- Being high in nonsocial, solitary situations
- Being unable to stop getting high
- Feeling a need for a drink or a drug to get through the day
- Becoming physically unhealthy
- Failing at school or on the job
- Thinking about liquor or drugs all the time
- Avoiding family or friends while using liquor or drugs

Any combination of these symptoms should be sufficient to alert you to the potential of a serious drug problem.

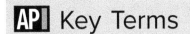 Key Terms

| addictive drugs | narcotics |
| depressants | psychoactive drugs |
| hallucinogens | stimulants |

## Class Discussion Ideas

**CURRENT DRUG USE PATTERNS IN THE UNITED STATES** Show students figures from the Substance Abuse and Mental Health Services Administration (SAMHSA) website (http://www.samhsa.gov). These are easily downloadable and will provide updates to the information in the text. An interesting question to ask students is "What is the most frequently used psychoactive drug?" The answer will surprise them—caffeine.

**CURRENT INFORMATION ON ALCOHOL ABUSE** More up-to-date information on alcohol abuse can be found on the National Institute of Alcohol Abuse and Alcoholism website (http://www.niaaa.nih.gov/). There also are a number of useful handouts and graphics for lecture that can be downloaded from this site.

## Activities

**DRUG USE STATS** Have students go to the U.S. Substance Abuse and Mental Health Services Administration website (http://www.samhsa.gov) and find answers to the following questions:
- Approximately what percentage of the U.S. population 12 years and older uses illicit drugs?
- Who is more likely to abuse illicit drugs—people over 35 or people under 35?
- What is the most commonly used illicit drug?

**ALCOHOL ADVERTISEMENTS** Have students complete *Handout: Alcohol Advertisements*.

**ATTITUDES TOWARD DRUGS** Have students complete *Handout: Attitudes Toward Drugs*.

**TYPES OF DRUGS** Have students choose one depressant drug, one stimulant drug, and one hallucinogenic drug and discuss the neural pathway the drug takes in the brain, what neurotransmitters the drug affects, the physiological problems that take place, and the psychological problems that take place. You can have the students do this activity individually or as a group.

**FACTS ABOVE THE INFLUENCE** Using Above the Influence website, http://abovetheinfluence.com/faqs/, create a "fact or fiction" discussion about the various answers to some compelling questions that often get asked about drug use. This is a great time to reintroduce the importance of critical thinking skills and help students understand their own experience in context with psychological research.

**MARIJUANA AND OTHER DRUGS DEBATE** Make four large signs titled (1) FOR, (2) AGAINST, (3) ON THE FENCE, and (4) THIS IS WHAT IT WOULD TAKE TO MAKE ME TO CHANGE MY POSITION. Tape a sign in each corner of the room. The topic to debate is: Should marijuana (or any psychoactive drug) be legal for medical purposes? Have students go to the corner that best describes their position. Next, ask each student to explain their position and instruct them to move to another corner should it change as more information is revealed. Usually a lively debate will ensue. Another idea is for students to research the topic before class and support their position with research and websites of interest.

**DRUG EDUCATION**  Research suggests that many common drug education programs are ineffective. Have students work in groups to create educational materials that they believe would effectively teach other students about drugs and alcohol.

**CAFFEINE CAPER**  Go on a caffeine hunt. Check out the ingredient lists for the beverages, painkillers, and snacks you typically consume. Which contain caffeine? Are you surprised by how much caffeine you ingest regularly?

## Discussion Questions

**DRUG USE**
- Why have drug education campaigns largely been ineffective in stemming the use of illegal drugs?
- Should the use of certain illegal drugs be made legal?
- Would it be more effective to stress reducing drug use rather than prohibiting it?
- Why do you feel people are so attracted to altered states of consciousness? In your answer, discuss both the physiological and psychological effects of drug use.

## Polling Questions

**IT'S LEGAL!**  Several states have legalized marijuana for medicinal purposes. However, some have even legalized it for recreational use. What's your stance? How many think it is acceptable to legalize marijuana for recreational purposes? What about medicinal purposes? Who thinks that by legalizing marijuana, more and more people will become addicted to it? What about driving: Who thinks there will be a bigger problem with people driving while under the influence of marijuana if it is legalized for recreational purposes? How many think that legalizing marijuana for any purpose will increase the number of users of the drug?

## Suggested Media

- *Alcoholics Anonymous:* http://www.aa.org.
- *Marijuana Anonymous:* http://www.marijuana-anonymous.org.
- *Narcotics Anonymous:* https://www.na.org.
- *National Institute on Alcoholism and Alcohol Abuse:* https://www.niaaa.nih.gov.
- *National Institute of Drug Abuse:* http://www.nida.nih.gov/.
- *Quitting cigarettes and laser therapy:* http://www.youtube.com/watch?v=prYUrhqmqtI
- Genetic Science Learning Center. (2013, August 30) Mouse Party. Retrieved July 26, 2019, from https://learn.genetics.utah.edu/content/addiction/mouse/

## Additional Readings

Agrawal, A., & Lynskey, M. T. (2008). Are there genetic influences on addiction: Evidence from family, adoption and twin studies. *British Journal of Addiction, 103*(7), 1069–1081.

Koob, G. F., Aarends, M. A., & Le Moal, M. (2014). *Drugs, addiction, and the brain.* Elsevier.

# AP Student Edition Answer Key

## AP Test Practice

### Section I: Multiple Choice

1. **C** *(Skill 1.A, Learning Target 2.P)*

2. **D** *(Skill 1.A, Learning Target 2.P)*

3. **E** *(Skill 1.B, Learning Target 2.Q)*

### Section II: Free Response

**A.**

Caffeine is a stimulant that causes arousal of the central nervous system. Symptoms associated with caffeine use include a rise in heart rate, blood pressure, and muscular tension.

Alcohol is a depressant that causes decreased arousal of the central nervous system. Symptoms associated with alcohol use include anxiety reduction, feelings of happiness, and loss of inhibition. Increased doses may make people feel emotionally and physically unstable, show poor judgment and act aggressively, and impair memory, processing speed, and speech. Significant doses can lead to passing out or alcohol poisoning.

Amphetamines are strong stimulants. In small doses amphetamines can lead to energy, alertness, talkativeness, heightened confidence, increased concentration, and reduced fatigue. There are also more negative side effects such as loss of appetite, increased anxiety, and irritability. Use of amphetamines over extended periods can lead to paranoia, suspiciousness, and/or decreased sex drive. Large quantities of this drug can lead to convulsions and death.

**B.**

Cocaine produces feelings of pleasure by blocking the reabsorption of leftover dopamine. As a result, the brain is flooded with dopamine-produced pleasurable sensations.

Use of MDMA can lead to long-term changes in serotonin receptors in the brain, disrupting thoughts and perception.

**C.**

Tolerance is the need for an increased dose of the addictive drug to produce the initial pleasurable affects. Methamphetamine users take it more frequently and in increasing doses.

Long-term use can lead to brain damage.

Withdrawal symptoms are the unpleasant symptoms associated with stopping the use of the addictive drug. Withdrawal symptoms associated with opioids include sweating, chills, abdominal cramps, insomnia, vomiting, and diarrhea.

# CHAPTER 6
# Learning

## AP Introduction

The understanding of human behavior is as much psychological as it is physiological. In this chapter the focus on how humans and other species learn by way of classical, operant, and observational learning will be introduced. A considerable amount of time should take place on the important researchers in the psychology of learning over the years. The unit may appear short but its importance in explaining behavior in authentic contexts, an important skill for students to master, is vital for success in the psychology course.

## AP Essential Questions

- How do we learn?
- How do our experiences influence our behaviors and mental processes?

## Module 17: Classical Conditioning

**AP Learning Targets:**

- Identify the contributions of key researchers in the psychology of learning.
- Interpret graphs that exhibit the results of learning experiments.
- Apply learning principles to explain emotional learning, taste aversion, superstitious behavior, and learned helplessness.
- Provide examples of how biological constraints create learning predispositions.
- Describe basic classical conditioning phenomena.
- Distinguish general differences between principles of classical conditioning, operant conditioning, and observational learning.

**Pacing:**

2 Blocks or 4 Traditional Class periods

# Module 18: Operant Conditioning

**AP Learning Targets:**

- Identify the contributions of key researchers in the psychology of learning.
- Interpret graphs that exhibit the results of learning experiments.
- Provide examples of how biological constraints create learning predispositions.
- Distinguish general differences between principles of classical conditioning, operant conditioning, and observational learning.
- Predict the effects of operant conditioning.
- Predict how practice, schedules of reinforcement, other aspects of reinforcement, and motivation will influence quality of learning.
- Suggest how behavior modification, biofeedback, coping strategies, and self-control can be used to address behavioral problems.

**Pacing:**

2 Blocks or 4 Traditional Class periods

# Module 19: Cognitive Approaches to Learning

**AP Learning Targets:**

- Identify the contributions of key researchers in the psychology of learning.
- Interpret graphs that exhibit the results of learning experiments.
- Describe the essential characteristics of insight learning, latent learning, and social learning.
- Distinguish general differences between principles of classical conditioning, operant conditioning, and observational learning.
- Identify the contributions of key researchers in cognitive psychology.

**Pacing:**

1 Block or 2 Traditional Class periods

# Module 17: Classical Conditioning

## AP Module Summary

In Module 17, classical conditioning is the area of focus and can be a tricky one. It is important that in this module you spend time reviewing the process and concepts of classical conditioning. Several practice activities and demonstrations have been provided to assist you with helping your students understand the stimulus-response relationship. When reviewing Ivan Pavlov's classical conditioning it is important to have students practice applying the concepts listed as examples in the course and exam description. Make sure to include the work of Robert Rescorla and his Contingency Theory of Classical Conditioning. If time does not permit you to do so in this module, his work can also be introduced in Module 19.

- *Learning* is a relatively permanent change in behavior that is brought about by experience. Habituation is the decrease in response to a stimulus that occurs after repeated presentations of the same stimulus. Example: We are primed for learning from the beginning of life.

**THE BASICS OF CLASSICAL CONDITIONING (SEE FIGURE 1)**  The first systematic research on learning was done at the beginning of the 20th century, when Ivan Pavlov developed the framework for learning called classical conditioning. *Classical conditioning* is a type of learning in which a neutral stimulus comes to elicit a response after being paired with a stimulus that naturally brings about that response.

Keeping in mind Pavlov's laboratory experiments with dogs, the basics of classical conditioning can be explained as follows:
- First, before conditioning, there are two unrelated stimuli: the ringing of a bell and meat. We know that normally the ringing of a bell does not lead to salivation but to some irrelevant response, such as pricking up the ears or perhaps a startle reaction.
- *Neutral stimulus (bell)* because it is a stimulus that before conditioning does not naturally bring about the response in which we are interested. We also have meat, which naturally causes a dog to salivate—the response we are interested in conditioning.
- *Unconditioned stimulus (UCS)* (Meat)
  - Because food placed in a dog's mouth automatically causes salivation to occur.
- *Unconditioned response (UCR) (Salivate)*—a natural, innate, reflexive response that is not associated with previous learning. Unconditioned responses are always brought about by the presence of unconditioned stimuli.
- After a number of pairings of the bell and meat, the bell alone causes the dog to salivate.
- *Conditioned stimulus (CS) (Bell)*
- *Conditioned response (CR) (Salivation)*

**APPLYING CONDITIONING PRINCIPLES TO HUMAN BEHAVIOR**  Although the initial conditioning experiments were carried out with animals, classical conditioning principles were soon found to explain many aspects of everyday human behavior. Emotional responses are especially likely to be learned through classical conditioning processes. In more extreme cases, classical conditioning can lead to the development of phobias, which are intense, irrational fears. Posttraumatic stress disorder (PTSD), suffered by some war veterans and others who have had traumatic experiences, can also be produced by classical conditioning. On the other hand, classical conditioning also relates to pleasant experiences. For instance, a particular fondness for the smell of a certain perfume or aftershave lotion because thoughts of an early love come rushing back whenever one encounters it.

**EXTINCTION (SEE FIGURE 2)**  *Extinction* occurs when a previously conditioned response decreases in frequency and eventually disappears. To produce extinction, one needs to end the association between conditioned stimuli and unconditioned stimuli. *Spontaneous recovery* or the reemergence of an extinguished conditioned response after a period of time and with no further conditioning.

**GENERALIZATION AND DISCRIMINATION** *Stimulus generalization* is a process in which, after a stimulus has been conditioned to produce a particular response, stimuli that are similar to the original stimulus produce the same response. The greater the similarity between two stimuli, the greater the likelihood of stimulus generalization. *Stimulus discrimination*, in contrast, occurs if two stimuli are sufficiently distinct from each other so that one evokes a conditioned response but the other does not. Stimulus discrimination provides the ability to differentiate between stimuli.

**BEYOND TRADITIONAL CLASSICAL CONDITIONING: CHALLENGING BASIC ASSUMPTIONS** Pavlov hypothesized that all learning is nothing more than long strings of conditioned responses; this notion has not been supported by subsequent research. According to Pavlov, the process of linking stimuli and responses occurs in a mechanistic, unthinking way.

Traditional explanations of how classical conditioning operates have also been challenged by John Garcia, a learning psychologist. He found that some organisms—including humans—were biologically prepared to quickly learn to avoid foods that smelled or tasted like something that made them sick. The surprising part of Garcia's discovery was his demonstration that conditioning could occur even when the interval between exposure to the conditioned stimulus of tainted food and the response of sickness was as long as 8 hours. Furthermore, the conditioning persisted over very long periods and sometimes occurred after just one exposure.

## AP Key Terms

| | |
|---|---|
| classical conditioning | neutral stimulus |
| conditioned response (CR) | spontaneous recovery |
| conditioned stimulus (CS) | stimulus discrimination |
| extinction | stimulus generalization |
| learning | unconditioned response (UCR) |
| higher-order learning | unconditioned stimulus (UCS) |
| contingencies | |

## AP Important People

Ivan Pavlov
Robert Rescorla
John B. Watson
John Garcia

## Class Discussion Ideas

### Describe Learning

- **What Does It Mean to Learn?** Engage your students in a healthy dialogue/debate on the meaning of learning. What does it mean to have learned something? Are students learning in your class? How do they know that they have learned something? Further your discussion about "knowing information" versus "learning information." You can comment on the process of learning and how most learning takes time. What is the impact of technology on learning? How does the scheduling of accelerated courses benefit the student from a learning perspective?
- **Basic Processes of Learning:** Right now you are habituated to dozens of stimuli—including the feel of clothing on your skin. Now you are sensitized to it. How so? **Discussion:** Is habituation learning? Ask students to think about their job. How much of what they do is automatic? That is, are they demonstrating habituation (they are oriented to what they do and are exposed to repeatedly) or learning?

**PAVLOV'S RESEARCH** Ivan Pavlov, a Russian physiologist, never intended to do psychological research. In 1904, he won the Nobel Prize for his work on digestion, testimony to his contribution to that field. Yet Pavlov is remembered not for his physiological research but for his experiments on basic learning processes—work that began quite accidentally.

Pavlov had been studying the secretion of stomach acids and salivation in dogs in response to eating varying amounts and kinds of food. While doing his research, he observed a curious phenomenon: Sometimes salivation would begin in the dogs when they had not yet eaten any food. Just the sight of the experimenter who normally brought the food or even the sound of the experimenter's footsteps was enough to produce salivation in the dogs. Pavlov's genius lay in his ability to recognize the implications of this discovery. He saw that the dogs were responding not only on the basis of a biological need (hunger) but also as a result of learning—or, as it came to be called, classical conditioning.

To demonstrate classical conditioning, Pavlov (1927) attached a tube to the salivary gland of a dog, allowing him to measure precisely the dog's salivation. He then rang a bell and, just a few seconds later, presented the dog with meat. This pairing occurred repeatedly and was carefully planned so that, each time, exactly the same amount of time elapsed between the presentation of the bell and the meat. At first, the dog would salivate only when the meat was presented, but soon it began to salivate at the sound of the bell. In fact, even when Pavlov stopped presenting the meat, the dog still salivated after hearing the sound. The dog had been classically conditioned to salivate to the bell.

For additional information about Pavlov:
http://www.nobelprize.org/nobel_prizes/medicine/laureates/1904/pavlov-bio.html.

## Little Albert

- **Discussion:** In a now infamous case study, psychologist John B. Watson and colleague Rosalie Rayner (1920) showed that classical conditioning was at the root of such fears by conditioning an 11-month-old infant named Albert to be afraid of rats. "Little Albert," like most infants, initially was frightened by loud noises but had no fear of rats. In the study, the experimenters sounded a loud noise whenever Little Albert touched a white, furry rat. The noise (the unconditioned stimulus) evoked fear (the unconditioned response). After just a few pairings of noise and rat, Albert began to show fear of the rat by itself, bursting into tears when he saw it. The rat, then, had become a CS that brought about the CR, fear. Furthermore, the effects of the conditioning lingered: Five days later, Albert reacted with some degree of fear not only when shown a rat, but also when shown objects that looked similar to the white, furry rat, including a white rabbit, a white sealskin coat, and even a white Santa Claus mask. (By the way, we don't know for certain what happened to Little Albert, and his fate remains a source of considerable speculation.) In any case, Watson, the experimenter, has been condemned for using ethically questionable procedures that could never be conducted today; Beck, Levinson, & Irons, 2009; Powell et al., 2014; Griggs, 2015). Discuss the Little Albert experiment in connection to the principles of classical conditioning and as a reminder of ethical guidelines.

- **Discussion:** Watson, perhaps the father of the behavioral movement, is best known for the infamous quote: "Give me a dozen healthy infants, well-formed, and my own specified world to bring them up in, and I'll guarantee to take any one at random and train him to become any type of specialist I might select—doctor, lawyer, artist, merchant—chief, and yes, even beggar-man and thief, regardless of his talents, penchants, tendencies, abilities, vocations, and race of his ancestors" (Watson, 1925, p. 82). Based on this quotation, what would this mean if you had an IQ of 100 and wanted to be a doctor? What if you lacked the ability for athleticism, as you were born small and weaker than most, but you wanted to be a professional football player? What would Watson say?

- **Discussion:** Students are generally interested in this story, and you may want to also talk about little Peter, a follow-up study done by Mary Cover Jones (1924) under Watson's supervision.

# Helpful Hints for Students

**Present the following hints to help make the relationships between stimuli and responses easier to understand and remember:**

- Conditioned = learned; and unconditioned = not learned
- An unconditioned stimulus leads to an unconditioned response.
- Unconditioned stimulus–unconditioned response pairings are unlearned and untrained.
- During conditioning, a previously neutral stimulus is transformed into the conditioned stimulus.
- A conditioned stimulus leads to a conditioned response, and a conditioned stimulus–conditioned response pairing is a consequence of learning and training.
- An unconditioned response and a conditioned response are the same (such as salivation in the example described earlier). However, the unconditioned response occurs naturally, whereas the conditioned response is learned.

**Don't forget to mention the other phenomena related to classical conditioning are:**

- Extinction
- Spontaneous recovery
- Stimulus generalization
- Stimulus discrimination
- Higher-order learning- when a conditioned stimulus is paired with a new neutral stimulus, creating a second (often weaker) conditioned stimulus.

# Activities

## Classical Conditioning Activities

- **Classical Conditioning Demonstration:** Collect these props: a small whistle and a squeezable "puff" maker (as is sold in ear wax cleaner kits).
    - Ask for a student volunteer. They should be about your height, and should not be wearing contact lenses.
    - Have the student stand squarely facing you, about 1 foot away. Set this up so that other students can see the volunteer's eyes.
    - Announce that you will now show how classical conditioning is done. You will show that you can condition the volunteer to blink their eyes in response to the whistle.
    - Put the volunteer at ease. Ask them where they are from, and then have the class applaud to that. Now show that they will not blink when you blow the whistle.
    - Then start conditioning—pair the whistle with the air puff about five or six times. On the next trial, just blow the whistle. Have the observers verify that the volunteer blinked, and then take your bows and applause!
    - This is a very uncontrolled situation, but what will help you have a successful result is to create the expectation that you will get a successful result—you are counting, in part, on the suggestibility of your subject. (While this is going on, you may want to have someone take a picture.)
    - After completing the demonstration, use this overhead to have the students review the relevant concepts:
        - The UCS was the: _____ (air puff)
        - The CS was the: _____ (whistle)
        - The UCR was the: _____ (eye blink)
        - The CR was the: _____ (eye blink)
    - *Extend the demonstration by having students think of how to apply the concepts: Acquisition, Extinction, Spontaneous Recovery, Generalization, Discrimination, and Higher-order learning.*

- **Classical Conditioning Demonstration:** Bring enough small paper cups with 1 tablespoon of powdered lemonade mix for each student in the class. Instruct each student not to drink anything and to remove gum before doing this activity. Tell students that every time you say "Pavlov," they are to lick their finger, dip it in the powdered lemonade, and put it on their tongue and swallow. Begin the activity by saying "Pavlov" every 15 seconds for 2 minutes. After 2 minutes, tell students to put down their cup but still not drink anything. Then begin introducing the idea of classical conditioning by defining the term and stating that it was accidentally uncovered by Pavlov. Pause and then ask students if they began salivating at the name *Pavlov*. Most students in your class will have salivated. Use this to illustrate the ideas of US, UR, CS, and CR. Source: Cogan, D., & Cogan, R. (1984). Classical salivary conditioning: An easy demonstration. *Teaching of Psychology, 11,* 170–171.)

**OTHER EXAMPLES OF CONDITIONING PHENOMENA** Ask students what or who they associate with a particular product—name a brand of athletic shoes, for example, or a certain soft drink or car. If students name a personality, icon, or abstraction to describe the product rather product features, then they are seeing the theory of behaviorism in action.

- **Classical Conditioning Experiences:** Have students complete *Handout: Classical Conditioning Experiences,* in which they analyze examples of classical conditioning.
- **Classical Conditioning Terms:** Use *Handout: Classical Conditioning Terms* as a way for students to better understand the terms that accompany classical conditioning. In this activity, the students read examples and identify the US, CS, UR, and CR in each of the examples.
- **Advertising:** In a group, have students design an advertisement using the principles of classical conditioning. As an alternative, have the group of students recall a specific advertisement and illustrate the principles of classical conditioning for that advertisement in a short presentation. To make this activity more interactive, have the group bring in the item that the advertisement is for to use as a prop during their presentation.

## Research Involving Classical Conditioning

- **Classical Conditioning and Psychological Disorders:** Have students search online for examples of current research involving classical conditioning, including research involving conditioning as a method for treating psychological disorders such as phobias or mood disorders.

## Discussion Questions

**EXAMPLES OF CLASSICAL CONDITIONING** Identify and describe an example of classical conditioning from your own life. Be sure to use the classical conditioning terminology to explain the example.
- Give an example of how waking up at 7:00 A.M. to the sound of an alarm clock describes acquisition, generalization, discrimination, extinction, and spontaneous recovery.
- Classical Conditioning and Your Pet: Ask students to think about their pet. Ask them what happens when they go into the kitchen. How do their fish respond when they walk over to the tank? Why do animals get excited by these mundane behaviors? Their pet has learned to associate these behaviors with food. If you want to continue this line of discussion, ask them about "false alarms." If they go into the kitchen repeatedly and then don't give their pet food, what happens? Ask students to provide additional examples of this learning by association (e.g., how have they trained their significant other?).

# **AP** Student Edition Answer Key

## AP Test Practice

### Section I: Multiple Choice

1. **E** *(Skill 1.C, Learning Target 4.A)*

2. **D** *(Skill 1.B, Learning Target 4.D)*

3. **A** *(Skill 1.A, Learning Target 4.F)*

## Section II: Free Response

**A.**

The conditioned response is the learned reaction. The conditioned response for Little Albert was the fear/crying when exposed to the white, furry rat.

The unconditioned stimulus is the unlearned cause. The unconditioned stimulus for Little Albert was the loud noise because it naturally caused fear.

Acquisition is the initial learning period when the neutral stimulus is being paired with the unconditioned stimulus. Acquisition occurred for Little Albert when the white, furry rat was paired with the loud noise.

Stimulus generalization is a process in which similar stimuli to the original conditioned stimulus produces the same conditioned response. Generalization occurred for Little Albert when objects that looked similar to the white, furry rat caused him to have a similar reaction and cry.

Extinction occurs when a conditioned response decreases because the conditioned stimulus is no longer paired with the unconditioned stimulus. Little Albert would experience extinction if his fear/crying decreased because the white, furry rat was no longer paired with the loud noise.

**B.**

Ethical flaws regarding the Little Albert experiment might include protection from harm (he was induced with fear), proper informed consent (he was an orphan and recently adopted), or proper debriefing. The research design was flawed because it did not have a control group and there was only one subject.

John B. Watson set out to condition a phobia in an emotionally stable infant. He proved emotional responses could be learned through classical conditioning. This work could be applied to anxiety disorders and their treatments.

# Module 18: Operant Conditioning

## AP Module Summary

The applicability of concepts in Module 18 on operant conditioning are far more relatable to students. In this unit students can easily think of examples found both at home and at school to help them with the mastery of the material. In this unit take some time to review the work of Edward Thorndike and B.F. Skinner, spending more time on the work of the Skinner. New to the course and exam description is the addition of positive and negative punishment. Many activities have been included and by taking the time to having students practice the application of the concepts can help ease their anxiety. When reviewing positive and negative reinforcement it helps to also review positive and negative punishment.

- *Operant conditioning* is learning in which a voluntary response is strengthened or weakened, depending on its favorable or unfavorable consequences. The organism "operates" on its environment to produce a desirable result.
- Unlike classical conditioning, in which the original behaviors are the natural, biological responses to the presence of a stimulus such as food, water, or pain, operant conditioning applies to voluntary responses, which an organism performs deliberately to produce a desirable outcome.

**THORNDIKE'S LAW OF EFFECT**  After conducting the cat-in-the-cage experiment (see **Figure 1**), Edward L. Thorndike observed the cat had learned that pressing the paddle was associated with the desirable consequence of getting food. Thorndike summarized that relationship by formulating the law of effect: Responses that lead to satisfying consequences are more likely to be repeated.

**THE BASICS OF OPERANT CONDITIONING**  Thorndike's early research served as the foundation for the work of one of the 20th century's most influential psychologists, B. F. Skinner (1904–1990).

The Skinner box was a chamber with a highly controlled environment that was used to study operant conditioning processes with laboratory animals (see **Figure 2**). Skinner, whose work went far beyond perfecting Thorndike's earlier apparatus, is considered the inspiration for a whole generation of psychologists studying operant conditioning.

**Reinforcement: The Central Concept of Operant Conditioning**

- *Reinforcement* is the process by which a stimulus increases the probability that a preceding behavior will be repeated.
  - Reinforcer is any stimulus that increases the probability that a preceding behavior will occur again.
    - **Primary reinforcer** satisfies some biological need and works naturally, regardless of a person's previous experience (e.g., food).
    - **Secondary reinforcer** is a stimulus that becomes reinforcing because of its association with a primary reinforcer (e.g., money).

**Positive Reinforcers, Negative Reinforcers, and Punishment (See Figure 3)**

- **Positive reinforcer** is a stimulus added to the environment that brings about an increase in a preceding response. If food, water, money, or praise is provided after a response, it is more likely that that response will occur again in the future.

- **Negative reinforcer** refers to an unpleasant stimulus whose removal leads to an increase in the probability that a preceding response will be repeated in the future. Negative reinforcement, then, teaches the individual that taking an action removes a negative condition that exists in the environment.

- **Punishment** refers to a stimulus that decreases the probability that a prior behavior will occur again. Unlike negative reinforcement, which produces an increase in behavior, punishment reduces the likelihood of a prior response. There are two types of punishment:
  - Positive punishment weakens a response through the application of an unpleasant stimulus.
  - Negative punishment consists of the removal of something pleasant.

Both positive and negative punishment result in a decrease in the likelihood that a prior behavior will be repeated.

**THE PROS AND CONS OF PUNISHMENT: WHY REINFORCEMENT BEATS PUNISHMENT** Punishment often presents the quickest route to changing behavior that, if allowed to continue, might be dangerous to an individual. Punishment has several disadvantages:

- For one thing, punishment is frequently ineffective, particularly if it is not delivered shortly after the undesired behavior or if the individual is able to leave the setting in which the punishment is being given.
- Physical punishment can convey to the recipient the idea that physical aggression is permissible and perhaps even desirable.
- Those who resort to physical punishment run the risk that they will grow to be feared.
- Can also reduce the self-esteem of recipients unless they can understand the reasons for it.
- Does not convey any information about what an alternative, more appropriate behavior might be.

To be useful in bringing about more desirable behavior in the future:

- Must be accompanied by specific information about the behavior that is being punished, along with specific suggestions concerning a more desirable behavior.

In short, reinforcing desired behavior is a more appropriate technique for modifying behavior than using punishment.

### Schedules of Reinforcement: Timing Life's Rewards (See Figure 4)

- *Schedules of reinforcement* refer to the different patterns of frequency and timing of reinforcement following desired behavior.
- *Continuous reinforcement schedule*—Behavior that is reinforced every time it occurs
- *Partial (or intermittent) reinforcement schedule*—Behavior that is reinforced some but not all of the time.
- Although learning occurs more rapidly under a continuous reinforcement schedule, behavior lasts longer after reinforcement stops when it is learned under a partial reinforcement schedule.

Partial reinforcement schedules can be put into two categories:
- *Fixed- and Variable-Ratio Schedules*—schedules that consider the number of responses made before reinforcement is given, called fixed-ratio and variable-ratio schedules,
  - *Fixed-ratio schedule*—reinforcement is given only after a specific number of responses.
  - *Variable-ratio schedule*—reinforcement occurs after a varying number of responses rather than after a fixed number.
- *Fixed- and Variable-Interval Schedules: The Passage of Time*—those that consider the amount of time that elapses before reinforcement is provided, called fixed-interval and variable-interval schedules.
  - *Fixed-interval schedule*—reinforcement for a response only if a fixed time period has elapsed, overall rates of response are relatively low.
  - *Variable-interval schedule*—time between reinforcements varies around some average rather than being fixed.

**DISCRIMINATION AND GENERALIZATION IN OPERANT CONDITIONING**  Just as in classical conditioning, operant learning involves the phenomena of discrimination and generalization. A discriminative stimulus signals the likelihood that reinforcement will follow a response. The phenomenon of stimulus generalization, in which an organism learns a response to one stimulus and then exhibits the same response to slightly different stimuli, occurs in operant conditioning.

**SHAPING: REINFORCING WHAT DOESN'T COME NATURALLY**  *Shaping* is the process of teaching a complex behavior by rewarding closer and closer approximations of the desired behavior. In shaping, you start by reinforcing any behavior that is at all similar to the behavior you want the person to learn. Later, you reinforce only responses that are closer to the behavior you ultimately want to teach. Finally, you reinforce only the desired response. Each step in shaping, then, moves only slightly beyond the previously learned behavior, permitting the person to link the new step to the behavior learned earlier.

**BIOLOGICAL CONSTRAINTS ON LEARNING: YOU CAN'T TEACH AN OLD DOG JUST ANY TRICK**  Not all behaviors can be trained in all species equally well. Instead, there are biological constraints, built-in limitations in the ability of animals to learn particular behaviors. The existence of biological constraints is consistent with evolutionary explanations of behavior. Clearly, there are adaptive benefits that promote survival for organisms that quickly learn—or avoid—certain behaviors. Additional support for the evolutionary interpretation of biological constraints lies in the fact that the associations that animals learn most readily involve stimuli that are most relevant to the specific environment in which they live.

**COMPARING CLASSICAL AND OPERANT CONDITIONING (SEE FIGURE 5)**  We have considered classical conditioning and operant conditioning as two completely different processes. The key concept in classical conditioning is the association between stimuli, whereas in operant conditioning, it is reinforcement. Furthermore, classical conditioning involves an involuntary, natural, innate behavior, but operant conditioning is based on voluntary responses made by an organism.

**APPLYING PSYCHOLOGY IN THE 21ST CENTURY: HOW UBER AND LYFT PUT THEMSELVES IN THE DRIVER'S SEAT**  Uber and Lyft both use learning principles to reinforce drivers to keep driving, a technique to help them manage the availability of their drivers. They are otherwise unable to control this availability and therefore present certain messages when drivers are about to log off that remind them to keep driving because they are close to earning another goal (e.g., "You're $20 away from $200. Are you sure you want to go offline?"). Uber also uses simple messages to encourage drivers to promote the company and recruit additional drivers. In addition, drivers can earn achievement badges. All of these are concrete behavioral tactics to reinforce drivers and retain their driver base.

**BECOMING AN INFORMED CONSUMER OF PSYCHOLOGY: USING BEHAVIOR ANALYSIS AND BEHAVIOR MODIFICATION**

- **Behavior modification** is a technique for increasing the frequency of desirable behaviors and decreasing the incidence of unwanted ones.
- **Behavior analyst** is a psychologist who specializes in behavior modification techniques. Participants in a behavior change program do, however, typically follow a series of similar basic steps that include the following:
  - Identifying goals and target behaviors
  - Designing a data-recording system and recording preliminary data
  - Selecting a behavior-change strategy
  - Implementing the program
  - Keeping careful records after the program is implemented
  - Evaluating and altering the ongoing program

Behavior-change techniques based on these general principles have enjoyed wide success and have proved to be one of the most powerful means of modifying behavior.

## 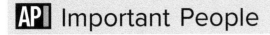 Key Terms

behavior modification

continuous reinforcement schedule

fixed-interval schedule

fixed-ratio schedule

negative reinforcer

operant conditioning

partial (or intermittent) reinforcement schedule

positive punishment

negative punishment

positive reinforcer

punishment

reinforcement

reinforcer

schedule of reinforcement

shaping

variable-interval schedule

variable-ratio schedule

## Important People

**B.F. Skinner**
**Edward Thorndike**

## Class Discussion Ideas

**BIOGRAPHY OF B. F. SKINNER** Burrhus Frederic Skinner (1904–1990) is one of the most famous, influential, and controversial figures in contemporary American psychology. He was born in the small railroad town of Susquehanna, Pennsylvania, in March 1904. After graduating from Hamilton College in 1926 with a degree in English, he tried writing but eventually gave it up because he felt he had nothing important to say. He became interested in psychology and earned his PhD from Harvard University in 1931.

He taught for several years at the University of Minnesota and Indiana University. During this time, he wrote two of his most important books—*The Behavior of Organisms* (1938) and a novel, *Walden Two* (1948), which is an account of a utopian society run in accordance with operant principles. Skinner returned to Harvard in 1948, where he remained until his death in August 1990.

Skinner made numerous contributions to the science of behavior. He strongly influenced the area of learning that he named operant conditioning. His Skinner box is now a standard apparatus for the experimental study of animal behavior. Much of his work involved the study of how reinforcement schedules influence learning and behavior. His *Beyond Freedom and Dignity* (1971) is a nonfiction examination of his utopian society in which he explains why we must understand how we control behavior in everyday life. In his 1987 book, *Upon Further Reflection,* Skinner presents his views on issues ranging from world peace and evolution to education and old age.

Source: Pettijohn, T. E. (1998). *Psychology: A ConnecText* (4th ed.). Dushkin/McGraw-Hill.

**BIOGRAPHY OF EDWARD L. THORNDIKE** Edward Lee Thorndike was born in Williamsburg, Massachusetts, in 1874. His mother was homemaker, and his father was a minister. After graduating from high school in 1891, he attended Wesleyan University, where he graduated in 1895. He then continued his education at Harvard University. In 1897, he left Harvard and began graduate work at Columbia University. Thorndike studied learning in cats and earned a PhD in psychology in 1898.

His dissertation resulted in his publication in 1898 of "Animal Intelligence" in *Psychological Review.* Thorndike observed trial and error learning in cats. He placed a cat in a small cage and observed it manipulate the environment in order to escape. Thorndike called this type of learning instrumental learning, stating that the individual is instrumental in producing a response.

After teaching for a year at the College for Women of Case Western Reserve in Cleveland, Ohio, Thorndike went to Teachers College at Columbia University, where he remained the rest of his academic career. He became more interested in human mental abilities, and in 1903, he published a monograph, "Heredity, Correlation and Sex Differences in School Abilities."

Thorndike was a prolific writer, publishing more than 450 articles and books. Some of his important publications include *Educational Psychology* (1903), *The Elements of Psychology* (1905), *The Fundamentals of Learning* (1932), and *The Psychology of Wants, Interests, and Attitudes* (1935).

He also worked on solving industrial problems, such as employee exams and testing. He was a member of the board of the Psychological Corporation. He served as president of the American Psychological Association in 1912. Thorndike died in 1949.

Source: Pettijohn, T. E. (1998). *Psychology: A ConnecText* (4th ed.). Dushkin/McGraw-Hill.

**COMPARISON OF CLASSICAL AND OPERANT CONDITIONING** An excellent study tool is to have students create a comparison chart for their notes to help with mastering the concepts of classical and operant conditioning.

Show students this comparison chart:

| Classical Conditioning | Operant Conditioning |
|---|---|
| Acquisition | Acquisition |
| Extinction | Extinction |
| Spontaneous recovery | Spontaneous recovery |
| Stimulus generalization | Stimulus generalization |
| Association between stimuli and responses | Reinforcement |
| Based on involuntary reflexive behavior | Based on voluntary behavior |

Source: Pettijohn, T. E. (1998). *Psychology: A ConnecText* (4th ed.). Dushkin/McGraw-Hill.

**SCHEDULES OF REINFORCEMENT** Use these examples:

| Schedule | Examples |
|---|---|
| Fixed ratio: rewards given after fixed number of responses | Getting a free coffee for every 10 cups that you buy at a local coffee house<br>Magazine subscription offer: buy 11 issues and get the 12th one for free<br>Being paid by commission |
| Variable ratio: rewards given after varying number of responses | Gambling (slot machine) is always the best example. |
| Fixed interval: rewards given after a fixed period of time | Exam is given every Friday in class. Studying occurs on Thursday night.<br>A store offers a sale or discount every Saturday. Weekly paycheck |
| Variable interval: rewards given after varying periods of time | A radio station offers free tickets at some point during the next hour, but you do not know when the offer will occur. |

# Activities

**DEMONSTRATION: SHAPING** You will need to arrange for a umbrella to be present in the classroom. Have it sitting unobtrusively off in an area in the classroom.

Select a volunteer. Ask the student to step outside of the room. When the volunteer is out of earshot, tell the class that they are going to use shaping to get the volunteer to open the umbrella and dance in a circle while holding it over their head. The students will do this by clapping as the volunteer gets closer to each desired step in a sequence. First, the volunteer will have to look at the umbrella. Then they will have to walk over to it and so on, until they open and dance while holding it over their head. The class will look at you, and you will cue them when to clap. After the volunteer performs the desired act, the clapping should stop and should not start again until the next higher level in the hierarchy is reached. After the desired behavior is performed, lead the class in a big round of applause for the volunteer. (While the volunteer is dancing with the umbrella, you may want to have someone take their picture.)

## Shaping and Successive Approximation

- **Shaping** Use *Handout: How Do You Shape Behaviors?* The goal of this activity is to have students demonstrate the concept of shaping. The students are given various behaviors and are supposed to describe how they would go about shaping them.

- **Shaping the Teacher** This activity gives students the opportunity to observe and then shape their teacher's behavior. For example, pacing behaviors can be shaped if every time the teacher paces to the left, students ask questions, stay awake, take notes, and look interested. If the teacher moves to the right, students yawn, take no notes, talk to other students, and generally ignore the professor. Ask the class members if they think they can shape you. Remind them to pick a simple behavior, then leave the room while they make their choice. Even with this introduction and with the full awareness of the teacher, they can be very successful. They may be able to shape you to write on the blackboard, look out of the window, or touch your ear. *Source:* Chisler, J. C. (2000). Conditioning instructor's behavior: A class project in psychology of learning. In M. E. Ware & D. E. Johnson (Eds.). *Handbook of Demonstrations and Activities in Psychology* (2nd ed.), pp. 137–139. Psychology Press.

**REINFORCEMENT** Positive reinforcement and negative reinforcement can be difficult concepts to grasp. The real-world examples and accompanying practice exercises on the following website should help to clarify the distinction for you: http://psych.athabascau.ca/html/prtut/reinpair.htm.

## Schedules of Reinforcement

- **Differences Between Primary and Secondary Reinforcers:** Students may have difficulty discriminating the differences between these two types of reinforcements. You can use the advertising example in the text (e.g., how reinforcers may acquire pleasant characteristics by virtue of their association with something that is inherently reinforcing, such as food or sex, in ads for sports cars, beer, beauty supplies, etc.). You can also discuss what types of reinforcers are most effective for different situations. For example, ask how to get class-mates to show up at different events: the answer is FREE FOOD (a primary reinforcer). How might you as a faculty member get students to attend class regularly? OFFER EXTRA CREDIT (a secondary reinforcer).

- **Partial Reinforcement:** Break the class into groups, and have each group come up with one example each for fixed-ratio schedules, variable-ratio schedules, fixed-interval schedules, and variable-interval schedules. The students will learn from each other by working together to come up with their examples. They will also be reviewing the various schedules as they complete the assignment.

- **Schedules of Reinforcement:** Use *Handout: Which Schedule Is It?* The goal of this activity is to have students read various scenarios from which they are to identify the schedule of reinforcement (positive or negative reinforcement, or positive or negative punishment). The students will gain knowledge with the various schedules of reinforcement. They will have to evaluate the example critically before determining which schedule of reinforcement it fits into.

- **Schedules of Reinforcement—Personal Examples:** Use *Handout: Schedules of Reinforcement.* The goal of this activity is to have students provide an original example from their daily life for each of the schedules of reinforcement.

# Punishment

- **Behavior Modification:** Use *Handout: How Do You Change Behavior?* In this activity, the students will have to choose a behavior from the ones listed on the assignment sheet, and they will have to use the principles of operant conditioning that were discussed in the chapter to change the behavior they chose.
- **Time-Out:** Have your class debate the effectiveness of "time-out" as punishment for children's bad behaviors. Students should be able to articulate examples of punishments and reinforcements as they argue their opinions about this topic. To add depth in the debate, ask students to reflect on cultural components of this argument and what place culture and social components have in learning.

## Discussion Questions

### Reinforcement and Punishment

- Why do psychologists prefer negative reinforcement to punishment as a way to shape behavior?
- What are examples of negative reinforcement in your life?
- What are examples of punishment in your life?
- Which is more effective in motivating you—negative reinforcement or punishment?
- Discuss alcohol addiction as it relates to reinforcement and punishment.
- Discuss how wearing sunglasses can be a form of positive reinforcement, negative reinforcement, positive punishment, and negative punishment. Do the same for smoking cigarettes.

**BEHAVIOR MODIFICATION** How should you best modify behaviors? Ask students how their parents reinforced and punished them. Which actions were most effective? Which were most ineffective? Skinner emphasized that reinforcement is a much more effective way of modifying behavior than is punishment. Specifically, using reinforcement to increase desirable behaviors works better than using punishment in an attempt to decrease undesirable behaviors. As another example, ask students to honestly report if they have ever driven while texting (speeding, not wearing a seatbelt, etc.). Then ask if they were ever caught in this act. What can government do to curb such behavior? Should it punish people with jail sentences, major fines, etc., or should it reward people each time they drive when not performing such behavior?

## Polling Questions

**POLLING QUESTION: PUNISHMENT** After John brings home a disappointing report card, his mother responds by taking away his cell phone. This is an example of:
a) Positive reinforcement
b) Negative reinforcement
c) Positive punishment
d) Negative punishment

**POLLING QUESTION: LEARNING PRINCIPLES—ABUSIVE TO ANIMALS (YOU DECIDE)** Service dogs and sniffer dogs have been trained to demonstrate excellent skills and amazing complex behaviors that you may not ever see from your house pet. Training dogs to detect blood sugar levels in humans through smell or having service dogs flush toilets for those who are disabled are among some of the most extraordinary skills these canines have mastered. How did they do it? Learning principles are incredibly powerful and influential. How many of you think it is acceptable to train service dogs to do such extraordinary behaviors? Imagine the extensive training programs these dogs go through. Who thinks we have crossed the line by training dogs in this manner, utilizing the same learning principles discussed in this chapter? How many of you think it is an invaluable service that these dogs provide and would consider it a privilege to either own or train one of these special animals?

## Applying Psychology in the 21st Century: How Uber and Lyft Put Themselves in the Driver's Seat

Answer Suggestions

- Using principles of learning to manipulate humans should be viewed as a positive influence. Perhaps it is ethical if manipulation is being used for good overall. Ethical considerations for experiments include informed consent, which is not being provided in this circumstance.

- The intermittent schedules of reinforcement have different outcomes. Fixed-ratio schedules create quick learning. Variable-ratio schedules lead to high rates of responses and resistance to exhaustion. Fixed-interval schedules create a scalloping effect. Variable-interval schedules produce steady rates of responses and take longer to extinguish after reinforcement ends.

## AP Test Practice

### Section I: Multiple Choice

1. **A** (Skill 1.B, Learning Target 1.E)
2. **B** (Skill 1.A, Learning Target 1.E)
3. **E** (Skill 1.B, Learning Target 1.E)

### Section II: Free Response

**A.**

Negative reinforcement is the removal of an unpleasant stimulus that leads to an increased behavior. Bella cleaned her bedroom (increased behavior) to remove her mother's nagging (unpleasant stimulus).

A fixed-interval schedule provides reinforcement for a response after a set time has elapsed. Bella cleaned her room (behavior) on Sunday mornings because she knew the consequence of her mom nagging would start on Sunday evenings (set time) if her room was not clean.

A secondary reinforcer is a stimulus that becomes reinforcing because it is associated with a primary reinforcer. Cory earned a secondary reinforcer of money for doing the garbage and recycling.

Operant conditioning of a superstitious behavior occurs when a random consequence alters a behavior that is not tied to the behavior. Johnny found money (consequence) when he wore striped socks (behavior). He now wears socks hoping for a similar consequence.

Positive punishment is the addition of an unpleasant stimulus that weakens a response. Kurt doesn't take out the garbage and recycling anymore (weakened response) because his brother always yelled at him (addition of an unpleasant stimulus).

**B.**

A biological constraint is a built-in limitation in the ability for an animal to learn a particular behavior. The puppy may learn new tricks, but biological constraints will prevent the puppy from learning to read or speak.

The evolutionary perspective views behavior as having been influenced by the genetic inheritance from our ancestors. The evolutionary perspective supports biological predispositions and constraints. There are survival benefits for organisms who quickly learn-or avoid-certain behaviors. Perhaps the puppy may be genetically predisposed to be fearful of certain stimuli.

# Module 19: Cognitive Approaches to Learning

## AP Module Summary

Module 19 introduces the role that cognitive processes have in how we learn. In this module it is important that students know the research of Albert Bandura (Social Learning), Edward Tolman (Latent Learning) and Wolfgang Kohler (Insight Learning). Please keep in mind that there will be some overlap in this module with other units, providing an excellent opportunity for review of material. And, if you ran out of time in module 17 and didn't review Robert Rescorla's work, this would be a great time to do so!

Some psychologists view learning in terms of the thought processes, or cognitions, that underlie it—an approach known as *cognitive learning theory*. In its most basic formulation, cognitive learning theory suggests that it is not enough to say that people make responses because there is an assumed link between a stimulus and a response—a link that is the result of a past history of reinforcement for a response. Instead, according to this point of view, people and even lower animals develop an expectation that they will receive a reinforcer after making a response. Two types of learning in which no obvious prior reinforcement is present are latent learning and observational learning.

**LATENT LEARNING (SEE FIGURE 1)** *Latent learning* holds that behavior is acquired but is not demonstrated until some incentive is provided for displaying it. Both humans and animals develop cognitive maps, which are mental representations of spatial locations and directions. For example, latent learning may permit a person to know the location of a kitchenware store at a local mall that they have frequently visited, even though they have never entered the store and do not even like to cook.

**OBSERVATIONAL LEARNING: LEARNING THROUGH IMITATION** According to psychologist Albert Bandura and colleagues, a major part of human learning consists of *observational learning*, which is learning by watching the behavior of another person or model. A social phenomenon—is often referred to as a social cognitive approach to learning. One crucial factor that determines whether we later imitate a model is whether the model is rewarded for their behavior. Models who are rewarded for behaving in a particular way are more apt to be mimicked than are models who receive punishment. Observing the punishment of a model, however, does not necessarily stop observers from learning the behavior.

For more information, see the "Neuroscience in Your Life: Learning Through Imitation" box in the text.

**VIOLENCE IN TELEVISION AND VIDEO GAMES: DOES THE MEDIA'S MESSAGE MATTER?** Most psychologists agree that watching high levels of media violence makes viewers more susceptible to acting aggressively. Violent video games have also been linked with actual aggression. In one of a series of studies by psychologist Craig Anderson and his colleagues, college students who frequently played violent video games, such as Postal or Doom, were more likely to have been involved in delinquent behavior and aggression. Frequent players also had lower academic achievement.

Several aspects of media violence may contribute to aggressive behavior. For one thing, experiencing violent media content seems to lower inhibitions against carrying out aggression. Exposure to media violence also may distort our understanding of the meaning of others' behavior, predisposing us to view even nonaggressive acts by others as aggressive. Finally, a continuous diet of aggression may leave us desensitized to violence, and what previously would have repelled us now produces little emotional response.

On the other hand, there are contrary research findings. For example, a recent meta-analysis of video game influences finds the effects of video games on aggression are not substantial.

Furthermore, some researchers argue that violent video games may produce certain positive results—such as a rise in social networking.

**EXPLORING DIVERSITY: DOES CULTURE INFLUENCE HOW WE LEARN?** Some psychologists, taking a cognitive perspective on learning, suggest that people develop particular learning styles, characteristic ways of approaching material, based on their cultural background and unique pattern of abilities. Learning styles differ along several dimensions. For example, one central dimension is relational versus analytical approaches to learning. People with a relational learning style master material best through understanding the "big picture" about something. They need to understand the complete picture of what they're studying before they understand its component parts.

In contrast, those with an analytical learning style do best when they first analyze the various components underlying an object, phenomenon, or situation. By developing an understanding of the individual parts, they are best able to grasp the full picture.

The conclusion that members of particular ethnic and gender groups have similar learning styles is controversial. Because there is so much diversity within each particular racial and ethnic group, critics argue that generalizations about learning styles cannot be used to predict the style of any single individual, regardless of group membership. Still, it is clear that values about learning, which are communicated through a person's family and cultural background, have an impact on how successful students are in school. One theory suggests that members of minority groups who were voluntary immigrants are more apt to be successful in school than those who were brought into a majority culture against their will. The theory suggests that the motivation to succeed is lower for children in forced immigration groups.

## **AP** Key Terms

**cognitive learning theory**
**latent learning**
**insight learning**
**observational learning**

## **AP** Important People

**Albert Bandura**
**Edward Tolman**
**Wolfgang Kohler**

# Class Discussion Ideas

**FOCUS OF COGNITIVE LEARNING THEORY** Emphasize the focus of cognitive learning theory on thoughts and expectations. Explain why this was an important departure from strict behaviorism.

## Observational Learning

- **Violence in the Media:** Raise the issue of whether violence on television, in the movies, and in video games affects young people and how. Include in this discussion the question of the effects of the behavior of well-known public figures such as politicians, sports personalities, pop stars, and movie celebrities.

# Activities

- **Latent Learning:** Ask the students to think about a time in their life when latent learning was evident. After they have written down an example of latent learning in their life, break the class into groups and have them share with others in their group the example they came up with for latent learning. The students will have to review the concept of latent learning in order to come up with their own examples and will learn from each other by sharing with the group.
- **Bandura's Approach:** Break the class into groups. Write various behaviors on the board such as riding a bike, jumping rope, washing dishes, and driving a car. Ask the groups to work their way through Bandura's four approaches that are discussed in this chapter as though they were observing another person acting out these behaviors. Ask the groups to choose two of the behaviors and discuss how they would go about imitating those behaviors.

**Blame the Video Game?** As an interactive assessment of student's understanding of the various principles of learning, create student teams and play "Blame the Video Game." The instructor will give one concept of learning (e.g., positive reinforcement), and student teams must come up with one example of this concept used in video games. Each team must come up with a unique video game and/or example that illustrates this concept, and their explanation must be correct in order to win points. Other teams can "steal" the points by refuting the explanation or showing how it is incorrect. If two teams use the same video game or example from the video game, then no team gets the points. These rules are similar to Scattergories, the family game by Hasbro Milton Bradley Company. Finally, ask students to discuss the impact video games are having on children based on the use of learning principles.

**Effects of Music Videos:** Have students complete *Handout: Images in Music Videos.*

- **Ideal Internship and Observation Learning:** Imagine that you are about to begin an internship in an organization that you would like to join someday as a professional. Use the processes of observational learning to describe your strategy for making the most of your internship.
- **Role Models and Observational Learning:** Have students complete *Handout: Effects of Role Models* on the effect of role models on their behavior.
- **Violence on Television:** Give students a homework assignment of watching television. Have them make note of different types of aggression they see in the course of one evening (you may wish to differentiate physical aggression versus relational aggression). Talk to students in the next class meeting about their observations. They will likely be surprised by just how much aggression they saw. Ask them how this might influence children (you can also talk about cartoon violence here).

# Discussion Questions

**WHAT IS THE DIFFERENCE BETWEEN LATENT LEARNING AND INSIGHT LEARNING?** Sixteen-year-old Sena has never driven a car before but has observed many of her friends drive. On her first attempt at driving, Sena shows remarkable skill and ability. What might explain Sena's ability?

Describe something you learned by insight. What led to your learning?

**IMPACT OF TELEVISION AND MOVIES ON AGGRESSION IN CHILDREN AND TEENS** What do you think are the effects of watching violent television programs and movies on children? Why?

- Reflect on some examples of ways in which observational learning has benefited you in your life. Are there instances in which observational learning has worked to your disadvantage?
- Do you think watching violence in movies and TV leads to aggressive behavior? Why or why not?
- How would you evaluate the argument that showing violence on television and in movies helps to reduce violence in children by showing them that they will be punished for this behavior?
- Can vicarious learning be beneficial? How?

# Polling Questions

**POLLING QUESTION: DON'T DOWNPLAY MY INSIGHT** Max Wertheimer's experiment on insight learning consisted of his telling children to find the area of a parallelogram. In one group, he told them a formula to solve the problem, but the other group did not receive the formula. The children who were given the formula were able to find the area, but they did not understand why it was the answer. Because not many of the children who were not given the formula knew how to find the area of a parallelogram, they figured out to cut the right triangles off the ends of the parallelogram and combine them to form a rectangle.

After this was done, Wertheimer gave both groups of students a set of transfer problems like the original but different in some way). The children who were not given the formula and understood how to find the area of the parallelogram did better on the transfer problems, whereas the children who received the formula and did not understand did worse. The children who were not given the formula used insight learning, which allowed them to see how to solve the problem.

Let's take a more personal look at insight learning. First, do you think you are insightful? What does that mean to you? How many of you think that insight learning is really just good guessing? Who in this room has had an experience in which you didn't really know how to do or solve something, then, like magic, you managed to figure it out? How many of you think that animals can exhibit insight learning? For those who answered yes, what examples can you give?

**POLLING QUESTION: VICARIOUS LEARNING** Do you believe that violent video games, TV shows, and movies have an impact on aggressive behavior?

# Suggested Media

*Bobo doll study:* https://www.youtube.com/watch?v=dmBqwWlJg8U. This clip includes an interview with Bandura along with footage from the original study.

- *Learning and Transfer Lab:* http://greenlab.psych.wisc.edu/.
- *Observational learning: Children See. Children Do,* http://www.youtube.com/watch?v=KHi2dxSf9hw.
- *Support monkeys:* http://www.monkeyhelpers.org/.

## Neuroscience in Your Life: Learning Through Imitation

Answer Suggestions

- The neuroscience or biological approach views behavior from the perspective of biological functioning. Another neural explanation for observational learning involves mirror neurons that fire when we perform a particular behavior and when we observe another person carrying out the same behavior.
- The independent variable is imitation of the experimenter because it is the variable being manipulated. The dependent variable is mu activity, a neural indicator of motor activity in the brain, because it is being measured.

## AP Test Practice

### Section I: Multiple Choice

1. **C** *(Skill 2, Learning Target 1.E)*
2. **A** *(Skill 1.A, Learning Target 1.C)*
3. **D** *(Skill 1.B, Learning Target 1.C)*

### Section II: Free Response

Latent learning is learning in which a new behavior is acquired but is not demonstrated until some incentive is provided for displaying it. Samantha knows the school rules, but waits to display them until she can earn some Skinner Bucks. In addition, Samantha knows the answer in class but only contributes to class discussions when there are points awarded for participation.

A cognitive map is a mental representation of a spatial location. Samantha has created a cognitive map of Behaviorism High School and can mentally locate her next classroom so she can make it to class on time.

Observational learning is learning by watching the behavior of another person. Samantha learned the school rules by watching her peers and teachers.

A secondary reinforcer is a stimulus that becomes reinforcing because it is associated with a primary reinforcer. Samantha can earn Skinner Bucks that can be turned in for other prizes.

The hippocampus plays an important role in learning and memory. Samantha's hippocampus helps her learn and remember her friends' names.

# CHAPTER 7
# Memory

## AP Introduction

The chapter on memory can be an excellent place to begin the school year. In this chapter students are introduced to the theories behind memory and what causes memory to fade. Due to the massive amount of vocabulary and the number of important people mentioned in this chapter, the study of memory early on can help your students apply many of the concepts introduced within this chapter. Knowing how memory works will provide them with tools that can be used throughout the school year, not just in psychology but in all courses. What would we do without memory? How would not having a memory impact our day to day existence? Who would we be without our memories?

## AP Essential Questions

- What roles do memory and thinking play in our behaviors?

## Module 20: The Foundations of Memory
### AP Learning Targets:

- Compare and contrast various cognitive processes.
- Describe and differentiate psychological and physiological systems of memory.
- Identify the contributions of key researchers in cognitive psychology.
- Outline the principles that underlie construction and encoding of memories.
- Outline the principles that underlie effective storage of memories.
- Describe strategies for retrieving memories.
- Describe and differentiate psychological and physiological systems of short- and long-term memory.

### Pacing:

1 Block or 2 Traditional Class period

## Module 21: Recalling Long-Term Memories
### AP Learning Targets:

- Describe and differentiate psychological and physiological systems of memory.
- Identify the contributions of key researchers in cognitive psychology.
- Describe strategies for retrieving memories.
- Describe strategies for memory improvement and typical memory errors.

### Pacing:

1 Block or 2 Traditional Class periods

# Module 22: Forgetting: When Memory Fails

**AP Learning Targets:**

- Identify the contributions of key researchers in cognitive psychology.
- Describe strategies for memory improvement and typical memory errors.
- Discuss the major diagnostic categories, including dissociative disorders, somatic symptom and related disorders, and trauma-and stressor-related disorders and their corresponding symptoms.

**Pacing:**

1 Block or 2 Traditional Class period

# Module 20: The Foundations of Memory

## AP Module Summary

In Module 20 a number of very important concepts are introduced when explaining memory. Several concepts are referred to in multiple ways for example, procedural memory is also referred to as implicit memory (example 5.B.3) and declarative memory is also referred to as explicit memory (example 5.B.6). It is important that you highlight this fact to students because both are specified in the new Advanced Placement Course and Exam Description Guide. In addition, the terms metacognition (example 5.A.4) and prospective memory (example 5.B.5) are listed but not included in the text. One key researcher, George A. Miller's work is briefly mentioned but doesn't include his name, this would be a important detail to add to your lesson on the foundations of memory. Finally, it is important to spend more time on the physiological systems (example 5.B.7) of memory. This is new and should not be overlooked.

The initial process of recording information in a form usable to memory, a process called *encoding*, is the first stage in remembering something. However, even if you remember something, you may still be unable to recall it when required because of a failure to retain it. Memory specialists speak of *storage*, the maintenance of material saved in memory. If the material is not stored adequately, it cannot be recalled later. Memory also depends on one last process—*retrieval*: material in memory storage has to be located and brought into awareness to be useful. In sum, psychologists consider *memory* to be the process by which we encode, store, and retrieve information (see **Figure 1**).

According to the three-system approach to memory that dominated memory research for several decades, there are different memory storage systems or stages through which information must travel if it is to be remembered. (see **Figure 2**). *Sensory memory* refers to the initial, momentary storage of information that lasts only an instant.

*Short-term memory* holds information for 15 to 25 seconds and stores it according to its meaning rather than as mere sensory stimulation.

*Long-term memory* a relatively permanent basis, although it may be difficult to retrieve.

**SENSORY MEMORY** *Sensory memory* can store information for only a very short time. If information does not pass into short-term memory, it is lost for good.

There are several types of sensory memories, each related to a different source of sensory information.

- Iconic memory reflects information from the visual system.
- Echoic memory stores auditory information coming from the ears.

In addition, there are corresponding memories for each of the other senses.

**SHORT-TERM MEMORY** Because the information that is stored briefly in sensory memory consists of representations of raw sensory stimuli, it is not meaningful to us. If we are to make sense of it and possibly retain it, the information must be transferred to the next stage of memory: short-term memory.

Maximum length of retention there is relatively short.

The specific amount of information that can be held in short-term memory has been identified as seven items, or "chunks," of information, with variations of plus or minus two chunks. A *chunk* is a group of familiar stimuli stored as a single unit in short-term memory.

At this point you would want to introduce George A. Miller and "The Magical Number Seven, Plus or Minus Two."

**REHEARSAL** The transfer of material from short- to long-term memory proceeds largely on the basis of *rehearsal*, the repetition of information that has entered short-term memory. Rehearsal accomplishes two things.

- As long as the information is repeated, it is maintained in short-term memory.
- Allows us to transfer the information into long-term memory.

If the information in short-term memory is rehearsed using a process called elaborative rehearsal, it is much more likely to be transferred into long term memory. *Elaborative rehearsal* occurs when the information is considered and organized in some fashion.

By using organizational strategies such as mnemonics, we can vastly improve our retention of information. *Mnemonics* are formal techniques for organizing information in a way that makes it more likely to be remembered.

**WORKING MEMORY** *Working memory* is the memory system that holds information temporarily while actively manipulating and rehearsing that information. Working memory is thought to contain a *central executive* processor that is involved in reasoning and decision making. The central executive coordinates three distinct storage-and-rehearsal systems: the visual store, the verbal store, and the episodic buffer (see Figure 4). Working memory permits us to keep information in an active state briefly so that we can do something with the information. Although working memory aids in the recall of information, it uses a significant amount of cognitive resources during its operation. In turn, this can make us less aware of our surroundings. Furthermore, stress can reduce the effectiveness of working memory by reducing its capacity.

This would be a good time to introduce students to selective versus divided attention.

**LONG-TERM MEMORY** Material that makes its way from short-term memory to long-term memory enters a storehouse of almost unlimited capacity. Evidence of the existence of long-term memory, as distinct from short-term memory, comes from a number of sources. For example, people with certain kinds of brain damage have no lasting recall of new information received after the damage occurred, although people and events stored in memory before the injury remain intact. Results from laboratory experiments are also consistent with the notion of separate short-term and long-term memory. The distinction between short- and long-term memory is also demonstrated by the fact that ability to recall information in a list depends on where in the list an item appears. For instance, in some cases, a primacy effect occurs, in which items presented early in a list are remembered better. In other cases, a recency effect is seen, in which items presented late in a list are remembered best.

**LONG-TERM MEMORY MODULES (SEE FIGURE 5)** One major distinction within long-term memory is that between declarative memory and procedural memory.

- *Declarative memory (or Explicit Memory)* is memory for factual information: names, faces, dates, and facts. Can be subdivided into:
  - *Semantic memory* is memory for general knowledge and facts about the world, as well as memory for the rules of logic that are used to deduce other facts.
  - *Episodic memory* is memory for events that occur in a particular time, place, or context.
- *Procedural memory* (or nondeclarative/Implicit memory) refers to memory for skills and habits.

*Include in this same place the comparison of effortful versus automatic processing

*This would be a great place to introduce students to the concept of prospective memory, which is not in the text but is important for the CED.

**THE NEUROSCIENCE OF MEMORY (SEE FIGURE 7)** The search for the *engram*, the term for the physical memory trace in the brain that corresponds to a memory, has proved to be a major puzzle to psychologists and other neuroscientists interested in memory. Using advanced brain scanning procedures in their efforts to determine the neuroscientific basis of memory formation, investigators have learned that certain areas and structures of the brain specialize in different types of memory-related activities. The *hippocampus*, a part of the brain's limbic system, helps to consolidate memories, stabilizing them after they are initially acquired. That information is subsequently passed along to the cerebral cortex of the brain, where it is actually stored. The amygdala, another part of the limbic system, also plays an important role in memory. The amygdala is especially involved with memories involving emotion.

**MEMORY AT THE LEVEL OF NEURONS** *Long-term potentiation* shows that certain neural pathways become easily excited while a new response is being learned. At the same time, the number of synapses between neurons increases as the dendrites branch out to receive messages. These changes reflect a process called *consolidation*, in which memories become fixed and stable in long-term memory. Memory traces are distributed throughout the brain. In short, the physical stuff of memory—the engram—is produced by a complex of biochemical and neural processes.

See the "Neuroscience in Your Life: The Building Blocks of Memory: Do You Have a Beyoncé Neuron in Your Brain?" box in the text for related information.

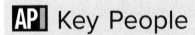 Key Terms

chunk

declarative memory (explicit)

episodic memory

long-term memory

memory

procedural memory (implicit)

rehearsal

semantic memory

semantic networks

sensory memory

metacognition

short-term memory

working memory

prospective memory

effortful processing

automatic processing

## **AP** Key People

George A. Miller

# Class Discussion Ideas

**REMEMBERING NAMES AND FACES** There are also a number of systems to remember names and faces, a useful skill for yourself to remember the names of your students. Here are some suggestions:

- Associate the name with a part of the face—such as "Larry" and "lip."
- Pay attention when you first hear the name—most people do not really listen when they meet someone for the first time.
- Pronounce the name and see how it is spelled—this gives you additional cues.
- Link the person's name with that of a celebrity—such as a woman named "Carly," who reminds you of Carly Simon or a song by Carly Simon.
- Ask again if you forget—try a different cue this time.

**OLFACTION MEMORY** Students often find olfactory cues to be an interesting subject. You may want to ask students if there are any smells that evoke strong memories for them. Then point out that one reason may be the location of the olfactory bulb in the limbic system (which is the same as the hippocampus).

# Activities

**THREE PROCESSES OF MEMORY**  Have students write down a memory. Next have them write down how this memory went through the three stages of encoding, storage, and retrieval. Go over the examples and discuss them as a class.

**CONSTRUCTIVE NATURE OF MEMORY**  Read the following words aloud at a rate of about one word per second:

BED, QUILT, DARK, SILENCE, FATIGUE, CLOCK, SNORING, NIGHT, TOSS, TIRED, NIGHT, TOSS, TIRED, NIGHT, ARTICHOKE, TURN, NIGHT, REST, DREAM

Ask students if they heard you say *aardvark*. They typically look at you like you are nuts. Next, ask them if they heard you say *sleep*. Many will raise their hands even though *sleep* is not on the list. Point out the constructive nature of memory. This is a variation on Deese (1959). Source: Deese. K. (1959). On the prediction of occurrence of particular verbal intrusions in immediate recall. *Journal of Experimental Psychology, 58*, 17–22.

**CLASSROOM DEMONSTRATION: IF YOU DON'T ENCODE, YOU CAN'T RETRIEVE IT, PART 1**  To show the importance of encoding, ask students to provide answers to these questions:

- Which color is on top on a stoplight?
- How many rows of stars are on the U.S. flag?
- Whose image is on a dime? Is he wearing a tie?
- What five words in addition to "In God We Trust" appear on most U.S. coins?
- When water goes down the drain, does it swirl clockwise or counterclockwise?

The point is that students have seen these stimuli thousands of times but because they did not think about the information, they cannot recall it.

(Answers are red; 9; F. D. Roosevelt with no tie; *United States of America* and *Liberty*; and water drains counterclockwise in the Northern Hemisphere.)

**CLASSROOM DEMONSTRATION: IF YOU DON'T ENCODE, YOU CAN'T RETRIEVE IT, PART 2**

- **Encoding Failure:**  Bring a $10 bill to class. Ask students what image appears on the back of a $10 bill (hold it up). Most students don't know. In fact, most people do not know. The answer is the U.S. Treasury. Ask students why they don't know. Often they will say that they don't need to know. This is another example of how we don't encode everything and that errors in encoding information do occur. Source: McDaniel, M. A. (2014). *Improving student learning: Moving from memory laboratory to the classroom.* NITOP presentation.
- **Imagery:**  Use *Handout: The Story of $E = mc^2$* as a way for students to use imagery to remember information. The students will be writing a story much like the one S. wrote for remembering an equation. The students should see how using imagery and mnemonics helps in remembering information.

**CLASSROOM DEMONSTRATION: CHUNKING**
- Ask for a volunteer or adapt this activity for the whole class.

Announce that you are going to prove that ordinary students can remember 15 letters without any difficulty.

Display this letter sequence for one second on a slide, and ask the volunteer or the class to say or write it down:

T WAN BAC BSC PRC IA

They will not remember more than four or five letters. Then display this letter sequence:

TWA NBA CBS CPR CIA

They will have no difficulty remembering it.

Show this picture for one second (or less, if possible).

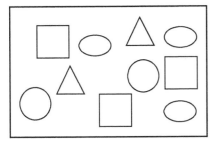

Ask students to recall which items were in the picture.

Then show this picture:

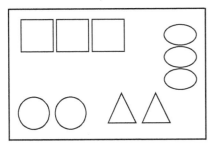

They should be able to say exactly which items were in this picture without any difficulty because the shapes are chunked.

- **Short-Term Memory:** Use *Handout: Chunking* as way for students to experience how chunking works. Students will see how their brains are already set up to chunk information that is familiar to them.
- **Short-Term Memory:** There are many variations of this exercise. Have students test their short-term memory abilities with the digit span task. Tell them you are going to say "ready" and then read a list of numbers. After you say "recall," they should write the list of numbers down. After signaling students, each time read the following list: 4432, 98325, 793627, 9963012, 10521904, and 563829610. Re-read the list so students can see what they got correct. Ask them at what point did this task begin to get difficult. Ask them what they think you could have done to help them remember the list better. This can lead into a discussion of chunking.

**SENSORY MEMORY** Play two lines of a song. Ask students if they heard the song. Next ask students to write down the lyrics of the song they heard. Students may get some of the words but not all of them, even though they told you that they did hear it. Next, run a PowerPoint slide show with 10 slides, each with a different number on it, and run them rather quickly. Have students write down the numbers they remember seeing. Students will probably remember some of the numbers but not all of them. Break the students into groups and have them compare their answers. Go over the correct answers as a class, and discuss how information in sensory memory, both echoic and iconic, only lasts for a few seconds.

**CLASSROOM DEMONSTRATION: WORKING MEMORY**
- To show how working memory is tested, use this demonstration:

Add up each of the following:

$3 + 2 = ?$

$7 - 4 = ?$

$6 - 2 = ?$

$5 + 1 = ?$

Now ask: What was the second digit mentioned in each arithmetic task?

- **Mnemonics:** Use *Handout: Mnemonic Devices* as a way for students to understand and practice how mnemonic devices work. In this activity, students have to come up with their own mnemonics for various sets of words. They also have to explain what mnemonic devices they used.

## Discussion Questions

**PERSONAL EXPERIENCE OF MEMORY LOSS**  Choose one recent situation in which you forgot (and later remembered) something important. Describe it briefly. Then use one of the theories of forgetting to explain:

- Why you forgot this
- What helped you remember it later
- How you could have avoided forgetting it

You may want to discuss developmental trends in memory systems. Most research shows that memory systems improve over childhood and remain fairly stable until very late adulthood and even there, with the exception of source memory, most people who are healthy and living an active life show no major deficit, save slower times. This also reinforces Hebb's "use it or lose it" law.

Have you ever walked into a room and could not remember why you went there? How do you retrieve that memory?

**LONG-TERM MEMORY**  To help students remember the different types of long-term memory, ask them to complete the following:

- Define the term *declarative memory* and give an example from your own life.
- Define the term *procedural memory* and give an example from your own life.
- Define the term *semantic memory* and give an example from your own life.
- Define the term *episodic memory* and give an example from your own life.

## Polling Questions

**IF YOU CAN'T ENCODE, YOU CAN'T RETRIEVE**  Use the questions from the above Classroom Demonstration: If You Can't Encode, You Can't Retrieve It—to assess students' memory and launch a discussion about the process encoding. Do you agree that people can have repressed memories? Have you ever had an experience that created a flashbulb memory?

## Suggested Media

- *How Does Your Memory Work?* Insight Media, 2008, 50:00.
- Case studies of people who suffer from memory problem are presented.
- *Memory.* Insight Media, 2001, 30:00. Several models of memory including encoding, storage, and retrieval stages are described.

- *The Mind.* 2nd ed. Teaching module #10, Pt. 1. "Life without memory: The case of Clive Wearing." Video File, 1999. Video posted to http://www.learner.org/resources/series150.html.
- The nature of memory and its importance are discussed.
- *The Mind.* 2nd ed. Teaching module #11, Pt. 2. "Clive Wearing: Living without memory." Video File, 1999. Video posted to http://www.learner.org/resources/series150.html.
- The relationship between brain damage and memory is described.
- *Pieces of Mind. Scientific American Frontiers*, PBS, 60:00.
- Alan Alda takes the viewer through many fascinating aspects of memory.

**POPULAR TELEVISION SHOW: *SEINFELD***

- A way to illustrate the principle "if you don't encode, you can't retrieve" is the *Seinfeld* episode *The Parking Garage (Season 3, Episode 6)* in which the characters forget where they parked their car and wander for hours in a parking garage while one of the characters carries a heavy package: http://en.wikipedia.org/wiki/The_Parking_Garage.
- https://www.youtube.com/watch?v=SUsUu3XRJ4I

**POPULAR MOVIES**

- **Anterograde amnesia** A number of movies have depicted anterograde amnesia, including *Finding Nemo, Finding Dory, Memento*, and *50 First Dates* starring Drew Barrymore, which is a lighthearted look at anterograde amnesia.
- ***The Man with the Seven Second Memory*** This documentary follows the story of Clive Wearing, a man with one of the worst documented cases of antergrade amnesia. His story provides a stark depiction of the realities of living with little to no short-term memory: https://www.youtube.com/watch?v=k_P7Y0-wgos.

# AP Student Edition Answer Key

## Neuroscience in Your Life: Superior Memory

Answer Suggestions

- The independent variable is memory training because it is the variable being manipulated. The dependent variable is memory capacity because it is being measured.
- Mnemonics are memory aids that enhance recall with organization, association, or meaning. Examples include method of loci, peg-word, acronyms, acrostics, chunking, or self-reference effect.

## AP Test Practice

### Section I: Multiple Choice

1. **B** *(Skill 1.A, Learning Target 5.B)*
2. **C** *(Skill 2, Learning Target 5.B)*
3. **A** *(Skill 1.B, Learning Target 5.G)*

### Section II: Free Response

Mnemonics are memory strategies that organize information to enhance recall. Kurt could use the method of loci and imagine the 70 items in a familiar location. He could also create an acronym for several words or create associations with the words.

Elaborative rehearsal utilizes meaning and leads to information being transferred to long-term memory because the information is considered and organized in some fashion. Kurt could invent a story connecting the material to his hometown to enhance his recall.

Chunking is grouping separate pieces of information to increase the amount of information held in short-term memory. Kurt could group ten words together at a time in order for the material to be learned in seven chunks.

Long-term potentiation is the strengthening of neural pathways resulting in improved memory. Kurt's training strengthened his neural pathways leading to better memory.

Primacy effect is where items presented at the beginning of the list are remembered better. Kurt will be able to remember the items at the beginning of the list better due to repetition so he should focus attention on the other words toward the end of his training.

# Module 21: Recalling Long-Term Memories

## **AP** Module Summary

In Module 21 you delve deeper into the study of memory specifically how one retrieves their memories and how those memories can be distorted. Though not much has been added to this specific area, the material is just as important in our understanding of memory. It is in this module where time should be spent covering the important research of Elizabeth Loftus.

**The tip-of-the-tongue phenomenon** is the inability to recall information that one realizes one knows—a result of the difficulty of retrieving information from long-term memory.

**RETRIEVAL CUES**  A *retrieval cue* is a stimulus that allows us to recall more easily information that is in long-term memory.

- In *recall* a specific piece of information must be retrieved.
- In contrast *recognition* occurs when people are presented with a stimulus and asked whether they have been exposed to it previously or are asked to identify it from a list of alternatives.
  - Recognition is generally a much easier task than recall (see **Figure 1** and **Figure 2**).

## Levels of Processing

One determinant of how well memories are recalled is the way in which material is first perceived, processed, and understood. The *levels-of-processing theory* emphasizes the degree to which new material is mentally analyzed. It suggests that the amount of information processing that occurs when material is initially encountered is central in determining how much of the information is ultimately remembered. According to this approach, the depth of information processing during exposure to material—meaning the degree to which it is analyzed and considered—is critical; the greater the intensity of its initial processing, the more likely we are to remember it.

## Explicit and Implicit Memory

- *Explicit memory* refers to intentional or conscious recollection of information.
- *Implicit memory* refers to memories of which people are not consciously aware but that can affect subsequent performance and behavior.
- *Priming* - One way that memory specialists study implicit memory and is a phenomenon in which exposure to a word or concept (called a prime) later makes it easier to recall related information.

**CONSTRUCTIVE PROCESSES IN MEMORY: REBUILDING THE PAST**  *Constructive processes* are processes in which memories are influenced by the meaning we give to events. When we retrieve information, the memory that is produced is affected not just by the direct prior experience we have had with the stimulus but also by our guesses and inferences about its meaning.

**MEMORY IN THE COURTROOM: THE EYEWITNESS OF TRIAL**  Research on eyewitness identification of suspects, as well as on memory for other details of crimes, has shown that eyewitnesses are apt to make significant errors when they try to recall details of criminal activity—even if they are highly confident about their recollections. One reason is the impact of the weapons used in crimes. When a criminal perpetrator displays a gun or knife, it acts like a perceptual magnet, attracting the eyes of the witnesses. As a consequence, witnesses pay less attention to other details of the crime and are less able to recall what actually occurred. The specific wording of questions posed to eyewitnesses by police officers or attorneys also can lead to memory errors (see **Figure 5**).

- **Children's Reliability:** The problem of memory reliability becomes even more acute when children are witnesses because increasing evidence suggests that children's memories are highly vulnerable to the influence of others. Children's memories are especially susceptible to influence when the situation is highly emotional or stressful.

**REPRESSED AND FALSE MEMORIES: SEPARATING TRUTH FROM FICTION** *Repressed memories* are apparent recollections of events that are initially so shocking that the mind responds by pushing them into the unconscious. Supporters of the notion of repressed memory (based on Freud's psychoanalytic theory) suggest that such memories may remain hidden, possibly throughout a person's lifetime, unless they are triggered by some current circumstance, such as the probing that occurs during psychological therapy. However, memory researcher Elizabeth Loftus maintains that so-called repressed memories may well be inaccurate or even wholly false—representing *false memory*.

For additional information on false memory, see the "Applying Psychology in the 21st Century: Remembering What Never Happened" box in the text.

**APPLYING PSYCHOLOGY IN THE 21ST CENTURY: MEMORIES CAN BE MADE TO BE MEANINGFUL** Memory errors occur frequently and can be a result of the fallacy of our own reconstructive memory processes. When we reconstruct memories, we add layers of interpretations, inferences, and assumptions that can embellish details, resulting in a memory that is, in part, imaginary. These types of memories can be particularly problematic when it comes to relying on eyewitness testimony. In the process of telling and retelling a meaningful memory, we embellish and alter the content to appeal to different listeners. Based on others' reactions, these embellishments reinforce themselves and are remembered strongly (Schacter, Guerin, & St. Jacques, 2011; Dunlop, Guo, & McAdams, 2016).

**EXPLORING DIVERSITY: ARE THERE CROSS-CULTURAL DIFFERENCES IN MEMORY?** Memory researchers suggest that there are both similarities and differences in memory across cultures. Basic memory processes such as short-term memory capacity and the structure of long-term memory—the "hardware" of memory—are universal and operate similarly in people in all cultures. In contrast, cultural differences can be seen in the way information is acquired and rehearsed—the "software" of memory. Culture determines how people frame information initially, how much they practice learning and recalling it, and the strategies they use to try to recall it.

## 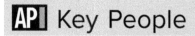 Key Terms

| | | |
|---|---|---|
| autobiographical memory | levels-of-processing theory | tip-of-the-tongue phenomenon |
| constructive processes | priming | deep processing |
| explicit memory | recall | shallow processing |
| flashbulb memories | recognition | |
| implicit memory | schemas | |

## AP Key People

**Elizabeth Loftus**

# Class Discussion Ideas

**EYEWITNESS FALLIBILITY SCENARIO FROM THE "WHEN EYES DECEIVE" VIDEO SEGMENT** See https://www.youtube.com/watch?v=MDq6vtdIS4M for reference.

Enlist a volunteer to serve as the "perpetrator." The volunteer should be as neutral as possible—that is, medium build, height, skin color, hair. He should wear a distinctive item of clothing, and his face should be at least partially covered.

Take photos of the perpetrator and four or five men of similar build and appearance. These will be used as the "lineup" photos.

Several days ahead of time, make sure that you leave in a prominent position on the desk or lecture podium the item that will be "stolen." That way, it will not seem obvious on the day of the theft. Also mention that there have been thefts recently in classrooms and that students should be careful. (This is generally true, so it is not bad to warn them.)

Practice how you will cue the perpetrator and how you will respond. Watch the video segment first so you can see how that was done and what accommodations you will need to make to your particular classroom. The best scenario is one where you do not react to the thief but react to the students in the class who react to the thief. You also should arrange to have a teaching assistant run after the perpetrator.

The following scenario has worked with some success:

Begin the class. At a preassigned point early in the lecture (at a certain word or time, such as when I say "implicit memory"), the perpetrator will come into the room, but you will have your back to him.

You will hear the perpetrator steal the object but will not see him. Instead, you will react to the students, who will scream out.

Then you put on an air of concern and fear.

After your confederate goes after the perpetrator, look at the class in shock and express your fright and surprise. Pause for a few seconds—and then indicate that the whole thing was a stunt. However, before the students talk or say anything, they should immediately write down on a sheet of paper everything they remember about the perpetrator such as his eye color, age, height, weight, hair color, skin color, clothing, and anything distinctive such as the "odd shape of his nose." Then show the "lineup" photos and have them write down the number corresponding to the perpetrator. I have used an adaptation of the *Law & Order* website image as a backdrop during the exercise.

Some examples from my students:

Jacket color (it was black)
The perp was wearing a blue sweater.
He had on a navy blue jacket.
He was wearing a big, puffy, black jacket.
He wore a white shirt.
He was wearing a gray, hooded sweatshirt.

Pants (he wore jeans)
He was wearing baggy pants.
He had on grayish-green pants.
He wore khaki pants.

Height (he was about 5'8")
He was 5'3".
Shortish
About 5'7"
Medium height
He was 6 feet tall.

Skin color (white)
He was Caucasian.
He was an African American guy.
He had olive skin.

## MEMORY SUGGESTIBILITY DEMONSTRATION

This is the Deese-Roediger-McDermott paradigm.

Tell students that you are going to implant a false memory. You will read a list of words and they are to recall as many from the list as they can. Then they will be given a recognition memory test. The list of words is:

| | |
|---|---|
| candy | honey |
| sour | soda |
| sugar | chocolate |
| bitter | heart |
| good | cake |
| taste | eat |
| tooth | pie |
| nice | |

Give them a minute to write down the words. Then present this recognition task:

Which words were on the list I read to you? Indicate "old" or "new" for each. For example:

taste (old word)
point (unrelated new word)
sweet (related new word)

Then score the data by having them raise their hands if they wrote down "old" and go through each of the items in order.

Most will raise their hands for *taste*, very few will for *point*, and then almost all the hands go up for *sweet*.

You can then ask how many people wrote down *sweet* on the recall test; roughly half will raise their hands.

The key to this experiment is that the lists all contain words that are strongly associated to category names of "sweet," hence implanting the false memory.

For more information, see Roediger, H.L. & McDermott K. B. (1995). Creating false memories: Remembering words not presented in lists. *Journal of Experimental Psychology, 21,* 803–814.

**SEVEN SINS OF MEMORY (SCHACTER, 2001)** Following are the "seven sins of memory" with brief definitions and examples. Add other examples from the student assignment on this topic. Also Schacter's book has a number of very interesting examples of each "sin."

- *Transience:* Simple forgetting.
- *Absentmindedness:* Insufficient attention at encoding stage. Example: you park your car at the mall but cannot find it when you go to leave because you did not really look at where you parked it when you arrived.
- *Blocking:* Inability to retrieve, like tip of the tongue. Example: forgetting the name of someone you know very well.
- *Misattribution:* Wrong source of information. You think that one person told you something, but in reality, someone else did.
- *Suggestibility:* Planting of false memory. The memory suggestibility demonstration above showed how this works.

- *Bias:* See oneself in a positive light. Students arrested for disorderly conduct over time, in memory, regard this as the fault of their friends or the police.
- *Persistence:* Intrusive recollections of past events. People with posttraumatic stress disorder continually re-experience the trauma.

Source: Schacter, D. (2001). *The seven sins of memory: How the mind forgets and remembers.* New York: Houghton Mifflin.

## Activities

### Levels of Processing Activity

**Have students complete this level of processing experiment (this also can be presented on slides to the class).**

Introduce the activity to students as follows:

This activity will test the effectiveness of depth of processing. You will be presented with a list of 20 words, one at a time. After each word, you will be given instructions for processing that word. Specifically, you will be asked either to count the number of syllables in some words or to rate the word for its pleasantness or unpleasantness. When you are finished with the entire list, you will be asked to remember as many of the words as you can. For example, if the word was *penguin* and your task was to count the number of syllables, you would say "two" to yourself. If the word was *penguin* and your task was to rate it for pleasantness or unpleasantness, you would have to think about the word and decide whether you thought of it as a more pleasant or more unpleasant word.

Show these words in this order with the instructions next to them:

School (count the number of syllables)

Trailer (rate the pleasantness or unpleasantness)

Elephant (rate the pleasantness or unpleasantness)

Bookcase (count the number of syllables)

Triangle (count the number of syllables)

Giraffe (rate the pleasantness or unpleasantness)

Table (count the number of syllables)

Sailboat (rate the pleasantness or unpleasantness)

Telephone (count the number of syllables)

Glasses (rate the pleasantness or unpleasantness)

Pencil (count the number of syllables)

Computer (count the number of syllables)

Book (rate the pleasantness or unpleasantness)

Television (count the number of syllables)

Calendar (rate the pleasantness or unpleasantness)

Watch (count the number of syllables)

Sandwich (rate the pleasantness or unpleasantness)

Zebra (count the number of syllables)

Wallet (rate the pleasantness or unpleasantness)

Shoe (rate the pleasantness or unpleasantness)

Then show this list and have students check the words that they recognize.

| | | |
|---|---|---|
| Ring | Date | Sailboat |
| Trailer | Platform | Television |
| College | Ship | Sandwich |
| Park | Square | Horn |
| Watch | Glasses | Lunch |
| Money | Dial | Bookcase |
| Shelf | Plates | Radio |
| Mouse | Pencil | School |
| Text | Computer | Elephant |
| Giraffe | Calendar | Sock |
| Telephone | Triangle | Shoe Lion |
| Table | Pen | Zebra |
| Wallet | Disk | |

Now show the list of correct words and have them count the syllables versus pleasantness rating list. There should be more correct words in the pleasantness rating list.

**LONG-TERM MEMORY** Use *Handout: What Type of Memory Is It?* as a way to give students experience in learning the various types of long-term memory and seeing how memories are organized.

### RETRIEVAL

**Serial Position Effect:** Write a list of 25 groceries on the board. Tell the students that they should study this list for about 5 minutes. After the 5 minutes have elapsed, either erase or cover the board and have the students write down as many of the items on the grocery list as they can remember. Give the students about 5 minutes or so to write down their answers. Next, show them the original list again and have them compare their answers to the correct list. Ask by a show of hands how many of them got at least the first 5 items correct, and then ask them how many of them got at least the last 5 items correct. Discuss with students how the answers they gave demonstrate the primacy and recency effects.

**Serial Position Effect:** Ask students to write down all the presidents of United States. You may want to remind students how many presidents we have had in the United States. Give them a few minutes to do this exercise. Typically, students write the first few and the last few presidents. This is a great example of the serial position effect. Source: Roediger, H. L., & Crowder, R. G. (1976). A serial position effect in recall of United States presidents. *Bulletin of the Psychonomic Society, 8,* 275–278.

**Recall and Recognition:** While this exercise is "culture bound," students will find it interesting. First, have students list the Seven Dwarfs. Next, ask them to pick out the names of the Seven Dwarfs from an array of names that you present via PowerPoint or another visual means. You may change names as you like. Below is a sample of the listing of the names of the dwarfs:

**GROUCHY, GABBY, FEARFUL, SLEEPY, SMILEY, JUNKIE, JUMPY, HOPEFUL, DROOPY, DOPEY, SNIFFY, WISHFUL, PUFFY, DUMPY, SNEEZY, LAZY, POP, GRUMPY, BASHFUL, CHEERFUL, TEACH, SHORTY, NIFTY, HAPPY, DOC, WHEEZY, STUBBY, SLEAZY**

Ask students if it was easier to list the names or to pick out the names. Typically, they will tell you that it is easier to pick out the names. You can introduce students to the topic of retrieval in this way. This is often a good time to discuss why students often prefer a multiple-choice exam to an essay-type exam. You may also want to ask students if they almost came up with a name but just couldn't. Students will quickly catch on what the tip-of-the-tongue phenomenon is all about.

**Memory and Emotion:** Some people remember more negative experiences and others remember more positive experiences in their lives. Ask students to take a few minutes and write down 10 memories of their childhood. Next, label the memories as positive, negative, or neutral. Have students calculate the number of positive, negative, or neutral memories. Are they surprised by the results of this exercise? Why or why not? You may also want to generate a class tally of the number of positive, neutral, or negative memories. This can lead to a nice discussion of emotion and memory. It can also lead to a discussion of forgetting and false memory.

**Memory Cues:** Ask students to list the 50 states. When the students are done, tell them you are not interested in how many states they wrote down. Tell them instead that you are interested in how they retrieved the states from their memory. They will begin to tell you they retrieved the names based on states in which they have lived, states they have visited, a visual map, the alphabet, sports teams, or region of the country. This is a great springboard to discussing the value of cues and how we tend to cue ourselves.

**Retrieval Exercise:** Divide the class into four fairly equal groups. Have each student take out a piece of paper and label it with their group number. Tell the class that they are going to hear a list of words and that they need to remember the words. According to Wertheimer (1981), the following list works well:

**Envelope, bex, nav, Carter, ruj, fet, textbook, nav, Nixon, fulfill, GEF, mandate, fet, 47, tal**

Instructors may also make up their own list; just be sure to include nonsense words, real words, and duplicates of some words or nonsense words. Note: pronounce and spell the nonsense syllables.

After you have read the list once, read it again in the same voice at the same pace. Following the second reading, ask ONLY Group 1 to write down as many words as they can remember. Continue class. After about 3 minutes, ask Group 2 to write down as many words as they can remember. Continue class. Again, after about 5 minutes, ask Group 3 to write down as many words as they can remember. Continue class for about 40 more minutes, then ask Group 4 to write down as many words as they can remember.

Which group remembered more words? Are real words remembered better than nonsense words? Are repeated words remembered better? Is there evidence of the serial position effect?

Source: Wertheimer, M. (1981). Memory and forgetting. In L. T. Benjamin & K. D. Lowman (Eds.). *Activities handbook for the teaching of psychology*, Volume 1 (pp. 75–76). Washington, DC: American Psychological Association.

**EYEWITNESS MEMORY DEMONSTRATION** There are many variations of this exercise. You may want to enlist the help of your teaching assistant or another confederate for a demonstration of how poor eyewitness testimony can be. Have the confederate come in during class and cause some form of disruption (maybe yell and then laugh or throw paper wads and then run out). Next, ask students to describe what they saw, how the person was dressed, hair color, etc. If you are in a large room, make sure the confederate comes into the room and is in long enough to draw attention. You may even want to ask your confederate not to wear socks and slightly roll up their pant legs. When you are asking the class to describe the person, you may want to add "even down to their socks." You can see if any students "construct" a memory of socks.

## Discussion Questions

**EYEWITNESS TESTIMONY** Should the criminal justice system put as much emphasis as it does on eyewitness testimony? What are some possible circumstances that could influence eyewitnesses to say they saw something they might not really have seen?

It is sometimes difficult to believe that our memories are not as accurate as we think. To test your ability to be a good eyewitness, visit one of the following websites:

http://www.pbs.org/wgbh/pages/frontline/shows/dna/

Did this exercise change your opinion of the accuracy of eyewitness testimony? Explain.

# Polling Questions

**REMEMBER ME?** Can a memory be forgotten and then remembered? Can a so-called memory be suggested and then remembered as true? These questions lie at the heart of the memory of childhood abuse issues and other experienced traumatic events. For a historical background to prompt deeper discussions, visit: http://www.apa.org/topics/trauma/memories. aspx. How many of you think that adults who remember past childhood abuse are telling the truth about the experiences? How many of you think that adults who remember past childhood abuse are making up these memories for a hidden motive? Who believes we have enough technology, research, and information to be able to see memories in the brain? How many would consider using a neuroimaging technique to verify whether a person was telling the truth or lying about a particular traumatic experience?

**JUST GOOGLE IT!** Without a doubt, technology has changed our world. New research is being conducted on the influence technology has on our memory. We've all had someone ask us a question that we didn't know the answer to or couldn't remember. So, what did you do? Did you Google it on your smartphone or use another devise to look up the answer? Are the days of remembering facts for the sake of pure knowledge over now that we have instant access to information from our devices? Within the last 3 days, how many of you have searched on the Internet for an answer to something that you probably should have known? Who feels less motivated to remember something now that you can access that information instantly while on the go? How many of you think that this method of accessing information (rather than memorizing it) has affected your ability to do well on a test or in a class? How many of you think that memorization takes too much time? Resource: Ambrose, S. H. (2010). Coevolution of composite-tool technology, constructive memory, and language. *Current Anthropology, 51*(S1), S135–S147.

**MEN VERSUS WOMEN—THE BEST MULTITASKER CHALLENGE** Ever wondered who is really better at multitasking? Just about everyone today is expected to engage in multitasking in one way or another. As we learned about memory, attention plays a very important role in what we remember and its accuracy. How many of you think that multitasking has interfered with your ability to remember some important detail because you were too busy to stop one task to focus on another? Though controversial, there is some research that suggests there are gender differences in multitasking ability. Who thinks that men are better at multitasking than women? (Indicate that those who don't respond think that women are better multitaskers than men.) Who thinks they are better at multitasking than their friends or family? (If the entire class thinks they are better, delve into this overconfidence a bit more.) Resource: Mäntylä, T. (2013). Gender differences in multitasking reflect spatial ability. *Psychological Science, 24*(4), 514–520.

# AP Student Edition Answer Key

## Applying Psychology in the 21st Century: Memories are Made to be Meaningful

Answer Suggestions

- Researchers could use emotionally significant events that happened on a large national scale with lots of evidence from the media. Then, researchers could interview participants after varying time periods to test for constructive processes.
- Increasing evidence suggests memory reliability is problematic for children as eyewitnesses because their memories are highly vulnerable to the influence of others. This is especially true for situations that are highly emotional or stressful.

# AP Test Practice

## Section I: Multiple Choice

1. **B** *(Skill 1.B, Learning Target 5)*

2. **A** *(Skill 3, Learning Target 5)*

3. **E** *(Skill 2, Learning Target 5)*

## Section II: Free Response

**A.**

Recognition is a retrieval process in which individuals can identify the answer from a list of alternatives. Maria will have an easier time identifying the burglar if she is provided a lineup with the burglar and several other choices.

At the deepest level of processing, information is analyzed in terms of its meaning. While witnessing the crime, Maria may have been deeply processing the burglar's appearance by making an association between the individual and someone she already knows. This deep level of processing will enhance her recall of the burglar.

**B.**

Schemas are organized bodies of information stored in memory that bias the way new information is interpreted, stored, and recalled. Maria used schemas to identify the burglar, which may lead to a false memory because schemas often consist of expectations in addition to the actual material.

Source amnesia occurs when an individual has a memory for some material but cannot recall where he or she encountered it. Maria may have source amnesia and accidently describe the burglar based on the crime movie she saw the night before.

Tip-of-the-tongue phenomenon is the inability to recall information that one realizes one knows. Maria might know who the burglar looked like but have difficulty retrieving that information right now.

Flashbulb memories are memories related to a specific, important, or surprisingly emotionally significant event. They are recalled easily and with vivid imagery, however, the details are often inaccurate. Maria witnessed a highly emotional event, therefore the details of the burglar might not be accurate.

# Module 22: Forgetting: When Memory Fails

## **AP** Module Summary

Similar to Module 21, Module 22 has little change but is just as important. The person of interest that students need to know is Herman Ebbinghaus. I highly recommend that you use this as a time to review proactive and retroactive interference along with anterograde and retrograde amnesia. The four concepts are tricky and have been on past AP exams. Amnesia will reappear in later modules, but introducing it here makes perfect sense.

The first attempts to study forgetting were made by German psychologist Hermann Ebbinghaus. The basic conclusion of his study was that there is almost always a strong initial decline in memory, followed by a more gradual drop over time (see **Figure 1**). Furthermore, relearning of previously mastered material is almost always faster than starting from scratch, whether the material is academic information or a motor skill such as serving a tennis ball.

## Why We Forget

- **Decay** is the loss of information in memory through nonuse.
- **Interference** - information stored in memory disrupts the recall of other information stored in memory.
- **Cue-dependent forgetting** - forgetting that occurs when there are insufficient retrieval cues to rekindle information that is in memory.

**PROACTIVE AND RETROACTIVE INTERFERENCE: THE BEFORE AND AFTER OF FORGETTING**  There are actually two sorts of interference that influence forgetting (see **Figure 3**).
- **Proactive interference** - information learned earlier disrupts the recall of newer material.
- **Retroactive interference** occurs when material that was learned later disrupts the retrieval of information that was learned earlier.

## Memory Dysfunctions: Afflictions of Forgetting

- *Alzheimer's disease* is a progressive brain disorder that leads to a gradual and irreversible decline in cognitive abilities.
- *Amnesia* is memory loss that occurs without other mental difficulties. There are two types of amnesia:
- *Retrograde amnesia,* memory is lost for occurrences prior to a certain event, but not for new events.
- *Anterograde amnesia,* memory is lost for events that follow an injury.

**BECOMING AN INFORMED CONSUMER OF PSYCHOLOGY: IMPROVING YOUR MEMORY**
Apart from the advantages of forgetting, most of us would like to find ways to improve our memories. Effective strategies for studying and remembering course material include the following:

- Use the keyword technique.
- Rely on organization cues.
- Take effective notes.
- Practice, practice, practice.
- Talk to yourself.
- Do not believe claims about drugs that improve memory.

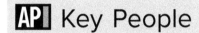 Key Terms

| | |
|---|---|
| Alzheimer's disease | interference |
| amnesia | Korsakoff's syndrome |
| anterograde amnesia | proactive interference |
| cue-dependent forgetting | retroactive interference |
| decay | retrograde amnesia |

**AP** Key People

Hermann Ebbinghaus

## Class Discussion Ideas

**TRICKS OF MEMORY EXPERTS** Present students with this strategy used by memory experts in which numbers are associated with letters:

| Number | Letter/Sound | Memory Aid |
|---|---|---|
| 1 | t, d | t has one downstroke |
| 2 | n | n has two downstrokes |
| 3 | m | m has three downstrokes |
| 4 | r | Four ends with r |
| 5 | L | Latin 50 = L |
| 6 | j, sh, ch | J reversed looks like 6 |
| 7 | k | Visualize a K drawn with two 7s |
| 8 | f, v | Cursive f has two loops like an 8 |
| 9 | p, b | P reversed looks like 9 |
| 10 | z, s | Zero starts with z |

This is the standardized mnemonic system used by memory experts. It has been optimized in order to make it easy to learn and use. Note that pairs of letters have been grouped together because of their phonetic similarity, such as t and d or p and b. If you are not familiar with phonetics, whisper the word *dog*. Notice that it sounds like "tok." This is how you can tell which sounds are phonetically similar.

Here are some rules about using the number alphabet:

- The alphabet is strictly phonetic. For example, the word *cough* should be thought of as KoF and translated to 78; *gem* is pronounced JeM and is thus 63.
- Double letters are not counted. For example, *butter* translates to B, T, and R (only one T).
- Three consonant sounds do not appear in the chart: W, H, and Y. Why, you ask? Good question! Good answer!
- Vowels are always ignored, as well as W, H, and Y mentioned above. The long word *hollow*, for example, contains just one useful letter: L.
- When creating words from consonants, vivid nouns usually work the best, rather than adjectives, verbs, or other related words.

There are other tips for this method. The source for this information was http://www.thememorypage.net/htiym3.htm, but it also can be found on other websites.

## Activities

**FORGETTING** Have students complete *Handout: Theories of Forgetting*.

**ENCODING FAILURE:** Have students write their answers to the following questions:

1. On a U.S. penny, which way does Lincoln's face point—to the left or to the right?

2. What is written below Lincoln's head?

3. What does it say above Lincoln's head?

4. What is to the right of Lincoln's face?

This assignment will show students that even though they think that they have encoded information, they may not have encoded everything. There are errors in encoding information.

**PROSPECTIVE MEMORY:** Break the class up into groups, and ask them to discuss and come up with two examples each of a time-based prospective memory and an event-based prospective memory. After completing the assignment, have the students discuss their examples with the rest of the class.

## Discussion Questions

### REPRESSED MEMORIES

- Do you agree that people can have repressed memories? Why or why not?
- What is the basis for the charge that therapists plant repressed memories in their clients?
- How do you think a repressed memory would affect a person's everyday functioning?

### PERSONAL EXPERIENCE OF MEMORY LOSS

- Why does it seem we remember more negative events than positive ones?
- What would life be like if you did not remember?
- Ask students if they would like to have the ability to never forget. In other words, they would always be able to remember everything that happened to them. Would they like to be able to do this? Why or why not? This might make a nice lead-in to the story of Jill Price.

## AP Student Edition Answer Key

## AP Test Practice

### Section I: Multiple Choice

1. **D** *(Skill 1.B, Learning Target 5)*

2. **E** *(Skill 1.B, Learning Target 5)*

3. **A** *(Skill 1.A, Learning Target 5)*

### Section II: Free Response

**A.**

The hippocampus is a brain part located in the limbic system involved in learning and memory. Patient H.M. had both hippocampi removed, which impacted his memory and ability to learn.

Explicit memory refers to intentional or conscious recollection of information. It can further be divided into semantic memory (general knowledge) and episodic memory (personal knowledge). Patient H.M. could not acquire new explicit memories. He could not remember the current president (semantic) or his birthdays (episodic).

Procedural memory (nondeclarative or implicit) is memory for skills and habits. Patient H.M.'s procedural memory stayed intact and he was able to learn new motor skills, such as completing a maze or mirror-drawing.

Anterograde amnesia involves loss of memory after an event. Patient H.M. was unable to form new memories after the surgery.

**B.**

The case study is an indepth interview and examination of one person or a group. An advantage of this research method is to gain an indepth understanding of rare conditions. Thanks to H.M. there is a better understanding of how brain damage impacts memory.

Ethical considerations require confidentiality or keeping a patient's name private. Henry Gustav Molaison's name was revealed after he died. His initials were used to protect his identity.

An MRI scan shows a computer-generated image of brain structures by using a powerful magnetic field. An MRI scan could be used on H.M. to show what brain structures were damaged and the extent of the damage after the surgery.

# CHAPTER 8
# Cognition and Language

## AP Introduction

The 2019 AP Psychology Course and Exam Description (CED) framework has added some specifics to the unit on Cognitive Psychology. The unit is a heavily weighted unit and should not be overlooked, spending more time on the topic of memory and then allowing some time to review the other areas. Also, the new CED has incorporated the study of intelligence into the unit of cognition. I recommend testing over intelligence separately from memory, thinking and language. In this unit students should begin to see some overlap with previously covered units, it all depends on the sequencing of units. It would be worth your time to see which areas can be incorporated into other units too, some suggestions have been made to help you out.

## AP Essential Questions

- What roles do memory and thinking play in our behaviors?

## AP Module Summary

Module 23 has students looking at thinking and reasoning. Nothing has been added to this specific topic therefore your instruction of this content can pretty much stay the same. It is recommended within this module that you spend some time reviewing the concepts of availability and representativeness heuristics both concepts have appeared on the AP exam in past years.

- *Cognitive psychology* is the branch of psychology that focuses on the study of higher mental processes including thinking, language, memory, problem solving, knowing, reasoning, judging, and decision making.
- Psychologists define *thinking* as brain activity in which we purposefully manipulate mental representations of information.

**MENTAL IMAGES: EXAMINING THE MIND'S EYE** *Mental images* are representations in the mind of an object or event. They are not just visual representations; our ability to "hear" a tune in our heads also relies on a mental image.

## Concepts: Categorizing the World

- *Concepts* are mental groupings of similar objects, events, or people. Concepts enable us to organize complex phenomena into cognitive categories that are easier to understand and remember.
- *Prototypes* are typical, highly representative examples of a concept that correspond to our mental image or best example of the concept (see **Figure 2**).

**REASONING: MAKING UP YOUR MIND**  Reasoning is the process by which information is used to draw conclusions and make decisions. It is only relatively recently that cognitive psychologists have begun to investigate how people reason and make decisions.

## Formal Reasoning

- *Deductive reasoning* is reasoning from the general to the specific.
- *Inductive reasoning* is reasoning from the specific to the general.

**ALGORITHMS AND HEURISTICS**  When faced with making a decision, we often turn to various kinds of cognitive shortcuts, known as algorithms and heuristics, to help us.

- *Algorithm* is a rule that, if applied appropriately, guarantees a solution to a problem.
- *Heuristic* is a thinking strategy that may lead us to a solution to a problem or decision, but—unlike algorithms—may sometimes lead to errors.
  - **Availability heuristic** involves judging the probability of an event on the basis of how easily the event can be recalled from memory.
  - **Representativeness heuristic** is estimating the likelihood of events in terms of how well they seem to represent, or match, particular prototyes; which can lead us to ignore relevant information.

**COMPUTERS AND PROBLEM SOLVING: SEARCHING FOR ARTIFICIAL INTELLIGENCE**  Computers are making significant inroads in terms of the ability to solve problems and carry out some forms of intellectual activities. According to experts who study artificial intelligence, the field that examines how to use technology to imitate the outcome of human thinking, problem solving, and creative activities, computers can show rudiments of humanlike thinking because of their knowledge of where to look—and where not to look—for an answer to a problem. They suggest that the capacity of computer programs (such as those that play chess) to evaluate potential moves and to ignore unimportant possibilities gives them thinking ability. Computers using artificial intelligence, such as Apple's Siri or Amazon's Alexa, are designed for tasks that require speed, persistence, and a huge memory. Artificial intelligence is also used to design algorithims to inform decision making about loan lending and other financial matters.

**APPLYING PSYCHOLOGY IN THE 21ST CENTURY: ARE OUR ATTENTION SPANS BECOMING SHORTER?**  Attention span has decreased from 12 seconds in 2000 to approximately 8 seconds in 2015. Attention is worse for those who consume more media, particularly those who frequently use tablets or smartphones (McSpadden, 2015). This may suggest that brains are evolving to pay attention to the most useful information and to task-switch more easily across multiple stimuli.

## AP Key Terms

| | |
|---|---|
| algorithm | inductive reasoning |
| availability heuristic | mental images |
| cognitive psychology | prototypes |
| concepts | representativeness heuristic |
| deductive reasoning | thinking |
| heuristic | |

# Class Discussion Ideas

**CONCEPTS AND PROTOTYPES** Compare answers among students from *Handout 1: Concepts and Prototypes.* Use this in the lecture to point out which concepts have clear prototypes and which do not.

**THE WASON SELECTION TASK** Although not discussed in the text, this classic logic problem is a fascinating one that has been analyzed in a number of psychological studies on reasoning.

The gist of the task is as follows:

Four cards are presented as follows:

The cards are labeled "D" or "K" on one side and "3" or "7" on the other.

A rule says that "if a card is D on one side then it is 3 on the other side."

Which cards need to be turned over to know whether this sample of cards is consistent with the rule?

The answer is "D" and "7."

If there is a 3 on the other side of D, this proves the rule of those two cards. If there is a D on the other side of 7, this violates the rule.

Researchers have found that people have a great deal more difficulty handling this rule when presented in the abstract than when presented in concrete terms: http://www.cep.ucsb.edu/socex/wason.htm.

For instance, if these are tickets purchased at a party where underage drinkers are not allowed to drink alcohol, the four cards showing would be:

D = Beer

K = Soda

3 = Age 21

7 = Under 21

Therefore, all "Beer" tickets should have "Age 21" on the back and no "Under 21" tickets should have "Beer" on the back. This problem is easier to solve than the D-K-3-7 problem.

## What's My Heuristic?

**Benefits of Heuristics:** You may want to spend some time going over the representativeness heuristic and availability heuristics. Remind students that all heuristics are fallible, but they allow us to make snap judgments quickly, and what we sacrifice for accuracy is the ability to make quick general appraisals. Point out the adaptive value of these devices. Both have strong survival implications.

**Statistical Heuristics:** Identify and describe a situation in which you have fallen prey to the availability heuristic. What factors affected your reasoning in this case?

# Activities

**HEURISTICS IN COGNITIVE MAPS** Illustrate the operation of heuristics in cognitive maps, which are mental representations of geographic spaces:

- Two days before this lecture, ask students to draw a map of their house. Specify which rooms or areas to include. On the day before the cognition lecture, collect the maps.

**CONCEPTS AND PROTOTYPES** Have students complete *Handout: Concepts and Prototypes.*

**LOGICAL REASONING: WORD PUZZLES** Here are some good word puzzles that will test the logical powers of your students.

A murderer is condemned to death. He has to choose between three rooms. The first is full of raging fires, the second is full of assassins with loaded guns, and the third is full of lions that have not eaten in three years. Which room is safest for him?

ANSWER: The third. Lions that have not eaten in 3 years are dead.

Two different plastic jugs are filled with water. How could you put all of this water into a barrel, without using the jugs or any dividers, and still tell which water came from which jug?

ANSWER: Freeze them first. Take the ice out of the jugs and put it in the barrel. You will be able to tell which water came from which jug.

What is black when you buy it, red when you use it, and gray when you throw it away?

ANSWER: Charcoal.

Can you name three consecutive days without using the words *Monday, Tuesday, Wednesday, Thursday, Friday, Saturday,* or *Sunday*?

ANSWER: Yesterday, today, and tomorrow.

**ALGORITHMS VERSUS HEURISTICS** Define the difference between algorithms and heuristics. Algorithms are slow but always generate the correct solution; heuristics are quicker but may lead to the wrong answer.

Examples:
1. Baking cookies.

*Heuristic*: Allison decides to bake chocolate chip cookies to take to her boyfriend's house for dinner. She calls her mother to find out the "family" recipe. Allison's mother tells her to take about a cup of butter, a bit of baking soda, two eggs, about a cup of brown sugar, and about the same amount of flour. Finally, add some chocolate chips.

*Algorithm*: Allison is nervous about making the cookies without having more exact amounts. She looks up a recipe in a cookbook and decides to use that one, which specifies how much to use of sugar, flour, butter, baking soda, and chocolate chips. The recipe also says exactly what order in which to add the ingredients.

Lecture demonstration:

What word can you form from this anagram?

ERET

The answer is *TREE*. Ask students if they tried all possible combinations before they reached the answer. This would be using an algorithm. It is possible to do this with a four-letter word.

Now show this:

LSSTNEUIAMYOUL

The answer is *SIMULTANEOUSLY*. Find out how many students tried all possible combinations. Chances are they did not, as this would be a much slower solution. Therefore, they had to use a heuristic.

# Statistical Heuristics

Give students these problems in class:

**Availability heuristic:** People judge events that they can remember easily as more common than events that they cannot remember.

   1. Which is more common—deaths from homicides or deaths from suicides?

ANSWER: Deaths from suicides. Newspapers place much more emphasis on deaths from homicides and therefore people can remember these deaths more readily and hence judge them as more frequent.

Another similar example is deaths from drowning versus deaths from fires. Drowning deaths are more frequent, but they do not get as much media attention.

   2. Which is more common in the English language: Words that begin with the letter "r" or words that have the letter "r" as the third letter?

ANSWER: Words that have the letter "r" as the third letter. People can remember words that begin with a letter more readily than they can remember words that have an embedded letter.

Vividness and distinctiveness also play a role. You are more likely to believe a friend who tells you a dramatic story about the problems he had with his Camry than all the positive ratings you read in consumer reports. Similarly, people are more likely to buy flood insurance after reading about floods than at any other time, even though the probability of a flood is no different than it was before the flood.

**Representativeness heuristic:** People tend to ignore base rates, and fail to seek out base rates when base rate information is needed to make reliable probabilistic judgments.

For example, people believe that coincidences are unlikely. Out of 30 people, there is a 70 percent probability that two will share the same birthday, but people think it is a coincidence when that occurs.

People will also believe that a sequence of the same six numbers is less likely to win in a lottery than a sequence of six different numbers even though they are equally likely.

   1. When flipping coins, which is the most likely sequence?

   HHHTTT

   HHHHHH

   TTTTTT

   HTHTHT

   HHTTHH

ANSWER: They are all equally probable; each coin toss is a separate event and each has a 50–50 chance of occurring.

   2. Imagine you just met a man named Steve. Steve is very shy and withdrawn, invariably helpful, but with little interest in people or in the world of reality. A meek and tidy soul, he has a need for order and structure, and a passion for detail. Is Steve more likely to be a librarian or a salesperson?

ANSWER: A salesperson. Statistically, there are far more salespeople than librarians in the workforce. Therefore, although Steve may seem to have the attributes of a librarian, the odds are far more likely that he is a salesperson.

**Representative heuristic:** You may want to ask students if this could be a serious error. Point out that racial profiling is an example of the representativeness heuristic and thus could have very serious errors associated with it.

## Polling Questions

**I'M NOT BLIND! I SEE EXACTLY WHAT I WANT TO SEE!** Let's talk about the bias blind spot, a concept that suggests even the smartest, deepest thinkers—the ones who are open minded and considerate of others—harbor a level of bias against others and even themselves. What do you think? Who thinks we are hard-wired (biologically) to create groups and show favoritism toward a certain set of individuals? Let's take a Social Attitudes test by Project Implicit: https://implicit.harvard.edu/implicit/. How many of you were surprised at your results?

## Suggested Media

- *Heuristics Demonstrations:* http://cat.xula.edu/thinker/decisions/heuristics/.
- *Thinker:* http://cat.xula.edu/thinker/decisions/heuristics/ranking. This site discusses decision making and errors:

## Additional Readings

Ariely, D. (2010). Predictably irrational, revised and expanded edition: The hidden forces that shape our decisions. Houghton-Mifflin.

Answer Suggestions

- There is a negative correlation between increased social media use and lowered attention span. Negative correlations tell us that as one variable increases, the value of the other decreases.
- Boredom can lead to increased creativity.

## AP Test Practice

### Section I: Multiple Choice

1. **A** *(Skill 1.B, Learning Target 5.I)*

2. **C** *(Skill 1.A, Learning Target 5.I)*

3. **A** *(Skill 1.B, Learning Target 5.I)*

### Section II: Free Response

Concepts are mental groupings of similar objects, events, or people that enable us to organize complex phenomena into cognitive categories that are easier to understand. Brian has a concept, or mental grouping, for a car. This will help him organize the different vehicle options so he can select a new car.

Prototypes are typical, highly representative examples of a concept. Brian may rely on a prototype (model) for each car brand (make) to help create a list of pros and cons when selecting a new car.

Inductive reasoning is reasoning from the specific to the general. Brian may use inductive reasoning and look at several models of cars (Fiesta, Mustang, or Taurus) and then form a conclusion about the broader brand (Ford). Or he might have had a problem while test driving a convertible (specific), so he concludes that all convertibles are problematic (general) and he should not purchase one.

Deductive reasoning is reasoning from the general to the specific. Brian may use deductive reasoning and start with a general theory, such as convertibles have problems. Then, he will derive a more specific hypothesis that he should not buy a Ford Mustang convertible because it will have problems.

An availability heuristic involves judging the likelihood of an event occurring on the basis of how easy it is to think of examples. Brian uses the availability heuristic and uses car commercials that readily come to mind when deciding what car to buy.

# Module 24: Problem Solving

## AP Module Summary

In module 24 the topic of cognition focuses on problem solving. Nothing new has been added to this specific area and just like with module 23 your instruction of this content can pretty much stay the same. It is recommended that time be spent on the concepts of convergent and divergent thinking. Both have appeared on the AP exam in the past. If you didn't introduce Wolfgang Kohler in the unit on Learning, this would be another opportunity for you to do so!

**PRODUCTION: GENERATING SOLUTIONS** In place of trial and error, complex problem solving often involves the use of heuristics, cognitive shortcuts that can generate solutions. Probably the most frequently applied heuristic in problem solving is a *means-ends analysis*, which involves repeated tests for differences between the desired outcome and what currently exists. Although this approach is often effective, if the problem requires indirect steps that temporarily increase the discrepancy between a current state and the solution, means-ends analysis can be counterproductive. For other problems, the best approach is to work backward by focusing on the goal, rather than the starting point, of the problem.

**INSIGHT: SUDDEN AWARENESS** Some approaches to generating possible solutions focus less on step-by-step heuristics than on the sudden bursts of comprehension that one may experience during efforts to solve a problem. In a classic study, the German psychologist Wolfgang Köhler examined learning and problem-solving processes in chimpanzees (see **Figure 7**). Köhler noticed the chimps exhibiting new behavior and called the cognitive process underlying the behavior *insight*, which refers to a sudden awareness of the relationships among various elements that had previously appeared to be independent of one another.

**IMPEDIMENTS TO SOLUTIONS: WHY IS PROBLEM SOLVING SUCH A PROBLEM?** Significant obstacles to problem solving can exist at each of the three major stages. Although cognitive approaches to problem solving suggest that thinking proceeds along fairly rational, logical lines as a person confronts a problem and considers various solutions, several factors can hinder the development of creative, appropriate, and accurate solutions.

**FUNCTIONAL FIXEDNESS AND MENTAL SET** The difficulty most people experience with the candle problem (see **Figure 8**) is caused by *functional fixedness*, the tendency to think of an object only in terms of its typical use. Functional fixedness is an example of a broader phenomenon known as *mental set*, the tendency for old patterns of problem solving to persist. A mental set is a framework for thinking about a problem based on our prior experience with similar problems. Mental set can affect perceptions as well as patterns of problem solving. It can prevent you from seeing beyond the apparent constraints of a problem (see **Figure 10**).

**INACCURATE EVALUATION OF SOLUTIONS** *Confirmation bias* is the tendency to prefer one's first hypothesis and ignore contradictory evidence that supports alternative hypotheses or solutions. Confirmation bias occurs for several reasons.

- Because rethinking a problem that appears to be solved already takes extra cognitive effort, we are apt to stick with our first solution.
- We give greater weight to subsequent information that supports our initial position than to information that is not supportive of it.

**CREATIVITY AND PROBLEM SOLVING** Despite obstacles to problem solving, many people adeptly discover creative solutions to problems.

**Creativity** is the ability to generate original ideas or solve problems in novel ways. Several characteristics are associated with creativity.

**Divergent thinking**, thinking that generates unusual, yet appropriate, responses to problems or questions.

**Convergent thinking**, which is thinking in which a problem is viewed as having a single answer and which produces responses that are based primarily on knowledge and logic.

**BECOMING AN INFORMED CONSUMER OF PSYCHOLOGY: THINKING CRITICALLY AND CREATIVELY** Research suggests that critical and creative thinkers are made, not born. Consider, for instance, the following suggestions for increasing critical thinking and creativity: Redefine problems, use subgoals, adopt a critical perspective, consider the opposite, use analogies, think divergently, think convergently, use heuristics, experiment with various solutions, and walk away.

## AP Key Terms

confirmation bias

convergent thinking

creativity

divergent thinking

functional fixedness

insight

means-ends analysis

## AP Key People

**Wolfgang Kohler**

## Class Discussion Ideas

### Approches to Solving Problems

**Four ways to obtain solutions:**

1. Trial and error—most primitive and time-consuming. For example, if you do not know how to use a remote control, you push every button until what you want happens.

2. Means-ends analysis—most frequently used. Involves heuristics. Example: Planning route to center of town around beltway.

3. Subgoals—divide problem into steps if possible—making a meal involves going through a set of subroutines so that everything is finished on time.

4. Insight—burst of comprehension ("aha" experience). For some reason, the word *aha* always draws a laugh.

### Types of Problems

**Anagrams (Arrangement problem):**

Here are some humorous anagrams. For an "anagram maker" website, go to http://www.wordsmith.org/anagram/.

listen = silent

dormitory = dirty room

schoolmaster = the classroom

Elvis = lives

slot machines = cash lost in 'em

conversation = voices rant on

The Hilton = Hint: hotel

snooze alarms = alas, no more Z's

Presbyterian = Best in prayer

eleven plus two = twelve plus one

debit card = bad credit

psychology = cop go shyly (not very funny, but relevant)

# Transformation Problem

Go to this Tower of Hanoi website: http://www.cut-the-knot.org/recurrence/hanoi.shtml.

Alternatively, you can purchase an inexpensive Tower of Hanoi and have a student volunteer try to solve it as a class demonstration.

This is a great time to discuss Gazzaniga's work on split brain and the problems folks have solving problems. You may want to show a clip of Gazzaniga with his patient talking about split brain: http://www.youtube.com/watch?v=ZMLzP1VCANo. Here is a clip of Gazzaniga discussing his early research: http://www.youtube.com/watch?v=0lmfxQ-HK7Y.

# Inducing Structure Problem

Give students this puzzle:

This is an unusual paragraph. I am curious how quickly you can find out what is so unusual about it. It looks so plain you would think nothing was wrong with it! In fact, nothing is wrong with it. Study it, and think about it, but you still may not find anything odd. But if you work at it a bit, you might find out. Try to do so without any coaching.

Write your answer here: _____

Answer: The letter "e," which is the most common letter in the English language, does not appear even once in the paragraph.

# Functional Fixedness

For an excellent example of functional fixedness or mental set, present these examples:

A construction detour leads you to take the long way around to get to your psychology class. After the construction is finished and the detour removed, you continue to go the long way around.

Overcoming functional fixedness can save your life: Jan Demczur, a window cleaner who was stuck on an elevator in the World Trade Center attack, was able to rescue himself and a group of people with him on the elevator by using his "squeegee" to open a hole in the wall.

A failure in logic also was involved in the World Trade Center construction. Although explicitly designed to withstand an airplane's impact, the engineers had not taken into account the effect of a full load of jet fuel.

**INSIGHT: MATCHSTICK ARITHMETIC** For another example of functional fixedness and insight, go to http://creativethinking.net/the-matchstick-problem/.

**CREATIVITY DEMONSTRATION: DIVERGENT THINKING** Guilford developed tests of creativity as part of his structure of intellect model. In the "Alternative Uses Task," the respondent answers questions such as "Name all the uses for a brick." Scoring is based on four dimensions: originality, fluency, flexibility, and elaboration. Ask students to provide answers to this question. Have them share their answers either by switching papers or contributing their answers while you write them down. Then have other students rate the uses along the four dimensions.

See this website: http://www.indiana.edu/~bobweb/Handout/d1.uses.htm.

**CONVERGENT THINKING** Traditional problems that have one correct solution provide examples of convergent thinking. An entertaining example of such a problem is: "I have two coins in my pocket that add up to $.30 in value. One of the coins is not a nickel. What is the other coin?" The answer is—a nickel! One of the coins is not a nickel, but the other one is.

## Impediments to Problem-Solving

**Mental set:**

A very silly example of this was suggested by Tammy Rahhal. Have the class repeat after you:

Coast

Coast

Coast

Then say: What do you put in a toaster?

The class will all shout out "Toast!"

Of course, that is ridiculous because you would put bread in a toaster, not toast.

## Activities

## Examples of Problem-Solving Terms

**PROBLEM SOLVING:** Tell the class that sometimes a problem-solving exercise just comes together in an "aha" moment often called insight. Write the words *you just me* on the board or another type of visual presenter. Ask students what this means. Typically, they look blankly at you. Provide a hint: "What is the relative position of *just*?" If you think of this problem in terms of the relative position, then the phrase "just between you and me" becomes obvious. Write the following on the board:

**stood**

**well**

**view**

What is communicated in these three words? If needed, give your students a hint. Tell them that stood is above well and both words are above view. With this reorganization most students will suddenly come up with "well understood overview." Source: Wertheimer, M. (1999). Reorganization and productive thinking. In L. T. Benjamin et al. (Eds.), *Activities handbook for the teaching of psychology* (Vol. 4). Washington, DC: American Psychological Association.

**DIVERGENT AND CONVERGENT THINKING:** Have students take 10 minutes to jot down all the uses for a cardboard box, including every possibility that they can think of, even if it seems unreasonable. Explain that this list is divergent thinking. Next, have students look the list over and determine which of the possible uses are most usual or most likely to be worthwhile. Explain that this is convergent thinking.

**DECISION MAKING:** Discuss decision making, especially the areas of decision making without awareness, confirmation bias, and hindsight bias. Have the students come up with an example from their own lives where these three concepts have played a part. Have them write down and explain the example. Next, break the class into groups and have them discuss their examples with the other students in the group. The students will get a better understanding of decision making when they come up with their own examples, and they will gain knowledge from the other students in their group by hearing their examples.

# Creativity

Have students read the article "Biological Basis for Creativity Linked to Mental Illness" in *Science Daily* (http://www.sciencedaily.com/releases/2003/10/031001061055.htm) and then find a scholarly article on this topic and write a brief review of the research.

**CREATIVITY AND PLAY:** Watch the video of Tim Brown's TED Talk on "Tales of Creativity and Play" (http://www.ted.com/talks/tim_brown_on_creativity_and_play?language=en) and consider using one of the examples discussed in the video in class or assign students to pick one activity and report their experience to the class on the following meeting.

**CREATIVITY:** Make copies of the Remote Associates Test or have students go to the website at http://www.cengage.com/collegesuccess/book_content/1413031927_santrock/ch05/ch05exe6.html and take the test. You could have students take the test individually or in groups and then discuss their findings.

**METACOGNITION** Ask students to engage in a metacognitive exercise. Ask them to think about their study habits from the last test. Did they work? What could they do differently to improve performance? This will not only demonstrate what metacognition is but also prove useful in their studying for the next exam.

# Discussion Questions

**APPLYING PSYCHOLOGY IN THE 21ST CENTURY: DOES PLAYING VIDEO GAMES IMPROVE YOUR THINKING?** Have students review the related box in their text and answer the following questions:

- Why might dividing the sample into nonplayers and frequent players exaggerate the effects of playing video games?
- When different studies reach very different conclusions like this, how can the question be resolved?

# Polling Questions

**CALLING ALL GENIUSES—YOUR PSYCHOTHERAPIST IS READY TO SEE YOU NOW** "Genius and insanity may actually go together, according to scientists who found that mental illnesses such as schizophrenia and bipolar disorder are often found in highly creative and intelligent people." Let's critically evaluate this statement. There is research that indicates a link between creativity and mental health; however, there is also research that suggests the opposite. So, what do you think? Given the numerous examples of creative geniuses and their reported mental health status, who thinks that those who are super intelligent are more likely to possess a psychological disorder? List four psychological disorders, and have students vote on the disorder most likely to be associated with creative genius. Collectively discuss why the disorder with the highest votes is perceived to be related to being a genius.

Do you consider yourself to be a creative person?

Do you believe that it is possible to test for creativity?

## Suggested Media

- *Curiosity.com:* https://curiosity.com/. Register for free on this website to access current videos and topics related to life-long learning, creativity and problem-solving.
- *Decision Making,* Khan Academy: https://www.khanacademy.org/science/health-and-medicine/executive-systems-of-the-brain/cognition-2014-03-27T18:40:04.738Z/v/decision-making.
- *Mindtools:* http://www.mindtools.com/pages/main/newMN_TMC.htm.

This site provides a test of problem-solving abilities and gives some problem-solving techniques.

**POPULAR MOVIES OR TELEVISION SHOWS: PROBLEM SOLVING** Show a scene from a movie such as *Cast Away,* in which Tom Hanks demonstrates the ability to avoid functional fixedness in escaping from the island where his airplane crashed. Alternatively, show a scene from the television show *Survivor* in which the contestants find novel ways to use familiar objects. The ABC show *Lost* also involves similar situations, especially in Season 1, when the survivors were challenged to make use of their crashed airplane to fashion living quarters for themselves.

## Additional Readings

Kotovsky, K., Hayes, J. R., & Simon, H. A. (1985). Why are some problems hard? Evidence from the tower of Hanoi. *Cognitive Psychology, 17,* 248–294.

## **AP** Student Edition Answer Key

### AP Test Practice

#### Section I: Multiple Choice

1. **A** *(Skill 1.C, Learning Target 5.C)*
2. **C** *(Skill 1.A, Learning Target 5.J)*
3. **E** *(Skill 1.B, Learning Target 5.K)*

#### Section II: Free Response
**A.**

Confirmation bias is the tendency to seek out information that supports one's initial hypothesis and ignore contradictory evidence. Mrs. Karlin uses confirmation bias when she finds articles to support her belief that misbehaving students should sit in the front of the classroom.

Convergent thinking is thinking in which a problem is viewed as having a single answer. Mrs. Karlin has convergent thinking because she can only think of putting misbehaving students in the front of class. She cannot generate multiple and unusual solutions.

Insight is the sudden awareness of a solution to a problem. Mrs. Karlin could suddenly find a solution for her third hour class, such as spreading the talkative students around the room.

**B.**

Positive reinforcement is when a pleasant stimulus is added to the environment that brings about an increase in a preceding response. When the misbehaving students talk, Mrs. Karlin provides attention (pleasant stimulus) that increases their misbehavior of talking out of turn.

Observational learning is learning by watching the behavior of others. Students are learning to misbehave and talk out of turn by watching others do this behavior in the classroom.

# Module 25: Language

## AP Module Summary

The study of language can be a dull one to cover. But, if you incorporate some of the activities along with the class discussion ideas, I'm sure you could make it an enjoyable learning experience! This module can be split up into two parts if time and student engagement is running short. For example, the development of human language can be added to the unit on human development. Leaving the remaining material to be presented with the unit on cognition. Or, you can keep it as is expecting students to know that cognition is memory, thinking, problem-solving, and language.

The use of *language*—the communication of information through symbols arranged according to systematic rules—is a central cognitive ability, one that is indispensable for us to communicate with one another. Not only is language central to communication, but it is also closely tied to the very way in which we think about and understand the world.

**GRAMMAR: LANGUAGE'S LANGUAGE** *Grammar*, the system of rules that determine how our thoughts can be expressed. Grammar deals with three major components of language:

- *Phonology* is the study of *phonemes*, the smallest basic units of speech that affect meaning, and of the way we use those sounds to form words and produce meaning.
  - ○ Example: "a" sound in *fat* and the "a" sound in *fate* represent two different phonemes in English.
- *Syntax* refers to the rules that indicate how words and phrases can be combined to form sentences. Every language has intricate rules that guide the order in which words may be strung together to communicate meaning.
- *Semantics*, the meanings of words and sentences. Semantic rules allow us to use words to convey the subtle nuances in meaning.

## Language Development: Developing a Way with Words

*Babbling* (3 mos.-1.5)—make speechlike but meaningless sounds

**PRODUCTION OF LANGUAGE:** By the time children are approximately 1 year old, they stop producing sounds that are not in the language to which they have been exposed. It is then a short step to the production of actual words. In English, these are typically short words that start with a consonant sound such as b, d, m, p, and t. Of course, even before they produce their first words, children can understand a fair amount of the language they hear. Language comprehension precedes language production.

After the age of 1 year, children begin to learn more complicated forms of language. By age 2, the average child has a vocabulary of more than 50 words. They produce two-word combinations, the building blocks of sentences, and sharply increase the number of different words they are able to use. Just 6 months later, that vocabulary has grown to several hundred words. At that time, children can produce short sentences, although they use *telegraphic speech*—sentences that sound as if they were part of a telegram, in which only essential words are used. Rather than saying, "I showed you the book," a child using telegraphic speech may say, "I show book."

By age 3, children learn to make plurals by adding *s* to nouns and to form the past tense by adding *-ed* to verbs. This skill also leads to errors, since children tend to apply rules inflexibly. *Overgeneralization* is the phenomenon by which children apply language rules even when the application results in an error.

# Understanding Language Acquisition: Identifying the Roots of Language

**Learning Theory Approaches: Language as a Learned Skill**

**LEARNING-THEORY APPROACH** suggests that language acquisition follows the principles of reinforcement and conditioning discovered by psychologists who study learning. This view suggests that children first learn to speak by being rewarded for making sounds that approximate speech. Ultimately, through a process of shaping, language becomes more and more like adult speech

*At this point if you have covered the unit on learning you can ask for the name of the psychologist who is known for the principles of reinforcement.

## Nativist Approaches: Language as an Innate Skill

The linguist Noam Chomsky argued that humans are born with an innate linguistic capability that emerges primarily as a function of maturation. According to his *nativist approach* to language, all the world's languages share a common underlying structure that is prewired, biologically determined, and universal. Chomsky suggested that the human brain has an inherited neural system that lets us understand the structure language provides—a kind of universal grammar.

*Interactionist approach* suggests that language development is both biological and social, produced through a combination of genetically determined predispositions *and* circumstances in one's social environment growing up that help teach language.

**EXPLORING DIVERSITY: TEACHING WITH LINGUISTIC VARIETY: BILINGUAL EDUCATION** How to appropriately and effectively teach the increasing number of children who do not speak English is not always clear. Many educators maintain that *bilingual education* is best. With a bilingual approach, students learn some subjects in their native language while simultaneously learning English. In contrast, other educators insist that all instruction ought to be in English from the moment students, including those who speak no English at all, enroll in school. In *immersion* programs, students are immediately plunged into English instruction in all subjects.

Although the controversial issue of bilingual education versus immersion has strong political undercurrents, evidence shows that the ability to speak two languages provides significant cognitive benefits over speaking only one language. Individuals who are bilingual have more linguistic tools for thinking because of their multiple-language abilities. In addition, the advantages of bilingualism start early: by the time bilingual children are 3 or 4 years old, their cognitive development is superior to that of children who speak only one language. Furthermore, speaking several languages changes the organization of the brain. See the "Neuroscience in Your Life: Being Bilingual Affects Processing in the Brain" box in the text.

Related to questions about bilingual education is the matter of biculturalism—that is, being a member of two cultures and its psychological impact. Some psychologists argue that society should promote an alternation model of bicultural competence. Such a model supports members of a culture in their efforts to maintain their original cultural identity as well as in their integration into the adopted culture. In this view, a person can belong to two cultures and have two cultural identities without having to choose between them.

## AP Key Terms

babble

grammar

interactionist approach (to language development)

language

learning-theory approach (to language development)

linguistic-relativity hypothesis

nativist approach (to language development)

overgeneralization

phonemes

phonology

semantics

syntax

telegraphic speech

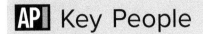 

**Noam Chomsky**

## Class Discussion Ideas

Although language can be a very dry topic (unless you are a specialist in this area), there are many ways to spice up this lecture by poking fun at our use of language through understanding ambiguities, puns, Freudian slips, and the nonverbal aspects of communication, as in dialects. Here are some ideas to incorporate into the lecture and, taken together, can easily occupy an entire class period.

**ANIMAL LANGUAGE**  This is a great time to ask students what they think about animal language. You may want to show a clip of the bee waggle dance: http://www.youtube.com/watch?v=-7ijl-g4jHg. Ask students what they feel are potential barriers to studying animal cognition and language. Ask if they think their dog is thinking. Communicating with other dogs? Engaging in reflective thinking? Problem solving and reasoning? Do they think that we are currently underestimating other species' abilities in thinking and overestimating our own? Another great clip on this is Susan Savage-Rumbaugh talking about her work with bonobos and language: http://www.ted.com/index.php/talks/susan_savage_rumbaugh_on_apes_that_write.html.

**LANGUAGE AND THINKING**  This is a good time to also point out that language and memory go hand in hand. You may also want to tie in for students the relationship between thought and language being the representation of things symbolically. Point out that Piaget and Vygotsky both argued that language is required for higher-order thinking. Ask students if they think metacognition, for example, would be possible without language.

**EVOLUTIONARY APPROACHES**  Ask students which approach to language acquisition they think best explains universal grammar. They should answer "nativist." Discuss evolutionary pressures that could pressure language to be selected for.

**VISUAL REPRESENTATION**  Hormones affect our way of thinking. Moderately high levels of testosterone, in both men and women, are associated with the ability to perform spatial and mental rotation tasks such as finding one's way around a new building or playing a three-dimensional video game. You may want to discuss the role of evolution in selecting a male bias in spatial thinking. Evolutionary psychology would suggest that the male advantage in spatial thinking comes from hunter-gatherer days when males would need to travel great distances and to hunt, skills that would require good mental rotation and spatial orientation.

**FERAL CHILDREN**  Discuss the case of Genie. Show part or all of the BBC's series on Genie. You may also want to mention the case of Itard's Victor, the first documented feral child. These cases support the critical period and illustrate the link between thought and language.

**GENIE**  Assign students to watch *The Mockingbird Don't Sing,* a 2001 movie based on the case of Genie. Have them write a paragraph on the interaction of species-typical genes in a species-atypical environment. Make sure they grasp that species-typical genes require a species-typical environment to develop in a species-typical manner.

**LEARNING A SECOND LANGUAGE**  Ask if there are any bilingual students in the room. Ask them if they think more in one language than another. You may also want to point out that early plasticity in the brain may also account for these differences.

**HUMOROUS INSTRUCTIONS** These state the obvious, so that although they are grammatically correct, they are semantically empty. Students will readily come up with other examples of their own:

In Microsoft Word: To undo the last action, click the Undo button.
On a Sears hair dryer: Do not use while sleeping.
On a bag of Fritos: You could be a winner! No purchase necessary. Details inside.
On a bar of Dial soap: Directions: Use like regular soap.
On some Swanson frozen dinners: Serving suggestion: Defrost.
On a hotel-provided shower cap in a box: Fits one head.
On Tesco's Tiramisu dessert: Do not turn upside down. (Printed on the bottom of the box.)
On Marks & Spencer's Bread Pudding: Product will be hot after heating.
On packaging for a Rowenta Iron: Do not iron clothes on body.
On Boots Children's Cough Medicine: Do not drive car or operate machinery.
On Nytol (a sleep aid): Warning: may cause drowsiness.
On a Korean-made kitchen knife: Warning: keep out of children.
On a string of Chinese-made Christmas lights: For indoor or outdoor use only.
On a Japanese food processor: Not to be used for the other use.
On Sainsbury's peanuts: Warning: contains nuts.
On an American Airlines packet of nuts: Instructions: open packet, eat nuts.
On a Swedish chainsaw: Do not attempt to stop chain with your hands.
On many promotional offers: Void where prohibited.
On a Knorr soup mix packet: To prepare with low-fat milk: Prepare as directed above using low-fat milk.

**STUPID SPORTS QUOTES** The following quotes are also semantically empty. They say nothing that is not patently obvious. Here is one of my favorites from a coach at my university on his thoughts about the weekend's game with Rhode Island:

> "We just have to keep playing the way we have. It's nice to be home. We know it will be another tough game. Rhode Island is a rival and a conference opponent. They've struggled a little and a win might turn their year around."

Others can be heard on sports commentaries:

- They didn't have their game face on.
- They didn't come out to play.
- We wanted it more.
- You've got to play with emotion.
- The game was closer than the score indicated.

Specific sports quotes are variants on these:

- "Any time Detroit scores more than 100 points and holds the other team below 100 points, they almost always win." (Doug Collins, sports commentator)
- "Ninety percent of this game is half mental." (Yogi Berra)
- "I ain't in no slump, I just ain't hittin'." (Yogi Berra)
- "I want to rush for 1,000 or 1,500 yards, whichever comes first." (New Orleans Saints running back George Rogers when asked about the upcoming season)
- "Nobody in football should be called a genius. A genius is a guy like Norman Einstein." (Football commentator and former player Joe Theismann)
- "I can't really remember the names of the clubs that we went to." (Shaquille O'Neal on whether he had gone to the Parthenon during his visit to Greece)
- "We can't win at home. We can't win on the road. As general manager, I just can't figure out where else to play." (Pat Williams, Orlando Magic general manager, on his team's 7–27 record in 1992)

**GOOD POLITICAL QUOTES** Politicians are also able to devise their own special brand of language:

"All the partisanship is on their side." (Senator Trent Lott)
"When I was coming up, it was a dangerous world and we knew exactly who the they were. It was us versus them, and it was clear who them was. Today, we're not so sure who the they are, but we know they're there." (President George W. Bush)
Their most important job "is not to be Governor or First Lady, in my case." (Presidential candidate George W. Bush)
"I've never professed to be anything but an average student." (Senator Dan Quayle)

**AMBIGUOUS OR OTHERWISE RIDICULOUS NEWSPAPER HEADLINES** There are many, many of these floating around on the Web. Here is a sampling:

Juvenile court to try shooting defendant
Red tape holds up new bridge
Deer kill 17,000
Chef throws his heart into helping feed needy
Arson suspect is held in massachusetts fire
Lansing residents can drop off trees
Prostitutes appeal to pope
Air head fired
Police begin campaign to run down jaywalkers
Safety experts say school bus passengers should be belted
Farmer bill dies in house
Iraqi head seeks arms
Shipping workers nabbed with Oscars
Sox fan accused of verbally abusing horse with anti-Yankee slur.
Tighter seat belt rule rejected
Eye drops off shelf
Teacher strikes idle kids
Squad helps dog bite victim
Enraged cow injures farmers with ax
Killer sentenced to die for second time in 10 years
Miners refuse to work after death
Kids make nutritious snacks
Local high school dropouts cut in half
Steals clock, faces time
Typhoon rips through cemetery: Hundreds dead
Two sisters reunited after 18 years in the checkout counter
Hospitals are sued by 7 foot doctors
Some pieces of Rock Hudson sold at auction
Include your children while baking cookies
Something went wrong in jet crash, expert says
Plane too close to ground, crash probe told
War dims hope for peace
If strike isn't settled quickly, it may last a while
Enfield couple slain: Police suspect homicide
Panda mating fails, veterinarian takes over
Soviet virgin lands short of goal again
Postal service to mail warning
Police arrest seven armed men

# Ridiculous Signs

DRIVE WITH CAUTION (as opposed to with reckless abandon?)
DRIVE SAFELY (same as above)
DUE TO RECENT PLUMBING CONCERNS, ONLY TOILET PAPER MAY BE FLUSHED DOWN TOILETS (in a bathroom)
SIGNS POSTED ON THIS GLASS WILL BE REMOVED IMMEDIATELY (sign on a window in a building, ironically next to a sign that says "Think")
VOID WHERE PROHIBITED

**FREUDIAN SLIPS** Mistakes in speaking are very common, estimated at one error for every 10 to 20 utterances. Although Freud believed that our unconscious desires are reflected in slips of the tongue, linguistics experts attribute these mistakes to such mundane processes as phonemic substitution. For example, sounds may be rearranged between two or more separate words, such as "snow flurries" becomes "flow snurries." Words may be rearranged, as in "passing the rusher" instead of "rushing the passer."

Some examples:

- "Yosef Burg, leader of the National Religious Party (in Israel), a Bedouin (instead of veteran) in Israeli politics" (*The New York Times,* Sept. 13, 1984).
- Misquote in a book review: "Your goal should be to help your daughter become a sexually active, healthy adult" (instead of—I assume—"sexually healthy adult") (*The New York Times,* March 19, 2001).
- At other times, though, a Freudian interpretation may hold some weight. At a meeting of a group of women's psychologists that I attended, the speaker stated, "We must work in condom" (rather than "in tandem").

Of course, the most famous Freudian slips were Spoonerisms, named after Reverend William A. Spooner, dean and warden of New College, Oxford, who uttered such memorable lines as "queer old dean" instead of "dear old queen" when referring to Queen Victoria.

**DIALECTS** Students find it amusing to hear about dialects, especially their own! Below is a list of Boston dialects. You can probably find some from your own part of the country as well:

*When we say . . . We mean . . . .*
bizah = odd
flahwiz = roses, etc.
hahpahst = 30 minutes after the hour
Hahwahya? = How are you?
cawkees = what we staht the cah with
shewah = of course
wikkid = extremely
yiz = you (plural)
popcahn = popular snack
bubblah = water fountain
haht dahgs = hot dogs

**INTONATIONS AND OTHER STYLISTIC IDIOSYNCRASIES** Point out that students often will end a verbal statement with a question mark (women are more likely to do this than men), so when you ask where someone is from, the answer sounds as though the person is not sure, as in "Shrewsbury?" Do you know where you are from, or are you asking? On my campus, people from Massachusetts are more likely to do this (because there are so many small towns), but people from the New York area rarely do, just stating "the Bronx." No questions there!

Another stylistic idiosyncrasy is to use the word *like* as every other word in a sentence.

Gestures, eye contact, and facial expressions are also fun to examine, often reflecting cultural influences (this ties into the video segment below).

**FOOT IN MOUTH AWARD** This website presents awards given in the United Kingdom for particularly bad use of language:
http://www.plainenglish.co.uk/awards/foot-in-mouth-award.html.

# Activities

**HUMOR IN LANGUAGE** Assign students the task of finding ambiguous headlines, humorous instructions, and quotes.

## Language in Other Species

- Talk to students about Irene Pepperberg's work with Alex the gray parrot. Do they think that Alex has language? Why or why not? You may want to show the clip about Alex the gray parrot and language at http://www.youtube.com/watch?v = WGiARReTwBw&feature = related.

- This may be a good time to ask students what they think about animal language and communication. Ask students what they feel are potential barriers to studying animal cognition and language. Ask if they think their dog is thinking. Communicating with other dogs? Engaging in reflective thinking/problem solving and reasoning? Do they think that we are currently underestimating other species' abilities in thinking and overestimating our own? It may be interesting to show "Orangutan Found to Mimic Human Speech," https://www.youtube.com/watch?v=dpoydpDHT8A.

# Discussion Questions

**THEORIES OF LANGUAGE DEVELOPMENT** Of the three theories of language development discussed in your text, which do you believe best explains how we learn language? Provide evidence from the text along with examples from your own life to support your position.

- Ask students to discuss how culture plays a role in language development.
- Ask students if males and females use language differently and why.
- Ask student why gender differences are so fascinating to people.
- Have students explain why some people talk a lot and others are quieter.

Most colleges and universities have a foreign language requirement for graduation. Is this a good idea? Why or why not? What are the advantages of bilingualism or multilingualism? In what ways might bilingualism or multilingualism increase thinking and creativity? Are there any disadvantages?

**THE INFLUENCE OF LANGUAGE ON THINKING: DO ALASKA NATIVES HAVE MORE WORDS FOR SNOW THAN TEXANS DO?** The contention that Alaska Native languages are especially abundant in snow-related terms led to the *linguistic-relativity hypothesis*, the notion that language shapes and, in fact, may determine the way people in a specific culture perceive and understand the world. According to this view, language provides us with categories that we use to construct our view of people and events in the world around us. Consequently, language shapes and produces thought.

On the other hand, suppose that instead of language being the cause of certain ways of thinking, thought produces language. The only reason to expect that Alaska Native languages might have more words for snow than English is that snow is considerably more relevant to Alaska Natives than it is to people in other cultures. Most recent research refutes the linguistic-relativity hypothesis and suggests, instead, that thinking produces language. New analyses of Alaska Native languages suggest that Alaska Natives have no more words for snow than English speakers. Still, the linguistic-relativity hypothesis has not been entirely discarded. A newer version of the hypothesis suggests that speech patterns may influence certain aspects of thinking. In short, although research does not support the linguistic-relativity hypothesis that language causes thought, it is clear that language influences how we think. It certainly is the case that thought influences language, suggesting that language and thinking interact in complex ways.

**DO ANIMALS USE LANGUAGE?** One question that has long puzzled psychologists is whether language is uniquely human or if other animals are able to acquire it as well. Many animals communicate with one another in rudimentary forms. Researchers have yet to demonstrate conclusively that animals use true language, which is characterized in part by the ability to produce and communicate new and unique meanings by following a formal grammar.

Psychologists, however, have been able to teach chimps to communicate at surprisingly high levels. Even more impressively, Kanzi, a bonobo, has linguistic skills that some psychologists claim are close to those of a 2-year-old human being. Kanzi's trainers suggest that he can create grammatically sophisticated sentences and can even invent new rules of syntax. Despite the skills primates such as Kanzi display, critics contend that the language such animals use still lacks the grammar and the complex and novel constructions of human language. Instead, they maintain that the chimps are displaying a skill no different from that of a dog that learns to lie down on command to get a reward.

## Polling Questions

Do you believe that animals are capable of learning and using language?

## Neuroscience in Your Life: Being Bilingual Affects the Brain

Answer Suggestions

- Possible hypotheses include: Spanish-English monolinguists have more grey matter volume in frontal and parietal brain regions than English monolinguists, or managing the use of two separate languages affects the structure and functioning of the brain.
- The frontal and parietal lobes are associated with executive control, including attention, inhibition, and short-term memory.

## AP Test Practice

### Section I: Multiple Choice

1. **D** (Skill 1.C, Learning Target 5.C)

2. **C** (Skill 1.A, Learning Target 5.S)

3. **B** (Skill 1.C, Learning Target 5.S)

### Section II: Free Response

**A.**

The independent variable is the variable being manipulated in the experiment. The learning method is the independent variable because it is being manipulated.

The operational definition of the dependent variable is the precise method of measurement. The operationally defined dependent variable is the score of 0-100 on the oral assessment.

Random assignment allows for cause-and-effect conclusions to be drawn. Also the learning method was being manipulated. Some participants received an electronic translator, while others received traditional learning methods.

A control group is the group participating in an experiment that receives no treatment. In this study it was the second group that received traditional methods of learning a language.

**B.**

Phonemes are the smallest unit of sound in speech. Young infants can distinguish and produce all 869 phonemes, but this ability declines after 6 to 8 months. The difficulty in pronouncing phonemes is one reason people have difficult learning other languages as they get older.

Universal grammar is the theory that humans are genetically prewired to learn language at certain times and in particular ways. Humans are born with an innate linguistic capability that emerges with maturation. However, as you get older it becomes more challenging to learn a new language.

A critical period is the time period when a skill can easily be acquired. Some theorists argue a critical period exists for language development early in life. Children are more sensitive to language cues and can easily acquire language.

# CHAPTER 9

# Intelligence

## AP Introduction

The topic of intelligence represents an integration of topics covered in the cognition unit—learning, memory, and problem solving. It is now included in the cognition unit and no longer a separate unit. Like many areas in psychology, it does not have a generally accepted definition. Theories of intelligence differ according to the number and organization of proposed abilities. Controversial areas in research on intelligence relate to questions of whether intelligence should be defined in terms of academic abilities alone and whether intelligence testing is biased against racial and ethnic minorities.

## AP Essential Questions

- What is intelligence and how can we study it to understand it?

## Module 26: What Is Intelligence

**AP Learning Targets:**

- Define intelligence and list characteristics of how psychologists measure intelligence.
- Discuss how culture influences the definition of intelligence.
- Compare and contrast historic and contemporary theories of intelligence.
- Identify the contributions of key researchers in intelligence research and testing.
- Explain how psychologists design tests, including standardization strategies and other techniques to establish reliability and validity.
- Interpret the meaning of scores in terms of the normal curve.

**Pacing:**

1 Block or 2 Traditional Class periods

## Module 27: Variations in Intellectual Ability

**AP Learning Targets:**

- Define intelligence and list characteristics of how psychologists measure intelligence.
- Describe relevant labels related to intelligence testing.

**Pacing:**

1 Block or 2 Traditional Class periods

# Module 28: Group Differences in Intelligence: Genetic and Environmental Determinants

## AP Learning Targets:

- Discuss psychology's abiding interest in how heredity, environment, and evolution work together to shape behavior.
- Define intelligence and list characteristics of how psychologists measure intelligence.
- Discuss how culture influences the definition of intelligence.
- Debate the appropriate testing practices, particularly in relation to culture-fair test uses.

## Pacing:

1 Block or 2 Traditional Class periods

# Module 26: What Is Intelligence?

## AP Module Summary

The term *intelligence* can take on many different meanings. People from different countries and cultural backgrounds tend to have varied ideas about what intelligence is. If, for instance, you lived in a remote part of the Australian outback, the way you would differentiate between more intelligent and less intelligent people might have to do with successfully mastering hunting skills, whereas to someone living in the heart of urban Miami, intelligence might be exemplified by being "streetwise" or by achieving success in business.

In contrast, people in Eastern cultures and some African communities view intelligence more in terms of understanding and relating to one another.

- *Intelligence* is the capacity to understand the world, think rationally, and use resources effectively when faced with challenges.

**THEORIES OF INTELLIGENCE: ARE THERE DIFFERENT KINDS OF INTELLIGENCE?** Early psychologists interested in intelligence assumed that there was a single, general factor for mental ability which they called **g,** or the **g-factor**. This general intelligence factor was thought to underlie performance in every aspect of intelligence, and it was the *g*-factor that was presumably being measured on tests of intelligence. More recent theories explain intelligence in a different light. Rather than viewing intelligence as a unitary entity, some psychologists consider it to be a multidimensional concept that includes different types of intelligence. This would be an excellent time to introduce Charles Spearman and his theory on intelligence.

**FLUID AND CRYSTALLIZED INTELLIGENCE** Some psychologists suggest that there are two different kinds of intelligence:

- *Fluid intelligence* is the ability to think logically, reason abstractly, and solve problems.
- *Crystallized intelligence* is the accumulation of information, knowledge, and skills that people have learned through experience and education.

In late adulthood, people show declines in fluid intelligence but not crystallized intelligence.

**GARDNER'S MULTIPLE INTELLIGENCES: THE MANY WAYS OF SHOWING INTELLIGENCE** Psychologist **Howard Gardner** has taken an approach very different from traditional thinking about intelligence and has developed a *theory of multiple intelligences*.

Gardner argues that we have a minimum eight different forms of intelligence, each relatively independent of the others: musical, bodily kinesthetic, logical-mathematical, linguistic, spatial, interpersonal, intrapersonal, and naturalist (see **Figure 1**). In Gardner's view, each of the multiple intelligences is linked to an independent system in the brain. Furthermore, he suggests that there may be even more types of intelligence, such as existential intelligence, which involves identifying and thinking about the fundamental questions of human existence.

**THE BIOLOGICAL BASIS OF INTELLIGENCE** Using brain-scanning methods, researchers have identified several areas of the brain that relate to intelligence. For example, the brains of people completing intelligence test questions in both verbal and spatial domains show activation in a similar location: the lateral prefrontal cortex. This area of the brain is critical to juggling many pieces of information simultaneously and solving new problems. In addition, higher intelligence is related to the thickness of the cerebral cortex. Similarly, tasks requiring different types of intelligence involve different areas of the brain. These findings suggest that there is a global "workspace" in the brain that organizes and coordinates information, helping to transfer material to other parts of the brain. In this view, the activity in the workspace represents general intelligence.

See the "Neuroscience in Your Life: What Makes Someone Intelligent?" box in the text.

**PRACTICAL AND EMOTIONAL INTELLIGENCE: TOWARD A MORE INTELLIGENT VIEW OF INTELLIGENCE**

*Practical intelligence* is intelligence related to overall success in living. Noting that traditional tests were designed to relate to academic success, psychologist **Robert Sternberg** points to evidence showing that most traditional measures of intelligence do not relate especially well to career success. Whereas academic success is based on knowledge of a specific information base obtained from reading and listening, practical intelligence is learned mainly through observation of others' behavior. People who are high in practical intelligence are able to learn general norms and principles and apply them appropriately. In addition to practical intelligence, Sternberg argues there are two other basic, interrelated types of intelligence related to life success: analytical and creative. *Analytical intelligence* focuses on abstract but traditional types of problems measured on IQ tests, while *creative intelligence* involves the generation of novel ideas and products.

- *Emotional intelligence* is the set of skills that underlie the accurate assessment, evaluation, expression, and regulation of emotions. It is the basis of empathy for others, self-awareness, and social skills. It encompasses the ability to get along well with others.

**ASSESSING INTELLIGENCE** *Intelligence tests* are tests devised to quantify a person's level of intelligence.

The idea that the size and shape of a person's head could be used as an objective measure of intelligence was put forward by **Sir Francis Galton**. Galton's motivation to identify people of high intelligence stemmed from personal prejudices. He sought to demonstrate the natural superiority of people of high social class by showing that intelligence is inherited. He hypothesized that head configuration, which is genetically determined, is related to brain size and, therefore, is related to intelligence. Galton's theories were proved wrong on virtually every count. However, Galton's work did have one desirable result: He was the first person to suggest that intelligence could be quantified and measured in an objective manner.

**BINET AND THE DEVELOPMENT OF IQ TESTS** The first real intelligence tests were developed by the French psychologist **Alfred Binet** (1857–1911). His tests followed from a simple premise: If performance on certain tasks or test items improved with chronological (physical) age, performance could be used to distinguish more intelligent people from less intelligent ones within a particular age group. On the basis of the Binet test, children were assigned a score relating to their *mental age*, the age for which a given level of performance is average or typical. Assigning a mental age to students provided an indication of their general level of performance. However, it did not allow for adequate comparisons among people of different chronological ages. A solution to the problem came in the form of the *intelligence quotient (IQ)*, a measure of intelligence that takes into account an individual's mental and chronological (physical) age. Although the basic principles behind the calculation of an IQ score still hold, today IQ scores are determined in a different manner and are known as deviation IQ scores. First, the average test score for everyone of the same age who takes the test is determined, and that average score is assigned an IQ of 100. Then, with the aid of statistical techniques that calculate the differences (or "deviations") between each score and the average, IQ scores are assigned (see **Figure 4**).

This would be an excellent time to introduce Lewis Terman and his contributions on intelligence research and testing.

**CONTEMPORARY IQ TESTS: GAUGING INTELLIGENCE** Remnants of Binet's original intelligence test are still with us, although the test has been revised in significant ways. Now in its fifth edition and called the Stanford-Binet Intelligence Scale, the test consists of a series of items that vary according to the age of the person being tested. The IQ tests most frequently used in the United States were devised by psychologist **David Wechsler** and are known as the Wechsler Adult Intelligence Scale-IV (commonly, the WAIS-IV) and a children's version, the Wechsler Intelligence Scale for Children-V (WISC-V). Because the Stanford-Binet, WAIS-IV, and WISC-V all require individualized, one-on-one administration, they are relatively difficult to administer and score on a large-scale basis. Consequently, there are now a number of IQ tests that allow group administration. However, sacrifices made in group testing may outweigh the benefits.

**RELIABILITY AND VALIDITY: TAKING THE MEASURE OF TESTS** Psychological tests are expected to have

- *Reliability*—that they measure consistently what they are trying to measure.
- *Validity*—actually measure what they are supposed to measure.

Test validity and reliability are prerequisites for accurate assessment of intelligence. Assuming that a test is both valid and reliable, one further step is necessary in order to interpret the meaning of a particular test-taker's score:

- *Norms* are standards of test performance that permit the comparison of one person's score on a test to the scores of others who have taken the same test.

Tests for which norms have been developed are known as *standardized tests*.

## AP Key Terms

| | |
|---|---|
| abstract versus verbal measures | mental age |
| crystallized intelligence | norms |
| emotional intelligence | practical intelligence |
| fluid intelligence | reliability |
| g or g-factor | speed of processing |
| intelligence | theory of multiple intelligences |
| intelligence quotient (IQ) | validity |
| intelligence tests | |

## AP Key People

| | |
|---|---|
| Charles Spearman | Francis Galton |
| Howard Gardner | Lewis Terman |
| Robert Sternberg | David Wechsler |
| Alfred Binet | |

## Class Discussion Ideas

**WHAT MAKES A GOOD INTELLIGENCE TEST?** Originally, Alfred Binet developed the intelligence test to predict future academic success. The value of an intelligence test to predict achievement depends on several important factors: validity, reliability, standardization, objectivity, and practicality.

Validity refers to the degree to which a test actually measures what it is intended to measure. A valid intelligence test would measure intelligence, not memory, speed, guessing ability, or vocabulary. Reliability is the degree to which a person's score at one time is the same at a different time. A reliable intelligence test would yield consistent scores from one time to the next.

Standardization is the process of obtaining a norm, or sample of scores representative of the population, and is necessary in interpreting a particular subject's score. For example, if a friend of yours tells you that they received a score of 179 on a test, how would you know whether this was a good score? It would help if you knew that the test contained a possible 200 points, the mean score was 125, and the range for the class was 75 to 190.

Psychologists standardize tests so that they can interpret individual test results. The first step is to define the population serving as the standardization group. For example, we might wish to know how an individual compares to other adult Americans, and so we would standardize the test on the American adult population. Or a population might include all high school seniors in Canada. After the population is identified, we need to obtain a norm, or representative sample, that will allow us to describe what the entire population is like.

An intelligence test should be objective. Objectivity ensures that a test's results are not affected by the personal feelings and biases of the examiner. Ideally, a test should be constructed so that any qualified person can administer and score it and obtain the same results as any other scorer.

An intelligence test should also be practical. Practicality provides that a test can be administered easily and scored in a reasonable amount of time. Chances are good that psychologists would not be interested in a new test requiring five people to administer and 16 hours to complete.

Tests that are valid, reliable, standardized, objective, and practical meet the general requirements for use. Developing intelligence tests that meet all of these requirements is a difficult task.

Source: Pettijohn, T. E. (1998). *Psychology: A ConnecText* (4th ed.). Dushkin/McGraw-Hill.

**ALFRED BINET'S BIOGRAPHY** Alfred Binet was born in 1857 in Nice, France. His parents divorced when he was young, and he was raised by his mother. He entered college with the goal of getting a medical degree but dropped out when he became interested in psychology. He never completed a degree but continued to read and study psychological topics.

In 1883, Binet accepted a position at a clinic at Salpetriere Hospital, where he worked with Jean Charcot, who was studying hypnosis at the time. In 1890, he resigned this position and spent time studying the cognitive abilities of his young daughters.

Binet began working at the Laboratory of Physiological Psychology at the Sorbonne and was appointed director there in 1894. He studied memory, thinking, hypnosis, handwriting, and perception. He also served as editor of the French psychological journal *L'Année Psychologique*.

In 1904, he began work on developing a test to identify students who needed special education because of their low level of intellectual functioning. Binet and his colleague Théodore Simon published the first intelligence scale in 1905.

During the next several years, Binet spent much of his time testing children and revising the intelligence test, first in 1908 and again in 1911, the year of his death. Binet's early work on intelligence testing has stimulated an enormous amount of research in this area of psychology.

Source: Pettijohn, T. E. (1998). *Psychology: A ConnecText* (4th ed.). Dushkin/McGraw-Hill.

**ROBERT STERNBERG'S BIOGRAPHY** Robert J. Sternberg was born in December 1949 in Newark, New Jersey. He attended Yale University, where he decided to major in psychology (even after earning a C in his introductory psychology course). After graduating (with high honors in psychology) in 1972, he entered Stanford University, earning his PhD in psychology in 1975.

Sternberg has been extremely influential in psychology, especially in the cognitive area of intelligence and the emotional area of love. The American Psychological Association awarded him a Distinguished Scientific Award for an Early Career Contribution to Psychology in 1981. Since then, he has received many honors in the discipline.

Sternberg recalls that he has had an interest in intelligence since he was in elementary school, where he experienced great test anxiety whenever he took intelligence tests. Throughout his career, he has conducted research in intelligence and thinking. He published an award-winning book, *Beyond IQ: A Triarchic Theory of Human Intelligence,* in 1987, and a collection of practical advice called *Successful Intelligence* in 1996.

In addition to his work on intelligence, Sternberg has developed a theory of love, as outlined in his 1988 book, *The Triangle of Love.* He feels that love is an important emotion that can be studied scientifically. He also published another book, *Love Is a Story: A New Theory of Relationships* (1998, Oxford University Press).

Robert Sternberg is currently professor of psychology at Yale University, where he has been since 1975.

Source: Pettijohn, T. E. (1998). *Psychology: A ConnecText* (4th ed.). Dushkin/McGraw-Hill.

## Activities

**GARDNER'S MULTIPLE INTELLIGENCES THEORY** Have students test their abilities on Gardner's forms of multiple intelligence, adopting the lecture ideas above as follows. (Instead of presenting the lecture ideas above, have students complete the tasks as an assignment or several short assignments.)

Note: These are not validated tests. They would not be used for any actual diagnosis but are opportunities for students to get a hands-on sense of the complexity of intelligence as defined by Gardner.

**Musical Intelligence** Have students work in pairs. One student can hum the tunes and the other can guess them.

**Interpersonal Intelligence** Choose one of the other seven forms of intelligence. Have the student complete the test for that one and then have the student compare their score on that test with self-rated intelligence on that scale on *Handout: Self-Rating of Multiple Intelligences*. The closer the score is to a high score on that scale, the greater the student's self-knowledge and hence intrapersonal intelligence.

Ask students to think about multiple intelligences. Which two areas do they believe are their strengths and weaknesses? Ask them to defend their answer.

Ask students how they feel about the concept of multiple intelligences. You may want to use the bodily kinetic in your discussion, as that is one of the most controversial aspects of the theory. Yes, it involves spatial cognition, but is that intelligence?

**Emotional Intelligence** Have students complete *Handout: Emotional Intelligence*.

Have students complete a self-assessment of their own emotional intelligence. One site that provides a short and free EQ quiz is www.ihhp.com/?page=freeEQquiz. Upon getting their results, have students identify what emotional intelligence is and its relationship to academic achievement and/or work productivity.

## Discussion Questions

**VALIDITY OF EMOTIONAL INTELLIGENCE** What happened the last time you did not "get your way" in dealing with a friend? How did you handle it?

Do you agree that the ability to delay gratification is an important part of emotional intelligence? Why or why not?

How do you think emotional intelligence compares to academic intelligence in importance in life success? Why?

## Suggested Media

- *Association for Psychological Science:* www.psych.hanover.edu/APS/teaching.html. This site has many teacher resources to link students to opportunities to participate in research or activities across the various subfields in the discipline.
- *Battle of the Brains: The Case for Multiple Intelligences.* Films for the Humanities and Social Sciences, 2007, 50:00. The importance of multiple intelligence is discussed in this film.
- *Intelligence theory.* www.intelltheory.com/. The site includes biographical profiles of people who have influenced the development of intelligence theory and testing.
- *Multiple intelligences research:* www.edutopia.org/multiple-intelligences-research.
- *Personality research:* www.personalityresearch.org/intelligence.html. *Shattering the bell curve:* Shaywitz, D. A., (2004, April 7). Shattering the bell curve. *Wall Street Journal,* www.online.wsj.com/articles/SB117736979316179649.
- *Sternberg's triachic theory of intelligence:* www.psychestudy.com/cognitive/intelligence/triarchic.

## **AP** Student Edition Answer Key

### Neuroscience in Your Life: What Makes Someone Intelligent?

Answer Suggestions

- A meta-analysis permits psychologists to combine many separate studies into one overall conclusion.
- Functional magnetic resonance imaging (fMRI) scans provide a detailed, three-dimensional computer-generated image of brain structures and activity.

### AP Test Practice

#### Section I: Multiple Choice

1. **D** *(Skill 1.A, Learning Target 5.L)*
2. **B** *(Skill 1.B, Learning Target 5.P)*
3. **C** *(Skill 1.A, Learning Target 5.Q)*

#### Section II: Free Response

General intelligence is the single, general factor for mental ability assumed to underlie intelligence. This intelligence is often represented by a single score on most academic intelligence tests.

Interpersonal intelligence is one of Howard Gardner's eight multiple intelligences and consists of the skills involved in interacting with others. This intelligence includes being able to be sensitive to the moods, temperaments, motivations, and intentions of others.

Practical intelligence, according to Robert Sternberg, is intelligence in terms of nonacademic, career, and personal success. It is often learned through observation of others' behavior and called "street smarts." This intelligence includes the art of building rapport and negotiating deals.

Emotional intelligence provides an understanding of what other people are feeling and experiencing and permits us to respond appropriately to others' needs. This intelligence includes responding appropriately and quickly to others' feelings in a high stress situation.

Crystalized intelligence relates to information, skills, and strategies learned through experience. This intelligence includes facts that we have learned and information that resides in our long-term memory.

# Module 27: Variations in Intellectual Ability

## AP Module Summary

An easy way to discuss the labels placed on individuals in society who have significantly impaired and/or advanced intellectual abilities is to review it while going over the bell curve (Figure 4). Lead a discussion while marking the curve, asking students do the same. Make sure to include standard deviations, WAIS and SAT scores too. This can serve as a great review of chapter 2 on psychological research. The concept savant syndrome has been added to the CED and should be included in your lectures related to intellectual ability.

More than 7 million people in the United States, including around 11 per 1,000 children, have been identified as far enough below average in intelligence that they can be regarded as having serious deficits. Individuals with low IQs (people with intellectual disabilities) as well as those with unusually high IQs (the intellectually gifted) require special attention if they are to reach their full potential.

**INTELLECTUAL DISABILITIES** *Intellectual disability* is a disability characterized by significant limitations in both intellectual functioning and in adaptive behavior, which covers many everyday social and practical skills, and originates before the age of 18.

**IDENTIFYING THE ROOTS OF INTELLECTUAL DISABILITIES** *Fetal alcohol syndrome*, produced by a mother's use of alcohol while pregnant. In some cases, intellectual disabilities begin after birth following a head injury, a stroke, or infections such as meningitis. However, the majority of cases of intellectual disabilities are classified as *familial intellectual disability*, in which no apparent biological defect exists but in which there is a history of intellectual disability in the family.

**APPLYING PSYCHOLOGY IN THE 21ST CENTURY: DOES A HIDDEN GENIUS LIE WITHIN US?** Savant syndrome has been understood as a set of extraordinary but narrowly focused mathematical, musical, or artistic abilities in developmentally disabled people who are otherwise intellectually impaired (Treffert, 2014). A small subset of savants acquired their abilities after a brain injury. This is considered acquired savant syndrome and may suggest that there are incredible abilities lying latent in our brains. To test this, researchers inhibited left hemisphere function while stimulating regions in the right hemisphere, which allowed 40% of participants to solve a previously unsolveable problem. Those participants in the control group were never able to solve the problem. There may be unknown brain abilities laying dormant until the right circumstance arises for them to be released.

**THE INTELLECTUALLY GIFTED** *Intellectually gifted* differ from those with average intelligence as much as individuals with intellectual disability, although in a different manner. Accounting for 2% to 4% of the population, they have IQ scores greater than 130. The intellectually gifted are most often outgoing, well-adjusted, healthy, popular people who are able to do most things better than the average person can. Although special programs attempting to overcome the deficits of people with intellectual disability abound, programs targeted at the intellectually gifted are rarer. Some approaches, however, have acknowledged that without some form of special attention, the gifted become bored and frustrated with the pace of their schooling and may never reach their potential.

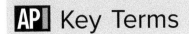 Key Terms

familial intellectual disability

fetal alcohol syndrome

intellectual disability

intellectually gifted

savant syndrome

## Class Discussion Ideas

**BACKGROUND ON INTELLECTUAL DISABILITY** Using the resources on the website of the Administration on Developmental Disabilities (www.acl.gov/programs/aidd/index.aspx), summarize current concerns, research findings, and issues.

Information can also be found at the National Organization on Disability site: www.nod.org/.

## Activities

**CAUSES OF INTELLECTUAL DISABILITY** Have students complete *Handout: Causes of Intellectual Disability,* in which they are asked to summarize causes of and prevention against intellectual disability.

**DISTRIBUTION IN IQ SCORES** You may want to show an overhead of the distribution and discuss how 95% fall within two standard deviations of the mean. You have 2.5% of the population in the two tails: the R tail being "gifted" and the L tail being "mentally retarded." Remind students that any significant developmental delay will result in testing at a lower IQ because the individual is being compared to others of the same age. You also may want to stress that because of the distribution, schools are only looking for the top 2.5% and bottom 2.5%, as 95% are within "normal" range. Thus, there is no need to give a long, full IQ test to most folks, as they will be within "normal" range. They only need to give full tests to kids who might fall out of the two standard deviations.

## Discussion Questions

**ATTITUDES TOWARD PEOPLE WITH INTELLECTUAL DISABILITY** What experiences have you had with people who have intellectual disability?

Do you believe that children with intellectual disability should be mainstreamed, or do you support the notion of full inclusion? Why?*

What are the challenges in daily life faced by people with intellectual disability?

How do social attitudes toward intellectual disability affect the daily lives of people with intellectual disability?

Note: The terms *mainstreaming* and *inclusion* are often used interchangeably. This inconsistency in usage has led to confusion about what educators mean when they talk about inclusion or full inclusion. Mainstreaming is the practice of educating the disabled student in the general education classroom. Inclusion is a newer term used to describe the placement of students in regular classes for all, or nearly all, of the school day; mainstreaming is often associated with sending a student from a special education class to a regular class for specified periods. Although in some inclusion models students are mainstreamed only part of the day, students in full inclusion programs remain in the general classroom for the entire day.

## Polling Questions

**INTELLECTUAL DISABILITIES** Do you attend a high school that mainstreams or fully includes students with intellectual disabilities?

## Suggested Media

- *Developmental disabilities:* www.cdc.gov/ncbddd/developmentaldisabilities.
- *Is Rain Man Syndrome Real?:* www.verywellhealth.com/the-rain-mans-disorder-savant-syndrome-2860421.
- *Catching Up With Rex. 60 Minutes. Savant Syndrome:* www.youtube.com/watch?v=cCF1xSgyKXg
- *MENSA:* www.mensa.org.
- *National Association for Gifted Children*: www.nagc.org/.

## AP Student Edition Answer Key

### Applying Psychology in the 21st Century: Does a Hidden Genius Lie Within Us?

Answer Suggestions

- Plasticity is the brain's ability to change in significant ways over the course of the life span through the addition of new neurons, new interconnections between neurons, and the reorganization of information processing areas.
- Random assignment is used to make cause-and-effect conclusions.

## AP Test Practice

### Section I: Multiple Choice

1.  **D** *(Skill 1.B, Learning Target 5.L)*
2.  **A** *(Skill 1.A, Learning Target 5.O)*
3.  **B** *(Skill 1.A, Learning Target 5.R)*

### Section II: Free Response

Intellectual disability is characterized by significant limitations in both intellectual functioning and adaptive behavior. Stephen has a moderate intellectual disability because his IQ score falls within the 40–54 range and he is experiencing limitations in adaptive behavior.

Savant syndrome is an island of extraordinary, but narrowly focused, ability amidst a developmental disorder or intellectual disability. Stephen is a savant. Despite an intellectual disability, he has an island of brilliance in calendar calculating.

Giftedness is a score than 130. Matt would be considered gifted with an IQ score of 140.

Lewis Terman conducted a longitudinal study of gifted children and found they were socially adjusted. Most likely Matt is physically, academically, and socially capable. These advantages will probably pay off in terms of career success for Matt when he gets older.

The *WISC-V* is an IQ test frequently used in the United States. Both boys have probably taken the *WISC-V* to identify their IQ score.

# Module 28: Group Differences in Intelligence: Genetic and Environmental Determinants

## **AP** Module Summary

The last module on intelligence is one that can stir up great discussion and reflective thought. The concept stereotype threat has been added to this area and should be included in your lecture. Several connections can be made between this module and modules presented in the social psychology chapter.

**EXPLORING DIVERSITY: CAN WE DEVELOP CULTURE-FAIR IQ TESTS?** In a *Culture-fair IQ test*, one that does not discriminate against the members of any minority group, psychologists have tried to devise test items that assess experiences common to all cultures or emphasize questions that do not require language usage. However, test makers have found this difficult to do because past experiences, attitudes, and values almost always have an impact on respondents' answers. Psychologists' efforts to produce culture-fair measures of intelligence relate to a lingering controversy over differences in intelligence between members of different racial and ethnic groups.

**IQ AND HERITABILITY: THE RELATIVE INFLUENCE OF GENETICS AND ENVIRONMENT** *Heritability* (see **Figure 1**), the degree to which a characteristic can be attributed to genetic, inherited factors. However, many psychologists reacted strongly to the arguments laid out in *The Bell Curve*, refuting several of the book's basic conclusions. One criticism is that even when attempts are made to hold socioeconomic conditions constant, wide variations remain among individual households. Blacks who are raised in economically enriched environments have IQ scores similar to whites in comparable environments. Drawing comparisons between different races on any dimension, including IQ scores, is an imprecise—potentially misleading or damaging—and often fruitless venture. By far, the greatest discrepancies in IQ scores occur when comparing individuals, not when comparing mean IQ scores of different groups.

This would be a great place to introduce students to the concept of *stereotype threat* and the implications it can have on an individual.

**ARE WE GETTING SMARTER IN THE 21ST CENTURY? WHY IQ SCORES ARE RISING** IQ tests are normed, which means that individual scores indicate performance on the test relative to the average score, which is set to 100. However, over the course of its roughly 100-year history, test designers have noticed something peculiar: They have had to repeatedly re-norm the test as the average score kept creeping up, gradually making it more and more challenging. The phenomenon has become known as the *Flynn effect,* named for a researcher who brought early attention to it.

**PLACING THE HEREDITY-ENVIRONMENT QUESTION IN PERSPECTIVE** There is no definitive answer to the question of the degree to which intelligence is influenced by heredity and by the environment. The more critical question is not whether hereditary or environmental factors primarily underlie intelligence, but whether there is anything we can do to maximize the intellectual development of individuals, so that each person to reach their potential.

## 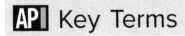 Key Terms

culture-fair IQ test

heritability

# Class Discussion Ideas

**GENETICS** Information on genetics can be obtained on this website: ghr.nlm.nih.gov/primer.

- **Heritability and IQ** When you talk about IQ heritability and the adoptee data, ask students what they think. Is there any third factor or confounding variables? YES! Remind students that adoption takes money. It also takes motivation. Thus, folks who adopt have money and really want kids.

**SAT VARIATIONS BY RACE AND ETHNICITY** An excellent discussion of variations in SAT scores by race and ethnicity can be found at www.pbs.org/wgbh/pages/frontline/shows/sats/etc/gap.html.

- **Reliability and Validity:** Students often have difficulty here. Try using the example of a scale. If you have a scale that is off by 10 pounds consistently, it would be reliable (that is, test retest would be high) but not valid; it isn't accurately measuring your weight. This is also a good time to point out that reliability is thought to be more important. If my scale is off (low validity), does it still have utility (usefulness)? Yes, it can still measure change, and I know that it is reliable, so that provides utility.

**RACE AND INTELLIGENCE** One of the most controversial issues in the relationship of heredity to intelligence concerns the issue of race. African Americans tend to score an average of 15 points lower on IQ tests than do whites (Bracken & colleagues, 1993). Although other minorities in the United States, including Mexican Americans and Native Americans, also sometimes score lower on standardized tests; one exception is the mathematical skills of Asian Americans (D'Ailly, 1992). Although there have been many explanations for these findings, Arthur Jensen (1969) caused a controversy in the academic community by suggesting that intelligence was due nearly exclusively (80 percent) to hereditary factors. And, more recently, the genetic theory of racial differences in intelligence was supported by Herrnstein and Murray (1994), but again, not without controversy. Let us take a look at the facts to try to understand what conclusions might be reached concerning race and intelligence.

As reported in the text, the correlation for IQs of identical twins reared together is .86, suggesting that heredity largely accounts for the similarity. There are other possible interpretations of the data. For example, the .86 correlation for identical twins reared together is actually determined by both genetic and environmental factors. These twins not only share identical genes, but they also share nearly identical environments. It could be argued that environment is contributing much more than the .14 figure first suggested by the data.

Keep in mind also that these correlations are for group data and tell us nothing about individual scores. Indeed, there is more variation within a particular race than between two races. Thus, we cannot make a prediction about an individual from this group data.

Since, until fairly recently, most intelligence tests were standardized for white, middle-class people, it is no wonder that other races do not score as well as whites. Indeed, it could be argued that the earlier versions of intelligence tests were invalid for measuring the intelligence of African Americans (Houston, 1990). The intelligence tests themselves could be biased. A number of attempts to construct a truly culture-fair intelligence test have shown only moderate success, and we are left with less than ideal testing instruments.

Studies have suggested that environmental differences that exist between races are extremely important in IQ determination. For instance, data from the Minnesota Transracial Adoption Study reported by Scarr and Weinberg (1983) found that when African American children were adopted by white families at an early age, their IQs were more similar to the white IQ average of 110, compared with an average of 90 for African American children reared in the black community. However, the African American adopted children still scored 6 points below the white children in the same family. Scarr and Weinberg concluded that genetic differences between the races cannot be used exclusively to explain IQ differences.

Source: Pettijohn, T. E. (1998). *Psychology: A ConnecText* (4th ed.). Dushkin/McGraw-Hill.

**ONLINE RESEARCH: RACIAL DIFFERENCES IN INTELLIGENCE** Have students conduct an online search for information on racial differences in intelligence. Ask them the following questions:

- Summarize the current data on racial differences in intelligence. Do such differences really exist?
- What might account for any differences in intelligence scores between groups?
- Do you believe that intelligence tests should be "culture fair," or should they take into account socialization and acculturation? Why?
- How might the results of research on racial differences in intelligence be misused by employers, educators, and policy makers?

**BELL CURVE** Show part or the entire interview with Charles Murray at www.youtube.com/watch?v=vMCjkfp_9JQ. Discuss with students what the authors are suggesting. What other factors could explain the data? The answer is SES. Remind students that regardless of whether they agree with the authors, it was a catalyst for Head Start, early neonatal interventions, WIC programs, etc. Discuss the effects of being poor on IQ.

**CULTURE-FAIR IQ TEST** A free culture-fair IQ test can be found on this website: www. highiqsociety.org/iq_tests/. Have students complete this test. Ask them to discuss the advantages and disadvantages of this type of test compared to a test based on verbal skills.

- **Cultural Bias in IQ Testing:** Have students do a search on the Internet for cultural bias in intelligence testing and write a short paper on the information they find. The students should discuss the pros (if any) and cons of cultural bias in intelligence testing. The next day, break the class into groups, and have them develop a 10-question quiz using what they think would be culturally biased questions.
- **Intelligence Testing and Bias.** To demonstrate the many forms of bias in intelligence testing, put the following on a PowerPoint:
  - Un metro es igual a cuantos centimetros?
  - Un Ferrari es al coche como la Alta Construa esta a _____?
  - Cuantos discipulos tuvo Jesucristo?
  - Quien era el anfitrion de *American Bandstand*?

Beyond demonstrating importance of language in intelligence testing, this shows many forms of cultural bias.

- One meter equals how many centimeters? (100) [culture, country]
- Ferarri is to car as haute couture is to ___? (Fashion) [socioeconomic]
- How many disciples did Jesus have? (12) [religion]
- Who was the host of *American Bandstand*? (Dick Clark) [Age, country]

## Activities

Have students ask a few friends to define the term *intelligent*. Do they describe intelligent people or intelligent behaviors? Do their definitions focus on cognitive or other abilities?

- **Nature versus Nurture:** Discuss with the class the differences between nature and nurture and how these ideas are very controversial in the area of intelligence. Break the students into groups, and have them randomly draw slips of paper with the words *nature* or *nurture* on them. Each group must then develop a debate strategy for arguing either for a nature influence or a nurture influence on intelligence. The following week have the groups debate both sides as a presentation.
- **Education:** This activity should make for a lively debate in class. Have students bring two good sources of research to support their views on the following: Should resources be spent mostly to bring everyone up to a level of proficiency, or should public schools focus on enhancing the education of those who are gifted? How much money would you be willing to pay in taxes every year to accomplish both?

# Suggested Media

- *Nonverbal IQ test:* www.youtube.com/watch?v=sThCoWH03HU&feature=related/

# AP Student Edition Answer Key

## AP Test Practice

### Section I: Multiple Choice

1. **D** *(Skill 1.B, Learning Target 5.L)*

2. **C** *(Skill 1.B, Learning Target 5.T)*

3. **A** *(Skill 1.A, Learning Target 5.T)*

### Section II: Free Response

To reduce cultural bias, psychologists have attempted to create a culture-fair IQ test that does not discriminate against any minority group. Test designers will need to create assessment items that will consider experiences common to all cultures and not require language usage.

The Flynn effect is the increase of IQ scores each decade. Test designers will need to repeatedly renorm the assessment to take into account the increase in scores.

Reliability is the consistency of an assessment measuring what it is trying to measure. Test designers should find a positive correlation between the scores when the assessment is first provided and then tested again.

Validity is the degree to which an assessment actually measures what it is supposed to measure. Test designers should check to make sure the assessment is measuring intelligence instead of some other construct.

Norms are standards of test performance that permit the comparison of one person's score on a test to the scores of others who have taken the same test. Test designers should create a standardized test that has norms. They can create norms by calculating the average score achieved by a specific group for whom the test was designed. The sample should be representative of the population to whom the test is directed.

# CHAPTER 10

# Motivation and Emotion

## **AP** Introduction

The topics of motivation and emotion are basic to psychology. Theories of motivation attempt to explain the "whys" of behavior; theories of emotion attempt to explain why we feel the way we do. Both areas share the quality of involving a variety of theoretical approaches. These approaches reflect the major perspectives in psychology ranging from biological to social. They also have important implications for the way that we feel about ourselves and our daily activities.

## **AP** Essential Questions

- What motivates us to think and act the way we do?
- Why do some people respond to stress in a healthier way than others?
- Why don't psychologists agree?

## Module 29: Explaining Motivation

**AP Learning Targets:**

- Identify and apply basic motivational concepts to understand the behavior of humans and other animals.
- Compare and contrast motivational theories, including the strengths and weaknesses of each.
- Identify contributions of key researchers in the psychological field of motivation and emotion.
- Discuss the biological underpinnings of motivation, including needs, drives, and homeostasis.

**Pacing:**

2½ Blocks or 4 Traditional Class periods

## Module 30: Human Needs and Motivation: Eat, Drink, and Be Daring

**Pacing:**

½ Block or 1 Traditional Class period

## Module 31: Understanding Emotional Experiences

**AP Learning Targets:**

- Identify contributions of key researchers in the psychological field of motivation and emotion.
- Compare and contrast major theories of emotion.
- Describe how cultural influences shape emotional expression, including variations in body language.

**Pacing:**

2 Blocks or 4 Traditional Class periods

# Module 29: Explaining Motivation

## AP Module Summary

In Module 29, the College Board has added more specific concepts to address the "whys" of behavior. The concept of the overjustification effect was added and should be included in your instruction when you review the concept of incentives. Additionally, self-efficacy has been included to the new course and exam description guide. Self-efficacy is one of those concepts that seems to appear in numerous chapters; therefore, depending on how you organize your course you may only need to review it and explain how it applies to motivation.

Several new concepts have been added to explain motivational theories. The arousal theory has always existed, however, now you should include with it the Yerkes-Dodson law. The new theories that have been added are the evolutionary theory of motivation, Maslow's theory (which most do anyway but now the CED is specifically including it) and the cognitive dissonance theory. This concept is also one that reappears in another unit and so it may just be a review for you and your students and to see how it can be applied to motivation.

- *Motivation* refers to the factors that direct and energize the behavior of humans and other organisms.

**INSTINCT APPROACHES: BORN TO BE MOTIVATED** *Instincts* are inborn patterns of behavior that are biologically determined rather than learned. According to *instinct approaches to motivation*, people and animals are born preprogrammed with sets of behaviors essential to their survival. Those instincts provide the energy that channels behavior in appropriate directions.

This would be a good time to review the *Evolutionary Theory of motivation*.

**DRIVE-REDUCTION APPROACHES: SATISFYING OUR NEEDS** *Drive-reduction approaches to motivation* suggest that a lack of some basic biological need (such as water) produces a drive to push an organism to satisfy that need (in this case, seeking water). A *drive* is motivational tension, or arousal, that energizes behavior to fulfill a need. Many basic drives, such as hunger, thirst, sleep, and sex, are related to biological needs of the body or of the species as a whole. These are called *primary drives*. Primary drives contrast with secondary drives in which behavior fulfills no obvious biological need. In *secondary drives*, prior experience and learning bring about needs.

**HOMEOSTASIS** *Homeostasis*, the body's tendency to maintain a steady internal state, underlies primary drives. Using feedback loops, homeostasis brings deviations in body functioning back to an optimal state. (See **Figure 1**.)

**AROUSAL APPROACHES: BEYOND DRIVE REDUCTION** According to *arousal approaches to motivation*, each person tries to maintain a steady level of stimulation and activity. As with the drive-reduction model, this approach suggests that if our stimulation and activity levels become too high, we try to reduce them. However, in contrast to the drive-reduction perspective, the arousal approach also suggests that if levels of stimulation and activity are too low, we will try to increase them by seeking stimulation. People vary widely in the optimal level of arousal they seek, with some people looking for especially high levels of arousal.

This would be an excellent time to share with students the Yerkes-Dodson law.

**INCENTIVE APPROACHES: MOTIVATION'S PULL** *Incentive approaches to motivation* suggest that motivation stems from the desire to obtain valued external goals, or incentives. In this view, the desirable properties of external stimuli—whether grades, money, affection, food, or sex— account for a person's motivation. Although the theory explains why we may succumb to an incentive (such as a mouth-watering dessert) even though we lack internal cues (such as hunger), it does not provide a complete explanation of motivation because organisms sometimes seek to fulfill needs even when incentives are not apparent. Consequently, many psychologists believe that the internal drives proposed by drive-reduction theory work in tandem with the external incentives of incentive theory to "push" and "pull" behavior, respectively.

This would be a great time to introduce students to the *Overjustification Effect*.

**COGNITIVE APPROACHES: THE THOUGHTS BEHIND MOTIVATION** *Cognitive approaches to motivation* suggest that motivation is the outcome of people's thoughts, beliefs, expectations, and goals. Cognitive theories of motivation draw a key distinction between intrinsic and extrinsic motivation. *Intrinsic motivation* causes us to participate in an activity for our own enjoyment rather than for any actual or concrete reward that it will bring us. In contrast, *extrinsic motivation* causes us to do something for money, a grade, or some other actual, concrete reward. We are more apt to persevere, work harder, and produce work of higher quality when motivation for a task is intrinsic rather than extrinsic.

A great time to introduce or to review self-efficacy and the cognitive dissonance theory. This concept is mentioned in several areas of psychology and may have already been introduced but, regardless, will be on the AP exam.

**MASLOW'S HIERARCHY: ORDERING MOTIVATIONAL NEEDS (SEE FIGURE 3)** Maslow's model places motivational needs in a hierarchy and suggests that before more sophisticated, higher-order needs can be met, certain primary needs must be satisfied. The basic needs are primary drives: needs for water, food, sleep, sex, and the like. To move up the hierarchy, a person must first meet these basic physiological needs. Safety needs come next in the hierarchy; Maslow suggests that people need a safe, secure environment in order to function effectively. Physiological and safety needs compose the lower-order needs.

Only after meeting the basic lower-order needs can a person consider fulfilling higher-order needs, such as the needs for love and a sense of belonging, esteem, and self-actualization.

- *Self-actualization*, the highest-level need, is a state of self-fulfillment in which people realize their highest potentials in their own unique way.

Maslow's hierarchy of needs is important for two reasons: It highlights the complexity of human needs, and it emphasizes the idea that until more basic biological needs are met, people will be relatively unconcerned with higher-order needs.

# **AP** Key Terms

| | |
|---|---|
| arousal approaches to motivation | instinct approaches to motivation |
| cognitive approaches to motivation | instincts |
| cognitive dissonance theory | motivation |
| drive | overjustification effect |
| drive-reduction approaches to motivation | self-actualization |
| evolutionary theory of motivation | self-efficacy |
| homeostasis | Yerkes-Dodson law |
| incentive approaches to motivation | |

# Class Discussion Ideas

**MOTIVATION DEFINED** Have students ask their friends and parents to define the word *motivation*, then compare those definitions of motivation with the way psychologists define and approach motivation. What are the similarities? What are the differences? How do the definitions of their friends differ from those of their parents? Why do they think all of these variations exist?

**MASLOW'S HIERARCHY OF NEEDS** One argument against Maslow's hierarchy is that the same behavior could serve to fulfill different needs for different people. For example, you might use food. Food is clearly a physiological need, but for some it can serve other functions such as love, security, safety, or achievement. Have students think of other behaviors that may fulfill multiple needs on the hierarchy.

Ask students to think about how mood affects daily behaviors, such as helpfulness. If they are in a good mood and another driver is trying to merge into their lane, what do they do? What about if someone yells for them to hold the elevator? Generally, if you're in a good mood, you are more helpful (you let people into your lane and frantically press the "open door" button or put your foot in the doorway to keep the elevator open). If you're in a bad mood, though, you may be less helpful (speeding up to prevent the merge and actively pushing the "close door" button).

**THE *AMAZING RACE* OR *SURVIVOR*** Use a segment from one of these television shows to point out that it is consistent with Maslow's theory to risk lower-order needs for the purposes of becoming self-actualized. Lower-order needs must be satisfied, but they may be set to one side for the purpose of achieving a higher goal.

# Activities

**APPLYING THEORIES OF MOTIVATION**

- **Assign** *Handout: Applying Theories of Motivation to Personal Accomplishments.*
- **Goal-Setting Exercise** To explore your own goals and sense of purpose, try the following activity. First, list the top five or 10 goals that you are trying to accomplish in your everyday behavior. Then write your responses to the following questions that Damon used in his interviews (Damon, 2008):
  - Do you have any long-term goals?
  - What does it mean to have a good life?
  - What does it mean to be a good person?
  - If you were looking back on your life now, how would you like to be remembered?

Finally, consider: Are your everyday goals leading to the fulfillment of your long-term dream? How are you working in your everyday behavior to achieve your grander purposes?

**MASLOW**

- **Maslow's Theory of Self-Actualization** Assign *Handout: Maslow's Theory of Self-Actualization.*
- **Intrinsic and Extrinsic Motivation** Discuss with the class the differences between intrinsic and extrinsic motivation. Have the students write down examples from their own life when they did something for intrinsic motivation and something else for extrinsic motivation. Break the class into groups, and have them discuss their examples.

**INCENTIVE THEORIES** Assign *Handout: Drive Versus Incentive Motivations in Advertising.*

# Discussion Questions

**MOTIVATION THEORY** Give examples of how various cultures view the motivation for going to college or going into the workforce.

**INTRINSIC AND EXTRINSIC MOTIVATION** Ask students the following questions:

- Name three sources of intrinsic motivation in your life.
- Name three sources of extrinsic motivation in your life.
- Do you agree that your creativity suffers if extrinsic rewards are provided for conducting activities that are intrinsically rewarding to you?

Ask students what motivates them. Is it food? (It usually is!) Understanding? Love? Ask them what motivates them *most*. If they are having a hard time getting started, talk to them about how clubs and organizations draw new members—they have events that advertise free food! How do landlords draw in new tenants? They offer cuts in rent or a month free. How do commercials get you to buy products? They promise physical attraction and love. In other words, they appeal to our basic needs.

**INTRINSIC AND EXTRINSIC MOTIVATION** Ask students what motivates them to perform well in school. It may be that they are not motivated to perform well in school, so you may want to have another example, such as what motivates them to do well at work. Get students to think about these motivators. This can be a nice lead-in to intrinsic and extrinsic motivation.

**INCENTIVE THEORY** To illustrate incentive theory, show TV or print advertisements that attempt to create a need in the viewer or reader for food, entertainment, or luxury items (going through the daily newspaper can provide ample examples, such as ads for jewelry, vacations, video games, digital equipment, or DVDs). Have students pay attention to the pop-up ads on social media sites and when browsing search engines. Ask students how advertisers manipulate our desires to sell their products (this can be done in conjunction with the student assignment on *Handout: Drive versus Incentive Motivations in Advertising*.

# Suggested Media

- *The Puzzle of Motivation,* TED Talks: www.ted.com/talks/dan_pink_on_motivation.html. Career analyst Dan Pink examines the puzzle of motivation, starting with a fact that social scientists know but most managers don't: Traditional rewards aren't always as effective as we think. Listen for illuminating stories—and, maybe, a way forward.
- *Napoleon Dynamite:* In the scene "I Want That," Napoleon's uncle uses a model sailboat as an incentive when he sells plastic dishware. This is an excellent example to show in class and probably will be for a number of years.

## AP Test Practice

### Section I: Multiple Choice

1. **D** *(Skill 1.B, Learning Target 7.A)*

2. **E** *(Skill 1.B, Learning Target 7.B)*

3. **B** *(Skill 1.A, Learning Target 7.E)*

### Section II: Free Response

Instinct theory suggests that people are preprogrammed with sets of behaviors essential to their survival. Instinct theory might say an individual works to gather resources, which is essential for their survival.

Arousal theory suggests that people try to maintain a steady level of stimulation and activity. Arousal theory might say an individual works to maintain a steady level of stimulation so they don't get bored.

Incentive theory suggests that people desire to attain external rewards. Incentive theory might say an individual works to earn the external reward of money. Intrinsic theory suggests that individuals participate in an activity for enjoyment rather than a concrete reward. Intrinsic theory might say an individual works for the love of the job.

# Module 30: Human Needs and Motivation: Eat, Drink, and Be Daring

## AP Module Summary

Module 30 allows for the introduction of eating disorders and how one is motivated to develop one. Included in this module is the specific motivational concept of achievement motivation. When introducing this concept you may want to ask students what drives them? Is their drive to be successful a reflection of their culture? What happens once they achieve whatever it is they are seeking to find success at doing?

**THE MOTIVATION BEHIND HUNGER AND EATING** *Obesity* is body weight that is more than 20 percent above the average weight for a person of a particular height. The most widely used measure of obesity is *body mass index (BMI)*, which is based on a ratio of weight to height. People with a BMI greater than 30 are considered obese, whereas those with a BMI between 25 and 30 are overweight. Projections are that, by 2030, 50% of U.S. residents may be obese. (Source: www.hsph.harvard.edu/obesity-prevention-source/obesity-trends/)

### BIOLOGICAL FACTORS IN THE REGULATION OF HUNGER (SEE FIGURE 2)

One important factor is change in the chemical composition of the blood. Changes in levels of:

- *Glucose*—a kind of sugar, regulates feelings of hunger.
- *Insulin*—a hormone, leads the body to store excess sugar in the blood as fats and carbohydrates.
- *Ghrelin*—a hormone communicates to the brain feelings of hunger. The production of ghrelin increases according to meal schedules as well as the sight or smell of food producing the feeling that tells us we are hungry and should eat.
- *Leptin*—obese individuals have a higher level of the hormone which appears to be designed, from an evolutionary standpoint it is to "protect" the body against weight loss, and is one biological explanation for obesity.

The brain's hypothalamus monitors glucose levels. Increasing evidence suggests that the hypothalamus carries the primary responsibility for monitoring food intake. Injury to the hypothalamus has radical consequences for eating behavior, depending on the site of the injury.

Although the important role the hypothalamus plays in regulating food intake is clear, the exact way this organ operates is still unclear. One hypothesis suggests that injury to the hypothalamus affects the *weight set point*, or the particular level of weight that the body strives to maintain, which in turn regulates food intake.

People seem destined, through heredity, to have a particular *metabolism*, the rate at which food is converted to energy and expended by the body.

**EATING DISORDERS** Weight-related disorders include:

- *Anorexia nervosa* - People may refuse to eat while denying that their behavior and appearance—which can become skeleton-like—are unusual. Anorexia nervosa mainly afflicts girls and women between the ages of 12 and 40, although both men and women of any age may develop it.
- *Bulimia* - Bulimia is a disorder in which a person binges on large quantities of food, followed by efforts to purge the food through vomiting or other means.

With regard to anorexia nervosa and bulimia, some researchers suspect a biological cause such as a chemical imbalance in the hypothalamus or pituitary gland, perhaps brought on by genetic factors. Furthermore, brain scans of people with eating disorders show that they process information about food differently from healthy individuals (see "Neuroscience in Your Life: When Regulation of Eating Behavior Goes Wrong"). Others believe that the cause has roots in society's valuation of slenderness and the parallel notion that obesity is undesirable. Finally, some psychologists suggest that the disorders result from overly demanding parents or other family problems. These disorders most likely stem from both biological and social causes, and successful treatment probably encompasses several strategies, including therapy and dietary changes.

**THE NEED FOR ACHIEVEMENT: STRIVING FOR SUCCESS** The need for achievement is a stable, learned characteristic in which a person obtains satisfaction by striving for and achieving challenging goals. People with a high need for achievement seek out situations in which they can compete against some objective standard—such as grades, money, or winning a game—and prove themselves successful. People high in achievement motivation generally choose tasks that are of intermediate difficulty. In contrast, people with low achievement motivation tend to be motivated primarily by a desire to avoid failure.

This would be a good time to introduce students to the concept of achievement motivation.

**MEASURING ACHIEVEMENT MOTIVATION** The instrument used most frequently for measuring a person's need for achievement is the Thematic Apperception Test (TAT). In the TAT, an examiner shows a series of ambiguous pictures (see **Figure 4**). The examiner tells participants to write a story that describes what is happening, who the people are, what led to the situation, what the people are thinking or wanting, and what will happen next. Researchers then use a standard scoring system to determine the amount of achievement imagery in people's stories.

**THE NEED FOR AFFILIATION: STRIVING FOR FRIENDSHIP** *Need for affiliation* is an interest in establishing and maintaining relationships with other people. People who have higher affiliation needs are particularly sensitive to relationships with others.

**THE NEED FOR POWER: STRIVING FOR IMPACT ON OTHERS** *Need for power* is a tendency to seek impact, control, or influence over others and to be seen as a powerful individual. People with strong needs for power are more apt to belong to organizations and seek political office than are those low in the need for power.

## AP Key Terms

achievement motivation

anorexia nervosa

bulimia

metabolism

need for achievement

need for affiliation

need for power

obesity

weight set point

## Class Discussion Ideas

**BIOPSYCHOSOCIAL CAUSES OF EATING DISORDERS** Present eating disorders in terms of a biopsychosocial model to indicate that there are interactions among the possible causes in the biological (genetic, biochemical), psychological (body image disturbances), and social (media) domains.

**PHYSICAL ACTIVITY IN THE UNITED STATES** Emphasize the importance of physical fitness. The current U.S. guidelines for physical activity can be found here: www.health.gov/paguidelines/. Have students discuss their own experiences in relation to the guidelines.

**HUNGER**

- **Blood Chemistry** Ask the students to explain how glucose, insulin, and leptin all play a role in hunger. Are they all interconnected, and if so, how?
- **Biology of Hunger** Hunger involves internal biological processes interacting with external, environmental ones. Ask students about their dining experiences with their families at home or at a restaurant. Chances are, they want vast quantities of food. Not long after dinner, when they may be still very full, they look in the refrigerator to see if the "food fairy" has delivered anything new. Why does this happen? It happens because that is their social, environmental cue. They finish dinner, then look in the refrigerator.

## Activities

**FAVORITE FOODS** Ask students to list their favorite foods. When did they first begin to eat these foods? How did these foods become their favorite foods? When do they typically eat their favorite foods? Do these foods evoke any memories?

**ANOREXIA NERVOSA** Show the movie *Killing Me Softly* to the class, and then discuss the various struggles of anorexics. Break the class into groups and have them discuss why some people become anorexic and others do not. Have them also discuss whether they believe the media and fashion industries are partly responsible for the diet problems that young girls encounter today. Have each group make and present an outline of their key discussion points.

**TAT RATINGS** Show students the TAT picture in the text (**Figure 4**) and instruct them to write a story in which they state what is happening and what the people involved are feeling and thinking. Then show this list of Murray's 15 needs and their definitions. Have students count the number of times they referred to one of these needs.

| Abasement | To surrender and submit to others, accept blame and punishment. To enjoy pain and misfortune. |
|---|---|
| Achievement | To accomplish difficult tasks, overcoming obstacles, and becoming expert. |
| Affiliation | To be close and loyal to another person, pleasing them and winning their friendship and attention. |
| Aggression | To forcefully overcome an opponent, controlling, taking revenge, or punishing them. |
| Autonomy | To break free from constraints, resisting coercion and dominating authority. To be irresponsible and independent. |
| Counteraction | To make up for failure by trying again, seeking pridefully to overcome obstacles. |
| Defendance | To defend oneself against attack or blame, hiding any failure of the self. |
| Deference | To admire a superior person, praising them and yielding to them and following their rules. |
| Dominance | To control one's environment, controlling other people through command or subtle persuasion. |
| Exhibition | To impress others through one's actions and words, even if these are shocking. |
| Harm avoidance | To escape or avoid pain, injury, and death. |
| Infavoidance | To avoid being humiliated or embarrassed. |
| Nurturance | To help the helpless, feeding them and keeping them from danger. |
| Order | To make things clean, neat, and tidy. |

| Play | To have fun, laugh, and relax, enjoying oneself. |
|------|------------------------------------------------|
| Rejection | To separate oneself from a negatively viewed object or person, excluding or abandoning it. |
| Sentience | To seek out and enjoy sensual experiences. |
| Sex | To form relationships that lead to sexual intercourse. |
| Succorance | To have one's needs satisfied by someone or something. Includes being loved, nursed, helped, forgiven, and consoled. |
| Understanding | To be curious, ask questions, and find answers. |

**MEDIA PROJECT** In groups, have students search for pictures, articles, blogs, or other media in newspapers, magazines, or online that relate to body image or that advertise diet plans or exercise routines. Then, have the groups present their findings to the class and write a paper summarizing their conclusions. What does the media portray as "sexy," "healthy," or "motivating"? How does culture play a role in the media portrayal of eating, exercise, and appearance?

## Discussion Questions

**CULTURAL CONTRIBUTIONS TO EATING DISORDERS** Have students complete *Handout: Cultural Contributions to Eating Disorders,* which asks students to examine cultural contributions to eating disorders.

**SELF-RATINGS OF NEEDS** Have students complete *Handout: Self-Ratings of Needs.* The key is shown at the bottom of the handout.

## Suggested Media

- *Anorexia's Living Face:* www.youtube.com/watch?v=aTljRxT_Y9g.
- *Center for Eating Disorders at Sheppard Pratt Hospital:* www.eatingdisorder.org/. This site has links for more information on eating disorders.
- *Dying to Be Thin.* Carle Medical Communications, 1989, 25:00. This video gives real-life stories about people recovering from bulimia nervosa and anorexia nervosa.
- *Perfect Illusions.* PBS: www.pbs.org/perfectillusions/aboutshow/watchvideo.html. This video does an excellent job of dealing with the relationship of anorexia nervosa and bulimia to issues within the family.

## Applying Psychology in the 21st Century: A Losing Battle for the Biggest Losers

Answer Suggestions

- Resting metabolism decreased with weight loss and it didn't rise over time. Even though you remain physically active, your body burns far fewer calories than before. Maintaining the new weight was impossible without a restrictive diet.
- There is no easy route to lose weight. Keep track of what you eat and exercise.

## AP Test Practice

### Section I: Multiple Choice

1. **E** *(Skill 1.A, Learning Target 7.A)*

2. **A** *(Skill 1.B, Learning Target 7.C)*

3. **E** *(Skill 1.A, Learning Target 7.C)*

### Section II: Free Response

**A.** Drive-reduction theory suggests that a lack of some basic biological need produces a drive to push an organism to satisfy that need. Eating happens because your body needs food, making you hungry and motivated to eat.

Drive-reduction theory suggests that a lack of some basic biological need produces a drive to push an organism to satisfy that need. Eating happens because your body needs food, making you hungry and motivated to eat.

Arousal theory suggests that people try to maintain a steady level of stimulation and activity. Eating maintains a steady level of stimulation so you don't get bored.

Maslow's hierarchy of needs suggests that needs must come in order. Eating fulfills the most basic physiological need.

**B.** A biological approach looks at the body for causes of behavior. Hunger could relate to blood chemistry or brain parts. Also, genetic factors could determine weight set-point or metabolism.

A social approach looks to the environment for causes of behavior. Hunger could relate to external cues, such as mealtimes, cultural food preferences, and other learned habits.

# Module 31: Understanding Emotional Experiences

## AP Module Summary

Much like in Module 29 where many theories of motivation are introduced, Module 31 does the same with emotion. This module explains why we feel the way we do; therefore, understanding the different theories can help students' understanding. Specific theories have been added and must be included in the study of emotion. The Course Exam and Description Guide now include the evolutionary theory (primary emotions), Richard Lazarus's appraisal theory, Joseph LeDoux's theory, Paul Ekman's research on cross-cultural displays of emotion, and the facial feedback hypothesis.

- *Emotions* are feelings that generally have both physiological and cognitive elements and that influence behavior.

**DETERMINING THE RANGE OF EMOTIONS: LABELING OUR FEELINGS** If we were to list the words in the English language that have been used to describe emotions, we would end up with at least 500 examples. One challenge for psychologists has been to sort through this list to identify the most important, fundamental emotions. Theorists have hotly contested the issue of cataloging emotions and have come up with different lists, depending on how they define the concept of emotion. In fact, some reject the question entirely, saying that no set of emotions should be singled out as most basic and that emotions are best understood by breaking them down into their component parts. Other researchers argue for looking at emotions in terms of a hierarchy, dividing them into positive and negative categories and then organizing them into increasingly narrower subcategories (see **Figure 1**). One difficulty in defining a basic set of emotions is that substantial differences exist in descriptions of emotions among various cultures.

**THE ROOTS OF EMOTIONS** Consider the experience of fear. The most likely reactions, which are associated with activation of the autonomic nervous system, include an increase in your rate of breathing, an acceleration of your heart rate, a widening of your pupils (to increase visual sensitivity), and a dryness in your mouth as the functioning of your salivary glands and, in fact, your entire digestive system ceases. At the same time, though, your sweat glands probably will increase their activity because increased sweating will help you rid yourself of the excess heat developed by any emergency activity in which you engage. Some theorists suggest that specific bodily reactions cause us to experience a particular emotion—we experience fear, for instance, because the heart is pounding and we are breathing deeply. In contrast, other theorists suggest that the physiological reaction results from the experience of an emotion. In this view, we experience fear and, as a result, the heart pounds and our breathing deepens.

This may be a good place to mention the evolutionary theories (primary emotions).

**THE JAMES-LANGE THEORY: DO GUT REACTIONS EQUAL EMOTIONS?** To William James and Carl Lange, who were among the first researchers to explore the nature of emotions, emotional experience is, very simply, a reaction to instinctive bodily events that occur as a response to some situation or event in the environment. James and Lange suggested that for every major emotion there is an accompanying physiological or "gut" reaction of internal organs—called a visceral experience. It is this specific pattern of visceral response that leads us to label the emotional experience. They proposed that we experience emotions as a result of physiological changes that produce specific sensations. The brain interprets these sensations as specific kinds of emotional experiences. This view has come to be called the *James-Lange theory of emotion* (see **Figure 2**).

**THE CANNON-BARD THEORY: PHYSIOLOGICAL REACTIONS AS THE RESULT OF EMOTIONS**  In response to the difficulties inherent in the James-Lange theory, Walter Cannon and later Philip Bard, suggested an alternative view (see **Figure 2**). The *Cannon-Bard theory of emotion* assumes that both physiological arousal and the emotional experience are produced simultaneously by the same nerve stimulus, which Cannon and Bard suggested emanates from the thalamus in the brain. Hence, it is not necessary for different emotions to have unique physiological patterns associated with them—as long as the message sent to the cerebral cortex differs according to the specific emotion.

**THE SCHACHTER-SINGER THEORY: EMOTIONS AS LABELS**  The *Schachter-Singer Theory* states that emotions are determined jointly by a relatively nonspecific kind of physiological arousal *and* the labeling of that arousal on the basis of cues from the environment (see **Figure 2**).

**CONTEMPORARY PERSPECTIVES ON THE NEUROSCIENCE OF EMOTIONS**  Advances in the measurement of the nervous system and other parts of the body have allowed researchers to examine more closely the biological responses involved in individual emotions. As a result, evidence is growing that specific patterns of biological arousal are associated with specific emotions. In addition, new research shows that the *amygdala*, in the brain's temporal lobe, plays an important role in the experience of emotions. Because neural pathways connect the amygdala, the visual cortex, and the hippocampus, some scientists speculate that emotion-related stimuli can be processed and responded to almost instantaneously.

This would be a great time to introduce the work of Richard Lazarus and Joseph LeDoux.

**MAKING SENSE OF THE MULTIPLE PERSPECTIVES ON EMOTION**  As new approaches to emotion continue to develop, it is reasonable to ask why so many theories of emotion exist and, perhaps more importantly, which one provides the most complete explanation. Emotions are such complex phenomena, encompassing both biological and cognitive aspects, that no single theory has been able to explain fully all the facets of emotional experience. Furthermore, contradictory evidence of one sort or another challenges each approach, and therefore no theory has proved invariably accurate in its predictions.

**EXPLORING DIVERSITY: DO PEOPLE IN ALL CULTURES EXPRESS EMOTION SIMILARLY?**
Why do people across cultures express emotions similarly? A hypothesis known as the *facial-affect program* gives one explanation. The facial-affect program—which is assumed to be universally present at birth—is analogous to a computer program that is turned on when a particular emotion is experienced. When set in motion, the "program" activates a set of nerve impulses that make the face display an appropriate expression.

The importance of facial expressions is illustrated by an intriguing notion known as the *facial-feedback hypothesis*. According to this hypothesis, facial expressions not only reflect emotional experience, but they also help determine how people experience and label emotions.

This would be a great time to introduce the research of Paul Ekman on cross-cultural displays of emotion.

## AP| Key Terms

Cannon-Bard theory of emotion

emotions

evolutionary theories (primary emotions)

facial-affect program

facial-feedback hypothesis

James-Lange theory of emotion

Schachter-Singer theory of emotion

## AP| Key People

William James

Stanley Schachter

Richard Lazarus

Joseph LeDoux

Paul Ekman

## Class Discussion Ideas

**JAMES-LANGE THEORY** Starting with James, provide context for his theory that emotion follows a physiological response by reading the following quote, which captures the theory very well:

My theory . . . is that the bodily changes follow directly the perception of the exciting fact, and that our feeling of the same changes as they occur IS the emotion. Common sense says we lose our fortune, are sorry and weep; we meet a bear, are frightened and run; we are insulted by a rival, are angry and strike. The hypothesis here to be defended says that this order of sequence is incorrect, that the one mental state is not immediately induced by the other, that the bodily manifestations must first be interposed between, and that the more rational statement is that we feel sorry because we cry, angry because we strike, and afraid because we tremble.

For more information, read Ellsworth, P. C. (1994). William James and emotion: Is a century of fame worth a century of misunderstanding? *Psychological Review, 101,* 222–229.

**IMPORTANCE OF THEORIES OF EMOTIONS** Theories exist with regard to emotions because, as with motivation, there are many possible causes.

- Highlight the pros and cons of the main theories in your lecture.
- Be sure to emphasize the key differences between the theories—this is often a difficult topic for students.
- Show students the following image: http://graphics8.nytimes.com/images/blogs/morris/posts/27morris_ekman_cd.jpg and ask them which person is showing a Duchenne smile.
- Show students the following site: www.jaschahoffman.com/ekmanLight.jpg. The images are of the South Fore people of New Guinea. Ask them to identify the emotions in each face.
- You may want to place students in groups. Have students discuss what is attractive in today's society versus in the 1920s, 1960s, and 1980s. What is similar? What is different? If students have Internet access, ask them to provide some images from each era.

**HELPFUL HINTS FOR STUDENTS** Use these hints to help students keep the theories straight:

James-Lange: Lange hits James and makes him angry (i.e., physiological changes precede emotions).

Cannon-Bard: A cannon goes off in your thalamus.

Schachter-Singer: A singer makes you happy.

# Activities

**HUMOR IN PSYCHOLOGICAL WELL-BEING** Discuss the role of humor in promoting psychological well-being. Can laughter improve the body's immune functioning and reactions to stressful events, as is sometimes claimed? If so, why? And if not, why not? If you feel comfortable with this, tell a few good psychology jokes. Ask the class how they feel about the role of laughter in their lives.

Here are some psychology and psychologist jokes: www.workjoke.com/projoke30.htm.

## THEORIES OF EMOTION

- **Theories of Emotion** After discussing the various theories of emotion in class, break the class into three groups. Assign each group one of the theories and have them do an Internet search for studies on these theories. Each group should find at least two studies on their assigned theory. Next, have them present to the class, describing the studies that were conducted on the theory they were assigned. This activity will give the students more indepth knowledge of the theories, and each group will learn from the other groups about the other two theories.
- **Emotional Intelligence** Some psychologists believe that the ability to identify and regulate one's emotions is a kind of intelligence. Emotionally intelligent people are also thought to be better at reading the emotional expressions of others. Have students do an online search for *emotional intelligence tests* and take some online quizzes or try the one at www.testyourself. psychtests.com/testid/3038. Ask them: Do you think you are emotionally intelligent? Does your performance on the test seem to reflect your actual experience? What is your opinion of the test you tried? Is there information on the site about its validity and reliability?

## FACIAL EXPRESSIONS

- **Facial Expressions:** Create a slide show of a variety of faces with different expressions. For each face, have students guess the emotion being expressed. Do students generally agree? Disagree? Use this to encourage discussion about expressing and understanding emotions.
- **Facial Feedback:** Break the students into pairs. Give a list of facial expressions to one of the students in each pair. Ask the students with the list to make the facial expression listed to show their partners. The partner should then write down what emotion they think the other student is feeling. Afterward, ask students to discuss their answers to see if they got them correct. Have the pairs share and compare their results in a whole-class discussion.
  - A fun spin to the above activity is to show students the clip from Seinfeld. In season 3, episode 1: "The Alternate Side" the line "these pretzels are making me thirsty!" is repeated several times. Have students recite the same line using Carol Izard and Paul Ekman's 10 basic emotions.
- **Facial Feedback:** Ask half of the class to suck on their pencil or pen for 1 minute. Ask the other half to bite on their pencil or pen (held horizontally) for 1 minute. After the minute has passed, ask them to indicate their mood on a scale of 1 (highly depressed) to 10 (ecstatic). Discuss the difference.
- **Emoticon Challenge:** Team up your students to see who can identify the emotions that emoticons are trying to represent. To prepare ahead, go to: www.sharpened.net/glossary/ emoticons.php and pick out some of your favorites to show the students. At the end of this activity, ask students if someone from a different country would have the same answers as they did. Also, what is the benefit of having these emoticons? And, can students think of a time when they used one of these icons and someone misunderstood or misinterpreted what they wrote?

# Discussion Questions

**ROLE OF EMOTIONS IN DAILY LIFE** Ask students if they believe that there are gender differences in emotion. Do men and women feel differently, or do they just demonstrate their emotions differently? Ask students to explain and provide examples. You might also want to point out how single examples sometimes fall into stereotypical categories.

- Why are emotions important in our daily lives?
- Do you feel that fear is an unpleasant emotion? Knowing that most people feel fear as an unpleasant emotion, how can fear be seen in a positive manner?
- What would be the benefits of learning to control our emotions?
- How does a person's expression of emotions influence what you think about that person? Why?

**HAPPINESS** Ask students what would make them happy. Winning the lottery? Finding true love? Getting straight As? Talk to them about the predictors of happiness.

**EMOTIONAL AROUSAL AND HORROR MOVIES** Show students a scene from a frightening movie (preferably not too gory). Ask them how they feel after watching the scene. What emotions are they experiencing? How much of their feelings can be attributed to physiological arousal and how much to their cognitive labeling of the situation?

**LIE DETECTORS AND NONVERBAL BEHAVIORS** What is your opinion about lie detectors? Do you think they can be fooled?

Give an example of a misunderstanding you have had with someone else based on misinterpreting someone's nonverbal behavior.

Are there any conditions that you feel justify employers giving employees a polygraph test?

To what extent are nonverbal behaviors culturally determined or are there universal behaviors in the way we express ourselves?

- **Measuring Arousal** Have the students do an Internet search on the pros and cons of using the polygraph test to determine if suspects are lying. Have them summarize the arguments for and against this practice. Ask them to give examples of confounding variables in polygraphy.

# Suggested Media

- *All About Happiness.* Insight Media, 2008, 39:00. This ABC News program explores happiness.
- *Achievement anxiety test:* http://www.psych.uncc.edu/pagoolka/TestAnxiety-intro.html. This test is a 19-item questionnaire consisting of a facilitating anxiety scale, which measures the degree to which test anxiety improves student performance, and a debilitating anxiety scale, which measures the interference effect of test anxiety.
- *Dan Goleman on emotional intelligence and social intelligence:* http://www.youtube.com/watch?v=nZskNGdP_zM&feature=related.
- *Emotional Brain: An Introduction to Affective Neuroscience.* Films for the Humanities and Sciences, 2010, 33:00. In this program, animations and fMRI images introduce students to the subcortical emotional circuits in the brain and chemical processes that produce emotional responses and contribute to decision making and mental health.
- *How Happy Are You?* http://www.youtube.com/watch?v=qv6xYmh4Y-w.
- *Paul Ekman:* http://www.paulekman.com/. Ekman has conducted a number of famous studies on facial expression of emotion. This site contains a summary of his studies and descriptions of his most recent research.

- *Rethinking Happiness.* (part of the series *This Emotional Life*). PBS, 2009, 60:00. This program explores what makes people happy and how to predict happiness. It also looks at resilience.
- *Sensation seeking:* http://www.coasterphotos.com/Videos/coastervideos.htm. Introduce the concept of sensation seeking by talking about extreme roller coasters.
- *Truth or lie:* http://www.truthorlie.com/. This home page for the Truth or Lie Polygraph Examination Agency offers frames on short articles about polygraph issues.
- *When Tempers Flare: A Guide to Understanding and Managing Anger.* Insight Media, 2004, 30:00. Anger management is discussed in this video.

## **AP** Student Edition Answer Key

## Neuroscience in Your Life: Emotion and the Brain
Answer Suggestions

- Universal emotions provide evidence for nature because they are innate biological reactions that help an individual survive. Basic emotions are expressed universally regardless of where individuals have been raised or their learning experiences.
- Reading emotions with brain scanning technology gets us one step closer to understanding how emotions work. Perhaps the technology could be used as a clinical tool to assist with therapy.

## AP Test Practice

### Section I: Multiple Choice
1. **C** *(Skill 1.C, Learning Target 7.F)*
2. **A** *(Skill 1.B, Learning Target 7.F)*
3. **C** *(Skill 1.A, Learning Target 7.G)*

### Section II: Free Response
**A.**

The Schachter-Singer theory suggests emotions are determined jointly by physiological arousal and its cognitive label, based on environmental cues. In this experiment, the participants experienced physical arousal from the epinephrine and then cognitively labeled their emotion based on the confederate in their room.

The independent variable is the variable being manipulated. In this experiment, the independent variable is the type of confederate the participant was exposed to. A confederate is an actor employed by a researcher who participates in an experiment, pretending to be a participant. In this experiment, the two confederates were employed by the experimenter to help influence real participants' emotions.

Deception is lying to participants and is sometimes necessary to prevent participants from being influenced by what they think a study's true purpose is. In this experiment, researchers used deception when they told participants they were receiving an injection of vitamin when it was really epinephrine.

Debriefing is an ethical consideration in which after an experiment is completed, participants receive an explanation of the study and procedures that were involved. In this experiment, researchers should debrief participants after the experiment and tell them about its purpose and that deception about a vitamin shot was used.

**B.**

The James-Lange theory suggests that an environmental event activates a visceral change that is then interpreted by the brain as an emotional response. A disadvantage of this theory is that visceral changes must occur rapidly for this theory to be true, yet certain kinds of visceral changes occur slowly. Also, physiological arousal does not always produce emotional responses, such as when jogging. Lastly, it is difficult to believe that the range of emotions we experience are the result of unique visceral changes.

The Cannon-Bard theory contends that both physiological arousal and an emotional experience are produced simultaneously and that the visceral experience does not necessarily differ among differing emotions. A disadvantage of this theory is that researchers now know that the hypothalamus and limbic system play a role in emotional experiences, not the thalamus. Also, the simultaneous occurrence of the physiological and emotional responses has yet to be demonstrated conclusively, allowing room for other theories of emotion.

# CHAPTER 11

# Sexuality and Gender

## **AP** Introduction

The topic of sexuality is of natural interest and concern to most students, so drawing students into any of the topics within this unit will not be a great challenge. The topic, therefore, provides an excellent opportunity to take an integrative approach in which biological, psychological, and social themes are brought together. The information in this unit can help them make decisions that could have a lasting impact in their lives.

## **AP** Essential Questions

- How do we perceive and understand ourselves?
- What motivates us to think and act the way we do?

## Module 32: Gender and Sex

**AP Learning Targets:**

- Describe how sex and gender influence socialization and other aspects of development.
- Articulate the impact of social and cultural categories on self-concept and relations with others.
- Describe processes that contribute to differential treatment of group members.

**Pacing:**

1 Block or 2 Traditional Class periods

## Module 33: Understanding Human Sexual Response: The Facts of Life

**AP Learning Targets:**

- Describe classic research findings in specific motivations.
- Discuss the biological underpinnings of motivation, including needs, drives, and homeostasis.

## Module 34: The Diversity of Sexual Behavior

**AP Learning Targets:**

- Identify contributions of key researchers in the psychological field of motivation and emotion.

**Pacing:**

1/2 Block or 1 Traditional Class period

# Module 32: Gender and Sex

## AP Module Summary

Module 32 has students looking at gender and the roles which society places upon each. This specific module is closely linked to Unit 6: Developmental Psychology in the new Course and Exam Description Guide released by the College Board. This is not new and depending on the structure of your course you may review this topic when in the Social Psychology unit.

- *Gender* is the perception of being male or female. Although there is a good deal of overlap (and sometimes confusion) between the concepts of sex and gender, they are not the same: *sex* typically refers to sexual anatomy and sexual behavior, whereas *gender* refers to one's sense of being a male or female. Sex is biological; gender is psychological and social.

**GENDER ROLES: SOCIETY'S EXPECTATIONS FOR WOMEN AND MEN** *Gender roles* are the set of expectations, defined by a particular society, that indicate what is appropriate behavior for men and women.

Gender roles also may produce *stereotyping*, judgments about individual members of a group on the basis of their membership in that group (see **Figure 1**). Stereotypes put pressure on people to fulfill the stereotypes, thus making gender equality a significant challenge throughout the world (see **Figure 2**).

**GENDER DIFFERENCES: MORE SIMILAR THAN DISSIMILAR** Not surprisingly, gender stereotyping, combined with other factors, results in actual behavior differences between men and women. Before we consider the nature of gender differences, however, it is important to keep in mind that men and women are more similar to one another in most respects than they are different.

**PERSONALITY FACTORS** One of the most pronounced differences between men and women lies in their degree of aggressive behavior. Furthermore, compared with men, women experience greater anxiety and guilt about their aggressiveness and are more concerned about its effects on their victims. Men generally have higher self-esteem than women do, although the difference is not large. Men and women differ in how positively they view their own abilities and how they estimate the probability of their future success. In general, women evaluate themselves more harshly than men (see **Figure 5**). The content of men's and women's speech also differs. For example, women's speech patterns lead others to view them as more tentative and less assertive. Women's and men's nonverbal behavior differs as well in several significant respects.

**COGNITIVE ABILITIES** No general differences exist between men and women in overall IQ scores, learning, memory, problem solving, and concept-formation tasks. A few differences in more specific cognitive areas have been identified, although other research has called into question the true nature of those differences—and even their existence.

**SOURCES OF GENDER DIFFERENCES: WHERE BIOLOGY AND SOCIETY MEET** Given the indisputable fact that sex is a biological variable, it would seem reasonable to look at factors involving biological differences between men and women. It is also true that people are treated differently on the basis of their sex from the time they are born. Consequently, we must take into account both biological and social factors when we try to understand the source of gender differences.

**BIOLOGICAL AND EVOLUTIONARY FACTORS** It is possible that exposure to particular hormones prior to birth affects brain development, making children favor toys that involve certain kinds of skills, such as those related to spatial abilities. For instance, in one study, scientists studied a group of girls whose mothers had accidentally taken drugs containing high levels of androgen, a male hormone, prior to their birth. Girls exposed to the androgens were more likely to play with toys that boys stereotypically prefer (such as cars) and less likely to play with toys girls stereotypically prefer (such as dolls).

Similarly, some evidence suggests that women perform better on tasks involving verbal skill and muscular coordination during periods when their production of the female sex hormone estrogen is relatively high. In contrast, they perform better on tasks involving spatial relationships when the estrogen level is relatively low.

Some psychologists argue that evolutionary forces lead to certain differences between men's and women's behavior. For example, David Buss and colleagues point to differences in the nature of jealousy between men and women. Men are more jealous in cases of sexual infidelity than in cases of emotional infidelity; women are more jealous in cases of emotional infidelity than in cases of sexual infidelity. According to Buss's controversial explanation, the root cause for the differences in jealousy lies in the evolutionary implications of sexual versus emotional infidelity for men and women. He argues that for males, sexual infidelity represents a threat to their ability to ensure that their children are actually their own. In contrast, females have no doubt that a child they carry through pregnancy is their own. However, their major concern is ensuring the male's protection and support during child rearing. Thus, to females, maintaining males' emotional attachment is crucial. Psychologists relying on the evolutionary approach also argue that similarities in the division of labor between men and women across different cultures suggest that sex differences are due to evolutionary factors. However, many critics question the assumptions of the evolutionary approach.

Psychologists Alice Eagly and Wendy Wood criticize evolutionary explanations for gender differences on different grounds. In their biosocial explanation of gender differences, they argue that one important source of gender differences is the difference in the physical capabilities of men and women.

The extent to which biological and evolutionary factors may underlie gender differences is an unanswered and highly controversial question. One thing is clear, however: Biological factors and evolutionary factors alone do not explain the complete range of differences between male and female behavior. To fully understand the source of gender differences, we also must consider the social environment.

**THE SOCIAL ENVIRONMENT** From the moment of birth, with blue blankets for boys and pink ones for girls, most parents and other adults provide environments that differ in important respects according to gender. Parents interact with their children differently, depending on their sex. For example, fathers play more roughly with their infant sons than with their infant daughters. Such differences in behavior (and there are many more) produce different socialization experiences for men and women. *Socialization* is the process by which an individual learns the rules and norms of appropriate behavior. It is not just parents, of course, who provide socialization experiences for children. Society as a whole communicates clear messages to children as they are growing up. Children's reading books traditionally have portrayed girls in stereotypically nurturing roles, whereas boys have been given more physical and action-oriented roles. Television, too, acts as a particularly influential source of socialization. Our educational system also treats boys and girls differently. For example, in elementary school, boys are five times more likely than girls to receive attention from classroom teachers. Socialization produces a *gender schema,* a mental framework that organizes and guides a child's understanding of information relevant to gender. On the basis of their schemas for appropriate and inappropriate behavior for males and females, children begin to behave in ways that reflect society's gender roles.

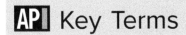 Key Terms

**gender**

**gender roles**

**gender schema**

**sexism**

**stereotyping**

# Class Discussion Ideas

**GENDER DIFFERENCES** The basic introduction to this topic involves defining the terms *sex, gender, sex role,* and *gender role.* Summarize the findings on gender differences in personality and cognitive abilities. Ask students to discuss the extent to which their observations in the text on these gender differences correspond to their own experiences.

**GENDER BIAS IN TOYS AND ADVERTISING** Use the results of the student assignments in class as a basis for discussing gender differences in toys and in advertising.

**GENDER DIFFERENCES IN EMPLOYMENT** Present data on gender differences in salary levels from the Bureau of Labor Statistics website: www.bls.gov/cps/.

# Activities

**LEARNING GENDER ROLES: BOY/GIRL GENDER SOCIALIZATION EXERCISE** This activity is a self-reflective opportunity as participants write and share short reflections about how their gender identities were informed through childhood messages about what it meant to be a boy or a girl. This activity can be used to introduce a discussion on gender socialization and oppression. Ask participants to write a short, one- to two-page reflective piece on the childhood memories and experiences that helped shape their gender identities and expressions. Ask them to address what messages they received as children about what it meant to be a boy or a girl. Also, ask them to discuss who sent those messages (parents, teachers, coaches, other kids, etc.).

**WHY I CHOOSE AND YOU CHOOSE DIFFERENT THINGS** Use *Handout: Choosy Genders*. This activity will help students understand how the evolutionary approach to gender development and mate selection currently impacts our behaviors, thoughts, and motivations. For each question, circle one answer. These situations represent choices that at some point we might have to make or have to think about making.

**A THEORETICAL DEBATE** In class, group students together, and assign each group one of the theories of gender development discussed in the text. Ask each group to identify why their theory is the "correct" theory of gender development and provide evidence of their position. Then, ask the groups to engage in a healthy debate about the applications of such theories. Finalize the discussion with a summary of an inclusive approach to gender and identity development.

**GENDER-AWARENESS DIARY** Keep a gender-awareness diary for a day. Try to become aware of every time you have an experience in which your gender matters to your life. From the moment you get up in the morning until you go to bed at night, if you are male, ask yourself, "Would I be doing this if I were a female?" If you are a female, ask yourself, "Would I be doing this if I were male?" When you see a female performing an activity, ask yourself, "Would this seem appropriate to me if a male were doing it?" Write down your thoughts and feelings about these activities, and reflect on the role of gender in your daily life.

## Gender Bias in Toys; Children and Gender Schemas

- **Gender Stereotyping in Toys:** Have students complete *Handout: Gender Stereotyping in Children's Toys*.
- **Children and Gender Schemas:** Have students interview two men and two women who are willing to spend some time answering the questions below. Do not deviate from the order of information.

  1. Do you want to know the gender of your baby before it is born? Why or why not?
  2. Would you allow your daughter to play with Barbie® dolls *and* toy cars? Why or why not?
  3. Would you allow your son to play with Barbie® dolls *and* toy cars? Why or why not?

- After, the students should write a two- to three-page summary including the answers to the following questions. Make sure they include references from the textbook or other sources that help explain their conclusions.

1. What was the most common response to the first question, "Do you want to know the sex of your baby before it is born?" Describe the most common explanations for their answers.
2. Did the men and women surveyed respond differently to Question 2? In other words, were the men more or less likely than the women to respond a particular way if their child were a boy versus a girl? Explain briefly.
3. How many of your respondents would allow a son to play with Barbie® dolls? Describe the most common explanations for their answers.
4. Based on your data, do you think your participants will have children who are more gender stereotyped or who are less gender stereotyped? Explain and support your answer with examples from your data.

## Gender Bias in Media

- **Gender Bias in Television Commercials:** Have students complete *Handout: Gender Bias in Commercials*. One theory about male versus female ads is that male ads are "simpler" in colors, storyline, and message. See if the students notice this difference in their analyses.
- **Media, Men, and Women:** Use *Handout: The Media and Men and Women* to brainstorm some images that come to the students' minds when they think about how the two genders are portrayed in the mass media, including TV and magazines. Write the words *Women* and *Men* on the board. Ask them to think about gender representations in news stories, feature articles, TV shows, and advertisements. Write their ideas under each heading. Ask students to discuss the impact that media has on gender identity and development.

## Discussion Questions

**FEMININITY AND MASCULINITY** How have the traditional American interpretations of femininity and masculinity changed, and why do you believe people are less inclined to hold typical gender-conformity attitudes?

**SEXUALITY IN THE MEDIA** How is sexuality represented in today's media? Do you think the depictions of relationships between partners are becoming more or less realistic than was true in the past?

- Think of current Hollywood couples. How do the media represent their relationships? Why is our society so fascinated by relationships among the "rich and famous"?
- How do you feel about sexual relationships among older adults? Do you think that sex becomes more or less satisfying as people get older? Why?

## Polling Questions

**"MILITARY, ATTENTION! DROP DOWN AND GIVE ME 20!"** Women have been serving in the military for years in noncombat roles. Now, however, the U.S. Defense Department has lifted this ban. How many of you think that women can perform in combat roles just as well as men? War doesn't discriminate—men and women are killed or wounded in the line of duty. Who thinks having a woman in a combat battalion is a liability to the group? How many of you think that boot camps should have separate training regiments and separate requirements for men and women? Who thinks that gays, lesbians, and transgendered individuals pose the same concerns as women do in the military?

**GENDER BIAS** Have you had an experience recently in which someone treated you a specific way because of your gender?

## Suggested Media

**TELEVISION PROGRAM: PORTRAYAL OF SEX IN THE MEDIA** Show an episode from a television comedy in which sex is discussed openly. Examples of popular shows are *Modern Family, Jane the Virgin, Grown-ish,* and *Riverdale.* Show a brief scene, and then ask students to comment on whether the portrayal of sexual relations was realistic or not. For an interesting contrast, show a scene from a sitcom from the 1960s or early 1970s.

## Additional Readings

Brown, C. S. (2015). Target is right on target about the use of gender labels. *Psychology Today: Beyond Pink and Blue.* www.psychologytoday.com/blog/beyond-pink-and-blue/201508/target-is-right-target-about-the-use-gender-labels.

## **AP** Student Edition Answer Key

### Neuroscience in Your Life: Do Women's Brains Differ from Men's?

Answer Suggestions

- Nonhuman males have more fear and aggression because they have a larger amygdala than nonhuman females.
- A meta-analysis combines the results of many separate studies into one overall conclusion. Replication is a critical activity, and many researchers believe that psychologists need to increase the number of studies that are replications of earlier research in order to have greater confidence in their findings.

## AP Test Practice

### Section I: Multiple Choice

1. **A** *(Skill 1.B, Learning Target 6.P)*
2. **E** *(Skill 1.C, Learning Target 6.P)*
3. **D** *(Skill 1.A, Learning Target 6.P)*

### Section II: Free Response

- The biological approach views behavior from the perspective of biological functioning. Researchers have investigated brain differences and hormones for reasons for gender differences.
- The evolutionary approach views behavior as being influenced by the genetic inheritance from our ancestors. Research on gender differences has pointed to differences in the nature of jealousy between men and women and the fear of sexual infidelity versus emotional infidelity. Evolutionary psychologists also argue that similarities in divisions of labor between men and women across different cultures suggest that sex differences are due to evolutionary forces. Male traits of being more aggressive, competitive, and prone to taking risks than women holds an evolutionary advantage.
- The social approach looks at the environment. According to the social learning theory, boys are taught and rewarded for performing the socially perceived appropriate behaviors for men, while girls are taught what society says is appropriate for women.
- The cognitive approach considers how people know, understand, and think about the world. Research on gender differences looks at the construction of gender schemas, or mental frameworks to organize and guide an understanding of gender. On the basis of their schemas for appropriate and inappropriate behavior for males and females, children begin to behave in ways that reflect society's gender roles.

# Module 33: Understanding Human Sexual Response: The Facts of Life

## AP Module Summary

Module 33 has students reviewing the biology of sex. Though not specified in the CED, this module contains the research of William Masters and Virginia Johnson and the sexual response cycle. A quick review of this is all that is necessary when addressing the research behind the motivational systems of sex. I often combine Modules 33 and 34 into one class period.

**THE BASIC BIOLOGY OF SEXUAL BEHAVIOR** Human sexual behavior, in comparison with animal behavior, is more complicated, although the underlying biology is not all that different from that of related species. The male and female sex organs are referred to as the *genitals* (see **Figure 1**). In males, for example, the testes begin to secrete *androgens*, male sex hormones, at puberty.

Women show a different pattern. When they reach maturity at puberty, the two ovaries begin to produce *estrogens,* female sex hormones. However, these hormones are not produced consistently; instead, their production follows a cyclical pattern. The greatest output occurs during *ovulation,* when an egg is released from the ovaries, making the chances of fertilization by a sperm cell highest.

Though biological factors "prime" people for sex, it takes more than hormones to motivate and produce sexual behavior. In animals, the presence of a partner that provides arousing stimuli leads to sexual activity. Humans are considerably more versatile; not only other people, but nearly any object, sight, smell, sound, or other stimulus can lead to sexual excitement.

**PHYSIOLOGICAL ASPECTS OF SEXUAL EXCITEMENT: WHAT TURNS PEOPLE ON?** If it was argued that the major human sex organ is the brain, in a sense that would be right. Much of what is considered sexually arousing in our society has little or nothing to do with our genitals; instead, it is related to external stimuli that, through a process of learning, have come to be labeled as erotic, or sexually stimulating. Sexual fantasies also play an important role in producing sexual arousal.

**THE PHASES OF SEXUAL RESPONSE: THE UPS AND DOWNS OF SEX** Although the kinds of stimuli that produce sexual arousal are to some degree unique to each individual, we all share some basic aspects of sexual responsiveness. According to pioneering work done by William Masters and Virginia Johnson (1966) who studied sexual behavior in carefully controlled laboratory settings, sexual responses follow a regular pattern consisting of four phases:

1. The *excitement phase,* which can last from just a few minutes to more than an hour, is the period in which an arousing stimulus begins a sequence that prepares the genitals for sexual intercourse.
2. In the *plateau phase,* maximum level of arousal is attained as the penis and clitoris swell with blood, and the body prepares for orgasm. *Orgasm* is the peak of sexual excitement, during which rhythmic muscular contractions occur in the genitals.
3. This is followed by the *resolution stage,* the interval after orgasm in which the body returns to its unaroused state, reversing the changes brought about by arousal.
4. *Refractory period* is a temporary period that follows the resolution stage and during which the male cannot develop an erection again.

## AP Key Terms

androgens

erogenous zones

estrogens

excitement phase

genitals

orgasm

ovulation

plateau phase

refractory period

resolution stage

## Suggested Media

- *Masters and Johnson:* www.kinseyinstitute.org/collections/archival/masters-and-johnson.php.

## Additional Readings

Burn, S. M. (2004). *Women Across Cultures.* (2nd ed.). New York: McGraw-Hill.

## AP Student Edition Answer Key

### AP Test Practice

#### Section I: Multiple Choice

1.  **B** *(Skill 1.A, Learning Target 6.P)*

2.  **E** *(Skill 1.C, Learning Target 6.P)*

3.  **A** *(Skill 1.A, Learning Target 6.P)*

#### Section II: Free Response

Androgens are male sex hormones secreted by the testes. Androgen production is fairly consistent.

Secondary sex characteristics are produced by androgens. Examples include growth of body hair and deepening of voice.

Estrogens are the female hormones produced by the ovaries. Great output of estrogens occurs during ovulation, when an egg is being released from the ovaries.

The sexual response cycle is the typical response when people become sexually excited. It follows four stages: excitement, plateau, orgasm, and resolution.

The refractory stage is the time period after the resolution stage during which the male cannot develop an erection again. It can last a few minutes to several hours. Women are able to cycle back to the orgasm phase and experience repeated orgasms. After the resolution stage, women return to a pre-stimulation state rather than entering the refractory stage like males.

# Module 34: The Diversity of Sexual Behavior

## AP Module Summary

In Module 34, the research of Alfred Kinsey is important to students' understanding of sexual motivation. With our ever changing society, I have found that students are displaying greater interest in understanding the topics of homosexuality, bisexuality, and transgenderism. There can also be, depending on the class, an interest in determining the causes of sexual orientation. Nothing new added has been added to the CED regarding motivation and sex.

**SURVEYING SEXUAL BEHAVIOR: WHAT'S HAPPENING BEHIND CLOSED DOORS?** For most of recorded history, the vast variety of sexual practices remained shrouded in ignorance. However, in the late 1930s, biologist Alfred Kinsey launched a series of surveys on the sexual behavior of people in the United States. The result was the first comprehensive attempt to see what people were actually doing sexually and was highlighted by the publication of Kinsey's landmark volumes, *Sexual Behavior in the Human Male* (Kinsey et al., 1948) and *Sexual Behavior in the Human Female* (Kinsey et al., 1953). Kinsey's work set the stage for later surveys. But due to political reasons (the use of government funding for sex surveys is controversial), surprisingly few comprehensive, large-scale, representative surveys—either in the United States or in other countries—have been carried out since Kinsey did his initial work.

**HETEROSEXUALITY** *Heterosexuality,* sexual attraction and behavior directed to the other sex, consists of far more than male-female intercourse. Kissing, petting, caressing, massaging, and other forms of sex play are all components of heterosexual behavior.

**HOMOSEXUALITY AND BISEXUALITY** *Homosexuals* are sexually attracted to members of their own sex, whereas *bisexuals* are sexually attracted to people of the same sex and the other sex. Many male homosexuals prefer the term *gay* and female homosexuals prefer the term *lesbian* because they refer to a broader array of attitudes and lifestyles than the term *homosexual,* which focuses on the sexual act. The exact number of people who identify themselves as exclusively homosexual has proved difficult to gauge; some estimates are as low as 1.1% and some as high as 10% (see the "Applying Psychology in the 21st Century: Estimating the Numbers: How Many People Are Gay or Lesbian?" box in the text). Although people often view homosexuality and heterosexuality as two completely distinct sexual orientations, the issue is not that simple. Pioneering sex researcher Alfred Kinsey acknowledged this when he considered sexual orientation along a scale or continuum with "exclusively homosexual" at one end and "exclusively heterosexual" at the other. In the middle were people who showed both homosexual and heterosexual behavior (see **Figure 4**). Kinsey's approach suggests that sexual orientation is dependent on a person's sexual feelings and behaviors, and romantic feelings.

**DETERMINING THE CAUSES OF SEXUAL ORIENTATION** Although there are a number of theories about what determines whether people are homosexual or heterosexual, none has proved completely satisfactory.

Some explanations for sexual orientation are biological, suggesting that there are genetic causes. Evidence for a genetic origin of sexual orientation comes from studies of identical twins. The studies found that when one twin identified himself or herself as homosexual, the occurrence of homosexuality in the other twin was higher than it was in the general population. Hormones also may play a role in determining sexual orientation.

Some evidence suggests that differences in brain structures may be related to sexual orientation. For instance, the structure of the anterior hypothalamus, an area of the brain that governs sexual behavior, differs between male homosexuals and heterosexuals. Similarly, other research shows that, compared with heterosexual men or women, gay men have a larger anterior commissure, which is a bundle of neurons connecting the right and left hemispheres of the brain. However, research suggesting that biological causes are at the root of homosexuality is not conclusive because most findings are based only on small samples of individuals.

Little evidence suggests that sexual orientation is brought about by child-rearing practices or family dynamics. Although proponents of psychoanalytic theories once argued that the nature of the parent-child relationship can produce homosexuality, research evidence does not support such explanations. Another explanation for sexual orientation rests on learning theory. According to this view, sexual orientation is learned through rewards and punishments in much the same way that we may learn to prefer swimming over tennis. Although the learning-theory explanation is plausible, several difficulties rule it out as a definitive explanation. Because our society has traditionally held homosexuality in low esteem, one ought to expect that the negative treatment of homosexual behavior would outweigh the rewards attached to it. Furthermore, children growing up with a gay or lesbian parent are statistically unlikely to be homosexual, which thus contradicts the notion that homosexual behavior may be learned from others.

Because of the difficulty in finding a consistent explanation for sexual orientation, we cannot definitively answer the question of what determines it. It seems unlikely that any single factor orients a person toward homosexuality or heterosexuality. Instead, it seems reasonable to assume that a combination of biological and environmental factors is involved.

**TRANSGENDER** *Transgender* is a broad term encompassing people whose gender identity, gender expression, or behavior does not conform to the sex to which they were assigned at birth. Transgender people may have male bodies but view their gender identity as female, or they may have female bodies and have a male gender identity. In other cases, transgender individuals may view themselves as a third gender (neither male nor female). In some cases, transgender individuals may seek sex-change operations in which their existing genitals are surgically removed and the genitals of the desired sex are fashioned.

Transgender issues have become increasingly prominent in recent years. For instance, schools, college campuses, and public facilities have struggled with how to best provide restrooms that address the needs of the transgender community.

Whereas transgenderism centers on gender identity concerns, some people are born having physical issues involving their genitals. An intersex person has an atypical combination of sexual organs or chromosomal or gene patterns.

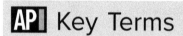 Key Terms

| bisexuals | homosexuals |
|-----------|-------------|
| heterosexuality | transgender |

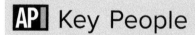 Key People

**Alfred Kinsey**

# Class Discussion Ideas

**DATA ON ATTITUDES TOWARD PREMARITAL SEX** The Kinsey Institute provides updates on surveys regarding attitudes and sexual behavior: www.indiana.edu/~kinsey/.

**GAY, LESBIAN, AND BISEXUAL ISSUES IN PSYCHOLOGY** Go to this APA website: www.apa.org/helpcenter/sexual-orientation.aspx, which presents information on gay, lesbian, and bisexual issues in psychology. Some issues to focus on are the following:

- Sexual orientation reflects multiple interacting factors.
- Sexual orientation is not considered to be a choice.
- Conversion therapy is not accepted in psychology.
- Importance of education against stereotypes and hate crimes

# Activities

**WHERE DOES SEXUAL ORIENTATION FIT INTO THIS?** Engage the classroom in a discussion using the following prompts or questions. This discussion should be introduced to the class using such terms as *respect* and *tolerance* for others' comments or thoughts.

- How would you define *heterosexual* or *homosexual* if someone isn't exactly male or female?
- What if their genitals are ambiguous?
- Do you base it on their legal status?
- How do you classify a transsexual woman partnered with a straight man?
- Does the definition depend on whether the transsexual woman has had gender reassignment or not?
- Does a straight man "become" homosexual through seeing and fancying a transsexual woman?
- Is it a mental illness to be different in this way?
- Is it a mental illness to be gay or lesbian? (Hint: It once was considered that way.)
- Do we need more than two gender roles or none at all?

**ATTITUDES TOWARD SEXUALITY IN THE MEDIA** The evolutionary psychology approach to gender suggests that men are more likely to seek women who are younger than they are and that women are more likely to seek older men with resources. Look at profiles on a dating website or app. Do the profiles' content support predictions about what men and women look for?

## Human Sexuality

**Survey on Human Sexuality:** Have students complete *Handout: Survey on Human Sexuality.*

- **Your Own Program:** Have students use *Handout: Your Own Program* to design a sex education program for children. Their plan should include goals, strategies for achieving their goals, and three to five resources they used to help develop their sex education plan.
- **A Sexual Double Standard:** Play the MTV documentary *Fight for Your Rights: The Double Standard in Sexuality.* This is a very modern, pop culture-infused take on how a double standard still exists in this culture when it comes to sexual behavior. After showing the video, have the class work in groups to identify the strengths and weaknesses of the documentary, along with any biases it appeared to have. If you cannot find this video, https://www.youtube.com/watch?v=baT3LWaSfuM is another link that can be used to illustrate the same concepts.
- **Trial by Jury or Psychologist:** Have students use *Handout: Trial by Jury or Psychologist* and determine how a judge or jury and a psychologist would interpret the behavior listed.

# Polling Questions

**Sex Is a Hot Topic** No matter where you turn today, and definitely on social media sites, sex, sexuality, and gender are hot topics. Let's consider why this is. Broadly speaking, how many of you believe that you hold very strong opinions on topics related to sex and sexual orientation? How many of you can identify where you have developed (or gotten) those opinions/beliefs from? Who thinks that we shouldn't even be talking about sex and sexual orientation because these topics are simply no one's business? How many of you think that social media sites have dramatized topics of debate on sexual orientation?

**Don't Teach My Kid That** Sex education in the schools has increasingly become a topic of conversations. With many influences, including political ones, how many of you think that the educational system should be responsible for teaching sex education to children? (List several age ranges, such as 5–7, 8–10, and 11–13.) From the ranges on the board, identify the age at which sex education should begin. Discuss any discrepancies and include content from the development chapter, as needed. Who thinks there should be an open, candid conversation about sex education curriculum that doesn't minimize the consequences of sexual behaviors?

# Suggested Media

- *Gay & Lesbian Alliance Against Defamation:* http://www.glaad.org.

- *Gay, Lesbian, and Straight Education Network:* https://www.glsen.org/. This valuable site has many links to resources that can be applied to various grade levels, including downloadable resource guides.

- *Healthy Place:* https://www.healthyplace.com/sex. This website includes topical discussions and external links related to sex issues in the community, positive sexual experiences, sexual disorders, and physical health concerns and sexual behavior.

- *Human Rights Campaign:* https://www.hrc.org. This is the website of the National Coalition of LGBT, which is committed to improving the health and well-being of lesbian, gay, bisexual, and transgender individuals and communities through public education, coalition building, and advocacy that focus on research, policy, education, and training.

- *The Kinsey Institute:* http://www.iub.edu/~kinsey/about/index.html. This website features links to other online resources, a FAQs section, and information on current research on sex, gender, and reproduction.

- *National LGBTQ Task Force:* http://www.ngltf.org/. This website is a good resource on gay and lesbian issues and explains how the task force is promoting individuals to take action.

- *The Science of Sexual Orientation. 60 Minutes,* CBS, 2006, 13:00. Researchers focus on twin studies to help understand the development of sexual orientation.

**TED TALK: WHY I MUST COME OUT** Geena Rocero, a transgender fashion model, gives a TED Talk that can help students understand gender identity and related concepts: https://www.ted.com/talks/geena_rocero_why_i_must_come_out.

# Additional Readings

Cherlin, A. J. (2013). Health, marriage, and same-sex partnerships. *Journal of Health and Social Behavior, 54*(1), 64–66.

McAnulty, R.D., & Burnette, M. (2006). *Sex and Sexuality, Volume 1: Sexuality Today: Trends and Controversies.* Westport: Greenwood Press.

# **AP** Student Edition Answer Key

## Applying Psychology in the 21st Century: Teen Sexting

Answer Suggestions

- Operational definitions are necessary for replication.
- The conclusions listed are from correlational studies, a research method that cannot determine a cause-and-effect relationship.

## AP Test Practice

### Section I: Multiple Choice

1. **D** *(Skill 1.C, Learning Target 6.P)*

2. **B** *(Skill 1.A, Learning Target 6.P)*

3. **D** *(Skill 1.A, Learning Target 7.D)*

### Section II: Free Response

Kinsey and colleagues interviewed thousands of Americans to learn about their sexual behavior. His research gave a more complete picture of contemporary sexual practices, such as masturbation, premarital sex, and marital sex. His research had problems, but few comprehensive studies have taken place since. Kinsey's surveys may have been biased and unrepresentative. His sample overrepresented college students, young people, well-educated individuals, urban dwellers, and people living in Indiana and the Northeast. It is unsure how many refused to participate in his survey. Also, participants may have lied about their private behavior.

Masters and Johnson found that the sexual response cycle follows a regular pattern consisting of four stages: excitement, plateau, orgasm, and resolution. They studied sexual behavior in carefully controlled laboratory settings. This method required participants who were not embarrassed to have sex in front of cameras. This may have created an unrepresentative and biased sample.

# CHAPTER 12

# Development

## AP Introduction

Developmental psychology is increasingly becoming a psychology of the life span rather than a psychology of children. This unit takes a life-span approach, covering cradle to grave. Themes to emphasize in the discussions based on these modules are the biopsychosocial nature of development (i.e., that development occurs in multiple domains) and that development occurs in a number of directions (i.e., not simply a trajectory of growth and decline). Although the last topic in the unit is death and dying, another possibility to consider is ending with the topic of "successful aging." Discussion ideas below contain suggestions for material to include on this topic.

## AP Essential Questions

- How do we perceive and understand ourselves?

## Module 35: Nature and Nurture: The Enduring Developmental Issue

**AP Learning Targets:**

- Differentiate types of research with regard to purpose, strengths, and weaknesses.
- Discuss psychology's abiding interest in how heredity, environment, and evolution work together to shape behavior.

**Pacing:**

½ Block or 1 Traditional Class period

## Module 36: Prenatal Development: Conception to Birth

**AP Learning Targets:**

- Explain the process of conception and gestation, including factors that influence successful pre-natal development.
- Discuss the interaction of nature and nurture (including cultural variations), specifically physical development, in the determination of behavior.

**Pacing:**

½ Block or 1 Traditional Class period

# Module 37: Infancy and Childhood

**AP Learning Targets:**

- Discuss the interaction of nature and nurture (including cultural variations), specifically physical development, in the determination of behavior.
- Discuss maturation of motor skills.
- Describe the influence of temperament and other social factors on attachment and appropriate socialization.
- Identify the contributions of major researchers in developmental psychology in the area of social development in childhood.
- Discuss the interaction of nature and nurture (including cultural variations), specifically social development, in the determination of behavior.
- Explain how parenting styles influence development.
- Explain the maturation of cognitive abilities (Piaget's stages, information process).
- Identify the contributions of major researchers in the area of cognitive development in childhood.
- Compare and contrast various cognitive processes.

**Pacing:**

2 Block or 4 Traditional Class periods

# Module 38: Adolescence: Becoming an Adult

**AP Learning Targets:**

- Discuss the interaction of nature and nurture (including cultural variations), specifically physical development, in the determination of behavior.
- Discuss maturation of motor skills.
- Discuss the interaction of nature and nurture (including cultural variations), specifically social development, in the determination of behavior.
- Discuss maturational challenges in adolescence, including related family conflicts.
- Characterize the development of decisions related to intimacy as people mature.
- Identify the contributions of key researchers in the area of adulthood and aging.
- Identify the contributions of major researchers in the area of moral development.
- Compare and contrast models of moral development.

**Pacing:**

1.5 Blocks or 2.5–3 Traditional Class periods

# Module 39: Adulthood

**AP Learning Targets:**

- Discuss the interaction of nature and nurture (including cultural variations), specifically physical development, in the determination of behavior.
- Discuss maturation of motor skills.
- Discuss the interaction of nature and nurture (including cultural variations), specifically social development, in the determination of behavior.
- Predict the physical and cognitive changes that emerge through the lifespan, including steps that can be taken to maximize function.
- Define intelligence and list characteristics of how psychologists measure intelligence.

**Pacing:**

½ Block or 1 Traditional Class period

# Module 35: Nature and Nurture: The Enduring Developmental Issue

## AP Module Summary

Module 35 takes a look at the research strategies used to better understand human development. Also included in this module is the study of twins, always a fascinating topic for students to discuss. Nothing is new or has been changed in the CED regarding nature-nurture.

*Developmental psychology* is the branch of psychology that studies the patterns of growth and change that occur throughout life. The *nature-nurture issue* is the degree to which environment and heredity influence behavior. Although the question was first posed as a nature versus nurture issue, developmental psychologists today agree that both nature and nurture interact to produce specific developmental patterns and outcomes.

Developmental psychologists agree that genetic factors not only provide the potential for specific behaviors or traits to emerge, but also place limitations on the emergence of such behaviors or traits. Developmental psychologists also agree that in most instances environmental factors play a critical role in enabling people to reach the potential capabilities that their genetic background makes possible.

**DETERMINING THE RELATIVE INFLUENCE OF NATURE AND NURTURE** Developmental psychologists use several approaches to determine the relative influence of genetic and environmental factors on behavior. Human twins serve as an important source of information about the relative effects of genetic and environmental factors.

- *Identical twins* (those who are genetically identical) display different patterns of development, those differences have to be attributed to variations in the environment in which the twins were raised.
- The most useful data comes from identical twins who are adopted at birth by different sets of adoptive parents and raised apart in differing environments.

**DEVELOPMENTAL RESEARCH TECHNIQUES** *Cross-sectional research* is a research method that compares people of different ages at the same point in time.

- Cross-sectional studies provide information about differences in development between different age groups.
- Cross-sectional research has limitations, however. For instance, we cannot be sure that the differences we might find are due to age differences alone.
- Instead, they may reflect differences of the cohorts represented. A cohort is a group of people who grow up at similar times, in similar places, and in similar conditions.

*Longitudinal research* asseses the behavior of one or more participants as the participants get older.

*Longitudinal studies* assess *change* in behavior over time, whereas cross-sectional studies assess *differences* among groups of people.

## AP Key Terms

cross-sectional research

developmental psychology

identical twins

longitudinal research

nature–nurture issue

# Class Discussion Ideas

**NATURE AND NURTURE** Point out that the debate of nature versus nurture is now nature AND nurture. The question is how much these factors interact in development.

**TWIN STUDIES** Explain that studies of identical twins raised in different environments allow us to compare the relative effects of nature and nurture. The following methods are used.

Monozygotic (identical) twins raised in the same environment are compared to:

- Monozygotic twins adopted by different parents and raised in different environments. Because they share genetic endowment, any differences between them must be due to the environment.
- Dizygotic (fraternal) twins raised in same environment. Differences between them must reflect genetics. The heritability index is used to calculate effect of genetics on a behavior.

**Research Methods Applied:** This section is a review of experimental design and research methods in psychology. Using PsycINFO or another search engine, provide students with peer-reviewed research articles that highlight cross-sectional and longitudinal study designs. Then in groups, ask students to describe the findings of the study as well as their significance to developmental psychology.

# Activities

**DEVELOPMENTAL PSYCHOLOGY AS LIFE-SPAN DEVELOPMENT** To get students thinking about development from a life-span perspective, have them work in teams to list changes that occur during each period of the lifespan. Ask students to list at least three changes or developments that characterize the following periods: prenatal, infancy, childhood, adolescence, and adulthood.

**DEVELOPMENTAL PROCESSES** Write various development changes that occur during life on the board. Break the class into groups, and have them discuss the physical, cognitive, and socioemotional processes that happen to an individual during the periods of time written on the board. The students will get an idea of what occurs during development and how development refers not only to physical changes, but also to other changes that occur.

# Discussion Questions

**NATURE AND NURTURE** Consider the factors that might determine when a child learns to walk. What kinds of environmental influences might be involved? What kinds of genetic influences might be involved?

Choose a personality trait that you believe describes you. How might nature and nurture have contributed to your personality? What kinds of environmental influences might be involved? What kinds of genetic influences might be involved?

# Polling Questions

**RESEARCH DESIGNS** If you wanted to study the development of language over time, which of the following research designs would you choose?

a. Cross-sectional

b. Longitudinal

## AP Test Practice

### Section I: Multiple Choice

1. **C** *(Skill 1.A, Learning Target 1.F)*

2. **A** *(Skill 1.A, Learning Targets 6.B)*

3. **E** *(Skill 1.A, Learning Target 6.B)*

### Section II: Free Response

Nature is the genetic cause of behaviors. Nature explains that a child's genetic makeup will determine when they will walk. According to maturation, the biological timeline is around one year.

Nurture is the environmental cause of behaviors. Nurture explains when a child will walk based on the child's experiences and the influence of parents, siblings, family, friends, and nutrition.

Cross-sectional studies compare people of different ages at the same point in time. To study walking, a cross-sectional study could compare children who are different ages (i.e., 9 months, 12 months, and 14 months) at the same time.

Longitudinal studies investigate behavior as the participants get older. To study walking, a longitudinal study could begin following a group of children at 9 months and continue to monitor their development until they turn 14 months.

# Module 36: Prenatal Development: Conception to Birth

## AP Module Summary

Module 36 is a biology lesson on human development. In this module, specifics such as the addition of teratogens have been added to the CED. Many students make connections with this module and their science courses and often have considerable background knowledge in the topic.

**THE BASICS OF GENETICS (SEE FIGURE 1)** The one-cell entity established at conception contains 23 pairs of *chromosomes*, rod-shaped structures that contain all basic hereditary information. One member of each pair is from the mother, and the other is from the father. Each chromosome contains thousands of *genes*—smaller units through which genetic information is transmitted. Either individually or in combination, genes produce each person's particular characteristics. Composed of sequences of *DNA* (deoxyribonucleic acid) molecules, genes are the biological equivalent of "software" that programs the future development of all parts of the body's hardware.

Some genes control the development of systems common to all members of the human species—the heart, circulatory system, brain, lungs, and so forth; others shape the characteristics that make each human unique, such as facial configuration, height, and eye color. The child's sex is also determined by a particular combination of genes (see **Figure 2**). Specifically, a child inherits an X chromosome from its mother and either an X or a Y chromosome from its father. When there is an XX combination, it is a female; an XY combination, develops as a male. Male development is triggered by a single gene on the Y chromosome; without the presence of that specific gene, the individual will develop as a female. As behavioral geneticists have discovered, genes are also at least partially responsible for a wide variety of personal characteristics, including cognitive abilities, personality traits, and psychological disorders.

### THE EARLIEST DEVELOPMENT

- *Zygote*—The zygote is the one-celled entity formed by the union of a sperm and an ovum.
- *Embryo*—Two weeks after conception, the zygote develops in to a multicellular organism and begins the *embryonic period*, which lasts from week 2 through week 8.
- *Fetus*—From week 8 and continuing until birth is fetal development. At the start of this period, the fetus has taken the recognizable form of its species and has developed major organs, though they are not yet fully functional.

**GENETIC INFLUENCES ON THE FETUS** A major cause of birth defects is faulty genes or chromosomes. Some of the more common genetic and chromosomal difficulties are: phenylketonuria (PKU), sickle-cell anemia, Tay-Sachs disease, and Down syndrome.

**PRENATAL ENVIRONMENTAL INFLUENCES (SEE FIGURE 3)** Environmental influences—the nurture part of the nature-nurture equation—also affect the fetus. Some of the more profound consequences are brought about by *teratogens*, environmental agents such as a drug, chemical, virus, or other factor that produce a birth defect. Among the major prenatal environmental influences on the fetus are through the mother and include: nutrition, illness, emotional state, use of drugs, alcohol, nicotine use, and exposure to second-hand smoke.

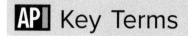 Key Terms

age of viability

chromosomes

embryo

fetus

genes

teratogens

zygote

## Class Discussion Ideas

**INFLUENCES ON THE FETUS** Summarize genetic and environmental influences, indicating their effects on the development of the fetus and whether they can be prevented or not. Below is detailed information to use as background for describing these influences.

### GENETIC FACTORS

- *Phenylketonuria (PKU)* is a genetic disorder in which a person's body cannot break down an amino acid called phenylalanine. Excess phenylalanine interferes with various metabolic processes in the central nervous system that lead to decreased production of neurotransmitters such as dopamine. The first behavioral signs of nerve cell damage are usually evident in an affected child within four to six months of birth.

- *Sickle-cell anemia* (SCA) and affects approximately 100,000 Americans. SCD occurs among about 1 out of every 365 Black or African-American births. SCD occurs among about 1 out of every 16,300 Hispanic-American births. About 1 in 13 Black or African-American babies is born with sickle cell trait (SCT). (https://www.ncbi.nim.nih.gov/books/NBK22238/)

- *Tay-Sachs disease* is a hereditary metabolic disorder that causes progressive mental and neurologic deterioration and results in death in early childhood. The disease is inherited as an autosomal recessive trait and occurs most commonly among people of eastern European (Ashkenazic) Jewish origin. Tay-Sachs infants appear normal at birth but become listless and inattentive during the first few months of life. As the disease progresses, the child loses motor abilities already gained, such as crawling and sitting, develops uncontrollable seizures, and is unable to lift its head or swallow. A cherry-red spot develops on the retina, and blindness and a general paralysis usually precede death. There is no treatment for the disease. (https://www.britannica.com/science/Tay-Sachs-disease)

- *Down syndrome* is a congenital disorder caused by extra genetic material from chromosome 21. The physical and cognitive impacts of Down syndrome range from mild to severe. Some common physical signs of the disorder include a small head, flattened face, short neck, up-slanted eyes, low-set ears, enlarged tongue and lips, and sloping underchin. Other characteristics of the disorder may include poor muscle tone, heart or kidney malformations (or both), and abnormal dermal ridge patterns on the palms of the hands and soles of the feet. Intellectual disability occurs in all persons with Down syndrome and usually ranges from mild to moderate. Congenital heart disease is found in about 40 to 60 percent of people with Down syndrome. https://www.britannica.com/science/Down-syndrome

### ENVIRONMENTAL FACTORS (ALSO CALLED TERATOGENS)

- *Rubella* (from http://www.daviddarling.info/encyclopedia/R/rubella.html): About 25 percent of babies whose mothers contract rubella during the first trimester of pregnancy are born with one or more birth defects, which, together, are referred to as congenital rubella syndrome. These birth defects include eye defects (resulting in vision loss or blindness), hearing loss, heart defects, intellectual disability, and, less frequently, cerebral palsy. Many children with congenital rubella syndrome are slow in learning to walk and to do simple tasks, although some eventually catch up and do well. The infection frequently causes miscarriage and stillbirth. The risk of congenital rubella syndrome from maternal infection drops to around 1 percent in the early weeks of the second trimester, and there is rarely any risk of birth defects when maternal rubella occurs after 20 weeks of pregnancy. Some infected babies have health problems that are not lasting. They may be born with low birth weight (less than 5.5 pounds), or have feeding problems, diarrhea, pneumonia, meningitis (inflammation around the brain), or anemia. Red-purple spots may show up on their faces and bodies because of temporary blood abnormalities that can result in a tendency to bleed easily. The liver and spleen may be enlarged.

- ○ Some infected babies appear normal at birth and during infancy. However, all babies whose mothers had rubella during pregnancy should be monitored carefully because problems with vision, hearing, learning, and behavior may first become noticeable during childhood.

- *Fetal alcohol syndrome:* Alcohol consumption during pregnancy—when it results in fetal alcohol syndrome—has emerged as one of the leading causes of intellectual disability. For additional information, see this website: http://www.cdc.gov/ncbddd/default.htm.

**Other drugs of abuse** Up-to-date information on the effects of prenatal exposure to cocaine, MDMA ("ecstasy"), methamphetamine, and heroin can be found on the National Institutes of Health Medline Plus website: http://www.nlm.nih.gov/medlineplus/pregnancyand substanceabuse.html.

## Activities

**EPIGENETICS** This is a good time to discuss the concept of epigenetics. A great site on pruning is: http://faculty.washington.edu/chudler/plast.html. I typically show clips from the PBS series *The Secret Life of the Brain*, including an overview of the series at http://www.pbs.org/wgbh/pages/frontline/shows/teenbrain/work/adolescent.html, and these episodes: (infant): http://www.pbs.org/wnet/brain/episode1/video.html; (child): http://www.pbs.org/wnet/brain/episode2/video.html; and (teenager): http://www.pbs.org/wnet/brain/episode3/video.html.

### INFLUENCES ON THE FETUS

- **Prenatal Influences:** Have students complete *Handout: Prenatal Influences*
- **Threats to the Fetus:** Have the students choose one of the three threats that were discussed in the textbook, such as teratogens, alcohol, or sexually transmitted infections. Have the students use the Internet to find various cases that describe these threats. The students should write a one- to two-page paper on the information they read. On the day the papers are due, break the class into groups and have them discuss which threat they chose and what information they found. The students will become more familiar with the threats to infancy and how they can be avoided. The students will also learn from others in their group about other threats that they had not chosen.
- **Lot in Life:** Brainstorm 15–20 real life situations (e.g. Your son was recently diagnosed as being autistic; You and your partner are expecting your first child and are told that there is a high probability that your child will be born with Down Syndrome.). Have students form groups of 3–4 and have them research and present the "Lot" and how best to deal with the situation. Then have students present their findings to the class.

## Polling Questions

**DRUG USE DURING PREGNANCY** Do you think it should be illegal to drink, use drugs, or smoke while pregnant?

## AP Test Practice

### Section I: Multiple Choice

1. **D** *(Skill 1.A, Learning Target 6.A)*

2. **E** *(Skill 1.B, Learning Targets 6.A)*

3. **E** *(Skill 1.A, Learning Target 6.B)*

### Section II: Free Response

A sensitive period is the time when organisms are especially susceptible to certain kinds of stimuli. The couple needs to be aware that the fetus is especially affected by the mother's use of drugs during the sensitive period before birth.

The embryo is the developing individual from 2–8 weeks. The couple's embryo is growing to about 1/5 of an inch and developing a heart, brain, intestinal tract, and other organs.

Age of viability is the point at which a fetus can survive if born prematurely. If the couple's fetus is born after 22 weeks, it is likely to survive.

PKU is a genetic disorder in which a child cannot produce an enzyme that is necessary for normal development. After birth the child will need to be tested for PKU. If the child has PKU, he will be placed on a special diet to help him develop properly.

A chromosome contains basic hereditary information. The couple's fetus will have 23 chromosomes from the mother and 23 chromosomes from the father.

# Module 37: Infancy and Childhood

## AP Module Summary

Module 37 covers an abundance of learning targets. New to the CED is the discussion of the interaction between nature and nurture on social development in the determination of behavior. This module is a big one and greater time should be spent covering the information within. Make sure to review *Albert Bandura, Konrad Lorenz, Harry Harlow, Mary Ainsworth, Diana Baumrind, Erik Erikson, Jean Piaget and Lev Vygotsky* and their theories of childhood development.

### The Extraordinary Newborn

**Reflexes:** A neonate is born with a number of *reflexes*—unlearned, involuntary responses that occur automatically in the presence of certain stimuli. Critical for survival, many of those reflexes unfold naturally as part of an infant's ongoing maturation.

- *Rooting reflex* causes neonates to turn their heads toward things that touch their cheeks—such as the mother's nipple or a bottle.
- *Sucking reflex* prompts infants to suck at things that touch their lips.
- *Gag reflex*—to clear the throat,
- *Startle reflex*—a series of movements in which an infant flings out the arms, fans the fingers, and arches the back in response to a sudden noise,
- *Babinski reflex*—a baby's toes fan out when the outer edge of the sole of the foot is stroked.

Infants lose these primitive reflexes after the first few months of life and replace them with more complex and organized behaviors. The typical baby rolls over by the age of about 3 months, sits without support at about 6 months, stands alone at about 11 months, and walks at just over a year old (see **Figure 1**).

**DEVELOPMENT OF THE SENSES: TAKING IN THE WORLD** Researchers have devised a number of ingenious methods that rely on the newborn's biological responses and innate reflexes to test perceptual skills. *Habituation* refers to the decrease in the response to a stimulus that occurs after repeated presentations of the same stimulus.

Infants' visual perception is remarkably sophisticated from the start of life. At birth, babies prefer patterns with contours and edges over less distinct patterns, indicating that they can respond to the configuration of stimuli. Furthermore, even newborns are aware of size constancy because they are apparently sensitive to the phenomenon by which objects stay the same size even though the image on the retina may change size as the distance between the object and the retina varies. In fact, neonates can discriminate facial expressions—and even imitate them (see **Figure 2**). In addition to vision, infants display other impressive sensory capabilities. Newborns can distinguish different sounds to the point of being able to recognize their own mothers' voices at the age of 3 days. They can also make the subtle perceptual distinctions that underlie language abilities. Moreover, they can recognize different tastes and smells at a very early age.

### Infancy Through Childhood

**Physical Development:** Children's physical growth provides the most obvious sign of development. During the first year of life, children typically triple their birth weight, and their height increases by about half. From age 3 to the beginning of adolescence at around age 13, growth averages a gain of about 5 pounds and 3 inches a year (see **Figure 3**). The physical changes that occur as children develop are not just a matter of increasing growth; the relationship of the size of the various body parts to one another changes dramatically as children age (see **Figure 4**).

**DEVELOPMENT OF SOCIAL BEHAVIOR: TAKING ON THE WORLD:**

- This would be a great time to introduce *Konrad Lorenz's* work regarding the critical period and imprinting.
- This would be a great time in which to introduce *Harry Harlow's* work on the area of social development.
  - *Attachment,* the positive emotional bond that develops between a child and a particular individual, is the most important form of social development that occurs during infancy. Developmental psychologists have suggested that human attachment grows through the responsiveness of infants' caregivers to the signals the babies provide, such as crying, smiling, reaching, and clinging. The greater the caregiver's responsiveness to the child's signals, the more likely it is that the child will become securely attached. Full attachment eventually develops as a result of the complex series of interactions between caregiver and child.

**Assessing Attachment:** Mary Ainsworth, the *Ainsworth strange situation* consists of a sequence of events involving a child and (typically) their mother. Initially, the mother and baby enter an unfamiliar room, and the mother permits the baby to explore while she sits down. An adult stranger then enters the room; after this, the mother leaves. The mother returns, and the stranger leaves. The mother once again leaves the baby alone, and the stranger returns. Finally, the stranger leaves, and the mother returns. Babies' reactions to the experimental situation vary drastically, depending, according to Ainsworth, on their degree of attachment to the mother:

- *Securely attached*—the mother is a kind of home base; they explore independently but return to her occasionally.
- *Avoidant* children do not cry when the mother leaves, and they seem to avoid her when she returns as if indifferent to her.
- *Ambivalent* children display anxiety before they are separated and are upset when the mother leaves, but they may show ambivalent reactions to her return.
- *Disorganized-disoriented*—these children show inconsistent and often contradictory behavior.

**The Father's Role:** Although early developmental research focused largely on the mother-child relationship, more recent research has highlighted the father's role in parenting—and with good reason: The number of fathers who are primary caregivers for their children has grown significantly, and fathers play an increasingly important role in their children's lives. Fathers engage in more physical, rough-and-tumble sorts of activities, whereas mothers play more verbal and traditional games, such as peekaboo. Despite such behavioral differences, the nature of attachment between fathers and children compared with that between mothers and children can be similar.

**Social Relationships with Peers:** By the time they are 2 years old, children become less dependent on their parents, more self-reliant, and increasingly prefer to play with friends. Initially, play is relatively independent: Even though they may be sitting side by side, 2-year-olds pay more attention to toys than to one another when playing. Later, however, children actively interact, modify one another's behavior, and exchange roles during play. Cultural factors also affect children's styles of play. Through play, children learn to take the perspective of other people and to infer others' thoughts and feelings, even when those thoughts and feelings are not directly expressed. Social interaction helps children interpret the meaning of others' behavior and develop the capacity to respond appropriately.

**The Consequences of Child Care Outside the Home:** Research on the importance of social interaction is corroborated by work that examines the benefits of child care out of the home, which is an important part of an increasing number of children's lives (see **Figure 6**). According to the results of a large study supported by the U.S. National Institute of Child Health and Development, children who attend high-quality child-care centers may not only do as well as children who stay at home with their parents, but in some respects they may actually do better. Children in child care are generally more considerate and sociable than other children, and they interact more positively with teachers. Especially for children from poor or disadvantaged homes, child care in specially enriched environments—those with many toys, books, a variety of children, and high-quality providers—may be more intellectually stimulating than the home environment. However, child care outside the home does not have universally positive outcomes. The key to the success of nonparental child care is its quality. High-quality child care produces benefits; low-quality child care provides little or no gain and may even hinder children's development.

**Parenting Styles and Social Development:** Parents' child-rearing practices are critical in shaping their children's social competence. According to classic research by developmental psychologist Diana Baumrind, four main categories describe different parenting styles (see **Figure 7**).

- *Authoritarian parents*—Rigid and punitive, value unquestioning obedience from their children. They have strict standards and discourage expressions of disagreement.
- *Permissive parents* give their children relaxed or inconsistent direction and, although they are warm, require little of them.
- *Authoritative parents* are firm and set limits for their children. As the children get older, these parents try to reason and explain things to them. They also set clear goals and encourage their children's independence.
- *Uninvolved parents* show little interest in their children.

The four kinds of child-rearing styles seem to produce very different kinds of behavior in children (with many exceptions, of course).

Children are born with a particular *temperament*—a basic, inborn characteristic way of responding and behavioral style. Some children are naturally easygoing and cheerful, whereas others are irritable and fussy or pensive and quiet. The kind of temperament a baby is born with may in part bring about specific kinds of parental child-rearing styles. In addition, children vary considerably in their degree of resilience, the ability to overcome circumstances that place them at high risk for psychological or even physical harm.

- At this point you may want to review *Albert Bandura's* Social Learning Theory. Check to see what connections students can make to social development and his theory.

**Erikson's Theory of Psychosocial Development:** Psychoanalyst Erik Erikson developed one of the more comprehensive theories of social development. *Psychosocial development* involves changes in our interactions and understanding of one another as well as in our knowledge and understanding of ourselves as members of society.

- **Trust-versus-mistrust stage** (ages birth to 1½ years), infants develop feelings of trust if their physical requirements and psychological needs for attachment are consistently met and their interactions with the world are generally positive.
- **Autonomy-versus-shame-and-doubt stage** (ages 1½ to 3 years), toddlers develop independence and autonomy if exploration and freedom are encouraged, or they experience shame, self-doubt, and unhappiness if they are overly restricted and protected.
- **Initiative versus-guilt stage** (ages 3 to 6). Children's desire to act independently conflicts with the guilt that comes from the unintended and unexpected consequences of such behavior.
- **Industry-versus-inferiority stage** (ages 6 to 12). Increasing competency in all areas, whether social interactions or academic skills, characterizes successful psychosocial development. In contrast, difficulties in this stage lead to feelings of failure and inadequacy.

**COGNITIVE DEVELOPMENT: CHILDREN'S THINKING ABOUT THE WORLD** *Cognitive development* is the process by which a child's understanding of the world changes due to their age and experience. Theories of cognitive development seek to explain the quantitative and qualitative intellectual advances that occur during development.

**Piaget's Theory of Cognitive Development:** Jean Piaget suggested that children around the world proceed through a series of four stages in a fixed order (see **Figure 8**). He maintained that these stages differ not only in the *quantity* of information acquired at each stage but in the *quality* of knowledge and understanding as well.

**Sensorimotor Stage: Birth to 2 Years:** During the sensorimotor stage, children base their understanding of the world primarily on touching, sucking, chewing, shaking, and manipulating objects. In the initial part of the stage, children have relatively little competence in representing the environment by using images, language, or other kinds of symbols. Consequently, infants lack what Piaget calls *object permanence*, the awareness that objects—and people—continue to exist even if they are out of sight.

**Preoperational Stage: 2 to 7 Years:** The most important development during the *preoperational stage* is the use of language. Children develop internal representational systems that allow them to describe people, events, and feelings.

- Preoperational children use *egocentric thought*, a way of thinking in which a child views the world entirely from their own perspective. Preoperational children think that everyone shares their perspective and knowledge. Preoperational children have not yet developed the ability to understand the **principle of conservation**, which is the knowledge that quantity is unrelated to the arrangement and physical appearance of objects (see **Figure 9**).

**Concrete Operational Stage: 7 to 12 Years:** Mastery of the principle of conservation marks the beginning of the *concrete operational stage*. According to Piaget, the concrete operational stage is characterized by logical thought and a loss of egocentrism. Although children make important advances in their logical capabilities during the concrete operational stage, their thinking still displays one major limitation: They are largely bound to the concrete, physical reality of the world.

**Formal Operational Stage: 12 Years to Adulthood:** The *formal operational stage* produces a new kind of thinking that is abstract, formal, and logical.

**Stages Versus Continuous Development: Is Piaget Right?** No other theorist has given us as comprehensive of a theory of cognitive development as Piaget. Still, many contemporary theorists suggest that a better explanation of how children develop cognitively can be provided by theories that do not involve a stage approach.

**INFORMATION-PROCESSING APPROACHES: CHARTING CHILDREN'S MENTAL PROGRAMS** To many developmental psychologists, changes in *information processing*, the way in which people take in, use, and store information, account for cognitive development. According to this approach, quantitative changes occur in children's ability to organize and manipulate information. Speed of processing increases with age as some abilities become more automatic. The speed at which children can scan, recognize, and compare stimuli increases with age. Memory also improves dramatically with age (see **Figure 10**). Memory capabilities are impressive at a very early age: Even before they can speak, infants can remember for months events in which they actively participated. Improvement in information processing relates to advances in *metacognition*, an awareness and understanding of one's own cognitive processes. Metacognition involves the planning, monitoring, and revising of cognitive strategies. Younger children, who lack an awareness of their own cognitive processes, often do not realize their incapacities. It is only later, when metacognitive abilities become more sophisticated, that children are able to know when they do not understand. Such increasing sophistication reflects a change in children's *theory of mind*, their knowledge and beliefs about the way the mind operates.

**Vygotsky's View of Cognitive Development: Considering Culture:** In an increasingly influential view, Vygotsky suggests that the focus on individual performance of both Piagetian and information-processing approaches is misplaced. Instead, he holds that we cannot understand cognitive development without taking into account the social aspects of learning.

- According to Vygotsky, the *zone of proximal development (ZPD)* is the gap between what children already are able to accomplish on their own and what they are not quite ready to do by themselves. In short, cognitive development occurs when parents, teachers, or skilled peers assist a child by presenting information that is both new and within the ZPD. This type of assistance, called *scaffolding*, provides support for learning and problem solving that encourages independence and growth.

## AP Key Terms

Egocentric thought

Formal operational stage

Habituation

Industry-versus-inferiority stage

Information processing

Initiative-versus-guilt stage

Metacognition

Neonate

Object permanence

Permissive parents

Preoperational stage

Principle of conservation

Psychosocial development

Reflexes

Sensorimotor stage

Temperament

Trust-versus-mistrust stage

Uninvolved parents

Zone of proximal development (ZPD)

## AP Key People

Mary Ainsworth

Harry Harlow

Konrad Lorenz

Diana Baumrind

Albert Bandura

Erik Erikson

Jean Piaget

Lev Vygotsky

# Class Discussion Ideas

Much of the material in this unit is self-explanatory, and students can read about the facts regarding infant development on their own.

**THE DEVELOPING INFANT AND CHILD** The newborn human brain is especially responsive to the specific world around it, allowing nurture to shape human nature. You may want to stress the idea of epigenetics. This is also a good time to point out that Piaget's theory is epigenetic in nature. That is, he believes that children are active and cause their own development as they interact with the world. Thus an impoverished environment (one with little chance for exploration with the baby stuck in a playpen or bounce seat all day) should lead to limited cognitive development. On the other hand, an environment that has many opportunities for exploration should lead to a more complex level of thought. You may want to have students discuss the ways to have a rich environment.

**BASICS OF VYGOTSKY'S THEORY** Concepts to emphasize in Vygotsky's theory are:

- Focus on social processes in development.
- Zone of proximal development—area of knowledge just beyond a child's abilities; according to Vygotsky, children learn best when they encounter information at this level.
- Scaffolding—adults and teachers present the kind of support for learning (within the ZPD) that enables the children to work independently but with help so that they can both solve problems and develop their cognitive abilities more generally.

**CLASS DEMONSTRATION: CONSERVATION** This activity is designed to show students that the ability to understand reversibility (in conservation) is not necessarily established by the age of 8. For this activity, you will need to bring into class a set of items in pairs that are the same or similar in amount but are different in their configuration.

For example:

1. Two differently shaped perfume bottles containing the same amount of perfume
2. Two 1-pound boxes of pasta boxes, one long and thin (spaghetti) and one wide and short (ziti)
3. Two cans of fruit that are of different weights, with the smaller one weighing more

Then ask for a volunteer to judge whether they are the same or different amounts. Chances are that the volunteer will make a few mistakes, demonstrating that conservation is not necessarily established by the age of 8 and that even adults can be fooled!

# Activities

**INFANCY, PIAGET, PARENTING STYLES**

- **Piaget's Conservation:** Have students complete *Handout: Everyday Examples of Conservation.*
- **Piaget's Stages of Cognitive Development:** Use *Handout: Which Stage Is It?* The students will read various statements and then decide during which of Piaget's stages of cognitive development the behavior is occurring.
- **Piaget:** This is a great time to discuss the educational implications of Piaget's work. Remind students that Piaget felt that peers only offered a state of disequilibrium and that was the only benefit. You may want to tie in Vygotsky's zone of proximal development as a counterperspective to this. You can also point out to students that Piaget believed children cause their own development. Montessori based her educational work on this perspective. You can show a clip of Montessori and her work: http://www.youtube.com/watch?v=q7a3Br6kPbU.

**GUEST SPEAKER**  Invite a parent of an infant or young child to class (if possible, have them bring their child with them). Based on the age of the child, ask the parent to discuss or demonstrate relevant concepts (e.g., with an infant, the topic could be reflexes; with an older child, it could be Piaget's stages). Have students work together to prepare questions ahead of time.

**HARRY HARLOW AND COMFORT**  Start by showing a clip of Harlow's work: http://www.youtube.com/watch?v=_O60TYAIgC4.

**ATTACHMENT**  Have students look at http://www.psych.uiuc.edu/~rcfraley/attachment.htm, which has a great overview of how infant attachment correlates with adult attachment styles. Then have them go to http://www.web-research-design.net/cgi-bin/crq/crq.pl to take a quick survey on adult attachment style (it even plots where they are on the graph). Then have them write a paragraph summarizing infant attachment styles, a paragraph on adult attachment styles, and finally a paragraph on if they feel this assumption of adult effects is correct, based on their score.

**PARENTING STYLES**  Have students interview three people outside of class about the parenting styles those people grew up with during childhood. The people they interview should be from three different cultural backgrounds. The students should then turn in an overview of what they found, along with a description of the parenting style in their household as they were growing up. The students will learn about various parenting styles. They will also learn about the differing parenting styles across cultures.

- Have students consider the style of parenting with which they were raised. Suggest that it might help to think of specific situations or moments when their parents did or did not put limits on their behavior. If they have one or more siblings, have them ask for their opinion too and determine if they agree with one another about their parents' style. Students should then give these definitions to their parents, and ask which, if any, describes them. Sometimes there are as many different views of a family as there are members of that family.

**CHILD'S PLAY**  A major part of any child's life is playing, and when kids are playing, they are often playing with toys. Using the information on perceptual and cognitive development reviewed in this chapter, design a toy that you think is a perfect fit for a child of 2 months, of 2 years, and of 10 years. With respect to the child's development, what features of the toy are especially good for the child of each age group.

# Discussion Questions

## THEORIES OF COGNITIVE DEVELOPMENT (PIAGET, INFORMATION PROCESSING, VYGOTSKY)

- Which theory of cognitive development do you most agree with? Why?
- How does each theory of cognitive development treat the role of social and cultural factors? Which theory gives the most emphasis to culture?
- If you were a teacher, how would you apply each of the three theories of cognitive development?
- As a parent, how would you handle your child asking for a cell phone or tablet to use and to play with?
- What limitations, if any, would you impose? And, does the age of the child change your answers? What evidence can you use to support your decisions?

# Polling Questions

**VIOLENCE DOESN'T BELONG HERE** It seems that more and more we are hearing about violence in our schools. Going to school provides very important developmental experiences that are necessary for children to grow up healthy physically, cognitively, and socially. In the wake of the Sandy Hook Elementary School shootings and other examples, what do you think? How many of you think that violence is more prevalent in schools than it ever has been before? How many of you think that the media and other social institutions are overly publicizing and making these situations more dramatic than necessary? Who thinks that children going to school are more fearful today of terror and violence than were previous generations?

# AP Student Edition Answer Key

## Neuroscience in Your Life: Emotional Responses in Infancy

Answer Suggestions

- Temperament is a basic, inborn characteristic way of responding and behaving. Since it is innate, it would be better explained by nature.
- The statistics show how much hemoglobin levels changed as blood went to active brain areas. Happy babies had a greater neural response to happy faces in the left frontal cortex. The results suggest that neural responses to emotional stimuli are related to an infant's temperament.

## AP Test Practice

## Section I: Multiple Choice

1. **C** *(Skill 1.A, Learning Target 6.B)*
2. **D** *(Skill 1.B, Learning Targets 6.C)*
3. **C** *(Skill 1.A, Learning Target 6.E)*

# Section II: Free Response

**A.**

Authoritative parents, according to Baumrind, are firm and set limits for their children, but they also reason and explain things to them. Children of authoritative parents tend to have high social skills and are likeable, self-reliant, independent, and cooperative.

Securely attached children, according to Ainsworth, employ the mother as a home base and explore independently. When the mother leaves, they are distressed, but they go to her when she returns. Children with a secure attachment tend to be more socially and emotionally competent, and are often cooperative, capable, and playful.

Contact comfort, according to Harlow, is the physical touch necessary for attachment. For the Harlow's monkey experiment, the cloth monkey provided greater comfort to the infants; milk alone was insufficient to create attachment.

Zone of proximal development (ZPD), according to Vygotsky, is the gap between what children are able to accomplish on their own and what they are not quite ready to do by themselves. When children are given information in their ZPD, they can increase their understanding or master a new task.

**B.**

Temperament is the inborn characteristic way of responding and behavioral style. A child's temperament, such as being difficult, may bring about a specific kind of child-rearing style that is not helpful for their development.

Egocentrism, according to Piaget, is a way of thinking in which a child views the world entirely from his or her perspective. Parents that don't understand egocentric thought may think that their child is selfish, which impacts their relationship in a negative way.

Autonomy-versus-shame-and-doubt according to Erikson is the period during which toddlers develop independence if exploration and freedom are encouraged, or they feel shame and self-doubt if they are restricted and overprotected. Parents need to provide a reasonable amount of control for their children to develop properly. If parents are overly controlling, their children will not develop a sense of control over their world and will experience shame, self-doubt, and unhappiness.

# Module 38: Adolescence: Becoming an Adult

## AP Module Summary

Just like Module 37, Module 38 is big and important to students' understanding of human development. The theories continue and several new ones are added. The research of Lawrence Kohlberg and Carol Gilligan on moral development should be an area of focus. Students should be made aware of how the theory on moral development corresponds to Piaget's stages of cognitive development. This may also be a good time to discuss depression and the rates among adolescents, keeping in mind that the seriousness and sensitivity of the topic should be of utmost importance.

*Adolescence* is the developmental stage between childhood and adulthood. It is a time of profound changes and, occasionally, turmoil. Considerable biological change occurs as adolescents attain sexual and physical maturity. At the same time and rivaling these physiological changes, important social, emotional, and cognitive changes occur as adolescents strive for independence and move toward adulthood.

**PHYSICAL DEVELOPMENT: THE CHANGING ADOLESCENT** *Puberty,* the period at which maturation of the sexual organs occurs, begins at about age 11 or 12 for girls, when menstruation starts. However, there are wide variations (see **Figure 1**). Sexual attraction to others begins even before the maturation of the sexual organs at around age 10. For boys, the onset of puberty is marked by their first ejaculation, known as spermarche. Spermarche usually occurs around the age of 13. The age at which puberty begins has implications for the way adolescents feel about themselves—as well as the way others treat them. The rate at which physical changes occur during adolescence can affect the way in which people are viewed by others and the way they view themselves.

**MORAL AND COGNITIVE DEVELOPMENT: DISTINGUISHING RIGHT FROM WRONG**

**Kohlberg's Theory of Moral Development:** According to Kohlberg, people pass through a series of stages in the evolution of their sense of justice and in the kind of reasoning they use to make moral judgments (see **Figure 2**). Largely because of various cognitive limitations, preadolescent children tend to think either in terms of concrete, unvarying rules or in terms of the rules of society. Adolescents, however, have typically reached Piaget's formal operational stage of cognitive development and can reason on a higher plane. Kohlberg suggests that the changes in moral reasoning can be understood best as a three-level sequence. His theory assumes that people move through the levels in a fixed order and that they cannot reach the highest level until about age 13—primarily because of limitations in cognitive development before that age. However, many people never reach the highest level of moral reasoning. In fact, Kohlberg found that only a relatively small percentage of adults rise above the second level of his model. One difficulty with the theory is that it pertains to moral judgments, not moral behavior. In addition, the theory applies primarily to Western society and its moral code; cross-cultural research conducted in cultures with different moral systems suggests that Kohlberg's theory is not necessarily applicable.

**Moral Development in Women:** One glaring shortcoming of Kohlberg's research is that he primarily used male participants. Furthermore, psychologist Carol Gilligan (1996) argues that because of men's and women's distinctive socialization experiences, a fundamental difference exists in the way each gender views moral behavior. According to Gilligan, men view morality primarily in terms of broad principles, such as justice and fairness. In contrast, women see it in terms of responsibility toward individuals and willingness to make sacrifices to help a specific individual within the context of a particular relationship. The fact that Gilligan's conception of morality differs greatly from Kohlberg's suggests that gender plays an important role in determining what a person sees as moral.

## SOCIAL DEVELOPMENT: FINDING ONE'S SELF IN A SOCIAL WORLD

**Erikson's Theory of Psychosocial Development: The Search for Identity:** Erikson's theory of psychosocial development emphasizes the search for identity during the adolescent years.

- *Identity-versus-role-confusion stage*—during this stage, a time of major testing, people try to determine what is unique about themselves. They attempt to discover who they are, what their strengths are, and what kinds of roles they are best suited to play for the rest of their lives—in short, their *identity*.

During the identity-versus-role-confusion period, an adolescent feels pressure to identify what to do with his or her life. Because these pressures come at a time of major physical changes as well as important changes in what society expects of them, adolescents can find the period an especially difficult one. The identity-versus-role-confusion stage has another important characteristic: declining reliance on adults for information with a shift toward using the peer group as a source of social judgments.

- *Intimacy-versus-isolation stage*—(from post-adolescence to the early 30s), this stage focuses on developing close relationships with others.
- *Generativity-versus-stagnation stage*—Generativity is the ability to contribute to one's family, community, work, and society and to assist the development of the younger generation.
- *Ego-integrity-versus-despair stage,* spans later adulthood and continues until death. People in this stage ask themselves if they have lived a meaningful life.

**Stormy Adolescence: Myth or Reality?** At one time, psychologists thought that most children entering adolescence were beginning a period filled with stress and unhappiness. Now, however, research shows that this characterization is largely a myth. The reality is that most young people pass through adolescence without great turmoil in their lives and that they get along with their parents reasonably well.

In most families with adolescents, the amount of arguing and bickering clearly rises. Most young teenagers, as part of their search for identity, experience tension between their attempts to become independent from their parents and their actual dependence on them.

One reason for the increase in discord during adolescence appears to be the protracted period in which children stay at home with their parents. Current social trends hint at an extension of the conflicts of adolescence beyond the teenage years because a significant number of young adults—known as *boomerang children*—return to live with their parents, typically for economic reasons, after leaving home for some period. Another source of strife with parents lies in the way adolescents think. Adolescence fosters *adolescent egocentrism*, a state of self-absorption in which a teenager views the world from his or her own point of view. Egocentrism leads adolescents to be highly critical of authority figures, unwilling to accept criticism, and quick to fault others. Furthermore, they develop *personal fables*, the belief that their experience is unique, exceptional, and shared by no one else. Finally, parent-adolescent discord occurs because adolescents are much more apt to engage in risky behavior than later in life. In large part, their riskiness is due to the immaturity of brain systems that regulate impulse control, some of which do not fully develop until they are in their mid-20s.

**Exploring Diversity: Rites of Passage: Coming of Age around the World:** It is not easy for male members of the Awa tribe in New Guinea to make the transition from childhood to adulthood. First come whippings with sticks and prickly branches both for the boys' own past misdeeds and in honor of those tribesmen who were killed in warfare. Next, adults jab sharpened sticks into the boys' nostrils. Then they force a 5-foot length of vine into the boys' throats until they gag and vomit. Finally, tribesmen cut the boys' genitals, causing severe bleeding.

Other cultures have less fearsome although no less important ceremonies that mark the passage from childhood to adulthood. For instance, when a girl first menstruates in traditional Apache tribes, the event is marked by dawn-to-dusk chanting. Western religions, too, have several types of celebrations, including bar mitzvahs and bat mitzvahs at age 13 for Jewish boys and girls, respectively.

In most societies, males are the focus of coming-of-age ceremonies. The renowned anthropologist Margaret Mead remarked, only partly in jest, that the preponderance of male ceremonies might reflect the fact that "the worry that boys will not grow up to be men is much more widespread than that girls will not grow up to be women." Men are forced to rely on culturally determined rituals to acknowledge their arrival into adulthood.

## 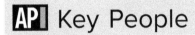 Key Terms

**Adolescence**

**Ego-integrity-versus-despair stage**

**Puberty**

**Generativity-versus-stagnation stage**

**Intimacy-versus-isolation stage**

**Identity**

**Identity-versus-role-confusion stage**

## 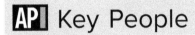 Key People

**Lawrence Kohlberg**

**Carol Gilligan**

## Class Discussion Ideas

As noted above, rather than repeat what many students already know about adolescence, focus on theories relevant to adolescence that may be more difficult for them to understand from their reading.

**ERIKSON'S THEORY OF IDENTITY** According to Erikson, identity is the major psychosocial issue of adolescence. Based on Erikson's theory, James Marcia proposed four types or statuses that characterize the identity–versus–identity–diffusion stage. In addition to the polar opposites of identity achievement versus identity diffusion, Marcia proposed that many adolescents achieve an identity without going through a crisis. He referred to this as "foreclosed." Another possibility is that adolescents remained in a prolonged state of crisis, called "moratorium."

Students can be asked these questions, which will give them an idea of which type they are:

- Have you chosen a college major?
- What led you to that decision?
- Did you consider any alternatives?
- If you have not chosen a college major, what are you doing to help you decide?

*Identity achievement:* Have a major, considered alternative before deciding on it

*Identity diffusion:* No college major, not particularly concerned about finding one

*Foreclosed:* Decided on a college major without going through a period of questioning

*Moratorium:* Trying to decide and very involved in trying to arrive at this decision

**KOHLBERG'S STAGES** Kohlberg developed his theory on the basis of interviews with adolescent boys. Starting with Piaget's theory, Kohlberg proposed that children's moral judgments reflect their cognitive abilities. They are able to see the relative pros and cons of different moral positions after they pass the stage of concrete operations. Compared with Piaget's theory, Kohlberg developed these ideas in much more detail, and although there are controversies associated with both the theory and the research on which it is based, Kohlberg's theory provides a comprehensive framework for understanding how we develop our sense of right and wrong.

# Activities

**MORAL DEVELOPMENT**

**Kohlberg's Moral Dilemma:** Although Kohlberg is most famous for the Heinz Dilemma (described in the text), he also used a variety of other moral dilemmas to measure development. Visit the following website and choose one of Kohlberg's dilemmas to share with your students: http://ww3.haverford.edu/psychology/ddavis/p109g/kohlberg.dilemmas. html. Have students work in pairs to answer the questions following the chosen dilemma.

**Kohlberg's Theory of Moral Development:** Use *Handout: Kohlberg's Theory of Moral Development* as a way for the students to become more familiar with Kohlberg's stages of moral development. The students will have to work through the stages with a moral dilemma that they decide on.

**Gender and Moral Development:** Gilligan argues that psychology has underestimated sex differences in development and thinking. Specifically, she argued that the traditional view of moral development (Kohlberg's) was unfair to women. She argued for a "caring" versus "justice" orientation as opposed to the Kohlberg's view. For more information, see http://www.stolaf.edu/people/huff/classes/handbook/Gilligan.html.

**The Adolescent Brain and the Legal System:** Have students go on the Internet and find a case in which the defense attorney argues that an adolescent should not be given the death penalty because of his or her immature brain development. Have the students write a one- to two-page paper about the case and their own personal opinion on the situation. In class, discuss with the students the cases they found and why the situation is debatable. The students will find some real-world situations that address the developing brains of adolescents, and they will have to think about their own views on the issue.

**Where Do I Fit In?** Using biculturalism and multiculturalism as a foundation for discussion, have students list where they think they fit in, in terms of ethic and cultural identities. Then, pair-share to converse on similarities and differences between cultures as well as comfort levels of confidence in ethnic identity development.

**Internet Addication Test:** Have students take the Internet Addiction Test (IAT):

# Discussion Questions

**RITES OF PASSAGE AND ADOLESCENCE** Describe a rite of passage that exists in your culture. If this is an event you have experienced, details can be added from your own life.

Explain your opinions about the media being responsible for how women feel about their weight and appearance. Do you think women will ever really accept the fact that gaining weight in adolescence is biologically determined?

Give an example from your own life in which adolescent egocentrism came into play.

# Polling Questions

**ADOLESCENCE** Do you believe that the conception of adolescence as a time of storm and stress is accurate?

# **AP** Student Edition Answer Key

## AP Test Practice

### Section I: Multiple Choice

1. **C** *(Skill 1.A, Learning Target 6.J)*

2. **B** *(Skill 1.A, Learning Targets 6.M)*

3. **C** *(Skill 1.C, Learning Target 6.N)*

### Section II: Free Response

Identity-versus-role-confusion is the period during adolescence of major testing to determine one's unique qualities. Adolescents confused about their role may lack a stable identity, become socially deviant, or have difficulty maintaining close relationships.

The postconventional stage of moral development is when moral issues are considered in terms of principles that are broader than the rules of the individual societies. Some adolescents can reason at this higher level and begin to understand that morality is not always black and white, and that conflict can exist between two sets of socially accepted standards. However, Kohlberg found that few individuals rise above the conventional level of morality.

Adolescent egocentrism is a state of self-absorption in which a teenager views the world from his or her own point of view. Egocentrism leads adolescents to be highly critical of authority figures, unwilling to accept criticism, and quick to fault others. It also makes them self-conscious because they believe they are the center of everyone's attention.

Personal fables are the belief that one's experience and beliefs are unique, exceptional, and shared by no one else. Personal fables make adolescents feel invulnerable to risks.

# Module 39: Adulthood

## AP Module Summary

In Module 39 the topic of adulthood takes center stage. Much of what students will read is fairly intuitive, especially if they have individuals in their life in this age group. There is some reintroduction to important concepts that students should know according to the CED, so this will serve as a great review. No additional changes have been made to this topic according the the CED.

*Emerging adulthood* is the period beginning in the late teenage years and extending into the mid-20s. During emerging adulthood, people are no longer adolescents, but they have not fully taken on the responsibilities of adulthood (see **Figure 1**).

**PHYSICAL DEVELOPMENT: THE PEAK OF HEALTH**  For most people, early adulthood marks the peak of physical health. From about 18 to 25 years of age, people's strength is greatest, their reflexes are quickest, and their chances of dying from disease are quite slim. Moreover, reproductive capabilities are at their highest level. Around age 25, the body becomes slightly less efficient and more susceptible to disease. Overall, however, ill health remains the exception; most people stay remarkably healthy during early adulthood.

During middle adulthood, people gradually become aware of changes in their bodies. They often experience weight gain. Furthermore, the sense organs gradually become less sensitive, and reactions to stimuli are slower. The major biological change that does occur during middle adulthood pertains to reproductive capabilities. On average, during their late 40s or early 50s, women begin *menopause*, during which they stop menstruating and are no longer fertile.

For men, the aging process during middle adulthood is somewhat subtler. There are no physiological signals of increasing age equivalent to the end of menstruation in women; that is, no male menopause exists. In fact, men remain fertile and capable of fathering children until well into late adulthood.

**SOCIAL DEVELOPMENT: WORKING AT LIFE**  The entry into early adulthood is usually marked by leaving one's childhood home and entering the world of work. People envision life goals and make career choices. In their early 40s, however, people may begin to question their lives as they enter a period called the *midlife transition*. Finally, during the last stages of adulthood, people become more accepting of others and of their own lives and are less concerned about issues or problems that once bothered them.

**PHYSICAL CHANGES IN LATE ADULTHOOD: THE AGING BODY**  *Genetic preprogramming theories of aging* suggest that human cells have a built-in time limit to their reproduction. These theories suggest that after a certain time cells stop dividing or become harmful to the body—as if a kind of automatic self-destruct button had been pushed. In contrast, *wear-and-tear theories of aging* suggest that the mechanical functions of the body simply work less efficiently as people age.

**COGNITIVE CHANGES: THINKING ABOUT—AND DURING—LATE ADULTHOOD**  At one time, many gerontologists would have agreed with the popular view that older adults are forgetful and confused. Today, however, most research indicates that this assessment is far from an accurate one of older people's capabilities.

In general, skills relating to *fluid intelligence* (which involves information-processing skills such as memory, calculations, and analogy solving) show declines in late adulthood (see **Figure 3**). In contrast, skills relating to *crystallized intelligence* (intelligence based on the accumulation of information, skills, and strategies learned through experience) remain steady and in some cases actually improve. Even when changes in intellectual functioning occur during later adulthood, people often are able to compensate for any decline. They can still learn what they want to learn; it may just take more time.

**MEMORY CHANGES IN LATE ADULTHOOD: ARE OLDER ADULTS FORGETFUL?** Most evidence suggests that memory change is not an inevitable part of the aging process. Even when people show memory declines during late adulthood, their deficits are limited to certain types of memory. For instance, losses tend to be limited to episodic memories that relate to specific experiences in people's lives. Declines in episodic memories can often be traced to changes in older adults' lives.

For instance, *Alzheimer's disease* is a progressive brain disorder that leads to a gradual and irreversible decline in cognitive abilities. Alzheimer's occurs when production of the *beta amyloid precursor protein* goes awry, producing large clumps of cells that trigger inflammation and deterioration of nerve cells. The brain shrinks, neurons die, and several areas of the hippocampus and frontal and temporal lobes deteriorate.

**THE SOCIAL WORLD OF LATE ADULTHOOD: OLD BUT NOT ALONE** Late adulthood brings significant challenges. People who have spent their adult lives working and then enter retirement bring about a major shift in the role they play. There is no single way to age successfully. According to the *disengagement theory of aging*, aging produces a gradual withdrawal from the world on physical, psychological, and social levels. According to the *activity theory of aging*, people who age most successfully are those who maintain the interests, activities, and level of social interaction they experienced during the earlier periods of adulthood. Activity theory argues that late adulthood should reflect a continuation, as much as possible, of the activities in which people participated during the earlier part of their lives.

Regardless of how people age, most engage in a process of *life review* in which they examine and evaluate their lives. Remembering and reconsidering what has occurred in the past, people in late adulthood often come to a better understanding of themselves.

# **AP** Key Terms

| | |
|---|---|
| Activity theory of aging | Genetic programming theories of aging |
| Alzheimer's disease | Life review |
| Disengagement theory of aging | Menopause |
| Emerging adulthood | Wear-and-tear theories of aging |

# Class Discussion Ideas

**INFORMATION ON MARRIAGE AND THE FAMILY** The U.S. Census Bureau's website contains recent demographic information on changing trends in the American family: http://www.census.gov/population/www/socdemo/hh-fam.html.

**CHANGING DEMOGRAPHICS ON AGING IN THE UNITED STATES AND THE WORLD** There is a wealth of data on aging in the United States. Some websites to check are:

- www.census.gov: The complete U.S. Census website—look for links on aging.
- www.cdc.gov/nchs: National Center for Health Statistics site has some links on aging, including:
  - http://www.cdc.gov/aging/: Focused solely on aging with links to other publications and data sources
  - http://www.cdc.gov/nccdphp/: Includes aging in the larger issue of chronic disease

**PHYSICAL AND COGNITIVE FUNCTIONING IN LATER LIFE** Discuss the roles of social attitudes toward aging on physical and cognitive functioning. Emphasize the importance of findings that show that older adults will "lose it" if they do not "use it." The National Institute on Aging has published a number of helpful online reports and articles on these topics: http://www.nia.nih.gov/.

**SUCCESSFUL AGING** Rather than ending the lecture with death and dying, closing with the topic of "successful aging" provides a more upbeat approach to life-span development. The Centers for Disease Control and Prevention (CDC) publishes an excellent series on "Healthy Aging" that can form the basis for this part of the lecture: http://www.cdc.gov/aging/.

Ask students to describe themselves at age 75. What will they be like physically, cognitively, socially, and emotionally? How do they feel about aging? Have students share their answers. Look for similarities, differences, and myths about aging in students' answers.

## Activities

**ATTITUDES TOWARD AGING**

- **Erikson's Adult Stages:** Ask students to come up with their own examples of situations that adults would go through in each of Erikson's adult stages
- **Future Self:** Set aside 15 minutes to have students write a brief essay as follows: Think about your life in the future, when you are 70 or 80 years old. Imagine that everything has gone as well as it possibly could, and you have achieved your life dreams. What is your life like at this stage? What things about you are the same at that age as they are for you now as a student of psychology? What things have changed? What is your best possible older adult self? How have aspects of your life today contributed to this "happily older after"?

## Discussion Questions

**DEATH AND DYING** How would you characterize our society's attitudes toward death and dying?

Should terminally ill patients have the right to choose when to end their lives? Why or why not?

What role can psychologists play in helping people adjust to death, both their own and the death of others close to them?

## Polling Questions

**TYING THE KNOT** Research indicates that people are waiting until they are older to get married. Let's explore this in more detail. How many of you plan to wait until you are older to get married? Who doesn't even plan on getting married? How many of you think that having a stable job or career is important prior to getting married? Who thinks that the online dating sites have impacted the marriage trends in the United States?

**WITH OR WITHOUT YOU** Let's consider all of the issues and research around parenting. Some will say it is a lot of work and can be very stressful, while others say that being a parent is the happiest part of their lives. So, let's vote on this topic. Who believes that being a parent is too stressful and often makes people less happy? Are people without children happier than people with children? Does being a parent require too much emotional energy to deal with everything else? Discuss these answers within the context of current literature on emotional well-being and parental happiness.

**AGING IS TRICKY BUSINESS, BUT I'VE GOT IT COVERED** Adult development is largely a conscious process. This means that as we get older, despite some changes, we are relatively in charge of how we handle new experiences, challenges, and emotional connections. There are really two ways of looking at aging: "doom and gloom" or "revitalization and reconnection." How many of you perceive the aging process as "doom and gloom," meaning that decline in physical, cognitive, and social development happens and there is really nothing you can do about it? How many of you think the opposite? Who thinks that a grandparent or older adult using technology is cool or really a good idea? How many of you think that companies such as Apple, Microsoft, and Samsung should make their technology products more user-friendly for older adults?

# **AP** Student Edition Answer Key

## Applying Psychology in the 21st Century: How Do Cognitive Abilities Rise and Fall as We Age?

Answer Suggestions

- Cross-sectional and longitudinal studies have found differences in the types of intelligences.
- Age-related changes in intellectual skills vary according to the specific cognitive ability in question. Individuals can maintain their cognitive skills with intellectual stimulation and exercise.

## AP Test Practice

### Section I: Multiple Choice

1. **C** *(Skill 1.A, Learning Target 6.L)*

2. **B** *(Skill 1.A, Learning Targets 6.L)*

3. **E** *(Skill 1.B, Learning Target 6.L)*

### Section II: Free Response

During early adulthood, there are physical peaks. People's strength is greatest, their reflexes are quickest, and reproductive capabilities are the highest.

During middle adulthood, there are gradual physical changes. People gain weight, their sense organs are less sensitive, and reaction time decreases. Women also experience menopause.

During late adulthood, physical appearance changes in more obvious ways. Hair thins and grays, skin wrinkles and folds, and height can slightly decrease. People experience sensory decreases, slow reaction times, and physical stamina changes.

During early adulthood, there are cognitive peaks of memory. People often create many first memories (i.e., work, marriage, family) during this time period. Cognitive and information processing speed is stable.

During middle adulthood, cognitive development remains steady with slight declines. People grow their crystallized intelligence. Cognitive speeds start to decline. Memory declines for episodic memories near the end of middle adulthood.

During late adulthood, some intellectual functioning declines. People experience declines in fluid intelligence, but their crystallized intelligence remains steady or even improves. Some older adults experience forms of dementia or Alzheimer's disease.

During early adulthood, social development is marked by leaving one's childhood home and entering the workforce. People also focus on developing close relationships during Erikson's intimacy-versus-isolation stage.

During middle adulthood, some individuals experience a midlife transition where they begin to question their lives. People take stock of their contributions to family and society during Erikson's generativity-versus-stagnation stage.

During late adulthood, individuals become more accepting of others and their own lives. People try to understand their accomplishments and failures during Erikson's ego-integrity-versus-despair stage.

# CHAPTER 13
# Personality

Personality is the pattern of enduring characteristics that produce consistency and individuality in a given person. Personality encompasses the behaviors that make each of us unique and that differentiate us from others. Personality also leads us to act consistently in different situations and over extended periods of time.

Like motivation, emotion, and intelligence, personality is characterized by a variety of theoretical approaches. In this unit, students will learn about personality as viewed by the major perspectives. Tying these lectures back to the opening unit on psychology's major perspectives will help students understand the roots of these theories, each of which is derived from one of those perspectives. In addition, the application of the theories to the area of personality assessment gives students concrete ways to understand how these theoretical perspectives influence the ways that psychologists attempt to describe and explain individual differences.

## AP Essential Questions

- What motivates us to think and act the way we do?
- Why do some people respond to stress in a healthier way than others?
- Why don't psychologists agree?

## Module 40: Psychodynamic Approaches to Personality

**AP Learning Targets:**

- Identify the contributions of major researchers in developmental psychology in the area of social development in childhood.
- Identify the contributions of major researchers in personality theory.
- Compare and contrast the psychoanalytic theories of personality with other theories of personality.

**Pacing:**

1 Block or 2 Traditional Class periods

## Module 41: Trait, Learning, Biological and Evolutionary, and Humanistic Approaches to Personality

**AP Learning Targets:**

- Identify the research contributions of major historical figures in psychology.
- Identify the contributions of key researchers in the psychology of learning.
- Identify and apply basic motivational concepts to understand the behavior of humans and other animals.
- Describe and compare research methods that psychologists use to investigate personality.
- Identify the contributions of major researchers in personality theory.
- Compare and contrast the behaviorist and social cognitive theories of personality with other theories of personality.
- Compare and contrast humanistic theories of personality with other theories of personality.
- Speculate how cultural context can facilitate or constrain personality development especially as it relates to self-concept.
- Compare and contrast trait theories of personality with other theories of personality.

**Pacing:**

1 ½ Block or 3 Traditional Class periods

## Module 42: Assessing Personality: Determining What Makes Us Distinctive

**AP Learning Targets:**

- Identify frequently used assessment strategies, and evaluate relative test quality based on reliability and validity of the instruments.

**Pacing:**

½ Block or 1 Traditional Class Period

# Module 40: Psychodynamic Approaches to Personality

## AP Module Summary

Module 40 introduces students to several big names associated with psychology. I personally would continue to include Karen Horney in your review of the psychoanalytic perspective even though her name does not appear in the Course and Exam Description Guide. Karen Horney is only one of several important women who have contributed to the study of psychology involving women's issues and culture and is important for students to know.

*Psychodynamic approaches* to personality are based on the idea that personality is primarily unconscious and motivated by inner forces and conflicts about which people have little awareness. The most important pioneer of the psychodynamic approach was Sigmund Freud. A number of Freud's followers, including Carl Jung, Karen Horney, and Alfred Adler, refined Freud's theory and developed their own psychodynamic approaches.

**FREUD'S PSYCHOANALYTIC THEORY: MAPPING THE UNCONSCIOUS MIND** *Psychoanalytic theory* posits that conscious experience is only a small part of our psychological makeup and experience. Freud argued that much of our behavior is motivated by the *unconscious*, a part of the personality that contains the memories, knowledge, beliefs, feelings, urges, drives, and instincts of which the individual is not aware.

**STRUCTURING PERSONALITY: ID, EGO, AND SUPEREGO** To describe the structure of personality, Freud developed a comprehensive theory that held that personality consists of three separate but interacting components:

1. The *id* is the instinctual and unorganized part of personality. From the time of birth, the id attempts to reduce tension created by primitive drives related to hunger, sex, aggression, and irrational impulses. The id operates according to the *pleasure principle* in which the goal is the immediate reduction of tension and the maximization of satisfaction.

2. The *ego,* which begins to develop soon after birth, strives to balance the desires of the id and the realities of the objective, outside world. In contrast to the pleasure seeking id, the ego operates according to the *reality principle* in which instinctual energy is restrained to maintain the individual's safety and to help integrate the person into society.

3. The *superego,* the final personality structure to develop in childhood, represents the rights and wrongs of society as taught and modeled by a person's parents, teachers, and other significant individuals. The superego helps us control impulses coming from the id, making our behavior less selfish and more virtuous.

**DEVELOPING PERSONALITY: PSYCHOSEXUAL STAGES** Freud also provided us with a view of how personality develops through a series of five *psychosexual stages* (see **Figure 2**) during which children encounter conflicts between the demands of society and their own sexual urges (in which sexuality is more about experiencing pleasure and less about lust).

- Failure to resolve the conflicts at a particular stage can result in *fixations*, conflicts or concerns that persist beyond the developmental period in which they first occur.
- Such conflicts may be due to having needs ignored or (conversely) being overindulged during the earlier period.

Psychosexual stages:

1. *Oral stage (Birth to 12 or 18 mos.)*—the baby's mouth is the focal point of pleasure. Sucking, eating, and biting anything they can put into their mouths. This behavior suggested that the mouth is the primary site of a kind of sexual pleasure and that

weaning (withdrawing the breast or bottle) represents the main conflict during the oral stage. If infants are either overindulged (perhaps by being fed every time they cry) or frustrated in their search for oral gratification, they may become fixated at this stage. Fixation at the oral stage might produce an adult who was unusually interested in oral activities—eating, talking, smoking—or who showed symbolic sorts of oral interests such as being "bitingly" sarcastic or very gullible ("swallowing" anything).

2. *Anal stage (12 to 18 months until 3 years)*—major source of pleasure changes from the mouth to the anal region, and children obtain considerable pleasure from both retention and expulsion of feces. If toilet training is particularly demanding, fixation might occur. Fixation during the anal stage might result in unusual rigidity, orderliness, punctuality, or extreme disorderliness or sloppiness in adulthood.

3. *Phallic stage (approx. age 3)*—interest focuses on the genitals and the pleasures derived from fondling them. If difficulties arise during this period, however, all sorts of problems are thought to occur, including improper sex-role behavior and the failure to develop a conscience.
   a. Children must also negotiate one of the most important hurdles of personality development: the *Oedipal conflict*—according to Freud, at this time the male unconsciously begins to develop a sexual interest in his mother, starts to see his father as a rival, and harbors a wish to kill his father and enjoy the affections of his mother—as Oedipus did in the ancient Greek tragedy. But because he views his father as too powerful, he develops a fear that his father may retaliate drastically by removing the source of the threat: the son's penis.
      i. *Castration anxiety*—the fear of losing one's penis, which ultimately becomes so powerful that the child represses his desires for his mother and identifies with his father.
   b. For girls, the process is different. Freud argued that girls begin to experience sexual arousal toward their fathers and begin to experience penis envy. Like males, they find that they can resolve such unacceptable feelings by identifying with the same-sex parent. At this point, the Oedipal conflict is said to be resolved, and Freudian theory assumes that both males and females move on to the next stage of development.

4. *Latency period (age 5 to 6)*—lasts until puberty, sexual interests become dormant, even in the unconscious.

5. *Genital stage (7 to death)*—focus is on mature, adult sexuality, which Freud defined as sexual intercourse.

## Defense Mechanisms

- *Defense mechanisms* are unconscious strategies that people use to reduce anxiety by distorting reality and concealing the source of the anxiety from themselves (see **Figure 3**).
- *Repression* is a primary defense mechanism in which unacceptable or unpleasant id impulses are pushed back into the unconscious.

**EVALUATING FREUD'S LEGACY** Many contemporary personality psychologists have leveled significant criticisms against psychoanalytic theory. Among the most important is the lack of compelling scientific data to support it. The lack of evidence is due, in part, to the fact that Freud's conception of personality is built on unobservable abstract concepts. Moreover, it is not clear that the stages of personality Freud laid out provide an accurate description of personality development. We also know now that important changes in personality can occur in adolescence and adulthood—something that Freud did not believe happened. The vague nature of Freud's theory also makes it difficult to predict how an adult will display certain developmental difficulties. Furthermore, Freud can be faulted for seeming to view women as inferior to men because he argued that women have weaker superegos than men and in some ways unconsciously yearn to be men. Finally, Freud made his observations and derived his theory from a limited population. His theory was based almost entirely on upper-class Austrian women living in the strict, puritanical era of the early 1900s who had come to him seeking treatment for psychological and physical problems. How far one can generalize beyond this population is a matter of considerable debate.

**THE NEO-FREUDIAN PSYCHOANALYSTS: BUILDING ON FREUD** A series of successors who were trained in traditional Freudian theory but later rejected some of its major points are known as *neo-Freudian psychoanalysts*. The neo-Freudians placed greater emphasis than Freud on the functions of the ego by suggesting that it has more control than the id over day-to-day activities. They focused more on the social environment and minimized the importance of sex as a driving force in people's lives. They also paid greater attention to the effects of society and culture on personality development.

**JUNG'S COLLECTIVE UNCONSCIOUS** Carl Jung, one of the most influential neo-Freudians, rejected Freud's view of the primary importance of unconscious sexual urges. Instead, he looked at the primitive urges of the unconscious more positively and argued that they represented a more general and positive life force that encompasses an inborn drive motivating creativity and more positive resolution of conflict. Jung suggested that we have a universal *collective unconscious*, an inherited set of ideas, feelings, images, and symbols that are shared with all humans because of our common ancestral past. This collective unconscious is shared by everyone and is displayed in behavior that is common across diverse cultures—such as love of mother. Jung went on to propose that the collective unconscious contains *archetypes*, universal symbolic representations of a particular person, object, idea, or experience. To Jung, archetypes play an important role in determining our day-to-day reactions, attitudes, and values.

**HORNEY'S NEO-FREUDIAN PERSPECTIVE** Karen Horney was one of the earliest psychologists to champion women's issues and is sometimes called the first feminist psychologist. Horney suggested that personality develops in the context of social relationships and depends particularly on the relationship between parents and child and how well the child's needs are met. She rejected Freud's suggestion that women have penis envy; she asserted that what women envy most in men is not their anatomy but the independence, success, and freedom women often are denied. Horney was also one of the first to stress the importance of cultural factors in the determination of personality.

**ADLER AND THE OTHER NEO-FREUDIANS** Alfred Adler, another important neo-Freudian psychoanalyst, also considered Freudian theory's emphasis on sexual needs misplaced. Instead, Adler proposed that the primary human motivation is a striving for superiority, not in terms of superiority over others but in terms of a quest for self-improvement and perfection. Adler used the term *inferiority complex* to describe adults who have not been able to overcome the feelings of inferiority they developed as children. Other neo-Freudians included Erik Erikson, whose theory of psychosocial development we discussed in earlier modules, and Freud's daughter, Anna Freud. Like Adler and Horney, they focused less than Freud on inborn sexual and aggressive drives and more on the social and cultural factors behind personality.

## 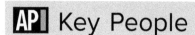 Key Terms

| | | |
|---|---|---|
| anal stage | id | phallic stage |
| archetypes | identification | psychoanalytic theory |
| collective unconscious | latency period | psychodynamic approaches to personality |
| defense mechanisms | neo-Freudian psychoanalysts | |
| ego | Oedipal conflict | psychosexual stages |
| fixations | oral stage | repression |
| genital stage | personality | superego |
| | | unconscious |

## Key People

| | | | |
|---|---|---|---|
| Alfred Adler | Sigmund Freud | Carl Jung | Karen Horney |

# Class Discussion Ideas

**OPENING CONSIDERATIONS** As was true with intelligence, this topic covers a theoretical construct that cannot be directly observed. The wealth of theories can frustrate some students, who seek clear-cut definitions and answers. By pointing out that each theory has something worthwhile to offer, you can address these concerns. Students can use these theories as a way to understand their own beliefs and assumptions about human nature.

Another feature of this topic that is important to emphasize is that what is covered in personality theories will be fundamental to understanding abnormal behavior and treatment, topics in which most students are very interested.

Ask students to consider what situations dominate their behaviors; for example, being in class. There are set scripts outlining how you behave: you sit down, take out paper and a pen, take notes, etc. If you go to a funeral, job interview, etc., you act in a particular fashion. Some situations, though, allow more flexibility (e.g., the beach, a coffee shop, a park, etc.).

Have students ask their primary caregiver about the type of temperament they displayed as a child. Have them provide at least three specific examples.

**FREUDIAN THEORY** Ideas regarding Freud's theory are most easily understood as falling into these categories:

- Structures of the mind (id, ego, superego)
- Defense mechanisms
- Stages of personality development

Emphasize that Freud developed his theory within the context of his clinical practice. However, he had the lofty ambition of creating a "science of the mind." Therefore, he used his patients as a way to test the components of his theory. This was both a strength and a limitation. As he was creating new ideas about personality, he was also gathering data from sources that were limited in time and place within the historical context of late-19th- and early-20th-century Vienna. Regardless of what students may think about the validity of his theory, Freud's ideas had a major impact on 20th-century (and beyond) culture.

**WHY FREUD?** Ask students about their opinions on Freud's theories. Do they think they are scientifically valid? Ask them why they think it is still important to study Freud. Should Freud be given much space in textbooks? Why or why not?

**NEO-FREUDIAN THEORY** Each of the neo-Freudians described in the chapter began their work as traditional psychoanalysts, but each found the theory too limiting. Jung was interested in the spiritual roots of personality; Adler in the relationship between the individual and society; and Horney rejected Freud's ideas about women but also felt that his theory did not place enough weight on social factors in development.

Here are specific bullet points for each theorist:

*Jung*

- Collective unconscious at the center of personality
- Made up of archetypes
- Healthy personality strives for balance

*Adler*

- Humans strive for self-improvement
- Inferiority complex the basis for neurosis

*Horney*

- Women not motivated by penis envy; instead, envy men's higher social status
- Emphasized discrepancy between real and ideal self

# Activities

## PSYCHODYNAMIC PERSPECTIVE

**Personality:** This activity makes for a nice lead-in to the topic of personality. Ask students who they are. Have them write down traits or characteristics that describe themselves. After they have done this, have them mark each trait as positive or negative. Are there any traits that they would like to change, and why? Where do they think personality comes from?

- **Personality Structures:** Use *Handout: Explaining the Id, the Ego, and the Superego* as a way for students to become more familiar with the differences between Freud's three personality structures. In this exercise, the students are given various scenarios or situations and have to describe how the id, the ego, and the superego would handle them.
- **Birth Order:** Ask students if they think Adler's theory on birth order fits their own personalities. Ask them if they believe the "spread" affects birth order. For example, if you are 10 years younger than your sibling, could you be considered a first-born? Ask them to defend their answers.
- **Jung's Shadow:** Darth Vader is a good example of Jung's shadow archetype. Ask students to come up with a list of other examples in literature, movies, and television. It may help to mention several fairy tales to help students get started.

**DEFENSE MECHANISMS IN EVERYDAY LIFE** Have students complete *Handout: Defense Mechanisms*.

# Discussion Questions

Ask students if they feel personality is based more on nature or nurture. Have them use their own experiences and personalities to back up their opinion. You can use the CPS clickers to poll the class on this to get the discussion underway.

**COMPARISON OF PERSONALITY THEORIES (WITH REGARD TO DEFENSE MECHANISMS)** Think of a recent instance in your life in which you used a particular defense mechanism. Describe what happened and which defense mechanism you used. Why do you think you used this defense mechanism?

Would your behavior be better explained by another personality theory? This can be incorporated to go with the activity and *Handout: Defense Mechanisms*.

# Suggested Media

- *Adler School of Professional Psychology:* http://www.adler.edu/.
- *The Jung Page:* http://www.cgjungpage.org/.
- *Neuropsychoanalysis:* http://www.neuropsa.org.uk/.
- *Sigmund Freud and the Freud Archives:* http://www.freudarchives.org/.

**POPULAR MOVIES: JUNGIAN ARCHETYPES** Show a scene from a movie illustrating archetypes such as *Star Wars* or *Lord of the Rings*. The Broadway musical *Into the Woods* is an excellent example of Jungian theory, as the characters are all archetypes. In addition, they seek greater balance within their personalities. Each looks in the "woods" (i.e., the unconscious) to find happiness, but instead almost each of the main characters is eaten by the Giant.

# Additional Readings

Leman, K. (2009). *The Birth Order Book: Why You Are the Way You Are*. Revell.

Mitchell, S.A., & Black, M. (2016). *Freud and Beyond: A History of Modern Psychoanalytic Thought*. Basic Books.

## AP Test Practice

### Section I: Multiple Choice

1. **D** *(Skill 1.B, Learning Target 7.K)*

2. **A** *(Skill 1.C, Learning Targets 7.K)*

3. **E** *(Skill 1.B, Learning Target 7.K)*

### Section II: Free Response

Fixations are concerns that persist beyond the typical developmental period. Anna's disorganization might be considered evidence that she is fixated in the anal stage.

Repression is a defense mechanism in which unpleasant impulses are pushed into the unconscious and forgotten. Anna might be experiencing repression when she pushes her anxiety-causing deadlines into the unconscious and forgets about them.

Rationalization is a defense mechanism in which people provide self-justifying explanations for their behavior. Anna might be rationalizing when she creates excuses for why her work is not completed on time.

The unconscious can be accessed through slips of the tongue, fantasies, and dreams.

# Module 41: Trait, Learning, Biological and Evolutionary, and Humanistic Approaches to Personality

## **AP** Module Summary

A substantial amount of time and focus should go into the review of Module 41. In this module students should be able to describe and compare the research methods used by completing the many activities that exist for each of the personality theories. The use of such inventories will help students master the learning target found in the new Course and Exam Description Guide. Make sure to review the Big Five personality factors and the work of Paul Costa and Robert McCrae.

Much of our own understanding of others' behavior is based on the premise that people possess certain traits that are consistent across different situations. Dissatisfaction with the emphasis in psychoanalytic theory on unconscious—and difficult to demonstrate—processes in explaining a person's behavior led to the development of alternative approaches to personality, including a number of trait-based approaches.

**TRAIT APPROACHES: PLACING LABELS ON PERSONALITY** *Traits* are consistent, habitual personality characteristics and behaviors displayed across different situations. *Trait theory* seeks to identify the basic traits necessary to describe personality. Trait theorists do not assume that some people have a trait and others do not; rather, they propose that all people possess certain traits but the degree to which a particular trait applies to a specific person varies and can be quantified.

**CATTELL AND EYSENCK: FACTORING OUT PERSONALITY** *Factor analysis* is a statistical method of identifying patterns among a large number of variables.

- Example, a personality researcher might ask a large group of people to rate themselves on a number of individual traits. A researcher can identify the most fundamental patterns or combinations of traits—called *factors*—that underlie participants' responses.

Using factor analysis, personality psychologist Raymond Cattell suggested that 16 pairs of traits represent the basic dimensions of personality (Sixteen Personality Factor Questionnaire, or 16 PF).

Another trait theorist, psychologist Hans Eysenck (1995), also used factor analysis to identify patterns of traits, but he came to a very different conclusion about the nature of personality. He found that personality could best be described in terms of just three major dimensions: (1) extraversion dimension relates to the degree of sociability; (2) neuroticism dimension encompasses emotional stability; and (3) psychoticism refers to the degree to which reality is distorted (see **Figure 1**). By evaluating people along these three dimensions, Eysenck was able to predict behavior accurately in a variety of situations.

## The Big Five Personality Traits

- At this point you would want to mention Robert McCrae and Paul Costa. A helpful mnemonic to review with students to aid them in their retention of the five traits is using O.C.E.A.N or CANOE.

For the last two decades, the most influential trait approach contends that five traits or factors—called the Big Five—lie at the core of personality (see **Figure 2**). Using factor analytic statistical techniques, a host of researchers have identified a similar set of five factors that underlie personality. The five factors are openness to experience, conscientiousness, extraversion, agreeableness, and neuroticism (emotional stability). A growing consensus exists that the Big Five represent the best description of personality traits we have today. Still, the debate over the specific number and kinds of traits—and even the usefulness of trait approaches in general—remains a lively one.

**EVALUATING TRAIT APPROACHES TO PERSONALITY** Trait approaches have several virtues. They provide a clear, straightforward explanation of people's behavioral consistencies. Furthermore, traits allow us to readily compare one person with another. However, trait approaches also have some drawbacks. For example, we have seen that various trait theories describing personality come to very different conclusions about which traits are the most fundamental and descriptive. The difficulty in determining which of the theories is the most accurate has led some personality psychologists to question the validity of trait conceptions of personality in general. Even if we are able to identify a set of primary traits, we are left with little more than a label or description of personality—rather than an explanation of behavior.

**LEARNING APPROACHES: WE ARE WHAT WE'VE LEARNED** The psychodynamic and trait approaches concentrate on the "inner" person—the fury of an unobservable but powerful id, or a critical set of traits. In contrast, learning approaches to personality focus on the external environment and how that determines and affects personality.

**SKINNER'S BEHAVIORIST APPROACH** According to the most influential learning theorist, B. F. Skinner, personality is a collection of learned behavior patterns. Similarities in responses across different situations are caused by similar patterns of reinforcement that have been received in such situations in the past. Strict learning theorists such as Skinner are less interested in the consistencies in behavior across situations than in ways of modifying behavior. Their view is that humans are infinitely changeable through the process of learning new behavior patterns.

**SOCIAL COGNITIVE APPROACHES TO PERSONALITY** Unlike other learning approaches to personality, *social cognitive approaches to personality* emphasize the influence of cognition—thoughts, feelings, expectations, and values—as well as observation of others' behavior, on personality. According to Albert Bandura, one of the main proponents of this point of view, people can foresee the possible outcomes of certain behaviors in a specific setting without actually having to carry them out. This understanding comes primarily through *observational learning:* viewing the actions of others and observing the consequences.

**SELF-EFFICACY** Bandura places particular emphasis on the role played by self-efficacy, the belief that we have the personal capabilities to master a situation and produce positive outcomes. Self-efficacy underlies people's faith in their ability to carry out a specific task or produce a desired result. People with high self-efficacy have higher aspirations and greater persistence in working to attain goals and ultimately achieve greater success than those with lower self-efficacy.

Compared with other learning theories of personality, social cognitive approaches are distinctive in their emphasis on the reciprocity between individuals and their environment. Not only is the environment assumed to affect personality, but people's behavior and personalities are also assumed to "feed back" and modify the environment.

**SELF-ESTEEM** *Self-esteem* is the component of personality that encompasses our positive and negative self-evaluations. It relates to how we feel about ourselves. Although people have a general level of self-esteem, it is not unidimensional. We may see ourselves positively in one domain but negatively in others. Self-esteem is strongly affected by culture. For example, in Asian cultures, having high relationship harmony—a sense of success in forming close bonds with other people—is more important to self-esteem than it is in more individualistic Western societies.

- This would be a good time to introduce the concept of self-concept and how cultural context can facilitate or constrain personality development. Make sure to introduce students to the concepts of collectivistic and individualistic cultures.

**EVALUATING LEARNING APPROACHES TO PERSONALITY** Because they ignore the internal processes, such as thoughts and emotions, traditional learning theorists such as Skinner have been accused of oversimplifying personality. Their critics think that reducing behavior to a series of stimuli and responses and excluding thoughts and feelings from the realm of personality leaves behaviorists practicing an unrealistic and inadequate form of science. Of course, some of these criticisms are blunted by social cognitive approaches, which explicitly consider the role of cognitive processes in personality. Still, learning approaches tend to share a highly deterministic view of human behavior, which maintains that behavior is shaped primarily by forces beyond the individual's control. Nonetheless, learning approaches have helped make personality psychology an objective, scientific venture by focusing on observable behavior and the effects of their environments.

**BIOLOGICAL AND EVOLUTIONARY APPROACHES: ARE WE BORN WITH PERSONALITY?** *Biological and evolutionary approaches to personality* suggest that important components of personality are inherited (see **Figure 4**). Personality tests indicate that, in major respects, genetically identical twins raised apart are quite similar in personality, despite having been separated at an early age. Furthermore, it is increasingly clear that the roots of adult personality emerge in the earliest periods of life.

*Temperament* is an inborn behavioral style and characteristic way of responding. Temperament encompasses several dimensions, including general activity level and mood. Some researchers contend that specific genes are related to personality. For example, people with a longer dopamine-4 receptor gene are more likely to be thrill-seekers than those without such a gene. See the "Neuroscience in Your Life: Wired to Be an Extrovert? The Biological Underpinnings of Personality" box in the text for additional information.

**HUMANISTIC APPROACHES: THE UNIQUENESS OF YOU** According to humanistic theorists, all the approaches to personality we have discussed share a fundamental misperception in their views of human nature. Instead of seeing people as controlled by unconscious, unseen forces (psychodynamic approaches), a set of stable traits (trait approaches), situational reinforcements and punishments (learning theory), or inherited factors (biological and evolutionary approaches), *humanistic approaches to personality* emphasize people's inherent goodness and their tendency to move toward higher levels of functioning. It is this conscious, self-motivated ability to change and improve, along with people's unique creative impulses, that humanistic theorists argue make up the core of personality.

**ROGERS AND THE NEED FOR SELF-ACTUALIZATION** The major proponent of the humanistic point of view is Carl Rogers (1971). Along with other humanistic theorists, such as Abraham Maslow, Rogers maintains that all people have a fundamental need for *self-actualization*, a state of self-fulfillment in which people realize their highest potential, each in a unique way. He further suggests that people develop a need for positive regard that reflects the desire to be loved and respected. Because others provide this positive regard, we grow dependent on them.

If the discrepancies between people's self-concepts and what they actually experience in their lives are minor, the consequences are minor. But if the discrepancies between one's experience and one's self-concept are great, they will lead to psychological disturbances in daily functioning. Rogers suggests that one way of overcoming the discrepancy between experience and self-concept is through the receipt of unconditional positive regard from another person—a friend, a spouse, or a therapist. *Unconditional positive regard* refers to an attitude of acceptance and respect on the observer's part, no matter what a person says or does. This acceptance, says Rogers, gives people the opportunity to evolve and grow both cognitively and emotionally and to develop more realistic self-concepts. In contrast, *conditional positive regard* depends on your behavior. In such cases, others withdraw their love and acceptance if you do something of which they do not approve. The result is a discrepancy between your true self and what others wish you would be, which leads to anxiety and frustration (see **Figure 5**).

**EVALUATING HUMANISTIC APPROACHES** Although humanistic theories suggest the value of providing unconditional positive regard toward people, unconditional positive regard toward humanistic theories has been less forthcoming. The criticisms have centered on the difficulty of verifying the basic assumptions of the approach as well as on the question of whether unconditional positive regard does, in fact, lead to greater personality adjustment. Humanistic approaches have also been criticized for making the assumption that people are basically "good"—a notion that is unverifiable—and, equally important, for using nonscientific values to build supposedly scientific theories.

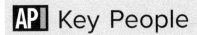 Key Terms

biological and evolutionary approaches to

humanistic approaches to personality

self-actualization

self-efficacy

self-esteem

social cognitive approaches to personality

temperament

trait theory

traits

unconditional positive regard

## **AP** Key People

Albert Bandura

Paul Costa

Robert McCrae

Abraham Maslow

Carl Rogers

## Class Discussion Ideas

**TRAIT THEORY** Ask students to think about what aggression is and the behaviors that make it up. Have them then label traits that may lead to such behaviors. This activity can help them see how multifaceted "traits" are.

Major theorists are Allport, Cattell, and Eysenck. They agreed that personality is made up of stable dispositions or dimensions along which people differ. Big Five or Five Factor Model theory incorporates other trait theories into a set of five. The Big Five or Five Factor Model traits are: openness to experience, conscientiousness, extraversion, agreeableness, and neuroticism. To remember these names, think of *OCEAN* or *CANOE* (or a canoe on the ocean!).

Here are brief descriptions of each trait:

- *Openness to experience:* Toleration for and exploration of the unfamiliar
- *Conscientiousness:* Degree of organization, persistence, and motivation in goal-directed behavior
- *Extraversion:* Capacity for joy, need for stimulation
- *Agreeableness:* One's orientation along a continuum from compassion to antagonism in thoughts, feelings, and actions
- *Neuroticism:* Proneness to psychological distress, excessive cravings or urges, unrealistic ideas

**Eysenck:** Have students take Eysenck's personality test at http://similarminds.com/eysenck. html. What did their results say about them? Do they feel their results are valid? You can have students do both activities three and four and compare their results.

**SELF-EFFICACY** In conjunction with *Handout: Defense Mechanisms*, indicate that self-efficacy is usually measured with regard to specific situations. You can have students choose one area of their lives for which they feel that performance is important and rate their self-efficacy for that area. This would take into account:

- Expectations for success or failure
- Self-assessments of abilities
- Evaluation of the challenges faced
- Past record of success or failure

Self-efficacy is applied to a variety of situations such as fears or phobias, stress, addictive behavior, achievement in school, career choice, and ability to recover from illness such as coronary heart disease.

# Activities

## HUMANISITIC PERSPECTIVES

**A Grinch's Personality Unfolded** Either in class or as an assignment, have students watch the 26-minute *How the Grinch Stole Christmas* video. Then either in groups or individually, have students apply the following personality theories to explain the Grinch: Freud, Jung, Adler, Horney, Maslow, and Rogers. Have students engage in analytical and critical thought on how the theory(ies) explain what we know about the Grinch. Modifications of this activity can be found and credited at: http://apcentral.collegeboard.com/apc/members/courses/teachers_corner/34494.html.

**The Big Five** Have students take the five-factor personality test at http://similarminds.com/bigfive.html. What did their results say about them? Do they feel their results are valid?

**Man's Best Friend** Ask students to consider their family's or a friend's pet. At some point, they have probably spoken of the pet as if it were human, allocating specific terms to explain how or why a pet behaves the way it does. Have them use the Big Five factors of personality to identify which traits the pet appears to be high or low on and why. Ask them to share their example with the class or present a more formal paper on the application of personality traits to animals.

**Self-Efficacy Scale** Have students complete the items in *Handout: Self-Efficacy Scale*. However, indicate that self-efficacy is also established for specific areas of abilities and is usually not measured as a general trait or quality.

**Self-Efficacy** Use *Handout: Make a Life Change* as a way for students to understand the steps involved in making a positive change. The students will choose an activity that they want to stop doing, and then they will work through the strategic steps discussed in the chapter for stopping this unwanted behavior.

## SURVEY ON LOCUS OF CONTROL

*Handout: Locus of Control Scale* contains a form of the measure that assesses an individual's tendency to seek reinforcement from internal or external sources.

**The Locus of Control** Have the students make a list of important behaviors, such as coming to class regularly, going to work, completing their homework, and so on. Next, have them discuss whether the locus of control for these behaviors is internal or external. How does a person switch from an external locus to an internal one, and why would they want to?

## BIOLOGICAL PERSPECTIVES

**Temperament** The *Kiersey Temperament Sorter* is a 70-item test that measures four pairs of preferences and can be used to develop 16 personality profiles. The pairs (based on Jung's dimensions) are:

- Extraversion–introversion
- Intuition–sensation
- Thinking–feeling
- Judging–perceiving

Use all of the items or select one pair such as extroversion-introversion to illustrate the concept of a continuum of bipolar dimensions. The scale is found in Kiersey, D., & Bates, M. (1984). *Please Understand Me: Character and Temperament Types*. Prometheus Nemesis Book Company.

**Eysenck** The Lemon Juice Experiment was devised by Hans Eysenck to demonstrate differences between the extrovert and the introvert by arousing salivation. Findings indicate that extroverts will require more juice to arouse salivation, compared to the introvert who needs just a couple drops to arouse salivation. Assign students to go to this link (hosted by the BBC): http://www.bbc.co.uk/science/humanbody/mind/articles/personalityandindividuality/lemons.shtml. Ask them to follow the link's directions and complete the experiment at home and be prepared to discuss the findings the next class period. You may want to assign this as a writing assignment.

**Trauma and Personality:** Engage the class in a healthy discussion about whether personality is "fixed" or whether it changes. How do they explain people who witnessed traumatic events as "being different from before?" Did that person's personality change? What about military personnel and war? Was the person "wired" to be a certain disposition or personality or did the impact of war change "who they are?"

## Polling Questions

**DROOLING IS COOL?** Ask students what relationship, if any, they think exists between one's level of introversion or extraversion and how much they drool. Most students will think that extraverts drool more. Then discuss Corcoran's (1964) research in this area (see Additional Readings), which says introverts drool more because of their higher baseline of arousal. You can link this to Eysenck's theories.

**MOVE OVER FREUD, SOCIAL MEDIA IS THE NEW THING** It is astonishing what people will post on social media sites. Think about the last time you read a post on Facebook or Twitter that shocked you. You said "I can't believe so-and-so posted that!" Now, consider personality psychology. How many of you think that social media has influenced people's expressions of their personality. Think about what you post: What do you think your postings say about you? How many of you think it is all right for a potential employer to access your social media sites before offering you a job? Who thinks that what we post on social media can be an insight into our unconscious motivations and anxieties?

**YOUR DENSITY... I MEAN, YOUR DESTINY** Alice Dreger works with people with unusual anatomies, such as conjoined twins and intersex people. In her observation, it's often a fuzzy line between male and female, among other anatomical distinctions. Which brings up a huge question: Why do we let our anatomy determine our fate? Watch Dreger's TED Talks video at http://www.ted.com/talks/alice_dreger_is_anatomy_destiny?language=en and vote on how many believe that we are a product of our biology. Who believes we can take control over who we are by changing the experiences we choose to have?

## Suggested Media

- Big Five Project Personality Test: http://www.outofservice.com/bigfive/.
- *PEN Model:* http://www.personalityresearch.org/pen.html.
- Personality Project: http://www.personality-project.org/readings-theory.html.
- Psychological science at work (Association for Psychological Science): http://www.psycho-logicalscience.org/news/minds-business.

**HUMOROUS TV SHOW: SATURDAY NIGHT LIVE** You can show "Great Moments in the Herstory of Psychology" with Dan Aykroyd as Freud and Laraine Newman as Anna from the first season of *Saturday Night Live.*

**OBSERVATIONAL LEARNING: BOBO DOLL STUDY** The Bobo doll study, conducted by Albert Bandura, is one of the original studies of observational learning in children. This video includes an explanation from Bandura himself along with footage from the experiment: https://www.youtube.com/watch?v=eqNaLerMNOE

**POPULAR TELEVISION SHOW: UNCONDITIONAL POSITIVE REGARD** Show a clip from the PBS children's show *Mister Rogers* to illustrate the theory of Carl Rogers (interesting coincidence!) in which the main character discusses the importance of children feeling good about themselves.

## Additional Readings

Bailey, S. (201, July 8). Can personality predict performance? *Forbes*. http://www.forbes.com/sites/sebastianbailey/2014/07/08/can-personality-predict-performance/#3851f0991fa0.

Barondes, S. (2011). *Making sense of people: Decoding the mysteries of personality*. FT Press.

Cain, S. (2012). *Quiet: The power of introverts in a world that can't stop talking*. Crown.

Carere, C., & Maestripieri, D. (Eds.). (2013). *Animal personalities: Behavior, physiology, and evolution*. Chicago: University of Chicago Press.

Hampson, S. E. (2012). Personality processes: Mechanisms by which personality traits "get outside the skin." *Annual Review of Psychology, 63*, 315.

Jaffe, E. (2013). The link between personality and immunity. *APS Observer, 26*, 27–30.

Kam, C., & Meyer, J. P. (2012). Do Optimism and pessimism have different relationships with personality dimensions? A re-examination. *Personality and Individual Differences, 52*(2), 123–127.

Loveland, J. M., Lounsbury, J. W., Park, S. H., & Jackson, D. W. (2015). Are salespeople born or made? Biology, personality, and the career satisfaction of salespeople. *Journal of Business & Industrial Marketing, 30*(2), 233–240.

Massen, J. J., & Koski, S. E. (2014). Chimps of a feather sit together: Chimpanzee friendships are based on homophily in personality. *Evolution and Human Behavior, 35*(1), 1–8.

Roberts, B. W., Berenbaum, H., Fraley, C., Newman, D., & Larson, R. (2012). Exploring the Link Between Conscientiousness and Positive Affect.

Shanahan, M. J., Hill, P. L., Roberts, B. W., Eccles, J., & Friedman, H. S. (2012). Conscientiousness, health, and aging: The life course of personality model.

Soto, C. J. (2015). Is happiness good for your personality? Concurrent and prospective relations of the big five with subjective well-being. *Journal of Personality, 83*(1), 45–55.

## AP Student Edition Answer Key

### Neuroscience in Your Life: The Neurological Underpinnings of Personality

Answer Suggestions

- The five-factor model, also called the Big Five, is supported by the trait approach.
- Using the results of a brain scan, we could make predictions about behaviors that correlate with the Big Five traits, such as conflict with others, optimism, psychological disorders, or longevity. A better understanding of the brain and the size of the cortex could also lead to new treatment methods.

### Applying Psychology in the 21st Century: Does Personality Shift from Generation to Generation

Answer Suggestions

- Longitudinal research is a method that investigates behavior as participants get older. Researchers in Finland looked at personality trends over time and how they related to income. The advantage of the longitudinal study is that it addresses the cohort effect.
- The Flynn effect is the increase of IQ scores each decade.

# AP Test Practice

## Section I: Multiple Choice

1. **B** *(Skill 1.B, Learning Target 7.L)*

2. **E** *(Skill 1.A, Learning Targets 7.O)*

3. **E** *(Skill 1.B, Learning Target 7.M)*

## Section II: Free Response

**A.**

Those who score high on conscientiousness tend to be careful, disciplined, and organized. If Tia is conscientious, she will carefully plan and study for her test to enhance her performance.

Unconditional positive regard is an attitude of total acceptance. If Tia receives unconditional positive regard from her friends and parents, this will allow her to do her best on the test and know her parents and friends will accept her no matter how she performs.

High self-efficacy is the belief that one can master a situation and produce positive outcomes. If Tia has high self-efficacy for the test, she will have greater persistence and increase her performance.

**B.**

Those who score high on neuroticism tend to be tense, anxious, and insecure. If Tia is neurotic, her anxiety may cause problems with her performance.

Regression is the defense mechanism in which people behave as if they are in an earlier stage of development. If Tia experiences regression, she may start to cry and give up. These less mature behaviors may lead to a decrease in performance.

# Module 42: Assessing Personality: Determining What Makes Us Distinctive

## AP Module Summary

The assessment of personality can be done throughout the unit on personality. The Course and Exam Description Guide have modified the language used to not be so specific, e.g. Minnesota Multiphasic Personality Inventory (MMPI). Now the examples of assessment strategies include personality inventory and projective tests.

Psychologists interested in assessing personality must be able to define the most meaningful ways of discriminating between one person's personality and another's. To do this, they use **psychological tests**, standard measures devised to assess behavior objectively. With the results of such tests, psychologists can help people better understand themselves and make decisions about their lives. Researchers interested in the causes and consequences of personality also employ psychological tests.

**EXPLORING DIVERSITY: SHOULD RACE AND ETHNICITY BE USED TO ESTABLISH NORMS?** The passions of politics may confront the objectivity of science when test norms are established, at least in the realm of standardized tests that are meant to predict future job performance. In fact, a national controversy has developed around the question of whether different norms should be established for members of various racial and ethnic groups. Critics of the adjusted norming system suggested that such a procedure discriminates in favor of certain racial and ethnic groups at the expense of others, thereby fanning the flames of racial bigotry. However, proponents of race norming continue to argue that norming procedures that take race into account are an affirmative action tool that simply permits minority job-seekers to be placed on an equal footing with white job-seekers. Furthermore, a panel of the National Academy of Sciences supported the practice of adjusting test norms. It suggested that the unadjusted test norms are not very useful in predicting job performance and that they would tend to screen out otherwise qualified minority group members. Job testing is not the only area in which issues arise regarding norms and the meaning of test scores. The issue of how to treat racial differences in IQ scores is also controversial and divisive.

**SELF-REPORT MEASURES OF PERSONALITY** Psychologists utilize *self-report measures* that ask people about their own behavior and traits (see **Figure 1**). One of the best examples of a self-report measure, and one of the most frequently used personality tests, is the *Minnesota Multiphasic Personality Inventory-2-Restructured Form (MMPI-2-RF)*. Although the original purpose of this measure was to identify people with specific sorts of psychological difficulties, it has been found to predict a variety of other behaviors. The test consists of a series of 338 items to which a person responds "true," "false," or "cannot say." The questions cover a variety of issues ranging from mood to opinions to physical and psychological health. There are no right or wrong answers. Instead, interpretation of the results rests on the pattern of responses. The test yields scores on 51 separate scales, including several scales meant to measure the validity of the respondent's answers (see **Figure 2**). The authors of the MMPI-2-RF, in order to determine what specific patterns of responses indicate, used a process that is typical of personality test construction—known as *test standardization*.

**PROJECTIVE METHODS** *Projective personality tests* are personality tests in which a person is shown an ambiguous, vague stimulus and asked to describe it or to tell a story about it. The responses are considered to be "projections" of the individual's personality. The best-known projective test is the *Rorschach test* involves showing a series of symmetrical stimuli (inkblots) to people who are then asked what the figures represent to them (see **Figure 3**). The *Thematic Apperception Test (TAT)* is another well-known projective test. The TAT consists of a series of pictures about which a person is asked to write a story. The stories are then used to draw inferences about the writer's personality characteristics.

**BEHAVIORAL ASSESSMENT** Psychologists subscribing to a learning approach to personality would be likely to object to the indirect nature of projective tests. Instead, they would be more apt to use *behavioral assessment*—direct measures of an individual's behavior designed to describe characteristics indicative of personality. Behavioral assessment is particularly appropriate for observing—and eventually remedying—specific behavioral difficulties, such as shyness in children. It provides a means of assessing the specific nature and incidence of a problem and subsequently allows psychologists to determine whether intervention techniques have been successful.

## AP Key Terms

behavioral assessment

Minnesota Multiphasic Personality Inventory-2-
    Restructured Form (MMPI-2-RF)

projective personality test

psychological tests

Rorschach test

self-report measures

test standardization

Thematic Apperception Test (TAT)

## Class Discussion Ideas

**PROJECTIVE MEASURES** Go to Wikipedia and download Rorschach test images to show to the class. Because these are now available online, it is no longer illegal to show them in a public setting such as the classroom.

The instructions for the Rorschach are to ask "What might this be?" Ask this question, and then have students write down three brief answers for each stimulus (separately). Note that scoring of these responses would occur along the following dimensions: (a) whether or not color is mentioned; (b) whether the answer takes into account the whole figure or a part of it; (c) if the figures are seen as two halves of a single figure, or as mirror images; (d) whether the images look like cartoon, comic, or animal-like figures. Although the Rorschach's validity is often questioned, these are the types of considerations given in assessments using standardized procedures.

## Activities

### SELF-TESTING OF THE BIG FIVE TRAITS

**Just One Personality** Have students take the self-assessing 41-question personality inventory found at http://www.41q.com/. Once they have completed it, the computer will synthesize their results and provide them some feedback. Ask them to print out their results and compare them to the Big Five factors. Then have them determine which traits they are higher or lower on. Do they consider the self-assessment accurate in terms of reliability and validity? Why or why not? Ask them to find an alternative personality test website and see if their results are similar on a different test. Have students report their findings to the class.

### PERSONALITY ASSESSMENT

**Self-Report Tests** Have the students compare the Five Factor assessment with the MMPI assessment and give examples of each.

**Projective Tests** Bring some examples of Rorschach inkblots into class. As you show them to the class, ask the students to write down their interpretations of them. After they complete this assignment, break the class into groups, and have the students share with the others in their group what they thought the inkblots were.

**Projective Tests** Show students Rorschach inkblots and TAT images and ask them what they see (e.g., http://www.deltabravo.net/custody/rorschach.php). Students really get into this.

**Thematic Apperception Test:** For a homework assignment, have the students make up various cards that tell a story in the way that the Thematic Apperception Test does. The next day, break the class into pairs, and have the students go through their cards with their classmates.

**CLASS DEMONSTRATION: THE "BARNUM EFFECT" OR PROBLEMS WITH SELF-REPORT INVENTORIES** The "Barnum Effect" refers to the tendency to place faith in generic feedback. The term is derived from the expression (wrongly) attributed to circus producer P. T. Barnum: "There's a sucker born every minute." For this demonstration, you will give students a generic personality inventory, such as the Marlowe-Crowne Social Desirability Scale (excerpted in *Handout: Barnum Effect*). Alternatively, you can make up an innocuous personality questionnaire with items that sound like those on the MMPI or the online Big Five questionnaire. For this demonstration to work, you must present the questionnaire as though it is known to have great validity and provides an accurate picture of an individual's personality. Give the questionnaire 2 weeks before the lecture so that students will not associate the questionnaire with the feedback. The guise for this is that it will take 2 weeks for the data to be analyzed. Have students complete the questionnaire on a machine scoring format (an Opscan or scantron sheet), with an ID number that they give to themselves but that you do not have access to. They should write this ID number down so that they can retrieve it later.

On the day that you are giving feedback, copy the feedback in the handout onto a sheet of paper and insert it into an envelope with the ID number on it. Hand this back to the students along with the rating sheet. Do not allow them to talk or share comments. (Ensure this by stating that the feedback is highly individualized and may contain very revealing facts. To protect themselves, they should keep it private.) Then collect their ratings. You should be able to scan them quickly to determine that the majority rate the applicability of the feedback as very high (you can calculate this later and report the actual number during the next class). In class testing of this demonstration, the percentages with ratings of 4 or 5 ranged from 70 percent to 80 percent. Then point out that the name of the questionnaire, the "SUCR," actually stands for "sucker," and that they have been victims of the Barnum Effect!

# Discussion Questions

Discuss the pros and cons of developing separate test norms for different racial and ethnic groups. Based on your list of pros and cons, draw a conclusion: Do you believe the testmakers should use one set of norms for everyone, or should norms depend on your racial and ethnic background?

# Suggested Media

- Locus of control scale: http://www.mccc.edu/~jenningh/Courses/documents/Rotter-locusofcontrolhandout.pdf.
- *Personality tests—Psychology Today:* https://www.psychologytoday.com/tests/personality.
- *Rorschach and Freudians:* https://www.youtube.com/watch?v=mUELAiHbCxc&app=desktop.
- *Rorschach test:* http://www.deltabravo.net/custody/rorschach.php.
- *TAT images:* http://web.utk.edu/~wmorgan/tat/tattxt.htm.

# Additional Readings

Archer, R. P., & Smith, S. R. (2014). *Personality assessment*. Routledge.

Mischel, W. (2014). *The marshmallow test: Mastering self-control*. Little, Brown, & Company.

# AP Student Edition Answer Key

## AP Test Practice

### Section I: Multiple Choice

1. **E** *(Skill 1.C, Learning Target 7.P)*

2. **A** *(Skill 1.B, Learning Targets 7.P)*

3. **D** *(Skill 1.A, Learning Target 7.I)*

### Section II: Free Response

**A.**

Projective tests use responses to an ambiguous stimulus in order to infer information about an individual's personality. Sam's responses to ambiguous stimuli would be used to reveal the unconscious aspects of his personality to see if he would be a good fit for the job.

Personality inventories are self-report tests that gather data about people by asking them questions about their own behavior. Sam's answers to multiple-choice questions would provide a list of traits that describe Sam to see if he would be a good fit for the job.

Behavioral assessments measure an individual's behavior used to describe their personality. Sam's behaviors would be observed in his current workplace to describe his personality and see if he would be a good fit for the job.

**B.**

The MMPI-2-RF is a widely used self-report test that identifies people with psychological difficulties and predict some everyday behaviors. Sam would be asked several true and false questions to predict his everyday behaviors in a workplace.

The Rorschach test involves showing a series of symmetrical visual stimuli to people who then are asked what the figures represent to them. Sam would be shown ambiguous inkblots and asked what the figures represent to him.

The Thematic Apperception Test (TAT) consists of a series of pictures about which a person is asked to write a story. Sam would be shown a picture and asked to write a story about it.

**C.**

The MMPI-2-RF has been standardized—a technique to validate personality test questions by studying the responses of people with known diagnoses. It was carried out on groups with different diagnoses to devise subscales that identified abnormal behavior.

Attempts to standardize the scoring of the Rorschach have frequently failed. However, it has been suggested that the reliability (consistency of scoring) and validity (degree a test measures what it is supposed to measure) of the Rorschach are great enough to provide useful inferences about personality.

# CHAPTER 14

# Health Psychology: Stress, Coping, and Well-Being

## AP Introduction

If this unit is taught during in sequence, students will be at a point in the semester at which the topic will be very relevant, as they will most likely be trying to meet deadlines for exams, papers, and other assignments. It is also quite likely that they are suffering the effects of sleep deprivation and hence are feeling more stressed than usual. The material in this chapter on how to cope with stress will definitely be of value. In addition, students find the topic of Type A behavior to be fascinating and of practical use.

## AP Essential Questions

- What motivates us to think and act the way we do?
- Why do some people respond to stress in a healthier way than others?
- Why don't psychologists agree?

## Module 43: Stress and Coping

**AP Learning Targets:**

- Discuss theories of stress and the effects of stress on psychological and physical well-being.
- Discuss the major diagnostic categories, including dissociative disorders, somatic symptoms and related disorders, and trauma- and stressor-related disorders and their corresponding symptoms.
- Identify contributions of key researchers in the psychological field of motivation and emotion.

**Pacing:**

½ Block or 1 Traditional Class period

## Module 44: Psychological Aspects of Illness and Well-Being

**AP Learning Targets:**

- Discuss theories of stress and the effects of stress on psychological and physical well-being.

**Pacing:**

½ Block or 1 Traditional Class period

## Module 45: Promoting Health and Wellness

**AP Learning Targets:**

- Distinguish the different domains of psychology.

**Pacing:**

½ Block or 1 Traditional Class period

# Module 43: Stress and Coping

## AP Module Summary

Of the three modules, Module 43 contains the material that students need to understand for the AP exam. In this module students are introduced to the work of Hans Selye and the General Adaptation Syndrome (GAS) and the three stages: alarm, resistance, exhaustion (ARE). I'm sure that some clever mnemonic can be made to help students encode the information into memory so that they can retrieve for use later.

*Health psychology* investigates the psychological factors related to wellness and illness, including the prevention, diagnosis, and treatment of medical problems. Health psychologists investigate the effects of psychological factors such as stress on illness. They examine the psychological principles underlying treatments for disease and illness. They also study prevention: how healthier behavior can help people avoid and reduce health problems such as stress and heart disease.

Health psychologists are among the primary investigators in a growing field called *psychoneuroimmunology,* or *PNI,* the study of the relationship among psychological factors, the immune system, and the brain. PNI has led to discoveries such as the existence of an association between a person's emotional state and the success of the immune system in fighting disease. In sum, health psychologists view the mind and the body as two parts of a whole human being that cannot be considered independently.

**STRESS: REACTING TO THREAT AND CHALLENGE** *Stress* refers to people's response to events that threaten or challenge them. Life is full of circumstances and events known as *stressors* that produce threats to our well-being. All of us face stress in our lives. Ultimately, our attempts to overcome stress may produce biological and psychological responses that result in health problems.

**CATEGORIZING STRESSORS** There are three general types of stressors:

- *Cataclysmic events* are strong stressors that occur suddenly and typically affect many people simultaneously.
- *Personal stressors* include major life events such as the death of a parent or spouse, the loss of one's job, a major personal failure, or even something positive such as getting married.
- *Background stressors,* or more informally, daily hassles, are the third major category of stressors (see **Figure 2**).

Some victims of major catastrophes and severe personal stressors experience *posttraumatic stress disorder,* or *PTSD,* in which a person has experienced a significantly stressful event that has long-lasting effects that may include re-experiencing the event in vivid flashbacks or dreams.

**THE HIGH COST OF STRESS** Stress can produce both biological and psychological consequences.

*Psychophysiological disorders* are medical problems that are influenced by an interaction of psychological, emotional, and physical difficulties. On a psychological level, high levels of stress prevent people from adequately coping with life. Their view of the environment can become clouded. In short, stress affects us in multiple ways. It may increase the risk that we will become ill, it may directly cause illness, it may make us less able to recover from a disease, and it may reduce our ability to cope with future stress.

**GENERAL ADAPTATION SYNDROME MODEL: THE COURSE OF STRESS** *General adaptation syndrome (GAS)* is a theory developed by Hans Selye that suggests that a person's physiological response to a stressor consists of three stages:

- *Alarm and mobilization*—occurs when people become aware of the presence of a stressor. On a biological level, the sympathetic nervous system becomes energized, which helps a person cope initially with the stressor.
- *Resistance*—the body is actively fighting the stressor on a biological level. If resistance is inadequate, people enter the last stage.
- *Exhaustion*—a person's ability to fight the stressor declines to the point where negative consequences of stress appear: physical illness and psychological symptoms in the form of an inability to concentrate, heightened irritability, or, in severe cases, disorientation and a loss of touch with reality.

**PSYCHONEUROIMMUNOLOGY AND STRESS** Focusing on the outcomes of stress, contemporary health psychologists specializing in PNI have identified three main consequences of stress (see **Figure 5**).

- First, stress has direct physiological results, including an increase in blood pressure, an increase in hormonal activity, and an overall decline in the functioning of the immune system.
- Second, stress leads people to engage in behaviors that are harmful to their health, including increased nicotine, drug, and alcohol use; poor eating habits; and decreased sleep.
- Third, stress produces indirect consequences that result in declines in health: a reduction in the likelihood of obtaining health care and decreased compliance with medical advice when it is sought.

**COPING WITH STRESS** Efforts to control, reduce, or learn to tolerate the threats that lead to stress are known as *coping*.

**Emotion-focused coping:** In emotion-focused coping, people try to manage their emotions in the face of stress by seeking to change the way they feel about or perceive a problem.

**Problem-focused coping:** Problem-focused coping attempts to modify the stressful problem or source of stress. Problem-focused strategies lead to changes in behavior or to the development of a plan of action to deal with stress.

One of the least effective forms of coping is avoidant coping. In *avoidant coping,* a person may use wishful thinking to reduce stress or use more direct escape routes, such as drug use, alcohol use, and overeating. Another way of dealing with stress occurs unconsciously through the use of defense mechanisms. *Defense mechanisms* are unconscious strategies that people use to reduce anxiety by concealing the source from themselves and others. Defense mechanisms permit people to avoid stress by acting as if the stress were not even there. Another defense mechanism used to cope with stress is *emotional insulation* in which a person stops experiencing any emotions at all and thereby remains unaffected and unmoved by both positive and negative experiences.

- This may also be a good time to introduce the work of Kurt Lewin and his motivational conflicts theory if you didn't already do so in the unit on motivation.

**LEARNED HELPLESSNESS** *Learned helplessness* occurs when people conclude that unpleasant or aversive stimuli cannot be controlled—a view of the world that becomes so ingrained that they cease trying to remedy the aversive circumstances even if they actually can exert some influence on the situation.

**APPLYING PSYCHOLOGY IN THE 21ST CENTURY: DOES USING FACEBOOK MAKE YOU FEEL BAD?** In a large sample study of adults, Facebook use (i.e., posts, clicks on posted links, "likes," and updated status messages) were associated with poorer life satisfaction and mental health. Although this association may be attributable to who seeks out Facebook to begin with, this study compared pre- and post-use scores and found that individuals felt worse after engaging with Facebook (Shakya & Christakis, 2017).

**SOCIAL SUPPORT: TURNING TO OTHERS** Our relationships with others also help us cope with stress. Researchers have found that *social support,* the knowledge that we are part of a mutual network of caring, interested others, enables us to experience lower levels of stress and better cope with the stress we do undergo.

Such support demonstrates that a person is an important and valued member of a social network. Similarly, other people can provide information and advice about appropriate ways of dealing with stress. Finally, people who are part of a social support network can provide actual goods and services to help others in stressful situations.

## 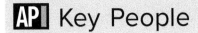 Key Terms

Background stressors ("daily hassles")

Cataclysmic events

Coping

General adaptation syndrome (GAS)

Hardiness

Health psychology

Learned helplessness

Personal stressors

Posttraumatic stress disorder (PTSD)

Psychoneuroimmunology (PNI)

Psychophysiological disorders

Resilience

Social support

Stress

## AP Key People

Han Selye

## Class Discussion Ideas

**THE NATURE OF STRESS** Begin by describing the biological and psychological consequences of stress.

*Biological consequences include:*

- Hormones (cortisol)
- Heart rate
- Blood pressure
- Skin conductivity (GSR)

Over time, the heightened levels of these consequences can lead to psychophysiological disorders.

*Psychological consequences include:*

- Distorted view of environment
- Extreme emotional responses
- Inability to handle new stressors

**Top Three Stressors:** Have students list three things that are currently causing them stress. Ask them to describe how they physically when they are under stress. Ask them to describe their thoughts and feelings when they are under stress. Next, ask them what they do to cope with stress. Finally, ask them what, if anything, they would like to do differently to cope with their stress.

**PSYCHONEUROIMMUNOLOGY** Stress is viewed as an interaction among:

- Central nervous system functioning
- Immune system
- Emotions

**Adaptive Value of Stress?** Is stress adaptive? You may want to discuss with students if they think there is an adaptive value to stress. What does it do that's good and helpful? For example, on the next exam, should they have some stress? What if they had none? Would they even study?

**Chronic Stress and Disease:** This is a good time to discuss incurable chronic health conditions and their effect on stress levels, not only for the person with the disease but also for family, friends, and caregivers. Ask students to think about any long-term incurable condition (e.g., cancer, diabetes, herpes, etc.). Keep in mind that many folks have difficulty adjusting to a diagnosis, as may their loved ones. This may actually even have greater impact on family, friends, and caregivers, as they may feel that "they have to be strong" for their loved one.

**Stress and Aging:** Stress makes your cells age faster. Ask students what physical changes in their appearance they notice about themselves when they are under stress. Ask how they recognize stress in their friends and loved ones.

**GENERAL ADAPTATION SYNDROME (GAS)** Ask students to describe stages with regard to specific stressors from their own lives. Ask them whether they have experienced these stages during exam time and how their health was affected.

An important qualification on this model is that the physiological reaction depends on the way the event is perceived.

**CATEGORIZING STRESSORS** Distinguish among cataclysmic, personal, and background stressors as follows:

- *Cataclysmic:* Strong stressors that occur suddenly and affect many people at once. Examples include the 2010 Haitian earthquake, 2004 tsunami, 2005 Hurricane Katrina, and so on. Choose a recent one to illustrate. (Hint to students to remember this term: Cataclysm sounds like chasm, and falling down a chasm would be a catastrophe.)
- *Personal:* Major life events that have immediate consequences that fade with time. Examples: see the College Stress Test (below).
- *Background:* Everyday annoyances that cause minor irritations but have no long-term effects unless continued or combined with other stressful event.

Point out that cataclysmic stressors often include personal stressors (the death of a loved one) and background stressors (after a fire or natural disaster, people have difficulties on a daily basis in terms of housing, work, and transportation). It is also important to point out that appraisal processes influence how these events are interpreted, as discussed below in terms of the Folkman and Lazarus model. People with strong religious convictions will see these stressful events as a test of their faith.

**MODEL OF COPING** Use this as the basis for a discussion of the Lazarus and Folkman model of coping:

Person-environment encounter (the potentially stressful situation) → Appraisal (of situation and ability to cope) → Emotion (stress or challenge) → Coping (problem-focused = change situation; emotion-focused = change emotion)

Point out that in this model, it is "all in the appraisal." There is no absolutely stressful event because one person's stress is another person's challenge. This makes the Lazarus model very different from the life events model in which individual differences in appraisal of events are not taken into account (as in the College Stress Test, above).

**TYPES OF COPING** Emotion-focused coping is characterized by the conscious regulation of emotions. It does not change the perception of the problem, but instead involves strategies such as accepting sympathy or looking at the bright side of the situation.

Problem-focused coping is characterized by the management of the problem or stimulus that caused stress. This strategy involves changing behavior or developing a plan of action, meaning that the perception of the problem that caused the stress is modifiable.

Some methods of coping do not fall into these two categories, specifically seeking social support and escaping from a stressful situation.

Indicate that the appropriateness of the coping method depends on the situation. Emotion-focused coping is more effective in situations that are not amenable to change; by contrast, problem-focused coping is more effective when the situation is modifiable. For example, emotion-focused coping would not be an effective way to prepare for an exam, but problem-focused coping would be.

**Emotion-Coping Strategies:** Ask students which emotion-focused coping strategies they use most often and which are most effective.

# Activities

**Stress Vulnerability Quiz:** Have students take the quiz at http://allpsych.com/tests/self-help/stresstest.html and print out their results (the results will appear in a pop-up box). Students can write a one- to two-page paper on their results and identify specific coping mechanisms that they can use to help decrease their vulnerability to stress.

**Final Exams Just Make Me Sick:** After learning about stress's effect on the immune system, create a seminar or workshop for students at your school that teaches them about the importance of coping strategies and ways to handle stress during final exam week. Present your ideas to the class.

**Stress:** Have students complete Holmes and Rahe's Social Readjustment Rating Scale (SRRS) at http://www.uccs.umn.edu/oldsite/lasc/handouts/socialreadjustment.html. Ask them if they think the values accurately represent different stressors. Why or why not?

**Stress:** Have students complete the Interactive Stress Scale at http://www.teachhealth.com/#stressscale. Ask them if they think the results are accurate for them.

### COPING CHECKLIST

**Methods of Coping:** Have students complete *Handout: Methods of Coping.*

### HOW DO YOU COPE?

- **How Do You Cope?** Have students complete *Handout: How Do You Cope?*, indicating methods they have used in a stressful situation.
- **Reducing Tension:** The following site offers three different breathing exercises: http://www.drweil.com/drw/u/ART00521/three-breathing-exercises.html. Have the students record how tense they feel before the breathing exercise. If possible, minimize classroom distractions. Next, teach the students how to perform Exercise 3. Have the students practice the exercise for about 5 minutes. Then ask them to record their tension level at the end of the exercise. Discuss the results in class and have those who are willing to share say if their tension levels changed at all. Ask the students what would stop them from practicing such an exercise daily.

### LOCUS OF CONTROL & ATTRIBUTION STYLE TEST
Have students go to http://psychologytoday.psychtests.com/cgi-bin/tests/transfer_ap.cgi?partner=pt&part=1&test=lc&AMT=9.95&item=Locus%20of%20Control%20Test%20-%20R and take the Locus of Control & Attribution Style Test—Revised. This gives you the opportunity to discuss the role that LOC has on explanatory styles and thus resiliency in the face of negative events.

### BURNOUT SURVEY
Have students complete *Handout: Burnout Survey.*

# Discussion Questions

**LEARNED HELPLESSNESS** Give an example of a time when you felt that you were a victim of learned helplessness. Describe this briefly.

- How did you feel about not being able to alter the outcome of the situation?
- What do you think people can do to overcome the feeling of learned helplessness?

# Suggested Media

- *American Institute of Stress:* http://www.stress.org.
- *Coping with Stress—CDC:* https://www.cdc.gov/features/copingwithstress/.
- *Health Psychology & Rehabilitation:* http://www.healthpsych.com/. This website offers research, viewpoints, and practical suggestions about health psychology.
- *Help! I'm Stressed.* Insight Media, 2012, 26:00. This program defines stress and looks at both positive and negative forms of stress. It describes the symptoms of stress and stress management techniques.
- *Selye on stress:* http://www.youtube.com/watch?v=YJCeDtNh_Aw.
- *20 Tips to Tame Your Stress:* https://psychcentral.com/lib/20-tips-to-tame-your-stress/.

# Additional Readings

Creswell, J. D., & Lindsay, E. K. (2014). How does mindfulness training affect health? A mindfulness stress buffering account. *Current Directions in Psychological Science, 23*, 401–407.

Epstein, R. (2011). Fight the FRAZZLED Mind. *Scientific American Mind, 22*(4), 30–35.

Greenberg, J. S. (2010). *Comprehensive stress management.* McGraw-Hill.

Lovallo, W. (2016). *Stress and health: Biological and psychological interactions.* Sage.

McGonigal, K. (2015). *The upside of stress: Why stress is good for you and how to get good at it.* Avery.

Sood, A. (2013). *The Mayo Clinic's guide to stress free living.* Da Capo Life Long Books.

Tummers, N. (2013). *Stress management: A wellness approach.* Human Kinetics.

Wolever, R.Q., Reardon, B. , & Hannan, T. (2016). *The mindful diet: How to transform your relationship with food for lasting weight loss and vibrant health.* Simon and Schuster.

# **AP** Student Edition Answer Key

## Neuroscience in Your Life: The Neuroscience of Resilience

Answer Suggestions

- Finding out if individuals who experience high levels of stress are predisposed to psychological disorders may lead to new therapeutic interventions.
- Questions might include: How large was the sample? Were both genders investigated? What were participants' ages (younger brains are more plastic)? What was the strength of the trauma? Was there previous trauma?

# Applying Psychology in the 21st Century: Does Using Facebook Make You Feel Bad?

Answer Suggestions

- Online social interactions might be problematic if only positive events are displayed. This might create an illusion that others are doing better than you and decrease your self-esteem. The benefits of online interactions include reinforcing real-world relationships and accessing social support.
- The research found that online social networking does not provide the same health benefits as real-world social networking. Constant use of Facebook was associated with poor life satisfaction and mental health.

# AP Test Practice

## Part I: Multiple Choice

1.  **E** *(Skill 1.A, Learning Target 7.H)*

2.  **A** *(Skill 1.A, Learning Target 7.H)*

3.  **D** *(Skill 1.B, Learning Target 7.H)*

## Part II: Free Response

**A.**

The alarm stage is when one meets and resists the stressor. When Ali enters alarm, her sympathetic nervous system will become energized so she can initially cope with the stressor. She may have increased blood pressure and increased hormone activity.

The resistance stage is when one copes and resists the stressor. When Ali enters resistance, her sympathetic nervous system will continue to actively fight the stressor by releasing more hormones.

The exhaustion stage is when negative consequences occur because coping is inadequate. When Ali enters this stage, she may get physically ill or have negative psychological symptoms, such as being irritable or unable to concentrate in her classes.

The immune system protects one's body. The stress Ali is experiencing may decrease the functioning of her immune system and she may end up catching a cold.

**B.**

Problem-focused coping attempts to modify the stressful problem. Ali may cope with her stress by creating a plan of action to have a parent deliver the project to school so she can still turn it in.

Defense mechanisms are unconscious strategies used to reduce anxiety. Ali might deal with her stress by rationalizing and creating an excuse for why she left the project at home.

Learned helplessness is a state in which people conclude that an aversive stimuli cannot be controlled and quit trying to remedy the situation. Ali may quit trying to submit her project for credit because she feels turning in the project is out of her control.

# Module 44: Psychological Aspects of Illness and Well-Being

## AP Module Summary

In Module 44 is where you will find more specific information that should be addressed. The new course and exam description guide has added specifics to the learning target e.g. stress related illnesses, Lewin's motivational conflicts theory and unhealthy behaviors. Much of the information is intuitive but regardless pointing out the relevance will help students identify and better recall for later use.

**THE AS, BS, AND DS OF CORONARY HEART DISEASE** The *Type A behavior pattern* is a cluster of behaviors involving hostility, competitiveness, time urgency, and feeling driven. In contrast, the *Type B behavior pattern* is characterized by a patient, cooperative, noncompetitive, and nonaggressive manner. The importance of the Type A behavior pattern lies in its links to coronary heart disease. Men who display the Type A pattern develop coronary heart disease twice as often and suffer significantly more fatal heart attacks than those classified as having the Type B pattern. Hostility is the key component of the Type A behavior pattern that is related to heart disease. Hostility is very toxic as it produces excessive physiological arousal in stressful situations. That arousal, in turn, results in increased production of the hormones epinephrine and norepinephrine as well as increases in heart rate and blood pressure. In addition, other types of negative emotions besides the hostility found in Type A behavior appear to be related to heart attacks. For example, psychologist Johan Denollet has found evidence that what he calls *Type D*—for "distressed"—behavior is linked to coronary heart disease. In this view, insecurity, anxiety, and the negative outlook Type Ds display put them at risk for repeated heart attacks.

**SMOKING** Genetics seems to determine, in part, whether people will become smokers, how much they will smoke, and how easily they can quit. However, although genetics plays a role in smoking, most research suggests that environmental factors are the primary cause of the habit. Greater exposure to smoking in media such as film also leads to a higher risk of becoming an established smoker. In addition, smoking a cigarette is sometimes viewed as a rite of passage for adolescents undertaken at the urging of friends and viewed as a sign of growing up.

Ultimately, smoking becomes a habit. People begin to label themselves smokers, and they become dependent physiologically as a result of smoking because nicotine, a primary ingredient of tobacco, is highly addictive. A complex relationship develops among smoking, nicotine levels, and a smoker's emotions in which a certain nicotine level becomes associated with a positive emotional state. As a result, people smoke in an effort to regulate both emotional states and nicotine levels in the blood.

**Quitting Smoking:** Because smoking has both psychological and biological components, few habits are as difficult to break. Some of the biochemical reactions to nicotine are similar to those to cocaine, amphetamines, and morphine. Furthermore, changes in brain chemistry brought about by smoking may make smokers more resistant to antismoking messages.

Among the most effective tools for ending the smoking habit are drugs that replace the nicotine found in cigarettes. Whether in the form of gum, patches, nasal sprays, or inhalers, these products provide a dose of nicotine that reduces dependence on cigarettes. Another approach is exemplified by the drugs Zyban and Chantix; rather than replacing nicotine, they reduce the pleasure from smoking and suppress withdrawal symptoms that smokers experience when they try to stop. Behavioral strategies, which view smoking as a learned habit and concentrate on changing the smoking response, can also be effective. In the long term, the most effective means of reducing smoking may be changes in societal norms and attitudes toward the habit.

## ![AP] Key Terms

**Type A behavior pattern**
**Type B behavior pattern**

## Class Discussion Ideas

**TYPE A AND TYPE B BEHAVIOR PATTERNS** Distinguish between these behavior patterns using this list:

*Type A behavior pattern:*

- Competitive
- Urgency about time
- Driven quality to one's work
- Hostile in verbal and nonverbal behavior

*Type B behavior pattern:*

- Not competitive
- Not urgent about time
- Not unusually aggressive or hostile

*Problems with Type A/Type B research:*

Point out that as compelling as the Type A-Type B distinction seems, there are still weaknesses in the literature. The main problem is that the data are correlational and other factors may be responsible for the apparent relationship between behavior and cardiovascular disease.

**HEALTH IN THE UNITED STATES** Describe the results of findings on health of the U.S. population, summarized in this graph from the Centers for Disease Control and Prevention report, *Health-Related Quality of Life*: http://www.cdc.gov/hrqol/index.htm.

*This was the measure used to assess health-related quality of life:*

- Would you say that in general, your health is excellent, very good, good, fair, or poor?
- Now thinking about your physical health, which includes physical illness and injury, for how many days during the past 30 days was your physical health not good?
- Now thinking about your mental health, which includes stress, depression, and problems with emotions, for how many days during the past 30 days was your mental health not good?
- During the past 30 days, for about how many days did poor physical or mental health keep you from doing your usual activities, such as self-care, work, or recreation?

**PREVALENCE OF CIGARETTE SMOKING IN THE UNITED STATES** The CDC has extensive resources on this topic: http://www.cdc.gov/tobacco/data_statistics/fact_sheets/youth_data/tobacco_use/index.htm.
The National Cancer Institute also has informative resources: https://www.cancer.gov.

**Why Smoke?** Ask why, if people know that smoking is unhealthy, they continue to smoke. Students may talk about addiction, association with pleasant things (eating, socializing, food, etc.), or a combination thereof. You may want to use this question to reinforce the idea of the biopsychosocial model and its effect on health.

# Activities

**TYPE A AND TYPE B BEHAVIOR PATTERNS QUESTIONNAIRE**

**Type A and B Behavior Patterns:** Have students complete *Handout: Type A and B Behavior Inventory.*

**Type A, Type B, and Type D Behavior:** Have the students write down the names of their immediate family members. Next, have the students determine if those family members are of Type A, Type B, or Type D. Direct the students to explain their choices.

**Type A:** Have students take the Type A test, comprised of 73 questions:

http://www.queendom.com/tests/access_page/index.htm?idRegTest=1126. Do they think the results are accurate? Why or why not?

**Quitting Smoking:** Have the students think of someone they know that has quit smoking. Ask the students to interview that person to find out how that person quit. Did he or she use any of the common methods discussed in the chapter? They should find out information such as how long it has been since the person last smoked and whether or not he or she still has cravings. Ask the students to write a brief one- to two-page paper summarizing the information they found.

# Discussion Questions

**TYPE A AND TYPE B BEHAVIOR** Do you know someone who shows the Type A behavior pattern? What is it like being around this person?

- Why might hostility be such an important component of the Type A behavior pattern?
- Would it be possible to help a Type A person become more like Type B? How might this be accomplished?
- Do you believe individuals in the United States experience more stress than those in other countries? Why or why not?
- Are individuals really responsible for the unhealthy life styles they may be living, considering how easy our society makes it to be unhealthy with fast-food restaurants, remote controls for televisions, easy car purchasing, gas prices that are low compared with those in other countries, and having most foods preprocessed for microwave cooking?
- What areas of psychology discussed in the textbook prior to the present chapter can contribute to health psychology? Explain.

# Suggested Media

- *American Cancer Association:* http://www.cancer.org/docroot/home/index.asp.
- *American Heart Association:* http://www.heart.org/HEARTORG/GettingHealthy/ StressManagement/HowDoesStressAffectYou/FAQs-About-Stress_UCM_307982_Article. jsp. The American Heart Association's FAQs on stress and heart disease can be found here.
- *Quit Smoking—CDC:* http://www.cdc.gov/tobacco/quit_smoking/index.htm. This is a part of the Center for Disease Control and Prevention's website. It has a lot of links, programs, and materials for quitting smoking.
- *Tips from Former Smokers Campaign—CDC:* http://www.cdc.gov/tobacco/campaign/tips/ about/campaign-overview.html.

**CANCER EDUCATIONAL VIDEOS** Web resources include videos on cancer prevention and survivor stories. Consult this website:

http://www.sciencedaily.com/videos/health_medicine/.

## Additional Readings

Borelli, L. (2016). How long will I live? Personality type influences physical health, life span. *Medical Daily.* http://www.medicaldaily.com/how-long-will-i-live-personality-type-influences-physical-health-life-span-396082.

Goliszek, A. (2014). Is there a cancer prone personality? *Psychology Today: How the Mind Heals the Body.* https://www.psychologytoday.com/blog/how-the-mind-heals-the-body/201411/is-there-cancer-prone-personality.

## AP Student Edition Answer Key

### AP Test Practice

#### Part I: Multiple Choice

1. **B** *(Skill 1.B, Learning Target 7.H)*

2. **C** *(Skill 1.A, Learning Target 7.H)*

3. **E** *(Skill 1.A, Learning Target 7.H)*

#### Part II: Free Response

**A.**

Positive emotions may help generate specialized "killer" cells that help control the size and spread of cancerous tumors.

Certain types of psychological therapy have the potential for improving quality of life and extending the lives of cancer patients by slowing the progression of the disease.

**B.**

Psychoneuroimmunology studies the relationship between psychological factors, the immune system, and the brain. Stress decreases the ability of the immune system to respond to disease, allowing cancer cells to spread more rapidly. Stress does this by decreasing the production level of disease-fighting white blood cells called lymphocytes.

Emotion-focused coping concentrates on managing emotions by seeking to change how one perceives a problem. Examples of emotion-focused coping for a cancer diagnosis include accepting sympathy from others and looking at the bright side of a situation.

Social support is being part of a mutual network of caring, interested others. After receiving a diagnosis of cancer, individuals may utilize their social support to provide information, advice, and physical aid. Social support also helps to lower stress levels and increases coping.

# Module 45: Promoting Health and Wellness

## AP Module Summary

The material in Module 45 serves as a reminder to students on how best to improve their psyiological and psychological well-being. The important work of Martin Seligman and positive psychology should be an emphasis of study. These concepts and research may have been covered in earlier modules and so specifically setting a day aside to review module 45 may be unnecessary. Chances are you may have discussed many of the details in this module when reviewing emotions.

**WELL-BEING AND HAPPINESS** What makes for a good life? Health psychologists are turning their spotlight on the question by investigating *subjective well-being*, people's sense of their happiness and satisfaction with their lives.

- This would be a good time to have students review the work of Martin Seligman and the approach of positive psychology.

### WHAT ARE THE CHARACTERISTICS OF HAPPY PEOPLE?

- *Happy people have high self-esteem.* Particularly in Western cultures, which emphasize the importance of individuality, people who are happy like themselves.
- *Happy people have a firm sense of control.* They feel more in control of events in their lives, unlike those who feel they are the pawns of others and who experience learned helplessness.
- *Happy individuals are optimistic.* Their optimism permits them to persevere at tasks and ultimately to achieve more.
- *Men and women generally are made happy by the same sorts of activities—but not always.* Most of the time, adult men and women achieve the same level of happiness from the same things, such as hanging out with friends.
- *Happy people like to be around other people.* They tend to be extroverted and have a supportive network of close relationships.

## AP Key Terms

**Subjective well-being**
**Positive Psychology**

## Class Discussion Ideas

**SUBJECTIVE WELL-BEING** Present these components of subjective well-being:

- High self-esteem
- Firm sense of control
- Optimism
- Enjoy being around other people

Show the relationship between subjective well-being or optimism and health (Cohen et al., 1999).

Optimists have better immune system functioning during high levels of short-term stress. However, when faced with chronic stress, they suffer more harmful immune system changes than pessimists. High expectations of the optimists may make them more vulnerable.

# Activities

**WELLNESS AND STRESS CONTROL**

- **Becoming Physically Active and Eating Right:** Ask students to keep a journal for a week on how many times they exercise and what activities they do. They should also write down what they eat during the day for breakfast, lunch, and dinner, as well as snacks. At the end of the week, ask the students to write a summary of what they found out about their eating habits and exercise habits. Discuss with the students what was in the chapter regarding varying the exercise routines and eating food from all four food groups. The students should gain some insight into their eating habits, noticing where they should make adjustments and improvements.

- **Personal Interview of Success:** Interview someone you know who has successfully quit smoking, or started an exercise program. Ask the person about his or her experience with each of the stages of change. Does the theory fit that person's experience? Why or why not?

- **Fact or Fiction Nutrition Game:** Have students play one of the games found at http://www.eatright.org/resource/food/resources/national-nutrition-month/national-nutrition-month-games. Once they have completed the game, the students will see their results. Have a dialogue about these results and discuss all of the misinformation that exists about eating healthy.

- **Smart Choices on the Go**: Using *Handout: Smart Choices on the Go!,* have students discuss their dining-out habits in groups. They should include the healthy and unhealthy habits in the discussion. Have a note-taker write down what the group discusses and then present to the rest of the class.

- **Don't Label Us:** Becoming a wise consumer of healthy food choices can be difficult. Either go to the grocery store or find some items in your household pantry, and take a very close look at what the label tells you about the food or product you are eating. Check expiration dates as well. Make sure you look up any words that you don't understand. Create a report to the class on your findings.

# Discussion Questions

Why do people engage in unhealthy behaviors even when they know it is unhealthy?

# Suggested Media

- *Eatright:* http://www.eatright.org. This Academy of Nutrition and Dietetics website on eating healthy includes interactive games, fact sheets, and other useful information regarding nutrition.
- *Healthy choices:* http://insight.kellogg.northwestern.edu/article/healthy_choices.
- *Why Some People Find Exercise Harder Than Others:* Emily Balcetis, TedxNewYork, 2014: http://www.ted.com/talks/emily_balcetis_why_some_people_find_exercise_harder_than_others.

# Additional Readings

Creswell, J. D., & Lindsay, E. K. (2014). How does mindfulness training affect health? A mindfulness stress buffering account. *Current Directions in Psychological Science, 23*, 401–407.

Tummers, N. (2013). *Stress management: A wellness approach.* Human Kinetics.

Wolever, R. Q., Reardon, B. , & Hannan, T. (2016). *The mindful diet: How to transform your relationship with food for lasting weight loss and vibrant health.* Simon and Schuster.

## AP Test Practice

### Part I: Multiple Choice

1.  **E** (Skill 1.A, Learning Target 7.H)

2.  **C** (Skill 1.A, Learning Target 7.H)

3.  **B** (Skill 1.A, Learning Target 7.H)

### Part II: Free Response

Positively framed messages are best for motivating preventative behavior. Jayden could share how skin cancer is curable if detected early and chances are reduced by using sunscreen.

Cultural values and expectations can contribute to barriers between patients and caregivers. Jayden could suggest that his classmates seek medical practitioners who are familiar with their culture in order to produce compliance with medical recommendations.

Set point for happiness is the belief that specific events may temporarily elevate or depress one's mood, but people ultimately return to their general level of happiness. Jayden could talk about how events, such as a grade or change in employment, will impact one's mood only temporarily.

# CHAPTER 15

# Psychological Disorders

## AP Introduction

For many students, the topic of abnormal psychology represents the high point of the course: what they have been waiting to learn all semester. Therefore, engaging student interest in the topic should not be a problem. The challenge is choosing which topics to focus on in this very rich area of content. Working within the structure of the perspectives in psychology will make this content easier for students to grasp because the basic parameters have already been laid down and developed in other chapters. Thus, presenting the possible causes for psychological disorders should be done in terms of those perspectives.

In terms of presenting the disorders, it is crucial to emphasize the role of *DSM-5* (the most recent version) in setting the stage for reliable diagnoses. *DSM-5* also provides a good organizing structure to use in presenting the disorders. Although there will not be time to devote sufficient attention to all disorders, you should be able to focus on one or two that are of particular interest to you to use in helping students gain a conceptualization of disorders as having multiple causes and (as discussed in the next chapter) multiple approaches to treatment.

## AP Essential Questions

- Why is psychological perspective necessary in the treatment of disorders?
- How are psychological disorders treated?

## Module 46: Normal Versus Abnormal: Making the Distinction

### AP Learning Targets:

- Describe and compare different theoretical approaches in explaining behavior.
- Recognize the use of the most recent version of the *Diagnostic and Statistical Manual of Mental Disorders (DSM)* published by the American Psychiatric Association as the primary reference for making diagnostic judgments.
- Describe contemporary and historical conceptions of what constitutes psychological disorders.
- Discuss the intersection between psychology and the legal system.
- Evaluate the strengths and limitations of various approaches to explaining psychological disorders.
- Identify the positive and negative consequences of diagnostic labels.

### Pacing:

1 Block or 2 Traditional Class periods

# Module 47: The Major Psychological Disorders

**AP Learning Targets:**

- Discuss the major diagnostic categories, including neurodevelopmental disorders, neuro-cognitive disorders, schizophrenia spectrum, and other psychotic disorders, and their corresponding symptoms.
- Discuss the major diagnostic categories, including anxiety disorders, bipolar and related disorders, depressive disorders, obsessive-compulsive and related disorders, and their corresponding symptoms.
- Discuss the major diagnostic categories, including dissociative disorders, somatic symptoms and related disorders, and trauma- and stressor-related disorders and their corresponding symptoms.
- Discuss the major diagnostic categories, including feeding and eating disorders, personality disorders, and their corresponding symptoms.

**Pacing:**

3½ Blocks or 7 Traditional Class periods

# Module 48: Psychological Disorders in Perspective

**No AP Learning Targets:**

**Pacing:**

½ Block or 1 Traditional Class period

Module 48 could be skipped in favor of spending extra time elsewhere

# Module 46: Normal versus Abnormal: Making the Distinction

## AP Module Summary

You will find much of Module 46 to be a review of the psychological perspectives. This review will serve as a valuable moment for students who are approaching the end of the course and preparing for the national exam. In this module students should now be able to clearly see how their understandings of the perspectives is important to the understanding of human behavior. The only change made to the new Course and Exam Description Guide is the specific reference to the newly revised Diagnostic and Statistical Manual of Mental Disorders.

If it was to be believed that a piece of writing could help us understand and ascertain to what degree a person is "normal," it would not be true. Casually examining a person's writing is insufficient to determine the degree to which that person is "normal." However, even when we consider more extensive samples of a person's behavior, we will find that there may be only a fine line between behavior that is considered normal and behavior that is considered abnormal.

**DEFINING ABNORMALITY** Because of the difficulty in distinguishing normal from abnormal behavior, psychologists have struggled to devise a precise, scientific definition of "abnormal behavior." For instance, consider the following definitions, each of which has adequacies and deficiencies:

- *Abnormality as deviation from the average:* To employ this statistically based approach, we simply observe what behaviors are rare or occur infrequently in a specific society or culture and label those deviations from the norm "abnormal."
- *Abnormality as deviation from the ideal:* An alternative approach considers abnormality in relation to the standard toward which most people are striving—the ideal.
- *Abnormality as a sense of personal discomfort:* A more useful definition concentrates on the psychological consequences of the behavior for the individual. In this approach, behavior is considered abnormal if it produces a sense of personal distress, anxiety, or guilt in an individual—or if it is harmful to others in some way.
- *Abnormality as the inability to function effectively:* Most people are able to feed themselves, hold a job, get along with others, and, in general, live as productive members of society. Yet there are those who are unable to adjust to the demands of society or function effectively.
- *Abnormality as a legal concept:* To the judicial system, the distinction between normal and abnormal behavior rests on the definition of *insanity,* which is a legal but not a psychological term. The definition of insanity varies from one jurisdiction to another. In some states, *insanity* simply means that defendants could not understand the difference between right and wrong at the time they committed a criminal act. Other states consider whether defendants are substantially incapable of understanding the criminality of their behavior or unable to control themselves.

Psychologists typically define *abnormal behavior* broadly as behavior that causes people to experience distress and prevents them from functioning in their daily lives.

**PERSPECTIVES ON ABNORMALITY: FROM SUPERSTITION TO SCIENCE (SEE FIGURE 1)** Throughout much of human history, people linked abnormal behavior to superstition and witchcraft. Individuals who displayed abnormal behavior were accused of being possessed by the devil or some sort of demonic god. Authorities felt justified in "treating" abnormal behavior by attempting to drive out the source of the problem. This typically involved whipping, immersion in hot water, starvation, or other forms of torture. Contemporary approaches take a more enlightened view. Today, six major perspectives are used to understand psychological disorders. These perspectives suggest not only different causes of abnormal behavior but different treatment approaches as well.

**MEDICAL PERSPECTIVE** The *medical perspective* suggests that when an individual displays symptoms of a psychological disorder, the fundamental cause will be found through a physical examination of the individual, which may reveal a hormonal imbalance, a chemical deficiency, or a brain injury.

**PSYCHOANALYTIC PERSPECTIVE** The *psychoanalytic perspective* holds that abnormal behavior stems from childhood conflicts over opposing wishes regarding sex and aggression. To uncover the roots of people's disordered behavior, the psychoanalytic perspective scrutinizes their early life history. However, there is no conclusive way to link people's childhood experiences with the abnormal behaviors they display as adults. Consequently, we can never be sure that specific childhood experiences can be linked to specific adult abnormal behaviors.

**BEHAVIORAL PERSPECTIVE** The *behavioral perspective* looks at the rewards and punishments in the environment that determine abnormal behavior and views the behavior itself as the problem. Using the basic principles of learning, behavioral theorists see both normal and abnormal behaviors as responses to various stimuli—responses that have been learned through past experience and are guided in the present by stimuli in the individual's environment.

**COGNITIVE PERSPECTIVE** The *cognitive perspective* suggests that cognitions (people's thoughts and beliefs) are central to a person's abnormal behavior. A primary goal of treatment using the cognitive perspective is to explicitly teach new, more adaptive ways of thinking.

**HUMANISTIC PERSPECTIVE** The *humanistic perspective* emphasizes the responsibility people have for their own behavior, even when such behavior is abnormal. Humanistic approaches focus on the relationship of the individual to society; it considers the ways in which people view themselves in relation to others and see their place in the world. The humanistic perspective views people as having an awareness of life and of themselves that leads them to search for meaning and self-worth. Rather than assuming that individuals require a "cure," the humanistic perspective suggests that they can, by and large, set their own limits of what is acceptable behavior.

**SOCIOCULTURAL PERSPECTIVE** The *sociocultural perspective* assumes that people's behavior—both normal and abnormal—is shaped by the society and culture in which they live. According to this view, societal and cultural factors such as poverty and prejudice may be at the root of abnormal behavior. Specifically, the kinds of stresses and conflicts people experience in their daily lives can promote and maintain abnormal behavior.

**CLASSIFYING ABNORMAL BEHAVIOR: THE ABCS OF *DSM*** Society has long placed labels on people who display abnormal behavior. Unfortunately, most of the time these labels have reflected intolerance and have been used with little thought as to what each label signifies. Providing appropriate and specific names and classifications for abnormal behavior has presented a major challenge to psychologists. It is not hard to understand why, given the difficulties discussed earlier in simply distinguishing normal from abnormal behavior. Yet psychologists and other care providers need to classify abnormal behavior in order to diagnose it and ultimately treat it.

- Bring up the role of confidentiality in diagnosing individuals.

***DSM-5:* DETERMINING DIAGNOSTIC DISTINCTIONS** One standard system, devised by the American Psychiatric Association, has emerged in the United States. Most professionals today use this classification system, known as the *Diagnostic and Statistical Manual of Mental Disorders, Fifth Edition (DSM-5),* to diagnose and classify abnormal behavior (American Psychiatric Association, 2013). The *DSM-5,* most recently revised in 2013, attempts to provide comprehensive and relatively precise definitions for more than 200 disorders. By following the criteria presented in the *DSM-5* classification system, diagnosticians use clients' reported symptoms to identify the specific problem an individual is experiencing. (**Figure 2** provides a brief outline of the major diagnostic categories; American Psychiatric Association, 2013.) Some practitioners have argued that this diagnostic approach is too heavily based on a medical model.

**CONNING THE CLASSIFIERS: THE SHORTCOMINGS OF *DSM*** When clinical psychologist David Rosenhan and eight colleagues sought admission to separate mental hospitals across the United States in the 1970s, each stated that he or she was hearing voices—"unclear voices" that said "empty," "hollow," and "thud"—and each was immediately admitted to the hospital. However, the truth was that they actually were conducting a study, and none of them was really hearing voices. Aside from these misrepresentations, everything else they did and said represented their true behavior, including the responses they gave during extensive admission interviews and their answers to the battery of tests they were asked to complete. In fact, as soon as they were admitted, they said they no longer heard any voices. In short, each of the pseudo-patients acted in a "normal" way (Rosenhan, 1973). Each of them was diagnosed as severely abnormal on the basis of observed behavior. Mental health professionals labeled most as suffering from schizophrenia and kept them in the hospital for 3 to 52 days, with the average stay of 19 days. Even when they were discharged, most of the "patients" left with the label *schizophrenia—in remission,* implying that the abnormal behavior had only temporarily subsided and could recur at any time. Most disturbing, no one on the hospital staff identified any of the pseudopatients as impostors—although some of the actual patients figured out the ruse.

**THE STIGMA OF LABELING** The results of Rosenhan's classic study illustrate that placing labels on individuals powerfully influences the way mental health workers perceive and interpret their actions. It also points out that determining who is psychologically disordered is not always a clear-cut or accurate process. Gender dysphoria (in which one's gender identity is in conflict with one's biological sex) provides a modern illustration of the dilemma between the pros of a formal diagnosis and the cons of patient labeling. For example, most medical insurance providers require a formal, specific diagnosis in order to provide health care coverage for procedures such as a sex change operation. Many individuals who experience a conflict between their gender identity and their biological sex object theoretically to the idea that their desire to be the other sex should be labeled a "disorder." Yet without a formal diagnosis, those same individuals may be forced to pay out-of-pocket for what is an expensive medical procedure. This diagnosis-based system of insurance coverage often creates a catch-22 for mental health care professionals: They must decide between potentially stigmatizing their clients by providing a formal diagnosis, implying some type of disorder, or leaving patients undiagnosed and potentially without the financial support necessary to receive important procedures that will significantly improve the clients' quality of life.

- This may be a point in the introduction to psychological disorders when you bring up the legal system and the use of the insanity defense.

## **AP** Key Terms

| | |
|---|---|
| abnormal behavior | humanistic perspective |
| behavioral perspective | medical perspective |
| cognitive perspective | psychoanalytic perspective |
| Diagnostic and Statistical Manual of Mental Disorders, Fifth Edition (DSM-5) | sociocultural perspective |

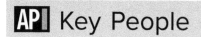
**David Rosenhan**

## Class Discussion Ideas

### SUMMARY OF HISTORY OF MENTAL ILLNESS

**Prehistoric times** Demonic possession was thought to cause psychological disorders. Based on evidence of trephined skulls, it was thought that prehistoric people tried to release the evil spirits by drilling a hole in the skull.

**Ancient Greece and Rome** The scientific approach emerged. The Greek physician Hippocrates sought a cause within the body. This approach continued through Roman times with the writings of the physician Galen.

**Middle Ages** Return to belief in spiritual possession and attempts to exorcise the devil out of the mentally ill. The mentally ill were thrown into prisons and poorhouses.

**Renaissance** Bethlem Royal Hospital was founded in London in 1247, as a priory dedicated to St. Mary of Bethlehem; it served as a site for the housing of people with psychological disorders. Also in this period, witch hunts took place, starting in the 1480s and continuing through the 1700s.

**1700s** Asylums became overcrowded and conditions deteriorated. By the 1700s, St. Mary's was known as "bedlam."

**1800s** Reform movements began in Europe and the United States:

- Benjamin Rush attempted to devise new methods of treatment (the "tranquilizing chair") based on scientific method.
- Dorothea Dix, a Massachusetts schoolteacher, originated the state hospital movement as a means of providing "moral treatment."

**Early to mid-20th century** Overcrowding again became prevalent in state mental hospitals. Extreme measures of treatment were used that many thought to be inhumane.

**Era of deinstitutionalization—late 20th century** Invention of antipsychotic medications in the 1950s made it possible for people with severe disorders to live outside institutions. President John F. Kennedy called for community mental health centers. However, this has not been completely effective as the problem of homelessness has arisen.

**DEFINING PSYCHOPATHOLOGY** You may want to point out to students that defining a disorder is no easy feat. For example, do you go with statistically unusual as the standard? If so, then how do you deal with intelligence? The bottom 2.5 percent are in the *DSM* as intellectually challenged, but the top 2.5 percent (the gifted portion) are not. Should they be? Then what do you do about disorders that are high in the general population, such as substance abuse?

Students generally have no problem brainstorming ideas about what abnormal is, but it is easy to challenge most of them. For example, let's use unusual behaviors. Are behaviors you don't see frequently necessarily abnormal? What if a student took off his or her shirt and started dancing on the bleachers in the stadium? It's not something you see every day, but as the tabloids show us, it's not something that people think is necessarily "abnormal." However, if it happened in class....

Another factor is cultural influences. It is important to remind students that speaking in tongues in a Pentecostal church is fine, but in another setting, it's probably not.

**"MADNESS" AND CREATIVITY: THE CASE OF VINCENT VAN GOGH** The case of Vincent van Gogh (1853–1890) provides an excellent opportunity to discuss the relationship between "madness" and creativity. Van Gogh is generally considered the greatest Dutch painter after Rembrandt. His reputation is based largely on the works of the last 3 years of his short 10-year painting career, and he had a powerful influence on expressionism in modern art. He produced more than 800 oil paintings and 700 drawings, but he sold only one during his lifetime. His striking colors, coarse brushwork, and contoured forms display the anguish of the mental illness that drove him to suicide.

Illustrate his case with examples of his late art works, completed while he was a patient at the asylum in Saint-Rémy. The Vincent van Gogh online museum can be found at: http://www.vangoghgallery.com/painting/main_az.htm.

**Discuss the diagnoses that have been ascribed to van Gogh over the years.** They are as follows:

Epilepsy

Schizophrenia

Suppressed form of epilepsy

Episodic twilight states

Epileptoid psychosis

Psychopathy

Psychosis of degeneration

Schizoform reaction

Cerebral tumor

Active luetic schizoid and epileptoid disposition

Phasic schizophrenia

Dementia praecox

Meningoencephalitis luetica

Psychotic exhaustion caused by creative effort

Atypical psychosis heterogeneously compounded of elements of epileptic and schizoid disposition

Phasic hallucinatory psychosis

Neurasthenia

Chronic sunstroke and the influence of yellow

Psychomotor epilepsy

Dromomania

Maniacal excitement

Turpentine poisoning

Hypertrophy of the creative forces

Acute mania with generalized delirium

Epileptic crises and attacks of epilepsy

Glaucoma

Frontotemporal dementia

Xanthopsia caused by digitalis (as treatment for mania)—seeing the world through a yellow haze

Numerous websites discuss van Gogh's condition and possible diagnoses; here is one: http://www.psych.ucalgary.ca/PACE/VA-Lab/AVDE-Website/VanGogh.html.

**Most recently, this diagnosis was published in the *American Journal of Psychiatry*:**

Vincent van Gogh (1853–1890) had an eccentric personality and unstable moods, suffered from recurrent psychotic episodes during the last two years of his extraordinary life, and committed suicide at the age of 37. Despite limited evidence, well over 148 physicians have ventured a perplexing variety of diagnoses of his illness. Henri Gastaut, in a study of the artist's life and medical history published in 1956, identified van Gogh's major illness during the last two years of his life as temporal lobe epilepsy precipitated by the use of absinthe in the presence of an early limbic lesion. In essence, Gastaut confirmed the diagnosis originally made by the French physicians who had treated van Gogh. However, van Gogh had earlier suffered two distinct episodes of reactive depression, and there are clearly bipolar aspects to his history. Both episodes of depression were followed by sustained periods of increasingly high energy and enthusiasm, first as an evangelist and then as an artist. The highlights of van Gogh's life and letters are reviewed and discussed in an effort toward better understanding of the complexity of his illness.

Source: Blumer, D. (2002). The illness of Vincent van Gogh. *American Journal of Psychiatry,* 159, 519–526. http://www.ncbi.nlm.nih.gov/entrez/query.fcgi?cmd=Retrieve&db=PubMed&list_uids=11925286&dopt=Abstract.

## THE *DSM-5*

- **Summarize the assumptions of the *DSM-5*:**
  - Descriptive, atheoretical

- **Present two areas of criticism of the *DSM-5*:**
  - Because it is descriptive, it does not address causes the way that medical diagnostic manuals do.
  - Dimensional ratings may be preferable.

## Activities

**VIEWS ON PSYCHOLOGICAL DISORDERS**  Have students complete *Handout: Views on Psychological Disorders.*

- Have students read more about illness anxiety disorder at the *Encyclopedia of Mental Disorders* (http://www.minddisorders.com/Flu-Inv/Hypochondriasis.html) and discuss how creativity factors into this disorder.
- Have a speaker from the counseling department at your school come and speak to your class. As high school students are at the peak age for the development of many disorders, counselors can answer student questions and review the support available. This may also increase students' awareness of diversity and disability.

**ABUSE AND BRAIN DAMAGE**  Remind students that perhaps being abused as a child may affect the development of the brain. That is, neglect and abuse no doubt affect the way the brain becomes wired. For example, let's take poor feeding habits. Would poor food choices affect the development of the brain? Further, witnessing extreme abuse of others or being in an aggression-charged environment would have effects on behavior as well.

**THEORETICAL APPROACHES**  Have students choose one psychological disorder from a list of the various disorders discussed in the chapter. Next, have them walk that disorder through the various theoretical perspectives and explain how each perspective (biological, psychological, and sociocultural) would describe and explain the disorder. The students should get a better understanding of each of the perspectives and perhaps how many of the disorders were described and treated according to the various perspectives.

**CHALLENGE YOUR THINKING**  Have students answer the following as a class discussion, small-group confab, or short essay: What is an appropriate label for someone with a psychological disorder? When are medical treatments appropriate for a psychological disorder? Finally, if a teacher suggested your child be tested for ADHD, what would you do?

**LIBRARY RESEARCH ON THE *DSM-5***

**The *DSM* Classification System**  Have the students again choose a psychological disorder from a list of disorders. Next, for a homework assignment, the students should go to the library or on the Internet and find a copy of the *DSM-5*. The students should describe what the *DSM-5* says about the disorder they have chosen. Through this process, the students will have a closer look at the *DSM* and its classification system. As they are looking up the disorder of their choice, they will also see other disorders listed and will probably look into these also.

# Discussion Questions

## PERSPECTIVES ON ABNORMALITY

- How does the medical perspective of abnormality compare with the behavioral neuroscience perspective in psychology? How are they the same, and how are they different?
- If you were a mental health professional, how would you integrate the best of each perspective in treating your clients?
- Which perspective is the *DSM-5* most closely associated with?
- Could the biological, psychological, and sociocultural factors behind psychological disorders all be correct, or is there only one factor that dominates? Explain.
- Why is it difficult for an individual with a psychological disorder to identify and find the correct treatment of a physical illness? What are some ideas for correcting this problem?
- How can society help individuals with psychological disorders overcome the stigma and labeling they face every day?

# Suggested Media

- *Asylum: A History of the Mental Institution in America.* Insight Media, 1989, 60:00. A history of mental institutions is presented.
- *Behavenet.com:* http://behavenet.com/capsules/. This website lists the major psychological disorders and the DSM-IV-TR criteria for each disorder.
- *Diagnostic and Statistical Manual of Mental Disorders (DSM-5):* http://www.dsm5.org/Pages/Default.aspx.
- *Eysenk and psychoticism:* http://www.trans4mind.com/personality/EPQ.html. This site provides an overview of traits Eysenk argued were parts of psychoticism. Eysenk has done considerable research on creativity and psychoticism and may be one of the leaders in this area.
- *Mental health:* Centers for Disease Control and Prevention: http://www.cdc.gov/mentalhealth/.
- *National Alliance on Mental Illness:* http://www.nami.org/.
- *National Institute of Mental Health (NIMH):* http://www.nimh.nih.gov/.

**POPULAR MOVIE: HISTORICAL PERSPECTIVES ON ABNORMALITY** *One Flew Over the Cuckoo's Nest* is the classic depiction of life in a psychiatric hospital in the late 1950s, when ECT was used as punishment.

- Depending on the community in which you serve, a parent/guardian permission slip may be required.

**TED TALK: WHAT'S SO FUNNY ABOUT MENTAL ILLNESS?** In this talk, Ruby Wax urges viewers to end the stigma that surrounds mental illness.

# Additional Readings

Costello, Victoria. (2012). *Scientific American Mind, 23*(1), 31–37.

Epstein, R. (2010). Are You Mentally Healthy? *Scientific American Mind, 21*(1), 58–61.

# AP Student Edition Answer Key

## AP Test Practice

### Part I: Multiple Choice

1.  **E** *(Skill 1.A, Learning Target 8.B)*

2.  **C** *(Skill 1.C, Learning Target 8.B)*

3.  **E** *(Skill 1.C, Learning Target 8.E)*

### Part II: Free Response

**A.**

Abnormal behavior includes deviation from the average or ideal, a sense of personal discomfort, the inability to function effectively, and legal conceptions. If Cheryl's behavior was personally distressing and caused dysfunction, it would be considered abnormal.

**B.**

The medical perspective assumes that physiological causes are at the root of psychological disorders. Sheryl's shyness would be caused by something physiological.

The behavioral perspective assumes that abnormal behaviors are learned responses. Cheryl's shyness would be caused by basic learning principles, such as reinforcement or observation.

The psychoanalytic perspectives argue that disorders stem from unconscious childhood conflicts. Cheryl's shyness would stem from unconscious childhood conflict.

The sociocultural perspective assumes that behavior is shaped by family, society, and culture. Cheryl's shyness would be caused by societal demands.

**C.**

The *DSM* has helped to increase the reliability and validity of categorizing diagnoses. Insurance companies often require a formal diagnosis from the *DSM* to provide coverage.

The *DSM* has been criticized for powerfully influencing mental health workers, relying too much on the medical perspective, compartmentalizing abnormal behavior into all-or-none categories, and providing labels that are dehumanizing and stigmatizing.

# Module 47: The Major Psychological Disorders

## AP Module Summary

Watchout! Module 47 will take some time and you could find yourself going down a rabbit hole if you're not careful. Students may benefit from a review of each of the Learning Targets listed focusing on one disorder from each and applying the perspectives to that disorder. Several disorders have appeared in previous units, e.g. neurodevelopmental disorders (Alzheimers), PTSD, and eating disorders, therefore very little, if any, time should be spent specifically on them. Finally, you will see reference to movies as a resource. I caution you when using film prior to the exam because valuable instructional time can be lost and confusion may lead to students not understanding the symptoms of the disorder being portrayed.

Each psychological disorder represents a very human set of difficulties that influence and in some cases considerably disrupt people's lives.

**ANXIETY DISORDERS** *Anxiety* is a feeling of apprehension or tension in reaction to stressful situations. There is nothing "wrong" with such anxiety. It is a normal reaction to stress that often helps rather than hinders our daily functioning. However, some people experience anxiety in situations in which there is no apparent reason or cause for such distress. *Anxiety disorders* occur when anxiety arises without external justification and begins to affect people's daily functioning.

**PHOBIC DISORDER** A *specific phobia* is an intense, irrational fear of a specific object or situation (see **Figure 1**). The objective danger posed by an anxiety-producing stimulus is typically small or nonexistent. However, to someone suffering from the phobia, the danger is great, and a full-blown panic attack may follow exposure to the stimulus. Phobic disorders differ from generalized anxiety disorders and panic disorders in that there is a specific, identifiable stimulus that sets off the anxiety reaction.

**PANIC DISORDER** In *panic disorder, panic attacks* occur that last from a few seconds to several hours. Unlike phobias, which are stimulated by specific objects or situations, panic disorders do not have any identifiable stimuli. Instead, during an attack, anxiety suddenly—and often without warning—rises, and an individual feels a sense of impending, unavoidable doom. Although the physical symptoms differ from person to person, they may include heart palpitations, shortness of breath, unusual amounts of sweating, faintness and dizziness, gastric sensations, and sometimes a sense of imminent death. After such an attack, it is no wonder that people tend to feel exhausted.

**GENERALIZED ANXIETY DISORDER** People with *generalized anxiety disorder* experience long-term, persistent anxiety and uncontrollable worry (see **Figure 2**). Sometimes their concerns are about identifiable issues involving family, money, work, or health. In other cases, though, people with the disorder feel that something dreadful is about to happen but cannot identify the reason and thus experience "free-floating" anxiety.

**OBSESSIVE-COMPULSIVE DISORDER** In *obsessive-compulsive disorder (OCD),* people are plagued by unwanted thoughts, called obsessions, or feel that they must carry out behaviors, termed compulsions, which they feel driven to perform. **Obsession** is a persistent, unwanted thought or idea that keeps recurring.

Example: A student may be unable to stop thinking that she has neglected to put her name on a test and may think about it constantly for the 2 weeks it takes to get the paper back.

- *Compulsions*—irresistible urges to repeatedly carry out some act that seems strange and unreasonable even to them.

Example: Repeatedly checking the stove to make sure all the burners are turned off, or more unusual, washing one's hands so much that they bleed.

**THE CAUSES OF ANXIETY DISORDERS AND OBSESSIVE-COMPULSIVE DISORDER**  The variety of anxiety disorders means that no single explanation fits all cases. Genetic factors clearly are part of the picture. Furthermore, a person's characteristic level of anxiety is related to a specific gene involved in the production of the neurotransmitter serotonin. This is consistent with findings indicating that certain chemical deficiencies in the brain appear to produce some kinds of anxiety disorder. Some researchers believe that an overactive autonomic nervous system may be at the root of panic attacks. Psychologists who employ the behavioral perspective have taken a different approach that emphasizes environmental factors. They consider anxiety to be a learned response to stress. Finally, the cognitive perspective suggests that anxiety disorders grow out of inappropriate and inaccurate thoughts and beliefs about circumstances in a person's world. According to the cognitive perspective, people's maladaptive thoughts about the world are at the root of an anxiety disorder.

### SOMATIC SYMPTOM DISORDERS

- *Somatic symptom disorders* are psychological difficulties that take on a physical (somatic) form but for which there is no medical cause. Even though an individual with a somatoform disorder reports physical symptoms, no biological cause exists, or if there is a medical problem, the person's reaction is greatly exaggerated.
- *Illness anxiety disorder* in which people have a constant fear of illness and a preoccupation with their health. These individuals believe that everyday aches and pains are symptoms of a dread disease. The "symptoms" are not faked; rather, they are misinterpreted as evidence of some serious illness.
- *Conversion disorders* involve an apparent physical disturbance, such as the inability to see or hear or to move an arm or leg (see **Figure 3**). The cause of such a physical disturbance is purely psychological; there is no biological reason for the problem.

**DISSOCIATIVE DISORDERS**  *Dissociative disorders* are characterized by the separation (or dissociation) of different facets of a person's personality that are normally integrated and work together. By dissociating key parts of who they are, people are able to keep disturbing memories or perceptions from reaching conscious awareness and thereby reduce their anxiety. Several dissociative disorders exist, although all of them are rare. *Dissociative identity disorder (DID)* (once called multiple personality disorder) displays characteristics of two or more distinct personalities, identities, or personality fragments. Individual personalities often have a unique set of likes and dislikes and their own reactions to situations. The diagnosis of dissociative identity disorder is controversial.

- *Dissociative amnesia* is another dissociative disorder in which a significant, selective memory loss occurs. Dissociative amnesia is unlike simple amnesia, which involves an actual loss of information from memory and typically results from a physiological cause. In contrast, in cases of dissociative amnesia, the "forgotten" material is still present in memory—it simply cannot be recalled. The term *repressed memories* is sometimes used to describe the lost memories of people with dissociative amnesia.
- *Dissociative fugue* is a form of amnesia in which a person leaves home suddenly and assumes a new identity. In this rare and unusual state, people take sudden, impulsive trips and adopt a new identity. After a period of time—days, months, or sometimes even years—they suddenly realize that they are in a strange place and completely forget the time they have spent wandering. Their last memories are those from the time just before they entered the fugue state.

**MOOD DISORDERS**  A *mood disorder* is a disturbance in emotional experience that is strong enough to intrude on everyday living.

**MAJOR DEPRESSIVE DISORDER**  *Major depressive disorder* is a severe form of depression that interferes with concentration, decision making, and sociability. People who suffer from major depression experience similar feelings, but the severity tends to be considerably greater. They may feel useless, worthless, and lonely, and they may think the future is hopeless and that no one can help them. They may lose their appetite and have no energy. Moreover, they may experience such feelings for months or even years. They may cry uncontrollably, have sleep disturbances, and be at risk for suicide. The depth and duration of such behaviors are the hallmarks of major depression.

**MANIA AND BIPOLAR DISORDER**

- *Mania* is an extended state of intense, wild elation. People experiencing mania feel intense happiness, power, invulnerability, and energy.
- *Bipolar disorder* is a disorder in which a person alternates between periods of euphoric feelings of mania and periods of depression. The swings between highs and lows may occur a few days apart or may alternate over a period of years. In addition, in bipolar disorder, periods of depression are usually longer than periods of mania.

**CAUSES OF MOOD DISORDERS**  Some mood disorders clearly have genetic and biochemical roots. In fact, most evidence suggests that bipolar disorders are caused primarily by biological factors. For instance, bipolar disorder (and some forms of major depression) clearly runs in some families, pointing to a genetic cause. Furthermore, researchers have found that several neurotransmitters play a role in depression.

Other explanations for depression have focused on psychological causes. For instance, proponents of psychoanalytic approaches see depression as the result of feelings of loss (real or potential) or of anger directed at oneself.

Behavioral theories of depression argue that the stresses of life produce a reduction in positive reinforcers. As a result, people begin to withdraw, which only reduces positive reinforcers further. Some explanations for mood disorders attribute them to cognitive factors. For example, psychologist Martin Seligman suggests that depression is largely a response to learned helplessness. Learned helplessness is a learned expectation that events in one's life are uncontrollable and that one cannot escape from the situation. As a consequence, people simply give up fighting aversive events and submit to them, which thereby produces depression. Clinical psychologist Aaron Beck has proposed that faulty cognitions underlie people's depressed feelings. Specifically, his cognitive theory of depression suggests that depressed individuals typically view themselves as life's losers and blame themselves whenever anything goes wrong.

Brain imaging studies suggest that people with depression experience a general blunting of emotional reactions. Other explanations of depression derive from evolutionary psychology, which considers how our genetic inheritance from our ancestors influences our behavior.

**DEPRESSION IN WOMEN**  Why does depression occur in approximately twice as many women as men—a pattern that is similar across a variety of cultures? One explanation suggests that the stress women experience may be greater than the stress men experience at certain points in their lives—such as when a woman must simultaneously earn a living and be the primary caregiver for her children. In addition, women have a higher risk for physical and sexual abuse, typically earn lower wages than men, report greater unhappiness with their marriages, and generally experience chronic negative circumstances. Furthermore, women and men may respond to stress with different coping mechanisms. Biological factors may also explain some women's depression.

**SCHIZOPHRENIA**  *Schizophrenia* refers to a class of disorders in which severe distortion of reality occurs. Thinking, perception, and emotion may deteriorate; the individual may withdraw from social interaction; and the person may display bizarre behavior. The symptoms displayed by persons with schizophrenia may vary considerably over time, and people with schizophrenia show significant differences in the pattern of their symptoms even when they are labeled with the same diagnostic category. The following characteristics reliably distinguish schizophrenia from other disorders:

- *Decline from a previous level of functioning:* An individual can no longer carry out activities he or she was once able to do.
- *Disturbances of thought and speech:* People with schizophrenia use logic and language in a peculiar way. Their thinking often does not make sense, and their logic is frequently faulty, which is referred to as a formal thought disorder.
- *Delusions:* People with schizophrenia often have delusions, firmly held, unshakable beliefs with no basis in reality. Among the common delusions people with schizophrenia experience are the beliefs that they are being controlled by someone else, they are being persecuted by others, and their thoughts are being broadcast so that others know what they are thinking.
- *Hallucinations and perceptual disorders:* People with schizophrenia do not perceive the world as most other people do. They also may have hallucinations, the experience of perceiving things that do not actually exist. Furthermore, they may see, hear, or smell things differently from others. In fact, they may not even have a sense of their bodies in the way that others do and have difficulty determining where their bodies stop and the rest of the world begins.
- *Inappropriate emotional displays:* People with schizophrenia sometimes show a lack of emotion in which even the most dramatic events produce little or no emotional response. Conversely, they may display emotion that is inappropriate to a situation.
- *Withdrawal:* People with schizophrenia tend to have little interest in others. They tend not to socialize or hold real conversations with others, although they may talk at another person. In the most extreme cases, they do not even acknowledge the presence of other people and appear to be in their own isolated world.

Usually, the onset of schizophrenia occurs in early adulthood. The *DSM-5* classifies the symptoms of schizophrenia into two types.

1. *Positive-symptom schizophrenia* is indicated by the presence of disordered behavior such as hallucinations, delusions, and emotional extremes. Those with positive-symptom schizophrenia clearly lose touch with reality.

2. *Negative-symptom schizophrenia* show disruptions to normal emotions and behaviors. For example, there may be an absence or loss of normal functioning, such as social withdrawal or blunted emotions.

**SOLVING THE PUZZLE OF SCHIZOPHRENIA: BIOLOGICAL CAUSES**  Because schizophrenia is more common in some families than in others, genetic factors seem to be involved in producing at least a susceptibility to or readiness for developing schizophrenia (see **Figure 7**). One biological hypothesis to explain schizophrenia is that the brains of people with the disorder may have a biochemical imbalance. For example, the dopamine hypothesis suggests that schizophrenia occurs when there is excess activity in the areas of the brain that use dopamine as a neurotransmitter. This hypothesis came to light after the discovery that drugs that block dopamine action in brain pathways can be highly effective in reducing the symptoms of schizophrenia. Some biological explanations propose that structural abnormalities exist in the brains of people with schizophrenia perhaps as a result of exposure to a virus during prenatal development (see the "Neuroscience in Your Life: Brain Changes with Schizophrenia" box in the text). Further evidence for the importance of biological factors shows that when people with schizophrenia hear voices during hallucinations, the parts of the brain responsible for hearing and language processing become active. When they have visual hallucinations, the parts of the brain involved in movement and color are active.

**SITUATIONAL CAUSES OF SCHIZOPHRENIA** Psychoanalytic approaches suggest that schizophrenia is a form of regression to earlier experiences and stages of life. Freud believed that people with schizophrenia lack egos that are strong enough to cope with their unacceptable impulses. They regress to the oral stage—a time when the id and ego are not yet separated. Some researchers suggest that schizophrenia is related to a family interaction style known as expressed emotion. Expressed emotion is an interaction style characterized by high levels of criticism, hostility, and emotional intrusiveness within a family. Some psychologists suggest that schizophrenia results from overattention to stimuli in the environment. Other cognitive experts argue that schizophrenia results from underattention to certain stimuli. Although it is plausible that overattention and underattention are related to different forms of schizophrenia, these phenomena do not explain the origins of such information-processing disorders.

**PREDISPOSITIONAL MODEL OF SCHIZOPHRENIA: THE DISORDER'S MULTIPLE CAUSES** Most scientists now believe that schizophrenia involves both biological and situational factors. The *predisposition model of schizophrenia* suggests that individuals may inherit a predisposition or an inborn sensitivity to schizophrenia. This genetic predisposition makes them particularly vulnerable to stressful factors in the environment, such as social rejection or dysfunctional family communication patterns. The stressors may vary, but if they are strong enough and are coupled with a genetic predisposition, they result in the appearance of schizophrenia. Furthermore, a strong genetic predisposition may lead to the onset of schizophrenia even when the environmental stressors are relatively weak.

**PERSONALITY DISORDERS** A *personality disorder* is characterized by a set of inflexible, maladaptive behavior patterns that keep a person from functioning appropriately in society. People with personality disorders frequently lead seemingly normal lives. However, just below the surface lies a set of inflexible, maladaptive personality traits that do not permit these individuals to function as members of society.

- *Antisocial personality disorder* (sometimes referred to as a sociopathic personality). Individuals with this disturbance show no regard for the moral and ethical rules of society or the rights of others. Although they can appear quite intelligent and likable (at least at first), upon closer examination they turn out to be manipulative and deceptive. Moreover, they lack any guilt or anxiety about their wrongdoing.

- *Borderline personality disorder* have problems regulating emotions and thoughts, display impulsive and reckless behavior, and have unstable relationships with others. They also have difficulty developing a secure sense of who they are. As a consequence, they tend to rely on relationships with others to define their identity. Individuals with borderline personality disorder often feel empty and alone, and they have difficulty cooperating with others.

- *Narcissistic personality disorder,* which is characterized by an exaggerated sense of self-importance. Those with the disorder expect special treatment from others while at the same time disregarding others' feelings. In some ways, in fact, the main attribute of the narcissistic personality is an inability to experience empathy for other people.

**DISORDERS THAT IMPACT CHILDREN** Almost 20 percent of children and 40 percent of adolescents experience significant emotional or behavioral disorders. For example, although major depression is more prevalent in adults, around 2.5 percent of children and more than 8 percent of adolescents suffer from the disorder.

Children do not always display depression the same way adults do. Rather than showing profound sadness or hopelessness, childhood depression may produce the expression of exaggerated fears, clinginess, or avoidance of everyday activities.

- *Attention-deficit hyperactivity disorder,* or *ADHD,* a disorder marked by inattention, impulsiveness, a low tolerance for frustration, and generally a great deal of inappropriate activity. Although all children show such behavior some of the time, it is so common in children diagnosed with ADHD that it interferes with their everyday functioning.

- *Autism spectrum disorder,* a severe developmental disability that impairs children's ability to communicate and relate to others, is another disorder that usually appears in the first 3 years and typically continues throughout life. Children with autism have difficulties in both verbal and nonverbal communication, and they may avoid social contact.

**OTHER DISORDERS**

- *Psychoactive substance use disorder* relates to problems that arise from the use and abuse of drugs. *Alcohol use disorders* are among the most serious and widespread problems.
- *Eating disorders* such as *anorexia nervosa, bulimia,* and *binge-eating disorder*
- Neurocognitive disorders are problems that have a purely biological basis, such as Alzheimer's disease and some types of developmental disabilities.

## **AP** Key Terms

antisocial personality disorder

anxiety disorder

attention-deficit hyperactivity disorder (ADHD)

autism spectrum disorder

bipolar disorder

borderline personality disorder

compulsion

conversion disorder

dissociative amnesia

dissociative disorders

dissociative fugue

dissociative identity disorder (DID)

generalized anxiety disorder

illness anxiety disorder

major depressive disorder

mania

mood disorder

narcissistic personality disorder

obsession

obsessive-compulsive disorder (OCD)

panic disorder

personality disorder

schizophrenia

somatic symptom disorders

specific phobia

## Class Discussion Ideas

**SCHIZOPHRENIA** You may want to introduce students to the neurodevelopmental hypothesis, which argues that early brain development gone awry may be causal in the development of schizophrenia. See biology online for a brief overview: https://www.biology-online.org/articles/advances_neurobiology_schizophrenia/neurodevelopmental_hypothesis_schizophrenia.html.

**ANXIETY DISORDERS**

- **PTSD:** Ask students about what kinds of events other than war can lead to PTSD. Point out that being a victim of a violent crime, for example, could lead to similar effects. What kinds of effects could this have on everyday life?
- **Phobias:** Ask students what they have a phobic response to. You may want to point out that having one phobia in a subtype—say, animal types—increases the probability of having another phobia in the same subtype (e.g., fear of spiders and snakes). You may want to show this clip of unusual phobias: http://www.youtube.com/watch?v=9rl7Lr6eDLc.
- **Biology as Destiny:** Those most likely to develop anxiety disorders are people with a genetic predisposition to anxiety, low levels of GABA, or the personality trait of neuroticism *and* who also experience chronic stress environments or abuse. Ask students to discuss the issue of biology being destiny. If they know that their partner has a history of a psychological disorder somewhere in his or her bloodline, should they panic about reproducing?

**AUTISM SPECTRUM DISORDERS** You may want to point out that the increase in the occurrence of autism spectrum disorder is most likely due to several factors—increased awareness, a broadening of the definition into "spectrum," a need to "label" a child to procure government-provided services for children with delays, and many others. Ask students to brainstorm other possible reasons for why the numbers have jumped.

Some people who have autism or Asperger's syndrome are called savants for their extreme giftedness in one domain, such as music or math. At this point, most students are thinking that this sounds great. Students tend to idolize actors, writers, musicians, and artists. Remind students that although savants show great creativity, the data overall supports that these increases in ability in one area are tied to severe deficits in other areas. For example, although it may sound to students that savants have these great spikes, they often cannot complete many aspects of independent living without help. Neuroatypicality including depressive stages and autism can be severely debilitating.

**FORMS OF PHOBIA** Show these terms and symptoms for a variety of types of phobias:

| Disorder | Symptoms |
|---|---|
| Panic disorder | Panic attacks occur without a specific trigger or stimulus |
| Agoraphobia | Fear of being in a situation in which escape is difficult and in which help for a possible panic attack would not be available |
| Ailurophobia | Fear of cats |
| Arachnophobia | Fear of spiders |
| Cynophobia | Fear of dogs |
| Equinophobia | Fear of horses |
| Insectophobia | Fear of insects |
| Ophidiophobia | Fear of snakes |
| Rodentophobia | Fear of rodents |
| Acrophobia | Fear of heights |
| Brontophobia | Fear of thunder |
| Claustrophobia | Fear of small, enclosed spaces |
| Mysophobia | Fear of dirt |
| Nyctophobia | Fear of darkness |

# Activities

## ABNORMAL PSYCHOLOGY IN THE MEDIA

- **Abnormal Psychology in the Media:** Have students complete *Handout: Abnormality in the Popular Media.*
- ***Girl, Interrupted*:** Have students watch *Girl, Interrupted* and write a two-paragraph synopsis of the disorders seen in the film. *Depending on the community in which you serve a parent/guardian permission slip may be required.
- **What Is Abnormal, Anyway?** Use *Handout: What Is Abnormal, Anyway?* The goal of this activity is for students to use the various aspects of the definition of abnormal (deviant, maladaptive, and distressful) to explain why they classified certain behaviors or thoughts as abnormal. Students should discuss their answers in groups to conclude that distinguishing what is abnormal is not always easy to do and the implications for such decisions have potentially lifelong consequences.

## ANXIETY DISORDERS

- **Anxiety Disorder:** Discuss with the students the difference between normal worrying and generalized anxiety disorder. Ask the students to write about a time when they were worried about something and how this type of worrying did not turn into generalized anxiety disorder. Ask them to explain what would have had to happen for the worrying to be considered a generalized anxiety disorder.

- **Anxiety Disorders:** Use *Handout: What Type of Anxiety or Anxiety-Related Disorder Is It?* The goal of this activity is for students to recognize the various anxiety disorders described in the chapter. The students will read through various examples and then identify which anxiety disorder is being described.
- **Messiness versus Hoarding Quiz:** Use *Handout: Is It Hoarding or Just Messiness?* Have students complete the quiz and in class discuss the answers. This quiz is adapted from the TV show *Hoarding: Buried Alive*: http://www.tlc.com/tv-shows/hoarding-buried-alive/games-and-more/hoarding-quiz.htm. You may also consider using excerpts from this show as illustrations of the disorder.
- **Obsessive-Compulsive Disorder (OCD):** Show the film *As Good as It Gets.* Have the students identify the obsessive and compulsive behaviors. Discuss these in class, describing as well what it must be like to live with OCD. Compare and contrast what was shown in the film and the symptoms of the disorder as they were described in the text reading. *Depending on the community in which you serve a parent/guardian permission slip may be required.

## MOOD DISORDERS

**Causes of Mood Disorders:** Have students choose one mood disorder from a list of the various disorders. Next, have them walk that disorder through the various causes and explain how each cause (biological, psychological, sociocultural, socioeconomic status, gender, and ethnic) would describe and explain the disorder. The students should get a better understanding of each of the causes.

## DISSOCIATIVE DISORDERS

- **Dissociative Amnesia:** Have students watch the movie *The Butterfly Effect,* which illustrates dissociative disorder. Then, either in a group discussion or through a written paper, students should identify the main features along with some of the challenges psychologists face with the diagnosis of the disorder. *Depending on the community in which you serve a parent/guardian permission slip may be required.
- **Dissociative Identity Disorder:** Show the movie *The Many Faces of Eve*, which discusses dissociative identity disorder. Afterward, break the class into groups to discuss the movie. Have the groups discuss the idea that some personalities are developed through therapy. *Depending on the community in which you serve a parent/guardian permission slip may be required.

## SCHIZOPHRENIA

- **Schizophrenia: Positive, Negative, and Cognitive Symptoms:** Use *Handout: Schizophrenia: Positive, Negative, or Cognitive Symptoms—What Type of Symptom Is It?* The goal of this activity is for students to become more familiar with the various types of symptoms found in schizophrenia. The students will read examples of individuals with schizophrenia and identify which set of symptoms is being described.
- **A "Normal Life" & Examples of Schizophrenia:** Show the film *A Beautiful Mind* that features John Nash, a Nobel Prize winner and professor at Princeton University. Have the students compare his life to the conception of a normal life. Afterward, break the class into groups to discuss the movie, focusing on the progression of schizophrenia in John Nash. *Depending on the community in which you serve a parent/guardian permission slip may be required.

**PERSONALITY DISORDERS** Use *Handout: Which Personality Disorder Is It?* The goal of this activity is for students to become more familiar with the various types of personality disorders. The students will read examples of individuals with a personality disorder and then identify which type of disorder is being described.

# Discussion Questions

**PERSPECTIVES ON SPECIFIC DISORDERS** Choose the psychological disorder that is of greatest interest to you and answer these questions:

- State which disorder it is and summarize its diagnostic criteria.
- Explain why this disorder is considered abnormal behavior.
- Compare two approaches to understanding this disorder (such as biological vs. sociocultural) and state which approach you prefer (and why).
- Compare and contrast the various forms of schizophrenia. Why are they all considered a form of schizophrenia?
- Is it possible that an individual with dissociative identity disorder can develop new personalities through the suggestion of a therapist?
- Compare and contrast the disassociated identity disorder with schizophrenia. What are the significant differences? If you had to have one of these disorders, which one would you prefer it be, and why?

Ask students to think about anorexia and bulimia. How do they think environmental factors such as media and the family can contribute to developing an eating disorder?

- **Technology Addiction?** Do you think a person can be addicted to technology? If a person is spending 10 or more hours online and it is interfering with their daily life, is that a problem? Is it a problem if a person constantly checks their phone? Be sure to have students defend their answer. This question often provides some lively debate, especially if a class has generational differences.

**MOVIE DEPICTIONS OF PSYCHOLOGICAL DISORDERS**

- Describe a movie character that you think is a good example of a psychological disorder. What disorder does this character represent? Why?
- Do you think that the movie did a good job or a bad job of depicting this disorder? Why?
- What impact do you think that movies can have on how people feel about psychological disorders?

# Polling Questions

**EVERYTHING'S A DISORDER** Two criticisms of the new *DSM-5* suggest that we will see an increase in the number of people being diagnosed with some psychological disorder: (1) Too many new categories of disorders have been added, some of which do not yet have consistent research support, and (2) there has been a loosening of standards for some existing diagnoses. What do you think about this? How many of you know someone who is diagnosed with a mental health disorder? With the changes in the *DSM-5*, how many of you think that more people will be diagnosed? Who thinks the increase in people suffering from mental health issues may suggest that some of the diagnoses are being labeled incorrectly? How many of you think that having more disorders listed in the *DSM-5* is a positive thing?

# Suggested Media

- *Anxiety Disorders Association:* http://www.adaa.org/.
- *Anxiety disorder:* http://www.brainexplorer.org/brain_disorders/Focus_Panic_disorder. shtml. A great biological site on anxiety disorder.
- *Bipolar: Life Between Two Extremes.* Telepool, 2010, 45:00. This program examines the lives of several people who struggle with bipolar disorder.

- *Bipolar:* http://www.youtube.com/watch?v=MBUOoQk0hhU. This clip describes bipolar disorder.
- *Bipolar:* http://www.youtube.com/watch?v=irt58wCWevI. The difficulty in diagnosing bipolar disorder is discussed in this clip.
- *The Brain and Schizophrenia:* http://www.youtube.com/watch?v=DL8mOHClb_w.
- *Dissociative identity disorder:* http://www.youtube.com/watch?v=gfiB82OUXf0. This CBS News clip provides a discussion of DID.
- *Eating disorders:* http://www.youtube.com/watch?v=aTljRxT_Y9g. This short piece focuses on Isabel Caro, who struggled with anorexia. She died shortly after this interview.
- *Eating disorders:* http://www.dailymail.co.uk/news/article-2012288/Rise-middle-aged-women-eating-disorders.html. This clip discusses the rise of eating disorders in middle-aged women.
- *Ellen Saks on "Seeing Mental Illness."* TED Talk: http://www.ted.com/talks/elyn_saks_seeing_mental_illness. Ellen Saks talks about her life with schizophrenia.
- *International Classification of Diseases (ICD-10):* http://www.who.int/classifications/icd/en/. Access to the classifications is free.
- *Manic depression:* http://www.youtube.com/watch?v=CxRLap9xLag. This clip features a doctor at Johns Hopkins who is living with manic depression.
- *Mental health:* U.S. Department of Health and Human Services https://www.mentalhealth.gov.
- *National Alliance on Mental Illness (NAMI):* http://www.nami.org/.
- *National Eating Disorders:* http://www.nationaleatingdisorders.org/. This website provides a wealth of information about eating disorders.
- *Obsessive-Compulsive Foundation:* http://www.ocfoundation.org. This website offers articles and links related to obsessive-compulsive disorders.
- *PhobiasList:* http://phobialist.com/. This is a list of many types of phobias.
- *PsychCentral:* http://www.psychcentral.com. This website offers information about various disorders.
- *Psych Web:* https://www.psywww.com/index.html.
- *Schizophrenia:* http://schizophrenia.com/.
- *Schizophrenia:* http://www.youtube.com/watch?v=f4R6jln_eZg&feature=related. This brief clip presents interviews of people with schizophrenia.
- *Schizophrenia:* http://www.youtube.com/watch?v=aBKSOxqu7CQ. This clip provides a brief overview of schizophrenia.
- *Schizophrenia:* http://www.youtube.com/watch?v=f4R6jln_eZg. This clip tells the stories of several people dealing with schizophrenia.
- *Schizophrenia:* http://www.youtube.com/watch?v=gGnl8dqEoPQ. Gerald, a schizophrenic, displays many symptoms of schizophrenia in this clip. The first few minutes provide a great demonstration of several schizophrenic symptoms.
- *Temple Grandin's website:* http://www.templegrandin.com/.
- *Trauma Information Pages:* http://www.trauma-pages.com. This site focuses on traumatic experiences—stress, PTSD, and mental health aspects of disaster.
- *Unusual phobias:* http://www.youtube.com/watch?v=9rl7Lr6eDLc.

**POPULAR MOVIES AND TELEVISION SHOWS** The following is a partial list of films and TV shows that portray characters with psychological disorders. *Depending on the community in which you serve a parent/guardian permission slip may be required.

- *As Good As It Gets:* Obsessive-compulsive disorder
- *A Beautiful Mind:* Schizophrenia (Media Resources has interview with Nash)
- *Benny & Joon:* Schizophrenia
- *Chicago:* Antisocial personality disorder in females (very unusual!)
- *Copycat:* Panic attacks and agoraphobia

- *Fatal Attraction:* Borderline personality disorder
- *The Fisher King:* Schizophrenia
- *Girl, Interrupted:* Borderline personality disorder (and/or depression)
- *Gone With the Wind:* Histrionic personality disorder
- *Heavenly Creatures:* Shared psychotic disorder
- *The Hours:* Major depressive disorder
- *I Am Sam:* Developmental disability
- *Iris:* Alzheimer's disease
- *King of Hearts:* Mental illness and society
- *Matchstick Men:* Obsessive-compulsive disorder
- *Memento:* Amnestic disorder
- *Monk:* Obsessive-compulsive disorder
- *Nurse Betty:* Dissociative fugue
- *Pollock:* Depression (and alcohol abuse)
- *Rain Man:* Autistic disorder
- *Silver Linings Playbook:* Multiple mental health illnesses including bipolar disorder
- *Single White Female:* Borderline personality disorder
- *The Soloist:* Schizophrenia
- *Still Alice:* Early-onset Alzheimer's disease
- *Sybil:* Dissociative identity disorder
- *Temple Grandin:* Autism
- *Three Faces of Eve:* DID and a forerunner to *Sybil*.
- *Vertigo:* Anxiety disorder (acrophobia)
- *The Virgin Suicides:* Depression in teens
- *What About Bob:* Borderline personality disorder

The television program *ER* provided an excellent example of bipolar disorder in the character of Abby's (the nurse) mother, played by Sally Field.

- The use of Hollywood produced films can make the teaching of this unit highly engaging. However, remember it is Hollywood and the accurate portrayal of mental illness may not be displayed in such a way. It is highly recommended that the time leading up to the national exam be for the study of psychology and what will be on the exam. I recommend using the movies listed in this module after the exam and/or as an extension to the learning that takes place at home.

## Hoarders

A&E broadcasts a reality-TV series on hoarders: http://www.aetv.com/shows/hoarders.

## Additional Readings

Abramowitz, J. S., & Jacoby, R. J. (2015). *Obsessive-compulsive disorder in adults*. Hogrege.

Angst, J. (2013). Bipolar disorders in DSM-5: Strengths, problems and perspectives. *International Journal of Bipolar Disorders,* http://www.journalbipolardisorders.com/content/pdf/2194-7511-1-12.pdf.

Brown, H. (2010). *Brave girl eating: A family's struggle with anorexia*. William Morrow.

Cockburn, P., & Cockburn, H. (2011). *Henry's demons: Living with schizophrenia, a father and son's story*. Scribner.

Fountoulaksi, K. N. (2015). *Bipolar disorder: An evidence-based guide*. Springer.

Fox-Kales, E. (2011). *Body shots: Hollywood and the culture of eating disorders*. State University of New York Press.

Freedman, R. (2010). *The madness within us: Schizophrenia as a neuronal process*. Oxford University Press.

Holland, J. (2009). *Weekends at Bellevue: Nine years in the psychiatric emergency room*. Bantam.

Hornbacher, M. (2009). *Madness: A bipolar life*. Boston: Mariner Books.

Howard-Taylor, L. (2009). *Biting anorexia: A firsthand account of an internal war:* New Harbinger.

Janicak, P. (2014). *Schizophrenia: Recent advances in diagnosis and treatment*. Springer.

Kaysen, S. (1994). *Girl, Interrupted*. Vintage.

Kelly, A. D. (2014). *The predatory lies of anorexia: A survivor's story*. Bettie Youngs Books.

Klein, T. (2011). *Coping with trauma-related dissociation: Skills training for patients and therapists*. W.W. Norton & Company.

Lilienfeld, S. O., & Arkowitz, H. (2010). Living with schizophrenia. *Scientific American Mind, 21*(1), 66–67.

Meyer, R. (2003). *Case studies in abnormal behavior* (6th ed.). Boston: Allyn & Bacon.

Montross, C. (2013). *Falling into the fire: A psychiatrist's encounters with the mind in crisis*. Penguin Press.

Nathan, D. (2011). *Sybil exposed: The extraordinary story behind the famous multiple personality case*. Free Press.

Oltmanns, T. F., Martin, M. T., Neale, J. M., & Davison, G. C. (2011). *Case studies in abnormal psychology*. Wiley.

Penney, D., & Stastny, P. (2008). *The lives they left behind: Suitcases from a state hospital attic*. Bellevue Literary Press.

Redfield-Jamison, K. (1997). *An unquiet mind: A memoir of moods and madness*. Vintage.

Redfield-Jamison, K. (2000). *Night falls fast: Understanding suicide*. Vintage.

Resnick, P. J. (2007). The Andrea Yates case: Insanity on trial. *Cleveland State Law Review, 55*(2), 147–156. http://engagedscholarship.csuohio.edu/cgi/viewcontent.cgi?article=1174&context=clevstlrev.

Singer, J. (2013). OCD: Getting the right treatment can be a challenge. PSYCHCENTRAL. Retrieved on September 28, 2013, from http://psychcentral.com/lib/ocd-getting-the-right-treatment-can-be-a-challenge/00017861.

Smith, D. (2013). *Monkey mind: A memoir of anxiety*. Simon & Schuster.

Westly, E. (2010). Different shades of blue. *Scientific American Mind, 21*(2), 30–37.

## Neuroscience in Your Life: Brain Networks Related to Memory Deficits in Schizophrenia

Answer Suggestions

- Negative symptoms are measured in this study. They show the removal or disruptions to normal emotions and behaviors, such as a decline in memory. Positive symptoms are indicated by the presence of disordered behavior, such as hallucinations or delusions.
- A control group is not exposed to the independent variable and it is used for comparison. In this study, the control group was the healthy patients without schizophrenia who were used for comparison.

## AP Test Practice

### Part I: Multiple Choice

1. **B** *(Skill 1.C, Learning Target 8.G)*

2. **C** *(Skill 1.A, Learning Target 8.F)*

3. **A** *(Skill 1.B, Learning Target 8.H)*

### Part II: Free Response

Phobias are linked to a specific stimulus, whereas GAD consists of "free floating" anxiety.

Bipolar consists of both lowered and elevated moods, whereas depression consists of only lowered mood.

DID is a nonpsychotic disorder and consists of more than one personality. Schizophrenia has a biological explanation, whereas DID is usually psychological.

# Module 48: Psychological Disorders in Perspective

## **AP** Module Summary

One out of two people in the United States is likely to suffer at some point in their lives from a psychological disorder. The significant level of psychological disorders is a problem not only in the United States. According to the World Health Organization, mental health difficulties are also a global concern (see **Figure 2**). Throughout the world, psychological disorders are widespread. Furthermore, there are economic disparities in treatment; more affluent people with mild disorders receive more and better treatment than poor people who have more severe disorders. In fact, psychological disorders make up 14 percent of global illness, and 90 percent of people in developing countries receive no care at all for their disorders. Also, the incidence of specific disorders varies significantly in other cultures.

**EXPLORING DIVERSITY: *DSM* AND CULTURE—AND THE CULTURE OF *DSM*** In most people's estimation, a person who hears voices of the recently deceased is probably a victim of a psychological disturbance. Yet some Plains Indians routinely hear the voices of the dead calling to them from the afterlife, and in their culture, that's considered perfectly normal. This is only one example of the role of culture in labeling behavior as "abnormal." In fact, among all the major adult disorders included in the *DSM* categorization, a minority are found across all cultures of the world. Most others are prevalent primarily in North America and Western Europe. Conversely, other cultures have disorders that do not appear in the West. For example, in Malaysia, a behavior called *amok* is characterized by a wild outburst in which a usually quiet and withdrawn person kills or severely injures another. Finally, *ataque de nervios* is a disorder found most often among Latinos from the Caribbean. It is characterized by trembling, crying, uncontrollable screams, and incidents of verbal or physical aggression. In sum, we should not assume that the *DSM* provides the final word on psychological disorders. The disorders it includes are very much a creation and function of Western cultures at a particular moment in time, and its categories should not be seen as universally applicable.

**BECOMING AN INFORMED CONSUMER OF PSYCHOLOGY: DECIDING WHEN YOU NEED HELP** We all experience a wide range of emotions, and it is not unusual to feel deeply unhappy, fantasize about bizarre situations, or feel anxiety about life's circumstances. It is the persistence, depth, and consistency of such behavior that set normal reactions apart from abnormal ones. On the other hand, many people do have problems that merit concern, and in such cases, it is important to consider the possibility that professional help is warranted. The following list of symptoms can serve as a guideline to help you determine whether outside intervention might be useful:

- long-term feelings of distress that interfere with your sense of well-being, competence, and ability to function effectively in daily activities
- occasions in which you experience overwhelmingly high stress accompanied by feelings of inability to cope with the situation
- prolonged depression or feelings of hopelessness, especially when they do not have any clear cause
- withdrawal from other people
- thoughts of inflicting harm on oneself or suicide
- a chronic physical problem for which no physical cause can be determined
- a fear or phobia that prevents you from engaging in everyday activities
- feelings that other people are out to get you or are talking about and plotting against you
- inability to interact effectively with others, preventing the development of friendships and loving relationships

# Activities

**WEB RESEARCH** Send students to the *Surgeon General's Report on Mental Health*: http://www.surgeongeneral.gov/library/mentalhealth/home.html. The report contains detailed information about the major psychological disorders. Give students instructions to report on a disorder that they personally find to be the most interesting. Have them briefly review the symptoms, causes, and prevalence of this disorder, then indicate how it differs among age groups (children, teens, adults, older adults). What are the prospects for the future of finding a cure for this disorder? (Skill 1.A)

An alternative is to send students to explore the website of the American Psychological Association: apa.org.

**EDUCATING OTHERS** Have students work together in teams to create educational materials (flyers, poster, video, etc.) geared toward students. These educational materials should focus on the signs that indicate an individual might need help. Have students focus on ways to encourage others to seek help when needed, something that can often be a struggle.

**COMBATING STIGMA**
**Stigma:** Before the section on stigma, you may want to ask students why they think negative biases exist about mental illness. Ask them what the "costs" are of the negative biases (e.g., not being hired for jobs). You may also want to ask students what they think is the greatest misconception that people have about the mentally ill and why this misconception is so prevalent. Finally, ask students what can be done to improve people's attitudes about those who have psychological disorders.

# Suggested Media

- *Journal of Abnormal Psychology:* http://www.apa.org/journals/abn/. Some free articles are available here.
- *Learning Resources Organization:* http://www.learner.org/resources/series60.html. Free copies of an
abnormal psychology video set are available here. You have to register first, but then you can play it
in the classroom.
- *Self-Quiz on Abnormal Behavior:* http://www.psywww.com/selfquiz/ch12mcq.htm
- *Suicide Awareness Voices of Education:* http://www.save.org/.

# Additional Readings

Arnold, C. (2012). Inside the wrong body. *Scientific American Mind, 23*(2), 36–41.

Miller, R. B. (2015). *Not so abnormal psychology: A pragmatic view of mental illness.* Washington, DC: American Psychological Association.

## Applying Psychology in the 21st Century: Is the Newest Generation of College Students More Psychologically Disordered Than Their Predecessors

Answer Suggestions

- There is less stigma, better treatments, and more awareness of services.
- There is more awareness of mental illness from community events, visible support of mental health (i.e., bracelets), and celebrities sharing their stories. There is more access to information of causes, symptoms, and treatments of mental disorders.

## AP Test Practice

### Part I: Multiple Choice

1. **D** *(Skill 1.A, Learning Target 8.B)*

2. **C** *(Skill 1.A, Learning Target 8.B)*

3. **A** *(Skill 1.A, Learning Target 8.A)*

### Part II: Free Response

Culture determines what disorders are listed in the *DSM*. Among all the major disorders included in the *DSM*, just a minority are found across all cultures of the world. Most of the listed disorders are found in North America and Western Europe. The *DSM-5* is recognizing culture-bound disorders.

Comorbidity is the appearance of multiple, simultaneous psychological disorders in the same person. For example, someone may be diagnosed with both depression and anxiety disorders.

The *DSM-5* has a comorbidity section under each major diagnosis.

Diagnostic labels provide a common language for therapists. However, labels can be stigmatizing and can influence the way mental health workers perceive and interpret a patient's actions.

# CHAPTER 16

# Treatment of Psychological Disorders

## **AP** Introduction

As was true for the unit on causes of and forms of psychopathology, this unit on treatment will capture student interest. Following the format established for the perspectives on abnormality in the previous unit, these modules can also be organized according to theoretical perspective in psychology. It is important to emphasize the multiple routes that exist to treatment and that most psychologists do not adhere to one form of therapeutic model. Instead, eclecticism and empirically validated treatments have become the norm in the practice of clinical psychology. It is also important to be sensitive to the fact that some students may be seeking treatment for disorders involving symptoms of depression or anxiety. Finally, giving students information about treatment may be vital in helping them to make decisions about seeking help, should they be suffering symptoms.

## **AP** Essential Questions

- Why is psychological perspective necessary in the treatment of disorders?
- How are psychological disorders treated?

### Module 49: Psychotherapy: Psychodynamic, Behavioral, and Cognitive Approaches to Treatment

**AP Learning Targets:**

- Describe the central characteristics of psychotherapeutic intervention.
- Identify the contributions of major figures in psychological treatment.
- Describe major treatment orientations used in therapy and how those orientations influence therapeutic planning.
- Summarize effectiveness of specific treatments used to address specific problems.
- Compare and contrast different treatment methods.

**Pacing:**

2 Blocks or 4 Traditional Class periods

# Module 50: Psychotherapy: Humanistic, Interpersonal, and Group Approaches to Treatment

**AP Learning Targets:**

- Describe the central characteristics of psychotherapeutic intervention.
- Identify the contributions of major figures in psychological treatment.
- Describe major treatment orientations used in therapy and how those orientations influence therapeutic planning.
- Summarize effectiveness of specific treatments used to address specific problems.
- Discuss how cultural and ethnic context influence choice and success of treatment (e.g., factors that lead to premature termination of treatment).
- Compare and contrast different treatment methods.

**Pacing:**

1 Block or 2 Traditional Class periods


# Module 51: Biomedical Therapy: Biological Approaches to Treatment

**Pacing:**

1 Block or 2 Traditional Class periods

# Module 49: Psychotherapy: Psychodynamic, Behavioral, and Cognitive Approaches to Treatment

## AP Module Summary

The new Course and Exam Description Guide now specify the treatment orientation: psychodynamic. It also goes further into stating that students should be able to compare and contrast the methods of rational-emotive, psychoanalytic/psychodynamic, client-centered, cognitive, behavioral, sociocultural, biopsychosocial, and cognitive-behavioral. Therefore, Module 49 is one on which a considerable amount of time should be spent. Finally, this is also the unit where the names of those who developed such techniques is also very important for students to know.

Psychologically-based therapy, or *psychotherapy,* is treatment in which a trained professional—a therapist—uses psychological techniques to help someone overcome psychological difficulties and disorders, resolve problems in living, or bring about personal growth. In psychotherapy, the goal is to produce psychological change in a person (called a "client" or "patient") through discussions and interactions with the therapist.

There are about 400 varieties of psychotherapy. Although the methods are diverse, all psychological approaches have a common perspective: They seek to solve psychological problems by modifying people's behavior and helping them obtain a better understanding of themselves and their past, present, and future. In light of the variety of psychological approaches, it is not surprising that the people who provide therapy vary considerably in their educational background and training (see **Figure 1**).

**PSYCHODYNAMIC APPROACHES TO THERAPY** *Psychodynamic therapy* seeks to bring unresolved past conflicts and unacceptable impulses from the unconscious into the conscious, where patients may deal with the problems more effectively.

- Based on Freud's psychoanalytic approach to personality
- Individuals employ defense mechanisms, psychological strategies to protect themselves from unacceptable unconscious thoughts and impulses. The most common being repression, which pushes threatening and unpleasant thoughts and impulses back into the unconscious impulses.

**PSYCHOANALYSIS: FREUD'S THERAPY** *Psychoanalysis* is the kind of psychotherapy in which the goal is to release hidden unconscious thoughts and feelings in order to reduce their power in controlling behavior.

- Tends to be a lengthy and expensive process, patients may meet with a therapist with considerable frequency, sometimes as much as 50 minutes a day, 4 to 5 days a week, for several years.
- In a technique called *free association,* patients say aloud whatever comes to mind, regardless of its apparent irrelevance or senselessness, and the analysts attempt to recognize and label the connections between what a patient says and the patient's unconscious.
- *Dream interpretation* is examining dreams to find clues to unconscious conflicts and problems.
  - *Manifest content*—moving beyond the surface description of a dream
  - *Latent content*—therapists seek its underlying meaning, which thereby reveals the true unconscious meaning of the dream.
  - *Resistance* is an inability or unwillingness to discuss or reveal particular memories, thoughts, or motivations.

Because of the close, almost intimate interaction between patient and psychoanalyst, the relationship between the two often becomes emotionally charged and takes on a complexity unlike most other relationships. *Transference* is the transfer of feelings to a psychoanalyst of love or anger that had been originally directed to a patient's parents or other authority figures.

**CONTEMPORARY PSYCHODYNAMIC APPROACHES** Few people have the time, money, or patience to participate in years of traditional psychoanalysis. Today, psychodynamic therapy tends to be of shorter duration and usually lasts no longer than 3 months or 20 sessions. The therapist takes a more active role than Freud would have liked by controlling the course of therapy and prodding and advising the patient with considerable directness.

**EVALUATING PSYCHODYNAMIC THERAPY** Even with its current modifications, psychodynamic therapy has its critics. In its longer versions, it can be time-consuming and expensive, especially in comparison with other forms of psychotherapy, such as behavioral and cognitive approaches. Ultimately, the most important concern about psychodynamic treatment is whether it actually works, and there is no simple answer to the question. Psychodynamic treatment techniques have been controversial since Freud introduced them. Part of the problem is the difficulty in establishing whether patients have improved after psychodynamic therapy.

**BEHAVIORAL APPROACHES TO THERAPY** *Behavioral treatment approaches* make use of the basic processes of learning, such as reinforcement and extinction, to reduce or eliminate maladaptive bahvior. These approaches make this fundamental assumption: Both abnormal behavior and normal behavior are learned. The goal of therapy is to change people's behavior to allow them to function more effectively.

**CLASSICAL CONDITIONING TREATMENTS**

- *Counterconditioning*
  - This would be a great time to introduce Mary Cover Jones.
- *Aversive conditioning* is a form of therapy that reduces the frequency of undesired behavior by pairing an aversive, unpleasant stimulus with undesired behavior.
- **Exposure Therapies**
  - This would be a great time to introduce Joseph Wolpe.
- **Systematic Desensitization** In *systematic desensitization,* gradual exposure to an anxiety-producing stimulus is paired with relaxation to extinguish the response of anxiety. The idea is to learn to associate relaxation with a stimulus that previously produced anxiety. The newest form of exposure therapy is virtual reality technology wherein clients wear virtual reality goggles that provide highly realistic depictions of stimuli that trigger anxiety. Once at the virtual site, a client can be treated with traditional systematic desensitization techniques.
- **Flooding Treatments** *Flooding* is a behavioral treatment for anxiety in which people are suddenly confronted with a stimulus that they fear. However, unlike systematic desensitization, relaxation training is omitted. The goal of flooding is to allow the maladaptive response of anxiety or avoidance to become extinct.

**OPERANT CONDITIONING TECHNIQUES** Some behavioral approaches make use of operant conditioning principles. These approaches are based on the notion that we should reward people for carrying out desirable behavior and extinguish undesirable behavior by either ignoring it or punishing it.

One example of the systematic application of operant conditioning principles is the *token system,* which rewards a person for desired behavior with a token such as a poker chip or some kind of play money that can later be exchanged for an actual reward. Contingency contracting, a variant of the token system, has proved quite effective in producing behavior modification. In *contingency contracting,* the therapist and client (or teacher and student, or parent and child) draw up a written agreement. The contract states a series of behavioral goals the client hopes to achieve. Behavior therapists also use *observational learning,* the process in which the behavior of other people is modeled, to systematically teach people new skills and ways of handling their fears and anxieties.

- This would be an excellent time to revisit the work of B.F. Skinner and would compliment the discussion of token systems.

**EVALUATING BEHAVIOR THERAPY** Behavior therapy works especially well for eliminating anxiety disorders, treating phobias and compulsions, establishing control over impulses, and learning complex social skills to replace maladaptive behavior. More than any of the other therapeutic techniques, it provides methods that nonprofessionals can use to change their own behavior. Critics of behavior therapy believe that because it emphasizes changing external behavior, people do not necessarily gain insight into the thoughts and expectations that may be fostering their maladaptive behavior. On the other hand, neuroscientific evidence shows that behavioral treatments can produce actual changes in brain functioning, which suggests that behavioral treatments can produce changes beyond external behavior.

**COGNITIVE APPROACHES TO THERAPY** *Cognitive treatment approaches* teach people to think in more adaptive ways by changing their dysfunctional cognitions about the world and themselves. Unlike behavior therapists, who focus on modifying external behavior, cognitive therapists focus on changing the way people think. Because they often use basic principles of learning, the methods they employ are sometimes referred to as the *cognitive-behavioral approach*. Cognitive therapy is relatively short term and usually lasts a maximum of 20 sessions. Therapy tends to be highly structured and focused on concrete problems.

One good example of cognitive treatment, *rational-emotive behavior therapy,* attempts to restructure a person's belief system into a more realistic, rational, and logical set of views. By adopting more accurate thought patterns, it is assumed that people will lead more psychologically healthy lives. Irrational beliefs trigger negative emotions, which in turn support the irrational beliefs and lead to a self-defeating cycle. Psychologist Albert Ellis calls it the A-B-C model in which negative activating conditions (A) lead to the activation of an irrational belief system (B), which in turn leads to emotional consequences (C) (see **Figure 3**).

Rational-emotive behavior therapy aims to help clients eliminate maladaptive thoughts and beliefs and adopt more effective thinking. To accomplish this goal, therapists take an active, directive role during therapy and openly challenge patterns of thought that appear to be dysfunctional.

Like rational-emotive behavior therapy, Aaron Beck's cognitive behavior therapy aims to change people's illogical thoughts about themselves and the world. Therapists urge clients to obtain information on their own that will lead them to discard their inaccurate thinking through a process of cognitive appraisal. In *cognitive appraisal,* clients are asked to evaluate situations, themselves, and others in terms of their memories, values, beliefs, thoughts, and expectations.

- Make sure to include the *Sociocultural method* when reviewing the different treatment methods.

**EVALUATING COGNITIVE APPROACHES TO THERAPY** Cognitive approaches to therapy have proved successful in dealing with a broad range of disorders, including anxiety disorders, depression, substance abuse, and eating disorders. The willingness of cognitive therapists to incorporate additional treatment approaches has made this approach a particularly effective form of treatment. At the same time, critics have pointed out that the focus on helping people to think more rationally ignores the fact that, in reality, life is sometimes irrational.

## AP Key Terms

aversive conditioning

behavioral treatment approaches

biomedical therapy

cognitive treatment approaches

cognitive-behavioral approach

flooding

psychoanalysis

psychodynamic therapy

psychotherapy

rational-emotive behavior therapy

sociocultural method

systematic desensitization

Aaron Beck

Albert Ellis

Sigmund Freud

Mary Cover Jones

B.F. Skinner

Joseph Wolpe

## Class Discussion Ideas

**MENTAL HEALTH PROFESSIONALS** Have a clinical psychologist, a psychiatrist, and a counselor come to the class to speak about their profession and about why they chose their particular profession over other mental health professions. Afterward, have the students ask questions and then write a one- to two-page paper summarizing the information from the speakers.

**PSYCHODYNAMIC THERAPY** The goal of psychodynamic therapy is to reduce anxiety by bringing conflicts and impulses into conscious awareness. Anxiety-producing areas may be long-hidden crises, trauma, or conflict.

One tool is free association, in which patients are told to say whatever comes to mind, regardless of its apparent irrelevance or senselessness (the "golden rule" of psychoanalysis). Unconscious forces can produce repression, which produces resistance in free association.

Dream interpretation is another important tool of the therapist.

Transference occurs as patients view the therapist as a parent, lover, or significant other in their past and apply the feelings they had for that individual to the therapist.

**BEHAVIORAL THERAPY** According to the behavioral model, causes of abnormal behavior are:

- failure to acquire adaptive skills.
- faulty learning of adaptive skills.

**MODIFICATION OF ABNORMAL BEHAVIOR** Modification of abnormal behavior involves:

- learning new behavior.
- unlearning maladaptive patterns.

Abnormal behavior is viewed as both a symptom as well as the problem.

### Classical conditioning approaches:

- Systematic desensitization - Progressively closer encounters with feared stimulus using counterconditioning (replacing fear with relaxation)
- Used for treating phobias, anxiety disorders, and sexual dysfunctions
- Example in the text is treating a fear of flying.

### Operant conditioning approaches:

- Token system - Person is rewarded for desired behavior with a tangible reward.
- Contingency contracting - Rewards are given for achieving specific goals.

### Cognitive therapy:

- In this form of therapy, the focus is on changing the way people think and behave.
- Rational-emotive approach (Ellis) - Attempts to restructure a person's belief system (get rid of the "musts")
- Cognitive-behavioral approach (Beck) - Attempts to change people's illogical thoughts about themselves

# Activities

**ATTITUDES TOWARD THERAPY** Have students complete *Handout: Attitudes Toward Psychotherapy.*

## BEHAVIORISM

- **Behaviorism** You may want to inform students that the reason behavioral and cognitive behavioral therapies are so popular now is: (1) their efficacy; (2) they are relatively short in duration; and thus, (3) they are less expensive. Ask students to generate examples of how a disorder could be learned and then how the behavioral perspective not only explains the disorder but also could "fix" it.
- **Behavior Therapies** Ask students to choose a phobia and then explain how systematic desensitization would be used in treating that phobia. Students will learn through experience how the steps in systematic desensitization work.

**COMPARISON OF THERAPY METHODS** Have students complete *Handout: Comparison of Therapy Methods.*

- **Cognitive Therapies** Use *Handout: Using REBT and Beck's Cognitive Therapy.* The students will read various scenarios of individuals who are upset with themselves over something they did. The students are to pretend that they are the therapist and treat the individual using either REBT or Beck's cognitive therapy.
- **Cognitive Therapy** Instruct students to write down the last circumstance that upset them. Next, have them list the kinds of thoughts they were thinking concerning the incident. If the thoughts were negative, ask them to change them to make them more realistic or positive. Finally, ask students to determine if they believe their thoughts can make them miserable. Why or why not?

# Discussion Questions

## BEHAVIOR THERAPY

- Have students select a behavior that they would like to modify and design a reinforcement therapy schedule to alter it. They should choose an undesirable behavior such as shyness, biting heir nails, snacking too much, or some other nervous habit.
- Define: What is this behavior?
- Identify a desired substitute behavior. Record their baseline, or normal frequency of showing the behavior.
- Decide on a reinforcer they find applicable. Reward themselves each time they show the desired behavior and withhold reinforcement when they show the undesired behavior. Record the results.
- Ask students: How difficult is it to apply behavior therapy to your own behavior? Why?

# Suggested Media

- *History of psychoanalysis and the case of Anna O*: http://www.youtube.com/watch?v=AUB85ISj4pM.

**POPULAR MOVIES: PSYCHOANALYSIS AND PSYCHOTHERAPY** Although unrealistic, the films *Analyze This* and its sequel *Analyze That* illustrate a type of psychoanalysis. The humor in these films is that in addition to the therapy conducted by the therapist, the client provides therapy to the therapist when he analyzes the reasons the therapist chose this career path. The film *Good Will Hunting* also portrays (albeit unrealistically) a complex relationship between a therapist and a client. *The Prince of Tides* also portrays therapy and raises ethical questions as well about client-therapist boundaries. *One Flew Over the Cuckoo's Nest* offers a classic depiction of a mental health center.

*Depending on the community in which you serve a parent/guardian permission slip may be required.

**POPULAR TELEVISION SHOWS** Several television series regularly include or focus entirely on therapy. For example, *The Sopranos* (available on DVD) includes many sessions between the lead character and his psychiatrist. Several episodes also include family therapy, couples therapy, and therapy with the adolescent son as well as sessions between the psychiatrist and her supervisor. In the second to last episode of the series, the psychiatrist violates confidentiality by naming her patient to guests at a dinner party—allowing for a discussion of ethics and therapy. Another HBO series, *In Treatment,* focuses exclusively on a therapist's practice. See www.hbo.com for series information.

*Depending on the community in which you serve a parent/guardian permission slip may be required.

# Additional Readings

Chiesa, M. (2010). Research and psychoanalysis: Still time to bridge the great divide? *Psychoanalytic Psychology, 27*(2), 99.

Ellis, A. A., & Dryden, W. (1987). *The practice of rational-emotive therapy.* New York: Springer Publishing Co.

Kurtz, M. M. (2013). A social salve for schizophrenia. *Scientific American Mind, 24*(1), 62–67.

Lipsey, M. W., & Wilson, D. B. (1993). The efficacy of psychological, educational, and behavioral treatment. *American Psychologist, 48,* 1181–1209.

# **AP** Student Edition Answer Key

## Neuroscience in Your Life: How Cognitive Behavioral Therapy Changes Your Brain

Answer Suggestions

- The sample consists of patients with social anxiety disorder.
- The independent variable is the treatment method (online cognitive behavioral therapy versus alternative methods), because it is being manipulated. The dependent variable is anxiety and structure and function of the amygdala, because both are being measured.

## AP Test Practice

### Part I: Multiple Choice

1. **E** *(Skill 1.A, Learning Target 8.K)*
2. **A** *(Skill 1.B, Learning Target 8.L)*
3. **E** *(Skill 1.C, Learning Target 8.L)*

## Part II: Free Response

A psychologist has a PhD or PsyD and will use talk therapy. A psychiatrist has a MD and can prescribe medication in addition to using talk therapy.

Systematic desensitization is a behavioral technique in which exposure to an anxiety-producing stimulus is paired with deep relaxation to reduce or eliminate anxiety. Kate and her therapist would begin by reviewing relaxation techniques. Next, they would create an anxiety hierarchy with the top of the pyramid consisting of Kate crossing a bridge. As Kate relaxes, she would be exposed to the first step of the hierarchy (i.e., imagining a bridge) and would gradually move upward until she crosses a bridge without anxiety.

Flooding is a behavioral technique in which people are confronted with a stimulus that they fear. Kate's therapist would take her to a bridge and expose her directly to her fear.

Rational-emotive behavior therapy is a cognitive technique in which dysfunctional thoughts are challenged in an attempt to restructure the belief system into a more realistic, rational, and logical set of views. Kate needs to restructure her negative thoughts about bridges into more positive healthy ones. Her therapist will directly confront her irrational thoughts about bridges and have her work on adopting a more realistic view of bridges.

# Module 50: Psychotherapy: Humanistic, Interpersonal, and Group Approaches to Treatment

## AP Module Summary

Module 50 is very much like Module 49. The new course and exam description guide goes further into stating that students should be able to compare and contrast the methods of rational-emotive, psychoanalytic/psychodynamic, client-centered, cognitive, behavioral, sociocultural, biopsychosocial, and cognitive-behavioral. A majority of students are able to understand the treatment methods of individual and group, therefore spending considerable amounts of time on them is not necessary. Mentioning Carl Rogers should also be a great review of previous units and then tying him to his approach on treating the individual may help with solidifying his work in the minds of students.

**HUMANISTIC THERAPY** *Humanistic therapy* is a therapy in which the underlying rationale is that people have control of their behavior, can make choices about their lives, and are essentially responsible for solving their own problems. Humanistic therapists believe that people naturally are motivated to strive for self-actualization.

**PERSON-CENTERED THERAPY** *Person-centered therapy* (also called client-centered therapy) aims to enable people to reach their potential for self-actualization. By providing a warm and accepting environment, therapists hope to motivate clients to air their problems and feelings.

Instead of directing the choices clients make, therapists provide what Carl Rogers calls unconditional positive regard—providing whole-hearted acceptance and understanding, and no disapproval, regardless of the feelings and attitudes the client expresses. Furnishing unconditional positive regard does not mean that therapists must approve of everything their clients say or do. Rather, therapists need to communicate that they are caring, nonjudgmental, and empathetic—that is, understanding of a client's emotional experiences.

**EVALUATING HUMANISTIC APPROACHES TO THERAPY** The notion that psychological disorders result from restricted growth potential appeals philosophically to many people. Furthermore, when humanistic therapists acknowledge that the freedom we possess can lead to psychological difficulties, clients find an unusually supportive environment for therapy. However, humanistic treatments lack specificity, a problem that has troubled their critics.

**INTERPERSONAL THERAPY** *Interpersonal therapy (IPT)* is short-term therapy designed to help patients control their moods and emotions by focusing on the context of their current social relationships. It typically focuses on interpersonal issues such as conflicts with others, social skills issues, role transitions (such as divorce), or grief. The approach makes no assumptions about the underlying causes of psychological disorders but focuses on the interpersonal context in which a disorder is developed and maintained.

**GROUP THERAPIES** In *group therapy,* several unrelated people meet with a therapist to discuss some aspect of their psychological functioning. People typically discuss with the group their problems, which often center on a common difficulty, such as alcoholism or a lack of social skills. Because several people are treated simultaneously in group therapy, it is a much more economical means of treatment than individual psychotherapy is. However, critics argue that group settings lack the individual attention inherent in one-on-one therapy and that especially shy and withdrawn individuals may not receive the attention they need in a group setting.

**FAMILY THERAPY** *Family therapy* involves two or more family members, one (or more) of whose problems led to treatment. However, rather than focusing simply on the members of the family who present the initial problem, family therapists consider the family as a unit to which each member contributes. Family therapists view the family as a "system" and assume that individuals in the family cannot improve without understanding the conflicts found in interactions among family members. One goal of this type of therapy, then, is to get the family members to adopt new, more constructive roles and patterns of behavior.

**SELF-HELP THERAPY** In many cases, group therapy does not involve a professional therapist. Instead, people with similar problems get together to discuss their shared feelings and experiences. For example, people who have recently experienced the death of a spouse might meet in a bereavement support group, or college students may get together to discuss their adjustment to college.

### EVALUATING PSYCHOTHERAPY: DOES THERAPY WORK?

**Is Therapy Effective?** This question requires a complex response. In fact, identifying the single most appropriate form of treatment is a controversial and still unresolved task for psychologists specializing in psychological disorders.

### EXPLORING DIVERSITY: RACIAL AND ETHNIC FACTORS IN TREATMENT: SHOULD THERAPISTS BE COLOR-BLIND?

This section explains the importance of taking people's environmental and cultural backgrounds into account during treatment for psychological disorders. In particular, members of racial and ethnic minority groups, especially those who are also poor, may behave in ways that help them deal with a society that discriminates against them. As a consequence, behavior that may signal psychological disorder in middle-class and upper-class whites may simply be adaptive in people from other racial and socioeconomic groups. For instance, characteristically suspicious and distrustful people may be displaying a survival strategy to protect themselves from psychological and physical injury, rather than suffering from a psychological disturbance.

In fact, therapists must question some basic assumptions of psychotherapy when dealing with racial, ethnic, and cultural minority group members. Clearly, therapists cannot be "color-blind." Instead, they must take into account the racial, ethnic, cultural, and social class backgrounds of their clients in determining the nature of a psychological disorder and the course of treatment.

## **AP** Key Terms

| | |
|---|---|
| family therapy | interpersonal therapy (IPT) |
| group therapy | person-centered therapy |
| humanistic therapy | spontaneous remission |

## Class Discussion Ideas

### HUMANISTIC THERAPY

**Three fundamental ideas are:**

- We have control over our behavior.
- We decide what kind of life to live.
- We must solve the difficulties that we encounter in our daily lives.

In humanistic therapy, the therapist is seen as a guide or facilitator. Psychological disorders are seen as resulting from lack of meaning in life and loneliness.

**Humanistic approaches include:**

- Client-centered therapy
- Nondirective methods
- Providing unconditional positive regard
- Goal is self-actualization

## Activities

**INTRODUCTION TO THERAPY** Facilitate a class discussion by asking students to consider how seeking therapy for a psychological disorder is a sign of strength and courage.

**FAMILY THERAPY** Use *Handout: Which Family Therapy Technique Is It?* The goal of this activity is for students to identify the various family therapy techniques discussed in this chapter.

## Discussion Questions

### COMPARISON OF THERAPY METHODS

- List three main differences between humanistic and psychoanalytic therapy (role of therapist, basic assumptions about human nature, interpretation of resistance and other "unconscious" phenomena).
- What advantages might there be for a therapist to be "genuine" rather than "neutral"? How would it make you feel to have a therapist who disclosed personal information?
- Why is humanistic therapy called "person-centered"?
- Would you agree that psychoanalysis is person-centered, even though it is not called this? Why or why not?
- Which of the various therapies discussed in this chapter would be the most successful for you? The least successful? Why?
- Why are there so many types of therapies to treat the same disorders?

### DEINSTITUTIONALIZATION
**Ask students the following questions:**

- What were the main causes of the deinstitutionalization movement?
- Some psychologists believe that clients were better treated in hospitals rather than community centers. Do you agree with this, or do you think that community centers are preferable?
- What are some of the problems involved in the current community treatment of people with serious mental illness?

If you were to become a therapist, which therapy technique would be your focus?

## Suggested Media

- *Happiness:* http://www.ted.com/index.php/talks/dan_gilbert_asks_why_are_we_happy. html. TED Talk by Harvard psychologist Dan Gilbert.
- *Person-centered therapy:* http://www.youtube.com/watch?v=Ew8CAr1v48M&feature=PlayLis t&index=6&list=PL9EA5A3049225F48F.
- *Phobias:* http://www.msnbc.msn.com/id/15221700/. In October 2006, the NBC *Today Show* broadcast a series in which the hosts confronted their fears. Unfortunately, they have not posted the segment in which Lester Holt is treated for snake phobia, but it is possible to view Campbell Brown (now of CNN) talk about her fear of cooking for her mother-in-law.

- *Intervention:* http://www.aetv.com/intervention. This A&E documentary series profiles addicts whose family and friends confront them in an intervention session.
- *Positive psychology:* http://www.ted.com/index.php/talks/martin_seligman_on_the_state_of_psychology.html. TED Talk with Martin Seligman on the state of psychology.
- *Psychotherapies:* National Institute of Mental Health https://www.nimh.nih.gov/health/topics/psychotherapies/index.shtml.
- *Psych Web:* http://www.psychwww.com/resource/bytopic/therapies.html.
- *Understanding Psychotherapy and How It Works* (APA): http://www.apa.org/helpcenter/understanding-psychotherapy.aspx.

## Additional Readings

Callahan, A., & Inckle, K. (2012). Cybertherapy or psychobabble? A mixed methods study of online emotional support. *British Journal of Guidance & Counselling, 40*(3), 261–278.

Epstein, R. (2011). Distance therapy comes of age. *Scientific American Mind, 22*(2), 60–63.

Gelso, C. J. (2011). Emerging and continuing trends in psychotherapy: Views from an editor's eye. *Psychotherapy, 48*(2), 182.

Lazarus, C. N. (2016, March 16). And the three best therapy methods are… . *Psychology Today: Think Well.*

Spring, B. (2007). Evidence-based practice in clinical psychology: What it is, why it matters, what you need to know. *Journal of Clinical Psychology, 63*(7), 611-631.

Sue, S., Zane, N., Hall, G. C. N., & Berger, L. K. (2009). The case for cultural competency in psychotherapeutic interventions. *Annual Review of Psychology, 60,* 525.

## AP Student Edition Answer Key

### Applying Psychology in the 21st Century: Click Here for Therapy

Answer Suggestions

- Longitudinal research of multiple aged patients with different disorders and perspectives. Cohort effects should be addressed. Research should explore how familiarity and increased use of technology impacts the effectiveness of online therapy.
- Online therapy is flexible, increases self-management, and is cost-effective; while traditional therapy allows the therapist to build a trusting relationship with the patient.

## AP Test Practice

### Part I: Multiple Choice

1. **E** *(Skill 1.C, Learning Target 8.Q)*
2. **C** *(Skill 1.A, Learning Target 8.L)*
3. **E** *(Skill 1.B, Learning Target 8.J)*

## Part II: Free Response

Nondirective counseling consists of therapists taking the role of guide or facilitator. They use techniques to help people understand themselves. The therapist will not interpret or answer Hannah's questions. Instead they will clarify or reflect on what Hannah said.

Person-centered therapy aims to enable people to reach their potential for self-actualization. The therapist will provide Hannah with an accepting environment in hopes that Hannah will share her problems and make healthy choices.

Empathy is understanding a client's emotional experiences. The therapist will communicate an understanding of Hannah's emotional experiences, which helps build a supportive relationship.

Humanistic therapies are appealing to many because they rest on free-choice. Therapy is supportive, which helps clients find solutions to their problems.

Humanistic treatments can be problematic because they lack specificity. They are probably the least scientific and theoretically developed approach to therapy. Also, they often work only for verbal patients.

# Module 51: Biomedical Therapy: Biological Approaches to Treatment

## AP Module Summary

The Course Exam and Description Guide specifies the biological perspective in the learning target that students are to master. Creating a table/chart for students to use when applying the biomedical treatments to the various disorders may prove to be helpful to students and save you time when reviewing the content in class. In this module it may also be helpful to review the neurotransmitters from the biological unit and the reuptake mechanisms and the concepts of agonists and antagonists.

*Biomedical therapy* relies on drugs and medical procedures to improve psychological functioning. Many therapists today take an *eclectic approach* to therapy, which means they use a variety of methods with an individual patient.

### Drug Therapy

*Drug therapy,* the treatment of psychological disorders through drugs, works by altering the operation of neurotransmitters and neurons in the brain (see **Figure 1**).

**ANTIPSYCHOTIC DRUGS** Probably no greater change has occurred in mental hospitals than the successful introduction in the mid-1950s of *antipsychotic drugs*—drugs used to reduce severe symptoms of disturbance, such as loss of touch with reality and agitation.

This dramatic change came about through the introduction of the drug chlorpromazine. Along with other similar drugs, chlorpromazine rapidly became the most popular and successful treatment for schizophrenia. Today, drug therapy is typically the preferred treatment for most cases of severely abnormal behavior and is used for most patients hospitalized with psychological disorders. The newest generation of antipsychotics, referred to as atypical antipsychotics, have fewer side effects; they include risperidone, olanzapine, and paliperidone. Most antipsychotics block dopamine receptors at the brain's synapses. Atypical antipsychotics affect both serotonin and dopamine levels in certain parts of the brain, such as those related to planning and goal-directed activity. Despite the effectiveness of antipsychotic drugs, the symptoms usually reappear when the drug is withdrawn.

**ANTIDEPRESSANT DRUGS** *Antidepressant drugs* are a class of medications used in cases of severe depression to improve a patient's mood and feeling of well-being.

Most antidepressant drugs work by changing the concentration of specific neurotransmitters in the brain. For example, *tricyclic drugs* increase the availability of norepinephrine at the synapses of neurons, whereas *MAO inhibitors* prevent the enzyme monoamine oxidase (MAO) from breaking down neurotransmitters. Newer antidepressants—such as Lexapro—are *selective serotonin reuptake inhibitors* (SSRIs). SSRIs target the neurotransmitter serotonin and permit it to linger at the synapse. Some antidepressants produce a combination of effects (see **Figure 2**). Finally, there are some newer drugs on the horizon. For instance, scientists have found that the anesthetic *ketamine* blocks the neural receptor NMDA, which affects the neurotransmitter glutamate.

The overall success rates of antidepressant drugs are good. In fact, antidepressants can produce lasting, long-term recovery from depression. In many cases, even after patients stop taking the drugs, their depression does not return. On the other hand, antidepressant drugs may produce side effects such as drowsiness and faintness, and there is evidence that SSRI antidepressants can increase the risk of suicide in children and adolescents.

**MOOD STABILIZERS** Mood stabilizers are used to treat mood disorders. For example, the drug *lithium,* a form of mineral salts, has been used very successfully in patients with bipolar disorders. Although no one knows definitely why, lithium and other mood stabilizers such as divalproex sodium (Depakote) and carbamazepine (Tegretol) effectively reduce manic episodes. However, they do not effectively treat depressive phases of bipolar disorder, so antidepressants are usually prescribed during those phases.

**ANTIANXIETY DRUGS** *Antianxiety drugs* reduce the level of anxiety a person experiences and increase feelings of well-being. They are prescribed not only to reduce general tension in people who are experiencing temporary difficulties but also to aid in the treatment of more serious anxiety disorders.

Antianxiety drugs such as Alprazolam and Valium are among the medications physicians most frequently prescribe. Although the popularity of antianxiety drugs suggests that they hold few risks, they can produce a number of potentially serious side effects. For instance, they can cause fatigue, and long-term use can lead to dependence.

**ELECTROCONVULSIVE THERAPY (ECT)** *Electroconvulsive therapy (ECT)* is a procedure used in the treatment of severe depression. In the procedure, an electric current of 70-150 volts is briefly administered to a patient's head, which causes a loss of consciousness and often causes seizures. Typically, health-care professionals sedate patients and give them muscle relaxants before administering the current; such preparations help reduce the intensity of muscle contractions produced during ECT.

ECT is a controversial technique. Apart from the obvious distastefulness of a treatment that evokes images of electrocution, side effects occur frequently. For instance, after treatment, patients often experience disorientation, confusion, and sometimes memory loss that may remain for months. Basically, therapists still use it because in many severe cases of depression, it offers the only quickly effective treatment. For instance, it may prevent depressed, suicidal individuals from committing suicide, and it can act more quickly than antidepressive medications.

One new and promising alternative to ECT is *transcranial magnetic stimulation (TMS)*. TMS creates a precise magnetic pulse in a specific area of the brain. By activating particular neurons, TMS has been effective in relieving the symptoms of major depression in a number of controlled experiments.

Another promising therapy, still in the early stages of development, is the use of implants placed deep inside the brain to provide a short jolt of electrical stimulation, a method called *deep brain stimulation (DBS)*.

**PSYCHOSURGERY** *Psychosurgery* is a brain surgery used to reduce the symptoms of mental disorder, but it is rarely used today. The initial form of psychosurgery, a *prefrontal lobotomy,* consisted of surgically destroying or removing parts of a patient's frontal lobes, which surgeons thought controlled emotionality.

Psychosurgery sometimes did improve a patient's behavior—but not without drastic side effects. Along with remission of the symptoms of the mental disorder, patients sometimes experienced personality changes and became bland, colorless, and unemotional. With the introduction of effective drug treatments—and the obvious ethical questions regarding the appropriateness of forever altering someone's personality—psychosurgery became nearly obsolete. However, it is still used in very rare cases when all other procedures have failed and the patient's behavior presents a high risk to the patient and others.

**BIOMEDICAL THERAPIES IN PERSPECTIVE** In some respects, no greater revolution has occurred in the field of mental health than biological approaches to treatment. As previously violent, uncontrollable patients have been calmed by the use of drugs, mental hospitals have been able to concentrate more on actually helping patients and less on custodial functions. Similarly, patients whose lives have been disrupted by depression or bipolar episodes have been able to function normally, and other forms of drug therapy have also shown remarkable results. Furthermore, new forms of biomedical therapy are promising.

Despite their current usefulness and future promise, biomedical therapies do not represent a cure-all for psychological disorders. For one thing, critics charge that such therapies merely provide relief of the symptoms of mental disorder; as soon as the drugs are withdrawn, the symptoms return. Biomedical therapies also can produce side effects that range from minor to serious physical reactions to the development of new symptoms of abnormal behavior. An overreliance on biomedical therapies may lead therapists to overlook alternative forms of treatment that may be helpful.

- This may be a good place to introduce/review the Biopsychosocial method for the treatment of disorders.

**COMMUNITY PSYCHOLOGY: FOCUS ON PREVENTION** *Community psychology* is a branch of psychology that focuses on the prevention and minimization of psychological disorders in the community. *Deinstitutionalization* is the transfer of former mental patients from institutions to the community.

Unfortunately, the promise of deinstitutionalization has not been met largely because insufficient resources are provided to deinstitutionalized patients. What started as a worthy attempt to move people out of mental institutions and into the community ended, in many cases, with former patients being dumped into the community without any real support. On the other hand, the community psychology movement has had some positive outcomes. Its emphasis on prevention has led to new approaches to psychological disorders.

## **AP** Key Terms

antianxiety drugs

antidepressant drugs

antipsychotic drugs

biopsychosocial method

community psychology

deinstitutionalization

drug therapy

electroconvulsive therapy (ECT)

mood stabilizers

psychosurgery

transcranial magnetic stimulation (TMS)

## Activities

**MEDICATION** Remind students of the controversy in medicating children for disorders such as ADHD. You may want to show *Frontline: The Medicated Child* (http://www.pbs.org/wgbh/pages/frontline/medicatedchild/) to get the discussion going. Ask them if they think children should receive medication for a disorder. You may want to remind them that unlike cholesterol, blood sugars, or HIV, the disorders commonly found in children (such as ADHD) cannot be tested for in a clear manner. This is where the controversy lies. Further, how does this carry over to adults?

**DRUG THERAPY** Use *Handout: Which Drug Will Help?* The goal of this activity is to familiarize students with the various psychoactive drugs used to treat psychological disorders. The students will be given a symptom and must identify the drug that would help with the disorder.

## Discussion Questions

- Would you consider the drug Antibuse, which is a drug for alcoholics to take to keep them from drinking, a form of aversive conditioning? Explain.
- What are the ethical concerns surrounding electroconvulsive therapy and psychosurgery?
- What are the ethical concerns for psychotherapy in general?
- How will you react if you are diagnosed with a psychological disorder?

**ATTITUDES TOWARD BIOMEDICAL THERAPIES** Ask students the following questions:

- Under what conditions do you think that clinicians should use biomedical therapies?
- How should biomedical therapies be combined, if at all, with psychotherapy?
- Do you agree or disagree that psychologists should have prescription privileges? Why or why not?
- Do you believe that the potential benefits of medical therapies outweigh the potential side effects?

## Suggested Media

- *Alternative therapies:* http://healthpsych.psy.vanderbilt.edu/alternative_therapy.htm.
- *Antidepressants:* https://medlineplus.gov/antidepressants.html
- *The Body:* http://www.thebody.com/pinf/drugbkix.html This site provides information about medications for a wide range of psychological disorders.
- *Brain-based therapies:* http://www.nami.org/Learn-More/Treatment/ ECT,-TMS-and-Other-Brain-Stimulation-Therapies
- *BrainPhysics:* http://www.brainphysics.com/ A great site on most of the disorders.
- *Childhood and adolescent mental health:* National Institute of Mental Health http://www. nimh.nih.gov/health/topics/child-and-adolescent-mental-health/index.shtml.
- *Deep Brain Stimulation*. ABC News, 2006, 20:00.
- Two patients undergoing deep brain stimulation for depression and OCD are followed in this DVD.
- *ECT*—Mayo Clinic: https://www.mayoclinic.org/tests-procedures/electroconvulsive-therapy/ about/pac-20393894.
- *Electroshock therapy:* http://www.ted.com/index.php/talks/sherwin_nuland_on_electro- shock_therapy.html. TED Talk by Dr. Sherwin Nuland.
- *fMRI studies on monks*: http://www.urbandharma.org/udharma8/monkstudy.html.
- *History of psychosurgery:* http://www.cerebromente.org.br/n02/historia/psicocirg_i.htm.
- *The Medicated Child*. PBS *Frontline:* http://www.pbs.org/wgbh/pages/frontline/ medicatedchild/.
- *Metrazol convulsive therapy:* http://www.youtube.com/watch?v=Fp8pY5wQ6nA. This brief clip demonstrates metrazol convulsive therapy. It may be useful if you are talking about the history of psychology and psychological treatments.
- *Numb: The Problems with Antidepressants*. Films for the Humanities and Sciences, 2011, 65:00. Discontinuing the use of antidepressants can be problematic, but many people tak- ing these drugs choose the painful withdrawal process, and subsequent depression, over the emotional numbness the meds can cause.
- *Transcranial magnet stimulation (TMS):* http://www.youtube.com/watch?v=stJFwxVH2_s.
- *Walter Freeman and the lobotomy:* http://www.youtube.com/watch?v=_0aNILW6ILk&feature =player_embedded#at=74.

## Additional Readings

Kaufman, M. (2005, January 5). Mediation gives brain a charge, study finds. *Washington Post,* p. A5.

## AP Test Practice

### Part I: Multiple Choice

1. **E** *(Skill 1.C, Learning Target 8.O)*

2. **C** *(Skill 1.A, Learning Target 8.P)*

3. **A** *(Skill 1.A, Learning Target 8.P)*

### Part II: Free Response

SSRIs block reuptake of serotonin, permitting the neurotransmitter to linger at the synapse. SSRI examples include *Fluoxetine (Prozac), Luvox, Paxil, Celexa, Zoloft,* and *nefazodone (Serzone)*.

Most antipsychotics block dopamine receptors at the brain's synapses. Antipsychotic examples include: *chlorpromazine (Thorazine), clozapine (Clozaril),* and *haloperidol (Haldol)*. Atypical antipsychotic examples include: *risperidone* and *olanzapine*.

Antianxiety medications increase the activity of GABA. Benzodiazepine examples include: *Valium* and *Xanax*.

# CHAPTER 17

# Social Psychology

## **AP** Introduction

**Social psychology** is the scientific study of how people's thoughts, feelings, and actions are affected by others. Social psychologists consider the kinds and causes of the individual's behavior in social situations. They examine how the nature of situations in which we find ourselves influences our behavior in important ways. Unlike personality psychology, which focuses on individual differences, social psychology examines the role of the group, culture, and context on behavior. There are many applications of the material in this unit that you can make to the student's everyday life, ranging from headline news items to group processes in the classroom and activities in student life. Tying the topics in this unit to earlier topics, you can point out how social cognition provides a perspective on the fallacies in our judgments about people, as in the fundamental attribution error. Social psychology also helps students learn ways to fight common tendencies toward stereotyping, discrimination, blind obedience, and being swayed by commercials, advertisements, and high-pressure sales tactics.

## **AP** Essential Questions

- How does the bias of a researcher affect their conclusions?

## Module 52: Attitudes and Social Cognition

**AP Learning Targets:**

- Speculate how cultural context can facilitate or constrain personality development, especially as it relates to self-concept.
- Apply attribution theory to explain motives.
- Identify important figures and research in the areas of attitude formation and change.
- Discuss attitude formation and change, including persuasion strategies and cognitive dissonance.
- Describe the processes that contribute to differential treatment of group members.

**Pacing:**

1 ½ Blocks or 3 Traditional Class periods

# Module 53: Social Influence and Groups

**AP Learning Targets:**

- Distinguish the different domains of psychology.
- Identify the contributions of key researchers in the areas of conformity, compliance, and obedience.
- Explain how individuals respond to expectations of others, including groupthink, conformity, and obedience to authority.
- Describe the structure and function of different kinds of group behavior.
- Predict the impact of the presence of others on individual behavior.

**Pacing:**

1 ½ Block or 3 Traditional Class periods

# Module 54: Prejudice and Discrimination

**AP Learning Targets:**

- Apply attribution theory to explain motives.
- Articulate the impact of social and cultural categories on self-concept and relations with others.
- Anticipate the impact of self-fulfilling prophecy on behavior.
- Predict the impact of the presence of others on individual behavior.
- Describe processes that contribute to differential treatment of group members.

**Pacing:**

4 Block or 2 Traditional Class periods

# Module 55: Positive and Negative Social Behavior

**AP Learning Targets:**

- Predict the impact of the presence of others on individual behavior.
- Describe processes that contribute to differential treatment of group members.
- Describe the variables that contribute to altruism and aggression.
- Describe the variables that contribute to attraction.

**Pacing:**

1 Block or 2 Traditional Class periods

# Module 52: Attitudes and Social Cognition

## AP Module Summary

In Module 52 some added attention needs to be given when reviewing several learning targets. For example the concepts of false consensus effect, confirmation bias, just-world hypothesis, and halo effect have now been specifically added. The elaboration likelihood model has been added which includes the central and peripheral routes to persuasion. Though the concept of bias has been seen throughout the course in several units, the concept itself has been added to the learning target having students describe the processes that contribute to differential treatment of group members. Finally, a specific learning target has been created for students to identify the important figures and research in the areas of attitude formation and change. Make sure to point out the work of Leon Festinger for this one.

Celebrity endorsements in advertisements are designed to mold or change our attitudes. Such commercials are part of the barrage of messages we receive each day from sources as varied as politicians, sales staff in stores, and celebrities—all of which are meant to influence us.

**PERSUASION: CHANGING ATTITUDES**  Persuasion is the process of changing attitudes, one of the central concepts of social psychology. *Attitudes* are evaluations of a person, behavior, belief, or concept. The ease with which we can change our attitudes depends on a number of factors, including:

- *Message source*
- *Characteristics of the message*
- *Characteristics of the target*

**ROUTES TO PERSUASION**  Recipients' receptiveness to persuasive messages relates to the type of information processing they use. Social psychologists have discovered two primary information-processing routes to persuasion: (see **Figure 1**).

1. *Central route processing* occurs when the recipient thoughtfully considers the issues and arguments involved in persuasion. In central route processing, people are swayed in their judgments by the logic, merit, and strength of arguments.

2. *Peripheral route processing* occurs when people are persuaded on the basis of factors unrelated to the nature or quality of the content of a persuasive message. Instead, factors that are irrelevant or extraneous to the issue, such as who is providing the message, how long the arguments are, or the emotional appeal of the arguments, influence them.

This is also known as the *Elaboration likelihood model.*

**THE LINK BETWEEN ATTITUDES AND BEHAVIOR**  Attitudes influence behavior. The strength of the link between particular attitudes and behavior varies, of course, but generally, people strive for consistency between their attitudes and their behavior. Furthermore, people hold fairly consistent attitudes. Ironically, the consistency that leads attitudes to influence behavior sometimes works the other way around: in some cases, our behavior shapes our attitudes. According to social psychologist Leon Festinger (1957), *cognitive dissonance* occurs when a person holds two contradictory attitudes or thoughts (see **Figure 2**).

**SOCIAL COGNITION: UNDERSTANDING OTHERS**

- *Social cognition* is the way people understand and make sense of others and themselves.
- *Schemas* are sets of cognitions about people and social experiences.

**ATTRIBUTION PROCESSES: UNDERSTANDING THE CAUSES OF BEHAVIOR** *Attribution theory* considers how we decide, on the basis of samples of a person's behavior, what the specific causes of that behavior are. Unlike impression formation, which focuses on how people develop an overall impression of others' personality traits, attribution theory asks the "why" question: Why is someone acting in a particular way? In seeking an explanation for behavior, we must answer one central question: Is the cause situational or dispositional?

- *Situational causes* are causes of behavior that are external to a person.
- *Dispositional causes* are causes of behavior brought about by a person's traits or personality characteristics.

**ATTRIBUTION BIASES: TO ERR IS HUMAN** Although attribution theory generally makes accurate predictions, people do not always process information about others as logically as the theory seems to suggest. In fact, research reveals consistent biases in the ways people make attributions. Typical biases include the following:

- *Halo effect:* The *halo effect* is a phenomenon in which an initial understanding that a person has positive traits is used to infer other uniformly positive characteristics. The opposite would also hold true.
- *Assumed-similarity bias:* Most people believe that their friends and acquaintances are fairly similar to themselves. But this feeling goes beyond just people we know to a general tendency—known as the *assumed-similarity bias*—to think of people as being similar to oneself even when meeting them for the first time.
- *Self-serving bias:* The *self-serving bias* is the tendency to attribute success to personal factors (skill, ability, or effort) and attribute failure to factors outside oneself.
- *Fundamental attribution error:* The *fundamental attribution error* refers to a tendency to overattribute others' behavior to dispositional causes and minimize of the importance of situational causes.

Behavioral economics is concerned with how individuals' biases and irrationality affect economic decisions. Rather than viewing people as rational, thoughtful decision makers who are impartially weighing choices to draw conclusions, behavioral economists focus on the irrationality of judgments.

- Make sure to include in the review of attribution biases the *Just-world hypothesis (phenomenon)*.

**EXPLORING DIVERSITY: ATTRIBUTION BIAS IN A CULTURAL CONTEXT: HOW FUNDAMENTAL IS THE FUNDAMENTAL ATTRIBUTION ERROR?** Attribution biases do not affect all of us in the same way. The culture in which we are raised clearly plays a role in the way we attribute others' behavior. For example, the fundamental attribution error is pervasive in Western cultures and not in Eastern societies. One reason for the difference may lie in the norms and values of Eastern society, which emphasize social responsibility and societal obligations to a greater extent than Western societies. In addition, the language spoken in a culture may lead to different sorts of attributions. The difference in thinking between people in Asian and Western cultures is a reflection of a broader difference in the way the world is perceived. Asian societies generally have a *collectivistic orientation*, a worldview that promotes the notion of interdependence. People with a collectivistic orientation generally see themselves as parts of a larger, interconnected social network and as responsible to others. In contrast, people in Western cultures are more likely to hold an *individualist orientation* that emphasizes personal identity and the uniqueness of the individual. They focus more on what sets them apart from others and what makes them special.

- This is a great time to review the concepts of *collectivistic* and *individualistic* cultures.

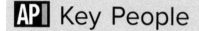
## Key Terms

assumed-similarity bias

attitudes

attribution theory

bias

central route processing

central traits

cognitive dissonance

collectivistic

dispositional causes (of behavior)

elaboration likelihood model

fundamental attribution error

halo effect

individualistic

just-world hypothesis (phenomenon)

peripheral route processing

schemas

self-serving bias

situational causes (of behavior)

social cognition

social psychology

## Key People

Leon Festinger

## Class Discussion Ideas

**SOCIAL PSYCHOLOGY** To begin the lecture on social psychology, ask students what social psychology means to them. Furthermore, ask them what sorts of topics social psychologists might discuss. Ask them how they think social psychology differs from sociology.

**DEMONSTRATION: COGNITIVE DISSONANCE EXPERIMENT** Below is another experiment I have taught using the format of "Great Moments in the History of Psychology."

The Festinger experiment is recreated as described in the text. Participant #1 is given a boring task of turning pegs in a board. Then, that participant is paid $1 and told to explain it as interesting to the next participant. The enthusiasm of Participant #1 is compared to that of Participant #2, who is paid $20 to do the same thing. Each participant is then asked how much he or she actually enjoyed the boring task, and Participant #1 says it was truly more interesting than does Participant #2.

This experiment shows what happens when dissonance is created between behavior (completing a boring task and saying you liked it) and attitudes (the task really was boring). Other forms of dissonance are:

- Smoking (the example used in the text)
- Not voting but believing in the importance of voting
- Believing lying is wrong but lying to get out of an unwanted responsibility
- Giving money to a cause that you do not support because a friend asks you to do so
- Buying an expensive item such as a digital camera or a computer and then reading later that that item was not as highly rated as another item
- Paying more for an item (such as a computer) at one store and finding that it could have been bought for less at another store (the dissonance is there only if you believe that it is good to save money)

**HALO EFFECT** An initial understanding that a person has positive traits is used to infer other personality characteristics. Ask students for examples from their own life.

# Activities

**SELF-SERVING BIAS** Ask the students to write down five examples of times when other people have probably used the self-serving bias. Next, break the class into groups, and have them share with each other the examples they came up with. They will learn from each other by examining the other students' examples.

**PERSUASION** Have students imagine they work for a large advertising firm and have a project due for a new brand of toothpaste. Ask them to use the methods of persuasion described in this chapter to say how they would try to convince people to use the new toothpaste.

## ATTITUDE MEASUREMENT

- **Attitudes Predicting Behavior:** Use *Handout: Can You Change Their Attitude?* The goal of this activity is for students to choose an issue or topic that they will try to change someone else's attitude about. The students will use the four questions discussed in the chapter to demonstrate how they would go about changing someone's attitude. They should also discuss how the people's attitudes are changed by using the four topics discussed in the chapter.
- **Attitudes:** Ask students to think about their attitudes on issues such as the right to bear arms, the growing scarcity of natural resources, health care, the death penalty, Social Security, etc. Assign an essay detailing how their view on one of the above issues influences their behavior. This can also make for a lively class discussion.

## COGNITIVE DISSONANCE

- **Cognitive Dissonance:** Use *Handout: Attitude Survey.* It is best to do this *before* beginning a lecture on cognitive dissonance. Ask students to complete the attitude survey first. Then ask students to turn the handout over and complete the behavioral survey. Be sure you *first* present the side that says *Attitude Survey.*
- After they are done, ask students to view their answers. Are there any discrepancies in their attitudes and in their behaviors? Students generally get the point of this exercise very quickly. In most cases, a majority of students will agree with or show positive attitudes toward the issue, but only a small minority will actually report behavior consistent with those attitudes. Source: Carkenord, D. M., & Bullington, J. (1993). Bringing cognitive dissonance to the classroom. *Teaching of Psychology, 20,* 41–43.

# Discussion Questions

## COGNITIVE DISSONANCE

- Provide an example of cognitive dissonance from your own experience.
- Do you agree that cognitive dissonance can cause attitude change? Why or why not?
- In general, how important is cognitive dissonance in everyday life? Why?

# Suggested Media

- *How to detect lies:* http://www.blifaloo.com/info/lies.php.
- *Paul Ekman, "Why We Lie":* http://www.youtube.com/watch?v=qGQf9O61cww.
- *Persuasion techniques:* http://www.as.wvu.edu/~sbb/comm221/primer.htm. This site offers information on a variety of persuasion techniques, with examples.
- *Self-serving bias:* http://www.youtube.com/watch?v=kjfSuOq6ReA&feature=related. This brief clip illustrates self-serving bias.
- *The Simpsons*: Moe takes a lie detector test: https://youtu.be/iQGwrK_yDEg.

- *Social Psychology Network:* http://www.socialpsychology.org/. This website is devoted to psychological research and teaching. It provides hundreds of links to other sources.

**TELEVISION COMMERCIALS** Show a television commercial that perhaps exemplifies a "bait and switch" method such as for used cars, furniture stores, electronic products, or jewelry. This is an excellent illustration of low-balling.

## Additional Readings

Haskins, J. (2015). The right to refuse service: Can a business refuse service to someone? *LegalZoom.*

Myers, D. (2012). *Social psychology,* 11th ed. McGraw-Hill.

Rosenberg, E. L. (Eds.) *What the face reveals: Basic and applied studies of spontaneous expression using the Facial Action Coding System (FACS)* (pp. 201–216). New York: Oxford University Press.

Smith, J. R., & Haslam, S. A. (2012). *Social psychology: Revisiting the classic studies.* Sage.

Stewart, D. W. (2015). *The handbook of persuasion and social marketing.* Praeger.

## **AP** Student Edition Answer Key

### AP Test Practice

#### Part I: Multiple Choice
1. **A** *(Skill 1.B, Learning Target 9.E)*
2. **B** *(Skill 1.B, Learning Target 9.A)*
3. **C** *(Skill 3, Learning Target 9.E)*

#### Part II: Free Response
The fundamental attribution error is the tendency to overestimate others' behavior due to dispositional causes and failure to recognize situational causes. Sonya used the fundamental attribution error when she assumed her teacher's disposition was happy and outgoing, as opposed to recognizing that the situation of being in the classroom might bring out those attributes.

People from individualist cultures are more likely to make the fundamental attribution error. Sonya is most likely from an individualist culture because she committed the FAE on her teacher.

The halo effect is a phenomenon in which an individual's positive traits are used to infer other positive traits. Sonya used the halo effect when she inferred that because her teacher was happy and outgoing in class she would also excel as an organized adviser after school.

The peripheral route of persuasion uses extraneous factors, such as emotional appeal or celebrity endorsements, to influence others. Sonya plans to use peripheral route of persuasion by using the familiarity of celebrities and the emotional appeal of their stories to persuade her peers to join the club.

# Module 53: Social Influence and Groups

## AP Module Summary

In Module 53 more specific concepts have been added to the learning targets. Students need to be aware of the specific contributions of key researchers in the areas of conformity, compliance, and obedience. The specific mentioning of Solomon Asch, Stanley Milgram and Philip Zimbardo is directly now correlated to this learning target whereas in the past it has been fairly generalized. A considerable amount of detail has been added to the learning target involving the predicting the impact of the presence of others on individual behavior and listing specific concepts: bystander effect, social facilitation, social inhibition, group polarization, deindividuation, diffusion of responsibility, reciprocity norms, social norms, and social traps.

Pressures to conform to others' behavior can be painfully strong and can bring about changes in behavior that otherwise never would have occurred. Conformity pressures are just one type of social influence. *Social influence* is the process by which social groups and individuals exert pressure on an individual, either deliberately or unintentionally. Social influence is so powerful, in part because groups and other people generally play a central role in our lives. As defined by social psychologists, **groups** consist of two or more people who (1) interact with one another; (2) perceive themselves as part of a group; and (3) are interdependent.

Groups develop and hold *norms*, expectations regarding behavior appropriate to the group. Groups exert considerable social influence over individuals that ranges from the mundane to the extreme.

This is a good place to connect the concept of **social norms** to the lecture.

**CONFORMITY: FOLLOWING WHAT OTHERS DO** *Conformity* is a change in behavior or attitudes brought about by a desire to follow the beliefs or standards of other people. Subtle or even unspoken social pressure results in conformity. The classic demonstration of pressure to conform comes from a series of studies carried out in the 1950s by Solomon Asch (see **Figure 1**).

**CONFORMITY CONCLUSIONS** Since Asch's pioneering work, literally hundreds of studies have examined conformity, and we now know a great deal about the phenomenon. Significant findings focus on:

- *The characteristics of the group:* The more attractive a group appears to its members, the greater its ability to produce conformity. Furthermore, a person's relative *status*, the social rank held within a group, is critical: The lower a person's status in the group, the greater the groups' power is over that person's behavior.
- *The situation in which the individual is responding:* Conformity is considerably higher when people must respond publicly than it is when they can do so privately.
- *The kind of task:* People working on ambiguous tasks and questions (those with no clear answers) are more susceptible to social pressure. In addition, tasks at which an individual is less competent than others in the group make conformity more likely.
- *Unanimity of the group:* Groups that unanimously support a position show the most pronounced conformity pressures. There are certain situations in which people with dissenting views have an ally in the group known as a *social supporter*, who agrees with them. Having just one person present who shares the minority point of view is sufficient to reduce conformity pressures.

**GROUPTHINK: CAVING IN TO CONFORMITY** *Groupthink* is a type of thinking in which group members share such a strong motivation to achieve consensus that they lose the ability to critically evaluate alternative points of view. Groupthink typically leads to poor decisions. Groups limit the list of possible solutions to just a few, and they spend relatively little time considering any alternatives once the leader seems to be leaning toward a particular solution. In addition, groups may fall prey to *entrapment*, a circumstance in which commitments to a failing point of view or course of action are increased to justify investments in time and energy.

- This would be a great time to include the concepts of *Group polarization* and *Social traps* to the review of content for this module.

**CONFORMITY TO SOCIAL ROLES** *Social roles* are the expectations for people who occupy a given social position. For example, the role of "student" comprises behaviors such as studying, listening to an instructor, and attending class. Like a theatrical role, social roles tell us what behavior is associated with a given position. Conforming to a social role can have a powerful consequence on the behavior of even normal, well-adjusted people and induce them to change their behavior in sometimes undesirable ways.

**COMPLIANCE: SUBMITTING TO DIRECT SOCIAL PRESSURE** When we refer to conformity, we usually mean a phenomenon in which the social pressure is subtle or indirect. But in some situations, social pressure is much more obvious with direct, explicit pressure to endorse a particular point of view or behave in a certain way. Social psychologists call the type of behavior that occurs in response to direct social pressure *compliance*.

Companies seeking to sell their products to consumers often use the techniques identified by social psychologists for promoting compliance. *Industrial-organizational (I/O) psychology,* a close cousin to social psychology, considers issues such as worker motivation, satisfaction, safety, and productivity. I/O psychologists also focus on the operation and design of organizations; they ask questions such as how decision making can be improved in large organizations and how the fit between workers and their jobs can be maximized.

**OBEDIENCE: FOLLOWING DIRECT ORDERS** Compliance techniques are used to gently lead people toward agreement with a request. In some cases, however, requests aim to produce *obedience,* a change in behavior in response to the commands of others. Although obedience is considerably less common than conformity and compliance, it does occur in several specific kinds of relationships. For example, we may show obedience to our bosses, teachers, or parents merely because of the power they hold to reward or punish us.

## 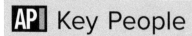 Key Terms

| | |
|---|---|
| bystander effect | obedience |
| compliance | social influence |
| conformity | social inhibition |
| group | social norms |
| group polarization | social supporter |
| groupthink | social traps |
| industrial-organizational (I/O) psychology | status |

## Key People

Solomon Asch

Stanley Milgram

Phillip Zimabardo

# Class Discussion Ideas

**CONFORMITY EXPERIMENT—SOLOMON ASCH** Subject was asked to judge the length of a line and compare it to three lines, A, B, and C (see **Figure 1**). The line was clearly the length of line A in this array, but confederates of the experimenter said it was the length of another line. The real subjects were more likely to conform to the judgments of the confederates. Groupthink is a variant of conformity.

**OBEDIENCE EXPERIMENT—STANLEY MILGRAM** A "teacher" was told by the experimenter to shock the "learner" for making mistakes. The learner was not seen by the teacher, but he made many mistakes in the experiment. Most of the "teachers" penalized the learners with the maximum level of shock.

- **Ethics and Milgram:** Remind students about the APA's ethical rules for experimentation. Ask students if they think that this study, exactly as it was conducted, would be allowed today. Why or why not? If they feel this was unethical, how would they suggest studying obedience?

**STUDY ON "THE POWER OF THE SITUATION"—PHILIP ZIMBARDO'S STANFORD PRISON EXPERIMENT** Stanford University students were arbitrarily divided into "prisoners" and "guards." The experiment had to be called off because the subjects all perceived it too realistically.

**HELPFUL HINTS FOR STUDENTS** To remember the differences among these experimenters, use these hints:

- Asch - He studied "conformi—tree" (an ash is a type of tree).
- Milgram - The finding that people were willing to torture others because they were following orders was pretty "grim."
- Zimbardo prison study - Prisons have "bars," as in his name.

**COMPLIANCE WITHOUT PRESSURE** Methods used to influence others to comply with requests, suggestions, or sales tactics include:

- The foot-in-the-door technique - Ask for a small favor and the person will be more likely to perform the large favor.
- The door-in-the-face technique - Ask for a large amount of money and then ask for how much you really want.
- The that's-not-all technique - Offer a product at an inflated price and then give an incentive, discount, or bonus that will make the deal seem more attractive when that was the original price anyway.
- The not-so-free sample technique - Offer a free sample and through the norm of reciprocity, the person will feel obligated to make a purchase.

Each of these methods relies on consistency of commitment, that people want to appear as though they are rational and make well-thought-out decisions.

Have students think of examples of each technique from their own lives.

**DEMONSTRATION: COMPLIANCE METHODS** Four methods of compliance can be illustrated in a "Deal or No Deal" format. Each one is acted out in an improvisational skit mode, and then students in the class have to guess which method they have just seen. To make the task more difficult, either illustrate only three of them or add low-balling, which is not included in the book, but which occurs when the participant agrees to the small favor (or amount of a purchase) and then before he or she actually engages in the behavior (e.g., does not buy the item but has only agreed to do so), the salesperson raises the price after "checking with my manager."

Once the game has begun, put the compliance methods up on the screen as an overhead so students know the choices.

**EXAMPLES OF EACH METHOD ARE AS FOLLOWS**

- Foot-in-the-door: A small favor is requested such as wearing a button endorsing a political candidate. After that, the person is more likely to spend hours making phone calls to raise money for that candidate.
- Door-in-the-face: As is done in my university's annual fund campaign, alums are called and asked to donate $1,000 when the desired contribution is $40.
- Not-so-free-sample: At a local grocer's, small cheese samples are handed out with the intention that recipients will buy the cheese.
- That's-not-all: A salesperson heaps on discounts for jewelry, arriving at a final price that is what was originally desired by the manager.
- Low-balling: The salesperson quotes a price that the consumer agrees to, but then the salesperson finds, after checking with the manager, that the final price will actually be higher (see any sales catalog such as Macy's, which offers an enormous number of "discounts.")

**THEFT REPORT**  Before students enter the classroom, set your purse, wallet, or briefcase on the desk. After students have arrived, tell them you forgot something and will be back in a few minutes. Have an accomplice then come in and take what you left. Return to the room and see how long it takes students to report the theft.

**STUDENT RESPONSE**  About 10 minutes into class, arrange for an accomplice to make noises outside the classroom as if they fell off their skateboard or tripped, etc., and hurt themselves. Continue class as if nothing happened and see how long it takes for students to respond.

**SOCIAL INFLUENCES ON PERFORMANCE**

- Social facilitation - The tendency to perform better on a task in front of an audience or when working with others than when working alone.
- Social loafing - The tendency to put in less effort when there are several people working together.
- Diffusion of responsibility - The greater the number of bystanders and shared responsibility, the less individual responsibility and the less individual help is given.

**Point out that social loafing applies to the amount of effort, and diffusion of responsibility applies to giving help.**

**SOCIAL FACILITATION OF COCKROACHES**  Students get a kick out of hearing about Zajonc, Heingartner, and Herman's (1969) social facilitation study with cockroaches. See Suggested Readings for a full citation.

**SOCIAL LOAFING ON GROUP PROJECTS**  Ask students for examples of when they have loafed or have been the victim of someone else's social loafing. Have them think about group work and group projects in class. Do they like this type of work? Why or why not?

- Include in this list the concept *Social inhibition & Bystander effect*.

**INGROUP-OUTGROUP BIAS**  People have a tendency to give members of their own group a positive evaluation and members of another group a negative evaluation. Examples of these can be derived from the student assignment on this topic.

# Activities

**ASCH'S CONFORMITY STUDY**

- **Have students complete the activity on this website:**
  http://www.mhhe.com/cls/psy/ch15/asch.mhtml.

Then ask them the following questions:

- At what point did you start to question your judgment?
- Do you think it was more or less convincing to have a computer provide feedback rather than peers? Why?
- How does the conformity experiment translate to real life? What does it say about human nature?

**CONFORMITY EXPERIMENT**  Have students design a test for conformity:

Arrange for several friends to do something unique and observe the reaction of others in the group. For instance, you might ask them to place their books on the floor rather than on their desks. Or they might hum a tune, giggle, stick their tongues out, look out the window, or, replicating the famous *Candid Camera* example, turn and face the rear in an elevator.

Then have students answer these questions:

- What percentage of bystanders conformed?
- Why do you think they did or did not?
- What did you learn about conformity?

**CONFORMITY**  Prior to class, cut a piece of string about 108 inches long. Before discussing conformity, tape the string to the wall or board. It is best to stagger the string and not hang it straight. Ask students to write down how long they think the string is in inches. Tell students not to put their names on their papers. Collect their papers. Ask a student volunteer to read the guesses while you write them on the board. There will most likely be a wide variety of answers. Next, ask students to publically tell you how long the string is in inches. Write down their responses. There is typically a wide range of answers with those that are the most bizarre and different from the norm dropping out. This is a nice way to demonstrate public and private responses in a conforming situation.

**SOCIAL FACILITATION EXPERIMENT**  Have students complete this experiment on social facilitation:

Print a series of letters (including consonants and vowels) on a sheet of paper. Make several copies. Ask half of your subjects to cancel (cross out) each of the vowels when seated in front of a group of people and the rest of the subjects to do it when alone. Time each subject until he or she cancels all of the vowels on the page.

Then have them record the performance of the students in the alone versus the social group.

Next, have students perform a difficult task—patting their heads while rubbing their stomachs, again, alone or in front of a group. Note in which condition students performed more effectively.

According to social facilitation theory, the subjects in front of a group should complete the first task in less time than those alone because it was easy, but they should perform more poorly on the second task in front of others rather than alone (with just an observer) because it is a more difficult task. An alternative to the head-stomach condition is shooting foul shots in a basketball hoop or juggling three small balls.

## GROUP INFLUENCE

- **Group Influence:** Break the class into groups, and have each group come up with an example of each of the following: deindividuation, social contagion, group performance, social facilitation, social loafing, and group interaction and decision making. After completing this assignment, have one member of each group come to the front of the class and discuss with the other students the examples their group decided on.

- **Deindividuation:** This is a classic in social psychology classes. Ask students to anonymously write down their response to this question. "If you could do anything humanly possible with complete assurance that you would not be detected or held responsible, what would you do?" Have student turn in their papers. After a discussion of deindividuation read the responses to the class. You will probably get a variety of answers from antisocial to prosocial. In my classes, I seem to get far more antisocial answers. Robbing a bank is always a very common response! Source: Dodd, D. (1985). Robbers in the classroom: A deindividuation exercise. *Teaching of Psychology, 12(2)*, 89–91.

**METHODS OF COMPLIANCE** Send students on a field trip in which they investigate methods of compliance. Have them visit several mall stores, including a department store, a jewelry store, an electronics store, and one "other" store. For each store, they should write down at least two examples of one of the sales compliance techniques. Then have them complete *Handout: Methods of Compliance.*

**OBEDIENCE** This exercise should be done prior to covering obedience in the social psychology class. You can do this yourself, or have another teacher walk into class and start moving students to different seats, then move them again, and give a student some money and ask them to go get you a soda. Do the students do what you ask or the other teacher asks? They typically do. Ask them why this happens. They usually say, "Because you are the teacher!" You can also use this as a lead into social psychology.

*Source:* Hunter, W. J. (1981). Obedience to authority. In L. T. Benjamin & K. D. Lowman (Eds.), *Activities handbook for the teaching of psychology, Volume 1* (pp. 149–150). Washington, DC: American Psychological Association. (Skill 1.B)

## Discussion Questions

**SOCIAL LOAFING** Social loafing sometimes occurs in group work. When you are working with other students on a project, how do you get all group members to participate equally?

**INGROUP-OUTGROUP BIAS**

- In what situations have you felt that you were the ingroup and others were the outgroup?
- How did you and the rest of your group treat the outgroup?
- In what situations have you felt that you were the outgroup and others were the ingroup?
- How did you feel at being a member of the outgroup?!

**CONFORMITY AND OBEDIENCE**

- Are there ways that conformity and obedience can be beneficial for a society? How might they be dangerous?
- How does your behavior change when you are with a particular group of people and why?
- What social movements have influenced your life and how?

# Suggested Media

- *Asch conformity study:* https://www.youtube.com/watch?v=NyDDyT1lDhA. Footage from this classic experiment.
- *Asch study reenactment:* http://www.youtube.com/watch?v=iRh5qy09nNw.
- *Brain Games:* http://channel.nationalgeographic.com/brain-games/episodes/peer-pressure/ The TV show *Brain Games* recreated the Asch experiment in the modern day: Note: Show these videos *after* you have had students try the task themselves (see Classroom Activities above).
- *Bystander effect:* http://www.youtube.com/watch?v=JozmWS6xYEw.
- *CBS News coverage on Wesley Autry, the New York subway hero:* http://www.youtube.com/watch?v=e9JcX2X7XnM.
- *Groupthink example:* http://www.psysr.org/about/pubs_resources/groupthink%20overview.htm.
- *Jonestown: The Life and Death of the People's Temple:* http://www.youtube.com/watch?v=IY3cx3U0gYE.
- *Kindness of Strangers.* ABC News, 2003, 15:00. This show explores bystander intervention in terms of when people will and will not help another in need.
- *Lab Conformity.* ABC News, 2006, 15:00. Conformity is discussed in this DVD, along with classic and modern studies.
- *Milgram's obedience study and* Ghostbusters *introduction:* http://www.youtube.com/watch?v=aB_lljnqkDw.
- *Obedience:* http://www.youtube.com/watch?v=HwqNP9HRy7Y. This brief clip discusses obedience to authority.
- *Obeying or Resisting Authority.* ABC News, 2007, 36:00. Jerry Burger, a professor at Santa Clara University, recreates the Milgram experiment with the help of *Prime Time*.
- *People Can and Do Help:* http://www.youtube.com/watch?v=dhGSczsf0tM. A man in a wheelchair falls onto the subway tracks and a bystander comes to his aid in this brief clip.
- *Quiet Rage: The Stanford Prison Experiment*. Insight Media, 50:00. The original footage from the Stanford Prison Experiment conducted by Phil Zimbardo.
- *Replication of Milgram's experiment by the BBC:* http://www.youtube.com/watch?v=BcvSNg0HZwk.
- *Stanford Prison Experiment website:* http://www.prisonexp.org/.
- *Stanley Milgram:* http://www.stanleymilgram.com/. This site provides a clear and concise description of the obedience studies carried out by Milgram. The site presentation is enhanced by the inclusion of photos that depict scenes of the original research project.
- *What Were You Thinking?* http://www.nbcnews.com/id/36787261/ns/dateline_nbc-the_hansen_files_with_chris_hansen/t/what-were-you-thinking/#.WA5kAdUrJQI. *Dateline NBC* documentary replicates several social psychology experiments.
- *Zimbardo's prison experiment:* http://www.ebaumsworld.com/video/watch/854678/. This clip portrays some original footage from the experiment.

**DAILY SHOW EPISODE** You can view Zimbardo's interview with Jon Stewart in which he discusses his book *The Lucifer Effect.* Stewart also makes comic remarks about his experience as a psychology major:
http://www.comedycentral.com/videos/index.jhtml?videoId=84518.

## Additional Readings

Cialdini, R. (2009). *Influence: Science and practice*. Pearson.

Cook, K. (2014). *Kitty Genovese: The murder, the bystanders, the crime that changed America*. New York: W. W. Norton.

Elias, S. M., & Pratkanis, A. R. (2006). Teaching social influence: Demonstrations and exercises from the discipline of social psychology. *Social Influence, 1*, 147–162.

Getlen, L. (2014, February 16). Debunking the myth of Kitty Genovese. *New York Post*.

Latané, B., Williams, K., & Harkins, S. (2006). Many hands make light the work: The causes and consequences of social loafing. In J. M. Levine & R. L. Moreland (Eds.). *Small Groups* (pp. 297–308). New York: Psychology Press.

Moore, R. (2009). *Understanding Jonestown and Peoples Temple*. Westport, CT: Praeger.

Riggio, H., & Garcia, A. L. (2009). The power of situations: Jonestown and the fundamental attribution error. *Teaching of Psychology, 36,* 108–112.

## AP Student Edition Answer Key

### AP Test Practice

### Part I: Multiple Choice

1. **E** *(Skill 3, Learning Target 9.F)*
2. **C** *(Skill 1.B, Learning Target 9.G)*
3. **A** *(Skill 1.B, Learning Target 9.E)*

### Part II: Free Response

Compliance is a change in behavior in response to direct social pressure. A technique to gain compliance is foot-in-the-door. After complying with a small and easy request, you agree to a larger request. Jay may first agree to wear the uniform shirt, but later agree to wear the whole outfit.

Conformity is a change in behavior brought about by the desire to follow the standards of others. Jay will conform by wearing the uniform because he wants to fit in at his new school.

Obedience is a change in behavior in response to the commands of others in authority. Jay will be obedient and wear his uniform if he is told to do so by an authority figure, such as his parents or teachers.

Cognitive dissonance is the mental conflict that occurs when a person holds two contradictory attitudes or thoughts. Jay will experience cognitive dissonance when he has to wear the uniform but dislikes it. To reduce his dissonance he may justify his behavior by saying the uniform really isn't that bad.

# Module 54: Prejudice and Discrimination

## **AP** Module Summary

In Module 54, more specific concepts have been added to the learning targets. A considerable amount of detail has been added to the learning target involving predicting the impact of the presence of others on individual behavior and listing specific concepts: in-group/out-group bias, reciprocity norms, social norms, social traps, prisoner's dilemma, conflict resolution, and superordinate goals. Finally, the learning target having students describe the processes that contribute to differential treatment of group members includes the specific concepts of: bias, discrimination, scapegoat theory, stereotype, out-group homogeneity bias, and mere-exposure effect.

A *stereotype* is a set of generalized beliefs and expectations about a specific group and its members. Stereotypes, which may be negative or positive, grow out of our tendency to categorize and organize the vast amount of information we encounter in our everyday lives.

Stereotypes can lead to *prejudice*, a negative (or positive) evaluation of a group and its members. For instance, racial prejudice occurs when a member of a racial group is evaluated in terms of race and not because of his or her own characteristics or abilities. Common stereotypes and forms of prejudice involve race, religion, ethnicity, and gender. Over the years, various groups have been called "lazy" or "shrewd" or "cruel" with varying degrees of regularity by those who are not members of that group.

Acting on negative stereotypes results in *discrimination*—behavior directed toward individuals on the basis of their membership in a particular group. Discrimination can lead to exclusion from jobs, neighborhoods, and educational opportunities, and it may result in lower salaries and benefits for members of specific groups. Discrimination can also result in more favorable treatment to favored groups.

Stereotyping not only leads to overt discrimination, but also can cause members of stereotyped groups to behave in ways that reflect the stereotype through a phenomenon known as the *self-fulfilling prophecy. Self-fulfilling prophecies* are expectations about the occurrence of a future event or behavior that act to increase the likelihood the event or behavior will occur.

**THE FOUNDATIONS OF PREJUDICE** According to *observational learning approaches* to stereotyping and prejudice, the behavior of parents, other adults, and peers shapes children's feelings about members of various groups. Likewise, young children learn prejudice by imitating the behavior of adult models. The mass media also provide information about stereotypes not just for children but for adults as well. When such inaccurate portrayals are the primary source of information about minority groups, it can lead to the development and maintenance of unfavorable stereotypes.

According to *social identity theory*, we use group membership as a source of pride and self-worth. Social identity theory suggests that people tend to be *ethnocentric,* viewing the world from their own perspective and judging others in terms of their group membership. However, the use of group membership to provide social respect produces an unfortunate outcome. In an effort to maximize our sense of self-esteem, we may come to think that our own group (our *ingroup*) is better than groups to which we do not belong (our *outgroups*). Consequently, we inflate the positive aspects of our ingroup—and, at the same time, devalue outgroups.

The most recent approach to understanding prejudice comes from an increasingly important area in social psychology: social neuroscience. *Social neuroscience* seeks to identify the neurological basis of social behavior. It looks at how we can illuminate our understanding of groups, interpersonal relations, and emotions by understanding their neuroscientific underpinnings. See the "Neuroscience in Your Life: The Prejudiced Brain, Race, and Empathy" box in the text.

- This may be a good time to introduce students to the *scapegoat theory & out-group homogeneity bias*.

**MEASURING PREJUDICE AND DISCRIMINATION: THE IMPLICIT ASSOCIATION TEST** Could you be prejudiced and not even know it? Probably yes, according to the researchers who developed a test that reveals hidden prejudice.

The Implicit Association Test, or IAT, is an ingenious measure of prejudice that permits a more accurate assessment of people's discrimination between members of different groups. The IAT uses the fact that people's automatic, instant reactions often provide the most valid indicator of what they actually believe. Having an implicit bias does not mean that people will overtly discriminate, which is a criticism that has been made of the test. Yet it does mean that the cultural lessons to which we are exposed have a considerable unconscious influence on us.

**REDUCING THE CONSEQUENCES OF PREJUDICE AND DISCRIMINATION** Following are the strategies that have proved effective in diminishing the effects of prejudice and discrimination:

- *Increasing contact between the target of stereotyping and the holder of the stereotype:* Research consistently shows that increasing the amount of interaction between people can reduce negative stereotyping. But only certain kinds of contact are likely to reduce prejudice and discrimination. Situations in which contact is relatively intimate, the individuals are of equal status, or participants must cooperate with one another or are dependent on one another are more likely to reduce stereotyping.
- *Making values and norms against prejudice more conspicuous:* Sometimes just reminding people about the values they already hold regarding equality and fair treatment of others is enough to reduce discrimination.
- *Providing information about the targets of stereotyping:* Probably the most direct means of changing stereotypical and discriminatory attitudes is education: teaching people to be more aware of the positive characteristics of targets of stereotyping.
- *Reducing stereotype threat:* Social psychologist Claude Steele suggests that many African Americans suffer from *stereotype vulnerability*, obstacles to performance that stem from their awareness of society's stereotypes regarding minority group members.
- *Increasing the sense of social belonging of ethnic minority students:* Although almost every college student faces feelings of inadequacy and uncertainty about belonging at the start of college, such feelings are especially strong for members of groups who are underrepresented and have been the targets of prejudice and discrimination. However, research shows that a simple intervention in which members of minority groups are made to understand that feelings of inadequacy are not unique to them—and that such feelings usually diminish with time—can help minority students increase their sense of social belonging.
- This may be a good time to introduce to students the concepts of the *Prisoner's dilemma, Conflict resolution* and *Superordinate goals*.

**APPLYING PSYCHOLOGY IN THE 21ST CENTURY: HELPING MORE WOMEN SUCCEED AS ENGINEERS**
Science, technology, engineering, and math (STEM) fields are challenging for women because they often encounter sexism, harassment, and hostility from their peers and even from their professors. These range from subtle to overt behaviors that often result in women leaving these fields (Nosek, Banaji, & Greenwald, 2002; Dennehy et al., 2018). Females paired with female mentors reported a greater sense of belonging in engineering, self-efficiacy, motivation, and intentions to pursue a career in engineering compared to those paired with a male mentor or no mentor at all (Dennehy & Dasgupta, 2017).

# AP Key Terms

conflict resolution

discrimination

ethnocentrism

out-group homogeneity bias

prejudice

prisoner's dilemma

social neuroscience

scapegoat theory

self-fulfilling prophecy

stereotype

superordinate goals

# Class Discussion Ideas

**PREJUDICE AND DISCRIMINATION** Ask students for examples of when they might have been the victims of prejudice or discrimination. This might include experiences being followed or harassed in retail stores.

**EVOLUTION AND ATTITUDES** Evolutionary forces explain certain inborn attitudes, but many of our attitudes come from experience. Ask students what attitudes they may have that they learned from others and which are evolutionarily predisposed. Ask students to share their experiences.

Have students discuss what a typical member of each of the following categories is like: men, women, teenagers, Republicans, Democrats, and any other category you feel is relevant. Explain to them that all their answers represent stereotypes that can potentially lead to prejudice and discrimination.

**U.S. EQUAL EMPLOYMENT OPPORTUNITY COMMISSION (EEOC)** Visit the website of the EEOC to receive the most current information on U.S. government policies and procedures to combat discrimination against targeted groups. http://www.eeoc.gov/.

# Activities

**RESEARCH PROJECT ON DISCRIMINATION**

- **Prejudice:** Break the class into groups. Each group will draw a piece of paper out of a hat. On each piece you will have written some prejudice such as age, sex, religion, race, etc. Give the students about 15 to 30 minutes to come up with different phrases and actions they can use to demonstrate that type of prejudice. After the allotted time, have the students perform the prejudice in front of the class. The other students in the class should try to figure out what type of prejudice the group is performing.

- **Stereotypes, Prejudice, and Discrimination:** Show the film *Crash* (R rated) or a variety of segments that show stereotypes, prejudice, and discrimination. While the students are viewing this film, have them identify on paper the stereotype and/or the prejudice portrayed and say how these have caused the discrimination. Discuss these observations in class. Finally, have the students brainstorm ways to overcome or change the negative attitudes, halt discrimination, and improve gender and interethnic relations. *Depending on the community in which you teacher a parent permission slip is recommended.

**IMPLICIT ATTITUDES TEST** Ask students to find out if they hold subtle and implicit prejudices by going to the website developed by Banaji, Greenwald, and Nosek: https://implicit.harvard.edu/implicit/demo/, then to the "Demonstrations Tests" link. Ask them to read the general information and then follow the "I wish to proceed" link, where they should choose one or more from many different forms of the IAT: race, religion, gender-science, sexuality, Arab-Muslim, age, and skin tone. Each one takes only about 10 minutes to complete. After they complete one version of the test, they will be provided with general results of how they did. Ask them if they think it is accurate.

## Discussion Questions

**THE "ISM'S"**

- Choose an "ism" about which you feel strongly (racism, sexism, ageism, heterosexism, etc.). Describe why this is an important area of discrimination.
- What do you think accounts for this area being an "ism"?
- How would you attempt to reduce discrimination against targets of this prejudice?

## Suggested Media

- *Breaking the Prejudice Habit:* http://breakingprejudice.org. This site includes activities and information about prejudice.
- *The Jigsaw Classroom:* http://www.jigsaw.org/. This page presents applications of the jigsaw technique for reducing prejudice and discrimination.
- *The Robber's Cave:* http://www.age-of-the-sage.org/psychology/social/sherif_robbers_cave_experiment.html. This page describes Sherif's Robber's Cave experiment and provides detailed account of the experiment.
- *Stereotype threat:* http://www.youtube.com/watch?v=tjn6ZSU_zS0. This clip presents an overview of the research on stereotype threat theory.
- *Understanding prejudice:* http://www.understandingprejudice.org. This site includes classroom activities, discussion springboards, and tips for instructors dealing with prejudice.
- *The Wave.* Insight Media, 1984, 46:00. This is a dramatized fictional account of a teacher who recreates his own "Third Reich" in a high school to demonstrate how Hitler gained power in Germany.

**PBS FRONTLINE: A CLASS DIVIDED**

- *A Class Divided,* PBS: http://www.pbs.org/wgbh/pages/frontline/shows/divided/etc/view.html. This special focuses on Jane Elliot's blue-eye/brown-eye exercise.
- The original brown eyes-blue eyes "experiment" is shown on this *Frontline* video: http://www.pbs.org/wgbh/pages/frontline/shows/divided/.

**TELEVISION AND POPULAR MOVIES: AGGRESSION, VIOLENCE, LOVE, AND PROSOCIAL BEHAVIOR**
Aggression and violence are themes of many television shows and popular movies. For example, the television show *Law & Order* often depicts violent crimes (and often presents these in a controversial manner). The movie *Bowling for Columbine* presents a view of violence in contemporary American society. Scenes from these shows or movies can be shown in class. Types of love are also illustrated in television shows and popular movies. Examples of friendship, romantic love, infatuation, empty love, and passion can readily be found in the current media. Examples of prosocial behavior may also be found in movies and news documentaries such as on *NBC Nightly News* "Making A Difference" segments.

## Additional Readings

Hassan, Y., Bègue, L., Scharkow, M., & Bushman, B. J. (2012). The more you play, the more aggressive you become: A long-term experimental study of cumulative violent video game effects on hostile expectations and aggressive behavior. *Journal of Experimental Social Psychology*.

Jackson, L. (2011). *The psychology of prejudice: From attitudes to social action*. Washington, DC: American Psychological Association.

Kahn, K. B., Spencer, K., & Glaser, J. (2013). Online prejudice and discrimination: From dating to hating. *The Social Net: Understanding Our Online Behavior*, 201.

Kernahan, C., & Davis, T. (2010). What are the long-term effects of learning about racism? *Teaching of Psychology, 37*, 41–45.

Lawson, T. J., McDonough, T. A., & Bodle, J. H. (2010). Confronting prejudiced comments: Effectiveness of a role-playing exercise. *Teaching of Psychology, 37*, 257–261.

Melchiori, K. J., & Mallett, R. K. (2015). Using *Shrek* to teach about stigma. *Teaching of Psychology, 42*, 260–265.

Morris, K.A., & Ashburn-Nardo, L. (2010). The Implicit Association Test as a class assignment: Student affective and attitudinal reactions. *Teaching of Psychology, 37*, 63–68.

Steele, C. (2011). *Whistling Vivaldi: How stereotypes affect us and what we can do*. New York: W. W. Norton.

Wing, Capodilupo, Torino, Bucceri, Holder, Nadal, & Esquilin (2007). Racial microaggressions in everyday life: Implications for clinical practice. *American Psychologist, 62*(4), 271–286. http://sph.umn.edu/site/docs/hewg/microaggressions.pdf.

## **AP** Student Edition Answer Key

## Neuroscience in Your Life: The Prejudiced Brain

Answer Suggestions

- Individuals who are employed in public service, such as law enforcement.
- Questions regarding the sample might include: age, education, socioeconomic status, country of origin, criminal activity in neighborhood they were raised, etc.

## Applying Psychology in the 21st Century: Helping More Women Succeed as Engineers

Answer Suggestions

- The independent variable is the type of mentor (female, male, none) because it is the variable being manipulated.
- Terms that could be used include stereotype threat and self-fulfilling prophecy. Stereotype threat is the perceived risk of confirming a stereotype, which leads to lowered performance. Self-fulfilling prophecies are expectations about the occurrence of a future event or behavior that act to increase the likelihood it will occur.

## AP Test Practice

### Part I: Multiple Choice

1. **C** *(Skill 1.B, Learning Target 9.C)*

2. **D** *(Skill 1.A, Learning Target 9.J)*

3. **D** *(Skill 1.B, Learning Target 9.J)*

## Part II: Free Response

**A.**

Teacher expectations caused a change in student IQ scores.

The dependent variable is measured as the score on the IQ test.

This study was experimental because random assignment was used and a variable was manipulated. One teacher received information about their students and the other did not.

**B.**

Stereotype threat is the perceived risk of confirming a stereotype, which leads to lowered performance. If students were reminded of a personal stereotype before taking the exam, it could increase their anxiety and impact their performance.

Self-fulfilling prophecies are expectations about the occurrence of a future event or behavior that act to increase the likelihood it will occur. The teacher's high expectations for their students led to increased performance.

Circadian rhythm is the biological processes that occur on a 24-hour cycle. Mental alertness follows a pattern throughout the day and students should not be tested in the late afternoon.

Mnemonics are strategies for organizing information in a way that makes the information more likely to be remembered. Students who create memory aids, such as acronyms, are more likely to transfer information into their long-term memory and improve their test performance.

# Module 55: Positive and Negative Social Behavior

## AP Module Summary

In Module 55, several of the changes that you introduce in Modules 53 and 54 will carry over. The Course and Exam Description Guide now have two separate learning targets for students to meet. One being focused on altruism and aggression and the other on interpersonal attraction.

**LIKING AND LOVING: INTERPERSONAL ATTRACTION AND THE DEVELOPMENT OF RELATIONSHIPS**
Nothing is more important in most people's lives than their feelings for others. Consequently, it is not surprising that liking and loving have become a major focus of interest for social psychologists. Known more formally as the study of *interpersonal attraction* or *close relationships*, this area addresses the factors that lead to positive feelings for others.

**HOW DO I LIKE THEE? LET ME COUNT THE WAYS** By far the greatest amount of research has focused on liking. Research has given us a good deal of knowledge about the factors that initially attract two people to each other. The important factors social psychologists consider are the following:

- *Proximity:* This is one of the more firmly established findings in the literature on interpersonal attraction: Proximity leads to liking.
- *Mere exposure:* Repeated exposure to a person is often sufficient to produce attraction. Interestingly, repeated exposure to any stimulus—a person, picture, song, or virtually anything—usually makes us like the stimulus more. Becoming familiar with a person can evoke positive feelings; we then transfer the positive feelings stemming from familiarity to the person him- or herself.
- *Similarity:* We tend to like those who are similar to us. Discovering that others have similar attitudes, values, or traits promotes our liking for them. Furthermore, the more similar others are, the more we like them. Because we experience a strong *reciprocity-of-liking effect* (a tendency to like those who like us), knowing that someone evaluates us positively promotes our attraction to that person.
- *Physical attractiveness:* For most people, the equation beautiful = good is quite true. As a result, physically attractive people are more popular than physically unattractive ones, if all other factors are equal.

**HOW DO I LOVE THEE? LET ME COUNT THE WAYS** As a first step to studying love, researchers tried to identify the characteristics that distinguish between mere liking and full-blown love. They discovered that love is not simply a greater quantity of liking but a qualitatively different psychological state. For instance, at least in its early stages, love includes relatively intense physiological arousal, an all-encompassing interest in another individual, fantasizing about the other, and relatively rapid swings of emotion. Similarly, love, unlike liking, includes elements of passion, closeness, fascination, exclusiveness, sexual desire, and intense caring. We idealize partners by exaggerating their good qualities and minimizing their imperfections. Other researchers have theorized that there are two main types of love: passionate love and companionate love. *Passionate (or romantic) love* represents a state of intense absorption in someone. It includes intense physiological arousal, psychological interest, and caring for the needs of another. In contrast, *companionate love* is the strong affection we have for those with whom our lives are deeply involved. The love we feel for our parents, other family members, and even some close friends falls into the category of companionate love. Psychologist Robert Sternberg makes an even finer differentiation between types of love. He proposes that love consists of three parts (see **Figure 1**):

- *Decision/commitment:* The initial thoughts that one loves someone and the longer-term feelings of commitment to maintain love.
- *Intimacy component:* Feelings of closeness and connectedness.
- *Passion component:* The motivational drives relating to sex, physical closeness, and romance.

According to Sternberg, these three components combine to produce the different types of love. He suggests that different combinations of the three components vary over the course of relationships.

**AGGRESSION AND PROSOCIAL BEHAVIOR: HURTING AND HELPING OTHERS** Drive-by shootings, carjacking, and abductions are just a few examples of the violence that seems all too common today. Yet, we also find examples of generous, unselfish, thoughtful behavior that suggest a more optimistic view of humankind. In fact, psychologists have found that microaggressions—small, daily slights, put downs, and insults, often perpetrated against members of marginalized groups based on race, gender, and sexual orientation—may be more harmful in the long run than are highly visible acts of aggression.

**HURTING OTHERS: AGGRESSION** Depending on the way we define the word, many examples of inflicted pain or injury may or may not qualify as aggression (see **Figure 4**). Most social psychologists define aggression in terms of the intent and the purpose behind the behavior. *Aggression* is intentional injury of, or harm to, another person. Not only do we hurt others through direct physical or verbal attacks, but we also can hurt people indirectly by doing such things as spreading rumors or by purposely ignoring someone.

**FRUSTRATION-AGGRESSION APPROACHES: AGGRESSION AS A REACTION TO FRUSTRATION** According to frustration-aggression theory, *frustration* (the reaction to the thwarting or blocking of goals) produces anger, which leads to a readiness to act aggressively. Whether actual aggression occurs depends on the presence of *aggressive cues*, stimuli that have been associated in the past with actual aggression or violence that will trigger aggression again. The stimuli that act as aggressive cues range from the most explicit, such as the presence of weapons, to more subtle cues, such as the mere mention of the name of an individual who behaved violently in the past.

**OBSERVATIONAL LEARNING APPROACHES: LEARNING TO HURT OTHERS** Taking an almost opposite view from instinct theories, which focus on innate explanations of aggression, *observational learning theory* emphasizes that social and environmental conditions can teach individuals to be aggressive. The theory sees aggression not as inevitable, but rather as a learned response that can be understood in terms of rewards and punishments. According to observational learning theory, people observe the behavior of models and the subsequent consequences of that behavior. If the consequences are positive, the behavior is likely to be imitated when observers find themselves in a similar situation.

**HELPING OTHERS: THE BRIGHTER SIDE OF HUMAN NATURE** Helping behavior, or *prosocial behavior* as it is more formally known, has been considered under many different conditions. There are certain factors that lead someone to help a person in need: One critical factor is the number of others present. When more than one person witnesses an emergency situation, a sense of diffusion of responsibility can arise among the bystanders. *Diffusion of responsibility* is the belief that responsibility for intervening is shared, or diffused, among those present. The more people who are present in an emergency, the less personally responsible each individual feels—and therefore the less help he or she provides. Although most research on helping behavior supports the diffusion of responsibility explanation, other factors are clearly involved in helping behavior.

According to a model of the helping process, the decision to give aid involves four basic steps (see **Figure 5**):

- Noticing a person, event, or situation that may require help.
- Interpreting the event as one that requires help: Even if we notice an event, it may be sufficiently ambiguous for us to interpret it as a nonemergency situation.
- Assuming responsibility for helping: It is at this point that diffusion of responsibility is likely to occur if others are present. Moreover, a bystander's particular expertise is likely to play a role in determining whether he or she helps.
- Deciding on and implementing the form of helping: After we assume responsibility for helping, we must decide how to provide assistance. Helping can range from very indirect forms of intervention, such as calling the police, to more direct forms, such as giving first aid or taking the victim to a hospital. Most social psychologists use a *rewards-costs approach* for helping to predict the nature of the assistance a bystander will choose to provide.

After determining the nature of the assistance needed, the actual help must be implemented. A rewards-costs analysis suggests that we are most likely to use the least costly form of implementation. However, this is not always the case: In some situations, people behave altruistically. *Altruism* is behavior meant to help another without regard for self-interest. People who intervene in emergency situations tend to possess certain personality characteristics that differentiate them from nonhelpers. For example, helpers are more self-assured, sympathetic, and emotionally understanding, and they have greater empathy (a personality trait in which someone observing another person experiences the emotions of that person) than are nonhelpers.

## AP Key Terms

aggression

altruism

catharsis

companionate love

diffusion of responsibility

interpersonal attraction (or close relationship)
   positive feelings for others; liking and loving

mere-exposure effect

passionate (or romantic) love

prosocial behavior

reciprocity-of-liking effect

## Class Discussion Ideas

**ATTRACTION** Ask students whether they think "opposites attract" or "birds of a feather flock together." Ask why and then explain that usually it is the latter.

**AGGRESSION**
**Instinct approaches:**

- Inborn, innate fighting urges
- Buildup is released through catharsis.

**Frustration-aggression approaches:**

- When a person is frustrated, this leads to a readiness to act aggressively. In the presence of aggressive cues, aggressive acts are more likely to be carried out.
- (Frustration $\rightarrow$ anger $\rightarrow$ readiness to act aggressively) + aggressive cues $\rightarrow$ aggression

**Observational learning approaches:**

- Social and environmental conditions influence readiness to respond aggressively.
- Aggression is a learned response through the observation of others.

**Aggression and Environmental Influences:** Aggression results from the interaction between genetic and social forces. Ask students what environmental factors have led them to aggressive actions.

**PROSOCIAL BEHAVIOR** Diffusion of responsibility leads individuals to keep from helping others during an emergency situation. However, we know that many people do engage in prosocial behavior. What factors might lead individuals to take action when needed to help?

Ask students how many of them have taken CPR classes. Ask them about the first thing they are taught to say to the "victim" (i.e., the dummy). Usually it's "Are you all right? Are you OK? YOU call 911" (said while pointing to one person). Why do we specify that one person is responsible for calling 911? Because if you don't, then people tend to look around for who is supposed to act, leading no one to act. This uncertainty is the result of diffusion of responsibility.

Ask students when the last time they helped someone was. Today? Yesterday? A week ago? Who did they help? Why? What did they do? You can also ask when the last time they received help was.

Ask students if they think altruism really exists. Ask for examples.

Watching someone you love experience pain activates components of physical pain circuitry in the brain. Ask students what they would find more painful: having each one of their toes broken or watching the person they love most in the world having his or her toes broken?

## Activities

### PROSOCIAL BEHAVIOR

- **Altruistic Behavior:** Show the class the documentary *39 Silent Witnesses: The Kitty Genovese Story* and then have them write a one- to two-page paper summarizing the documentary. They should also discuss whether times have changed since the Kitty Genovese incident or whether the same results would occur today. The students should also discuss how they feel about helping behavior and whether they have ever been guilty of not helping someone because they thought someone else would help.
- **Altruism:** Ask students to perform an act of kindness. Following the act, have students write a brief paper describing the act, the recipient's reaction, and their own reaction. Ask students to share their reactions with the class. This can provide a good discussion of prosocial behavior. Source: Radmacher, S. (1997, January 19). Social psychology projects. Teaching in the psychological sciences (TIPS-Online Discussion Group).
- **Altruism:** To begin the discussion, ask students what was the last act of altruism they did and why. Next, facilitate a class discussion with the following: Is altruism a puzzle to be solved or a natural expression of human nature? As a homework assignment extension to this discussion, have students find research to support their opinion.

### NEWSPAPER RESEARCH ASSIGNMENT

**Have students find an example of prosocial behavior from a newspaper article. Ask the following questions:**

- What was the behavior involved in this example?
- Why do you think the individual involved engaged in the behavior?
- What can we learn from this example that might encourage others to behave in a prosocial manner as well?

**AGGRESSION** Use *Handout: What Is the Cause of Aggression?* In this activity, the students will read various scenarios of aggressive behavior and determine whether a biological, psychological, or sociocultural cause is behind that behavior.

### LOVE AND LONELINESS

- **Types of Love:** Have students complete *Handout: Identifying Types of Love.*
- **What Makes a Happy Relationship?** Ask students to interview the happiest couple they know. Have them ask the partners individually about the things that they think help make their relationship work. Then have students examine their notes and determine how the characteristics of their "ideal" couple's relationship compare with the findings of research on close relationships.

## Discussion Questions

### ATTRACTION

- Ask students if they believe that "beauty is in the eye of the beholder." Ask them to defend their answer.

### AGGRESSION

- Which theory of aggression is most useful in helping to control violence? Why?
- Analyze a news story in which an aggressive act occurred according to the theories of aggression.

### PROSOCIAL BEHAVIOR

- What would make a person more likely to help in an emergency?
- How can diffusion of responsibility be lessened?

## Suggested Media

- *Attractiveness:* http://www.youtube.com/watch?v=ZuometYfMTk. This clip in the *Science of Attraction* video series portrays the halo effect.

**POPULAR MOVIES** The movie *Shrek* deals with issues of attractiveness and appearance in contemporary society.

# Additional Readings

Patzer, G. L. (2011). *The power and paradox of physical attractiveness*. BrownWalker Press.

Young, L., & Alexander, B. (2012). *The chemistry between us: Love, sex, and the science of attraction*. Penguin.

# AP Student Edition Answer Key

## AP Test Practice

### Part I: Multiple Choice

1. **A** *(Skill 1.B, Learning Target 9.J)*

2. **A** *(Skill 1.B, Learning Target 9.K)*

3. **E** *(Skill 1.A, Learning Target 9.L)*

### Part II: Free Response

**A.**

Mere exposure says we tend to like items we are familiar with. Jacob has had repeated contact with his neighbors, so has probably grown to like them.

Self-fulfilling prophecies are expectations about the occurrence of a future event or behavior that act to increase the likelihood it will occur. If Jacob expects the children to behave, they are more likely to behave. According to self-fulfilling prophecy, they will live up to his expectations.

**B.**

Diffusion of responsibility explains why in certain situations, the larger the number of bystanders the less likely you are to help someone in trouble. If Jacob was with a large group of friends, it would be less likely that a friend would help him because they would assume someone else would help and they are not responsible.

Altruism is behavior meant to help another person without regard for self-interest. A friend might express altruism and step into the street to help Jacob. His friend would be putting himself at risk and helping out of genuine concern for others.

Ingroup bias is the tendency to favor members from your own group over others. Jacob's friends are more likely to offer him assistance because he is part of their friend group.

# AP PSYCHOLOGY PRACTICE TEST ANSWER KEY

## Section I • ⏱ 1 hour and 10 minutes • Number of Questions: 100

1. Creativity seems to be associated with
   A. **divergent thinking.**
   B. old age.
   C. narrowed focus.
   D. high intelligence.
   E. extrinsic motivation.

2. The defense mechanism called sublimation protects us from painful emotions by
   A. allowing us to pretend certain events never happened.
   B. enabling us to attribute to others embarrassing feelings we have.
   C. enabling us to bury deep in our memory painful events of the past.
   D. enabling us to retreat to an earlier stage of life when life was simpler.
   E. **allowing us to transform negative energy into positive and useful outcomes.**

3. Which of the following produces a graph that displays wave patterns?
   A. an fMRI image
   B. **an electro-encephalogram device**
   C. an CAT scan
   D. a PET scan using radioactive sugar molecules
   E. lesioning

4. In his Stanford Prison Experiment, Philip Zimbardo discovered that his subjects
   A. suffered from schizophrenia, because some experienced hallucinations.
   B. provided evidence for the existence of the mere exposure effect.
   C. **assumed stereotypical social roles.**
   D. assumed gender roles more appropriate for the opposite sex.
   E. exhibited post-conventional moral reasoning.

5. Mark's retired grandmother decided to study art history at a university, as she put it, "just for fun." She is demonstating
   A. extrinsic motivation.
   B. **intrinsic motivation.**
   C. social-cognitive theory.
   D. drive-reduction theory.
   E. the James-Lange theory.

6. Francesca wanted to make an apple-cinnamon cake, but her recipe was smudged and she could not read how much cinnamon to put in the mix. To resolve this problem, she added one teaspoon of cinnamon to the mix, then tasted it. It wasn't quite right so she continued to add one teaspoon at a time, tasting after each addition, until she had a cake that tasted right. Which problem solving technique was she using?
   A. Heuristic
   B. **Algorithm**
   C. Insight
   D. State-dependent
   E. Confirmation bias

7. The ability to read a word despite it missing letters is related to the concept of
   A. top-down processing.
   B. bottom-up processing.
   C. difference threshold.
   D. depth perception.
   E. **perceptual constancy.**

8. Stress has all of the following direct physiological effects EXCEPT
   A. elevated blood pressure.
   B. decreased immune functioning.
   C. **decreased fatigue.**
   D. increased hormonal activity.
   E. psychophysiological conditions.

9. Since environment generally has little effect on eye color, we can say that eye color has a high degree of
   A. variability.
   B. reliability.
   C. introspection.
   D. **heritability.**
   E. determinism.

10. The type of reinforcement schedule likely to produce the longest-lasting behavior is a(n)
    A. **interval schedule.**
    B. ratio schedule.
    C. intensity schedule.
    D. variable schedule.
    E. implied schedule.

11. Conversion disorder and illness anxiety disorder are classified as
    A. mood disorders because they all have an element of depression.
    B. somatic symptom disorders because they are all caused by neurotransmitter deficits.
    C. anxiety disorders because they all feature impaired reality testing.
    D. mood disorders because they all include an element of mania.
    E. somatic symptom disorders because they all have physical features that are not caused by medical conditions.

12. Conditioning is most effective if the neutral stimulus
    A. precedes the unconditioned stimulus.
    B. precedes the conditioned stimulus.
    C. follows the unconditioned stimulus.
    D. follows the conditioned stimulus.
    E. occurs at the same time as the conditioned stimulus.

13. The ability to "bounce back" from life's problems, disappointments, and failures is termed
    A. resilience.
    B. self-efficacy.
    C. self-serving bias.
    D. competence.
    E. psychotherapeutic efficacy.

14. If a weightlifter can distinguish 50 lbs. from 55 lbs half of the time, then, according to Weber's Law, she
    A. will be able to distinguish 20 lbs. from 21 lbs. 50% of the time.
    B. will be able to distinguish 70 lbs. from 77 lbs. 50% of the time.
    C. will not be able to 20 lbs. from 25 lbs. 50% of the time
    D. will be able to distinguish 90 lbs. from 95 lbs. 50% of the time.
    E. will not be able to distinguish 60 lbs. from 67 lbs. 50% of the time.

15. An individual who displays an exaggerated sense of self-importance is exhibiting symptoms of
    A. an antisocial personality disorder.
    B. a narcissistic personality disorder.
    C. a borderline personality disorder.
    D. an attention-deficit hyperactivity disorder.
    E. an autism spectrum disorder.

16 Place theory provides a better explanation for the sensing of
    A. low-frequency sounds.
    B. high-frequency sounds.
    C. medium-frequency sounds.
    D. loud sounds.
    E. soft sounds.

17. Developmental psychologists use this term to describe the biologically programmed process by which infants develop motor skills such as rolling over, sitting, standing, and walking.
    A. Growth spurts
    B. Attachment
    C. Developmental graduation
    D. Maturation
    E. Motor skills learning

18. A therapist working from the cognitive perspective would likely
    A. be most concerned about the patient's family relationships.
    B. focus on incentives that motivate the patient's current behavior.
    C. help the patient identify and change dysfunctional thoughts.
    D. analyze a patient's dreams in order to explain the patient's unconscious conflicts.
    E. assist the patient in meeting his social and ego needs.

19. Giving a test or assessment to a group of students, and, one month later, giving it to them again is a method of establishing that the test has
    A. norms.
    B. adaptive testing.
    C. mental age.
    D. validity.
    E. reliability.

20. Which theory provides a neuroscience explanation of dreams?
    A. Unconscious wish fulfillment
    B. Activation-synthesis
    C. Dreams-for-survival
    D. Circadian rhythm
    E. Memory consolidation

21. Which of the following methods of brain research involves placing sensors on the skull to record brain activity?
    A. PET scan
    B. fMRI
    C. EEG
    D. CAT scan
    E. Lesioning

22. In Erikson's theory of social development individuals who fail to successfully resolve trust and identity issues may have difficulty later in
    A. earning a living.
    B. having children.
    C. making moral decisions.
    D. forming intimate relationships.
    E. thinking abstractly.

23. Jeffrey does poorly in school because he works until midnight every night to help support his family. When a teacher accuses him of being "just plain lazy," the teacher
    A. is probably using reciprocal determinism.
    B. has committed the fundamental attribution error.
    C. is using a peripheral route to persuasion to motivate Jeffrey.
    D. is using variable reinforcement on Jeffrey.
    E. is using the self-serving bias to cover up her poor teaching skills.

24. In Freud's terms, material that is easily recalled to the conscious mind is stored in
    A. the unconscious.
    B. as collective unconscious.
    C. the preconscious.
    D. the superego.
    E. the tranference conscious.

25. In late adulthood, individuals often show declines in what type of intelligence?
    A. Crystallized intelligence
    B. Fluid intelligence
    C. Practical intelligence
    D. Emotional intelligence
    E. Interpersonal intelligence

26. One's vestibular sense is in his or her
    A. ears.
    B. nose.
    C. eyes.
    D. skin.
    E. mouth.

27. Split-brain patients have undergone surgery to sever the
    A. optic chiasm.
    B. cerebellum.
    C. corpus callosum.
    D. optic nerve.
    E. sensory cortex.

28. A concept is
    A. an example of habituation.
    B. an example of bottom-up processing.
    C. the equilavent of feature abstraction.
    D. a collection of items that fit a schema.
    E. a heuristic algorithm.

29. A charitable organization tries to solicit contributions by showing TV commercials with celebrities endorsing the organization. The organization is using
    A. the celebrity heuristic.
    B. confirmation bias.
    C. the peripheral route to persuasion.
    D. an algorithm.
    E. the self-serving bias.

30. Incoming math majors at a university are given a math aptitude test. The university found a strong positive correlation between the incoming scores and the students' math GPA after two years. The university concluded that
    A. the test has predictive validity.
    B. the test has reliability.
    C. the test has adaptive testing.
    D. the test has mental age.
    E. the test has norms.

31. Unconditional positive regard is generally associated with
    A. Freud's psychoanalysis.
    B. Beck's cognitive therapy.
    C. Jones's behavior therapy.
    D. Rogers's person-centered therapy.
    E. psychopharmacology.

32. When children first begin to babble, at only a few months of age, they voice
    A. phonemes that are found only in the language spoken in the home.
    B. only a few, easily-pronounced phonemes.
    C. most of the morphemes found in the home language.
    D. phonemes from almost every language in the world.
    E. only phonemes from the correct language "family" - such European Romance languages.

33. As Megan anxiously prepares to step onstage to deliver the commencement speech, her heart is racing, her mouth is dry, and her pupils are fully dilated. Which part of her nervous system is in control?
    A. Endocrinatic
    B. Parasympathetic
    C. Skeletal
    D. Sympathetic
    E. Muscular

34. A highly skilled architect or sculptor probably has, according to Howard Gardner's theory of intelligence, a high level of
    A. spatial intelligence.
    B. 3-D intelligence.
    C. intrapersonal intelligence.
    D. naturalistic intelligence.
    E. bodily kinesthetic intelligence.

35. If a dog learns to associate a tone with being fed, the dog will salivate when it hears the tone. If the dog later hears a slightly higher pitched tone and salivates in response to the second tone, then a researcher can say that which of the following has occurred?
    A. Stimulus discrimination
    B. Spontaneous recovery
    C. Operant conditioning
    D. Stimulus deferment
    E. Stimulus generalization

36. As long as sales remain above the daily quota, a sales manager rewards his staff using the variable interval reinforcement schedule by
    A. giving each employee a $10 bill on Friday.
    B. giving the best seller of the week an extra $20 on Friday.
    C. occassionally buying lunch, once every week or so.
    D. giving the employees $10 every time sales exceed quota for five consecutive days.
    E. firing the least productive employee every month.

37. A student watched patrons at a sporting event and noted whether they more often went to the food concession stands during time-outs or when there was action on the field. Which type of research is this?
    A. Survey
    B. Correlational
    C. Naturalistic observation
    D. Clinical observation
    E. Experimental

38. Most professionals use the APA's *DSM* for what purpose?
    A. Define different therapy techniques
    B. Classify and define psychological disorders
    C. Establish the history of the different disorders
    D. List causes of psychological disorders
    E. Explain the theoretical basis of different therapies

39. Cognitive psychologists are likely to be interested in how
    A. you choose a college major.
    B. you feel about your college's football team.
    C. you process fear in your brain.
    D. you use your sense of depth perception.
    E. your heart rate changes when an attractive person walks by.

40. An individual who has a male body but views their gender identity as female may consider themselves
    A. transgender
    B. androgynous
    C. bisexual
    D. feministic
    E. intersexual

41. A reuptake inhibitor is likely to have the effect of
    A. raising the threshold for firing a neuron.
    B. increasing the amount of a neurotransmitter in the synapse.
    C. increasing the intensity of a neuron's firing.
    D. decreasing the amount of a transmitter in the synapse.
    E. lowering the threshold for firing a neuron.

42. Jennifer noticed that her husband, who snored heavily, often stopped breathing as he slept and then, after 30 to 45 seconds of not breathing, gasped for breath. She is concerned that he may be suffering from
    A. night terrors.
    B. insomnia.
    C. excessive REM sleep.
    D. sleep apnea.
    E. sleep tremors.

43. One reason that the validity of projective personality tests is questioned is that
    A. projective tests always have objective scoring criteria.
    B. psychologists who administer projective tests have extensive training in scoring them.
    C. projective tests are administered only by psychiatrists.
    D. most projective tests require some subjective scoring.
    E. an individual may score differently on two separate administrations of a projective test.

44. Because Celia's absolute threshold for hearing is eight decibels, it is likely that she will hear what percentage of sounds that are exactly eight decibels?
    A. 100%
    B. 0%
    C. 10%
    D. 90%
    E. 50%

45. When group members share such a strong motivation to achieve consensus that they lose the ability to critically evaluate alternative points of view, this is known as
    A. group polarization.
    B. gate control theory.
    C. prejudice.
    D. groupthink.
    E. ingroup bias.

46. When a four-year-old was asked to decide whether a row of four narrowly-spaced pennies or a row of four widely-spaced pennies had more coins, he said the widely-spaced row had more. This indicates that he has not yet developed
    A. egocentrism.
    B. conservation of number.
    C. telegraphic speech.
    D. conservation of length.
    E. the Babinski reflex.

47. Roger Sperry is primarily known for his work in
    A. split-brain research.
    B. personality.
    C. reuptake processes.
    D. feature detection in vision.
    E. social facilitation.

48. What type of memory is an episodic memory?
    A. Implicit memory
    B. Explicit memory
    C. Procedural memory
    D. Sensory memory
    E. Semantic memory

49. The Rosenhan study, in which normal people reported briefly experiencing a single symptom of schizophrenia, illustrated the fact that
    A. schizophrenia is a pervasive disorder in modern society.
    B. schizophrenia is easily treated with modern therapeutic methods.
    C. a mental set can interfere with proper diagnosis.
    D. many schizophrenics lie about their symptoms.
    E. older people are more likely than younger people to report symptoms of schizophrenia.

50. Before engaging in animal psychology research, a university professor would likely have to
    A. design his research so that no animal suffered any pain in the research.
    B. obtain approval from the Federal Psychology Licensing Board.
    C. provide the animals a comfortable retirement when he finished.
    D. ensure that he used only male animals in his research.
    E. obtain approval of his research from an Institutional Review Board or similar body.

51. The motor cortex devotes the most resources to which parts of the body?
    A. Muscles requiring very fine movement, such as in the lips and fingers
    B. The most important muscles, such as the heart and lungs
    C. The largest and strongest muscles
    D. The muscles furthest from the brain, such as those in the legs and feet
    E. The autonomic muscles

52. The area of central focus on the retina is called the
    A. cornea.
    B. aqueous humor.
    C. blind spot.
    D. fovea.
    E. ganglion cell.

53. Henry has a crush on a girl in his school, but she did not know him and never seemed to notice him. Because Henry understood the mere exposure effect, he decided to
    A. look up her online profile.
    B. join the swim team.
    C. join a club in which she is active.
    D. send her an anonymous note.
    E. work out to improve his physique.

54. In the basement of their home, a toddler and mother see a spider. The toddler is curious about the spider until the mother screams in terror, grabs the child tightly, and runs from the home, screaming, her heart beating wildly as she pants for breath between screams and sobs. Because of the mother's terror, the child also becomes terribly afraid of spiders. Assuming this phobia is established in the child by classical conditioning, what is the unconditioned stimulus in this scenario?
    A. The spider
    B. The basement
    C. The child's fear
    D. The toddler's curiousity
    E. The mother's fearful behavior

55. As people age, their resting metabolism tends to
    A. remain relatively constant.
    B. increase for men, and decrease for women.
    C. increase for women, and decrease for men.
    D. increase for both men and women.
    E. decrease for both men and women.

56. Which of the following drugs may produce mild euphoria and general relaxation, and in some cases, hallucinations, delusions and paranoia, though it is usually not physically addicting?
    A. Amphetamines
    B. Morphine
    C. Marijuana
    D. Stimulants
    E. Barbiturates

57. What does it mean if the results of an experiment are statistically significant?
    A. No difference was found between conditions
    B. The research was very important
    C. The research was conducted by a famous researcher
    D. Researchers are confident that they have confirmed their hypothesis
    E. The results have not been replicated

58. Which of the following research results regarding adolescent maturation is true?
    A. Menopause is associated with the start of puberty
    B. Sex characteristics develop at the end of puberty
    C. Puberty for boys is usually earlier than girls
    D. Early maturation is favorable for boys
    E. Early maturation is favorable for girls

59. The Big 5 personality traits consist of the following traits EXCEPT
    A. conscientiousness.
    B. neuroticism.
    C. optimism.
    D. extraversion.
    E. agreeableness.

60. According to the Cannon-Bard theory, which of the following is true?
    A. Arousal and the emotion are simultaneous.
    B. The emotion precedes the arousal.
    C. The arousal precedes the emotion.
    D. Arousal of sufficient intensity inhibits the emotion.
    E. Arousal includes a simultaneously-occuring cognitive event.

61. Angela wanted to try a new restaurant. She went to the restaurant's website, where she found dozens of glowing reviews from other patrons. She decided that the restaurant must be good, and she quickly made a reservation. It appears that Angela used
    A. self-serving bias.
    B. an algorithm.
    C. confirmation bias.
    D. expectations bias.
    E. hindsight bias.

62. In Hans Selye's theory of stress, the highest level of reaction to stress occurs in the
    A. initiation stage.
    B. the exhaustion stage.
    C. the resistance stage.
    D. the alarm stage.
    E. the extinction stage.

63. Though he hadn't ridden a bicycle in many years, George's grandfather quickly regained the skill of doing so when he began riding for exercise in his 70s. George's grandfather apparently has a functioning
    A. state memory.
    B. flashbulb memory.
    C. eidetic memory.
    D. iconic memory.
    E. procedural memory.

64. In Freudian theory, the process of projecting onto one's therapist the emotions felt earlier in life, especially toward parents, is called
    A. accommodation.
    B. the Electra Complex.
    C. identification.
    D. insight maintenance.
    E. transference.

65. Which of the following is a true statement?
    A. The hypothesis generally predicts that the dependent variable is affected by the independent variable.
    B. The dependent variable and the independent variable are interchangeable in most research.
    C. The random variable is the cause of both the independent variable and the dependent variable.
    D. Dependent variables are generally not used in psychology research.
    E. The independent variable is always affected by the dependent variable.

66. In the graph above illustrating the strength of a classically conditioned response, which of the following shows the conditioning process that is occuring in the phase from point A to point B?
    A. Spontaneous recovery
    B. Acquisition
    C. Extinction
    D. Variable reinforcement
    E. Generalization

67. The scores on a national psychology test are normally distributed. The mean of the test is 75 and the standard deviation is 15. What percentage of the test-takers scored between 60 and 90?
    A. Less than 1%
    B. About 2.5%
    C. About 34%
    D. About 57%
    E. About 68%

68. The fact that children who are blind from birth can make facial expressions appropriate to the emotional situation is reason to believe that
  A. expressions of basic emotions are attributable to social learning.
  B. facial expressions differ dramatically across cultures.
  C. facial expressions are subject to the James-Lange theory.
  D. expression of basic emotions is genetic in nature, not learned.
  E. such children cannot be representative of all children and therefore we cannot generalize about their abilities.

69. Three of Suzanne's friends know a lot about cell phones. When Suzanne purchases her phone, she buys the same brand that her friends have purchased. This is an example of
  A. obedience
  B. deindividuation
  C. groupthink
  D. social facilitation
  E. conformity

70. A way to treat bed-wetting in older children is to provide a special pad for the child to sleep on. The pad sounds an alarm and wakes the child if the child wets it. This method, which uses classical conditioning, has proven successful. What is the unconditioned response in this method?
  A. The alarm
  B. Bed-wetting
  C. Waking up
  D. Ending the habit of bed-wetting
  E. The feeling of a full bladder

71. Which endocrine gland produces Human Growth Hormone?
  A. Testes
  B. Hypothalamus
  C. Adrenal
  D. Pituitary
  E. Parathyroid

72. Students who continually fail in school classes and have difficulty forming personal relationships might
  A. suffer from deindividuation.
  B. be excessively optimistic.
  C. have an internal locus of control.
  D. experience learned helplessness.
  E. have high expectations of themselves.

73. Which of the following variables could not be used in correlational research?
  A. Age
  B. Gender
  C. Income
  D. Height
  E. Weight

74. An individual diagnosed with autism spectrum disorder who displays extraordinary memory skills would be known as
  A. conscientious.
  B. intellectually disabled.
  C. a prodigy.
  D. a savant.
  E. a genius.

75. The Freudian process by which a child incorporates the behavior and attitudes of the same-sex parent into his or her own personality is called
  A. transference.
  B. imitation.
  C. imprinting.
  D. identification.
  E. unconscious development.

76. The afterimage effect is explained by
  A. the opponent-process theory.
  B. accommodation.
  C. Weber's Law.
  D. the trichomatic theory.
  E. Helmholtz's Law.

77. Professor O'Doyle is conducting an experiment to determine whether or not drinking pomegranate juice before a test has an effect on students' scores on the test. Which of the following describes an operational definition for the dependent variable in this research?
  A. The amount of juice consumed before the test
  B. The students' post-test estimates of their scores
  C. The mean of the students' scores
  D. The difficulty of the test
  E. 6 oz. of juice consumed 40 minutes before the test

78. This researcher conducted a number of studies in which a mother and small child were left in a room. A stranger then entered the room and the mother left for a short period, before returning. The researcher was
  A. Mary Cover Jones.
  B. Mary Ainsworth.
  C. John Garcia.
  D. Robert Rescorla.
  E. Aaron Beck.

79. When a teacher gives her young students gold stars for good scores on a spelling test, she is using the principle of
    A. negative reinforcement.
    B. stimulus identification.
    C. stimulus generalization.
    D. reverse punishment.
    E. positive reinforcement.

80. Which classic experiment researched the concept of obedience?
    A. Zimbardo's prison study
    B. Milgram's shock study
    C. Asch's line study
    D. Ainsworth's strange situation study
    E. Pavlov's dog study

81. Antipsychotic drugs work by blocking what type of receptors at the brain's synapses?
    A. Serotonin
    B. Glutamate
    C. GABA
    D. Dopamine
    E. Norepinephrine

82. In a study conducted in the 1930s, a psychologist surveyed hotel and restaurant owners in California, asking them if they would serve Chinese immigrants to California. Nearly all said they would not serve the Chinese. Later, the psychologist sent a Chinese-American couple who spoke fluent English and dressed in American clothes to the establishments. Nearly all served the couple. The psychologist concluded from this study
    A. that racism was common in California in the 1930s.
    B. that confirmation bias had affected the couple's treatment.
    C. that the fundamental attribution error affected the couple's treatment.
    D. that there was no discrimination in Califormia in the 1930s.
    E. that attitudes do not always predict behavior.

83. For an experiment in how U.S. high school students learn best, Mr. Abercrombie gave the girls in his class written material on Freud to read. He gave the boys the same written material to read plus a video to watch on the same material. Later, he tested both groups, and when the boys scored higher on the test, he concluded that U.S. high school students learn best with two forms of study materials. One problem with this experiment is that
    A. he used neither random sampling nor random selection.
    B. he had too many dependent variables.
    C. he had too many independent variables.
    D. he used random sampling, but not random selection.
    E. he included no random variables.

84. The rooting reflex in infants occurs when
    A. the infant's cheek is stroked.
    B. the infant is preparing to walk.
    C. strangers interrupt the child's caregiver.
    D. an infant is tired.
    E. the caregiver leaves the room.

85. Young parents who hope to raise confident, self-reliant, independent children might do well to adopt
    A. an authoritarian parenting style.
    B. an authoritative parenting style.
    C. a permissive parenting style.
    D. an uninvolved parenting style.
    E. a "helicopter" parenting style.

86. One advantage of group therapy over individual therapy is
    A. that most patients prefer it.
    B. that many styles of therapy are more effective in groups.
    C. that patients' tendencies to conform make it likely that all in the group will improve.
    D. that the therapist can exploit the self-serving bias more effectively in a group.
    E. that it is more cost effective, because the therapist can work with more patients each day.

87. Phineas Gage has been of interest to psychologists because it appears that
    A. his thalamus was damaged, thus accounting for his vision problems.
    B. the connection between his amygdala and frontal cortex was damaged, thus accounting for his emotional problems.
    C. he became, as a result of his injury, a split-brain patient.
    D. his sensory cortex was damaged, thus accounting for his inability to smell after the accident.
    E. his temporal lobe was damaged, accounting for his inability to speak after the accident.

88. Which of the following is likely to become a flashbulb memory?
    A. What you had for lunch yesterday
    B. The title of your 8th grade math textbook
    C. Your first kiss
    D. The capital of Montana
    E. Part of a song you heard today on the car radio

89. According to Robert Sternberg's theory of intelligence, a person with high creative intelligence is likely to be able to
    A. adjust quickly to novel situations.
    B. solve simple addition and subtraction problems easily.
    C. recall the capitals of all 50 states.
    D. make friends easily.
    E. achieve a high score in Conscientiousness on a Big 5 test.

90. Forensic psychology is the field in which psychologists
    A. investigate and solve crimes.
    B. profile serial killers.
    C. interact with the legal system.
    D. train FBI agents in profiling techniques.
    E. interpret lie detector tests in criminal investigations.

91. Penny is a young infant who is irritable, easy to upset, and difficult to soothe. She would be best described as having a difficult
    A. excitement phase.
    B. attitude.
    C. temperament.
    D. attachment.
    E. gender identity.

92. Who was known for looking at head size to measure intelligence?
    A. Alfred Binet
    B. Howard Gardner
    C. David Wechsler
    D. Lewis Terman
    E. Francis Galton

93. In a correlation study comparing daily yogurt intake with blood sugar levels, the results showed an r value of -.12. This indicates
    A. that yogurt causes increased blood sugar level.
    B. that yogurt causes decreased blood sugar level.
    C. that there is a slight negative relationship between yogurt intake and blood sugar level.
    D. that there is a slight positive relationship between yogurt intake and blood sugar level.
    E. that there is no relationship at all between the two.

94. Which statistic represents the strongest relationship between two variables?
    A. r = 0
    B. r = .75
    C. r = −.90
    D. p = 1
    E. p = .05

95. A student who frequently enrolls in difficult courses because he finds them challenging and therefore rewarding to master exhibits a high level of
    A. extrinsic motivation.
    B. self-efficacy.
    C. reciprocal determinism.
    D. neuroticism.
    E. extraversion.

96. In Chomsky's theory of language acquisition, children's ability to make sense of language
    A. is acquired through classical conditioning.
    B. is voluntarily developed cognitive ability.
    C. is rarely affected by genetics.
    D. is acquired through operant conditioning.
    E. is a facility humans are born with.

97. If a culture generally expects males to be more aggressive and less overtly emotional than females, then boys who are more aggressive and less emotional can be said to be conforming to
    A. gender roles.
    B. gender identities.
    C. sexual typing.
    D. sexual scripting.
    E. cultural identities.

98. He showed that an important feature of a conditioned stimulus is the extent to which it predicts the likelihood of the unconditioned stimulus's appearance, as, for example, in taste aversions.
    A. Robert Rescorla
    B. Edward Tolman
    C. F. Skiner
    D. John Garcia
    E. Albert Bandura

99. A psychologist who studies ways that the elderly adapt to physical limitations in their lives is probably working in which of the following domains of psychology?
    A. Clinical
    B. I/O
    C. Developmental
    D. Psychometric
    E. Experimental

100. In drive-reduction theory, drives are always associated with
    A. instincts.
    B. emotional arousal.
    C. physiological needs.
    D. psychological needs.
    E. stress levels.

# Section II • ⏱ 50 minutes • Number of Questions: 2

*Directions:* You have 50 minutes to answer both of the following questions. It is not enough to answer a question merely listing facts. You should present a cogent argument based on your critical analysis of the question posed.

1. Mary is planning a trip to Europe after her first year of college. She plans to fly to Europe from her home in Chicago. She will travel by train in Europe and stay in hostels. She is excited that she will be able to experience new cultures and see the museums and tourist sights of Europe.

   For each of the following concepts, define (or describe) the concept AND explain how the concept would affect Mary's enjoyment of her trip.

   - Stereotype

   - Diffusion of responsibility

   - Conformity

   - Altruism

   - Motion parallax

   - Top-down processing

   - Place theory

   - Circadian rhythm

2. Explain how the first term in the following pairs causes, affects, facilitates, or improves the second. Definitions alone are not enough to score a point; you must address the relationship between the terms.

   - practice – self-efficacy

   - assimilation – schema

   - latent content – insight

   - refractory period – neuron

   - interneuron – reflex

   - operational definition – dependent variable

   - feature detection – perception

   - evolutionary psychology – mate selection